The Bedford Guide for College Writers

Other books by X. J. Kennedy and Dorothy M. Kennedy

The Bedford Reader, Second Edition
Knock at a Star: A Child's Introduction to Poetry

Other books by X. J. Kennedy

Nude Descending a Staircase, poems
Mark Twain's Frontier (with JAMES CAMP), text-anthology
Growing into Love, poems
Bulsh, a poem
Breaking and Entering, poems
Pegasus Descending, A Book of the Best Bad Verse
  (with JAMES CAMP and KEITH WALDROP), anthology
An Introduction to Poetry, Sixth Edition
Messages: A Thematic Anthology of Poetry
Emily Dickinson in Southern California, poems
Celebrations after the Death of John Brennan, a poem
One Winter Night in August, poems for children
The Phantom Ice Cream Man, poems for children
Three Tenors, One Vehicle
  (with JAMES CAMP and KEITH WALDROP), song lyrics
An Introduction to Fiction, Fourth Edition
Literature: An Introduction to Fiction, Poetry, and Drama, Fourth Edition
Tygers of Wrath: Poems of Hate, Anger, and Invective, anthology
Did Adam Name the Vinegarroon? poems for children
The Owlstone Crown, a novel for children
Hangover Mass, poems
French Leave: Translations
Cross Ties: Selected Poems
The Forgetful Wishing Well: Poems for Young People
Brats, poems for children

The Bedford Guide
for College Writers

X. J. KENNEDY *and* **DOROTHY M. KENNEDY**

A BEDFORD BOOK

St. Martin's Press • NEW YORK

Library of Congress Catalog Card Number: 86–60631

Manufactured in the United States of America

9

f   e   d

For information, write St. Martin's Press, Inc.,
175 Fifth Avenue, New York, NY 10010

Editorial Offices: Bedford Books *of* St. Martin's Press,
29 Commonwealth Avenue, Boston, MA 02116

ISBN: 0–312–07116–7

Book design: Sandra Rigney, The Book Department, Inc.
Cover design: Richard Hannus

Acknowledgments

Ed Anger. From "Junk Food Made Our Country Great." Reprinted by permission of *Weekly World News,* January 1, 1985.

James H. Austin. From "Four Kinds of Chance." © 1974 *Saturday Review* Magazine. Reprinted by permission.

Russell Baker. "The Art of Eating Spaghetti" from *Growing Up* by Russell Baker. Copyright © 1982 by Russell Baker. Published by Congdon & Weed, Inc. Reprinted by permission of Contemporary Books, Inc.

Elizabeth Bishop. From "In the Village" in *Collected Prose* by Elizabeth Bishop. Copyright © 1984 by Alice Methfessel. Reprinted by permission of Farrar, Straus & Giroux, Inc.

Suzanne Britt. "The First Person" from *Show and Tell* by Suzanne Britt. Morning Owl Press, Raleigh, NC. Copyright © 1983. Reprinted by permission of the author.

Nigel Calder. "Coffin of the Dinosaurs" from *The Comet Is Coming* by Nigel Calder. Copyright © 1980 by Nigel Calder. Reprinted by permission of Viking and Penguin Inc. and Elizabeth Calder.

(Continued on page 530)

Preface:
To the Instructor

So many textbooks for college writing now abound that when anyone brings still another into the world, you have a right to demand an apology.

In the past, both as writers of textbooks and as textbook users, we have felt that conventional textbooks on writing have addressed only vaguely and partially the needs of the freshmen we know. Groping both for ideas and for language, students at the beginning of their college careers need much more than just advice on how to write; they need experience in writing—as soon as possible. This book, written with those freshmen in mind, was the inevitable result of such convictions.

Like a few other recent books, *The Bedford Guide for College Writers* seeks to bring into the classroom the findings of contemporary research in composition. We try to show the beginning college student that writing is not a lockstep chore, but an often exciting process—or constellation of processes. Writing, we suggest, is not the laborious construction of something to say, but the lively and sometimes surprising act of thinking while working with language.

This view is hardly original, and yet perhaps this book can lay claim to some originality. At its heart are the five chapters in Part II, "A Writer's Resources," designed to set students to recalling, observing, reading, conversing, and imagining. Our hope is that if students will learn to draw on those five fundamental resources, they will realize how many ideas they already have on hand or can discover readily. If they do, then they need never be at a loss for words.

The students for whom we write tend to see their freshman English course as having nothing to do with their other courses or with the world beyond the classroom. To show them that in fact it does have practical value, each of the book's central chapters ends with a section called "Applying What You Learn." This section contains sample paragraphs by both student and professional writers on a variety of subjects—everything from tax law to chemistry, from child psychology to environmental studies. It seems to us that students will be motivated to write better if they are assured that what they learn in composition courses is applicable in their other courses and in their future professions.

How This Book Is Built

The table of contents will speak for itself, but let us briefly explain the reasons for its main features. Part One offers an introduction to writing for all kinds of college courses, not merely for the freshman course in composition. The book opens with a short and we believe honest account of the writing processes, giving the history of an actual student's experience. In Part One, which students may be asked to read outside of class, we offer practical suggestions for fulfilling assignments and meeting deadlines in all sorts of college writing situations. Attention is paid to the familiar problem of getting started and (if need be) unblocking, to working with peer editors, to writing with a computer.

Beginning in Part Two, we suggest writing assignments for the student to fulfill. The arrangement of each of twelve chapters (4 through 15) is uniform. You will always find:

1. Two short readings, one by a professional writer, one by a student, to show readers the nature of each task. Following each selection, questions are designed not merely to analyze what the writers have written but to provoke students to original thought.

2. A writing assignment general enough to let students define it for themselves and so become personally involved.

3. Detailed guidance in generating ideas, shaping a draft (with suggestions for planning), and rewriting (with suggestions for editing). Writing being a recursive activity, we do not pretend that it always proceeds in these three stages. We keep the stages few and flexible, the better to show how often they may overlap, how a writer will sometimes backtrack (say, from rewriting to generating more ideas) or leap ahead from one stage to another.

4. Other assignments in case you prefer one of them to the main assignment or want more assignments.

5. "Applying What You Learn"—a short discussion to show how writers used each writing procedure in other college courses and in the world beyond college.

Later, two of the chapters on research writing (16 and 18) and a chapter on writing about literature (21) observe substantially the same arrangement. We varied the arrangement a little, though, because to do so seemed to make more sense.

When you come to Part Three, "Writing to Explain," you may well think, "Aren't these the same old modes of discourse?" Please inspect these chapters critically; you will find comparison and contrast, process analysis, and the other modes presented not as inexorable monoliths but as ways of thought that naturally occur in certain writing tasks. Like the chapters before them, these five discussions all center on process: each traces the writing of an assignment. These discussions, by the way, go a step beyond those in the first and second editions of *The Bedford Reader,* where the modes are presented more as models than as mental processes.

In Part Four's two chapters on persuasive writing, the student will set forth an opinion and argue for an action. "A Note on Reasoning" offers a brief introduction to both traditional and recent logical methods.

In Part Five, four chapters on writing from research plunge the student into both library and field research. One chapter (17) gives a detailed tour of a typical library's reference facilities. Most textbooks warn students that research writing demands an approach quite different from that used for other writing tasks. But we suggest that when your students write a research paper, they make no such violent break with everything they know. They do, however, need to document their sources. The mechanics of documentation have been placed in a separate chapter, permitting easy reference.

A reference manual, the "Strategies" section (Part Seven) contains detailed, specific advice, both new and old. We see *The Bedford Guide for College Writers* as a transitional book for a transitional moment. By including the "Strategies," we hope to serve both the instructor who wishes some detailed treatment of recent concerns, such as nonlinear outlining and avoiding sexist usage, and the instructor who seeks help in teaching traditional outlining and the writing of thesis sentences. Perhaps the advice of Pope may still apply:

> Be not the first by whom the New are tried,
> Nor yet the last to lay the Old aside.

For some writing tasks, we believe, the practice of writing a thesis sentence still makes excellent sense. So does outlining in order to lay out a complicated task or to revise a paper riddled with confusion.

We have tried to write this book as plainly and readably as we knew how. Still, it is a working book, one to be used in writing and then cast aside, not an object to be kept and dusted on a shelf.

Thanks

Writing this book, like writing a freshman essay, has been a learn-as-you-go experience. Painfully, we have had to unlearn a few assumptions about writing that we had distilled from classic textbooks or had been taught. We have had to return to what we know in our bones about writing—at least, what we think we know. We have learned a good deal, besides, from many writers, teachers, and researchers. Some of these debts will be apparent, but let us acknowledge in particular the inspiration and the work of Ann E. Berthoff, Patricia Bizzell, Kenneth Burke, Edward P. J. Corbett, Frank J. D'Angelo, Janet Emig, Ken Macrorie, Donald Murray, William G. Perry, Jr., Carl Rogers, and Frank Smith.

Once in a decade a ground-breaking textbook appears: in 1985, it was *The St. Martin's Guide to Writing* by Rise B. Axelrod and Charles R. Cooper. We are indebted to this book for its method of setting assignments, then escorting the student through them. Not only a rhetoric but a reader and a handbook, Axelrod and Cooper's book will not soon be replaced, even though later textbook writers, like us, may have learned from it.

In the past four years, the advice and the insights of many people have changed our manuscript from a cautious and misapprehension-ridden draft into a book that, whatever its shortcomings, more truly reflects how writing is generally written—or so we feel. Our leading mentors have been three: Mike Rose, of the University of California, Los Angeles, who set out to educate us (by mail) in composition theory; John J. Ruszkiewicz of the University of Texas, Austin; and Robert A. Schwegler of the University of Rhode Island. These friendly but demanding critics read every manuscript page from the start of our project to its finish. They gave generous guidance all the way, corrected errors and wrong emphases, and many times wrote in thoughts of their own, which we often appropriated.

We owe deep thanks also to Donald McQuade of the University of California, Berkeley, for his detailed comments on our earliest plans and to Robert Rudolf, University of Toledo. For reading, criticizing, and demolishing our first draft—in addition to Professors Rose, Ruszkiewicz, and Schwegler—we are indebted to Jane Aaron; Robert DiYanni of Pace University; Diana Hacker of Prince Georges Community College; Clayton Hudnall of the University of Hartford; Thomas P. Miller of Southern Illinois University, Carbondale; and James C. Raymond of the University of Alabama, currently editor of *College English*. Later, as our manuscript improved, we also received much detailed, page-by-page criticism from Patricia Bizzell of the College of the Holy Cross; Richard L. Larson of City University of New York, recently editor of *College Composition & Communication;* Sonia Maasik of the University of California, Los Angeles (who supplied illustrations from her wide reading); Shirley Morahan of Northeast Missouri State University; and Nancy Sommers and Jo Tarvers of Rutgers University. All gave us more wisdom than we could put into writing, but without them, this book would not exist. To Professor Morahan we owe a further, deeper debt. From her experience as director of composition at Northeast Missouri, she has written the *Instructor's Manual to Accompany The Bedford Guide for College Writers,* which gives a firsthand account of this book in action.

Brave instructors tried our tentative assignments in their classes and provided the written results, often illuminating. We have especially to thank Lin Haire-Sargeant of Boston University and Dale Peterson and Frieda Gardner of Tufts University. Patricia Gilmore-Jaffe and Bonnie Lisle of the University of California, Los Angeles, let us read writing by their students. Others who made valuable suggestions include William Kelly of Bristol Community College and Judith Stanford of Merrimack College. Among students who took time to share their writing experiences, we are especially grateful to Jane Betz, Jennifer Bowe, Lisa Chickos, Rose Anne Federici, Jamie Merisotis, and Jeffrey Ting.

Chickos's research paper and several of the other student essays came to us from the Bedford Contest for Student Writing. Susan Osborn of Rutgers University helped select promising material from the contest's files. Among the instructors who fostered essays now included or quoted in this book are

X. Theodore Barber of New York University; Patrice Ficociello of the University of Cincinnati; Marilyn J. Frank of Harper College; Joan Frederick of James Madison University; Leonard D. Groski of LaRoche College; Sandra Handsher of Indian Valley College; Donna Jones of Georgia Southern College; Laura H. Miller, formerly of Indiana University of Pennsylvania; Laura Novo of Columbia University; Jeff Skoblow of University of California, Los Angeles; Fred Strebeigh of Yale University; Kim Anne Thomas, formerly of the University of Alabama, and Jeanne Walker of Chaffey Community College.

Peter L. Knox shared his experience in writing for professional journals of law. We owe thanks also to the Trustees of the Boston Public Library for cooperation in supplying materials and in permitting us to photograph them.

Not least, we thank publisher Charles H. Christensen for his constant advice and unswerving faith in this book. At many times, lesser faiths would have been shaken. Associate Publisher Joan Feinberg coordinated the whole project; she criticized plans, headings, and manuscript, worried with us (and about us), patiently guided, goaded, and inspired. Elizabeth M. Schaaf saw the book into print and solved its problems of art and photography. Barbara Flanagan edited copy, and Kathryn Blatt proofread pages. Steve Scipione lent his kindly intelligence; he and Andrew Christensen and Mary Lou Wilshaw fought the battle of permissions. Nancy Lyman prepared publicity: no mean feat, for the book changed even as she wrote. Matthew Carnicelli, Jane Dominik, Karen S. Henry, Christine Rutigliano, Julie Shevach, and Rebecca Saunders lent aid and counsel.

To Dorothy Kennedy's former students at the Ohio University and the University of Michigan; to XJK's at Michigan, the University of California, Irvine, the University of North Carolina, Greensboro, and Tufts University—thanks for letting us learn from your writing. Last, we deeply thank three college students and two high school students in our immediate family for their extensive help and advice: Kathleen, David, Matthew, Daniel, and Joshua. In their presences, living students could never be far from our minds.

Contents

The Bedford Guide for College Writers

Introduction:
What Is Writing?

Unlike parachute-jumping, writing is an activity that you can go ahead and try without first learning all there is to it. You learn to write by writing. In truth, nothing that anybody can tell you about it can help you so much as learning on the job. That is why in this book we will put you in various writing situations and say, "Go to it."

Still, when confronted with a writing task, most people feel reluctant to plunge in. In the words of Donald H. Graves, who studied people's attitudes toward writing for the Ford Foundation, most of us look on an obligation to write as an obligation to go to an uncomfortable, stuffed-shirt high-society ball: "The first concern is to be dressed properly. The second is not to say anything wrong. And the third is to get out of there as quickly as possible."

Why do most people see writing as such a grim duty? They worry that they won't write well. They have a troubling notion that their words really ought to come out sounding at least as intelligent as the Declaration of Independence. Afraid that they will stick their feet into their mouths, spell words wrong and commit grammatical errors, say stupid things and make themselves look like idiots, they are stricken wordless. If they are college students, they perhaps dread that their instructor, like a cat in wait for a mouse, just yearns to get hold of their writing and rip it to shreds. Besides, they fervently want to get A's. Then they'll prove to the folks at home that the tuition money was justified. As a result, they twist themselves into such an uptight state that they can hardly bear to set anything down on paper at all. "Desire to write grows with writing," said the sixteenth-century scholar Erasmus. To *want* to write, a writer has to begin.

Most college writers would do well to lower their standards. At least, when they first sit down to write, assignment in hand, they need not expect perfection from the start. Many veteran writers, even professionals, write stupid, confused stuff when they commence a writing task. What distinguishes them from beginners is that, having written a bunch of trash, they work long and hard to turn it into treasure.

By treasure, we don't mean writing that is merely error-free. Some writers tie themselves into knots by trying to revise each sentence as soon as it is born,

1

trying to make it Scripture-perfect before going on to the next. Sometimes they catch all the errors but miss something more important: their trains of thought. To be sure, when you are writing a letter for a serious purpose (to get it published in a newspaper or to land a job), you'll want to eliminate errors. If your letter bears eight misspellings and a coffee-cup ring, it won't bowl anybody over. Yet some elements in writing—especially college writing—matter far more than neatness and correctness. In college writing, to demonstrate that you are learning matters greatly; so does generating ideas of your own. Why worry if your first draft isn't neat? Cross things out, draw arrows, and move things from place to place. Scissor your draft to pieces; then Scotch-tape those pieces together in a stronger order. We know writers whose early drafts look like rag rugs that bulldogs have been chewing on. But all a reader sees is the final version.

The life of a writer, most people expect, is a silent and solitary activity—a matter of wearing out a chair bottom in a lonely room. For some writers, that's how it is; but for others, it is nothing of the kind. Some talk to themselves. They groan, they shriek, they yell, "Holy smoke! What a great sentence!" Some pace back and forth like tigers in cages; or like Mark Twain, who placed his writing desk next to a pool table, they tinker with sentences in their heads while listening to a ball ricochet back and forth and click into other balls and finally plop into a pocket—like a sentence that reaches its goal. Some spring up and vent their feelings to friends or roommates, read passages aloud to them, and demand, "Is that rotten? Is that any good?" All these are ways of fulfilling the writer's task.

Writing, then, isn't like building pyramids, a matter of piling up paragraphs like granite blocks. It's a matter of thinking and rethinking in words. How do most writers write? Like sculptors who sling down a lump of clay, they pound it and pat it and see a shape in it. They produce chaos, find sense in it, and get that sense across to someone else.

Whether performed in repose or in a sweat, writing tends to be a matter of dashing off, crossing out, leaping ahead, backtracking, correcting, adjusting, questioning, trying a different approach, failing, trying yet another approach, failing, trying still another approach, making a breakthrough, working and reworking, scrubbing, polishing—and perhaps, in the end, looking up the spellings of a bunch of suspicious-looking words. It is a job that Maxine Hong Kingston, who writes of Chinese-American life, compares to gardening in Hawaii: a little time spent in planting, much time spent in "cutting and pruning and hacking back." At moments writing can be a drudgery worse than scrubbing soup kettles; at other times, a sport full of thrills. It can be like whizzing downhill on a couple of well-greased skis, never knowing what you will meet around a bend.

Many people arrive in college with the notion that they shouldn't set down an idea until they have first thought it all out. This notion can paralyze them. But writing isn't an affair of copying down what you read from your mental TelePrompTer. What is it, then? French writer André Gide has given an account of his experience: "Too often before I write a sentence I find myself waiting for it to take shape in my mind. Far better I grasp it by the end that first presents itself, whether head or tail; and then, not knowing the rest of it, give a yank. The rest will follow."

This method of thinking in the act of writing (and not merely beforehand) can yield surprising results. Thoughts tend to come while the words flow down to paper, for while the fingers type or spur a racing pencil, the head keeps on working right along. "Thoughts," says Canadian language researcher Frank Smith, "are created in the act of writing, which changes the writer just as it changes the paper on which the text is produced."

Changes the writer! The phrase is worth emphasizing. Imagine—what you write can change, correct, and enlarge your mind. Often, an idea you have discovered in the process of writing will leap out and startle you. As English novelist E. M. Forster, author of *Passage to India*, put the experience, "How do I know what I think until I see what I say?" Asked how she wrote a poem, Anne Sexton said, "I will fool around on the typewriter. It might take me ten pages of nothing, of terrible writing, and then I'll get a line, and I'll think, 'That's what I mean!' "

That sense of revelation may come unexpectedly, or, with a little prodding, it can begin early—even while you are still pinning down your topic. You can read *like a writer*. With a tentative idea in mind, you look around purposefully, to see what other writers have written about it. Professional writers often spend more time in thinking and in looking for material than they do in placing words on a page. Sometimes you write *while* you collect material. Sometimes new ideas come while you revise.

So plunge in. Throw some words on paper and listen to them hit. Later on, you can cross out, add, rearrange; you can watch your ideas become stronger and sharper and clearer before your eyes. Don't fear that your readers expect your writing to be dazzling at the start, or at all times. No writer is brilliant all the time. That's why writers have wastebaskets.

Using This Book

The Bedford Guide for College Writers encourages you to write better by actually writing.

To make the book easy to use, it is divided into seven major parts. At the beginning of each part, a short note alerts you to what follows immediately. In this fashion, the book explains what it is doing as it goes along.

Part One is basic: "How Writers Write." You'll also find in it advice for meeting familiar challenges: facing assignments, coping with deadlines, getting started. In addition, this section offers advice on working with your fellow student writers and on writing with a word processor.

Then, in the succeeding parts, each containing two or more chapters, we suggest assignments for writing a paper of your own. In each chapter, you will meet examples of both professional writing and student writing. Then comes the assignment, followed by detailed guidance through it: in generating ideas, shaping a draft, and rewriting. Other possible assignments are suggested. Finally, the chapter shows how what you have just learned can be useful in your college (and later) writing.

Part Two is the heart of the book. It suggests five answers to the questions every college writer wrestles with: "What to write about?" and "What to say?" To find ideas and material, we claim, you have five useful resources: remembering, observing with your own eyes (and other senses), reading, talking with people, and imagining. The chapters in Part Two will start you writing from those resources.

The book goes on to deal with most kinds of college writing: explaining, persuading, doing research (whether in the library or in the field), taking essay exams, criticizing literature. There is also a chapter on business writing, some of it useful in college.

At the end of the book, Part Seven, "Strategies," functions as a sort of tool kit handily carried in the trunk. It presents an array of useful advice on specific ways to generate ideas, draft, and rewrite. These include such techniques as brainstorming (or rapidly listing ideas), keeping a journal, outlining, stating a thesis, giving examples, beginning and ending, cutting, and many more. Browse through the Strategies part at your leisure. Then you'll be able to consult it whenever it might be helpful. Finally, the Appendix tells you how to format your manuscript (if your instructor hasn't told you that already).

Because writing a paper, like a strenuous game of basketball, is hard work, we'd like to give you all the support we can muster. So, no doubt, does your instructor, someone closer to you than any textbook writers. But like coaches, instructors and textbook writers can improve your game only so far. Reading our advice on how to write won't make you a writer. You'll learn more, and find much more satisfaction, when you take a few sentences to the hoop and make some points yourself.

How Writers Write

In this section, we offer you a brief tour through the writing processes. The first chapter provides a vivid sense of what most writers go through when they write. You can compare other writers' experiences with your own. Here you will find no prescribed formula for writing but a rough account of what almost all writers do sooner or later. You will also find "The Story of an Essay": a true account of how one student writer fulfilled a writing assignment. (Right at the start, he ran into an obstacle. But you'll see how his paper turned out.)

As no one need tell you, writing in college presents challenges, and the second chapter in this section is designed to help you survive them: assignments that may appear unappetizing, deadlines that look impossible to meet, and that age-old challenge of every writer—how to get started in the first place. We offer a list of suggestions, some practical, a few slightly far-out, all of which have improved the quality of life for writers we know.

That you are not alone as a writer, that you can draw on the help and good counsel of other student writers (as well as your instructor), is the gist of the third chapter, "Peer Editing." In it you will find tips both for reading another student's paper and for profiting from another student's advice.

Last in this section, we supply a detailed note on that revolutionary way in which many writers now write: with the aid of a computer. This note is no more than a terse introduction to the subject. If you are already an old hand with a word processor, step past it. If you are only now thinking of making a word processor's acquaintance, you may find some of our hints useful.

CHAPTER 1

Understanding the Writing Processes

If you could observe a thousand writers at their desks—or at notebooks they juggle while riding a bus, or at word processors—you would probably find no two of them exactly alike in their working methods. Still, you could make generalizations. Sooner or later you would probably find that all thousand writers do things that are more or less the same.

They generate ideas. They find a promising idea, either by discovering one or by inventing an idea of their own. They try to find material to express it with.

They shape language. They give order to their thoughts and they make a rough draft. Through more drafts, they make their ideas clearer. (Perhaps, while they shape, they find still more ideas and material.)

They rewrite. They revise and polish, turning an early draft or drafts into readable copy.

Those stages don't always follow like dog after cat after rat. As a writer yourself, you can skip around, taking up parts of the job in any order you like. Editing—combing through your copy to fix small flaws, substituting a better word here and there—usually comes toward the very end. But you might, while collecting material to write about, feel an urge to play around with a sentence until you get it perfect. In so doing, you would leap from the discovery stage to revising and editing; then you might go back to discover more material. In the processes of writing—and they are various—all you can expect is that chaos will come before order.

Let's look at these flexible stages more closely. You'll want a general understanding of them now. In later chapters, as we try to help you fulfill assignments, this book will guide you through them again and again.

GENERATING IDEAS

This stage involves first finding what to write about and then finding what to write.

Discovering What to Write About

Finding something you really want to write about is half the task. You might begin by thinking along some line you feel a warm desire to pursue. Perhaps the general assignment you have been given ("Write about some trend in current lifestyles," or whatever) will give you your first clues. Make yourself comfortable and think. You can take notes while you ponder, scribble down a few possibilities.

Find a topic you honestly *want* to pursue, and words will flow. In a warm and funny memoir you can read in Chapter 4, Russell Baker tells how he became a real writer only when he stopped trying to please his teacher and started pleasing himself. To his great surprise, he delighted his teacher too. In discovering what to write, first look around close to home. Alert writers stand ready to find valuable material anywhere. When the English writer G. K. Chesterton simply hauled out the contents of his pockets and described what he found, the result was an essay that has lasted for seventy years. The Georgia writer Flannery O'Connor wrote a memorable article on peacocks from observing the birds in her farmyard.

If, as so often happens in college, an instructor hands you a very specific writing assignment that looks at first glance of no personal concern to you, you face the challenge of making it your own. (In "Writing to an Assignment," on p. 23 in Chapter 2, we offer some advice on meeting this challenge.)

Discovering Material

Once you glimpse your topic, one that seems promising, you start to seek material. You search your memory, perhaps observe things; you read purposefully, along the line of inquiry you wish to pursue. You talk with people, perhaps use your imagination. You start piling up notes. At first, you probably just throw your material into a heap without worrying yet about its shapeliness. Joseph Epstein, who writes magazine essays regularly, is a habitual heaper-up of material before he writes. As soon as he discovers his general topic, he starts collecting in a folder everything he meets that has some connection with it: quotations, anecdotes, titles of other books and articles on the same topic to be looked into, his own thoughts. As days go by, he adds notes from his reading, observations, sentences, "fugitive thoughts that come in the shower, before falling asleep, or at other inopportune times." When he finally sits down to write, he sits down to a folder packed with things to say—some of them already well worded. Epstein's method assumes, though, that you have days or weeks to prepare to write. It won't work for a writing assignment due tomorrow, although it might work if you are writing a term paper.

Whether you have much time or little, five basic resources—recalling, observing, reading, conversing, imagining—can help you gather material. You might consider these questions (and jot down answers):

1. What have you experienced along these lines? Have you ever heard of this topic before? If so, where? What do you know about this already? How

does it relate to you? (For more specific guidance in answering these fruitful questions, see Chapter 4.)

2. Is there anything you could go see—or hear, smell, touch, or taste—that might add information? (See Chapter 5.)

3. Where can you find something to read along these lines that might give you more ideas of your own or might supply some necessary facts and figures? (See Chapter 6.)

4. Who would know something about this topic? Will that person talk with you? Is there anyone nearby you might ask, "Do you know anything about . . . ?" (See Chapter 7.)

5. What fresh ways of looking at this topic can you imagine? How would it look to another person? (See Chapter 8.)

All the while you look for material, you're writing. You're *thinking on paper:* jotting notes, scribbling rough thoughts and summaries of things, perhaps writing (and smoothing right there and then) a few sentences to use in your finished paper. The task of generating ideas and information doesn't always stop before a paper is written. Some writers, without prior thought or a previous search for material, *start* with what they know (however much or little), write a draft, and *then* look around for material to flesh it out and make their ideas clear. Others find when they revise that a certain point needs more evidence. Then back they will go to discovering again. Whatever your writing habits, all the while you are discovering ideas and information, you'll want to keep your pencil busy.

SHAPING A DRAFT

Having discovered a burning idea to write about (or at least a smoldering one), having discovered thoughts and information with which to set it forth, you sort out what matters most and arrange it so that main points seem to follow. If right away it appears that your paper has one main point to make and that all your material is going to express that point, you're lucky. It would help to try to state that point in writing, to step back from your material and say, "All right, here's what I'm getting at." But if no one main point has emerged, never mind: you might find one as you work along. Some ideas aren't burning ideas to begin with; only when you start revising do they catch fire.

Expect to allow ample time for planning (organizing material in advance) and drafting (writing in the rough rather than in the smooth) and rewriting. If you think you won't need to start writing on an assignment until 3:30 A.M. the night before it is due, you're probably lost. You might need to write not only a first draft but two or more drafts. The novelist Philip Roth once said that when he starts a new book, he has to write many pages before he comes to "a paragraph that's alive." At that moment he tells himself, "Okay, that's your beginning, start there," and he discards all he had previously written: just a warm-up exercise.

You can arrange the notes you have, sorting them into piles of ideas that go together. Taking notes on index cards may help you shape your paper; they are easy to shuffle and deal. Some writers, instead of making a formal outline, write on a card each point they want to make and then arrange the cards in an order. Some writers plan with scissors, grouping and taping together similar ideas or ideas that seem to follow. Some writers have a simple outline, perhaps just a list of the points they will make. If you make an outline, stand ready to change it as more ideas occur. Some writers compile a list of the main points they're going to make. Some use a planning technique called *clustering*, described by novelist and historian William Manchester: "I write a word in the center of the page. Then I circle it with other words until a pattern appears." (For more advice on clustering, see p. 474 in Part Seven.)

How much time should you spend in planning? The more complex your subject, the more planning time it will probably call for. But we suggest that you leave some of your draft unplanned, or only roughly planned, so that you don't take all the fun and surprise out of the job. "It does little good," says poet and essayist David Greenhood, "to be wholly certain before going ahead with writing. . . . Nobody can blueprint spontaneity. Without that, we work like copyists."

When your writing task is an investigative paper—a research paper, the kind that calls for much gathering of material—you write with a pile of notes at your elbow. Such a pile can be comforting. You feel sure you'll have something to say. But don't let all those notes you took dominate you. You may find that your paper will be more lively if, in writing your draft, you don't even look at your notes. It is easy to get bogged down in recopying all of them, and you may feel tempted to include everything you have written down just because you went to the work of taking each note and hate to waste it. Sometimes this attitude results in a paper containing too much extraneous information, thrown in just because the writer wants to prove he went to the library and looked it up. Calvin Trillin tells how he writes magazine articles about murderers: he comes home with a pile of newspaper clippings, brochures, photographs, and Xerox copies of court transcripts, and with a notebook bulging with handwritten notes from conversations. His next move is to write from memory—without looking at the pile—a first draft so sloppy that he calls it not a draft but "a vomit-out." At least this rough document sketches a shape for his material and helps him see meaning in it.

Don't take our word that in drafting it's better to ignore notes than to consult them until you check out our advice against your own experience. Maybe you're a born consulter. Try both methods and see which works better for you. But in general, we suggest you try drafting at a brisk pace. If you are not a touch typist, better write in longhand. The hunt-and-peck system might make you concentrate more on finding the keys than on finding the ideas. If the right word won't come, if you need some bit of information from a note that isn't right in front of you, don't stop writing; just leave space to add the missing piece later.

Let your draft run long. Most writers find it is easier, later, to cut than to expand. Leave yourself time to revise. For most college papers on challenging topics, you will need to write not one draft but two or more. You may have to throw out your first attempt and start over because a stronger, clearer idea has occurred to you. That was what student Drew Cook found himself doing in his paper on James Bond (p. 14). You can expect to keep discovering ideas while you plan and while you draft. By all means, welcome them.

REWRITING

When you read a story, a memoir, or an essay—say by pioneer feminist Tillie Olsen—you might think that her words had flowed forth without effort. But if you could see her early drafts, you would find them full of crossings-out and second thoughts and hard work, just like yours. "In baseball," says play-wright Neil Simon, "you only get three swings and you're out. In rewriting, you get almost as many swings as you want and you know that, sooner or later, you'll hit the ball." (Sometimes, of course, you don't have time to keep swinging—as when a sociology report is due in the morning.)

When at last you complete a draft, you might well think that all your hard work is done, that nothing remains but to fix a few spelling errors. That isn't revising, though—that's only proofreading. For most skilled writers, the time of revising is when work begins in earnest. Indeed, the last draft (whether a second or a tenth) may still be only a detailed sketch to which the writer has yet to give shape and substance.

Revision—the word means "seeing again"—may take place at any time you are writing, at any moment you stop writing to reread. All the while you plan and draft, you make alterations in your original conception: change your plans, decide to put in or leave out, shift things, connect, disconnect, connect things in new ways. In revising, you don't just revise words—you sometimes revise the way you think, the way you see.

How deeply you revise may depend on the complexity of your writing job and on your familiarity with your material. To write a short memoir of an incident that took place on the beach last summer or to observe and describe a familiar room probably won't take as much revising as a long term paper for an economics course: "Changing Attitudes Toward the Protective Tariff, 1920–1987." As a rule, you don't rewrite a journal or a diary kept for your own eyes only or trouble to polish a casual letter to a friend. But after you write a draft of anything worth dressing up in its Sunday best, you generally revise. Much depends on whom you're writing for and what your purpose is.

Imagining a reader's reactions to your work can help you revise. Some writers try to define their audiences very carefully; others are content simply to reread their own work as a hard-to-please reader might do. If you're writing a letter to a friend, then you have a definite person in mind: you know what interests him or her, what reactions are likely. Your awareness that you have a friendly reader makes writing easy. But often you can't know your reader personally. When you write a letter applying for a job with a large firm or government agency, you have only a vague notion of your reader. When you write a poem or a short story, who knows who will read it? You write for people out there, whoever they are, and for yourself. In such situations, when you reread your work you try to step into the shoes of some other intelligent person—someone like yourself. You read to see if what you say is clear, to see if you (the reader) are interested in what you (the writer) say. Catherine Drinker Bowen, a celebrated historian, kept a sign pinned over her writing desk: "Will the reader turn the page?" If she wasn't sure the reader would bother, she revised.

Revising sometimes calls you over to a hostile reader's side, to sit in the seat of the scornful. Leo Rosten, humorist and novelist, urges writers to see their work as an *unfriendly* reader might look at it: "You have to put yourself in the position of the negative reader, the resistant reader, the reader who doesn't surrender easily, the reader who is alien to you as a type, even the reader who doesn't like what you're writing. You must make sure you are communicating—really communicating—getting something from your mind and emotions into his." Rosten's advice is good and hard-hitting, but we suggest you apply it only when your paper is nearing its finish. When your ideas first start to flow, you don't want to be mercilessly critical of them. You want to lure them forth, not tear them apart, or they might go back into hiding.

Revising need not be a solitary activity. At this stage, the opinion of another reader besides yourself, perhaps your instructor, may be of help to you. Another valuable, sometimes even pleasant way to revise is to trade papers with a fellow student or students, getting (and giving) reactions and suggestions. Often called peer-editing, this useful exchange might also be called peer-reading or peer-evaluating, for if it is truly useful, it goes much deeper than editing, which is mainly a matter of correcting surface mistakes and rearranging words. (We'll offer more suggestions for reading a fellow writer's work beginning on p. 36.)

Some writers like to read their work aloud to a friend. Others tape-record it and listen to it; unable to see their spelling mistakes, they can concentrate on the quality of their ideas.

If you can put aside your previous draft for a few hours or a day or more, you can then reread it with fresh eyes—and with a sharp pencil. Cross out the weak parts, add, substitute words, move things around (with an arrow or with the appropriate command in your word processing program) and put them in other places. If you discover newer and better ideas, don't hesitate to throw out some or all of what you have done and begin again.

For some college writers, revising and editing look like terrible chores, but that isn't how all writers see them. After writing a great pile of rough versions of poems that still needed months of hard labor, poet William Butler Yeats, looking forward to his toil, wrote to a friend: "What bliss!" Revision, he said, not only drafting, may be inspired. Perfecting a piece of writing may be somewhat like perfecting a film. Explaining how he makes movies, Swedish director

Ingmar Bergman told an interviewer, "I never edit while shooting. I'd find it too depressing. Besides, editing, for me, is a sort of erotic pleasure. I like to save it up."

Writers who claim they don't revise. Some writers claim they revise little or not at all. As a journalist in the eighteenth century, Samuel Johnson single-handedly wrote a whole weekly newspaper of debates in Parliament—without time to rewrite. Anthony Trollope, an English novelist, called revising "a waste of time." A recent writer who has publicly scorned revision is William F. Buckley, author of a children's book written in four hours. In truth, such writers do indeed revise—they revise in their heads as they go along. They seem able to shoulder the terrible burden of getting things right without further drafts. Such writers are usually long-experienced. Still, most writers, even veterans, are more fallible. Like Larry Bird or Magic Johnson, they don't sink every shot and don't mind coming back around to try again.

Editing and proofreading. Most writers need to give their work a final going-over: editing it, or tightening nuts, and proofreading it, or picking nits. Although he considered revising a waste of time, Anthony Trollope believed in editing and proofreading. Before sending anything to print, he would reread it three times. Most writers find, like Trollope, that editing comes late in the process of writing. Unlike revising, editing isn't concerned with the more crucial tasks of arranging your ideas in the strongest order, developing ideas further, changing your whole direction (if need be), making clear your attitude toward what you're saying. Editing just smoothes the surface of what you have said. Not that editing is a trivial pursuit. In certain sentences, the choice of a single word, even the location of a comma, can alter the meaning of the whole. But don't worry prematurely about editing. First, draft and revise.

Some writers combine drafting with editing; that is, they edit their work at any old time, as they go along. When they weary of sticking to a line of inquiry, they rest by tinkering with small flaws in their work's surface. Refreshed, having left a few sentences perfect, they go back to the hard part again. But dangers lurk in this practice: you can get so preoccupied with pulling weeds or picking flowers that you can lose sight of the crop to be harvested.

Editing, then, entails doing to your work what a publisher's editor would do to it: correcting any flaws that might stand in the way of your reader's enjoyment and understanding. For the most part, this means paying close attention to your choice and arrangement of words, checking grammar, rethinking punctuation. In editing, repairs generally accomplish the following:

Get rid of surplus baggage.

Replace jargon with standard English (replace *deprioritize* with *give less importance*, the verb *impact* with *effect* or *influence*) and sexist words with nonstereotyped words (replace *poetess* with *poet, mankind* with *humankind).*

Replace phrases that might annoy readers with phrases that are generally accepted (substituting for *less people* the preferred form *fewer people*).

Fix grammar: make subjects agree with verbs, pronouns agree with what they stand for.

Rearrange words into a stronger, clearer order.

Proofreading, generally the last step of all, is a term for reading finished material for mechanical flaws (such as a word misspelled or a keyboard error). Newspapers and other publishers hire proofreaders to read everything set in type (or on software) before it is printed. Proofreading may seem a relatively unimportant step in writing a short story, but in scientific writing it may be crucial. Errors in the application of scientific knowledge, as biologist Ruth C. Wilson has remarked, could mean a trip to Mars instead of to the moon; a proofreader's error in a report of a chemical spill could mean the difference between life and death.

In college writing, fortunately, proofreading rarely carries such fearful responsibility. It means giving your paper one last look, with a dictionary at your elbow, checking any doubtful spellings and correcting any typing mistakes.

Such are the stages of writing—not fixed, lock-step stages, but each one likely to come at some moment in writing most papers. We have set them forth as we have known them, but we wonder if you now feel encumbered by too much advice. If you do, forget everything we have said and just write.

Screenwriter and once-popular novelist Jack Woodford made a memorable remark: "The only way to learn to write is to write at least one million lousy words and throw them away." In this course, you won't be asked to write a million words. There won't be time. More likely, you will be asked to write a few thousand. Although in only a few weeks the course can't teach you everything about writing, it can show you how to take charge of your writing and start making it stronger, clearer, and more readable. In so doing, you will find that you aren't merely playing with words. You're thinking on paper.

THE STORY OF AN ESSAY

Drew Cook's freshman English instructor left the assignment open wide. She allowed students plenty of room to explore its possibilities:

Examine the relationship between you and another person (other than a lover or a spouse) or between you and some object important to you. Write to introduce yourself to the other members of this class or (if you prefer not to concentrate on yourself) to introduce them to one of your interests.

Starting out at this stage of initial discovery, Cook turned over in his mind a few possibilities. This assignment wasn't going to be much like his writing tasks in the College of Business. What to write about? He didn't want to concentrate on himself, and he didn't feel much like writing about a friend or relative. He decided to explore his relationship to a character on screen and in fiction who had intrigued him ever since he was a kid: Ian Fleming's master sleuth James Bond.

He began by recalling the first time he had set eyes on Bond. He still vividly remembered the exciting graphics and action shots that had opened the film *Dr. No.* He drafted, crossed out, changed words, and then typed out this trial paragraph:

```
     The screen goes dark.  Suddenly, a pulsating, stac-
cato music fills the theater.  A white dot moves, off and
on, horizontally across the screen in time with the mu-
sic.  The dot stops at the right side of the screen and
grows in size.  Twisting, swirling lines snake pinwheel-
fashion around the dot to end at its edges.  A hatted man
appears in the center, walking casually to the left of
the dot.  The man whirls unexpectedly and fires a handgun
directly at the audience!  A curtain of bright red begins
to drip downwards, covering the scene, and the white dot,
now red, wavers and sinks out of sight.  The audience re-
alizes it has been looking down a gun barrel, and another
James Bond screen adventure has begun.
```

Now *there* was a great opening. A little heavy on the adjectives, maybe—but right away, any reader who read it ought to feel hooked. Cook went on:

```
     My first experience with the world of James Bond be-
gan in 1963 when, at the age of 10, I "accidentally on
purpose" saw the film Dr. No, the first of the 007 screen
adventures.  A friend of mine and I stayed after the Sat-
urday morning kiddie movie (a Jerry Lewis comedy, I
believe) . . .
```

There his draft trailed off, and his typewriter rattled to a stop. To say any more about his personal relationship to James Bond was going to be difficult. He didn't want to psychoanalyze himself. He had a great many other things to say about Fleming's hero that wouldn't fit into the frame of a personal experience.

Aimlessly, he picked up pen and set out in a different direction:

The popularity of the films grew. They included more and more outrageous technological gadgets.

More and more struck him as confusing. He didn't mean numbers of gadgets, he meant "increasingly sophisticated." He crossed out *more and more* and made the change. Shouldn't he illustrate those technological gadgets? It occurred to him that some other writer might have written something helpful about the Bond stories. This hunch proved correct. A half hour in the library turned up articles in *Time* and *Newsweek* and a book, *James Bond in the Cinema*, by critic James Brosnan. This reading supplied him with a list of all the Bond films and their dates. He took notes. Some personal sidelights about Ian Fleming caught his fancy, so he recorded them. He didn't know yet whether he would use them, but he saved them. He returned to drafting with typewriter. He wrote two versions of another sentence and after more crossing out made it read:

```
        At first, in Dr. No (1962), Bond is reluctant to ex-
    change his trusted Beretta automatic pistol ("No stopping
    power" sneers the armorer) for a̶ ̶m̶o̶r̶e̶ ̶p̶o̶w̶e̶r̶f̶u̶l̶ undoubtedly
    superior -gun Walther PPK.  By Thunderball (1965), the
    fourth film in the series, Bond accepts without question
    an incredible artillery . . .
```

Things were moving fast. Hastily, Cook dashed off four more pages of stray thoughts. No, this essay definitely was going to be about something larger than his own ten-year-old admiration for agent 007. But what *would* it be about? He had so many things to say! .

At this point, his instructor asked to see a draft of his essay so far and a rough outline of the way he intended to go on with it. Cook set down the main points he had come up with. At that moment, they didn't quite follow in any order. He summed up what others had said about the Bond films:

```
        The critics were quick to point out the elements of
    sex, snobbery (Bond had an appreciation for the better
    things in life as far as clothes, food, wine, cigarettes,
    cars, and the like were concerned), and sadism in the
    books, complaining that Bond's morals were "indistin-
    guishable from the villain's."
```

Out of his notes, he quarried a revealing quotation from Fleming himself:

```
     Fleming began work on his first novel in 1952 at his
vacation retreat house in Jamaica "as a counter-irritant
or antibody to my hysterical alarm at getting married at
the age of 43."
```

For an outline, Cook turned in a list of statements he still wanted to make:

```
I plan to continue to describe a brief history of the
books--
     1.   that Fleming continued to write the books, ap-
prox. 1 a year from 1953-64 totaling 13 in all.
     2.   that the reading public slowly grew and eventu-
ally the Bond books were impatiently awaited by their
public much like Conan Doyle's Sherlock Holmes books
were.
     3.   that the film rights were sold and the films
were started by two very astute businessmen-producers.
     4.   that actor Sean Connery was perfectly cast as
Bond, this being the main factor, along with the many
other important aspects of the films, that ensured their
popularity and success.
     5.   that because of cold war climate in the world,
the Bond secret agent espionage syndrome was widely
accepted.
     6.   several "heavyweight" comments on Bond (by John
F. Kennedy, John Kenneth Galbraith).
     7.   wish-fulfillment aspects of Bond's popularity.
```

This seemed a great deal to attempt in an essay of 600 to 800 words. The instructor, Patrice Ficociello, wrote Cook a comment that confirmed suspicions he had been coming to himself:

> As well-chosen points of summary, both of Fleming's budding career and of the first novel, this stands very nicely. But what is the point you are after? Without a forming concept your outline will inflate into either a critical biography of Fleming or a hasty summary of all the novels with a nod to Sean Connery's portrayal of Bond.

Cook did more thinking. At the same time, he went back to Brosnan's book. A statement he came across, by the English writer Kingsley Amis, gave him a clue:

"We don't want to have Bond to dinner, or go golfing with Bond, or talk with Bond. We want to be Bond!" Yes, but why? After carefully pondering Amis's remark, Cook wrote some more paragraphs. When he glanced back over what he had done, one paragraph stood out. He made a jubilant note to himself, pointing to it.

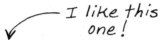

I like this one!

Why so popular? The 1950s have often been called "the decade of dull" and by the early 1960s the western world in particular was coming out of a sort of postwar hibernation. Rampant technology, changing sexual mores, a rising standard of living all contributed greatly to the popularity of Fleming's libidinous, discriminating hero.

Cook decided that, despite the liveliness of the facts he had turned up about Sean Connery and the astute film producers, his real subject was the vast appeal of James Bond to a worldwide audience. The sidelights about Ian Fleming weren't going to fit in, not even that lively quotation about the author's honeymoon. His original opening, that razzle-dazzle paragraph about how *Dr. No* began, had to go. Although he liked it, it now seemed decoration. The whole essay was moving in a different direction from the one Cook had imagined when he'd begun. As it took shape on paper, the course of his thinking was shifting, and he found himself altering his plans. As it was turning out, the essay was exploring something deeper and more interesting than just his own excitement as a ten-year-old watching his first Bond movie.

Revising and at the same time amplifying the main point he now found himself driving toward—the reasons for Bond's success—Cook wrote three more drafts of his paper. Here is the final version he turned in.

007: License to Kill--and Thrill
Drew Cook

During the 1960s, there existed a literary and cinematic phenomenon of international proportions that by
mid-decade had firmly established its subject as the most
popular mythological and technological hero of modern
times--James Bond, secret agent 007, the suave superspy
of the British Secret Service.

James Bond was the creation of Ian Fleming, a former
newspaper correspondent and Royal Navy commander who had
served in Naval Intelligence during World War II. In
all, Fleming wrote thirteen James Bond thrillers before
his death in 1964 at the age of fifty-six. Fleming did,
however, live to see Bond become a fantastically successful and profitable genre, a money-making machine that
sold millions of copies of his books and an even greater
number of theater tickets to the film versions of the
Bond adventures. The James Bond films, with the inherent
ability of the medium to reach a wider audience than the
books, had a much larger impact and made Bond a household
word.

Why were the James Bond films so popular? To begin
with, they were pure cinematic entertainment in the classic sense, fast-moving, thrilling adventure stories,
beautifully photographed on exotic locations and elaborate sets, with an assortment of stunningly attractive
women, evil villains, sophisticated gadgetry, and an appealing hero. The early films benefited from the perfect
casting of actor Sean Connery as Bond. A former athlete,
Connery moved through the films with a self-assured, sar-
donic style that proved to be a main ingredient of the
Bond character. Connery also handled the physical aspects of the role quite well--the fight scenes were ani-
matedly violent and realistic, a far cry from the usual
telegraphed punches and falls.

Certainly Bond was a fantasy figure in the tradition
of the mythical hero. As John Brosnan states in his excellent book <u>James Bond in the Cinema</u>, Bond is ". . . a
superman who can overcome all the odds and is never afflicted by self-doubt, anxiety, or feelings of insecur-
ity. In this day and age, when the individual feels
increasingly powerless and in the grip of forces beyond
his control, the attraction of such fantasies is obvious." The last sentence of Brosnan's statement brings
up the question of modern man's attempts to deal with the
never-ending, always amazing, sometimes frightening advances in technology that have characterized the growth
of the postwar western world.

Although the public had been largely enthusiastic
about reaping the rewards of this new technology, there
was also a growing feeling of confusion and mistrust, the
feeling of being out of control of one's destiny that
Brosnan spoke of. Certainly this feeling of helplessness
could also be attributed to the threat of "The Bomb" and
the possibility of nuclear war.

James Bond, on the other hand, was seemingly quite
comfortable with this new technology and used it time and
again in the films. Interestingly, the popularity of the
Bond series grew with the inclusion, in each successive
film, of an increasingly sophisticated number of seemingly outrageous gadgets, a technological arsenal which
Bond manipulated with an amused, detached, but deadly efficient precision.

In point of fact, a careful study of the Bond films
reveals a parallel of this modern-day love-hate, rejec-
tion-reliance of technology. The Bond films always had a
set-piece where the armorer, or equipment officer, presented Bond with the newest weapon or gadget. At first,
in <u>Dr. No</u> (1962), Bond is reluctant to exchange his
trusted Beretta automatic pistol ("No stopping power,"
sneers the armorer) for an undoubtedly superior Walther

```
PPK.  In From Russia with Love (1963), Bond listens with
amusement as "Q" presents him with a special attaché
case, complete with hidden money belts, concealed throw-
ing knives, a folding sniper rifle, and an exploding
tear-gas cannister.  By Goldfinger (1964), Bond is openly
bored and skeptical as "Q" shows him his machine-gunned,
smoke-screen-equipped, ejector-seated sports car.  "An
ejector seat! You're joking!" Bond says incredulously. "I
never joke about my work, 007," deadpans "Q" the techni-
cian.  By the time of Thunderball (1965), Bond has com-
pletely accepted the gadgetry and takes it without
question.  Finally, in You Only Live Twice (1967), Bond
directly requests "Little Nellie," a tiny autogyro loaded
down with every conceivable type of weaponry.
     Bond's reluctance to accept his experiences with,
and his ultimate embrace of, the new technology is an im-
portant part of his appeal, and the audience could feel a
kind of kinship with the otherwise mythological hero.
Significant, too, was the fact that those seemingly "out-
rageous" gadgets were closely based on experimental
models, working prototypes, or were actual working pro-
duction items.  Futuristic, fantastic new things used to
be described as being "Buck Rogers" after the science
fiction film serials of the 1930s.  In the 1960s, "James
Bond" came to mean the same thing.
```

Where were some of those lively sidelights he had found? Though they did not fit into the finished paper, those beginnings helped Drew Cook achieve his later insights: they helped him understand what he honestly wanted to write about. Resolutely, he cut them. If the paper has lost some of its original glitter (like that flashy paragraph about the white dot and the man firing a gun at the audience and the bit about Fleming's honeymoon), it has gained in strength and depth by hewing to a single line of inquiry.

All in all, the writing that went into this paper takes up thirty-four sheets, not counting pieces of scratch paper that got lost along the way. We don't really know everything that went on in Drew Cook's mind, but from the evidence of his random writing, reading notes, drafts, and revisions, we have inferred the story of his essay.

The first essay you write may unfold in a way different from that of "007: License to Kill—and Thrill." No two writers write the same way, and perhaps your instructor won't demand an outline or won't look at your paper until you finish it. Still, it is likely that, at some moment when you write a college essay, you will find your thoughts changing and your view expanding as you discover more evidence. Like Drew Cook, you may find yourself retracing your steps, changing your whole original idea, gritting your teeth, and crossing out passages you cherish. And like him, you may end up with a paper to turn in with pride.

Writing Exercises

1. In one or two paragraphs, relate the history of the best thing you ever wrote: the piece of writing that, more than any other you have written so far, gave you the most pleasure and satisfaction. Perhaps it was a personal letter, a diary, a poem or story you wrote strictly for your own pleasure, a contribution to a newspaper, an assignment for school. Why did it please you? Did it please or displease any readers? What, if anything, did you learn from writing it?

2. In the manner of Drew Cook, write a short analysis of a character or personality popular in films, television, comics, fiction, or the concert stage. Try to explain the source of that character's appeal.

3. Using the topic suggested in Exercise 2 (a short analysis of a popular character) or some other topic that interests you, start listing ideas and information about it. The five basic kinds of questions useful to discovering material (given on p. 8) will help you make your list. If your list looks promising, keep writing—it might turn into a finished paper.

CHAPTER 2

Meeting Challenges

WRITING TO AN ASSIGNMENT

Most of us write well about whatever we are experts in, whether it be cars, football, Mozart, ice cream, misery and happiness, chemistry, or downtown Salt Lake City. Usually we are willing—sometimes eager—to write about what we know well. For this reason, many English courses (and this textbook) offer you writing assignments with many possibilities. They hope to give you room, within the broad and generous limits of the writing task, to find something you care to say, perhaps already know something about.

But what if your instructor hands you a topic you think you don't know anything about and don't give a hoot about, either?

This problem may arise in any of your college courses. In that case, you'll need to spend time turning it around and around, looking for a way into it that appeals to you. Ask yourself, "What do I know about this topic?" or "What's this got to do with me?" Try jotting down whatever there is in the topic that most interests you. Often a dull-looking topic will reveal intriguing angles if you look at it hard enough. *The more boring your topic appears, the more you will need to find out about it.*

To interest a reader, you first have to interest yourself. Usually, as you discover more and more thoughts and information, you come to care more for your topic. You start to become an expert in it. Even if it looks as unpromising as "A Defense of the Tent Caterpillar" or "Causes for the Growth of Loom-Manufacturing in Antebellum South Carolina," it may hold hope. Some writers can wax hot on a topic like that and rivet us to our seats. (For readers interested in forestry or textiles, those topics just might be captivating.)

If you can find a way to get involved in your assignment, you will write more readily. Anyone who honestly wants to say something can be eloquent. In local newspapers, letters to the editor often show many a writer who hasn't gone through college sounding off with great force and clarity about some cause dear to his or her heart, like mosquito control or the infrequency of trash collections. On the eve of his execution for a crime he claimed he didn't commit, Bartolomeo Vanzetti, though he could barely write in English, wrote letters to his son that have been included in literature anthologies.

Before you start collecting material, make sure the assignment is absolutely clear to you, and if it isn't, go back to your instructor and ask questions. Talking over an assignment with your fellow students may also help rouse your own interest in it and get your own idea-machine going. Usually in an assignment (or in class), an instructor will direct you toward sources for all the material you will need. Sometimes you can discover what you already know about an assigned topic by *brainstorming:* rapidly listing all the ideas the topic brings to mind. If, say, the topic is "Ideas of Virtue" for a philosophy course, such a list might begin like this:

> Virtues?
> Generosity
> Honesty
> Helpfulness
> Sense of humor
> Bill Cosby has this
> Devotion to duty
> Saints
> Heroes
> George Washington—couldn't lie
> My brother—saved a child from drowning

The list might go on and on. Looking it over, a writer might circle or check likely-looking ideas, cross off unpromising ones. Other strategies to discover ideas and information might help, such as a news reporter's questions—Who are we talking about? What did that person or those persons do? When did they do it? Where? Why? How? (For more advice about brainstorming and a reporter's questions, see pp. 457 and 464 in Part Seven.)

Exploring an assigned topic with an open mind is the best way to find out whether it is truly a mind-deadener or (more likely) has fascinating angles in it. For finding material, we will have more suggestions for you in Part Two of this book, "A Writer's Resources."

WRITING TO A DEADLINE

In college, as in journalism and in the world of business, an assignment is usually due on a fixed date. For some people, fixed dates are dragons. Every college instructor is familiar with the chronic procrastinator, the student who, even without having a serious illness or a death in the family, can never turn in a paper by its due date but who begs for extension after extension and ends up taking a reduced grade or an incomplete mark in the course. Students who procrastinate like that may have a special problem: a chronic inability to get started in their writing or to get restarted once they bog down. If you have this problem, take a look at our suggestions for getting words to flow (these are coming up later in this chapter, in the section "Starting to Write").

Even if you are not a chronic procrastinator, deadlines can pose challenges. Pressed to deliver, you are always racing the red hand around the clock. Some students believe in the value of a desperate last-minute work spurt and so always put off writing anything until the last moment. They won't begin a term paper until the night before it is due. This method may focus your attention on the job, but it can make you feel like someone about to be hanged. It also robs you of the time you need for revising and so prevents you from turning in your best work. Desperate last-minute work spurts can grow bags under your eyes or lead to a reliance on caffeine and other stimulants. Instead, you can form a few helpful habits and attitudes.

To avoid all-night writing sessions, you can set your own deadline at least two days ahead of the instructor's. Take it seriously—mark it on your calendar and try to meet it, or come close to it. Two days' spare time can do wonders for your writing. You will then have leisure to take a last look, perhaps do one more draft. You can carefully edit and proofread your paper before you let go of it.

In Chapter 1, we mentioned Joseph Epstein, who before writing an essay collects notes, thoughts, scraps of reading, slowly accumulating his material over weeks or months. Obviously, if you have a paper due on Thursday, you won't have leisure to build such an extensive collection. Even so, you may be able to apply a simplified, accelerated version of the Epstein method. On separate note cards or on separate sheets, write any points you know you want to make in your essay. To this collection, you can add any other material you have. Don't take time to recopy everything; a note card that indicates what point to make and where to find it ("Freud, page 155") may be all you will need. In a short time, you will find yourself with a pile of things worth saying. Most writing goes faster if you have such ideas and don't have to waste time chewing your pencil. Long preparation makes for faster writing.

An advantage of planning with the aid of note cards is that you can easily arrange the cards into any order. You can stack them according to logic—making points follow in sequence, bringing together points that relate to one another—or perhaps according to their dramatic effectiveness—placing the most important point first or saving it for last. And with note cards you can save planning time: your stack of cards, arranged in order, may be all the outline necessary.

Another way to write a paper quickly is to think out in your head the main points you want to make and then write a rough draft. That draft may not be smooth enough to turn in, but perhaps one further draft will be.

Fast writing, by the way, isn't necessarily bad writing, nor is writing always good just because it is put together slowly and with agony. William Faulkner, a believer in getting a job done, declared, "There are some kinds of writing you have to do very fast, like riding a bicycle on a tightrope." The faster you write, though, the more time you had better save for careful proofreading.

In truth, there's no getting around the fact that good writing is time-consuming. Allow it as much time as possible. A rule of thumb may be to expect any writing job to take 50 percent more time than you'd generously figure for it.

STARTING TO WRITE

For most writers, the hardest part of writing comes first: the moment when you confront a blank sheet of paper. Fortunately, you can do much to get ready for it. Sometimes a simple trick or a playful change of your writing circumstances will ease you over that hard part and get you smoothly rolling along.

Experienced writers have many tested techniques to get moving. Many of the suggestions that follow may strike you as useless and far-out, even silly, but all have worked for some writers. Some work for us, and we hope a few will work for you.

Unless getting started is never a problem for you, in which case you can just skip to p. 36, we invite you to browse through this list. We've sorted the suggestions into three kinds:

1. Setting up circumstances in which you feel comfortable and ready to write
2. Preparing your mind
3. Making the start of a writing job gamelike and enjoyable

You may care to check or underline or highlight any suggestions that look useful. You're the only writer who can know which ideas might work for you. Help yourself to a few of the more promising.

Setting up Circumstances

Your physical surroundings can make your life as a writer harder—or easier. Why not, then, give them some attention? In making the following suggestions, we assume that it helps to create occasions when you feel like writing and that it helps to set up a routine.

Get comfortable. We don't just mean turn on a bright light because it's good for your eyes; why not create an environment? If you can write only with your shoes off or with a can of Orange Crush, by all means set yourself up that way. Some writers need a radio blaring heavy metal, others need quiet. Circumstances that put you in the mood for writing can encourage you.

Exhaust your excuses. Most writers are born experts at coming up with reasons not to write; and if you are one of those writers, you might find that it helps to run out of reasons. Is your room annoyingly jumbled? Straighten it. Drink that can of soda, sharpen those pencils, throw out that trash, make that phone call home. Then, your mind swept clean, you might have to give in and write. (If, after you go through all these steps, you still have good excuses not to write, jot down a list of them. At least you will then be writing.)

Yield to inspiration. Classical Greek and Roman critics held that a goddess called a Muse would gently touch a poet and leave him inspired. Whether or not you believe in divine inspiration, sometimes ideas, images, metaphors, or vague but powerful urges to write will arrive like sudden miracles. Good writers stay alert for them. When they come, even if you are taking a shower or getting ready to go to a movie, you are wise to yield to impulse and set aside everything else and write. You will find, then, that words will flow with little exertion. Don't feel guilty if friends think you a hermit for declining that movie date. You may be a hermit, but at least you'll be a hermit with a finished paper. If that movie is irresistible, jot down enough notes to rekindle your idea later when you can go back to it.

Relocate. Try writing in an unfamiliar place: a bowling alley, a bar, a bus station. Passers-by will wonder what you are doing there, scribbling away. Their curiosity might cause you to concentrate hard on your writing, just to show them that you aren't crazy but know what you're doing. We have heard of whole novels written in a cafeteria in midtown Manhattan.

Write in the library. See if you can find a quiet corner where you can work surrounded by heads bowed in concentration. These good examples may start you concentrating too. Keep away from any corner of the library where a bull session is raging.

Write on a schedule. Many writers find that it helps to have a certain predictable time of day to write. This method won't work for all, but it worked marvels for English novelist Anthony Trollope, a crack-of-dawn writer. Each day at 5:30 A.M., Trollope, before he dressed, would seat himself at his writing table, place his watch before him, spend half an hour rereading his work of the previous day, and then write 250 words every fifteen minutes until he had done his daily stint of 2,500 words. His literary labors over at 8:30, he would then set off to his job at the General Post Office. "I have found," he noted dryly, "that the 250 words have been forthcoming as regularly as my watch went." (He wrote more than sixty books.) Trollope may have been an extreme and compulsive scheduler, but there is much to be said for forming the habit of writing daily. Over the desk of John Updike, a prolific writer of our own day, hangs the motto *Nulla dies sine linea* ("Never a day without a line"), a saying of the Roman writer Pliny. Even if you can't write every day, it may help to declare, first thing in the morning, "All right, today from 11 to 12 I'll sit down and write."

Defy a schedule. On the other hand, if you write on a schedule and your work isn't going well, break out of your usual time frame. If you are an afternoon writer, write in the morning. Try writing in the small hours when the world is still.

Write early in the morning. Before you are wholly awake, your stern self-critic might not be awake yet either. (When you edit and proofread, though, you might want to be fully awake.) Poet Donald Hall likes to get up at dawn and start writing poems. He says that, his mind being closer to dream, the results are often more surprising and intriguing. Perhaps you might just find yourself staring at blank paper wishing for breakfast, but this technique is worth at least one try.

Write in bed. This technique might help you relax and get more work done—provided you can keep your eyes open. At the helm of Britain during World War II, Winston Churchill usually did a morning's work in bed, reading dispatches and answering them, conducting an extensive correspondence with his generals. Marcel Proust, the French novelist, also liked to write while horizontal.

Change activities. When words won't come, do something quite different from writing for a while. Walk, run, throw a Frisbee, work out at the gym. Exercise refreshes a tired brain with a shot of brand-new oxygen. Sometimes it helps to eat lunch, take in a movie, check out an art exhibit, listen to music, take a nap, or go down to the corner store and watch the cold cut slicer. Sometimes while you're not even thinking about the writing task before you, your unconscious mind will be working on it. And when you come back to it, with any luck, something will have been accomplished.

Switch instruments. Change the way your writing feels, looks, and sounds when it hits paper. Are you a typist? Try writing in longhand. If you are an inveterate penman, type for a change. Try writing with a different kind of pencil or pen: a colored felt-tip, say, or an erasable pen. Try writing on note cards (which are easy to shuffle and rearrange) or on colored paper (yellow second-sheets, by the way, are cheaper than typing paper). Have fun playing around with the physical means of writing. Perhaps you'll hit upon a new medium you'll enjoy much more. (Have you written with a word processor? For more about computer-assisted writing, see p. 43.)

Preparing

When a skeptic said that scientific discoveries happened merely because the discoverers were lucky, Louis Pasteur replied, "Chance favors the prepared mind." Among ways for writers to prepare their minds, here are only a few.

Discuss your plans. Collar any nearby listener: roommate, student down the hall, spouse, parent, friend. Tell the other person why you want to write this particular paper, what you're going to put into it, how you're going to lay out your material. If the other person says, "That sounds good," you'll be encouraged; but even if the reaction is a yawn, at least you will have set your own thinking in motion.

Shrink your immediate job. Break the writing task into several smaller parts and oblige yourself (for now) to do only the first one. It would look hard to hike cross-country, less hard if you knew you had to go only twenty miles by the first night. Similarly, writing a 1000-word paper, you might get going faster if you vow to turn out, say, just the first three paragraphs.

Freewrite. That is, just start out writing a bunch of stuff nonstop. You might start by writing your topic (if you have one) at the top of your paper and then listing the thoughts about it that first come to mind. Or you might just start writing any old thing. Because you will find yourself thinking as you freewrite, any old thing will often find that it wants to head in a certain direction. This method of writing is somewhat like the method that Spanish artist Joan Miró said he practiced in his work: "Rather than starting out to paint something, I begin painting and as I paint, the picture begins to assert itself, or suggest itself under my brush." Don't worry that what you write won't be admirable. Perhaps it won't be, but it may start suggesting a topic. (For more suggestions about freewriting and about still another useful technique, brainstorming, see pp. 459 and 457 in Part Seven.)

Write an angry letter to your instructor. Tell that (you can think of a name) just what you think of him or her for making you write a piece of foolish trash you don't want to write, that you're never going to write, that you wouldn't write in a million years. Tell that instructor and indeed the whole college what to do with their crummy college degree. Then, having vented your ire, keep writing. (When you turn in your finished paper, leave that letter out of it.)

State your purpose. In a sentence or a few lines, set forth what you want your paper to achieve. Are you trying to tell a story? If so, what is that story trying to do—prove a point or perhaps simply entertain? Are you trying to explain something? Win a reader over to your way of thinking? Sometimes doing this will define your job and bring blurred thoughts into focus. (For more about stating your purpose, see "Stating a Thesis" on p. 469.)

Read for fun. Read whatever you feel like reading. The step from reading to writing becomes shorter. Even when you're just reading for kicks, you start to involve yourself with words. Who knows, you might by pure accident (which tends to happen to some writers) hit upon something useful to your paper.

Read purposefully. If you have a topic, or an area to search for one, set out to read what's been written about it. As you read, take notes. Naturally, the more you know about your topic, the more securely you will feel on top of it and ready to write.

Try the carrot-and-stick. This method may work when inspiration is on strike. Like a donkey encouraged to plod toward his destination by a juicy carrot suspended in front of his teeth, promise yourself a reward. Keep it simple: a trip to the vending machine, a walk in the open air, a phone call to a friend, a fifteen-minute visit to a neighbor, a TV show—but only when you arrive at some moment in your labors at which you will truly feel you have earned your reward.

Seek a provocative title. Write down ten or twenty possible titles for your paper and then, looking over them, decide if any one sounds strikingly good to you. If so, you will probably be encouraged to write something rather than let such a promising title go to waste.

Keep a daily journal. Use the journal to record your experiences as a writer. You don't want to make this a huge project; we know you have other things to do. But you might be surprised how scribbling in a journal for fifteen minutes a day will nourish your writing. A small (5-by-7-inch) spiral-bound or looseleaf notebook is a nice, unintimidating size. Setting words down on a page becomes an everyday routine. In this, your writer's journal, you might note any writing problems you run into (and overcome), any ideas for things you'd like to write, any reactions to your writing you get from other people, any writing strategies that work well for you, anything about how to write that dawns on you. Journals can be kept for many purposes: a journal to record your reading and your reactions to it, a journal to track your progress in any course you take, a journal in which to save any stray thoughts you care to remember. (For more detailed suggestions about journals, see p. 461 in Part Seven.) For a student paper that emerged from a journal kept for a biology class, see Sandy Messina's "Footprints: The Mark of Our Passing" (p. 69).

Start a commonplace book. According to the *Oxford English Dictionary*, this is a book "in which one records passages or matters to be especially remembered or referred to." It's a scrapbook in which you store any brief piece of writing that strikes you as funny, awesome, wise, or in any other way memorable. You can write it down, photocopy it, or clip it and paste it in. The poet W. H. Auden kept a wonderful commonplace book, published as *A Certain World* (New York: Viking, 1970). The goal of your own commonplace book is to give you a better-stocked head. In dry seasons when you stare emptily at a piece of paper, you can leaf through such a ledger (or scroll through such a document) and find fresh ideas in it. Aside from its usefulness when you have to write and don't yet have a topic, keeping a commonplace book encourages you to pay a little loving attention to what you read, whether it be a thought of Plato, a thought of the comic-strip character Zippy, a Salada tea-bag tag, or the message inside a fortune cookie.

Doodle. At least you'll be pushing a pencil, even if you are only drawing rabbits, stick figures, or goofy faces. Who can tell? As you sit with pencil in hand, words might start to flow.

Meditate. True meditation takes training. If you haven't had any, just sit in a quiet place and contemplate your own breathing. Listen to it, trying not to think about anything at all. Thoughts will keep cropping up, but imagine that an invisible scissors is slicing them off as fast as they can sprout. The scissors needs to stay invisible, or else you will get interested in watching it work. Another mind-clearing method is to say over and over to yourself some simple word like *om, wow, who,* or *whee.* After fifteen or twenty minutes of being a fruitful blank, your mind will be refreshed. Thoughts will come, and you can start writing them.

Making a Start Enjoyable

Some writers find that if they can just make the art of writing start out playfully, like a game, they will find themselves at work before they know it.

Time yourself. Try being an Anthony Trollope: set out your watch, alarm clock, or egg timer and vow to finish a page of draft before the buzzer sounds or your time expires. Don't stop for anything—if you find yourself writing drivel, which you can always cross out later, just push on. This is a way to prompt yourself to hurry, if your natural bent is to dawdle.

Slow to a crawl. If such speed quotas don't work for you—and some people might find them a source of sheer paralysis—time yourself to write with exaggerated laziness, completing, say, not a page every fifteen minutes, but a sentence. Maybe your speed will improve. At least you'll have a sentence.

Begin badly—on purpose. For fun, begin by writing a deliberately crummy sentence, full of mistakes and misspellings and fuzzy mush-headedness. Then cross it out and write another, better sentence. This technique may help you clear the false starts out of the way quickly so that from then on, your paper can only improve.

Begin on scrap paper. There is something intimidating about a blank white sheet of paper that may have cost two or three cents. Some writers feel reluctant to mess up such a beautiful item. A bit of advice on that score comes from John Legget, novelist, biographer, and former director of the Writer's Workshop at the University of Iowa. To write preliminary notes, he uses the back of an old envelope or other scrap paper from his wastebasket. In this way, he told an interviewer, he is able to get started, feeling no guilt about "spoiling a nice piece of paper with my thoughts."

Tape-record yourself. Talk a first draft of your paper into a tape recorder. Then play it back. Then write. Unless you are a skilled stenographer (and you have one of those tape recorders with a stop pedal that may be turned off and on easily while you type), you probably would find it hard to transcribe your spoken words, but this technique can sometimes set your mind in motion.

Imagine you're giving a speech. On your feet, in front of an imaginary cheering crowd, spontaneously utter an opening paragraph. Then—quick!—write it down.

Write in a role. Pretend you are someone else (your instructor? your best friend? a screen star? some writer whose work you know well?) and write in that person's voice. Or invent an imaginary character and write as that character would. (Be careful to invent a character who might naturally write about your topic. An essay for an economics course, on supply and demand, might well be written in the person of a farmer or a small businessperson but might not go well if written from a punk rocker's point of view.) William York Tindall, a literary scholar and critic, once confided that he had been unable to write his doctoral dissertation, couldn't get a handle on it, until one day he hit upon the notion of writing it as though he were Edward Gibbon, cool and cynical author of *The Decline and Fall of the Roman Empire*. Once he tried on Gibbon's voice, Tindall said, his own writing took off at a brisk clip.

Try on the language of a writer you admire. Spend a few minutes copying in longhand or on your typewriter a piece of finished writing by somebody else. Pick a page or a paragraph you honestly enjoy and admire. To see those good words flowing out in your own handwriting or typewriting may spur you, too, to write. But if you find that this activity just clams you up, stop. (This suggestion is offered merely as a warmup exercise. You aren't going to use the other writer's words in your paper, of course, unless you quote them or clearly acknowledge them.)

Try the Great Chef method. According to legend, the great French chef Escoffier, by smelling a dish of food, could analyze it for its ingredients and then go into his kitchen and duplicate it. In similar fashion, analyze a paragraph by another writer—pick a paragraph you admire—and cook up a new paragraph of your own from its ingredients. Substitute your words for the other writer's, but keep the same number of sentences and keep each about the same length. If the other writer starts with a question, you start with a question. If the other writer uses a quotation, you use a quotation at the same place. The result will smell somewhat like the original, only different.

Write with excessive simple-mindedness. Do a whole paragraph or a whole paper the way a six-year-old talks: in plain, short, simple sentences. Karin

Mack and Eric Skjei, in *Overcoming Writing Blocks,* call this technique "Dick-and-Janing":

> Remember the first books of childhood, with their familiar characters and simple declarative sentences? "See Spot run. Hear Jane laugh. See Zeke rake leaves." Entire stories told in sentences of less than five words each. When you face an especially delicate or difficult writing assignment, you can get the skeleton of a rough draft started by reducing the first few paragraphs to Dick-and-Janese.

Dick-and-Janing works like this. Let's suppose you're writing an essay on some complex topic, say, "Television: Its Influence on Family Life." You might begin: "Television is fun. It brings families together. They all watch *Miami Vice*. Television is bad. Nobody talks. Nobody says how was your day. They watch Don Johnson's day . . . " and so on. Now, you wouldn't want to turn in a paper written like that; your readers would think you were still in third grade. But you have something down on paper that you can retool. You can combine some of those simple sentences and subordinate less important ideas to more important ones, and you can insert helpful transitions (see p. 486 in Part Seven).

Address a sympathetic reader. Write as if you were writing to a close friend. You might even begin, "Dear Friend, How's the home town treating you? I am writing a paper for an English class that I think you might like to read"—and so on. (You can always cross out that beginning later.) If you have a picture of that friend, place it in front of you.

Begin writing the part you find most appetizing. Novelist Bill Downey, in a book of advice on writing, urges writers to tackle jobs for which they feel the most excitement. "This makes writing different from childhood," he observes, "when we were forced to eat our vegetables first and then get our dessert. Writers are allowed to have their dessert first" (*Right Brain . . . Write On!*, Englewood Cliffs, NJ: Prentice-Hall, 1984). When you begin a writing task, try skipping the tough-looking steak for a while and start with the brownie. Set down the thoughts that come most readily to mind. Lo and behold, you'll have a beginning—something down on paper. Those early thoughts may coax forth other thoughts. Thoughts are like rabbits. If one brave one will step out of the underbrush, others may venture out too.

Restarting

When you have to write a long or demanding essay that you can't finish at one sitting, a special challenge often will arise. If a writing task drags on and on, sometimes you may return to it only to find yourself as clammed-up as before you began. You tromp your starter and nothing happens. Your engine seems reluctant to turn over. In such a fix, don't call AAA for a jump-start—try the following suggestions for getting back on the road.

Reread what you have written. When you return to work, spend a few minutes rereading what you have already written. This method was a favorite of Ernest Hemingway, who, even when writing a novel, would begin a day's work by rereading his manuscript from page 1. Trollope urged this technique on any beginning writer: "By reading what he has last written, just before he recommences his task, the writer will catch the tone and spirit of what he is then saying, and will avoid the fault of seeming to be unlike himself." (Just don't let rereading become a way to evade the writing itself.)

Try snowplowing. *Snowplowing* is the term invented by Jacqueline Jackson in her book about writing (and other things) *Turn Not Pale, Beloved Snail.* When you reach a point in a writing job that stops you cold—an obstinate passage or paragraph that won't come right—you imitate a snowplow and charge ahead through the difficulty:

> The plow gets to the bank and can't push it any farther. Then it goes back, revs up, comes barreling along the plowed snow, hits the bank and goes through—or at least a little farther.
>
> I reread the earlier paragraphs . . . and approach the impasse pretending it isn't there. I want to take it by surprise. Then when I'm suddenly upon it, I swerve: I don't reread it, for this would keep me in the same old rut. Instead I start writing madly, on the strength of the new thrust. This often gets me a few sentences farther, sometimes right through the bank.

Pause in midstream. End a writing session by breaking off in mid-sentence or mid-paragraph. Just leave a sentence trailing off into space, though you may know perfectly well what its closing words should be. That way, when you return to your task, you can sit down and start writing again immediately.

Leave yourself hints for how to continue. Maybe you're tired—it's been a long day, and you can't write any more. Quit, but if your head still holds any notions you have not yet expressed, jot down quick notes for them. In a few words, tell yourself what you think might come next. Then, when you come back to work, you will face not a blank wall but some rich and suggestive graffiti.

Writing Exercises

1. Toss off a quick, spontaneous paragraph describing your favorite writing situation. Where do you like to write? When? Do you have any helpful props or special circumstances you need in order to perform? If you like, imagine an ideal writing situation.

2. The next time you're obliged to fulfill a writing assignment (for this class or for another), try three or four of the methods we suggest in this chapter—ones you haven't tried before. Then report, in a paragraph for each, how successful or unsuccessful you found them.

3. Write an imaginary assignment for this course or any other in which you try to conceive the dullest, the most demanding, the most mind-crushing writing task that

ever was called for. Then, just to prove to yourself that as a writer you can do practically anything, write an opening paragraph in response to it. If it is too mind-crushing to write a whole paragraph about, at least write an opening line. After you do this exercise, most college writing assignments, by comparison, ought to seem a pleasure.

4. Make a list of any of your own methods for starting to write (or getting restarted) that you have found helpful. Compare your list with the lists of other students in your class. Has anybody found any good methods of breaking the ice that this book doesn't mention?

CHAPTER 3

Working with Fellow Writers: Peer Editing

Once you have written a first draft, you face the task of shaping your paper into its final, most readable form. How do you know what needs improving and changing? You may in fact be quite pleased with your draft as it stands and feel reluctant to imagine that it needs anything further done to it. At this point you may be wise to submit your paper to other student writers—your peers.

For many student writers, it comes as a pleasant surprise to find how genuinely helpful fellow students can be. Asked to read an early draft, they respond to a paper, signal strengths in it, and offer constructive suggestions. In doing so, they explicitly guide a writer in revising. When you are the writer, this process gives you a very real sense of having a living, breathing, supportive audience nearby.

Some instructors make peer evaluation a regular part of a course. They ask students to form small groups—often three or four people—and to read and respond to one another's writing in class. Other instructors ask that the reading and responding be done at home. In some classes, each member of the small group receives a photocopy of the writer's first draft, marks it up, and returns it to the instructor. By this system the instructor monitors the whole process, collects all the comments, and passes them on to the writer to use in revising the draft. Giving reactions to other writers becomes part of each student's process of learning to write better. In fact, students are graded not only on their writing but also on their skill as editors. Often the instructor will ask the student who gets the comments to grade the commentators or at least give them written responses in return. As a rule, all comments on a paper are set down in writing, not merely discussed in class. And so, when the author of the paper goes home to revise it, she or he has a record of the suggestions and can think each one over carefully.

If your instructor does not require peer editing, you can arrange it on your own. Enlist one or more peers to read your work and comment on it. You can provide the same service in return. Should the students you recruit be willing to read and react but reluctant to write comments for you, at least you can have them go through your draft with you, pointing out what they distrust—and admire. If you work that way, be sure you write down any suggestions any reader makes. Otherwise you may forget them by the time you're ready to revise.

SERVING AS A READER

What does it take to be a helpful, supportive reader? Once you see what such a reader goes through and serve as a reader and commentator yourself, perhaps you'll better appreciate any reactions you get to your own writing.

It might go without saying, but we'll say this anyway: approach your fellow writer's work in a friendly way. Remember, you aren't out to pass godlike judgment on your peer's effort ("What confused garbage!"). Your purpose is to give honest, intelligent appreciation—to help make the other writer aware of what's written right, not only what's written wrong. When you find fault, you can do so by making impartial observations—statements that nobody can deny. A judgmental way to criticize might be "This paper is confused. It keeps saying the same thing over and over again." But a more useful comment might be more specific: "Paragraph five makes the same point as paragraphs two and three" (which observation suggests that two of the three paragraphs might be eliminated).

Your job isn't merely to notice misspelled words or misused semicolons (although it can't hurt to signal any that you see). Bend your mind to deeper matters: to what the writer is driving at, to the sequence of ideas, to the apparent truth or falsehood of the observations, to the quantity and quality of any evidence, to the coherence or unity of the paper as a whole.

For help in looking for things like that, skim the following checklist of reader's questions. Not all these points will apply to every paper. We've given more questions here than you'll usually want to ask.

FIRST QUESTIONS

What is my first reaction to this paper?

What is this writer trying to tell me? What does he or she most want me to learn?

What are this paper's greatest strengths?

Does it have any major weaknesses?

QUESTIONS ON MEANING

Do I understand everything? Is there any information missing from this draft that I still need to know?

Is what this paper tells me worth saying, or does it only belabor the obvious? Does it tell me anything I didn't know before?

Is the writer trying to cover too much territory? Too little?

Does any point need to be more fully explained or illustrated?

When I come to the end, do I find that the paper has promised me anything it hasn't delivered?

Could this paper use a down-to-the-ground revision? Would it benefit from a different topic altogether—one the writer perhaps touches but doesn't deal with?

QUESTIONS ON ORGANIZATION

Has the writer begun in such a way that I'm interested? Am I quickly drawn into the paper's main idea? Or can I find, at some point later in the paper, a better possible beginning?

Does the paper have one main idea, or does it struggle to handle more than one? Would the main idea stand out better if anything were removed?

Might the ideas in the paper be more effectively rearranged in a different order? Do any ideas belong together that now seem too far apart?

Does the writer keep to one point of view—one angle of seeing? (If he starts out writing as a college student, does he switch to when he was a boy without telling me? If he starts out as an enemy of smoking, does he end up as an advocate?)

Does the ending seem deliberate, as if the writer meant to conclude at this point? Or does the writer seem merely to have run out of gas? If so, what can the writer do to write a stronger conclusion?

QUESTIONS ON LANGUAGE AND WRITING STRATEGIES

Do I feel this paper addresses *me?* Or does the writer appear to have no idea who might be reading the paper?

At any point in the paper, do I find myself disliking or objecting to a statement the writer makes, to a word or a phrase with which I'm not in sympathy? Should this part be kept, whether or not I object, or should it be changed?

Does the draft contain anything that distracts me, that seems unnecessary, that might be struck?

Do I get bored at any point and want to tune out? What might the writer do to make me want to keep reading?

Can I follow the writer's ideas easily? Does the paper need transitions (words and phrases that connect), and if it does, at what places?

Does the language of this paper stay up in the clouds of generality, referring always to *agricultural commodities* and *legality*, never to *pigs' feet* and *parking tickets?* If so, where and how might the writer come down to earth and get specific?

Do I understand all the words the writer uses, or are there any specialized words (such as scientific words or dialect) whose meaning needs to be made clearer?

LAST QUESTION

Now that I have lived with this paper for a while and looked at it closely, how well does it work for me?

To show the author just where you had a reaction, write comments on the margins of the paper. Then at the end write some overall comment, making any major, general suggestions. Let your final comment sum up the paper's strong and weak points. It can hardly be all good or all bad. Vague blame or vague praise won't help the writer. Don't say, "I liked this essay a lot because I can relate to it." True, such a response might be better than nothing: it might make the author feel glad. But "That example in paragraph nine clarified the whole point of the paper for me" might make the author feel glad for good reason.

What does a helpful overall comment look like? Here is the way Maria Mendez responded to a draft of a paper by Jill Walker that ended up being titled "Euthanasia and the Law":

> Jill—
>
> The topic of this paper interested me a lot, because we had a case of euthanasia in our neighborhood. I didn't realize at first what your topic was—maybe the title "Life and Death" didn't say it to me. Your paper is full of good ideas and facts—like the Hemlock Society to help mercy-killing. I got lost when you start talking about advances in modern medicine (paragraph 6) but don't finish the idea. To go into modern medicine thoroughly would take a lot more room. Maybe euthanasia is enough to cover in five pages. Also, I don't know everything you're mentioning ("traditional attitudes toward life and death"). I could have used an explanation there— I'm from a different tradition. On the whole, your paper is solid and is going to make us agree with you.
>
> Maria

LEARNING AS A WRITER

You, the writer whose work is in the spotlight, will probably find you can't just sit back and enjoy your fans' reactions. To extract all the usefulness from the process of peer reviewing, you'll need to play an active part in discussing your work. Probably your readers will give you many more specific reactions if you question them, directing their attention to places in your paper where you especially want insights. This will help them do a good job for you. Get at specific issues, get at the *whys* behind their responses. Ask pointed questions like these *in writing* for your critics to think about:

> When you read my conclusion, are you convinced that I'm arguing for the one right solution to this problem? Can you imagine any better solution?
>
> Paragraph four looks skimpy—only two short sentences. What could I do to make it longer?

How clear is my purpose? Can you sum up what I'm trying to say? What steps can I take to make my main point hit home to you?

You may already know that something is wrong with your early draft. Express any doubts you have. Point out to your readers what parts you found difficult to write. Ask them what *they* would do about any deficiencies.

The best editors are sympathetic but tough. Ask yours not to be too easy on you. Let them know that when you go back to your paper it will not be merely to make cosmetic repairs but, if need be, to make deep structural changes in what you have written. You might even get, from their reactions, new ideas you didn't have before. They may also have some tips about where to find more, and more valuable, material.

Occasionally students worry that asking another student, no wiser or brighter than themselves, to criticize their work is like asking the blind to lead the blind. It's true that you have to accept such help judiciously. Sometimes it will strike a reader that something is wrong with a piece of writing. Not wanting to seem unhelpful, the reader—although not knowing a surefire remedy—will make a suggestion anyway to show that he or she is trying to help. You want to be wary about following all the suggestions you receive. While some of them may help, others may lead down a dead-end street. At times when a reader finds fault with your work, you may want to make some change but not necessarily the very change your critic suggests.

Make a list of the suggestions you receive. You may find that some will cancel out others. Let your instincts operate: do any of the suggestions seem worth trying? The important thing in taking advice and suggestions is to listen to your critics but not be a slave to them. You have to feel that, after all, you're the boss.

It takes self-trust to take criticism with profit. The final decision about whether or not to act on the advice you get from your fellow students is solely up to you. If you feel that one person's suggestions have not helped at all, you would be wise to get a second opinion, and maybe a third. When several of your readers disagree, only you can decide whose suggestions to follow.

A PEER EDITOR IN ACTION

The following brief history points out how effectively a fellow student can help a revision. First, consider this early draft of an opening paragraph for the essay "Why Don't More People Donate Their Bodies to Science?" by Dana Falk, writing in a tandem course in English and sociology.

```
The question of why more organs and body parts are
not donated "to science"--that is, for the use of organ
transplants, medical research, and college education, is
a puzzling one. As I have learned through my research,
```

```
it is also a multidetermined one.   There are a plethora
of reasons that prevent there from being enough organs to
go around, and in this paper I shall examine a number of
the reasons I have uncovered, trying to evaluate the ef-
fectiveness of efforts to alleviate the shortage and sug-
gest possible alternate approaches myself. Primarily,
though, we will simply look at the factors that prevent
health professionals from being able to supply body parts
each and every time a donor is needed.
```

Falk showed her paper to a fellow student, Pamela Kong, who jumped at once on the opening sentence. "This could be rephrased as a question," she suggested, and she wrote "AWKWARD" next to the sentence that begins "There are a plethora of reasons that prevent their being. . . ." "That sentence was pretty bad!" Falk later realized. Kong zeroed in on the stilted word *multidetermined* (apparently meaning "having several causes") and called for a clearer announcement of where the paper was going to go. After reading Kong's comments and doing some hard thinking of her own, Falk recast her opening paragraph to read:

```
    The gap between the demand for human organs and
their current supply is ever-widening.  With the intro-
duction of cyclosporine, an immunosuppressant, the suc-
cess rate of transplants is way up, yet this bright spot
is clouded by the fact that many potential donors and
their families resist giving away their body parts,
creating an acute shortage.  Why is it that people so
fear giving their bodies to science?  My goal is to exam-
ine the causes of the shortage of transplantable organs
and to review some possible solutions.
```

As you'll see if you compare the two passages, Falk's language becomes more concrete and definite with the use of two figures of speech. Now we have an "ever-widening gap" and a "bright spot" that is "clouded." The added detail about the newly successful drug lends the paper fresh authority—and no longer does the writer have to trumpet "my research." Pam Kong's suggestion to turn the question into an actual one (with a question mark) lends life to the sentence that now begins "Why is it that people so fear. . . ." The announced plan for the rest of the paper, now placed at the end of the paragraph, points toward everything that will follow. In the revision, the pronoun *I* has disappeared—not that there is anything wrong with saying "I," but perhaps its omission indicates that the writer is involved less with herself and more with her subject. This hard-working job of rewriting (which continued throughout the whole paper) drew Falk's English instructor, Jeff Skoblow, to remark: "Your revising powers have grown formidable." No doubt some of the credit belonged to Pam Kong as well.

As your writing skills continue to develop, you may find yourself relying less on your peers and more on your own ability to analyze your early drafts. When you ask yourself what is right or wrong with your own paper, you can employ the very same list of questions you used in evaluating other writers' papers. And when you learn to answer those questions searchingly, you'll become your own most valuable reader.

Writing Exercises

1. To gain dry-run practice in working on a student paper before trying your skills on a paper by a student you know, select from the table of contents any student-written paper in this book and write a detailed reaction to it. Do this in the form of a short letter or note to the writer. If you and others in your class work on the same paper, compare your comments. What did you notice in the paper? What did you ignore that others noticed?

2. For a paper written by a fellow student, exchange a paper of comparable length that you have written in response to a college writing assignment. Both of you should write each other at least several hundred words of suggestions and reactions. Exchange comments and then sit down together and discuss your experiences. What did you find out about writing? About peer editing?

A Note on Word Processing

Some writers think word processing the greatest aid to handling words since Gutenberg made movable type. Others think they can write just as well with a pencil. Today on many campuses, students have the opportunity to make up their own minds about this new way to write, if they aren't already familiar with it. This chapter offers a few suggestions about word processing for anyone who would like to give it a try. Most college writers quickly take to it. Many find that for the first time, writing a paper becomes fun, like playing a video game: spewing out words like bursts of ray gun fire, swiftly changing direction, and zapping unwanted paragraphs.

A drawback, let us first admit, is cost. Most word processing programs call for a computer with at least 64K of memory, software (the word processing program and disks), and an electronic printer. All that equipment is expensive, and it takes up room. To their credit, some colleges have made it possible for students to buy or rent at reduced cost a computer with the necessary software to process words (that is, by the way, all a "word processor" is). Other colleges offer a facility where students can reserve time at a computer to write papers and where a printer prints them out. (Some facilities ask students to print only final drafts: paper and ribbons are also expensive.) What facilities does your college offer? Ask around.

Varieties of Hardware

In many campus libraries or writing laboratories, you can write at a keyboard that connects to a large mainframe computer system. Within its mighty brain, this college-wide behemoth stores a word processing program. If you write at an individual workstation, two kinds of computer may serve: a PC (or personal computer) and a dedicated word processor (or "small office system," such as the IBM Displaywriter or the DECmate). The first of these, the PC, is more familiar to most computer users. To process words, it needs software—that is, a disk containing a program sold under trade names such as WordStar (a popular program that takes some practice to use), Letter Perfect, Screenwriter

43

II, or the Bank Street Writer (this last one is a program written simply enough for schoolchildren to use). To make these programs work, you have to learn a series of commands. This may seem intimidating, but anyone who can learn to type, it is safe to say, can learn to use a word processor.

The other kind of computer, the dedicated word processor, is designed especially for its purpose. It sports keys specially reserved for certain commands (with the names of the commands lettered on them: Cut, Paste, Upper Case, Underline, Bold Face, Delete Word, Delete Character). These specialized keys make it unnecessary to learn a great number of special commands. Such a computer is designed to be used in offices by secretaries, who need only brief training. It costs more than a PC, and most devoted hackers (or computer lovers) find it a more boring thing, for it is limited in what it can do. With a PC, you can tackle all sorts of tasks—even balance your checkbook, play video games, or chart your biorhythms; but with a dedicated word processor, all you can do is the few jobs it's dedicated to. It is easy to learn, but it keeps giving you cumbersome instructions even when you don't need them anymore. As one professional systems analyst, Max ben Aaron, has remarked, "It's like trying to ride an adult bike with training wheels."

Printers usually come in two varieties: daisy wheel printers, whose printing is hard to tell from an electric typewriter's, and dot matrix printers, which form characters out of tiny dots. The printing of most dot matrix printers is a little harder to read, although some can be instructed to strike each letter twice, producing darker and more solid-looking copy. They're faster than daisy wheel printers, and they cost less. Newer than either of these traditional printers, expensive high-speed printers now spray ink or use laser beams to produce work of handsome letter quality.

What Is Word Processing Like?

"Everything you write comes out in a state of flux!" one writer complained, on first trying word processing, and went back to his typewriter. At first, for a writer accustomed to typing or pushing a pen, word processing may seem unnerving. You don't place marks directly on paper, where they stay put, to be corrected only by erasing or crossing out and rewriting or retyping. You arrange words in easily altered structures visible on a screen—or only partially visible. Because most screens display only about twenty-four lines at a time, some as few as sixteen, there will be parts of what you write that you won't be able to reread without summoning, or "scrolling," your work backward or forward. What the writer directly produces is a set of orders for a printer to obey.

Word processing might seem ideal for any writer who, like poet Gowan McGland in the film *Reuben, Reuben,* maintains that what he hates most about writing is the paperwork. But paper is still an essential element in the process— it is where the words end up. Besides, as a piece of writing goes through successive drafts, from time to time the writer may want the computer to print it out as hard copy (computerese for words on paper).

An advantage in word processing is that you can throw down thoughts not in a strict sequence, but in whatever order they come to mind. Then you can move them around and arrange them as seems best. Of course, you can do this kind of planning and revising with paper and scissors, too, but word processors encourage it. They enable you to write an outline, then flesh it out on screen, working on it until it turns into a finished essay before your eyes. The process is a little like making a stew, adding an ingredient at a time, stirring and blending and cooking everything to a consistent thickness, all in the same pot. Without retyping or recopying, you can pick something up—a word, a phrase, a paragraph, several paragraphs, a few pages—and set it down elsewhere in a better place. When you come across additional material, you can squeeze it right in where you want it, again without recopying. If you want to change a word throughout what you are writing, you tell the computer to search out that word and replace it each time it occurs. Unlike people who type on typewriters, writers who write with word processors may become more willing to draft quickly, less fearful of making mistakes.

And yet some college writers testify that a word processor makes them care more about getting things letter-perfect. Computers are sticklers for accuracy. Some students also find that to write in front of a glowing screen helps concentrate their attention. Fascinated, as if playing a video game, they stay aboard a train of thought for many miles.

For most brands of computer, programs are now available to aid in writing tasks. Valuable to writers whose phrases seem old as the hills, a cliché detector will automatically comb through prose and pick out stale phrases for freshening. Programs will even check your spelling for you: these work by matching what you write against words in an invisible dictionary. Unfortunately, they are no substitute for human proofreading. Even the wisest spelling-check program won't complain about certain errors: if you accidentally type *her* instead of *here*, the program won't see it as a mistake, for in its dictionary *her* is a perfectly good word. Still other programs check your grammar, show you what you did wrong, and suggest what to do about it. On the user's screen, IBM's word processing program Epistle will indicate a poorly structured sentence in red, alert the writer to the problem (or the broken grammatical rule) in blue, and suggest a correction in green. Such aids may help take the weight of editing and proofreading off the writer and free the mind for more essential things. Some instructors continue to expect a research paper to have footnotes (although the recent *MLA Handbook*, followed in this book, shows how to document sources without any footnotes). Software can format footnotes and fit them neatly at the bottom of the page where they belong.

Many word processing programs include an abbreviation feature—useful, say, if you will need to mention the name Peter Ilyich Tchaikovsky fifteen times in your essay. Instead of typing all those letters each time, you just type a special key followed by a *T* or an asterisk (or anything you've chosen) whenever you want it, and—presto!—the whole name will appear.

Some programs count words, so you can tell whether you are up to your assigned quota. Most programs will automatically drop in an identifying title at the top of each page, at the same time numbering the pages for you. One word processing program, called Nota Bene, will see that what you write conforms to any of five manuals of style, including the *MLA Handbook*, and will automatically format it for you. In practically every word processing program, you can search and replace—a feature useful if, in revising or editing, you think of a better word and want to substitute it at each place where an earlier word occurs.

Writers who use word processors have widely different writing styles. Many prefer to write, rewrite, and edit entirely on screen, not even touching a piece of paper until they print out their finished product. Some like to set down alternative versions of a sentence or paragraph and look at them, decide which to keep, and destroy the rest. Others use some combination of word processing and more conventional technology. These writers still write a first draft in longhand and then copy over their stuff on a word processor for revising or editing. Others write on screen, print out the product, see what it looks like in black and white, then revise in pen or pencil, and finally go back to the word processor to make alterations. If you do all your work on screen, it may be wise to create a copy of the old document or print it out before beginning to edit it. Then, if you ever want to go back to something you've revised, you have a spare copy of it. If you like to revise a printout in pencil, you can triple-space or print it out with an unnaturally wide margin and so give yourself plenty of revising room.

Even while you read, you can take notes. Instead of transcribing them laboriously on index cards, you can put them right on the floppy disk—lay them right into what you're writing or make a separate file of them on the same disk (from which you can summon them at will). Some computers and software programs enable you to produce graphs and even graphic illustrations quickly and efficiently.

Disadvantages (Besides Cost)

Despite all these benefits, word processing has drawbacks. Some writers, according to William Zinsser, miss the satisfaction of being able to rip a page out of the typewriter "and crumple it in a fit of frustration or rage." A trouble with writing with a stream of electrons is that the stream may dry up, if, say, your roommate plugs in a hair dryer while you have your word processor going and blows a fuse. Poof!—there goes your term paper. Some people worry terribly about accidentally erasing what they have written, and this makes them fearful of writing with a computer. These fears may be greatly exaggerated, unless you live in some place where the power is continually failing, like a Caribbean island, or where fuses continually blow, like a college dormitory. The answer to this problem, if it worries you, is to keep filing (or "saving") your work frequently. Whenever you come to a blank moment and want to knock off writing and vegetate for a while, save what you've written: transfer it out of the computer's memory to the disk. In two years of writing with word processors, we have lost only two pieces of copy—one because of a human blunder that deleted a whole page, the other because of a momentary power failure.

So literal-minded is a computer that it will follow instructions any sensible human being would know enough to ignore. Hit a wrong key and you can transform a whole page to CAPITAL LETTERS—an obvious mistake, but the computer merely does what you tell it to. More devastating blunders are possible. You can lift out a paragraph or a page and save it in the computer's memory, fully intending to set it down in another place. Then you can get so absorbed in working on some other paragraph that you forget what you have lifted out. On some systems it is even possible, when you store something new, to erase by accident the piece you have previously lifted out and stored in memory. Because (unlike writing on paper) any words you remove become invisible, you are usually wise, any time you move something, to deliver it promptly to its destination.

To guard against accidentally wiping out something you have written, it is good policy, every time you knock off work, to make a backup copy of the disk you have been working on. Another idea is to print out everything you write, turning it into hard copy, no longer fluid but fixed.

A temptation is to fall in love with the beautiful printouts you get before they are thoroughly revised. They look so flawless that you can regard them as done before they are. Still another temptation, when your work isn't going well, is to spend your time editing: tinkering with the surface of your work and trying to prettify it instead of coping with the large and demanding revisions that may be necessary. One way to get around this temptation is to switch off your screen or twist up the darkness control until the words you write become unreadable. Keep writing even though you can't see your words. When you want to reread (and edit), then and only then take a look at them.

Because your screen will probably display only twenty-four lines at a time, you may find it hard to hold in mind an entire piece of writing. In a long composition, large changes that involve several paragraphs may be harder to envision than if you had before you a stack of typed pages, which you could glance over in a flash. Of course, when you want to ponder several parts of your long document, you can scroll backward and forward; but then you have to hold in mind all that becomes invisible. The remedy for this problem (if you find it a problem) is to print out everything. Then you can ponder structural changes and other possible deep revisions much more easily and indicate with a pencil where you have work to do.

Some writers become garrulous blabbers when they take to word processing. Finding to their surprise that they are enjoying writing, they run on and on. At one business firm, after word processors had been provided for the whole staff, the management found the people happily writing not brief memoranda but endless dissertations. Will a word processor turn you into a blabber?

We suspect that it only makes you a more extreme case of the kind of writer you are already. If you are the sort who likes to fuss, word processing makes fussing easier. If you tend to jaw on and on, it will make you more loquacious by the yard, leading you to grind out vapid passages of word processorese. If you love concision, it will spur you to zap out the fat, make you all the more terse. You may have to keep yourself from sounding like a telegram.

Enthusiasts of word processing sometimes argue that to write with a computer is a more congenial way to think in language than to write with a typewriter or a pen. The latter, they charge, tends to direct the flow of words in a straight line, through the slow, laborious recopying of draft after draft. The latter process requires a writer to retype or recopy good passages left unchanged as well as those that need rewriting—a process that differs from that of the mind, which corrects only things that need correcting. The human mind seems to think in a nonlinear way. It stores up odd fragments of information at any old time, on any old subject; it leaps like a grasshopper from one idea to another idea far removed. Word processing seems tailor-made for such a mind. It enables a writer to shape easily the amorphous blob of a first thought. All these arguments may hold true, but it is still hard to carry a word processor and a printer around in your pocket.

Technology doesn't hold still. Recently, programs called "thought processors" or "idea processors" have been developed under trade names such as Framework, ThinkTank, and Freestyle. These allow you to enter random ideas and information and then sort all your material into an organized outline. Although programs to help you write a rough draft are becoming available, no program will ever do all your thinking for you. The mind of a computer remains relatively simple. Computer programs have been developed that will roughly translate simple scientific prose (after a fashion), but these programs often stumble, especially over any figurative language, such as metaphors ("Life is a bowl of cherries" or "Life is a can of worms"). One computer, told to translate the English proverb "Out of sight, out of mind" into literal Russian, dutifully complied. But when translated back into English, the proverb came out with an entirely different sense: "Invisible and insane."

If we regard computers as the simple tools they are, then with their aid we may be able to think—by writing—more swiftly and easily. More readily able to recall information, we may more readily deal with ideas of greater complexity. But the ideas have to be ours. A computer has no mind, no power to originate, no imagination at all—even though we call its spacious files a memory.

PART TWO

A Writer's Resources

With the blank page staring, the clock ticking away, and the writing assignment due tomorrow for a college course, you face a familiar challenge: What to say?

Fortunately, in seeking information and in creating ideas, you have five tremendous resources. In the following five chapters, you'll see how to put them to work for you in typical college writing assignments. None of these resources will be new to you. Already, you are adept in recalling *what you know and in* observing *the world around you. By this moment in your life, you're accustomed to* reading *and to* conversing *with people. And you have had plenty of experience with the richest resource of all:* imagining. *What you'll read in this book will only strengthen your skills at using these resources and show you how to channel them into your writing.*

At the start of each chapter, we offer illustrations by two good writers—a college student and a professional writer—who go to the same resource for ideas. Then we suggest a writing assignment: large and roomy, not narrowly specific, leaving you free to discover a topic you care about. We offer advice to help you in that quest, if you feel the need for any. We pose questions which, if you like, you can ask yourself. We offer you this guidance throughout the whole shifting, tentative, surprise-filled process of writing: through discovering, planning, and drafting; through multiple drafts, editing, and proofreading. By doing so, we hope to provide you with a trusty support system.

You don't need to separate these familiar resources of recalling, observing, reading, conversing, and imagining. While you write, you can draw on any of them, at any moment. If, for a psychology course, you find yourself writing about Sigmund Freud's Interpretation of Dreams, *suppose you recall an unforgettable dream you had, one that will illustrate a point you're making. Unless your assignment has specified, "Keep your own dreams out of this," why not go ahead and recall? Putting these lively resources to work for you should give you more ideas to express than you'll have space.*

CHAPTER 4

The Uses of Memory: Writing from Recall

To write from recall means to write from memory. Memory is the richest resource a writer has, and the handiest. For many kinds of college writing, it will be your most valuable source of material.

Often, when you need an appealing subject to write about, you will find it in your memory. This is clearly the case in an English course when you are asked to write of a personal experience, of a favorite place, of a memorable person. But even when an instructor assigns you a subject that at first glance seems to have nothing to do with you, your memory is the first place to look. Suppose you have to write a paper for a psychology course about how advertisers play on our fears. Begin with what you remember. What ads have sent chills down your back? (We recall a tire ad that showed the luckless buyer of an inferior product stuck with a blowout on a remote road on a stormy night, while the Frankenstein monster bore down on him.)

Memory, of course, is only one of your resources (along with observation, reading, conversation, and imagination). All by itself, it may not give you enough to write about. Sometimes your recollections will be fuzzy and will need checking. But whenever you need to start writing, you will rarely go wrong if you start by jotting down on paper anything memorable.

LEARNING FROM OTHER WRITERS

In this chapter you will be invited to write a whole paper from recall. First, let's illustrate what we mean by looking at two good samples of writing—one by a professional writer, one by a college student. We begin with an excerpt from columnist Russell Baker's autobiography, *Growing Up,* because autobiographical writing so clearly demonstrates the uses of recall. Searching memory, of course, is paramount for writers who set out to disclose something about their own lives and, in retrospect, to analyze them. The best of such writing, as the Baker selection shows, deals not only with what happened to the writer but also with the *meaning* of what happened.

Baker, in this memoir of his youth, first recalls what it was like to be sixteen in urban Baltimore, just beginning to wonder what to do with his life.

THE ART OF EATING SPAGHETTI
RUSSELL BAKER

The only thing that truly interested me was writing, and I knew that sixteen-year-olds did not come out of high school and become writers. I thought of writing as something to be done only by the rich. It was so obviously not real work, not a job at which you could earn a living. Still, I had begun to think of myself as a writer. It was the only thing for which I seemed to have the smallest talent, and, silly though it sounded when I told people I'd like to be a writer, it gave me a way of thinking about myself which satisfied my need to have an identity. 1

The notion of becoming a writer had flickered off and on in my head since the Belleville days, but it wasn't until my third year in high school that the possibility took hold. Until then I'd been bored by everything associated with English courses. I found English grammar dull and baffling. I hated the assignments to turn out "compositions," and went at them like heavy labor, turning out leaden, lackluster paragraphs that were agonies for teachers to read and for me to write. The classics thrust on me to read seemed as deadening as chloroform. 2

When our class was assigned to Mr. Fleagle for third-year English I anticipated another grim year in that dreariest of subjects. Mr. Fleagle was notorious among City students for dullness and inability to inspire. He was said to be stuffy, dull, and hopelessly out of date. To me he looked to be sixty or seventy and prim to a fault. He wore primly severe eyeglasses, his wavy hair was primly cut and primly combed. He wore prim vested suits with neckties blocked primly against the collar buttons of his primly starched white shirts. He had a primly pointed jaw, a primly straight nose, and a prim manner of speaking that was so correct, so gentlemanly, that he seemed a comic antique. 3

I anticipated a listless, unfruitful year with Mr. Fleagle and for a long time was not disappointed. We read *Macbeth*. Mr. Fleagle loved *Macbeth* and wanted us to love it too, but he lacked the gift of infecting others with his own passion. He tried to convey the murderous ferocity of Lady Macbeth one day by reading aloud the passage that concludes 4

> . . . I have given suck, and know
> How tender 'tis to love the babe that milks me.
> I would, while it was smiling in my face,
> Have plucked my nipple from his boneless gums. . . .

The idea of prim Mr. Fleagle plucking his nipple from boneless gums was too much for the class. We burst into gasps of irrepressible snickering. Mr. Fleagle stopped.

"There is nothing funny, boys, about giving suck to a babe. It is the— the very essence of motherhood, don't you see." 5

He constantly sprinkled his sentences with "don't you see." It wasn't a 6
question but an exclamation of mild surprise at our ignorance. "Your pronoun needs an antecedent, don't you see," he would say, very primly. "The
purpose of the Porter's scene, boys, is to provide comic relief from the
horror, don't you see."

Late in the year we tackled the informal essay. "The essay, don't you 7
see, is the . . ." My mind went numb. Of all forms of writing, none seemed
so boring as the essay. Naturally we would have to write informal essays.
Mr. Fleagle distributed a homework sheet offering us a choice of topics.
None was quite so simpleminded as "What I Did on My Summer Vacation,"
but most seemed to be almost as dull. I took the list home and dawdled
until the night before the essay was due. Sprawled on the sofa, I finally
faced up to the grim task, took the list out of my notebook, and scanned
it. The topic on which my eye stopped was "The Art of Eating Spaghetti."

This title produced an extraordinary sequence of mental images. Surg- 8
ing up out of the depths of memory came a vivid recollection of a night in
Belleville when all of us were seated around the supper table—Uncle Allen,
my mother, Uncle Charlie, Doris, Uncle Hal—and Aunt Pat served spaghetti
for supper. Spaghetti was an exotic treat in those days. Neither Doris nor
I had ever eaten spaghetti, and none of the adults had enough experience
to be good at it. All the good humor of Uncle Allen's house reawoke in my
mind as I recalled the laughing arguments we had that night about the
socially respectable method for moving spaghetti from plate to mouth.

Suddenly I wanted to write about that, about the warmth and good 9
feeling of it, but I wanted to put it down simply for my own joy, not for
Mr. Fleagle. It was a moment I wanted to recapture and hold for myself. I
wanted to relive the pleasure of an evening at New Street. To write it as I
wanted, however, would violate all the rules of formal composition I'd
learned in school, and Mr. Fleagle would surely give it a failing grade. Never
mind. I would write something else for Mr. Fleagle after I had written this
thing for myself.

When I finished it the night was half gone and there was no time left 10
to compose a proper, respectable essay for Mr. Fleagle. There was no choice
next morning but to turn in my private reminiscence of Belleville. Two
days passed before Mr. Fleagle returned the graded papers, and he returned
everyone's but mine. I was bracing myself for a command to report to Mr.
Fleagle immediately after school for discipline when I saw him lift my paper
from his desk and rap for the class's attention.

"Now, boys," he said, "I want to read you an essay. This is titled 'The 11
Art of Eating Spaghetti.' "

And he started to read. My words! He was reading *my words* out loud 12
to the entire class. What's more, the entire class was listening. Listening
attentively. Then somebody laughed, then the entire class was laughing, and
not in contempt and ridicule, but with openhearted enjoyment. Even Mr.
Fleagle stopped two or three times to repress a small prim smile.

I did my best to avoid showing pleasure, but what I was feeling was 13
pure ecstasy at this startling demonstration that my words had the power
to make people laugh. In the eleventh grade, at the eleventh hour as it
were, I had discovered a calling. It was the happiest moment of my entire

school career. When Mr. Fleagle finished he put the final seal on my happiness by saying, "Now that, boys, is an essay, don't you see. It's—don't you see—it's of the very essence of the essay, don't you see. Congratulations, Mr. Baker."

For the first time, light shone on a possibility. It wasn't a very heartening   14 possibility, to be sure. Writing couldn't lead to a job after high school, and it was hardly honest work, but Mr. Fleagle had opened a door for me. After that I ranked Mr. Fleagle among the finest teachers in the school.

This forthright recollection can speak for itself, but here are questions to help you see how Baker has written it and what central meaning he is driving at.

Questions to Start You Thinking

1. In your own words, state what Baker believes he learned in the eleventh grade about the art of writing. What incidents or statements help identify this lesson for readers of the essay? Tell what lesson, if any, you learned from the essay.

2. What is the effect, in paragraph 3, of Baker's many repetitions of the words *prim* and *primly?* What other devices does Baker use to make vivid his characterization of Mr. Fleagle? Why do you think the author uses so much space to portray his teacher?

3. What does the quotation from *Macbeth* add to Baker's account? Had the quotation been omitted, what would have been lost?

The next essay was written by a student, Robert Schreiner. He was asked to recall a significant event from his childhood. Notice the vividness of the details he includes. As you read and ponder Schreiner's recollection, pick out those details that bring the incident alive for you.

WHAT IS A HUNTER?

ROBERT G. SCHREINER

What is a hunter? This is a simple question with a relatively straight-   1 forward answer. A hunter is, according to *Webster's New Collegiate Dictionary,* a person that hunts game (game being various types of animals hunted or pursued for various reasons). However, a question that is just as simple but without such a straightforward answer is What characteristics make up a hunter? As a child, I had always considered the most important aspect of the hunter's person to be his ability to use a rifle, bow, or whatever weapon was appropriate to the type of hunting being done. Having many relatives in rural areas of Virginia and Kansas, I had been exposed to rifles a great deal. I had done extensive target shooting and considered myself to be quite proficient in the use of firearms. I had never been hunting, but

I had always thought that since I could fire a rifle accurately I would make a good hunter.

One Christmas holiday, while we were visiting our grandparents in 2 Kansas, my grandfather asked me if I wanted to go jackrabbit hunting with him. I eagerly accepted, anxious to show off my prowess with a rifle. A younger cousin of mine also wanted to come, so we all went out into the garage, loaded two .22 caliber rifles and a 20-gauge shotgun, hopped into the pickup truck, and drove out of town. It had snowed the night before and to either side of the narrow road swept six-foot-deep powdery drifts. The wind twirled the fine crystalline snow into whirling vortexes that bounced along the icy road and sprayed snow into the open windows of the pickup. As we drove, my grandfather gave us some pointers about both spotting and shooting jackrabbits. He told us that when it snows, jackrabbits like to dig out a hollow in the top of a snowdrift, usually near a fencepost, and lie there soaking up the sunshine. He told us that even though jackrabbits are a grayish brown, this coloration is excellent camouflage in snow, for the curled-up rabbits resemble rocks. He then pointed out a few rabbits in such positions as we drove along, showing us how to distinguish them from exposed rocks and dirt. He then explained that the only way to be sure that we killed the rabbit was to shoot for the head and, in particular, the eye, for this was on a direct line with the rabbit's brain. Since we were using solid point bullets, which deform into a ball upon impact, a hit anywhere but the head would most likely only wound the rabbit.

My grandfather then slowed down the pickup and told us to look out 3 for the rabbits hidden in the snowdrifts. We eventually spotted one about thirty feet from the road in a snow-filled gully. My cousin wished to shoot the first one, so he hopped out of the truck, balanced the .22 on the hood, and fired. A spray of snow erupted about a foot to the left of the rabbit's hollow. My cousin fired again, and again, and again, the shots pockmarking the slope of the drift. He fired once more and the rabbit bounced out of its hollow, its head rocking from side to side. He was hit. My cousin eagerly gamboled into the snow to claim his quarry. He brought it back holding it by the hind legs, proudly displaying it as would a warrior the severed head of his enemy. The bullet had entered the rabbit's right shoulder and exited through the neck. In both places a thin trickle of crimson marred the gray sheen of the rabbit's pelt. It quivered slightly and its rib cage pulsed with its labored breathing. My cousin was about to toss it into the back of the pickup when my grandfather pointed out that it would be cruel to allow the rabbit to bleed slowly to death and instructed my cousin to bang its head against the side of the pickup to kill it. My cousin then proceeded to bang the rabbit's head against the yellow metal. Thump, thump, thump, thump; after a minute or so my cousin loudly proclaimed that it was dead and hopped back into the truck.

The whole episode sickened me to some degree, and at the time I did 4 not know why. We continued to hunt throughout the afternoon, and, feigning boredom, I allowed my cousin and grandfather to shoot all of the rabbits. Often, the shots didn't kill the rabbits outright so they had to be killed against the pickup. The thump, thump, thump of the rabbits' skulls against the metal began to irritate me, and I was strangely glad when we turned around and headed back toward home. We were a few miles from the city limits when my grandfather slowed the truck to a stop, then backed up a few yards. My grandfather said he spotted two huge "jacks" sitting in the sun in a field just off the road. He pointed them out and handed me the .22, saying that if I didn't shoot something the whole afternoon would have been a wasted trip for me. I hesitated, then reluctantly accepted the rifle. I stepped out onto the road, my feet crunching on the ice. The two rabbits were about seventy feet away, both sitting upright in the sun. I cocked and leveled the rifle, my elbow held almost horizontal in the military fashion I had learned to employ. I brought the sights to bear upon the right eye of the first rabbit, compensated for distance, and fired. There was a harsh snap like the crack of a whip, and a small jolt to my shoulder. The first rabbit was gone, presumably knocked over the side of the snow-drift. The second rabbit hadn't moved a muscle; it just sat there staring with that black eye. I cocked the rifle once more and sighted a second time, the bead of the rifle just barely above the glassy black orb that regarded me so passively. I squeezed the trigger. Again the crack, again the jolt, and again the rabbit disappeared over the top of the drift. I handed the rifle to my cousin and began making my way toward the rabbits. I sank into powdery snow up to my waist as I clambered to the top of the drift and looked over.

On the other side of the drift was a sight that I doubt I will ever forget. 5 There was a shallow, snow-covered ditch on the leeward side of the drift and it was into this ditch that the rabbits had fallen, at least what was left of the rabbits. The entire ditch, in an area about ten feet wide, was spattered with splashes of crimson blood, pink gobbets of brain, and splintered fragments of bone. The twisted corpses of the rabbits lay in the bottom of the ditch in small pools of streaming blood. Of both the rabbits, only the bodies remained, the heads being completely gone. Stumps of vertebrae protruded obscenely from the mangled bodies, and one rabbit's hind legs twitched spasmodically. I realized that my cousin must have made a mistake and loaded the rifle with hollowpoint explosive bullets instead of solid ones.

I shouted back to the pickup, explaining the situation, and asked if I 6 should bring them back anyway. My grandfather shouted back, "No, don't worry about it, just leave them there. I'm gonna toss these jacks by the side of the road anyway; jackrabbits aren't any good for eatin'."

Looking at the dead, twitching bodies I thought only of the incredible 7 waste of life that the afternoon had been, and I realized that there was much more to being a hunter than knowing how to use a rifle. I turned and walked back to the pickup, riding the rest of the way home in silence.

Questions to Start You Thinking

1. Where in the essay do you first begin to suspect the nature of the writer's feelings toward hunting? What in the essay or in your experience led you to this perception? Are other readers likely to have had a similar response? Why or why not?

2. What details in Schreiner's essay contribute to your understanding of his grandfather? From what the writer says about him, how would you characterize him?

3.   How did the writer's understanding of himself change as a result of his hunting lesson? Would the change in outlook presented in the essay be any less evident if the first paragraph were omitted? How else might the essay be strengthened or weakened by cutting out the opening paragraph?

LEARNING BY WRITING

The Assignment

Write about a personal experience that took place at one moment in your life and that changed how you acted, thought, or felt from that moment on. What is important in this paper is to narrate the experience so vividly and clearly that your readers will have no doubts about the importance the experience had for you.

To enable you to look back on this experience with a little distance and detachment, we suggest you pick an event that happened outside your head. An encounter with a person who for some reason greatly influenced you, or with a challenge or obstacle, will be far easier to look back on (and to make vivid for your reader) than a subjective, interior experience like a religious conversion or falling in love. Those are memorable experiences all right, but to write about them presents large and special difficulties—probably more than you will need to face here.

Some memorable student papers we have read have recalled experiences like those that follow—some heavy, some light:

A woman recalled beginning dance lessons with an older teacher who at first seemed harsh but who turned out to be a true friend.

A woman recalled her childhood fear that her mother, injured in a car crash, would no longer be able to take care of her. (The fear proved groundless.)

A woman recalled how, as a small girl, she sneaked into a nun's room, out of curiosity stole some rosary beads, and discovered that crime does not pay.

A man recalled meeting a Native American who taught him a wider view of the natural world.

To help you fulfill this assignment, let's consider: What does writing from personal experience call for?

Generating Ideas

You may find that the minute you are asked to write about a significant experience in your life, the perfect incident will come to mind and you'll be ready to start on your first draft. If that is the case, start writing. Most writers, though, will need a little time in which to shake down their memories. If you are such a writer, the following suggestions may help.

Probably what will come to you first will be recent memories, but give long-ago memories time to surface, too, in whatever fragmentary order they occur. Novelist Willa Cather once said, "Most of the basic material a writer works with is acquired before the age of fifteen." As we might infer from her many stories based on memories of growing up on the plains of Nebraska, she was well aware of the value of searching memory. You, too, may find that early memories provide rich sources of material to write about.

Be ready for any recollections that well up at unexpected moments. Often, when you are busy doing something else—observing the scene around you, talking with someone, reading about someone else's experience—the activity can trigger a surprise recollection from the past. When a promising one surfaces, write it down. It may be the starting point for the paper you want to write.

As you rummage the storehouse of your memory, if any incidents stand out, if any now appear particularly stressful, funny, valuable in what they taught you, try reliving them—seeing, touching, hearing, and feeling them. Perhaps, like Russell Baker, you found unexpected success when you ignored what you thought you were supposed to do in favor of what you really wanted to do. Perhaps, like Robert Schreiner, you learned something important about yourself from a painful experience. If nothing much surfaces, you might want to prod your memory with the following questions.

DISCOVERY CHECKLIST: SEARCHING YOUR MEMORY

- Did you ever break a rule or rebel against authority in some memorable way? Did you learn anything from your actions? If so, what?
- What were the causes and the results of the worst fight you ever had?
- Did you ever succumb to peer pressure? Were the results of going along with the crowd good or bad? What did you learn from the experience?
- Did you ever regard a person in a certain way and then find you had to change your opinion of him or her?
- Did you ever have to choose between two equally attractive or equally dismal alternatives? What made the choice hard for you? What factors led you to decide as you did? Were you ultimately happy or unhappy with your choice?
- Did you ever make a serious error in judgment that led to disaster—or maybe to unexpected good fortune?
- Did you ever, as Robert Schreiner did, have a long-held belief or assumption challenged and toppled? Did you experience having one of your prejudices shattered?
- Was there ever a moment in your life when you decided to reform, to adopt a whole new outlook? In retrospect, would you characterize your attempt as successful, unsuccessful, laughable, painful, or what?
- Was there ever a moment in your life when you found, as Russell Baker did, that something you did just took off and seemed to do itself, and the result pleased you mightily, and perhaps pleased others, and you felt you had really learned something?

You might still think, "My life hasn't had any moments important enough to write about." If you continue to have difficulty turning up a meaningful experience, perhaps some other means of discovery might serve you. Spend ten or fifteen minutes *freewriting*—simply writing as fast as you can whatever comes into your head, regardless of whether it seems to have anything to do with the subject at hand. If you think you have nothing to say, write "I have nothing to say" over and over, until ideas come. They will come. Don't worry at all about spelling, punctuation, coherence, or anything else. Most of what you set down that way may have to be thrown out, but you may be delightfully surprised, when you read over what you have written, to find in it the germ of a good paper. (For more about freewriting, see p. 459 in Part Seven.)

Brainstorming, alone or as part of a classroom exercise, is another good way to jog your memory. When you brainstorm, you try to come up with as many ideas as you can, without any thought for their practical applications. Start with a suggestive word or phrase—"fight," "painful lesson," "peer pressure"— and list under that word or phrase as many ideas as occur to you through free association. Put them down in the random order in which they come to you. Later you can see if anything on your list suggests a fruitful direction in which to send your thoughts. (For more about brainstorming, see p. 457 in Part Seven.)

Try reading. Browse in the autobiography of some famous person. (Helen Keller, Maya Angelou, and Alec Guinness are only a few authors of memorable autobiographies.) See the brief story told by Mahatma Gandhi in his autobiography (quoted on p. 494) and what he learned from it. As you will find from reading, not every decisive experience is earthshaking—Gandhi learned a profound lesson from giving himself a bad haircut.

At any moment, one or several possible incidents to write about might occur to you. Write them down. Under each general possibility, start a list in which you record, in whatever order your thoughts occur, what you remember about it. Ask yourself whether you feel the same about the event now as you did when it took place—or has the passage of time changed the way you view what happened? Ask the *reporter's questions* that journalists, who call them the "five *W*'s and an *H*," find useful in their work:

Who was there?

What happened?

When did it happen?

Where did the event or events take place?

Why?

How did the event or events happen?

Any one of these questions can lead to further questions—and, so, to further discovery. Take, for instance, "Who was there?" If there were people besides yourself involved in the incident, you might also ask: What did they look like? What information about them would a reader have to know in order fully to appreciate the point of your story? (Remember Mr. Fleagle in Baker's reminiscence.) What did the people do? What did they say? Can you remember, or approximate, what they said? If so, might their words supply a lively quotation for your paper? Or take the question "What happened?" Think about that, and you might also ask: What were your inmost thoughts as the event took place? At what moment did you become aware that the event was no ordinary, everyday experience? Or weren't you aware of that until later—perhaps only now that you are writing about it? (For more advice about putting these questions to work for you, see "Asking a Reporter's Questions" on p. 464.)

Once you have a promising incident in mind, one you think might develop into a strong paper, imagine yourself writing it. You'll want to feel sure you can be honest in your presentation of the incident. If you find it too embarrassing to tell the whole truth, you might be better off choosing some other recollection.

As we find out in a psychology course, the memory does not only retain, it also drops. Particularly if an experience was very intense and painful, you may find that your brain has deep-sixed a few items it would gladly be rid of. So it may be that you will want to check your recollections of an experience against the recollections of anyone else who was there. If possible, talk to a friend or family member. See that person, or phone him or her. Did you keep a diary at the time? If so, you might glance into it and refresh your memory. Was the experience public enough (such as a riot or a blizzard) to have been recorded in a newspaper or a news magazine? If so, you can read up on it in a library. These are *possible* sources of material. Of course, if your experience didn't get written up in the papers, you may end up having to rely on your naked, unaided memory after all.

As you ponder your memories, one incident will probably begin to seem more fruitful than the others. When that happens, you can forget about the less promising, at least for the time being, and pursue the one with the most possibilities.

Shaping a Draft

Now, how will you tell your story? If the one experience you want to write about is burning in your mind, it may be that you can start right in and write a draft, without advance planning, instead planning and writing simultaneously, shaping your story as you go along. Such a method might work for a personal memoir like this. But whether or not you plan and draft at the same time, you'll find it reassuring to have at your elbow all the jottings you scribbled down as you searched your memory.

Most writers find that being able to consult a page or two of notes, even if some of them seem confused, trivial, or tangential, eases the way in to writing a first draft. Search through those notes, indicating with a check mark or any other attention-getter which of them you think will contribute life and energy to your story. Even now, as you transcribe and amplify your rough notes, you may find a new recollection arising. Write it down. The more material you discover, the easier it will be to come up with a good, full list. Too much material is more helpful than too little.

In any case, some simple outline may help. Because you'll be recalling an event, you may simply want to put what happened in sequence before you begin to write. The result will be a simple scratch outline that you can consult as you draft your paper. (For more advice on outlines, see p. 476 in Part Seven.) All the while you plan, keep writing. When you regard planning as a writing activity, when you keep crossing out and adding and shifting things around, you can usually dredge up more and more of what you know.

Although you can organize your draft in any way that you wish, you'll probably find that the simplest way to recount an experience is chronologically: relating events in the order in which they occurred. In doing so, you take the King's advice to the White Rabbit in *Alice's Adventures in Wonderland:* "Begin at the beginning, and go on till you come to the end: then stop." It is possible, of course, to begin in the middle of a story, at an exciting or interesting moment, and then by a flashback to tell your readers what else they need to know. This method is sometimes valuable for getting an arresting opening or for stressing (by putting it first) something you think especially crucial. But a good rule of thumb, in relating an experience, is to set down events chronologically—unless you see a good reason to set them down in some other way. However you proceed, the sequence of events has to be clear. You'll need transitions of time—at least brief phrases that tell when each event took place ("last Saturday," "seconds earlier"). (For more advice on transitions, see p. 486 in Part Seven.)

How can you best make your story come alive for your readers? Look again at Russell Baker's account of Mr. Fleagle teaching *Macbeth* and at the way Robert Schreiner depicts his cousin putting the wounded rabbits out of their misery. Both writers have done what good novelists and story writers do: they have not merely told us what happened, they have *shown* us, by creating scenes that we can see in our mind's eye. As you tell your story, you might include at least two or three scenes of your own. Show your readers exactly what happened, what was said, who said it. How did the other people react? Were there any sounds that contributed to the scene? Smells or tastes or textures that you want to record? (For more information about recounting an incident effectively, see "Telling a Story" on p. 493.)

Good fiction writers, and writers of true stories as well, know how to keep readers (or listeners) wondering, "What happened next?" They dole out essential information a little bit at a time so that readers have to keep reading or listening until the end to find out what they want to know. Both Baker and Schreiner save the meaning of the experience they share with us for the end of their accounts. You can decide as you write whether you think that's the best place to discuss your own story's meaning in your life.

How should your paper begin? How should it end? Many good writers work on their endings first, their beginnings last. You can write a draft in any order that suits you. The important thing is to put into words—any words, at first—what you want to say, what you think will interest and involve your reader.

Often, an account of a personal experience needs no lengthy introduction: it starts with something happening and then the writer fills in whatever background a reader needs to know. Richard Rodriguez, for instance, begins *Hunger of Memory,* a memoir of his bilingual childhood, with an arresting sentence:

> I remember, to start with, that day in Sacramento, in a California now nearly thirty years past—when I first entered a classroom, able to understand about fifty stray English words.

With such a limited vocabulary, we wonder, how will the child get along? The opening hooks our attention. In the rest of his essay, Rodriguez fills us in on his family history, on the gulf he came to perceive between the public language (English) and the language of his home.

Rewriting

After you have written an early draft and have put it aside for a day or two (or, if time is tight, for a few hours), read it over as if seeing it for the first time.

When you revise, ask: What was so memorable about this experience? Do you get that across? Have you made it come alive, by recalling it in sufficient concrete detail? Notice again Robert Schreiner's attention in his second paragraph to the world outside his own skin: his close recall of the snow, of the pointers his grandfather offered about the habits of jackrabbits and the way to shoot them. If you're recalling a fire, make your reader smell the smoke. If you're writing about a sailboat ride on a windswept lake, give your reader's stomach the quease. As you revise, keep recalling. Perhaps there are vivid details still buried in your memory, waiting to rise to the light.

Your purpose in your paper is to show that this experience was a crucial one in your life. So when you look back over your draft, make sure that this importance stands out. Ask again the question you probably asked yourself when you began: How did this experience alter your life? Have you got something in there about how life (or your view of it) has been different ever since? Pay a little extra attention to this major point. Be sure that the difference you point to is genuine and specific. Don't ramble on insincerely about "significances" that don't reflect the incident's real impact on you.

Here are some other questions for you to ask as you go over your paper.

REVISION CHECKLIST: WRITING FROM RECALL

- Is there a place in the draft that would have made a better beginning?
- As you go through the manuscript, do you find yourself wanting to keep on reading, to see what happens next?
- If there is dialogue, does it have the ring of real speech? Read it aloud. Try it on a friend.
- If the events are not recorded in chronological order, is it easy to follow the organization you have chosen? Do transitions of time make the sequence of events clear?

- Do you stick to the point? Does the draft contain extraneous thoughts, ideas, or events that ought to be struck out? (Draw a single line through any such wandering prose.)
- Have you paid enough attention to what is most dramatic, instructive, or revealing?

In the light of the answers to the questions you have asked yourself, rewrite. Keep at it until you know you've told your story and recorded its impact as well as you know how. This may take more than one new draft. It may take several.

Then go over your paper one last time. Check it carefully for mechanical errors. Even the names of people and places you know well may need to be checked. Writing a paper about a remembered trip to New York, a high school student once consistently referred to "the Umpire State Building." Any encyclopedia could have put that writer straight—if the writer had had enough self-doubt to look up the name. But don't agonize over the likelihood that you might make a spectacular boner. All writers do.

When you have made all the changes you need to make, retype or recopy or print out your paper—and hand it in.

Other Assignments

1. Choose a person outside your immediate family who had a marked effect on your life, either good or bad, and jot down ten details about that person that might help a reader understand what he or she was like. In searching your memory for details, consider the person's physical appearance, way of talking, and habits as well as any memorable incidents. When your list is finished, look back to "The Art of Eating Spaghetti" to identify the kinds of detail Baker used in his portrait of Mr. Fleagle, paying particular attention to the kinds of detail you might have included in your list but didn't. Then write a paper in which you portray that person and detail the nature of his or her impact on you.

2. Write a paper in which you remember a place you were once fond of—your grandmother's kitchen, a tree house, a library, a locker room, a clubhouse, a vacation retreat, a place where your gang got together. Try to emphasize why this place was memorable. What made it different from every other place? Why was it important to you? Do you ever now think back on it? What do you feel when you remember it? (No sentimental gush, now. But don't be afraid to set down honest feeling.)

3. Write a paper in which, from memory, you inform your readers about some traditional ceremony, ritual, or observation familiar to you. Such a tradition can pertain to a holiday, a rite of passage (confirmation, bar or bas mitzvah, fraternity or sorority initiation), a sporting event, a special day on your college calendar. It might be a family custom. Explain the tradition, making use of whatever information you recall. How did the observation or custom originate? Who takes part? How has the tradition changed through the years? What does it add to the lives of those who observe it?

APPLYING WHAT YOU LEARN:
SOME USES OF WRITING FROM RECALL

Autobiographers and writers of informal essays rely extensively on recall. All of us depend on recall in much of our informal, everyday writing—when we pen a letter to friends or family members, when we write out directions for someone who doesn't know where we live, when we make a diary entry, when we fill out an accident report or an application form.

Students of creative writing often find themselves reaching into their memories for experiences to write about. Recall is also an important resource for the kind of paper in which you, the expert, are asked to explain how to do something—train a puppy, drive a car, build a coffee table, make a speech, hunt for edible mushrooms. But recall also plays a role in the writing you are asked to do for classes other than English. In most papers written for a college course, you are expected to investigate, to explain an idea, or to argue. Clearly it's not enough merely to recount a personal experience, but personal experience does have a place in academic writing as support for exposition and argument. Rebecca Shriver, a student who had spent a year living and working in St. Thomas, added life and verisimilitude to her research paper analyzing cultural differences between the Virgin Islands and the United States by including not only material gathered from books and periodicals but also this telling recollection:

> Among the first things an American in the Virgin Islands will notice are the driving and the drivers. St. Thomas retains the custom, a carryover from Danish rule, of driving on the left-hand side of the road. Drivers are extremely aggressive, vocal, and heedless of others. West Indians, especially the cab drivers, virtually own the road. They stop for minutes at a time at the bottom of steep hills to chat with friends or to pick up hordes of workers. The streets resound with honks and screams as drivers yell obscenities at each other. Hitchhikers, too, are aggressive. It is nothing to notice a West Indian jumping into the back of one's truck, or schoolchildren who will tap on one's window, soliciting a ride.
>
> The mind-set of left-hand driving surfaces in an unusual way: walking habits. Since St. Thomians are so used to driving on the left, they also walk on the left, and an American who is unused to this will find himself bumping into a lot of West Indians on the sidewalk.

The writer used this recollection to make an important point: that recognizing and understanding cultural differences provide the keys to understanding. In an article called "Sex and Size," biologist Stephen Jay Gould makes effective use of recollection to ease his readers into a seven-page essay on a challenging subject. (Linnaeus [1707–1778], a Swedish botanist, originated the system of classifying organisms in established categories.)

> As an eight-year-old collector of shells at Rockaway Beach, I took a functional but non-Linnaean approach to taxonomy, dividing my booty into "regular," "unusual," and "extraordinary." My favorite was the common slipper limpet, although it resided in the realm of the regular by virtue of

its ubiquity. I loved its range of shapes and colors, and the pocket underneath that served as a protective home for the animal. My appeal turned to
fascination a few years later, when I both entered puberty and studied some
Linnaean taxonomy at the same time. I learned its proper name, *Crepidula
fornicata*—a sure spur to curiosity. Since Linnaeus himself had christened
this particular species, I marveled at the unbridled libido of taxonomy's
father.

When I learned about the habits of *C. fornicata*, I felt confident that I
had found the key to its curious name. For the slipper limpet forms stacks,
smaller piled atop larger, often reaching a dozen shells or more. The smaller
animals on top are invariably male, the larger supporters underneath always
female. And lest you suspect that the topmost males might be restricted to
a life of obligate homosexuality by virtue of their separation from the first
large female, fear not. The male's penis is longer by far than its entire body
and can easily slip around a few males to reach the females. *Crepidula
fornicata* indeed: a sexy congeries.

Then, to complete the disappointing story, I discovered that the name
had nothing to do with sex. Linnaeus had described the species from single
specimens in museum drawers; he knew nothing of their peculiar stacking
behavior. *Fornix* means "arch" in Latin, and Linnaeus chose his name to
recognize the shell's smoothly domed shape.

Disappointment finally yielded to renewed interest a few years later
when I learned the details of *Crepidula*'s sexuality and found the story
more intriguing than ever, even if the name had been a come-on. *Crepidula*
is a natural sex changer, a sequential hermaphrodite in our jargon. Small
juveniles mature first as males and later change to female as they grow
larger. Intermediate animals in the middle of a *Crepidula* stack are usually
in the process of changing from male to female.

Usually you have to research your subject in some depth before you can
write an acceptable paper about it. You need to rely on resources other than
memory. Yet even as you approach an academic writing assignment, a research
paper, or an argument on a topic, you can *begin* by writing down your own
relevant experiences. Whether or not you use them in your finished paper, they
can help direct your research. Often you *will* use them, as Shriver and Gould
did, in conjunction with more academic sources. A student who has worked in
a day-care center can add vigor and authority to a sociology paper on day care
in the United States today by including a few pertinent illustrations based on
that experience. Or, if you are the person writing the paper and you lack
personal experience with day care, you can illustrate a point or two with lively
anecdotes remembered from your reading or from having talked with someone
with firsthand experience. In a paper for a course in corporate ethics, your
next-door neighbor's gleeful account of a hostile takeover, divulged at the last
block party you attended, might hammer home the point you're making more
effectively than any statistic. An economics paper about the recent growth of
the fast-food industry could benefit immeasurably from an incident remembered from your harried days behind the counter at a McDonald's. If you grew

up in an urban ghetto, your recollections might lend enormous impact to a paper arguing for or against a particular city planning proposal.

Virtually every paper, no matter what it sets out to accomplish, stands to benefit from apt, vivid examples and illustrations. When you set out to include such examples and illustrations in your writing, your memories can prove as valuable as hidden treasure.

CHAPTER 5

The Evidence of Your Senses: Writing from Observation

Most writers, we said in the last chapter, begin to write by recalling what they know already. But sometimes when they sit down to write, they look around the storehouse of the brain only to find rows of empty shelves. In that case, a writer has another likely resource: observation.

Not enough material to write about? Try opening your eyes—and your other senses. Observing means taking in not only what you can see but also what you can hear, smell, touch, and taste. It means directing and concentrating your attention. It usually means seeing and sensing *analytically;* that is, by breaking the reports of your senses into parts and selecting those parts that seem important to the job at hand. In writing an account of a football game for a college newspaper, you might incidentally take in the crisp, white, buttery-smelling popcorn being sold and the rough, splintery feel of a wooden seat. But you might want to concentrate instead on something else you observed: which players scored.

Some writing consists almost entirely of observation: on-scene news reporting, clinical reports, travel books and diaries, accounts of laboratory and field experiments, descriptive writing (in both fiction and nonfiction) that evokes in words a person, place, or thing. To *describe* is to render a person, place, or thing in words exact and clear, based on sensory evidence. Usually, you write a description for either of two purposes: (1) to convey information without bias or emotion or (2) to convey it *with* feeling. In writing with the first purpose in mind, you write an *objective* (or *impartial* or *functional*) *description*. You observe your subject carefully, describe it exactly, and leave your emotions out. Here, for instance, is an objective description of a typical Morgan, a breed of horse for saddling or harnessing, taken from Pers Crowell's reference book *Cavalcade of American Horses.*

> In viewing the ideal type, we are impressed most by its stocky appearance, almost the extreme opposite of the rangier Thoroughbred. The head is rather short and broad, with heavy jaw, and exceedingly short ears set well apart. The eyes and nostrils are prominent, and the bones of the head are well modeled, giving an appearance of alert intelligence. The neck is

relatively shorter than that of most other breeds, and we become aware of its decided crest and heavy muscles. It is deep from the withers to the breast at its point of attachment to the shoulders. The throat latch is not as slender as in the Thoroughbred or American Saddle Horse. The neck rises up, giving a lofty carriage to the head. The shoulders are powerful, with a considerable degree of slope. Naturally, the withers do not appear as bony and prominently defined as in some rangier breeds. The back is short and broad, owing to the well-sprung ribs which round out into the deep, broad chest and body. The coupling of the hindquarters and the body at the point of the loins is short and strong. Moreover, there is no indication of a drawn-in, or "waspish," waist at the flanks. These points are important when considering the Morgan's superior weight-carrying ability and easy-keeping quality.

Crowell's purpose here is clearly practical: to help the reader recognize a type of horse. And so he describes in detail a typical Morgan horse, not an individual, and he sets forth characteristics of the breed. His observations give us a definite impression: that the Morgan is a serviceable, practical animal—a good weight carrier, easy to care for. Writing for an audience familiar with horses, Crowell uses specialized terms: *throat latch, well-sprung*. In the exactness of his observations and in his praise for the breed, we may detect an affection for Morgans, but Crowell doesn't seek to give us his personal feelings. He organizes his description with beautiful simplicity. He starts with the horse's head and works back to the hindquarters—thereby ensuring that he doesn't overlook anything.

The other kind of descriptive writing is *subjective* (or *impressionistic*) *description*, the kind that freely shows biases and personal feelings. Here is a portrait of a draft horse standing in a Nova Scotia blacksmith's shop, acquiring new shoes. It is from a memoir, "In the Village," by the poet Elizabeth Bishop.

> His harness hangs loose like a man's suspenders; they say pleasant things to him; one of his legs is doubled up in an improbable, affectedly polite way, and the bottom of his hoof is laid bare, but he doesn't seem to mind. Manure piles up behind him, suddenly, neatly. He, too, is very much at home. He is enormous. His rump is like a brown, glossy globe of the whole brown world. His ears are secret entrances to the underworld. His nose is supposed to feel like velvet and does, with ink spots under milk all over its pink. Clear bright-green bits of stiffened froth, like glass, are stuck around his mouth. He wears medals on his chest, too, and one on his forehead, and simpler decorations—red and blue celluloid rings overlapping each other on leather straps. On each temple is a clear glass bulge, like an eyeball, but in them are the heads of two other little horses (his dreams?), brightly colored, real and raised, untouchable, alas, against backgrounds of silver blue. His trophies hang around him, and the cloud of his odor is a chariot in itself. At the end, all four feet are brushed with tar, and shine, and he expresses his satisfaction, rolling it from his nostrils like noisy smoke, as he backs into the shafts of his wagon.

Bishop's purpose, it seems, is not (like Crowell's) to depict a general type of horse. Instead, she seeks to portray one draft horse in a way that will bring him alive. Her writing, you'll notice, abounds in visual images: the horse's loose-hanging harness, the "clear bright-green bits of stiffened froth, like glass" around his mouth; and, like Pers Crowell, she depicts the horse's markings and their coloration. From Bishop's observations, we get a definite central impression: that this work horse is tranquil and happy. The loose parts of the horse's harness jingle ("say pleasant things to him"); he is "very much at home," "he expresses his satisfaction." Apparently Bishop's observations aren't detached and impersonal; she regards the horse as a friend.

Perhaps what most clearly distinguishes these two passages of horse observation is the *language* each writer selects. Pers Crowell's words are exact and literal: used in their conventional dictionary senses and capable of simple interpretation. Bishop, on the other hand, employs colorful and inventive figures of speech: she calls the horse's markings *medals*—inventing a *metaphor*, a figure of speech that likens one thing to another without stating the companion directly. She uses other figurative comparisons: a loosened harness is like a man's suspenders; the horse's rump is like a globe of the world; and his odor advances before him like a stately chariot. Evidently Bishop is both observing and imagining. (Figurative language can lend much life to subjective writing. If this matter interests you, see "Growing a Metaphor" on p. 495 in Part Seven.) Notice that Bishop uses not only her eyes but also her ears (the harness jingles, the horse snorts) and her nose ("the cloud of his odor"). This vivid description, appealing to several senses, comes close to capturing in all dimensions the living horse.

Both Pers Crowell's and Elizabeth Bishop's ways of writing about a horse serve valuable ends. Bishop affords us delight. But if we want to identify a Morgan horse, we should read Crowell.

LEARNING FROM OTHER WRITERS

Now let's read two *complete* essays by writers who write from observation: a college student and a professional. Both their essays arise from the western American desert, but there the resemblance ends. As both will show, good writing from observation does more than list sensory evidence: it makes sense of something. First is the student paper, written by Sandy Messina, who was invited to submit the same paper to both a course in freshman composition and another course—in this case, environmental biology.

FOOTPRINTS: THE MARK OF OUR PASSING
SANDY MESSINA

No footprints. No tracks. No marks. The Navajo leave no footprints 1 because their shoes have no heels to dig into the earth's womb. They have a philosophy—walk gently on mother earth; she is pregnant with life. In the spring, when the earth is ready to deliver, they wear no shoes at all.

As I walk across the desert, I look at my shoes etch the sand dune. 2 There they are following me: the telltale prints left on the brown earth. Each footprint has a story to tell, a story of change, a story of death. Many lives are marked by our passing. Our steps can bring death to the life of a flower, the life of a forest, the life of a friendship. Some of our passages can bring death to the life of a nation.

I see my prints dug deeply into the spawning grounds of the desert 3 lavender, the evening primrose, the desert sunflower, and the little golden gilia. Life destroyed. Birth aborted. There under each mark of my passing is death. The fetuses—seeds of desert color, spring glory, trapped just below the surface waiting parturition—crushed into lifelessness. Man walks heavily on the earth.

He tramples across America, leaving giant footprints everywhere he 4 goes. He fills swamps, furrows hillsides, forms roads, fells trees, fashions cities. Man leaves the prints of his lifelong quest to subdue the earth, to conquer the wilderness. He pushes and pulls and kneads the earth into a loaf to satisfy his own appetites. He constantly tugs at the earth, trying to regulate it. Yet, man was not told to regulate, restrict, restrain the Garden of Eden but to care for it and allow it to replenish itself.

I look at my own footprints in the sand and see nearby other, gentler 5 tracks. Here on the sandy hummock I see prints, soft and slithery. The snake goes softly on the earth. His willowy form causes no tyranny. He has no need to prove his prowess: he graciously gives warning and strikes only in self-defense. He doesn't mar the surface of the earth by his entrance, for his home is found in the burrows of the other animals.

The spidery prints of the roadrunner, as he escapes with a lizard dan- 6 gling from his beak, show that he goes mercifully on the earth. He does not use his power of flight to feed off wide distances but instead employs his feathers to insulate his body from high temperatures. He takes suste-nance from the earth but does not hoard or store it.

The wood rat scrambles over the hillock to burrow beneath the Joshua 7 tree. His clawed plantigrade feet make sensitive little marks. He is caring of the earth. He doesn't destroy forage but browses for food and eats cactus, food no other animal will eat. His home is a refuge of underground run-ways. It even provides protection for his enemy the snake, as well as for himself, from the heat of the day. He never feels the compulsion to be his own person or have his own space but lives in harmony with many other animals, under the Joshua tree.

The Joshua tree, that prickly paragon that invades the desolation of 8 desert, welcomes to its house all who would dwell there. Many lives depend on this odd-looking creature, the Joshua tree. It is intimately associated with the moth, the lizard, the wood rat, the snake, the termite, the woodpecker, the boring weevil, the oriole. This spiky fellow is hospitable, tolerant, and kind on the earth. He provides a small world for other creatures: a world of pavilion, provision, protection from the harsh desert.

Unlike the Navajo's, my prints are still there in the sand, but not the 9
ruthless furrows I once perceived. My musings over nature have made my
touch upon the earth lighter, softer, gentler.

Man too can walk gently on the earth. He must reflect on his passing. 10
Is the earth changed, bent and twisted, because he has traveled there, or
has he considered nature as a symphony he can walk with, in euphony? He
need not walk heavily on the earth, allowing the heat of adversity and the
winds of circumstance to destroy him. He can walk gently on the earth,
allowing life to grow undisturbed in seeming desert places until it springs
forth.

Questions to Start You Thinking

1. "Footprints: The Mark of Our Passing" begins not with observation, but with a
    paragraph written from memory. Look again at this opening and list things the
    writer recalls about the Navajo. Why doesn't she plunge right in and immediately
    start to observe? Of what use to her essay is this first paragraph?

2. In paragraph 2, how is the writer's way of walking across the earth seen as different
    from the Navajo way? Paragraph 3 isn't observation, but what does the writer ac-
    complish in it? With paragraphs 4, 5, and 6, the writer returns to observing—for
    what purpose?

3. In the end, how has the process of observing her own footprints changed the
    writer's behavior? How would she change the behavior of the rest of us?

4. What specialized words suggest that this essay was written for a readership familiar
    with biology (her instructor and her fellow students)? Would you blast this essay
    for using too much *jargon*, or technical terminology (discussed on p. 520)? How
    readily does Messina communicate her ideas to a general reader? Does her essay
    consist primarily of objective or subjective description?

Now here is another, much different piece of writing from observation: an
article that sets out to depict the marriage industry in Las Vegas. Joan Didion
wrote it in 1967 for a wide, unspecialized audience—the readers of the *Saturday
Evening Post*, a magazine of general circulation.

MARRYING ABSURD
JOAN DIDION

To be married in Las Vegas, Clark County, Nevada, a bride must swear 1
that she is eighteen or has parental permission and a bridegroom that he
is twenty-one or has parental permission. Someone must put up five dollars
for the license. (On Sundays and holidays, fifteen dollars. The Clark County
Courthouse issues marriage licenses at any time of the day or night except
between noon and one in the afternoon, between eight and nine in the
evening, and between four and five in the morning.) Nothing else is required. The State of Nevada, alone among these United States, demands

neither a premarital blood test nor a waiting period before or after the issuance of a marriage license. Driving in across the Mojave from Los Angeles, one sees the signs way out on the desert, looming up from that moonscape of rattlesnakes and mesquite, even before the Las Vegas lights appear like a mirage on the horizon: "GETTING MARRIED? Free License Information First Strip Exit." Perhaps the Las Vegas wedding industry achieved its peak operational efficiency between 9:00 p.m. and midnight of August 26, 1965, an otherwise unremarkable Thursday which happened to be, by Presidential order, the last day on which anyone could improve his draft status merely by getting married. One hundred and seventy-one couples were pronounced man and wife in the name of Clark County and the State of Nevada that night, sixty-seven of them by a single justice of the peace, Mr. James A. Brennan. Mr. Brennan did one wedding at the Dunes and the other sixty-six in his office, and charged each couple eight dollars. One bride lent her veil to six others. "I got it down from five to three minutes," Mr. Brennan said later of his feat. "I could've married them *en masse*, but they're people, not cattle. People expect more when they get married."

What people who get married in Las Vegas actually do expect—what, in the largest sense, their "expectations" are—strikes one as a curious and self-contradictory business. Las Vegas is the most extreme and allegorical of American settlements, bizarre and beautiful in its venality and in its devotion to immediate gratification, a place the tone of which is set by mobsters and call girls and ladies' room attendants with amyl nitrite poppers in their uniform pockets. Almost everyone notes that there is no "time" in Las Vegas, no night and no day and no past and no future (no Las Vegas casino, however, has taken the obliteration of the ordinary time sense quite so far as Harold's Club in Reno, which for a while issued, at odd intervals in the day and night, mimeographed "bulletins" carrying news from the world outside); neither is there any logical sense of where one is. One is standing on a highway in the middle of a vast hostile desert looking at an eighty-foot sign which blinks "STARDUST" or "CAESAR'S PALACE." Yes, but what does that explain? This geographical implausibility reinforces the sense that what happens there has no connection with "real" life; Nevada cities like Reno and Carson are ranch towns, Western towns, places behind which there is some historical imperative. But Las Vegas seems to exist only in the eye of the beholder. All of which makes it an extraordinarily stimulating and interesting place, but an odd one in which to want to wear a candlelight satin Priscilla of Boston wedding dress with Chantilly lace insets, tapered sleeves and a detachable modified train.

And yet the Las Vegas wedding business seems to appeal to precisely that impulse. "Sincere and Dignified Since 1954," one wedding chapel advertises. There are nineteen such wedding chapels in Las Vegas, intensely competitive, each offering better, faster, and, by implication, more sincere services than the next: Our Photos Best Anywhere, Your Wedding on a Phonograph Record, Candlelight with Your Ceremony, Honeymoon Accommodations, Free Transportation from Your Motel to Courthouse to Chapel and Return to Motel, Religious or Civil Ceremonies, Dressing Rooms, Flowers, Rings, Announcements, Witnesses Available, and Ample Parking. All of these services, like most others in Las Vegas (sauna baths, payroll-check cashing, chinchilla coats for sale or rent) are offered twenty-four hours a day, seven days a week, presumably on the premise that marriage, like craps, is a game to be played when the table seems hot.

But what strikes one most about the Strip chapels, with their wishing 4 wells and stained-glass paper windows and their artificial bouvardia, is that so much of their business is by no means a matter of simple convenience, of late-night liaisons between show girls and baby Crosbys. Of course there is some of that. (One night about eleven o'clock in Las Vegas I watched a bride in an orange minidress and masses of flame-colored hair stumble from a Strip chapel on the arm of her bridegroom, who looked the part of the expendable nephew in movies like *Miami Syndicate*. "I gotta get the kids," the bride whimpered. "I gotta pick up the sitter, I gotta get to the midnight show." "What you gotta get," the bridegroom said, opening the door of a Cadillac Coupe de Ville and watching her crumple on the seat, "is sober.") But Las Vegas seems to offer something other than "convenience"; it is merchandising "niceness," the facsimile of proper ritual, to children who do not know how else to find it, how to make the arrangements, how to do it "right." All day and evening long on the Strip, one sees actual wedding parties, waiting under the harsh lights at a crosswalk, standing uneasily in the parking lot of the Frontier while the photographer hired by The Little Church of the West ("Wedding Place of the Stars") certifies the occasion, takes the picture: the bride in a veil and white satin pumps, the bridegroom usually in a white dinner jacket, and even an attendant or two, a sister or a best friend in hot-pink *peau de soie*, a flirtation veil, a carnation nosegay. "When I Fall in Love It Will Be Forever," the organist plays, and then a few bars of Lohengrin. The mother cries; the stepfather, awkward in his role, invites the chapel hostess to join them for a drink at the Sands. The hostess declines with a professional smile; she has already transferred her interest to the group waiting outside. One bride out, another in, and again the sign goes up on the chapel door: "One moment please—Wedding."

I sat next to one such wedding party in a Strip restaurant the last time 5 I was in Las Vegas. The marriage had just taken place; the bride still wore her dress, the mother her corsage. A bored waiter poured out a few swallows of pink champagne ("on the house") for everyone but the bride, who was too young to be served. "You'll need something with more kick than that," the bride's father said with heavy jocularity to his new son-in-law; the ritual jokes about the wedding night had a certain Panglossian character, since the bride was clearly several months pregnant. Another round of pink champagne, this time not on the house, and the bride began to cry. "It was just as nice," she sobbed, "as I hoped and dreamed it would be."

Questions to Start You Thinking

1. Where does Didion begin to observe? How much of this essay consists of observation?

2. "But Las Vegas seems to offer something other than 'convenience'; it is merchandising 'niceness' . . . to children who do not know how else to find it, how to make

the arrangements" (paragraph 4). Which of Didion's observations seem to bear out this insight?

3. Reflect on the scene in the concluding paragraph: the wedding party in the restaurant. Imagine a little of this couple's story *before* the moment Didion observes. Imagine a little of it as it might unfold, say, a year later. Then reflect again on that original scene. What do Didion's observations of it reveal?

4. Would you call Didion's attitude toward Las Vegas and its marriage chapels sneering and contemptuous? Is she wholly negative? How would you characterize her view of the city and its wedding industry?

LEARNING BY WRITING

The Assignment

Station yourself in some nearby place where you can mingle with a group of people, a group gathered together for some reason or occasion. Observe their behavior and in a short paper report on it. Then offer some insight. What is your main impression of the group?

This assignment is meant to start you observing closely, so we suggest you don't write from long-ago memory. Go somewhere nearby, today or as soon as possible, and open your senses. Write for your fellow students. Jot down what you can immediately see and sense. You may wish to take notes right there on the scene or minutes after you make your observations.

Although you need not praise or blame this group, please do so if you wish. In any case, after you have set forth your observations in detail, try to form some general impression of the group or come to some realization about it.

Notice how these people affect one another, how they respond. Which individuals stand out in the group and seem to call for an especially close look? What details (of their dress, actions, speech, body language) make you want to remember them? Four students writers made these observations:

One student recently did an outstanding job of observing a group of people nervously awaiting a road test for their driver's licenses. (She also observed them when they crossed the finish line—in most cases, triumphantly.)

Another observed a bar mitzvah celebration that reunited a family for the first time in many years.

Still another, who works nights in the emergency room of a hospital, observed the behavior of the resulting community of people that abruptly forms on the arrival of an accident victim (including doctors, nurses, orderlies, the patient's friends or relatives, and the patient himself or herself).

A fourth student observed a knot of people that formed on a street corner to inspect a lunar moth perched on a telephone pole (including a man who viewed it with alarm, a wondering toddler, and an amateur entomologist).

Expect to take at least two typewritten or three handwritten pages to cover your subject.

Generating Ideas

Setting down observations might seem a cut-and-dried task, not a matter of discovering anything. But to Joan Didion it is true discovery. "I write," she says, "entirely to find out what I'm thinking, what I'm looking at, what I see and what it means."

How do you discover such meaningful sense-evidence? First, you need to find a subject to observe. What groups of people come together for a reason? Get out your pencil and start brainstorming—listing rapidly and at random any ideas that come to mind (a technique often useful in getting started; for more advice about it, see p. 457). Here are a few questions to help you start your list.

DISCOVERY CHECKLIST: OBSERVING

- What people get together to take in some event or performance? (Spectators at a game, an audience at a play or concert—you go on.)
- What people get together to participate in some activity? (Worshipers at a religious service, students in a discussion class. . . .)
- What people assemble to receive advice or instruction? (A team receiving a briefing from a coach, actors, musicians, or dancers at a rehearsal. . . .)
- What people form crowds while they are obtaining something or receiving service? (Shoppers, students in a dining hall or student union, patients in a waiting room. . . .)
- What people get together for recreation? (People at a party, at a video arcade. . . .)

After you make your list, go over it and put a check mark next to anything that appeals to you as a writer. What are your own interests? Are there any nearby places where you'd like to spend time? Are there any groups you'd enjoy mingling with?

Maybe you won't know what you want to write about until you put yourself in the situation of an observer. You may soon find you have picked a likely group to observe—or you may instead find that you're getting nowhere and want to move on to another location. This site might be a city street or a hillside in the country, a college building or a campus lawn, a furiously busy scene— an air terminal, a fast-food restaurant at lunch hour, or a student hangout—or one on which only two or three people are idling—sunbathers, or dog walkers, or Frisbee throwers. Go plunge into the world beyond your sleeping quarters and see what you will see. Move around in the group, if possible. Stand off in a corner for a while, then mix in with the throng. Get different angles of view. You will see more that way.

Sandy Messina's essay "Footprints" began as a journal entry. In her biology course, Sandy was asked to keep a *specialized* journal in which to record her thoughts and observations on the subject, environmental biology. When she looked back over her observations of a desert walk, a subject stood out—one wide enough for a paper that she could submit to her English course as well. As you can see from her final version, to keep such a journal or notebook, occasionally jotting down thoughts and observations, creates a trove of material ready and waiting for use in more formal writing. (For further thoughts on journal keeping, see p. 461.)

The notes you take on your subject—or tentative subject—can be taken in any old order or methodically. One experienced teacher of writing urges her students to draw up an "observation sheet"[1] to organize their note taking. To use it, fold a sheet of paper in half lengthwise. On the left make a column (which might be called Objective) and list exactly what you saw, in an impartial way, like a zoologist looking at a new species of moth. Then on the right make a column (called Subjective), and list your thoughts and feelings about what you observed. For instance, an observation sheet inspired by a trip to observe people at a beach might begin this way:

OBJECTIVE	SUBJECTIVE
Two kids toss a red beach ball while a spotted dog chases back and forth trying to intercept it.	Reminds me of when I was five and my beach ball rolled under a parked car. Got stuck crawling in to rescue it, cried, had to be calmed down, dragged free. Never much liked beach ball after that.
College couples on dates, smearing each other with suntan lotion.	Good way to get to know each other!
Middle-aged man eating a foot-long hot dog. Mustard drips on his paunch. "Hell! I just lost two percent!"	Guy looks like a business executive: three-piece-suit type, I bet. But today he's a slob. Who cares? The beach brings out the slob in everybody.

As your own list grows, it may spill over onto a fresh sheet. Write on one side of your paper only: later, you can more easily organize your notes if you can spread them out and look at them all in one glance. An order may emerge. Even in this sample beginning of an observation sheet, some sense is starting to take shape. At least, the second and third notes both suggest that the beach is where people come to let their hair down. That insight might turn out to be the main impression that the paper conveys. For this writing assignment, an

[1] Myra Cohn Livingston, *When You Are Alone It Keeps You Capone* (New York: Atheneum, 1973), pp. 18–25. For this idea, Livingston credits her teacher at Sarah Lawrence College, Horace Gregory.

observation sheet seems an especially useful device. The notes in column one will trigger more notes in column two. Observations, you will find, start thoughts and feelings moving.

The quality of this finished paper will probably depend not on how much you rewrite but on the truthfulness of your observations. If possible, while you write keep looking at your subject. Sandy Messina is a good, exact observer of nature: the details of the snake's "soft and slithery" print in the sand, the wood rat's "clawed plantigrade feet" (a technical word: *plantigrade* means walking with both sole and heel touching the ground).

Have you captured not just sights, but any sounds, touches, odors? A memorable *image*, or evocation of a sense experience, can do wonders for a paper. In his memoir *Northern Farm*, naturalist Henry Beston observes a remarkable sound: "the voice of ice," the midwinter sound of a whole frozen pond settling and expanding in its bed:

> Sometimes there was a sort of hollow oboe sound, and sometimes a groan with a delicate undertone of thunder. . . . Just as I turned to go, there came from below one curious and sinister crack which ran off into a sound like the whine of a giant whip of steel lashed through the moonlit air.

Apparently Beston's aim in this passage is to report the nature of ice from his observations of it, and yet (like poet Elizabeth Bishop) he writes accurate language that arrests us by the power of its suggestions. He writes figuratively: he finds unexpected likenesses in two things that in most ways seem dissimilar—ice and a whip. But a sharp observer, even if his or her language is usual, will pick out a detail that conveys volumes. "John the Printer," in Robert Hershon's poem of the same name, has an eye for such a meaningful detail:

> . . . Guy across the street
> from me is in the Mafia
>
> How do you know, I say
>
> When they first moved in,
> he says, one Sunday morning,
> I look across the street and I see
> the lawn being mowed by
> two guys in three-piece suits
> and snapbrim hats

When British journalist and fiction writer G. K. Chesterton wrote of ocean waves, he was tempted at first to speak of the "rushing swiftness of a wave"— a usual phrase. But instead, as he tells us in his essay "The Two Noises," he dusted off his glasses and looked at a real wave toppling.

> The horrible thing about a wave is its hideous slowness. It lifts its load of water laboriously. . . . In front of me that night the waves were not like water: they were like falling city walls. The breaker rose first as if it did not wish to attack the earth; it wished only to attack the stars. For a time it stood up in the air as naturally as a tower; then it went a little wrong in its outline, like a tower that might some day fall.

How closely can you observe? Of these two copies of woodcuts by the sixteenth-century German artist known only by his signature, The Master I. B. with the Bird, one is the original, the other a forgery. Art critic William M. Ivins, Jr., remarked: "In this original the lines have intention and meaning. In

From this memorable description we get one main impression: that the wave's collapse is slow. Chesterton underscores this main impression with figurative language. He likens a wave to things that take their time: to a weight lifter, falling walls, a tower that may take years to collapse.

How do you notice memorable details? Observe long and hard, and write and write—if possible, while still observing. When you're done observing, review your notes. Take time to think them over.

the copy . . . the lines have lost their intention. They have all the characteristics of careless and unintelligent but laborious tracing." Which is which? The solution is on page 86.

Shaping a Draft

Having been writing, however roughly, all the while you've been observing, you will now have some rough stuff to organize. If you have made an observation sheet, you can mark it up: you can circle whatever looks useful. Or, having written down your various ideas just as they came, you can use the strategy of *clustering*—you can draw lines to connect ideas that go together. (For more about this useful strategy, see p. 474.)

Maybe you can plan best while rewriting your preliminary notes into a draft. Then you'll be throwing out details that don't matter, leaving those that do. That is a highly efficient kind of planning. But perhaps you are the kind of writer who feels more confident after having mapped out everything in advance. Such writers love an outline. (If you are one, see "Outlining" on p. 476.)

How do you map out a series of observations? One simple way—and you could map this out in a simple scratch outline—would be to proceed spatially. In observing a landscape, you might move from left to right, from top to bottom, from near to far, from center to periphery. One of these methods might be as good as any other. However, your choice may well depend on what you are trying to do.

You might see (or feel) a reason to *move from the most prominent feature to the less prominent*. If you are describing a sketch artist at work, say, the most prominent and interesting feature to start with might be the artist's busy, confident hands. If you are describing a basketball game, you might start with the action under a basket.

Or you might *move from specific details to a general statement of an overall impression*. In describing Fisherman's Wharf in San Francisco, you might start with sellers of shrimp cups and souvenir fishnets, tour boats loading passengers, and the smell of frying fish, and go on to say, "In all this commotion and commerce, a visitor senses the constant activity of the sea."

Or you could *move from common, everyday features to the unusual features you want to stress*. After starting with the smell of frying fish and the cries of gulls, you might go on: "Yet this ordinary scene attracts visitors from afar: the Japanese sightseer, perhaps a fan of American prison films, making a pilgrimage by tour boat to Alcatraz."

Perhaps your most important planning will take place as you answer the question, What main insight or impression do I want to get across? To ask yourself this question may help you decide which impressions to include and which to omit. Joan Didion's "Marrying Absurd" leaves us with a definite impression that the Las Vegas marriage chapel scene is full of absurd incongruities. (If Didion had any further thoughts on the natural beauties of Las Vegas, she sliced them from her final version.)

Rewriting

What if, when you look over your draft, you find that in observing some people you skimped, and now you need still more notes? If the group hasn't dispersed and a return trip is still possible, return to the scene. Professional journalists continually make such follow-ups. Sticklers for accuracy, they want to write from observation and not trust only to memory. Your rewriting, editing, and proofreading will all prove easier if you have taken good, accurate notes on your observations. Clearly, that is what Joan Didion did in Las Vegas: she must have copied down (or photographed) highway signs and other advertisements for marriage chapels. The ads she quotes sound authentic. If you have any doubts about your notes, go back to the scene and check them.

Not all writers rewrite in the same way. Some start tinkering early, perfecting little bits here and there. Even back in her original version of "Footprints," a few sheets of rough notes, Sandy Messina started making small improvements. In her first draft, she had written:

> Each of us must learn to walk gently on the earth. We must quit pushing and pulling and kneading it into a loaf to be our own bread.

Right away, she realized that by calling the earth "a loaf" she had already likened it to bread. So she crossed out "be our own bread" and substituted "suit our own appetites." She also crossed out verbs one at a time, as they occurred, until a strong verb came along.

> We ~~moved~~ ~~marched~~ trooped across America, leaving our giant footprints.

To test your draft, to see what parts need work when you rewrite, you might ask these questions.

REVISION CHECKLIST: WRITING FROM OBSERVATION

- Have you gathered enough observations to make your subject understandable to your reader? Do any observations need to be checked for accuracy?
- Does your paper leave the reader with a clear overall impression of your subject? (Try your draft on a fellow student and see what impression, if any, you have put across.)
- If you are writing a description, do you mean it to be subjective or objective? (Your reader should be able to tell. Remember that a subjective description, like an objective description, may include plenty of accurate specific details, as Elizabeth Bishop's portrait of the work horse demonstrates.)
- If you are writing a subjective description, allowing your feelings to show, what might you do with the *language* of your paper? Would any figures of speech—and comparisons—lend life? (See "Growing a Metaphor" on p. 495.)
- If you are writing an objective description, have you kept your emotional reactions in the background? (Even though you may have observed with feeling, you'll want to leave your enthusiasm or your anger out of your written work.) Do you report only what another person, observing the same subject from the same physical situation, might see too?
- Have you observed with *all* your senses? (Smell isn't always useful, but it might be.)

Other Assignments

1. To develop your own powers of observation, follow Sandy Messina's example. Go for a walk, recording your observations in two or three detailed paragraphs. Let

your walk take you either through an unfamiliar scene or through a familiar scene perhaps worth a closer look than you normally give it (such as a supermarket, a city street, or an open field). Avoid a subject so familiar that it would be difficult for you to see it from a fresh perspective (such as a dormitory corridor or a parking lot). Sum up your impression of the place, including any opinion you form by your close observations.

2. Just for fun, here is a short, spontaneous writing exercise that might serve as a warmup for a long assignment. Lin Haire-Sargeant of Tufts University, whose students enjoyed the exercise, calls it "You Are the Detective." She asked her students to begin the assignment that very day after class and to turn it in by 4:05 P.M.

> Go to a nearby public place—burger joint, library, copy center, art gallery—and select a person who catches your eye, who somehow intrigues you. Try to choose someone who looks as if she or he will stay put for a while. Settle yourself where you can observe your subject unobtrusively. Take notes, if you can do so without being observed yourself.

> Now, carefully and tactfully (we don't want any fistfights or lawsuits) notice everything you can about this person. The obvious place to start would be with physical characteristics, but focus on other things too. How does the person talk? Move? What does body language tell you?

> Write as if the person is going to hold up a bank ten minutes from now, and the police will expect you to supply a full and accurate description of him or her.

3. Observe some bird, animal, or object and record what you see in a paragraph as long as necessary.

4. Observe a subject in two different ways, each for a different purpose. For instance, you might write two descriptions, one subjective and one objective. You might observe a friend or someone in your family (1) objectively, as a photographer might view him or her, and then (2) subjectively, as you see that person—with feeling.

Or describe your hometown: first as a sociologist or geographer writing an objective, impartial description of the place; and then as if you were trying to persuade tourists to visit it.

For this task, you might find it helpful to make up an observation sheet (as recommended on p. 76).

5. Joan Didion writes from the perspective of a tourist, an outsider alert to details that reveal the distinctive character of places and people. If in the past year you, as an outsider, have visited some place, jot down from memory any details you noticed that you haven't been able to forget. Or spend a few minutes as a tourist right now. Go to a busy spot on or off campus and, in a few paragraphs, record your observations of anything you find amusing, surprising, puzzling, or intriguing.

Ask your instructor whether, for this assignment, you might write not a finished essay but a single draft. The idea would be to display your observations in the rough. If you and your instructor think it shows promise, it might be the basis for a later, more polished paper.

6. From among the photographs on the following pages, select one to observe. In a paragraph or two, capture in words its most memorable features. Does the photograph have any center that draws your attention? What main impression or insight does the picture convey to you? See if you can put a sense of the picture into the mind of a reader who hasn't seen it at all.

APPLYING WHAT YOU LEARN:
SOME USES OF WRITING FROM OBSERVATION

Like recalling, observing can be a rich resource for almost anything you will ever write. Indeed, we can't think of a kind of writing that doesn't call for the testimony of your senses, except, perhaps, theoretical mathematics. But in college (and immediately beyond) you may meet the following kinds of writing in which observation is especially necessary.

Many college courses designed to prepare students for a professional career involve field trips. In such courses, you are often expected to observe closely and later to write up your observations in a report. A sociology class (or maybe a class in prelaw) might visit a city police court on a Saturday morning to hear the judge trying the spouse beaters, drug pushers, streetwalkers, and peeping Toms hauled in on Friday night. A journalism class might visit the composing room of a large daily newspaper to see how a front page is made up. A class in early childhood education might visit a nursery school or a day-care center to observe how members of the staff direct activities, cope with fistfights and other problems, and try to instill good social attitudes. One student we know visited the Folger Shakespeare Library in Washington for a Shakespeare course and in a term paper reported his observations of the life-size Elizabethan stage. For a fine arts course, you might be asked to visit a museum to observe a painting and analyze it.

Much writing in scientific and technical courses consists of description. In a report for a chemistry or biology course, you might be asked to report your observations of a laboratory experiment ("When the hair was introduced into the condensing dish, bacteria collected in its follicles ... "); in zoology, to observe the behavior of animals. Here is a good illustration of scientific description from *Gorillas in the Mist*, written by Dian Fossey, a zoologist who for many years studied mountain gorillas in Rwanda, Africa. She records what a typical gorilla looks like at birth, based on her observations of scores of infant gorillas.

> The body skin color of a newly born gorilla is usually pinkish gray and may have pink concentrations of color on the ears, palms, or soles. The infant's body hair varies in color from medium brown to black and is sparsely distributed except on the dorsal surfaces of the body. The head hair is often jet black, short, and slick, and the face wizened, with a pronounced protrusion of the nasal region, giving a pig-snouted appearance. Like the nose, the ears are prominent, but the eyes are usually squinted or closed the first day following birth. The limbs are thin and spidery, and the digits typically remain tightly flexed when the baby's hands are not grasping the mother's abdominal hair. The extremities may exhibit a spastic type of involuntary thrusting movement, especially when searching for a nipple. Most of the time, however, a gorilla infant appears asleep.

In a college course in technical writing, and in many occupations, you are expected to write physical descriptions of objects, mechanisms, places of work, terrains, and other things. These descriptions are usually not written for the pleasure they give. In technical writing, descriptions are generally not ends in themselves; rather, they serve a purpose. Richard J. Councill, chief geologist for the Seaboard System Railroad, turned in a report on two possible building sites in New Hanover County, North Carolina, for the use of a client of the railroad— a company deciding where to build a plant. Because the decision to build rested on whether adequate supplies of groundwater would be available, Councill wrote (in part):

> Both sites are characterized by rolling, sparsely wooded fossil sand dunes attaining a maximum elevation of 25–30 feet and lowlands ranging from near 0 feet to 10 feet. Depending upon elevation, the total thickness of the dunes is 45 to 60 feet. The surface and subsurface materials are essentially homogenous and consist of interbedded strata of fine to medium quartz sand, fine to coarse sand containing thin clayey sand and clay seams. Beneath these geologically young materials are intercalated beds of fine to very coarse quartz sand, glauconite, thin discontinuous broken shell beds, and clay-silt beds of the Pee Dee formation.
>
> Both the younger and older sites contain appreciable amounts of water available to wells, but the older Pee Dee site generally contains highly mineralized water, often analyzing upward to 3,000 parts per million chloride and almost equal amounts of other dissolved solids. As a source of industrial water the lower site must be dismissed. However, the overlying younger materials in the upper site provide a substantial aquifer for supplying large amounts of groundwater of good quality.

In this kind of writing, no doubt immensely valuable to decision making, the writer sets forth observations mingled with judgments and recommendations. Evidently he bases his observations on tests he made: drillings and excavations to examine subsurface materials.

If, when launched on a career in business, science, or medicine, you are called on to write reports, you may find the writing of objective description necessary. Evidently, it serves practical purposes (helping in choosing a building site, evaluating the results of an experiment, or studying a patient's condition). But *subjective* description can do more than give pleasure: it also can serve usefully. In arguing that a city's parks need more attention, that voters should authorize funds for more police and more maintenance workers, a writer might appeal to readers' emotions. In so doing, an angry or sorrowful description of a playground littered with broken bottles might be persuasive. Both kinds of writing from observation, subjective description and objective, have the power to change the world.

Solution to the Problem of the Two Woodcuts

If you identified the woodcut on page 79 as the original by the Master I. B. with the Bird, your powers of observation are excellent. If you were wrong, don't feel alone: in his scholarly book, *The Woodcuts of the Master I. B. with the Bird* (Berlin, 1894), art historian F. Lippmann also mistook the forgery for the original.

CHAPTER 6

The Printed Word:
Writing from Reading

"A shut book," according to a saying, "is only a block of paper." So is an open book, until a reader interacts with it. Did you ever observe someone truly involved with a book? From time to time you might notice that reader put down the book to doubt, to ponder, or to dream; maybe pick it up again, jot notes, underline or star things, leaf backward for a second glance, sigh, mutter, fidget in discomfort, nod approvingly, perhaps laugh aloud, or disgustedly slam the book shut and reach for another. Such a reader gets involved, mixes in, interacts with the printed page, and reads with an individual style. Not all readers are so demonstrative. Some sit quietly, intently, hardly moving a muscle, and yet they too may be interacting, deeply involved.

The act of reading is highly personal in still another sense. Do all readers extract the same things from the same reading? Surely they don't. *The Divine Comedy,* said T. S. Eliot, has as many versions as that classic poem has readers. The point is not that a book can mean any old thing you want it to, but that each reader, like each visitor to a city, has different interests and so comes away with individual memories. Listening to a class discussion of a textbook all have read, you may be surprised by the range of insights reported by different readers. If you missed some of those insights when you read alone, don't feel crestfallen. Just contribute whatever insights may come to you. Other students, you'll find, may be equally surprised by what you saw—something they missed entirely.

As a reader, you can participate in dialogues with other writers. Enter in and be the cocreator of the text; bring it alive. Then you can put your own side of the dialogue into writing. This chapter will give you practice and guidance in doing so. To interact with print and let it nourish your writing, you have to do some thinking, of course. English philosopher John Locke makes the point memorably: "Reading furnishes our mind only with materials of knowledge; it is thinking [that] makes what we read ours."

Reading, then, is one of a college writer's richest resources. Often, you go to books or journals seeking to stimulate your own ideas. Like flints that strike against one another and cause sparks, readers and writers provoke one another.

Sometimes you read in search of a topic to write about. Sometimes, when you already have a topic, you seek more ideas. Sometimes, when you have enough ideas, you turn to other writers to help you explain them or to back them up with examples and evidence. Sometimes you read because you have ideas you want to test. Reading revises your ideas.

LEARNING FROM OTHER WRITERS

Let's look at two examples of writing evidently inspired by careful, thoughtful reading: first, an essay by David Quammen, whose wide reading contributes depth and breadth to his many writings on science. Though he gathers ideas from other sources, he also—as you'll see—propels himself from what he reads into a fresh view of his own. Originally, Quammen wrote this essay for the May 1983 issue of *Outside,* a magazine for general readers to which he contributes a regular column called "Natural Acts." By the way, if Quammen starts you thinking while you read, go ahead and respond. Asterisk things, underline, put in your comments.

A REPUBLIC OF COCKROACHES:
WHEN THE ULTIMATE EXTERMINATOR
MEETS THE ULTIMATE PEST
DAVID QUAMMEN

In the fifth chapter of Matthew's gospel, Christ is quoted as saying that   1
the meek shall inherit the earth, but other opinion lately suggests that, no,
more likely it will go to the cockroaches.

A decidedly ugly and disheartening prospect: our entire dear planet—   2
after the final close of all human business—ravaged and overrun by great
multitudes of cockroaches, whole plagues of them, whole scuttering herds
shoulder to shoulder like the old herds of bison, vast cockroach legions
sweeping as inexorably as driver ants over the empty prairies. Unfortunately
this vision is not just the worst Kafkaesque fantasy of some fevered pessi-
mist. There is also a touch of hard science involved.

The cockroach, as it happens, is a popular test subject for laboratory   3
research. It adapts well to captivity, lives relatively long, reproduces quickly,
and will subsist in full vigor on Purina Dog Chow. The largest American
species, up to two inches in length and known as *Periplaneta americana,*
is even big enough for easy dissection. One eminent physiologist has written fondly: "The laboratory investigator who keeps up a battle to rid his rat
colony of cockroaches may well consider giving up the rats and working
with the cockroaches instead. From many points of view the roach is practically made to order as a laboratory subject. Here is an animal of frugal
habits, tenacious of life, eager to live in the laboratory and very modest in
its space requirements." Tenacious of life indeed. Not only in kitchen cup-
boards, not only among the dark corners of basements, is the average

cockroach a hard beast to kill. Also in the laboratory. And so also it would be, evidently, in the ashes of civilization. Among the various biological studies for which cockroaches have served as the guinea pigs—on hormone activity, parasitism, development of resistance against insecticides, and numerous other topics—have been some rather suggestive experiments concerning cockroach survival and atomic radiation.

Survival. Over the centuries, over the millennia, over the geologic epochs and periods and eras, that is precisely what this animal has proved itself to be good at. The cockroach is roughly 250 million years old, which makes it the oldest of living insects, possibly even the oldest known air-breathing animal. Admittedly "250 million years" is just one of those stupefying and inexpressive paleontological numbers, so think of it this way: Long before the first primitive mammal appeared on earth, before the first bird, before the first pine tree, before even the reptiles began to assert themselves, cockroaches were running wild. They were thriving in the great humid tropical forests that covered much of the Earth then, during what geologists now call the Carboniferous period (because so much of that thick swampy vegetation was eventually turned into coal). Cockroaches were by far the dominant insect of the Carboniferous, outnumbering all other species together, and among the most dominant of animals. In fact, sometimes this period is loosely referred to as the Age of Cockroaches. But unlike the earlier trilobites, unlike the later dinosaurs, cockroaches lingered on quite successfully (though less obtrusively) long after their heyday—because, unlike the trilobites and the dinosaurs, cockroaches were versatile. 4

They were generalists. Those primitive early cockroaches possessed a 5 simple and very practical anatomical design that remains almost unchanged in the cockroaches of today. Throughout their evolutionary history they have avoided wild morphological experiments like those of their near relatives, the mantids and walking sticks, and so many other bizarrely evolved insects. For cockroaches the byword has been: Keep it simple. Consequently today, as always, they can live almost anywhere and eat almost anything.

Unlike most insects, they have mouthparts that enable them to take 6 hard foods, soft foods, and liquids. They will feed on virtually any organic substance. One study, written a century ago and still considered authoritative, lists their food preferences as "Bark, leaves, the pith of living cycads [fern palms], paper, woollen clothes, sugar, cheese, bread, blacking, oil, lemons, ink, flesh, fish, leather, the dead bodies of other Cockroaches, their own cast skins and empty egg-capsules," adding that "Cucumber, too, they will eat, though it disagrees with them horribly." So much for cucumber.

They are flattened enough to squeeze into the narrowest hiding place, 7 either in human habitations or in the wild. They are quick on their feet, and can fly when they need to. But the real reason for their long-continued success and their excellent prospects for the future is that, beyond these few simple tools for living, they have never specialized.

It happens to be the very same thing that, until recently, could be said 8 of *Homo sapiens.*

Now one further quote from the experts, in summary, and because it 9 has for our purposes here a particular odd resonance. "Cockroaches," say two researchers who worked under sponsorship of the United States Army, "are tough, resilient insects with amazing endurance and the ability to recover rapidly from almost complete extermination."

It was Jonathan Schell's best-selling jeremiad *The Fate of the Earth,* 10 published in 1982, that started me thinking about cockroach survival. *The Fate of the Earth* is a very strange sort of book, deeply unappealing, not very well written, windy and repetitious, yet powerful and valuable beyond measure. In fact, it may be the dreariest piece of writing that I ever wished everyone in America would read. Its subject is, of course, the abiding danger of nuclear Armageddon. Specifically, it describes in relentless scientific detail the likelihood of total human extinction following a full-scale nuclear war. In a section that Schell titles "A Republic of Insects and Grass," there is a discussion of the relative prospects for different animal species surviving to propagate again after mankind's final war. Schell takes his facts from a 1970 symposium held at Brookhaven National Laboratory, and in summarizing that government-sponsored research he says:

> For example, the lethal doses of gamma radiation for animals in pasture, where fallout would be descending on them directly and they would be eating fallout that had fallen on the grass, and would thus suffer from doses of beta radiation as well, would be one hundred and eighty rads [a standard unit of absorbed radiation] for cattle; two hundred and forty rads for sheep; five hundred and fifty rads for swine; three hundred and fifty rads for horses; and eight hundred rads for poultry. In a ten-thousand-megaton attack, which would create levels of radiation around the country averaging more than ten thousand rads, most of the mammals of the United States would be killed off. The lethal doses for birds are in roughly the same range as those for mammals, and birds, too, would be killed off. Fish are killed at doses of between one thousand one hundred rads and about five thousand six hundred rads, but their fate is less predictable. On the one hand, water is a shield from radiation, and would afford some protection; on the other hand, fallout might concentrate in bodies of water as it ran off from the land. (Because radiation causes no pain, animals, wandering at will through the environment, would not avoid it.) The one class of animals containing a number of species quite likely to survive, at least in the short run, is the insect class, for which in most known cases the lethal doses lie between about two thousand rads and about a hundred thousand rads. Insects, therefore, would be destroyed selectively. Unfortunately for the rest of the environment, many of the phytophagous species [the plant-eaters] ... have very high tolerances, and so could be expected to survive disproportionately, and then to multiply greatly in the aftermath of an attack.

Among the most ravaging of those phytophagous species referred to 11 by Schell is an order of insects called the Orthoptera. The order Orthoptera includes locusts, like those Moses brought down on Egypt in plagues. It also includes crickets, mantids, walking sticks, and cockroaches.

Ten thousand rads, according to Schell's premises, is roughly the aver-   12
age dosage that might be received by most living things during the week
immediately following Armageddon. By coincidence, 10,000 rads is also the
dosage administered to certain test animals in a study conducted, some
twenty-four years ago, by two researchers named Wharton and Wharton.
The write-up can be found in a 1959 volume of the journal *Radiation
Research*. The experiment was performed under the auspices, again, of the
U.S. Army. The radiation was administered from a two-million-electron-volt
Van de Graaff accelerator. The test animals were *Periplaneta americana,*
those big American cockroaches.

Remember now, a dose of 180 rads is enough to kill a Hereford. A   13
horse will die after taking 350 rads. The average lethal dose for humans
isn't precisely known (because no one is performing quite such systematic
experiments on humans, though again the Army has come closest, with
those hapless GIs forced to ogle detonations at the Nevada Test Site), but
somewhere around 600 rads seems to be a near guess.

By contrast, cockroaches in the laboratory dosed with 830 rads rou-   14
tinely survive to die of old age. Their *average* lethal dose seems to be up
around 3,200 rads. And of those that Wharton and Wharton blasted with
10,000 rads, *half* of the group were still alive two weeks later.

The Whartons in their *Radiation Research* paper don't say *how much*   15
longer those hardiest cockroaches lasted. But it was long enough, evidently,
for egg capsules to be delivered, and hatch, and for the cycle of cockroach
survival and multiplication—unbroken throughout the past 250 million
years—to continue on. Long enough to suggest that, if the worst happened,
cockroaches in great and growing number would be around to dance on
the grave of the human species.

With luck maybe it won't happen—that ultimately ugly event foreseen   16
so vividly by Jonathan Schell. With luck, and with also a gale of informed
and persistent outrage by citizenries more sensible than their leaders. But
with less luck, less persistence, what I can't help but envision for our poor
raw festering planet, in those days and years after the After, is, like once
before, an Age of Cockroaches.

If Quammen had written for a specialized scientific periodical like the
Journal of Comparative Zoology, he would have been expected to document
very carefully every idea or quotation he took from another writer. With the
aid of footnotes, endnotes, or other citations, he would have directed any curious reader to the very page he used—as we'll show you how to do in Chapter
16, "Writing from Library Research." But because he wrote for a general magazine, Quammen indicated rather more sketchily whenever he quoted or borrowed ideas. When later he collected his essays into a book, he cheerfully
admitted to having "cannibalized fact and reaped understanding" from other
writers. He then took pains to list his sources, as many as he could remember.
Here is his list for "A Republic of Cockroaches." It will give you a sense of the

reading he did in writing his essay—less than the writer of a scientific research paper might do, perhaps, but a reasonable amount for anyone writing an informal essay addressed to general readers.

PARTIAL SOURCES

Cornwell, P. B. *The Cockroach.* London: Hutchinson, 1968.

Guthrie, D. M., and A. R. Tindall. *The Biology of the Cockroach.* New York: St. Martin's Press, 1968.

Miall, L. C., and Alfred Denny. *The Structure and Life-History of the Cockroach* (Periplaneta orientalis). London: L. Reeve, 1886.

Rau, Phil. "The Life History of the American Cockroach, *Periplaneta americana* Linn. (Orthop.: Blattidae)." *Entomological News* 51 (1940).

Schell, Jonathan. *The Fate of the Earth.* New York: Alfred A. Knopf, 1982.

Wharton, D. R. A., and Martha L. Wharton. "The Effect of Radiation on the Longevity of the Cockroach, *Periplaneta americana,* as Affected by Dose, Age, Sex, and Food Intake." *Radiation Research* 11 (1959).

Questions to Start You Thinking

1. How did you respond to this essay? What did you star, question, underline, or comment on in the margin while you read?

2. What passages in "A Republic of Cockroaches" reveal Quammen's purpose in writing? What main idea is he driving at?

3. Apparently, Quammen was inspired by a paragraph in Jonathan Schell's *The Fate of the Earth,* and he then did further reading about cockroaches. Where in his essay does he appear to go beyond Schell and his other sources to contribute something original?

4. If, like Quammen, you had found yourself goaded to write after reading the paragraph from Schell's book that is quoted in this essay, in what other direction might your thoughts possibly have taken you? Would *your* essay have gone into detail about cockroaches?

"Write a comment on a book or article you have read recently," the writing class assignment asked, "something that has aroused a strong response in you or prompted you to do some further thinking." Rose Anne Federici had already been assigned to read a medical book on eating disorders for her course in nursing education. As she read, looking for passages that encouraged "further thinking," one page stood out for her. Her reflections about it sent her thoughts beyond the book's immediate subject and crystallized into this paper.

CONFLICTING MESSAGES: A LOOK AT A GENERATION TORN TWO WAYS
ROSE ANNE FEDERICI

I belong to a generation constantly torn in two directions. This realization came to me unexpectedly as I was reading *Eating Disorders: The*   1

Facts by Suzanne Abraham and Derek Llewellyn-Jones (Oxford: Oxford University Press, 1984). These two medical writers ask why eating disorders are so prevalent among young women. Many people my age become victims of anorexia, or self-starvation, while others overeat to the point of obesity and become victims of bulimia, or abnormal craving for food.

Why does this happen? The writers offer several possible explanations. One is that women in our society today are bombarded by two conflicting messages—eat and don't eat. Growing confused, a person may go to either extreme, becoming a dieter who wastes away or a foodaholic. It is in the media, the writers point out, where we often find the two messages coming at us at once. In almost any women's magazine, right after an article on a sensational new diet guaranteed to help us lose weight comfortably with little effort or willpower, we get a recipe for a delectable chocolate cake or a creamy sauce. A television commercial shows us a diet drink or a low-calorie cereal followed by another commercial for a burger joint or pizzeria. One minute, we receive the message that a woman's lifework is to be thin so as to be healthy, happy, and loved by everyone. The next minute we are told that eating not only satisfies the appetite but also fulfills many inner wants. It is sensuous fun, which every woman has a right to. Sometimes, Abraham and Llewellyn-Jones add, the contradictions beamed forth from television are reinforced by contradictory messages in the home.

> The social (and usually family) pressures are also contradictory: you must eat everything other people give you but you must not get fat.
>
> The provision of food is seen in our culture as a major sign of caring; and sharing food at a meal is seen as one of the prime social contacts. These cultural imperatives place a burden on a mother to provide abundant quantities of food, and on her loving daughter or son to eat that food. It is not surprising that in the face of the psychological bombardment of two contradictory messages, most young women diet.

The writers suggest other possible explanations for eating disorders, but this one started me thinking. I believe these writers are on to something important, and not only important for health care and preventive medicine. I suddenly realized that in our society, people are constantly being bombarded by contradictory messages, not only about eating but about almost everything. For example, advertisers constantly make appeals that tug us in two different directions. A television commercial tells us to get outdoors and explore the wilds of America. However, while we are roughing it and getting close to nature we are supposed to be living in a camper with a TV set, a microwave oven, and the other comforts of home. The same discount store ad in the newspaper that invites us to get plenty of exercise with a set of weights also tells us to take life easy with an automatic garage door opener.

Many of these conflicting messages are beamed at people of college age. We are told to assert our individuality—but to do so by wearing a name brand of makeup, or Jams, or Jordache jeans. How we can display our very own personalities when we are wearing what everyone else wears, we are not told. On television news and talk shows, glamorous unmarried mothers—Farrah Fawcett and Tatum O'Neal, for example—are presented as stars worthy of our admiration. Recently, the same channels that feature such shows have been running public service messages aimed at unmarried women and girls: "Don't get pregnant."

Often our parents and teachers tell us one thing, and television another. "Study hard and you will achieve success," I am told every time I go home. Meanwhile, on TV, I keep seeing people who are considered successes even though they have probably never opened a book. They simply buy a lottery ticket and they win a million dollars, or they record one hit song and become rich for life. Other conflicting messages bombard me every time I go home—"Study hard in college" and "Why don't you get out and meet people and enjoy yourself?"

In *Mademoiselle* magazine, an interview presents a woman for us to admire. After starting her own business, she has scored a huge success and now has twenty employees. At the same time she has a husband and three children. She maintains a "gracious home" and gives dinner parties. There may be many miracle workers like that woman, but for me the two messages—be a successful executive, be a wonderful wife and mother—point in different directions. I wonder if there is not a built-in conflict in the whole idea of becoming a big success and still being a loving person, able to spend time with family and friends. Being both is not impossible, but for me it would be hard to achieve.

I realize that even on a national level, conflicting messages are broadcast. We throw a big birthday party for the Statue of Liberty while doing our best to limit the number of immigrants allowed to enter the United States. We pride ourselves that we deinstitutionalize the mentally ill, but we do it by sending them out onto the streets while refusing to give them the skills and the support to make it on their own. We criticize the quality of our schools but pay our public school teachers very little. We spend money for "Star Wars" missiles and at the same time call for world peace. In the name of democracy, we send financial and military aid to corrupt governments in other lands. No wonder that, although I do not suffer from anorexia or bulimia, I have an increasing sense that I belong to a generation torn in different directions.

Questions to Start You Thinking

1. What did Rose Anne Federici herself add to the idea that she found in the book *Eating Disorders?*
2. What other contradictory messages are you familiar with from magazine and television advertising, from films, or from the news?
3. Do you agree that all the messages Federici cites are necessarily contradictory? Can't one diet most of the time, yet on special occasions eat a sliver of chocolate cake?

LEARNING BY WRITING

The Assignment

This assignment invites you to do some reading that will enlarge your area of knowledge. It asks you to reflect on what you read, arrive at some original insight or observation that stems from what you have read, and then write a paper in which you use your reading as the point of departure for your own ideas.

For at least five days, keep a reading journal in which you react each day to one essay, magazine article, or chapter of a book that sends your thoughts in some new and interesting direction. Then look over your journal and select the most promising entry. Develop it into a paper in which you share with your readers what you learned, your insights, your further ideas. Hand in your journal along with your paper.

Among the thoughtful papers we have seen in response to this assignment are these:

A man who had recently read about the economic law of supply and demand set out to explain that law by describing the behavior of both sellers and customers at a yard sale.

A woman, having read in her sociology textbook about the changes that city neighborhoods in the United States typically undergo in the course of fifty to a hundred years, thought about the changes that had taken place in a neighborhood she knew well and decided that the textbook's generalizations applied imperfectly.

A man, after having read and thought about George Orwell's classic essay "Shooting an Elephant," agreed with the writer that whole governments can act unwisely, seemingly for no better reason than to save face. He used as his main example U.S. policy toward Vietnam in the 1960s and 1970s.

A man, inspired by Gradgrind, the tyrannical and shortsighted schoolmaster in Charles Dickens's novel *Hard Times,* humorously insisted he had encountered as much mindlessness in the elementary school he had attended as in Gradgrind's classroom.

A woman, appalled by newspaper accounts of the 1986 nuclear disaster at Chernobyl in the Soviet Union, weighed the risks inherent in nuclear power against possible benefits to humankind.

Generating Ideas

Reading for ideas. What will you read to fulfill this assignment? Why not go to the library and browse through several current magazines, such as *The Atlantic, Harper's, New Republic, Commentary, Ms.,* and others likely to contain articles to spur you to thought. Never mind *People, Sporting News,* and other magazines written mainly to entertain. You want good, meaty articles, conducive to reflection; if they are a bit difficult to understand and need to be read twice, so much the better. Try not to start out with ideas you already have, looking only for confirmation. You'll do better if you stay open to fresh ideas that your readings may unexpectedly trigger.

What have you read lately that has started you thinking and wondering? Classics like Sigmund Freud's *The Interpretation of Dreams,* Rachel Carson's *The Sea Around Us,* or Henry David Thoreau's *Walden* bristle with challenging ideas. And why not draw on some reading you've been assigned for another course? It may be a chapter in a textbook, an essay in a reader used in your college English course, or a book assigned for outside reading. We suggest you mix your choices. Try one of each: a classic, a current magazine article, a chapter from a textbook, the letters of some famous person, a thought-provoking short story, a book about art or music—whatever engages your interest. That way, your journal will contain a variety of possibilities from which you can choose the topic for your paper.

As you begin your search for promising material, keep in mind that you're reading with a purpose, not just to enjoy yourself. You can't afford the luxury of reading everything word by word; skip, skim, and sample things. Should something prove thought-provoking, you can then read it more closely. When reading things for possible material, try reading just the first two paragraphs and the last two paragraphs. Those will probably alert you to the main points the writer makes. When you look into books to see if they're worth reading, skim through the first chapter and the last chapter. Then, if the book looks helpful, you can spend more time with it.

Once you have zeroed in on a likely chapter, article, or essay, read slowly and carefully, giving yourself plenty of time to think between the lines. Try to discern the writer's opinions, even if they are unstated. Don't just soak up opinions and information. Criticize. Question. Wonder. Argue back. Dare to differ with the author whose work you're reading. Most printed pages aren't holy writ; you can doubt them. Opinions you don't agree with can be valuable if they set your own thoughts in motion.

Read with pencil in hand and, if you're one of those people who find it helpful (not everyone does), react in writing. Write brief notes to yourself (if you're using library materials), or mark up the text (if you own the book or magazine or have made a photocopy of it). This technique will focus your attention. Underline phrases and sentences that contain essentials. Star things you think are important. Make cross-references: "Contradicts what he said on p. 17." Jot thoughts in the margin. Besides helping you participate while you read, such notes are a wonderful help in reviewing what you have read. Keep testing the writer's assumptions against what you already know and believe. Put question marks next to those assertions that seem flawed or untrue. You can scribble "Bull!" or "Idiocy!" in a margin. You can also use your pencil to applaud silently when a writer confirms your hunch or reveals an exciting new idea: "Right on!" or "Good!" When you question something, write in your question ("True in all cases?" "Other explanations possible?" "These figures still accurate today?"). You'll be reading and writing simultaneously.

Don't hesitate to talk over what you read with a friend whose mind you respect, one who doesn't swallow everything uncritically. Point out passages in your reading that you could use help in interpreting. The right to ask your fellow students for their views, as well as to ask your instructor, comes when you pay your tuition.

On the facing page, you can see how Rose Anne Federici reacted when she read Suzanne Abraham and Derek Llewellyn-Jones's *Eating Disorders: The Facts*.

Eating disorders — the facts

THE SOCIAL EXPLANATION

In Western culture two contrasting messages about food and eating are offered by society, and particularly by the media. The first message is that a slim woman is successful, attractive, healthy, happy, fit, and popular. To become slim, with all that this implies, is deemed to be a major pursuit of many women. The second message is that eating is a pleasurable activity which meets many needs in addition to relieving hunger, and women have a right to have these needs met. In women's magazines these two contrasting messages tend to appear inextricably mixed. In nearly every issue the magazines publish 'exciting' new diets which 'guarantee weight loss with minimum discomfort or motivation', and these diets are often followed by recipes for, and superb photographs of, luscious cakes and foods with rich sauces. It is difficult to watch television without being confronted by an advertisement for a substitute diet-food alternating with a fast food advertisement, or its equivalent. The social (and usually family) pressures are also contradictory: you must eat everything other people give you but you must not get fat.

The provision of food is seen in our culture as a major sign of caring; and sharing food at a meal is seen as one of the prime social contacts. These cultural imperatives place a burden on a mother to provide abundant quantities of food, and on her loving daughter or son to eat that food. It is not surprising that in the face of the psychological bombardment of two contradictory messages, most young women diet. Some become 'foodaholics' and develop bulimia. Others become preoccupied with food and the avoidance of weight gain, developing bulimia or anorexia nervosa. Some decide that dieting is too disturbing to their way of life and return to eating more food than they require, becoming obese. These women may also find obesity protective against acceding to current social attitudes to sexuality, which they fear. Hidden in a fat body, they give the message that they are not attractive and do not want to form a sexual relationship.

"don't eat"
&
"eat"

YES!

Other contradictory messages we receive?

28

By the way, she had a perfect right to mark up the copy: it was an assigned textbook in her nursing education course. She had made few marks until she came to the passage about contradictory messages. Then, recognizing a page she wanted to study closely, she scored the passage about messages, put a star by it, underlined main points, summarized the two messages ("don't eat" & "eat"), and exclaimed YES! in the margin beside a comment that reminded her of her own family. Finally, at the bottom of the page, she scribbled a question to prompt further thinking. We don't say you need to mark up every page you read so intensively. Evidently, Federici recognized that here was an especially valuable page, with an idea she would surely want to write about.

Keeping a reading journal. As the assignment suggests, keep a journal of thoughts that arise in response to your reading. Each day, after reading and thinking about the day's selection, dash out a few sentences. What do you put into a journal entry? Well, first (and this is easy), put in the title and author of any material you discuss. If as you read you come across passages you especially admire, copy them into your journal. Along with summaries and direct quotations, include your own reactions. (If you scribbled notes as you read, these will be easier to put together.) See if you can arrive at any further insight.

This is what Rose Anne Federici did in preparing to write her essay. Shortly after she found herself interacting with this passage, Federici felt elated. In the last place she might have looked for it—a textbook for her nursing course—she had discovered a really interesting criticism of the society in which we live. This suggestion cast light not only on people who gorge or starve themselves, but on advertising, political pronouncements, and family life as well. Excited, Federici jotted her thoughts in her notebook. We give them here to illustrate a typical, spontaneous entry in a reading journal, like the one that our assignment calls for.

> "Don't eat" and "Eat"—contradictory messages. I'm pretty sure we receive other c.m.s all the time.
> What about the line on mental health? Yesterday in nursing class lecturer talked about how mental patients are "deinstitutionalized"—this saves cost and is supposed to be good for them. But they are turned loose on the streets without money or support. They get in trouble, commit crimes.
> There's the line I get handed at home—"Study hard" vs. "Why don't you get out and meet people?"
> Do advertisers sometimes contradict themselves? What about politicians? I want to find some more examples. How many conflicting messages are there in our society?

As you start writing your own reading journal, you might ask these questions.

DISCOVERY CHECKLIST: RECORDING YOUR READING

- How would you state what the writer takes for granted? If a writer begins, "The serious threat of acid rain was dismissed with a collective yawn in Washington again last week," then evidently he or she assumes that acid rain is a serious menace and that legislators, too, should take it seriously.
- Do you agree with what the author has said? Does it clash with anything you hold dear? Does it question anything you take for granted?
- Do the writer's assertions rest on evidence? What kind of evidence? Statistics? The results of surveys? Quotations from authorities? Historical facts? Photographs? Are you convinced?
- With what do you disagree? Why?
- If you doubt the writer's statements, can you test them against anything you know or can find out?
- From any facts the writer presents, what inferences can you draw? If the writer musters facts that lead to an inescapable conclusion, might any conflicting evidence be mustered? A portrait of an unfriendly country that showed all its citizens to be rapists, drunks, and drug addicts would leave much out; evidently a different view would be possible.
- Has anything you read opened your eyes to new possibilities, new ways of looking at the world?
- Has the writer failed to tell you anything you wish you knew? If so, what?

If in your journal you write the answers to at least some of these questions, you'll have valuable thoughts on hand when you start drafting your paper.

Shaping a Draft

Faced now with your five journal entries, how do you decide which to expand into a paper? First, ask yourself which entry most interests you. Second, ask which of your reflections would most interest your possible readers—your fellow students and your instructor. As you look over your journal entries, decide which most clearly seems to say something. Which arrives at a conclusion, however tentative? That's the one to develop.

If, before you begin to draft, you feel the need for more ideas than there are in your journal entry, backtrack for a while. Look back over what you have read and do more thinking. One of the strengths of Rose Anne Federici's paper is its convincing array of examples. After she wrote her journal entry, Federici decided it looked a little skimpy. She wished she might discover other contradictory messages. "I thought of the one about deinstitutionalizing the mentally ill but refusing to help them," she recalls, "and the one about 'get good grades but get out and see people'—I'd heard that one before. I knew there must be lots of other contradictory messages, but at first it was hard to think of any."

After a solitary, fruitless attempt at brainstorming, Federici had a conversation with three other students. She told them of her assignment, shared her preliminary thoughts, and asked, "What other contradictory messages have you heard lately?" They creased their brows and came up with ten further examples. Some of their ideas didn't fit Federici's specifications. It seemed easy enough to think of differing messages coming from two different sources—such as health warnings that say "don't smoke" and tobacco ads that say "go ahead." A more difficult task, it seemed, was to become aware of contradictory messages that come from the same source: the ad for a camper that urges "rough it in the wilds" and at the same time invites the buyer to bring along a microwave oven. Still, two or three of her friends' examples proved useful, and to her relief she found that talking about her problem had launched her thoughts again. As Federici began to draft, looking over her notes on her brainstorming session and on her conversation, new examples occurred to her.

You may find that the best way to organize your paper is just to start writing, putting down your thoughts in whatever order they come to you. Once you have a draft written, you can always juggle its parts if you want to. You may want to work with your inspiring source in front of you, or you may prefer to write a draft without referring to your source so that you can focus on your own ideas. You may feel you need a detailed outline. Some writers find it helpful, before they begin putting details into place, to formulate a thesis statement, a sentence that sets forth the main idea they want to develop in their paper. If writing down a statement of your purpose in advance seems a good way to get your words flowing, by all means do it. If, on the other hand, you're the kind of writer whose thesis tends not to emerge until you've struggled with your ideas in writing for a while, just write. You can always formulate a thesis statement after your purpose has become clear to you, just to assure yourself that your paper does make a point. (For more about writing a thesis sentence, see p. 469.)

In general, identify any source of an idea or quotation right away, as soon as you mention it in your writing. You can do this informally, as David Quammen does in "A Republic of Cockroaches." It is enough in an informal paper to say, "Renowned feminist Betty Friedan states this idea convincingly in *The Feminine Mystique,*" and then quote Friedan. (Chapter 19 discusses the proper way to *formally* document writing that you do from reading, as you must do in writing a college research paper or in writing an article for a specialized or professional journal, and also the proper way to cite every page of another writer from which you derived something.) The first law of writing from reading is to acknowledge fully and honestly your debt to the writer from whom you derived anything, whether it be a quotation, information, or an idea. You can acknowledge your sources in any of three ways.

Quoting. When an author expresses ideas in a way so incisive, so brilliant, or so memorable that you want to reproduce those words exactly, you can quote them word for word. Direct quotations add life and color and the sound of a speaking voice. If you leave out part of a quotation, indicate the omissions with an ellipsis—three dots (. . .). If the ellipsis occurs at the beginning or end of a sentence, it contains *four* dots. Why leave anything out? Usually because, if left in, it would be too boring or cumbersome or distracting or needlessly long—perhaps because it adds some information that mattered to the author, but doesn't matter to the point you are making.

Nutshelling. Also called *summarizing,* this is a useful way to deal with a whole paragraph or section of a work when what you're after is just the general drift. To save time and space and to focus on the idea, you don't want to quote word for word. Without doing violence to an idea, you put it in a nutshell: you express its main sense in a few words—*your own words.* Jonathan Schell's long paragraph on gamma radiation, which Quammen quotes, is a summary of research conducted at Brookhaven National Laboratory.

Paraphrasing. This skill involves restating an author's ideas. When you put the author's thoughts into your own words, don't let the author's words keep slipping in. The style in paraphrasing, as in nutshelling, has to be yours. If some other writer says, "President Wilson called an emergency meeting of his cabinet to discuss the new crisis," and you say, "The President called on his cabinet to hold an emergency meeting to discuss the new crisis," that isn't far enough removed from the original. You could put quotation marks around the original sentence, although it seems unmemorable, not worth quoting word for word. Or, better, you could write: "Summoning his cabinet to an emergency session, Wilson laid forth the challenge before them." If you have dealt carefully with the material, you won't have to put quotation marks around anything in your paraphrase.

In Rose Anne Federici's "Conflicting Messages," you'll find all three methods in action: quotation, nutshell, and paraphrase. In her second paragraph, introducing the idea she had discovered in the book she read, Federici sums it up in a nutshell:

> One [explanation for eating disorders] is that women in our society today are bombarded by two conflicting messages—eat and don't eat. Growing confused, a person may go to either extreme, becoming a dieter who wastes away or a foodaholic.

Then, apparently feeling the need to explain more fully, she immediately goes on to paraphrase the writers' entire discussion of the two messages, with their illustrations from women's magazines and television advertising. Thus, without borrowing the writers' very language, she produces a new version true to their ideas. Better than quoting at great length, paraphrasing here serves her purposes. Freely, she arranges the writers' points in a different order, making the idea "contradictory messages" stand last in her own paragraph—and so giving it greater emphasis. She even invents specific examples where the original writers are vague: instead of their somewhat puzzling "a fast food advertisement, or its equivalent" (whatever its equivalent is!), she bravely and faithfully sub-stitutes "commercial for a burger joint or pizzeria." Paraphrasing a British book, she thus retains its sense while making its examples recognizably American.

Her essay clearly gains, too, from an appropriate quotation. In her third paragraph, she quotes four sentences from her original—for what reason? "Be-cause," she explains, "I wanted to keep the exact words about the mother and her loving daughter or son. Besides, I didn't know how to paraphrase 'cultural imperatives.' I could have said 'the dictates of society' or something, but that didn't sound as good. 'Cultural imperatives' was wonderful, and I wanted to leave it alone." (You can compare her nutshell and her paraphrase with the original text she read, reproduced on p. 97.)

How do you condense another writer's thoughts? Before you paraphrase or nutshell, we suggest that you do the following.

1. Read the original passage over a couple of times. You can underline key parts or note them.
2. Without looking at it, try to state its gist—the point it makes, the main sense you remember.
3. Then go back and reread the original one more time, making sure you got its gist faithfully. Revise your paraphrase as necessary.

To paraphrase, incidentally, has another use: it is one way to understand a knotty passage that has baffled you. You can try to paraphrase it in writing, or perhaps just paraphrase it mentally.

Rewriting

Perhaps, as you look over your draft, you will feel the need to read further. Would your paper be stronger if it had more facts, statistics, or other evidence? Take the trouble to do additional reading. David Quammen, inspired by Jona-than Schell's paragraph to picture Armageddon as a victory for cockroaches, apparently found that to make his vision effective, he had to read the work of several scientists knowledgeable about cockroaches. No one expects you to read as much as he did in the time that you have. We don't ask you at this point to write a research paper, though it is possible that something you read might lead to thoughts that can develop into one at some future date. For this assign-ment, just have enough facts and information at your disposal to state your ideas with confidence and authority.

As you read and write at the same time, you may find your views changing. If you rearranged your ideas drastically since starting to write, cosmetic changes may not be enough—you may have to revise thoroughly. To see how much your ideas have changed since you first wrote your journal entry, you might try to state (to yourself or in writing) what insight you had then, what insight you have now.

In looking back over your paper, you might ask the following questions.

REVISION CHECKLIST: WRITING FROM READING

- Where in your paper do you find evidence, examples, and illustrations that are too thin and undeveloped to support your assertions? Return to your original source or do some more reading and discover any more worthwhile material.
- Have you given emphasis to major points in the work you read? Or did you get sidetracked and deal with the writer's incidental points, skipping over what really matters?
- If you see any long stretches without a quotation, can you come up with a good, lively direct quotation to break the monotony? Look over your reading and see where it might be helpful (and interesting) to quote a writer's very words.
- Would it ever help to state the other writer's ideas in a nutshell or to paraphrase?
- Did you make clear what you took from your source or sources?

In writing from reading, you have certain minor but important responsibilities when you proofread your final draft. If you have used any direct quotations, check them against the original. In copying a quotation into your paper, it's easy to omit something, perhaps something essential. Of course, your main concern will be to make sure you've produced a paper in which you convey to your readers some of the power and joy of thinking, not only with the prompting of another writer, but also by thinking on your own.

Other Assignments

1. Read several comments on a recent news event by columnists and commentators in magazines and newspapers. Find two writers who disagree in their analyses. Decide which view you favor and explain it in a few paragraphs. In making your decision, you may find that you need to read still more, to know as much about the event as possible.

2. Write a letter to the editor of your local newspaper in which you take exception to the recent conduct of some world leader or celebrity as reported in the paper or to some column the newspaper printed recently. By referring to what you have read, make the grounds of your complaint clear enough so that even someone who didn't read the article you're criticizing will know what you're talking about.

3. To give yourself practice in skeptically analyzing what you read, study whatever story in a recent tabloid newspaper such as the *National Enquirer, Weekly World News,* or the *Star* seems to you the hardest to believe. Where was the story said to take place? What reliable witnesses were there? How could a skeptic verify the truth of the story? What inferences can you draw about the story, the reporter, and the newspaper that printed it?

4. Compare two history books in their accounts of a celebrated event—the Declaration of Independence, the bombing of Hiroshima, or any other event you wish to read more about. One of the books should be recent, the other at least thirty years old. Describe the differences in the two versions. How do you account for them?

APPLYING WHAT YOU LEARN:
SOME USES OF WRITING FROM READING

In college, writing from your reading is an activity you'll take part in almost daily. Many instructors, to encourage you to read and write continually, will ask you to keep a notebook of your reading and occasionally may ask you to turn it in for inspection. Writing about your reading, as you often do in taking tests and examinations, is intended to demonstrate your mastery of it. (For advice about writing essay examinations, see Chapter 20.)

Sometimes you may be called on to summarize a part of a book or textbook or an article. But usually instructors won't want you just to parrot your reading— they'll expect you to think along with it, perhaps dispute it, criticize it, sift it for what is valuable, add more ideas yourself. In a sociology course student Lisa Berry was asked to read a book by J. Allen Whitt and then write a paper answering the question "Does the concept of the 'Cadillac commuter system' (a system that primarily serves elites), applied by Whitt to the San Francisco BART system, apply as well to the Los Angeles transportation system?" Her response, entitled "L.A.'s Non-Cadillac System," begins:

> Compton. Santa Monica. Topanga Canyon. Three very diverse areas— environmentally, economically, and racially—yet all share a common bond in their need for transportation to and from downtown Los Angeles. Many of the suburbs house workers who commute to the central city daily. *Urban Elites and Mass Transportation* by J. Allen Whitt (1981) addresses the issue of mass transportation, asking who develops such systems and whom the system serves. From his analysis of the San Francisco transit line, Whitt claims that the BART system benefits the affluent fraction of the urban population who work in downtown San Francisco. In comparing the Los Angeles freeway system with BART, I had the feeling of trying to compare apples and oranges. The two plans provide different forms of transportation, but more important, the cities are drastically dissimilar in structure: Los Angeles is one of the most dispersed and San Francisco one of the most highly concentrated cities in the United States.

This paper is typical of a grade A book report in sociology. Berry starts by quickly placing the discussion in a context: how different communities all need to be served by a city highway system or mass transit system. She sums up Whitt's book in a two-sentence nutshell and then proceeds to set forth her own view.

For other college writing assignments, reading will be just one of your resources. An education course, to take an instance, might ask you to combine reading and observing: to watch a toddler for an hour a day over the course of a week, keep a detailed record of her appearance and her actions, compare those with what is average for a child of her age (information you would find by reading), and then draw some conclusions about her behavior. By writing, you draw what you read into your ever-growing fund of general knowledge. By reading, you nourish what you write.

At home or in high school you may have met general magazines like *Newsweek* and *National Geographic,* which most literate readers can take pleasure in. But later in college, many of your courses will oblige you to read periodicals of a different kind: journals written and read by trained specialists. Many specialists, from physicists to physicians, write articles for others in their field, sharing what they know. Doctors and other health professionals report new diseases or new treatments; scientists and technicians advance new theories; literary critics make fresh ventures into literary criticism; historians address other historians, enlarging on knowledge of the past, perhaps reinterpreting it. As part of your training in a special discipline, you may be introduced to *The Journal of Comparative Behavior, Nature, Educational Research, American Journal of Sociology, PMLA,* or *Foreign Affairs.* You will often be asked to report on an article, reading it critically, perhaps summarizing or paraphrasing its essentials, and finally adding a thoughtful comment. Though hard work, such an assignment will plunge you into professional language and habits of thought.

Many a learned article, whether in the sciences or the humanities, will begin with a short review of previous research, which the writer is about to dash to pieces. In some professional journals, though, summary or paraphrase of other writing may be an end in itself. Attorney Peter L. Knox, who in addition to practicing his profession writes articles about pension tax laws for professional journals such as *Taxation for Accountants* and the *Journal of Taxation,* says that writing for him is often a matter of reading difficult writing (like rulings of the Tax Court and the *Internal Revenue Manual*) and condensing it in plainer prose—"expressing in an organized, somewhat literary form a set of complex rules." You can see how such an article might greatly help other tax lawyers struggling to understand a long, crucially important entry about changing a pension plan, as in this example from *Final and Temporary IRS Regulations*:

> **§ 1.401(b)-1   Certain retroactive changes in plan   [TD 7437, filed 9-23-76].**
>   **(a)   *General rule.***   Under section 401(b) a stock bonus, pension, profit-sharing, annuity, or bond purchase plan which does not satisfy the requirements of section 401(a) on any day solely as a result of a disqualifying provision (as defined in paragraph (b) of this section) shall be considered to have satisfied such requirement on such date if, on or before the last day of the remedial amendment period (as determined under paragraphs (c), (d) and (e) of this section) with respect to such disqualifying provision, all provisions of the plan which are necessary to satisfy all requirements of sections 401(a), 403(a), or 405(a) are in effect and have been made effective for all purposes for the whole of such period.

The entry goes on like that for three and a half large pages of fine print divided into subsections, some with roman numerals. Bewildering as such material may be—probably no one reads IRS regulations for entertainment—thousands of a client's dollars may be riding on an attorney's ability to interpret that entry correctly. In an article explaining the passage to his fellow pension plan professionals, Knox helpfully begins, "Section 401(b) provides a way for retirement plans to be retroactively corrected" and goes on to tell how it is generally applied. Obviously, the law could not function without its interpreters, who translate its complex language into simpler directives that people can follow.

Besides, the interpreters foresee difficulties that can arise in real life when professionals try to apply the law. No mere exercise in translation, such specialized nutshelling and paraphrasing, it seems, calls for hard, even imaginative, thought.

We have been viewing books and articles as *immediately* useful sources of ideas and information. But sometimes there is a time lag: you read Melville's novel *Moby-Dick* or Thorstein Veblen's *The Theory of the Leisure Class* and, although your reading isn't immediately useful to the paper you have to write for geology, something from it remains with you, perhaps nothing but a phrase, an example, a stray idea, a way of constructing a sentence. Perhaps months later, when you are writing another paper, for any course, it returns to the forefront of your mind. In truth, writing from reading is useful to you in ways we haven't begun to indicate. We hold this truth to be self-evident: that the better you read—the more alertly, critically, questioningly—the better you write.

Reading is, in fact, the way you are most likely to sense the powers that language holds. You grow familiar with the forms of written language; you learn phrases useful to connect things, to gesture, to look back on what you have written, to look forward to what you still have to say. You absorb the vocabulary and habits of thought of your chosen field of work and make them your own. You see how skilled writers prove and demonstrate, evaluate, explain, select useful details, assert, affirm, deny, try to convince.

Indeed, some psychologists and students of writing believe that there is no way to learn to write well but to read excellent, effective writing and to try to do likewise. Do so, and in your own writing your reading will truly prove to be your richest, most inexhaustible resource.

CHAPTER 7

What People Say: Writing from Conversation

"When you don't know what to write about, go talk to somebody." That advice, given years ago by a high school English teacher, still holds true. If *conversation* is the spoken exchange of facts, thoughts, and feelings, then in conversing you both give and receive. In conversation you can find out things you didn't know you knew. By speaking your *own* thoughts and feelings, you shape them and define them in words.

Still, we would guess that if you can cultivate the art of listening to others, you'll find out even more. Listen closely to an hour's discussion between a class and an anthropology professor, and you might get enough material for a whole paper. Just as likely, you might get a paper's worth of information, thoughts, and feelings from a five-minute exchange with a mechanic who relines brakes. Both may be experts. We are surrounded, too, by people who are rewarding to know and to write about even if they aren't experts.

As this chapter will suggest, you can direct a conversation, ask questions to elicit what you want to find out. You do so in that special kind of conversation called *interviewing*. Newspaper reporters, as you know, interview people continually, and college writers can do so as well. An interview is a conversation with a purpose: usually to find out what the other person knows about a subject or to help you know the other person.

LEARNING FROM OTHER WRITERS

We include here two fine character studies whose writers relied heavily on face-to-face encounters with people. These people are not celebrities, but ordinary people who, merely by living their lives in their own way and showing a willingness to talk, have provided their interviewers with stories to tell and enlightening views. The student essay by Michael R. Tein was written for a college English course.

FLOWERS FOR CHAPEL STREET

MICHAEL R. TEIN

Few people on New Haven's Chapel Street ever notice Louie Weisser.   1
He presses his round back to the cement storefront, his hands reach deep
into his pockets rattling his change, and he surveys his flowers. He sells
them from a pushcart the way he saw done on the Lower East Side of New
York City where he was born 72 years ago. He wears the same clothes
almost every day: a burgundy knit-collar shirt, a stained tan V-neck, baggy
herringbone trousers, and cloth lace shoes. A blue nylon hunting cap with
earflaps hugs his head. It seems to be sewn right into his sparse scalp with
the threads of hair that remain. His cropped mustache has browned under
his nostrils from the smoke of thousands of cigarettes. Louie draws a Lucky
Strike from its box and crimps the pack's edge so the remaining smokes
stay huddled together. The cellophane crinkles as he shoves them back into
his pocket. "I started smokin' these 'cause my father smoked 'em. I used
to steal them from him when I was a kid."

Louie isn't much of a flower man. He drove a local bus for 38 years   2
("a couple million miles, I would figure") before he started to help out his
son's infant flower business. His brother "got a B.S. and M.S. and all that"
and was graduated from Yale, class of 1927. Lou thinks that he might have
prospered in business but has no regrets. Someone has to be the working
man.

Louie's years make him a remnant. He misses the five-cent cup of coffee   3
and the quarter pack of Luckys, but what he remembers most is the prejudice. His brother's credentials could only get him a job driving his father's
laundry truck. "Are you Jewish?" job interviewers asked. "Well, we don't
hire Jews." Lou's former employer, the Connecticut Transit bus company,
spurned blacks from the payroll. "It was strictly a white man's job. Now
they got women, blacks, they got everything now. They have quotas, they
gotta. It's a law now. It's not that they wanna do it, they're forced to do it."
He remembers going into a diner as a youth and having the waitress refuse
to serve his black friend. "So we all walked out, in protest you know, to
say 'the hell with you.' We were kids, we almost started a riot there, you
know, my younger days." He laughs. "Ain't that stupid."

Louie cannot fathom stereotypes. "They say that all the Jews have money,"   4
he remarks. "That's not true. You look at the millionaires in this country
and how many Jews do you find? Kennedys aren't Jewish, the Rockefellers
aren't Jewish. Why do they say the Jews have money? We never hurt, robbed,
or stole from anybody."

Lou balks at any distinction between races or religions. He married a   5
Protestant and his two sons were baptized at Trinity Church a block away
on the New Haven Green. "Just live up to those ten commandments and
you've got it made." he says. "Everybody was Jewish before the advent of
Christ. Christians came from the word 'Christ' and Christ was Jewish. I'm
modernized," Lou proclaims. "I don't even go to *shul* anymore."

A few times each day, Louie ventures into the Copper Kitchen for a   6
cup of coffee and a buttered Danish. He smokes a cigarette, spins his ashtray
back and forth, and tries to work out the day's crossword, which he never

finishes. He files it in his back pocket. He eyes his cart through the luncheonette entrance. Maybe a customer will come, maybe not. "You may be wise, but I'm Weisser," he shrugs his shoulders. "I got these old jokes." Lou chuckles to himself as he waves his cigarette at the waitress to signal for a refill.

Louie peddles all day until about six o'clock. The construction work 7 clouds the street with its refuse, jackhammers pound the pavement, and Yale students scurry by beneath the shadow of Vanderbilt and Bingham Halls. Lou is oblivious to the tumult. His flowers are his Garden of Eden. With each rose or swamp lily ("believe it or not, a swamp lily") that he sells, his innocent, toothy, stubble-lined smile reveals that this flower is his message of love and relief to a world which is far too complex, a world which has swept him along, rudderless, in its current. His family sailed from Russia to "the United States of America—the land of opportunity." The terms are still interchangeable for him. Lou was not the smart one. He drove a bus while his brother studied chemistry. His sons are grown. One is a teacher. The other is now his employer in the flower business. He worships both their achievements and failures, and his eyes bulge out and shine when he speaks of them.

Lou's eyes are his most remarkable feature. The years have pushed 8 them back into the folds of skin, and a yellow film coats the veiny whites. Each iris glows a deep purple. Once, his eyes might have been a hazel or blue, but they have filtered out so much darkness from his world that the residue seems to persist. He sees only good.

"I made friends with these people," Louie points to the stores behind 9 him. "I don't hurt anybody or block anything." Lou sets a high premium on friends. He needs them. An old black man shuffles along behind Lou. A crumpled hat wraps his head. He smiles at Lou through crooked and rotting teeth as he pushes a grocery cart containing fifteen or so discarded cans. "That's my friend Richard. He looks about my age. He used to work in a restaurant washing dishes, now he's on social security." Richard does not beg. He returns New Haven's cans for the five-cent deposit, and Lou respects him for that. He pities the young bums who ask him for dimes to buy cheap wine. After a while he stops giving. "I don't think that I should support that."

Lou is a terrible businessman. His heart beats with the people and not 10 with the buck. His son tells him to charge two dollars per rose; "for you, one dollar," Louie says. But with Louie, "for you" includes almost everyone, that is to say, all of his friends.

So Lou Weisser smiles and talks to Chapel Street, and Chapel Street 11 buys his flowers. The buses roll by, stores open and close, but few are able to pass without a word to Lou. "I'm really not the important part here," he says. "I'm just the background."

Questions to Start You Thinking

1. Where in his essay does Tein rely directly on conversation with his subject? Summarize what you think the old man's words reveal about his values and his outlook on life.

2.   Go back to "Flowers for Chapel Street" and reread it quickly, looking for answers to these questions about Tein's strategies as a writer: (a) Which of the resources other than conversing (recalling, reading, observing, imagining) does Tein employ? (b) Which of Louie Weisser's physical characteristics does the writer choose to emphasize?

3.   In paragraph 10, Tein calls Louie "a terrible businessman." To what extent is this a negative criticism of the man?

4.   In its early drafts, "Flowers for Chapel Street" had one sentence added to its conclusion: "On the contrary, Lou, more like the director." Why do you think Tein removed it? Which ending do you prefer?

William Least Heat Moon's conversation with Barbara Pierre, in St. Martinville, Louisiana, appears in the author's acclaimed *Blue Highways* (1982), aptly subtitled *A Journey into America*. The author, a "mixed-blood" who signs himself with a translation of his Sioux tribal name, wrote his book after traveling through the country on small roads, visiting and talking with unsung people wherever he encountered them.

A VIEW OF PREJUDICE

WILLIAM LEAST HEAT MOON

Because of a broken sealed-beam headlight and Zatarain's Creole Mustard, an excellent native mustard, I met Barbara Pierre. I had just come out of Dugas' grocery with four jars of Zatarain's, and we almost collided on the sidewalk. She said, "You're not from St. Martinville, are you? You can't be." 1

"I'm from Missouri." 2

"What in the world are you doing here? Got a little Huck Finn in you?" 3

"Just followed the bayou. Now I'm looking for the Ford agency." 4

"Coincidences. I work there. I'll show you the way." 5

She was a secretary at the agency and took classes at the University of Southwestern Louisiana in Lafayette when she could. I asked about St. Martinville, but she had to start working before we could say much. 6

"Here's an idea," she said. "Come by at noon and we can have lunch at my place. I live in the project on the other side of the bayou." 7

I picked her up at twelve. She asked about the trip, especially about Selma and how things were as I saw them. "A white man griped about changes, and a black said there weren't enough changes to gripe about." 8

"That's us too. What we want is slow coming—if it's coming at all. Older blacks here are scared of whites and won't do much for change if it means risk. Others don't care as long as everything gets smothered over with politeness by whites. Young blacks see the hypocrisy—even when it's not there. But too many of them are juked on drugs, and that's where some of this town wants us." 9

"Don't any whites here try to help?" 10

"A few, but if a white starts helping too much, they get cut off or shut 11 down by the others and end up paying almost the price we do. Sure, we got good whites—when they're not scared out of showing sympathy."

On Margaret Street, she pointed to her apartment in a small one-story 12 brick building. Standard federal housing. As we went to the door, a shadowy face watched from behind a chintz curtain in another apartment.

"See that? Could be the start of bad news," she said. 13

"Maybe I should leave. I don't want to cause trouble for you." 14

"Too late. Besides, I live my own life here. I won't be pushed. But it'll 15 come back in some little way. Smart remark, snub. One old white lady kicks me at the library. Swings her feet under the table because she doesn't want my kind in there. I could break her in two, she's so frail. She'll be kicking like a heifer if she gets wind of this."

Barbara Pierre's apartment was a tidy place but for books on the sofa. 16 "You can see I still use the library even with the nuisances. The kicking bitch hides books I return so I get overdue notices and have to go prove I turned the book in. I explain what's going on, but nothing changes. Simplest thing is trouble."

"That's what I heard in Selma." 17

"I'm not alone, but sometimes it seems like a conspiracy. Especially in 18 little towns. Gossip and bigotry—that's the blood and guts."

"Was that person who just looked out the window white?" 19

"Are you crazy? Nobody on this end of Margaret Street is white. That's 20 what I mean about us blacks not working together. Half this town is black, and we've only got one elected black official. Excuse my language, but for all the good he does this side of the bayou, he's one useless black mofo."

"Why don't you do something? I mean you personally." 21

"I do. And when I do, I get both sides coming down on me. Including 22 my own family. Everywhere I go, sooner or later, I'm in the courtroom. Duplicity! That's my burning pot. I've torn up more than one court of law."

We sat down at her small table. A copy of *Catch-22* lay open. 23

"Something that happened a few years ago keeps coming back on me. 24 When I was living in Norristown, outside Philadelphia, I gained a lot of weight and went to a doctor. She gave me some diet pills but never explained they were basically speed, and I developed a minor drug problem. I went to the hospital and the nuns said if I didn't sign certain papers they couldn't admit me. So I signed and they put me in a psychiatric ward. Took two hellish weeks to prove I didn't belong there. God, it's easy to get somebody adjudicated crazy."

"Adjudicated?" 25

"You don't know the word, or you didn't think I knew it?" 26

"It's the right word. Go on." 27

"So now, because I tried to lose thirty pounds, people do a job on my 28 personality. But if I shut up long enough, things quiet down. Still, it's the old pattern: any nigger you can't control is crazy."

As we ate our sandwiches and drank Barq's rootbeer, she asked whether 29 I had been through Natchitoches. I said I hadn't.

"They used to have a statue up there on the main street. Called the 30 'Good Darkie Statue.' It was an old black man, slouched shoulders, big

Barbara Pierre in St. Martinville, Louisiana

possum-eating smile. Tipping his hat. Few years ago, blacks made them take it down. Whites couldn't understand. Couldn't see the duplicity in that statue—duplicity on *both* sides. God almighty! I'll promise them one thing: ain't gonna be no more gentle darkies croonin' down on the levee."

I smiled at her mammy imitation, but she shook her head. "In the sixties I wanted that statue blown to bits. It's stored in Baton Rouge now at LSU, but they put it in the wrong building. Ought to be in the capitol reminding people. Preserve it so nobody forgets. Forgives, okay—but not forgets."

"Were things bad when you were a child?"

"Strange thing. I was born here in 'forty-one and grew up here, but I   33
don't remember prejudice. My childhood was warm and happy—especially
when I was reading. Maybe I was too young to see. I don't know. I go on
about the town, but I love it. I've put my time in the cities—New Orleans,
Philly. Your worst Southern cracker is better than a Northern liberal, when
it comes to duplicity anyway, because you know right off where the cracker
crumbles. With the Northerner, you don't know until it counts, and that's
when you get a job done on yourself."

"I'd rather see a person shut up about his prejudices."   34

"You haven't been deceived. Take my job. I was pleased to get it.   35
Thought it was a breakthrough for me and other blacks here. Been there
three weeks, and next Wednesday is my last day."

"What happened?"   36

"Duplicity's what happened. White man in the shop developed a bad   37
back, so they moved him inside. His seniority gets my job. I see the plot—
somebody in the company got pressured to get rid of me."

"Are you going to leave town?"   38

"I'm staying. That's my point. I'll take St. Martinville over what I've seen   39
of other places. I'm staying here to build a life for myself and my son. I'll
get married again. Put things together." She got up and went to the window.
"I don't know, maybe I'm too hard on the town. In an underhanded way,
things work here—mostly because old blacks know how to get along with
whites. So they're good darkies? They own their own homes. They don't
live in a rat-ass ghetto. There's contentment. Roots versus disorder." She
stopped abruptly and smiled. "Even German soldiers they put in the POW
camp here to work the cane fields wanted to stay on."

We cleared the table and went to the front room. A wall plaque: 40

OH LORD, HELP ME THIS DAY
TO KEEP MY BIG MOUTH SHUT.

On a bookshelf by the window was the two-volume microprint edition of
the *Oxford English Dictionary,* the one sold with a magnifying glass.

"I love it," she said. "Book-of-the-Month Club special. Seventeen-fifty.   41
Haven't finished paying for it though."

"Is it the only one in town?"   42

"Doubt it. We got brains here. After the aristocracy left Paris during the   43
French Revolution, a lot of them settled in St. Martinville, and we got known
as *Le Petit Paris.* Can you believe this little place was a cultural center only
second to New Orleans? Town started slipping when the railroad put the
bayou steamers out of business, but the church is proof of what we had."

"When you finish the college courses, what then?"   44

"I'd like to teach elementary school. If I can't teach, I want to be a   45
teacher's aide. But—here's a big 'but'—if I can make a living, I'll write
books for children. We need black women writing, and my courses are in
journalism and French. Whatever happens, I hope they don't waste my
intelligence."

She went to wash up. I pulled out one of her books: *El Señor Presidente*   46
by Guatemalan novelist Miguel Asturias. At page eighty-five she had underlined two sentences: "The chief thing is to gain time. We must be patient."

On the way back to the agency, she said, "I'll tell you something that 47 took me a long time to figure out—but I know how to end race problems."

"Is this a joke?"   48

"Might as well be. Find a way to make people get bored with hating 49 instead of helping. Simple." She laughed. "That's what it boils down to."

Questions to Start You Thinking

1. What feelings about her town and about the people in it does Barbara Pierre reveal as she talks? What reasons does she give for wanting to stay in St. Martinville?

2. Based on evidence from the essay, what proportion of his conversation with Pierre would you say the author has included? For what reasons do you think he omitted the rest?

3. To what extent does the author's conversation with Pierre provide insights into more than individual personality?

4. Imagine that you have a chance to interview Barbara Pierre. Make a list of ten questions that you would ask her, questions that either extend topics covered in William Least Heat Moon's essay or that cover areas on which you think Pierre's comments might be interesting.

LEARNING BY WRITING

The Assignment

Write a paper about someone you know, a paper that depends primarily for its content on a conversation you have with that person. You may write about any acquaintance, friend, or relative whose traits, interests, activities, background, or outlook on life you think will interest your readers. It need not be anyone remarkable. What matters is to show as thoroughly as you can this person's character and personality as revealed through his or her conversation—in other words, to bring your subject alive.

Among student papers we have read that grew out of a similar assignment were the following.

A man wrote about a high school science teacher who had quit teaching for a higher-paying job in the computer industry only to return three years later to the classroom.

A man wrote about an acquaintance who had embraced the hippie lifestyle in the 1960s by "dropping out" of mainstream society.

A woman recorded the thoughts and feelings of a discouraged farmer she had known since childhood.

A man wrote what he learned about one woman's aspirations when he interviewed the most ardent feminist he knew.

To help you get started on this assignment, consider the following question: What does writing a paper that depends on conversation call for?

Generating Ideas

Preparing for an interview. It may be that the minute you read the assignment, an image of the perfect subject will flash into your brain. If that's the case, consider yourself lucky and go at once in search of that person to set up an appointment. If, on the other hand, you draw a blank at first, you'll need to spend a little time casting about for a likely person to interview. As you begin examining the possibilities, you may find it helpful to consider one or more of the following questions:

DISCOVERY CHECKLIST: INTERVIEWING

- Of the people you know, which ones do you most enjoy talking with?
- Are you acquainted with anyone whose life has been unusually eventful, stressful, or successful? If not, don't be discouraged. Even unspectacular lives, as Tein and Least Heat Moon demonstrate, can make interesting reading.
- Among the people you know, which have passionate convictions about society, politics, sex, childrearing, or any other topic on which you'd expect them to hold forth in lively words? A likely subject may be someone actively engaged in a cause.
- Do you know anyone who has traits you particularly respect and admire— or deplore?
- Is there anyone whose background and life history you would like to know more about?
- Is there anyone in your area whose lifestyle is utterly different from your own and from that of most people you know?
- Is there anyone whose line of work you'd like to know more about?

You might list the names of a few people you'd like to portray and then set out to strike up an informal conversation with one or two of them. In the course of such an exchange, you can see whether your prospective source has the time and the inclination to grant you an interview. It's important, as you cast about for a subject, to make sure that the person you choose to interview can talk with you at some length—an hour, say. That should be enough time for you to conduct a thorough interview without tiring out the person you're talking with and yourself as well.

You'll want to ascertain, too, that this person has no objections to appearing in your paper. If you sense any reluctance on your prospective subject's part, probably your wisest course is to go in search of a new subject. There's no reason to make your task unnecessarily difficult.

There's something to be gained, too, from trying to schedule the interview on your subject's own ground: his or her home or workplace. As we've seen from both Tein's and Least Heat Moon's essays, an interviewer can learn a great deal from the objects with which a person surrounds himself or herself, and a written interview stands to gain a great deal of life when observations about such objects are included.

If you're shy about approaching someone for an interview, you can take comfort in the fact that many interviewers share your apprehension. Remind yourself that most people will be flattered by your interest in them and their lives. When you interview someone, you acknowledge that person as an expert. Your sincere interest in what your subject says will help you forget your initial timidity.

The interview will go better, too, if when you meet your subject at the appointed time, you come prepared with some questions to ask. Give these careful thought. What kinds of questions will encourage your subject to open up? Questions about the person's background, everyday tasks, favorite leisure-time activities, hopes, and aspirations are likely to bring forth answers that you'll want to record. Sometimes a question that asks your subject to do a little imagining will elicit a revealing response. (If your house were on fire, what are the first objects you'd try to save from the flames? If you were stranded on a desert island, what books would you like to have with you? If you could be any animal in the world, which one would you choose to be?) You won't be able to find out everything there is to know about the person you're interviewing. You'll have to focus on whatever aspect of that person's life you think will best reveal his or her character. Good questions will enable you to lead the conversation where you want it to go and get it back on track when it strays too far afield. Such questions will also help you avoid awkward silences. Here are some of the questions Michael Tein had scribbled down before going to see Louie Weisser, a man with whom he seems to have had only a slight acquaintance:

Where do you live?
Does your family live in New Haven?
When is business best?
Where do you get your flowers?
Who are your customers?
Does the construction bother you?
Does the noise bother you?
Is this the best street corner?
Any trouble with robbers?
Competition?
What got you involved in the flower business?

Probably Tein didn't have to use all those questions. One good question can get some people going for hours. Some experts insist that four or five are enough to bring to any interview, but we believe it's better to err on the side of too many than too few. If, when you're actually talking with your subject, some of the questions you wrote strike you as downright silly, you can easily skip them. Some of Tein's questions would have elicited very brief answers.

Others—like "What got you involved in the flower business?"—clearly inspired Louie to respond at length and with enthusiasm.

Conducting an interview. Michael Tein also demonstrates his awareness of a few other useful interviewing techniques: he was willing to be surprised, willing to let the conversation occasionally stray down interesting byways. He knew that interviews are basically disorganized affairs. Sometimes the key question, the one that takes the interview in its most rewarding direction, is the one the interviewer didn't write down in advance, one that simply grew out of something the subject said. Tein allowed Louie to answer some questions he hadn't even asked, and he really *listened* to what Louie was saying. William Least Heat Moon, in the account of his conversation with Barbara Pierre, demonstrates both the same flexibility and the same genuine interest in his subject. Of course, if the conversation heads toward a dead end, you can always bring it back by volunteering, "But to get back to what you were saying about. . . . "

During his interview, Least Heat Moon does something else that will later add vividness to his chapter about Barbara Pierre. In her apartment he uses his eyes as well as his ears. He observes. He notices what's in the room—books on the sofa, an open copy of *Catch-22* on the table, a wall plaque, an edition of the *Oxford English Dictionary*, a Guatemalan novel in which Pierre had underlined two sentences. He asks about those that interest him, and he works Pierre's answers into his account. When you conduct an interview, you too can notice and ask about distinctive items in the subject's environment. It may encourage your subject to reveal facets of his or her personality you wouldn't have thought to ask about.

Sometimes a question you thought would inspire an animated answer won't interest your subject as much as you'd hoped it would. Sometimes the person you're interviewing may seem reluctant to answer a question, especially if you're unwittingly trespassing into private territory. Don't badger. If you have the confidence to wait silently for a bit, you might be rewarded with some surprising and valuable information. But if the silence persists, just go on to the next question.

To tape-record or not to tape-record? Many interviewers advise against bringing a tape recorder to an interview on the grounds that sometimes it inhibits the person being interviewed. Too often, it makes the interviewer lazy about really concentrating on what the subject is saying. Too often, the objections go, it tempts the interviewer simply to quote the rambling conversation as it appears on the tape without shaping it into good writing. If you do bring a tape recorder to your interview, be sure that the person you're talking with has no objections to its presence. Arm yourself as well with a pad of paper and a pen or a few sharp pencils just in case the recorder malfunctions or the tape runs out before the interview ends. And don't let your mind wander. Martha Weinman Lear, a former editor with the *New York Times Magazine*, tape-records interviews but at the same time takes notes. "With the notes I hit all the high points, everything I know I want to use in the story. Then I can go back to expand on those points without having to listen to four hours of tapes, three-and-a-half hours of which might be garbage."[1]

Many interviewers approach their subjects without a tape recorder, with only paper and pen or pencil so that they can take notes unobtrusively as the interview proceeds. However, you won't be able to write down everything the person says as he or she is talking. It's more important to look your subject in the eye and keep the conversation lively than to scribble down everything he or she says. But be sure to record on the scene whatever you want to remember in exact detail: names and dates, numbers, addresses, whatever. If the person you're interviewing says anything that is so memorable that you want to record it exactly, it's perfectly all right to stop looking your subject in the eye long enough to jot down the speaker's words just as he or she said them. Put quotation marks around them so that when you transcribe your notes later, you can lift those words just as they are and put them, quoted, into your paper.

What about a telephone interview? It may sound like an easy way to work, but it will probably be less valuable than talking with your subject in person. You won't be able to duplicate by phone the lively interplay you can achieve in a successful face-to-face encounter. You'll be unable to observe the subject's possessions and environment, which so often reveal a person's personality, or see your subject's smiles, frowns, or other body language. Meet with your subject in person if at all possible. The freshness such an encounter can lend your writing will be well worth the effort.

Shaping a Draft

As soon as the interview ends, rush to the nearest available desk or table and write down everything you remember but were unable to record during the conversation. It's imperative to do this while the conversation is still fresh in your mind. Few interviewers can remember for very long exactly what went on during an interview. The questions you took with you into the interview will guide your memory, as will any notes you took while your subject talked. A tape recorder, if you used one, can also refresh your memory.

After you write down whatever you remember from the interview, you'll have a jumble of material, probably more than you can use: impressions of your subject, thoughts and opinions expressed during your meeting, direct quotations, descriptions of the "props" you noticed in the room and perhaps asked about. The more material you gathered during the interview, the richer and more revealing your jottings are sure to be.

If you now have plenty of material and feel you know what matters, you are ready to start writing your first draft immediately. You have a good notion of what to include, what to emphasize, what to quote directly, what to sum up.

[1]Quoted in "The Art of Interviewing," text of a symposium, *The Author's Guild Bulletin* June–July 1982, p. 17.

But if your notes seem a confused jumble, you may need to approach your first draft more slowly. What are you to do with the bales of material you have amassed during the interview? Inevitably, much of what you collected will be "garbage," as Martha Weinman Lear calls it. Does that mean you should have collected less? No, it simply means that as you plan, you have to find a way to zero in on what is most valuable and useful and be willing to throw out the rest.

How do you do this? Why not start by making a list of those details you're already pretty sure you want to include? To guide you as you sift and evaluate your material, you may find it useful to ask yourself a few questions.

> What part of the conversation gave you the most insight into your subject's character and circumstances?
>
> Which of the direct quotations you wrote down reveal the most about your subject? Which are the most amusing, pithy, witty, surprising, or outrageous?
>
> Which of the objects that you observed in the subject's environment provided you with valuable clues about your subject's interests?
>
> What, if anything, did your subject's body language reveal? Did it give evidence of discomfort, pride, self-confidence, shyness, pomposity?
>
> Did the tone of voice of the person you interviewed tell you anything about his or her state of mind?
>
> Is there one theme, one emphasis that runs through the material you have written down? If so, what is it?

You can organize your material in whatever order seems coherent and sensible. If you have a great deal of material and if, as often happens, your subject's conversation tended to ramble, you may want to emphasize just one or two things about him or her: a dominant personality trait, the person's views on one particular topic, the influences that shaped the views he or she holds today. More than likely your notes will reveal some dominant impression around which to organize your portrait.

As interviews go, William Least Heat Moon's is a bit unusual in that, without in any way detracting from his subject, the author reveals much about himself as well. Michael Tein concentrates exclusively on what Lou Weisser has told him. You can decide at the outset which alternative you prefer for your own paper. Probably it's easier to leave yourself out and concentrate on your subject. That way you have to concern yourself with only one side of the conversation.

As you write, you may find yourself unable to read your hasty handwriting, or you may discover you need some crucial bit of information that somehow escaped you when you were taking notes during the interview. In such a case, telephone the person you interviewed so that you can check out what you need to know. Have your questions ready so that you need take no more of your subject's time than necessary.

At the beginning of your paper, can you introduce the person you interviewed in a way that will frame him or her immediately in your reader's mind?

A quotation, a bit of physical description, a portrait of your subject at home or at work can bring the person immediately to life.

From time to time you'll want to quote your subject directly. You may not always be able to do this perfectly (unless you've taped your interview) but you should try to be as accurate as you possibly can. Don't put into quotation marks something your subject couldn't possibly have uttered. Sometimes you may care to quote a whole sentence or more, sometimes just a phrase. In either case, you should integrate what your subject has said into your own prose as smoothly as possible. Tein does this creditably in paragraph 2 of "Flowers for Chapel Street":

> His brother "got a B.S. and M.S. and all that" and was graduated from Yale, class of 1927.

Only the words in quotation marks are actually Louie's, and they make clear the old man's rather casual attitude toward academic achievement. In the rest of the paragraph, Tein merely sums up much of what Lou has told him. Throughout his paper he moves gracefully back and forth between direct quotation and summing up.

In *Reporting*, a collection of interviews, noted reporter Lillian Ross suggests that when you quote directly the person you have interviewed, you work hard to "find the quotations that get to the truth of what that person is. That does not mean that you make up quotations. Somewhere along the line, in the time you spend with your subject, you will find the quotations that are significant— that reveal the character of the person, that present as close an approximation of the truth as you can achieve." Keep writing until you believe you have come as close to that truth as it's possible to come.

Rewriting

Wait a few hours or a few days before you look again at the early draft you have written. As you pick it up to read it over, keep in mind that what you set out to do when you wrote it was to bring alive for your reader the person you interviewed. Your main task now is to make sure you have succeeded in doing that. This brief self-quiz may help you in reviewing your work.

REVISION CHECKLIST: WRITING FROM CONVERSATION

- Have you merely skimmed over what the person said to you, or have you been careful to represent the conversation in enough detail to reveal a unique individual, worth paying attention to?
- Are some statements you quoted of lesser importance, better suited to summing up or indirect quotation ("He said that he had suffered enough") than to direct quotation ("He said, 'I have suffered enough' ")? Should some of what you merely summed up be given greater prominence?
- Have you included details that show what your subject most cares about?

- Have you put in a few of your own observations, inspired perhaps by objects you noticed in the place where the interview was conducted?
- Do the person's voice, bearing, and gestures come through in your writing?
- Read the direct quotations out loud. Do they sound likely to have come out of the mouth of the person you're portraying?
- Do the things he or she says reveal personality, character, mood?
- If any of your classmates are acquainted with your subject, do you think they would be able to recognize him or her from what you have written, even if the person's name were omitted from your account? Find out.
- Does any of the material you put into your paper strike you now as drivel? If so, be merciless about getting rid of it.
- Do any additional details, left out of your early draft, now seem worth putting in after all? If so, it's not too late to find a place for them and add them. Skim over your interview notes or listen again to selected parts of your tape recording for material whose significance may not have struck you while you were deciding what to include.
- Could your paper have a stronger beginning?
- What can you strike out?

If you find it hard to criticize your own work, ask a friend to read your draft and suggest how to make the portrait more vivid, clear, and honest. Peer criticism is often the most useful kind.

Be sure that any quotations you use fit smoothly into your own prose and that you've used quotation marks with care. For instance, whenever you find that only part of a long sentence needs to be quoted directly, make sure that where you have omitted words, you have substituted an ellipsis (...)—three dots that show where omissions have occurred—and that the sentence that contains the ellipsis makes sense. Suppose you want to quote Marta, who was interviewed by anthropologist Oscar Lewis for his landmark study of a poor Mexican family, *The Children of Sanchez* (New York: Random House, 1961). Marta said, "I had been living in the Casa Grande, but there was an argument with Delila and I moved to my aunt Guadalupe's again, this time staying until just before Trini was born." Say that you want to quote just part of that sentence in your paper. You might do it like this: "I had been living in the Casa Grande, but there was an argument with Delila and I moved to my aunt Guadalupe's ... staying until just before Trini was born." The sentence is faithful enough to the original so that it doesn't distort the speaker's words, but the three dots indicate that something has been omitted.

Occasionally you may have included a quotation within a quotation, as Lewis does a little later in his interview with Marta, who says, "When Guadalupe had gone begging Prudencia to let them stay in a corner of her room, she was told, 'My house is yours, but there is no room for your son.' " When you quote your subject quoting someone else, your subject's words appear in regular quotation marks, the other person's in *single* quotes. If your written interview, like William Least Heat Moon's, contains dialogue, be sure to start a new paragraph each time a new person speaks.

Whenever you, the writer, want to emphasize something your subject didn't, underline the material and add "emphasis mine" in brackets:

"I've always believed that if you bring children into the world, you owe them <u>at least twenty years of yourself</u>" [emphasis mine].

As you can see from these illustrations, quoting from conversation requires special attention to punctuation, and you should check your paper carefully for mechanical errors before you hand it in.

Other Assignments

1. Write a paper based on an interview with at least two members of your extended family about some incident that is part of your family lore. You may find yourself amused to notice that different people's accounts of the event don't always agree. If you can't reconcile them, combine them into one vivid account, noting that some details may be more trustworthy than others. Give credit to your sources. The paper that results might just be worth saving for posterity.

2. Interview someone who is in a line of work you think you might like to enter yourself. Find out what this person recommends you do to prepare for the job that interests you. Then write a paper detailing your subject's advice.

3. Interview a mother you know to find out what it was like for her to give birth and write a paper in which you discuss her reactions to the event. (To ask pertinent questions, you may have to do some background reading to find out what the usual childbirth practices are in this country today, what objections have been raised about them in recent years, and what alternatives are available.) Ask what the mother might do differently if she were able to relive the experience.

4. After briefly questioning fifteen or twenty students on your campus to find out what careers they are preparing for, write a short essay summing up what you find out. Are students at your college more intent on earning a lot of money than on other pursuits? How many of them are choosing lucrative careers because they have to pay back huge college loans? Are any of them unhappy with the direction they have chosen? Provide some quotations to flesh out your survey. From the information you have gathered, would you call your classmates gross materialists? Idealists? Practical people?

APPLYING WHAT YOU LEARN: SOME USES OF WRITING FROM CONVERSATION

Interviewing is a familiar tool of many writers in the world beyond college. Biographers, when they write about someone living, often conduct extensive interviews with their subject in order to guarantee accuracy. Usually they interview friends, relatives, and other associates to round out their picture of a person. Likewise, news reporters and commentators often rely on interviews with "informed sources" (generally public officials, some of whom don't want to be named). Another familiar kind of interview is that in which some author, actor, or political figure airs his or her views on a variety of subjects. Such interviews are written by people who have talked with their subjects, sometimes by telephone but usually face to face, and have carefully recorded for their own use what was said. Later they try to provide their readers with the most revealing, engaging, or outrageous opinions their subjects have expressed.

In college, you may sometimes write a profile of a person in which you try to capture your subject's character or personality—as the main writing assignment in this chapter invited you to do. But often in college writing you find yourself interviewing people not because you are interested in their personalities but because you want to find out what they know. You might be called on to write an investigative paper dependent at least in part on knowledge not available in print. (For detailed information about such papers, see Chapter 18.) The world is full of people who have firsthand experience with whatever you need to find out.

A memorable quotation from such an expert can lend great life and conviction to a factual paper or article. To write "The Superstars of Heart Research" for *Boston* magazine, reporter Philip Zaleski gathered information by talking with surgeons and scientists, or, as in the following paragraph, with an official of a national health organization.

> "If you ever want to alter people's lifestyles," says Barnie Duane of the American Heart Association, "let them watch a coronary bypass. It's the most horrendous thing I've ever seen. I watched my first one at Massachusetts General with a bunch of kids. Some of them fainted. We observed from a glass dome just four feet above the head of the surgeon, so we had a perfect view. Two teams of doctors worked simultaneously. One stood at the patient's feet, cutting a huge vein out of his leg. The other stood at his chest, ripping open the sternum with a saw—*zip!* Then they cracked open his ribs with giant clamps—*snap! snap! snap!* The surgeons lifted out a damaged artery and held it up to our view and squeezed. Cholesterol squirted out like toothpaste from a tube. It's guaranteed to change your life."

In professional scholarly research, dozens of interviews may be necessary. The five sociologists who wrote the much-acclaimed *Habits of the Heart: Individualism and Commitment in American Life* (Berkeley: University of California Press, 1985) used as their sources not only books and periodicals but also extensive interviews with both ordinary citizens and professionals in various fields. Note how this example from a chapter written by Ann Swidler enlivens its discussion with pointed, informative quotations that read like spoken words:

> Asked why she went into therapy, a woman summed up the themes that recur again and again in accounts by therapists and their clients: "I was not able to form close relationships to people, I didn't like myself, I didn't love myself, I didn't love other people." In the therapeutic ideology, such incapacities are in turn related to a failure fully to accept, fully to love, one's self.

As the therapist Margaret Oldham puts it, many of the professionally trained, upper-middle-class young adults who come to her, depressed and lonely, are seeking "that big relationship in the sky—the perfect person." They want "that one person who is going to stop making them feel alone." But this search for a perfect relationship cannot succeed because it comes from a self that is not full and self-sustaining. The desire for relatedness is really a reflection of incompleteness, of one's own dependent needs.

Before one can love others, one must learn to love one's self. A therapist can teach self love by offering unconditional acceptance. As a Rogersian therapist observes, "There's nobody once you leave your parents who can just say you are O.K. with us no matter what you do." He continues, "I'm willing to be a motherer." ... Another, more behavioristic therapist concurs, saying he works by "giving them just lots of positive reinforcement in their selves; continually pointing out things that are good about them, feeding them with it over and over again." Thus the initial ingredient in the development of a healthy, autonomous self may be love from the ideal, understanding surrogate parent-lover-friend—the therapist. Unlike that of lovers, and friends, however, the purpose of the therapist's love is not to create a lasting relationship of mutual commitment, but to free people of their dependence so that ultimately they can love themselves.

CHAPTER 8

The Mind's Eye: Writing from Imagination

"Imagination," said Albert Einstein, "is more important than knowledge." Coming from a theoretical physicist who widened our knowledge of the universe, the remark is worth remembering. When we speak of "imaginative writing" we usually mean stories, poems, or plays. And yet storytellers, poets, and playwrights have no monopoly on imagination. Scientists, economists, and historians need it, too; so do authors of college reports, blue book exams, and research papers.

In one familiar sense of the word, imagining is nothing but daydreaming— imagining yourself wafted from a cold and rainy city street to a sunny beach in the tropics, for example. Enlarging that definition a little, the *Shorter Oxford Dictionary* calls imagination "forming a mental concept of what is not actually present to the senses ... of actions and events not yet in existence." That is a narrow and limited definition of imagining, all right as far as it goes. Still, for many imaginative writers and artists, imagination is a far larger, more wonderful resource. It is nothing less than a "magical power," in the view of poet and critic Samuel Taylor Coleridge, one that can reveal in familiar objects "novelty and freshness." Sometimes it brings new things into existence by combining old things that already exist. The painter Salvador Dali, whose specialty is dreamlike landscapes, may drape melted watches over tree branches, but the building blocks of his visions are watches that tick and trees that shed their leaves. Among writers, even Lewis Carroll, whose Alice books seem remote from actual life, drew the stuff of his fantastic adventures from his friendship with a real child and from real persons in England. (His portrait of the Mad Hatter resembles one Theophilus Carter, an eccentric Oxford furniture dealer.) Instead of creating out of thin air, imaginative writers often build from materials they find at hand. "The imagination," said poet Wallace Stevens, "must not detach itself from reality."

As many writers have testified, imagining is often playful: a fruitful kind of fooling around. Ursula LeGuin, writer of science fiction, calls imagination "the free play of the mind." In her essay "Why Are Americans Afraid of Dragons?" she explains:

By "free" I mean that the action is done without an immediate object of profit—spontaneously. That does not mean, however, that there may not be a purpose behind the free play of the mind, a goal; and the goal may be a very serious object indeed. Children's imaginative play is clearly a practicing at the acts and emotions of adulthood; a child who did not play would not become mature. As for the free play of an adult mind, its result may be·*War and Peace*, or the theory of relativity.

Though the result may not be Leo Tolstoy's classic novel or Einstein's theory, a college writer will find that such free play with language and ideas can be valuable and productive—and fun besides.

The imagination works in unpredictable, seemingly hit-or-miss ways, and it doesn't work like reasoning. When we reason, we often *analyze:* break processes into steps and things into parts. But when we imagine we often *synthesize:* combine things that may never have been combined before. Writing a paper for an English course, an imaginative student drew upon Nietzsche's philosophy to explain why people get tattooed—thus bringing together two far-apart sets of knowledge.[1] In reasoning, we proceed step after step, often setting out from basic premises or assumptions and proceeding from evidence to logical conclusions. Seeing an empty robin's nest on a low branch, feathers on the ground, and the footprints of a cat, we might logically reason, from the premise that cats stalk birds, that this was an instance of such a familiar hunt: a hungry cat seeking a meal climbed the tree and caught a robin. In imagining, we are more likely to take guesses, make intuitive leaps, and arrive at surprising conclusions. Imagining the story of the cat and the bird, we might envision the robin swooping down, snatching up the cat, and flying off with it—an unlikely story, but one more memorable. Or we might imagine a baby bird falling out of its nest and a passing cat, at the time not even hunting for a meal, just happening to find it—an explanation just as likely as the logical one based on the premise that cats stalk birds. In reasoning, we also make abstractions: we move from concrete details like birds' nests, feathers, and footprints to general ideas like "nature" or "the indifferent cruelty of the animal world." But imagining often works the other way around. It prefers, over abstractions like "nature," Smokey the cat and the empty nest woven of twigs, dried grass, and a bit of red twine—right now, in the present moment.

LEARNING FROM OTHER WRITERS

It appears that, to be a whole writer and a whole human being, each of us needs both a logical, analytical mind and what Shakespeare called "the mind's eye"—the faculty of envisioning. In this chapter, we don't presume to tell you how to imagine. We only suggest how to use any imagination you have already.

[1]For the text of this paper, see David A. Christman, "Nietzsche and the Art of Tattooing," *Student Writers at Work, Second Series,* ed. Nancy Sommers and Donald McQuade (New York: Bedford Books/St. Martin's Press, 1986).

To begin, here are two examples of imaginative writing, the first by a professional scientist and the second by a student of education. Recently, Alan Lightman, who teaches astronomy and physics at Harvard University, has been writing remarkably clear essays on science for a general audience. In the essay that follows, where does Lightman begin imagining? For what purpose? With what results?

TIME TRAVEL AND PAPA JOE'S PIPE
ALAN P. LIGHTMAN

When astronomers point their telescopes to the nearest large galaxy, 1
Andromeda, they see it as it was two million years ago. That's about the time Australopithecus was basking in the African sun. This little bit of time travel is possible because light takes two million years to make the trip from there to here. Too bad we couldn't turn things around and observe Earth from some cozy planet in Andromeda.

But looking at light from distant objects isn't real time travel, the in- 2
the-flesh participation in past and future of Mark Twain's Connecticut Yankee or H. G. Wells's Time Traveler. Ever since I've been old enough to read science fiction, I've dreamed of time traveling. The possibilities are staggering. You could take medicine back to fourteenth-century Europe and stop the spread of plague, or you could travel to the twenty-third century, where people take their annual holidays in space stations.

Being a scientist myself, I know that time travel is quite unlikely ac- 3
cording to the laws of physics. For one thing, there would be causality violation. If you could travel backward in time, you could alter a chain of events with the knowledge of how they would have turned out. Cause would no longer always precede effect. For example, you could prevent your parents from ever meeting. Contemplating the consequences of that will give you a headache, and science-fiction writers for decades have delighted in the paradoxes that can arise from traveling through time.

Physicists are, of course, horrified at the thought of causality violation. 4
Differential equations for the way things should behave under a given set of forces and initial conditions would no longer be valid, since what happens in one instant would not necessarily determine what happens in the next. Physicists do rely on a deterministic universe in which to operate, and time travel would almost certainly put them and most other scientists permanently out of work.

But even within the paradigms of physics, there are some technical 5
difficulties for time travel, over and above the annoying fact that its existence would altogether do away with science. The manner in which time flows, as we now understand it, was brilliantly elucidated by Albert Einstein in 1905. First of all, Einstein unceremoniously struck down the Aristotelian and Newtonian ideas of the absoluteness of time, showing that the measured rate at which time flows can vary between observers in relative motion with respect to each other. So far this looks hopeful for time travel.

Einstein also showed, however, that the measured time order of two 6
events could not be reversed without relative motions exceeding the speed

of light. In modern physics the speed of light, 186,000 miles per second, is a rather special speed; it is the propagation speed of all electromagnetic radiation in a vacuum, and appears to be nature's fundamental speed limit. From countless experiments, we have failed to find evidence of anything traveling faster than light.

There is another possible way out. In 1915 Einstein enlarged his 1905 7 theory, the Special Theory of Relativity, to include the effects of gravity; the later theory is imaginatively named the General Theory of Relativity. Both theories have remarkably survived all the experimental tests within our capability. According to the General Theory, gravity stretches and twists the geometry of space and time, distorting the temporal and spatial separation of events.

The speed of light still cannot be exceeded locally—that is, for brief 8 trips. But a long trip might sneak through a short cut in space created by gravitational warping, with the net result that a traveler could go between two points by one route in less time than light would require by another route. It's a little like driving from Las Vegas to San Francisco, with the option of a detour around Death Valley. In some cases, these circuitous routes might lead to time travel, which would indeed raise the whole question of causality violation.

The catch is that it is impossible to find any concrete solutions of 9 Einstein's equations that permit time travel and are at the same time well behaved in other respects. All such proposals either require some unattainable configuration of matter, or else have at least one nasty point in space called a "naked singularity" that lies outside the domain of validity of the theory. It is almost as if General Relativity, when pushed toward those circumstances in which all of physics is about to be done away with, digs in its heels and cries out for help.

Still, I dream of time travel. There is something very personal about 10 time. When the first mechanical clocks were invented, marking off time in crisp, regular intervals, it must have surprised people to discover that time flowed outside their own mental and physiological processes. Body time flows at its own variable rate, oblivious to the most precise hydrogen maser clocks in the laboratory.

In fact, the human body contains its own exquisite timepieces, all with 11 their separate rhythms. There are the alpha waves in the brain; another clock is the heart. And all the while tick the mysterious, ruthless clocks that regulate aging.

Nowhere is the external flow of time more evident than in the space- 12 time diagrams developed by Hermann Minkowski, soon after Einstein's early work. A Minkowski diagram is a graph in which time runs along the vertical axis and space along the horizontal axis. Each point in the graph has a time coordinate and a space coordinate, like longitude and latitude, except far more interesting. Instead of depicting only where something is, the diagram tells us when as well.

In a Minkowski diagram, the entire life history, past and future, of a 13 molecule or a man is simply summarized as an unbudging line segment. All this on a single piece of paper. There is something disturbingly similar about a Minkowski diagram and a family tree, in which several generations, from long dead relatives to you and your children, move inevitably downward on the page. I have an urgent desire to tamper with the flow.

Recently, I found my great grandfather's favorite pipe. Papa Joe, as he was called, died more than fifty years ago, long before I was born. There are few surviving photographs or other memorabilia of Papa Joe. But I do have this pipe. It is a fine old English briar, with a solid bowl and a beautiful straight grain. And it has a silver band at the base of the stem, engraved with three strange symbols. I should add that in well-chosen briar pipes the wood and tobacco form a kind of symbiotic relationship, exchanging juices and aromas with each other, and the bowl retains a slight flavor of each different tobacco smoked in the pipe.

Papa Joe's pipe had been tucked away in a drawer somewhere for years, and was in good condition when I found it. I ran a pipe cleaner through it, filled it with some tobacco I had on hand, and settled down to read and smoke. After a couple of minutes, the most wonderful and foreign blend of smells began wafting from the pipe. All the various tobaccos that Papa Joe had tried at one time or another in his life, all the different occasions when he had lit his pipe, all the different places he had been that I will never know—all had been locked up in that pipe and now poured out into the room. I was vaguely aware that something had got delightfully twisted in time for a moment, skipped upward on the page. There *is* a kind of time travel to be had, if you don't insist on how it happens.

Questions to Start You Thinking

1. "Time travel is quite unlikely according to the laws of physics," Lightman admits in paragraph 3. How, then, do you account for his essay about time travel? For what apparent purpose or purposes does he write? Is Lightman's essay mere entertainment, or does it tell you anything you didn't know before? If so, what?

2. Does the author's emphasis on Papa Joe's pipe at the end of his essay seem misplaced? What does the pipe have to do with time travel?

3. Review the discussion of imagining that opens this chapter. How does Lightman's essay demonstrate imagining?

Student Jennifer Bowe faced this challenging assignment: "Imagine your ideal college. Conceive it to fit your own wishes and deepest desires. Then describe it in writing. Perhaps this college might bring together the strong points of several real colleges—faculty, curriculum, location, facilities, or other prominent features—in a new combination. Propose a philosophy for your college, one that might lead to original methods of instruction."

To generate ideas, Bowe first took part in a two-hour brainstorming session with three of her peers. She scribbled eight pages of ideas, pondered them, and then wrote. The following paper, though lighthearted, makes interesting criticisms of conventional methods of instruction. Besides, it proposes an experiment: let professors teach and students learn without any time spent in class.

IF I COULD FOUND A COLLEGE

JENNIFER BOWE

Welcome to Sundial College. Jennifer Bowe, founder. (That's me, that 1
statue on horseback in front of the administration building.)

When you visit the campus of Sundial for the first time, you notice 2
something strange. The position of the sun never changes, for Sundial
College takes its name from its design, which is as unique as its educational
philosophy. The whole campus rests on an enormous disk that rotates with
the sun, almost imperceptibly, so that the sun always shines down on the
college from the same direction. Rather than rising in the east and setting
in the west, the sun appears to rise straight up and set straight down again.
This odd design is not merely an advertising gimmick to make the college
sound unique; it is quite practical. Classrooms are built to receive maximum
sunlight at all times, thus saving in heating costs more than enough to pay
for running the giant motor that turns the campus. Students reading on the
lawn do not need to keep moving their blankets to stay in the sun or the
shade. Greenhouses stay sunny all day long. Night Owl Hall, the dorm for
people who like to stay up late, has its back to the sun, so that its late
sleepers will receive no unwanted morning light. Lark Hall, for early risers,
lights up with the dawn. Out of necessity, the Astronomy Department is
located just outside the central disk, so that its instruments are in harmony
with the rest of the earth. At the hub of the campus wheel is a great sundial—fixed, keeping faithful time.

Sundial College operates on the philosophy that college should prepare 3
one to think independently. It believes that the best kind of learning takes
place outside of class. For this reason, there are no classes. I insisted on
making this experiment when I founded the college. In classes where students talk a lot, too much time is spent on chatter. I have heard some great
lectures, but they have been frustrating. When you try to take notes on a
lecture, you just get all the names spelled wrong. I believe you can obtain
knowledge faster and more accurately by reading a book.

Sundial students take only one course at a time, so as to concentrate 4
on it without being distracted by other courses. Each course lasts from two
to six weeks, as long as necessary. On the first day of a course, each student
visits the professor, who hands out a reading list and some writing assignments. The college library is open day and night and has bunk beds for
people to take naps. Access to the professors is easy. Each student has a
weekly appointment with the professor (the one whose course he or she
is now taking) to ask questions and receive feedback on reading and writing
assignments.

In this college without classes, does the student lack the stimulus of 5
classroom-type discussion? On the contrary, group discussions among students in a course take place daily, outdoors in the sun, so that students can
freely talk together without being graded on what they say. At the end of
the course there is a test, not graded but marked pass or fail. If a student
fails, he or she goes to the instructor, who finds out whether the student
didn't do the work or didn't understand it. Those who fail get a second

chance. If they fail again, they receive no credit for the course. None of the courses prepares students for careers; the courses only train their minds. I admit that careers are naturally important to some students, and an active work-study program finds paying jobs for those who want to take off and work for a semester.

The students come from every walk of life and from every country. The 6 faculty, brilliant people in their twenties and a few older scholars, come from all over the world. Enthusiasm for teaching, not famous publications, is the most important criterion in hiring them. More than half are women. All have to be approved by a student council before they are rehired. Besides these regular faculty, a group of "wandering scholars" spend their time roaming around campus engaging students in intellectual bull sessions. Some are famous scholars retired from other universities; some are just brilliant bums who can talk interestingly and stimulate students to think.

Although the campus stays fixed in its place in the sun, it is always in 7 a whirl of exciting activity. Each student sets time aside for strolling around the campus taking in events. Foreign films, good Hollywood films, and documentaries of all kinds run day and night in a ten-screen theater. Lectures, plays, and concerts are held at all hours. A computer room has every kind of educational software. Rooms with VCRs contain thousands of videotapes. Everything is designed to keep the student body thinking at all times.

The Sundial experience, of course, is not entirely an intellectual one. 8 There is a lively social life. When I founded Sundial, I insisted on no fraternities, because frats induce vomiting, especially at their beer parties. There aren't any sororities either, to divide the student body into castes. The students at Sundial are unified in spirit, and campus parties and barbecues leave nobody out in the cold. An essential center of society is the campus pub. Sundial's has dark brown walls, booths with vinyl cushions, a dart board, Sundialburgers (with a slice of onion for the gnomon), and several of the "wandering scholars" always hanging around challenging students to argue with them. A friendly old proprietor named Curly, who has been on the scene for thirty-five years, gives out sympathy and five-dollar loans to students short of cash.

Sports are laid-back and informal. The teams are really just clubs, which 9 anyone may join. I don't believe in sensational football and basketball teams with star players, supported on money given by the alumni. Alumni always like to support sports teams because they can't cheer for students in class taking tests.

To finance such a college without alumni support is not easy. Luckily, 10 in founding Sundial I had several billion dollars to endow it with. My continued generosity keeps the tuition fees down to about half those at a community college. Financial aid for those who need it is available and is the highest in the country. No scholarships need to be repaid, no part-time work is required, and substantial travel bonuses are given to students who have to come a long way.

In fact, Sundial is such a pleasant place that it has one serious problem: 11 how to make everyone go home for the summer. However, its problem has a built-in solution. Once again, the design of its revolving campus proves the wisdom and foresight of its founder. When the school year ends, the dorms are locked, keeping everyone outside. Then the huge disk of Sundial College accelerates, faster and faster, reaching a dizzying speed, until every last student takes off.

Questions to Start You Thinking

1. In what remarks does Jennifer Bowe seem to be kidding? Which does she apparently mean us to take seriously?

2. What features of Sundial College appeal to you? Do any strike you as mistakes?

3. If you were designing your own ideal college, how would you state its philosophy?

LEARNING BY WRITING

The Assignment

Write your thoughts in answer to a question that begins "What if . . . ?"

You might imagine a past that unfolded differently: for instance, "What if the airplane had never been invented?" You might imagine a reversal of present-day fact: "What if men had to bear children?" Or you might imagine an event in the future: "What if the U.S. and the U.S.S.R. were to reach agreement on gradual and total nuclear disarmament?"

Formulate such a "What if" supposition and envision in specific detail a world in which the supposition were true.

Unless your instructor encourages you to do so, don't write a story. To be sure, you could conceivably write this paper as science fiction. In answer to the question "What if time travel were possible?" you might begin: "As I walked into Me-opolis in 2500 A.D., the mayor rushed up to me. 'A terrible plague of headaches has struck our city!' he shouted. Luckily, I still had my bottle of Tylenol from the twentieth century. . . ." But unless your instructor encourages you to attempt fiction, write imaginative *nonfiction.*

To help you start imagining, here are some topics that students generated for this assignment. Some may reveal interesting dimensions in your possible major field of study; some are less serious.

A DIFFERENT PAST

What if the Equal Rights Amendment had become law?

What if the South had won the Civil War?

What if continental drift had never taken place, and the Americas, Africa, and Eurasia were still one connected land mass?

What if *Homo sapiens* had not straightened up, but still walked on all fours? (One first thought: Basketball rims would be lower.)

What if Sigmund Freud had never lived?

A DIFFERENT PRESENT

What if no one needed to sleep?

What if knees bent the other way? (How would chairs, cars, and bicycles have to be redesigned?)

What if smoking were good for you?

What if the human eye could perceive only two dimensions?

What if it were possible to travel backward in time? If you could do so, to what earlier eras would you go? (Alternative: What if you could meet any six prominent persons who ever lived? Whom would you choose?)

A POSSIBLE FUTURE

What if a woman were elected the next president of the United States?

What if the United Nations were to create and control a powerful army?

What if a space station, capable of sustaining hundreds of people, were placed in orbit?

What if the salaries of all teachers in public schools and colleges were increased by fifty percent, effective immediately?

What if legislation were passed limiting couples to two children?

Generating Ideas

Those lists were intended only to help you begin your own list of likely "What if's." In making your own list of "What if" questions, you may find it helpful to brainstorm, either by yourself or (as Jennifer Bowe did) with the aid of a group. Sometimes two or three imaginations are better than one. (For helpful tips on brainstorming, see p. 457.)

To help you in generating "What if's," here are a few questions.

DISCOVERY CHECKLIST: IMAGINING POSSIBILITIES

- What event in history has always intrigued you?
- What common assumption—something we all take for granted—might be questioned or denied? (It might be a scientific opinion, such as the influential view of the surgeon general that smoking is injurious to health.)
- What future event do you most look forward to?
- What present-day problem or deplorable condition do you wish to see remedied?

Jot down as many "What if" questions as you can think of, do some trial imagining, and then choose the topic that seems most promising. Say you pick as your topic "What if the average North American life span were to lengthen to more than a century?" You might begin by reflecting on some of the ways in which society would have to change. When ideas start to flow, then, pencil in hand, start listing them. No doubt a lengthened life span would mean that a greater proportion of the populace would be old. Ask questions: How would that fact affect doctors and nurses, hospitals, and other medical facilities? How might city planners respond to the needs of so many more old people? What would the change mean for retail merchants? For television programming? For the social security system?

Reading some imaginative writing can stimulate your own imagination. If you would like examples of "What if" writing that imagines a different past, you might read Virginia Woolf's thoughts in answer to the question "What if Shakespeare had had a sister?"—and if she had been an equally gifted playwright, what might have been her fate? (See Woolf, *A Room of One's Own;* New York: Harcourt Brace Jovanovich, 1981.) Another classic is James Thurber's speculation "If Grant Had Been Drinking at Appomattox" (in *92 Stories;* New York: Avenel Books, 1985, pp. 223–26). For "What if" writing that imagines a different present—one in which women can have wives—see Judy Syfers's essay "I Want a Wife" (in *The Bedford Reader;* New York: Bedford Books/St. Martin's Press, 1985, and many other anthologies). "What if" writing that envisions a possible future include Alvin Toffler's *Future Shock* (New York: Random House, 1970) and Jonathan Schell's *The Fate of the Earth* (New York: Alfred A. Knopf, 1982).

Although there are no fixed rules to follow in imagining, all of us tend to imagine in familiar ways. An acquaintance with these ways may help you fulfill your assignment.

Shifting perspective. In imagining, a writer sometimes thinks and perceives from another person's point of view. At one moment in imagining her ideal college, Jennifer Bowe stops and realizes that many students, unlike herself, want a college to prepare them for a career. She then alters her concept of Sundial College to include a work-study program. For a research paper in a course in European history, writing of the French Revolution, one student tried to imagine what it was like to be a citizen of Paris in 1789. That might have been a "What if" paper in answer to the question "What if you could be Parisian at the time of the French Revolution?" In writing your "What if" paper, you too may find yourself consciously shifting to the perspective of a person in a radically changed world.

Shifting perspective, by the way, is a kind of imagining every writer needs to cultivate. When you revise, you try to see your own work through the eyes of a reader who hasn't met your words before. Many writers also, as they plan or as they write, imagine a possible audience.

Envisioning. Imagining what might be, seeing in the mind's eye and in graphic detail, is the process of envisioning. A writer might imagine a utopia or ideal state, as did Thomas More in *Utopia* (1516), or an anti-utopia, as did George Orwell in his 1948 novel of a grim future, *1984.* By envisioning, you can conceive of other possible alternatives: to imagine, say, a different and better way of treating illness, of electing a president or a prime minister. The student who wrote about the French Revolution by imagining life in Paris in 1789 not only had to shift perspective but also to envision. Historian Arthur M. Schlesinger, Jr., considers such an effort essential: "A historian who does not make the imaginative effort to reproduce the emotional, spiritual, and moral atmosphere of the historical period is likely to miss the main point of the period."

Sometimes in envisioning, you will find a meaningful order in what had seemed a chaotic jumble. Leonardo da Vinci, in his notebooks, tells how, when starting to conceive a painting, he would gaze at an old stained wall made of various stones until he began to see "landscapes adorned with mountains, rivers, rocks, trees, plains, . . . combats and figures in quick movement, and strange expressions of faces, and outlandish costumes and an infinite number of things." Not everyone might see that much in a wall, but da Vinci's method is familiar to writers who have worked in an imaginative way—who also have looked into a confused and random array of stuff and envisioned in it a meaningful arrangement. Your "What if" assignment, in requiring you to conceive of a different world in the past, present, or future, calls for envisioning. Take plenty of time to generate a list of convincing details to root your vision in the ground.

Synthesizing. As we mentioned at the start of this chapter, synthesizing (generating new ideas by combining previously separate ideas) is the opposite of analyzing (breaking down into component parts). In synthesizing, a writer brings together materials, perhaps old and familiar materials, and fuses them into something new. A writer makes fresh connections. When synthesizing, as Coleridge points out, the mind balances and reconciles opposites, unites disparate, even clashing, materials. Surely this is what the student did who combined in one essay tattooing and Nietzsche's philosophy. Surely Picasso also achieved a synthesis when, in making a metal sculpture of a baboon and needing a skull for the animal, he clapped on the baboon's neck a child's toy car. With its windshield like a pair of eyes and its mouthlike bumper, the car didn't just look like a baboon's skull: it *became* one. To take a famous illustration of a scientist who made a discovery by imagining, the German chemist Friedrich Kekulé rightly guessed the structure of the benzene molecule when, in reverie, he imagined a snake swallowing its own tail. In a flash he realized that the elusive molecule was a ring of carbon atoms, not a chain, as earlier chemists had believed. Surely to bring together the benzene molecule and a snake was a feat of imaginative synthesis.

By the process of synthesizing, writers make *metaphors:* statements that point to a striking similarity in two things otherwise dissimilar. Often a metaphor is a statement that a thing *is* something apparently unlike it: "an ocean wave is a rolling pin of water." Literally, of course, a wave isn't a rolling pin: no one would use a wave to flatten pie crust, but it too is a cylinder that rolls. Mark Twain makes a fresh metaphor when he says a writer needs to seek "that elusive and shifty grain of gold, the right word." No doubt he drew that imaginative figure of speech from reality: from recalling his experience as a prospector panning for gold.

A written metaphor, like those examples, can be brief, expressed in a few words. It can also be book length, like Herman Melville's novel *Moby-Dick,* which likens a whale to (among other things) the vast, indifferent universe. Jennifer Bowe, in her paper in this chapter, develops a metaphor throughout her whole essay: in the name of Sundial College and in the physical description of its unorthodox campus. "In writing, as in life," said Eudora Welty, "the connections of all sorts of relationships and kinds lie in wait of discovery, and give out their signals to the Geiger counter of the charged imagination." (For more about this useful way of seeing and writing, read "Growing a Metaphor," p. 495.)

If we don't tell you exactly how to draw connections and make metaphors like Melville, envision like Leonardo, or shift perspective like the student who assumed the view of a Parisian of 1789, please don't accuse us of copping out. Some things cannot totally be reduced to rule and line, and imagination is one of them. (A proverb may be to the point here: "The wind in the grass cannot be taken into the house.") But we hope you will accept that imagining is a practical, everyday activity of which you are fully capable. The more you write, the more firmly you can trust your own imagination. And the more words you put on paper, the more often you will find that in the act of writing you can discover surprising ideas, original examples, unexpected relationships. You will do so only if you stay actively involved with language, that endlessly fascinating stained wall that invites you to find fresh shapes in it.

Shaping a Draft

We hope we haven't given you the impression that all imagining takes place *before* you write. On the contrary, you'll probably find yourself generating more ideas—perhaps more imaginative and startling ideas—in the act of writing.

Though in writing a "What if" paper you are freely imagining, you'll still need to lay out your ideas in a clear and orderly fashion so that readers can take them in. Some writers prefer to outline (as we discuss on p. 476). However, you might find that in fulfilling this assignment all the outline you will need is a list of points not to forget. If in writing your "What if" paper you enjoy yourself and words flow readily, by all means let the flow carry you along. In that happy event, you may be able to plan at the same time that you write your first draft.

To help your reader envision your imagined world just as vividly as you do, your "What if" could use an engaging (and convincing) opening. Alan Lightman's "Time Travel and Papa Joe's Pipe" has such a beginning: in his first paragraph, Lightman arrests us with an illustration of how astronomers, in a sense, actually witness an earlier time. This introductory illustration makes us almost willing to suppose, for the moment, that time travel may indeed be possible. In beginning to write her essay on Sundial College, Jennifer Bowe reported that her hardest problem was to introduce "the basically wacky idea" of a campus built on a turntable. "I didn't know how I'd ever get anybody to believe in that campus," she said, "so I tried to describe it in detail, keeping a straight face." In relying on concrete specifics (such as her detail about the perpendicular sunrise), Bowe makes her description of Sundial's campus ring almost true. Like Lightman and Bowe, use specific details and concrete examples. You'll need to make your vision appear tangible, as if it really could exist.

The ending of Bowe's paper, too, works well. It pushes to an incredible extreme the notion of a campus built on a turntable. If we have been persuaded to accept the possibility of such a revolving campus, carried along by the writer's serious discussion of novel teaching methods, the ending takes us by surprise. Perhaps we laugh, feeling as though a rug had been yanked out from under us. This is an effective surprise ending. Bowe might instead have written a paper with a bad, contrived, disappointing surprise ending (as we warn you against in "Other Assignments" on p. 139). (For still more advice about introductions and conclusions, see pp. 489 and 491.)

Often, imaginative writing appeals to the mind's eye. For some accessible picture-filled writing, see the sports pages of a daily newspaper. Sports writer Bugs Baer once wrote of fireball pitcher Lefty Grove: "He could throw a lambchop past a wolf." Dan Shaughnessy in the *Boston Globe* described a contemporary pitcher, Roger Clemens: "Watching the Mariners try to hit Clemens was like watching a stack of waste paper dive into a shredder." Notice the striking, imaginative connections those writers draw between pitching and dissimilar things. Such language isn't mere decoration: it points to a truth and puts vivid pictures in the reader's "mind's eye." (For more about writing with *images*— language that evokes sense experiences, not always sight—look back over pp. 77–78.)

Imagination isn't always a constant flame: sometimes it flickers and wavers. If in shaping your draft you find that you get stuck and that words don't flow, you may find it helpful to shift your perspective. Try imagining the past, present, or future *as if you were somebody else.* Perhaps you will then see possibilities in your topic that didn't occur at first. Also helpful may be the ordinary kind of perspective-shifting all writers do now and then. Take a walk, relax, do something else for a while. Then return to your draft and try to look at it with a *reader's* eyes. Or ask a fellow student to read what you've done so far—not to criticize it minutely at this point, but to offer suggestions: What do you say next? Sometimes even a useless suggestion, one you'll only disagree with, can show you the way to go.

Rewriting

Try your paper on a peer reader and see if at any point your vision becomes starry-eyed beyond belief. If your reader has doubts ("Aw, come off it"), look for places where more details might help flesh out your imaginings. As Jennifer Bowe reread her first draft, which she had typed, she thought of additional details: the scholarly bums who wander around provoking intellectual conversation, the Sundialburger with the onion casting a shadow. She added these details in pen, later incorporating them into her final version. Do you need more detail in places, to make your vision clear and convincing? Then make yourself comfortable and do some more imagining.

A minor problem in envisioning may be to keep your verb tenses straight. As she imagined her ideal college, Jennifer Bowe found herself waffling back and forth between the future tense ("you *will notice* something strange") and the conditional ("the huge disk of Sundial College *would accelerate*"). Aware of this problem, she went through her draft and changed all tenses to the present. She had hit upon the simplest solution. In envisioning your imaginary world, why not hold it in the mind's eye as though it now exists?

The belief of poet William Butler Yeats—that inspiration can come in re-writing as well as in writing—may hold true when you write your "What if" paper. As you revise, you may find fresh and imaginative ideas occurring for the first time. If they occur, by all means let them in.

While you review your paper, you might consider the following points.

REVISION CHECKLIST: WRITING FROM IMAGINATION

- Is your vision consistent? Do all the parts of your vision get along with all the others? Or is some part discordant, needing to be cut out?
- Does your paper at any point need more information about the real world? If so, where might you find it: what can you read, whom can you talk with, what can you observe?
- Have you used any facts that need verifying, any words that need checking? (Jennifer Bowe recalls: "I was glad about finding the right name for the upright hand in the middle of a sundial—the *gnomon*. I didn't know what to call it until I looked up *sundial* in my dictionary and found a picture of a typical sundial, with the names of its parts.")
- What difficulties did you run into in writing your "What if"? Did you over-come them? Are any still present that bother you? If so, what can you do about them?
- Is this vision plausible? Could the world you imagine possibly exist? What physical details, vivid description, images, and illustrations can you add that will make your vision seem real?

Other Assignments

1. Like Jennifer Bowe, author of "If I Could Found a College," imagine an ideal: a person, place, or thing that to your mind would be virtually perfect. Shape this ideal to your own desires. Then describe it in writing. Perhaps this ideal might combine the best features of two or three real people, places, or things. Set forth your vision in writing as if you are trying to be useful to someone attempting to achieve something excellent for a practical reason: to improve himself or herself, to build a new town or city or college from the ground up.

    If, like Bowe, you envision your ideal college, you will have a decision to make early. Will you imagine a college as conceivably it could exist today (if you too had several billion dollars)? Or will you imagine a college of the future, which could be more nearly perfect (utilizing what science has not yet discovered)? If your ideal could exist only in the future, will you imagine the near future (say, 2000 A.D.) or a more remote future?

In describing your ideal person, city, or college, you may be tempted to build up to a surprise ending. It might seem a great trick to reveal at the end (surprise, surprise!) that your ideal city is really good old Topeka, the best place on earth, or that your ideal mother is really your own real-life mother after all. But it probably won't be a convincing way to write your paper. Nothing that exists is ideal. Simply to describe what exists won't take any imagining.

2. Imagine two alternative versions of your own future, say ten years down the road: the worst possible future you could have and the best possible. Describe each in detail. This assignment may help you in making long-term plans. (If you would prefer not to limit your vision to your own future, imagine the future of your hometown or city, your region, or your country.)

3. Recall the way you envisioned something before you experienced it; then describe the reality you found instead. For instance: "My Dream of College and the Reality," "The London I Expected and the London I Found," "A Eurythmics Concert I Looked Forward To and What I Got." Your expectations, of course, might be good or bad; the reality might be a disappointment or a pleasant surprise. But if possible, pick some topic about which your ideas changed drastically. Write to show your fellow students how your mental picture changed. They might be interested because their mental pictures might coincide with yours (before or after your change).

4. Draw a connection between two things you hadn't ever thought of connecting before. Start with something that interests you—running, moviegoing, or sports cars—and try relating it to something remote from it. Connect it to rainstorms, travel, or children's play. See what both have in common and then explain their similarity in two or three paragraphs: "The Pleasures of Running in Rain," "Moviegoing: Traveling Vicariously," "Sports Car Buffs as Grown-up Players with Toys," or whatever more appealing topic you can generate.

5. Here are a few short exercises designed to limber your imagination.
    a.   By penciling a big *X,* divide a sheet of paper into quarters. In each quarter draw a person, a bird, an animal, a fanciful monster, a machine, or anything else you wish. Diversify the drawings: don't draw birds in all four squares; mix up your subject matter. A wildly assorted mixture will work well for this. The drawings, which can be comic or serious or both, don't need to be of museum quality; they are only for your own use. When you are done, contemplate your four drawings. Then write a one-page story that brings all four subjects together.
    b.   Envision the place where you have lived for the largest part of your life. Then visualize how it would have looked a hundred years ago or (if you like) how it will look a hundred years from now. Write a passage or paragraph rapidly, setting down any details you can see in your mind's eye.
    c.   Divide a sheet of paper into two columns. Write in the left column the names of a list of objects that (for no special reason) please you, intrigue you, or make you laugh. You might make this list from both memory and immediate observation—by just looking around. Then in the right column, for each object complete a sentence that makes a metaphor. For instance, one such list might begin:

    An ant carrying something
    My poodle
    A sailboat
    Althea's elbows

Write rapidly, without trying to be brilliant. Compare each object with another object far removed from it, in which you can find some similarity. The list might then give rise to metaphors such as these:

> An ant carrying something is a piano mover.
> My poodle is a barking marshmallow.
> A sailboat is a bird with one wing.
> Althea's elbows are a couple of unripe strawberries.

Not all your metaphors will be worth keeping; not all will make sense to anyone else. You have to expect some kernels not to pop. But if you get any metaphors you like, why not share them with the class? (Metaphors like these, incidentally, are sometimes poems in their infancy. If any metaphor turns you on, by all means keep writing—whether in prose or in verse.)

d.   Here is an exercise involving wordplay and other free play of the imagination. Choose a noun with interesting sounds or suggestions, a word or phrase you don't use daily: *luminosity, tyrannosaur, potato mashers, chromosome, platypus,* or perhaps a name such as *Amazon, Peter Ilyich Tchaikovsky.* Then rapidly write a series of statements, each beginning with that word or phrase. The statements need not follow logically or tell a story. Example:

> Peter Ilyich Tchaikovsky was always too shy to ask the prom queen for a date.
> Peter Ilyich Tchaikovsky attempted to fly by flapping his arms but usually fell on his face.
> Peter Ilyich Tchaikovsky couldn't cross the Delaware standing up in a rowboat like George Washington—the Delaware was always frozen and the rowboat leaked.

So far, without deliberate effort on the writer's part, connections are emerging: Peter Ilyich Tchaikovsky is becoming a distinctive and consistent character. That is how the imagination often operates. Our example may be absurd, but it exhibits a truth. "Language," says teacher and researcher Ann Berthoff, "enables us to make the meanings by whose means we discover further meanings."

APPLYING WHAT YOU LEARN: SOME USES OF WRITING FROM IMAGINATION

Imagination, we have suggested, is tremendously useful in much college writing, not only in a creative writing course. In scholarly writing, imagination is essential—as scholarly writers keep insisting. The surest guide to the past, declares historian L. P. Curtis, Jr., is imagination:

> Imagination at its best should prompt the historian to try different techniques and even different models . . . just as the complete mountaineer learns how to cope with different kinds of rock, snow, and ice as well as weather conditions and climbing companions. ("Images and Imagination in History," in *The Historian's Workshop: Original Essays by Sixteen Historians*)

French philosopher of history Paul Veyne would agree. Because a historian has to infer the motives of persons long dead, the writing of history is a difficult and uncertain business. Understanding the past, Veyne argues, is often a matter of imaginatively "filling in" what cannot be completely documented. In the field of geography, according to Robert W. Durrenberger in *Geographical Research and Writing,* a student who wishes to do research needs most of all to develop imagination. "Admittedly, an individual cannot be taught how to be creative," Durrenberger concedes. "But he can observe those who are creative and be on the lookout for new and original approaches to the solutions of problems."

To show you how you can usefully apply the ways of imagining to your college (and later) writing, let's consider them one at a time: shifting perspective, envisioning, and synthesizing.

Shifting perspective. The next time you are given an assignment in another course, try looking at the entire topic through someone else's eyes—someone unlike yourself. This method may or may not prove useful, but it is worth trying. For instance, in writing a term paper in economics, one student effectively changed lenses. First he looked at government aid to disadvantaged people in urban ghettos, thinking and writing first as a liberal (his own conviction) and then—by an act of imagination—thinking and writing as a conservative. Fortunately, he knew a conservative well: his uncle, in whose familiar voice he was able to write part of the paper. He concluded that neither liberals nor conservatives have all the answers to the problems of low-income people in cities but that liberals have a clearer plan of action. (His uncle read the paper and disagreed vehemently.)

You'll find this way of imagining often at work in specialized and professional writing, such as on a reading list for a course. Here, for example, is science writer Garrett Hardin taking a skeptical look at some prevalent popular assumptions. In this passage from *Naked Emperors: Essays of a Taboo-Stalker,* Hardin shifts perspectives. He imagines that an economist asks an ecologist, "Would you plant a redwood tree in your back yard?" When the ecologist says that he would, the economist charges him with being a fool—in economic terms.

> The economist is right, of course. The supporting economic analysis is easily carried out. A redwood tree can hardly be planted for less than a dollar. To mature [it] takes some two thousand years, by which time the tree will be about three hundred feet high. How much is the tree worth then? An economist will insist, of course, on evaluating the forest giant as lumber. Measured at a man's height above the ground, the diameter of the tree will be about ten feet, and the shape of the shaft from there upward is approximately conical. The volume of this cone is 94,248 board feet. At a "stumpage" price of 15 cents a board foot—the approximate price a lumberer must pay for a tree unfelled, unmilled, untransported—the tree would be worth some $14,000.
>
> That may sound like a large return on an investment of only one dollar, but we must not forget how long the investment took to mature: 2,000

years. Using the exponential formula to calculate the rate of compound interest we find that the capital earned slightly less than one-half of 1 percent per year. Yes, a man would be an economic fool to put his money into a redwood seedling when so many profitable opportunities lie at hand.

Hardin, of course, is being unfair to economists, many of whom are undoubtedly capable of feeling awe before a giant redwood. But his momentary shift to the strict dollars-and-cents point of view enables him to conclude that, if we care for the future and for our descendants, we sometimes need to act without regard for economics.

Envisioning. Some of the most challenging assignments you'll meet in a college course will set forth a problem and ask you to envision a solution. This question, from a final examination in an economics course, asks the student to imagine a better procedure:

> As we have seen, methods of stabilizing the dollar have depended on enlisting the cooperation of large banks and foreign governments, which has not always been forthcoming. Propose a better, alternative way for our own government to follow in protecting the value of its currency from severe fluctuations.

An effective answer to that question would be based on facts that the student has learned. What the exam question tries to provide is not just practice in recalling facts but also training in bringing them together and applying them.

In a research paper written in spring 1986, "Space Law: Rules of the Moon," student Daniel St. Hilaire considered problems and envisioned solutions. He proposed answers to legal questions likely to be crucial in the future: Should discoverers of resources on the moon be allowed to keep them? Should probes be allowed for a scientific purpose (which might involve quarrying and removing material), or should international law protect the moon's existing surface? (And how should the law define a scientific purpose?) Besides studying existing international agreements applying to the moon, St. Hilaire had to envision future conflicts and problems and suggest ways in which the law might deal with them.

A writer with a lively "mind's eye" is seldom at a loss for an illustration. In "Self-Defense," an essay explaining to women readers how the law views protecting oneself against attack, Arthur R. Miller envisions an imaginary (but typical) incident:

> Now, let's suppose a week after graduation from self-defense school, you get off the bus one night and start walking home. Suddenly a man comes up and grabs you and starts to wrestle you to the ground. You use your newly acquired expertise to knock him flat on his back. Obviously you can't be convicted of assault. This is a clear case of self-defense, since you acted to protect yourself from physical attack. A court most likely would conclude that you used reasonable force to repel the attacker, especially since you did not employ deadly force.

In envisioning an ideal, as Jennifer Bowe does in her Sundial College paper, a writer sets up an imagined goal, perhaps also begins thinking how to achieve it. In his epoch-opening speech in Washington, D.C., on the 1963 centennial of Lincoln's Emancipation Proclamation, Martin Luther King, Jr., set forth his vision of an unsegregated future:

> I have a dream that one day on the red hills of Georgia the sons of former slaves and the sons of former slave owners will be able to sit down together at the table of brotherhood. . . . I have a dream that my four little children will one day live in a nation where they will not be judged by the color of their skin but by the content of their character.

Synthesizing. Combining unlike things (such as Nietzsche's philosophy and tattooing) and drawing unexpected connections may result in a lively and revealing paper. Usually, a writing assignment in a course will not ask you to relate extremely distant things. More likely you will be asked to compare and contrast things with apparent similarities: the work of two painters, two sociologists' theories.

Still, in explaining almost anything, an imaginative writer can make metaphors and draw connections. Sylvan Barnet, in *A Short Guide to Writing About Art* (Boston: Little, Brown, 1985), questions whether a period of art can be entirely "Gothic" in spirit. To make a highly abstract idea clear, he introduces a brief *analogy,* an extended metaphor that likens the unfamiliar thing to something familiar:

> The very term *Gothic period* is a historian's invention, an attempt to impose order. Having imposed this simplification, the historian then begins to feel a bit uneasy and distinguishes between Early Gothic and Late Gothic, or between Spanish Gothic and English Gothic, and so on. Is there really an all-embracing style in a given period? One can be skeptical, and a simple analogy may be useful. A family often consists of radically different personalities: improvident husband, patient wife, one son an idler and the other a go-getter, one daughter wise in her choice of a career and the other daughter unwise. And yet all may have come from the same culture.

Though the differences between Spanish Gothic and English Gothic art may be unknown to us, we immediately grasp the idea of the family whose members exhibit a wide variety of character traits. (An analogy may also be written at greater length and in greater detail, and a writer may need to devote a whole essay to it.)

To be sure, imagining has practical applications beyond the writing of college papers and scholarly articles. Asked why World War I took place, Franz Kafka, one of the most influential writers of our century, gave a memorable explanation: the war was caused by a "monstrous lack of imagination." Evidently if we are to survive, we would do well to imagine both World War III and its alternatives—not only the consequences of the problems we now face, but also the solutions.

Further Writing Assignments: Combining Resources

Any of the five resources shown in the past five chapters—recalling, observing, reading, conversing, imagining—may be useful to you in virtually any college paper you write. We have been taking them one at a time, asking you to write papers using mainly one resource. But in some of the most interesting writing you will do, now and later in life, you will want to use any resource you can tap.

Here are assignments that tap more than one resource.

Recalling and Observing

Visit and describe a place long familiar to you, a place that has undergone changes over the years. These changes may be external and visible, or they may have occurred in *you*: in the way you now see the place, as opposed to the way it once seemed to you. Make comparisons between the way the place is now and how it used to be.

Recalling and Observing

Like Joan Didion, who observes the wedding chapel scene in "Marrying Absurd" (p. 71), have you ever been in a place you thought fake, tacky, or depressingly pretentious? If so, what did you observe at the time that gave you such an impression? Write a short description, recalling what you observed.

Recalling and Reading

Recall a subject you know well—a sport, a business, a film or current television program, a city. Then find out what another writer has had to say about it. (Recent numbers of the *Readers' Guide to Periodical Literature* in your library's reference room will lead you to promising magazine articles.)

In a short paper that you'd be willing to have your fellow students read, compare the writer's view of the subject with your own knowledge drawn from recall. What does the writer tell you that you find enlightening? What do you know from your own experience that the professional writer left out?

Recalling, Observing, and Conversing

What changes have taken place in television programs for children and young people since you were a child? Discuss some of those changes with a group of your fellow students. What changes in society—in manners and attitudes—do they mirror?

Perhaps you can observe reruns of "The Brady Bunch" or "The Partridge Family," recall "Mr. Rogers" or "Captain Kangaroo," or any other programs you used to watch. How, you might inquire, do the script writers regard women? How has the American family changed over the years? Do most families still enjoy the sit-down-together family dinner at home? Is the loving, uniformed servant like the Brady's Alice a familiar figure in many households today? (It might be risky to assume that she was familiar back then.) Are there programs on the air today with which you might compare these beloved antiques? Twist that dial, probe, ponder. Since you were eight years old, what shifts have taken place in the national consciousness?

Reading and Conversing

Browse through a few articles in current magazines. (The magazines need not be *Time* or *Newsweek;* why not look around your library's periodicals room and meet an interesting magazine or professional journal you hadn't known before?) Keep browsing until you find an article that provokes you to strong feeling. Maybe it will anger you, disturb or frighten you, or make you wonder how any writer could be that dumb. Make a photocopy of the article.

Write your interpretation of the article. What message does it convey? What does it demonstrate?

Next, show the article to another student. Ask him or her to read it closely and discuss it with you. Compare your interpretations; see whether either of you missed anything interesting.

Finally, write a second account of what you now think the article is saying. If your original interpretation hasn't changed (or, if you like, even if it has), write an answer or retort to the writer.

Observing and Imagining

Do writing assignment 2 on page 82—observing, like a good detective, another person in a public place without that person observing you. Then add the following step:

Piece together the person's probable situation at home or on the job. Feel free to speculate. What do you think your subject does in everyday life, when you aren't around to observe?

Reading and Imagining

Read a news account of an event in a distant country. Then put yourself in the shoes of the people affected: imagine that this event has taken place in your own neighborhood. How would the event affect you and people you know?

Reading, Observing, and Imagining

Here is the opening of an article, "The Tactile Land," by naturalist Robert Finch in *Sanctuary* magazine, a publication of the Massachusetts Audubon Society. Read it and briefly react to it, and try it on your own experience. Try observing something and reporting it as Finch reports the mother's caress. If you were to take Finch's kind of observing to heart, how might it change your view of the world?

Several years ago, as I sat in a maternity clinic waiting room anticipating the birth of my second child, I happened to see a young mother across the way just as she reached out and, in a purely unconscious gesture, casually caressed the head of her little boy, just beyond his ear. Because I had performed that same unconscious parental gesture hundreds of times, I not only saw the movement of her hand but felt it—felt the curve of the child's head, the fine texture of the hair, the swirl and dip of the crown, the hollow behind the ear, the small, soft, fleshy fold of ear lobe. From unpremeditated and forgotten affection there now rose, with this sight, palpable ripples of remembered feeling, tactile memories surfacing to color, warm, and revivify this simple visual scene. It was real to me, this tracing of the child's head by the woman; it enriched not only the present moment, but gave back to me parts of my own life that had gone unrecognized at the time.

That was the first time I became strongly aware of the great difference between merely observing an action or a scene and seeing it infused with the memory of tactile and emotional sensation. Drugs and danger, we are told, can heighten or expand the senses, but it seems to me that life is vivid to us primarily insofar as we have previously insinuated ourselves into it and gives us back a part of ourselves as we behold it in others in just such numerous, characteristically small ways.

Recalling, Observing, Reading, and Conversing

What does a professional critic of architecture think of a contemporary shopping mall? Barrie B. Greenbie makes this comment in his study *Spaces: Dimensions of the Human Landscape*. Read the passage critically. How well do Greenbie's observations fit any mall or malls you know?

The term *mall,* which used to mean a large, outdoor, public place, now refers to such a place under a roof. In some ways, the good shopping centers have returned the market street to the pedestrian better than have the central business districts of towns because the cars are left outside. A few of these shopping malls are as colorful and interesting as any other bazaars. A number of studies, including one in which I participated, have shown that people go to them as much for sociability as to purchase necessities. Youth gangs, which used to hang out around the neighborhood candy store, now drag race over to the local shopping plaza and hang out there.

The typical design of shopping centers calls for one or more large department stores as "anchors" (really magnets), between which are strung the smaller stores for so-called impulse shopping. Not only are they a place for strolling and people-watching, but for many community functions, such as charity fund drives, which used to be associated with central business districts. The shops generally do not have the personality of those operated by individual proprietors; most mall developers will rent space only to chains, which are viewed as being more reliable tenants than single-owner stores. The merchandise tends to be monotonously similar, with emphasis on products for youth. Most such emporiums do not offer the unique sense of place and the sensual variety of an old city center, but they are nevertheless very sociable promenades. . . . Their greatest weakness, as compared with lively pedestrian spaces downtown, is that they have no visible relationship to a larger exterior environment. That has been given over to parking. For example, the shopping mall which is the major public node of the "new town" of Columbia, Maryland, is as bleak on the outside as any warehouse, perhaps more so. Inside, however, it is an elegant commercial plaza, with pedestrian streets surrounded by lively architecture and spaces that can only be described as parks.

Discuss this passage in class or outside of class. Try to state what Greenbie apparently feels toward shopping malls 'and toward old city centers. In the usual designs or arrangements of places where people may shop, stroll, and congregate, what does he admire? What does he condemn?

In a paragraph or two based on your own recollections and observations, nourished too from your class discussion or conversation, write for or against Greenbie's view of a typical shopping mall of today. Don't hesitate to set forth your own likes and dislikes.

Recalling, Observing, Reading, Conversing, and Imagining

Recall an event of national or international significance that took place in your own lifetime: a disaster, an important discovery or breakthrough, a famous trial, whatever. Discuss the event with your peers to compare memories of it. Do some background reading so that you're sure you've got the facts straight, list some visible results that followed from this event, and then, in writing, imagine ways in which the world would now be different if the event had never occurred.

PART THREE

Writing to Explain

Most college writing assignments call on you to explain—that is, to set forth in your own words your own understanding of something you have studied or read. On an exam in economics, you might be asked to list the effects of the Hawley-Smoot tariff on trade relations. For sociology, you might find yourself explaining why the United States has a literacy problem. For geology, you might set forth how to classify mineral specimens or explain the stages by which a river forms a delta. For a business course, you might be asked to explain how to file for a patent; for French literature, to compare and contrast Sartre and Camus as philosophers.

Outside of class, you keep on explaining. Perhaps a friend in Alaska urges you to quit school and join him in digging for prehistoric animal bones preserved in permafrost. In a letter, you might present your reasons for staying put. Perhaps you're an expert in some special knowledge. You've stumbled on an original proof in math, and your instructor asks you to write out (and explain) your demonstration of it. You're a motorcycle aficionado, invited to write an article for the college paper comparing two leading makes of machine. All these writing jobs call for expository writing: writing that makes matters plain to readers who want to know.

To explain clearly and effectively is a learnable skill. In the next five chapters, we'll set forth five often-used methods for explaining while you write. The methods aren't like trusty card tricks, sure to work on an audience. Nor are they ends in themselves; they have no meaning until you put them to use. At times, you'll find these methods valuable in writing anything from a paragraph to a whole term paper. Essentially, they are ways to advance a purpose: to make valuable things understandable to others and to yourself.

CHAPTER 9

Setting Things Side by Side: Comparing and Contrasting

Which city—Dallas or Atlanta—has more advantages and more drawbacks for a young single person thinking of settling down to a career? How does the IBM personal computer stack up against a Macintosh for word processing? As songwriters, how are Bruce Springsteen and Bob Dylan similar and dissimilar? Such questions invite answers that set two subjects side by side.

When you compare, you point out similarities; when you contrast, you discuss differences. In writing assignments that ask you to deal with two complicated subjects, usually you will need both to compare *and* contrast. Taking Springsteen and Dylan, you might find that each has traits the other has—or lacks. In writing about the two, you wouldn't absolutely have to conclude that one is great and the other inferior. You might look at their differences and similarities and then conclude that they're two distinct composer-performers, each with an individual style. Of course, such fence-straddling papers can seem to lack heart; if you had a passionate preference for either Dylan or Springsteen, you'd want to voice it. In a paper whose main purpose is to judge between two subjects (as when you'd recommend that a young single person move either to Dallas or to Atlanta), you would look especially for positive and negative features, weigh the attractions of each city and its faults, and then stick your neck out and make your choice.

In daily life, all of us frequently compare and contrast, as when we decide which menu selection to choose, which car (or other product) to buy, which magazine to read in a waiting room, which college course to sign up for. Though in making such everyday decisions we do not usually commit our reasoning to paper, comparing and contrasting (and weighing evidence for and against) are familiar habits of thought. Used in writing, this dual method is easy to follow.

LEARNING FROM OTHER WRITERS

Let's see, for instance, how Maria A. Dixon sets two famous tennis stars side by side. In a paper written for an English course, she was asked to use the method of comparing and contrasting to show how two individuals are distinctive in character.

A TOTALLY DIFFERENT RACKET

MARIA A. DIXON

It was quiet as they entered center court. Each braced herself for the 1
ultimate confrontation. Simultaneously, they armed themselves, glancing
occasionally at their coaches for last-minute instructions. Within seconds,
the grunts and groans of human exertion could be heard by every spectator.
It seemed unreal that two women could turn a lonely strip of grass into a
virtual battleground; yet as Chris Evert Lloyd and Martina Navratilova clashed,
each realized that the stakes were high. For one, this would be the day of
her coronation as the queen of modern tennis and for the other a year of
being dubbed "the second greatest woman in tennis."

Remarkable as it seems, these two women have dominated women's 2
tennis for more than ten years. Although each of their careers has reached
great heights, these two women are exact opposites. Perhaps the greatest
differences are in their personal backgrounds, their personalities, and their
styles of playing tennis.

For Chris Evert Lloyd, the world was her piece of cake and all she had 3
to do was eat it. Tall, slim, and blond, she led the typical South Florida
beauty's life, where debutante balls and country club living were not luxuries but traditions. Her father, a rich Miami businessman, encouraged his
daughter to play by building her tennis courts and giving her customized
rackets.

When Chris entered the ranks of professional tennis, she immediately 4
became a crowd favorite. With her girl-next-door looks, she was nicknamed
"the darling" by the press. Soon she became more popular than old favorites like Billie Jean King and Yvonne Goolagong, causing them eventually
to fade into the background. Not only popular among the crowd and the
press, she was considered a great "catch" by many of the men on the tour.
During the early years of her career, she dated several top-ranking players
before she finally settled down with Englishman John Lloyd.

The only nickname given to Chris that she still dislikes is "Ice Princess"; 5
however, it is this name that truly defines her personality on and off the
court. Regardless of her position in a match, she remains passionless and
cool until the end of the game. In her post-game interviews she answers
questions crisply, with an air of aloofness, never going into more detail
than needed. Only occasionally is there a smile that covers her face or a
glimpse of humor in her manner. Usually we see only her emotionless
mask.

It is this stoic mask that has extended itself into her style of tennis. Like 6
her personality, her game is basic and passionless. By playing baseline
tennis, she relies on high-percentage shots to carry her to victory. Her style
consists of a series of long rallies that eventually lull her opponents to sleep
as well as emphasize the grace and elegance of "tennis à femme."

If life for Martina Navratilova was going to be a piece of cake, then she 7
would have to be the baker. Unlike Chris, Martina grew up in a middle-
class household in Czechoslovakia. For her, there were no debutante balls
or country club dinners, only endless hours of helping her family stay above

the poverty line. Her family considered tennis a waste of time; therefore, she had to learn tennis with a borrowed racket and an old cobblestone backboard.

"The Blimp" was the nickname given to Martina when she arrived on 8 the pro circuit. She was overweight, had masculine features, and was hostile to everyone. Her tennis game was inconsistent, although she was consistent in being defeated by Chris Evert Lloyd. Personal problems besieged her from every angle. She had defected from her homeland, and rumors developed that she had had a homosexual relationship. By the end of 1978, she was seen as the biggest laughingstock in professional tennis. Yet, underneath, Martina knew she had the ability to be a great player. She hired a team of specialists known as "Team Navratilova" to help transform her raw talent into a polished weapon. With advice from her coach, physical therapist, and nutritionist, she proceeded to set the world of tennis ablaze.

The word "volatile" comes to mind when describing Martina's person- 9 ality. Although she plays with an almost machinelike precision from the first serve to the last, Martina shows her emotions vividly. If she feels that things are not going her way, she never hesitates to sound off, though she usually tends to find the lighter side of the situation, and occasionally she clowns with the crowd. During her post-match interviews, she is witty and often insightful about her competitors.

Like Chris, Martina's style is nothing more than an extension of her 10 personality. Her style, called "Navratolism," is fast-paced, aggressive, and often intense. Frequently, she dashes to the net, producing shots that can only be reproduced by her. Her style is unique in women's tennis because it is a man's style. She was taught by a man to serve like a man, volley like a man, and be athletic like a man. While Chris lulls her opponents to sleep, Martina exhausts hers with extreme intensity and constant motion.

The crowd stands in tribute to the figures below and continues to cheer 11 as the silent women slowly walk toward the center of the court, appearing for an instant to be two weary warriors of the past. As they clasp their hands firmly, they exchange a look of exhaustion and yet, at the same time, one of challenge, for both women realize that the outcome of their next confrontation could be a totally different racket.

Questions to Start You Thinking

1. To what extent is Maria Dixon concerned with the two tennis stars as players? To what extent as people?

2. Does the writer appear to favor one of the stars, or is she impartial? On what evidence do you base your answer?

3. What other pairs of well-known people (in any walk of life) can you think of whose similarities and differences might shed light on them as individuals?

This professional essay, first published in 1972, has remained timely. Notice that the way this author organizes his comparison is different from the way Dixon organizes hers.

ANGLO vs. CHICANO: WHY?

ARTHUR L. CAMPA

The cultural differences between Hispanic and Anglo-American people 1
have been dwelt upon by so many writers that we should all be well informed about the values of both. But audiences are usually of the same
persuasion as the speakers, and those who consult published works are for
the most part specialists looking for affirmation of what they believe. So,
let us consider the same subject, exploring briefly some of the basic cultural
differences that cause conflict in the Southwest, where Hispanic and Anglo-
American cultures meet.

Cultural differences are implicit in the conceptual content of the lan- 2
guages of these two civilizations, and their value systems stem from a long
series of historical circumstances. Therefore, it may be well to consider
some of the English and Spanish cultural configurations before these Eu-
ropeans set foot on American soil. English culture was basically insular,
geographically and ideologically; was more integrated on the whole, except
for some strong theological differences; and was particularly zealous of its
racial purity. Spanish culture was peninsular, a geographical circumstance
that made it a catchall of Mediterranean, central European and north African
peoples. The composite nature of the population produced a marked re-
gionalism that prevented close integration, except for religion, and led to
a strong sense of individualism. These differences were reflected in the
colonizing enterprise of the two cultures. The English isolated themselves
from the Indians physically and culturally; the Spanish, who had strong
notions about *pureza de sangre* [purity of blood] among the nobility, were
not collectively averse to adding one more strain to their racial cocktail.
Cortés led the way by siring the first *mestizo* in North America, and the
rest of the conquistadores followed suit. The ultimate products of these
two orientations meet today in the Southwest.

Anglo-American culture was absolutist at the onset; that is, all the dom- 3
inant values were considered identical for all, regardless of time and place.
Such values as justice, charity, honesty were considered the superior social
order for all men and were later embodied in the American Constitution.
The Spaniard brought with him a relativistic viewpoint and saw fewer moral
implications in man's actions. Values were looked upon as the result of
social and economic conditions.

The motives that brought Spaniards and Englishmen to America also 4
differed. The former came on an enterprise of discovery, searching for a
new route to India initially, and later for new lands to conquer, the fountain
of youth, minerals, the Seven Cities of Cíbola and, in the case of the mis-
sionaries, new souls to win for the Kingdom of Heaven. The English came
to escape religious persecution, and once having found a haven, they settled
down to cultivate the soil and establish their homes. Since the Spaniards
were not seeking a refuge or running away from anything, they continued
their explorations and circled the globe 25 years after the discovery of the
New World.

This peripatetic tendency of the Spaniard may be accounted for in part 5 by the fact that he was the product of an equestrian culture. Men on foot do not venture far into the unknown. It was almost a century after the landing on Plymouth Rock that Governor Alexander Spotswood of Virginia crossed the Blue Ridge Mountains, and it was not until the nineteenth century that the Anglo-Americans began to move west of the Mississippi.

The Spaniard's equestrian role meant that he was not close to the soil, 6 as was the Anglo-American pioneer, who tilled the land and built the greatest agricultural industry in history. The Spaniard cultivated the land only when he had Indians available to do it for him. The uses to which the horse was put also varied. The Spanish horse was essentially a mount, while the more robust English horse was used in cultivating the soil. It is therefore not surprising that the viewpoints of these two cultures should differ when we consider that the pioneer is looking at the world at the level of his eyes while the *caballero* [horseman] is looking beyond and down at the rest of the world.

One of the most commonly quoted, and often misinterpreted, char- 7 acteristics of Hispanic peoples is the deeply ingrained individualism in all walks of life. Hispanic individualism is a revolt against the incursion of collectivity, strongly asserted when it is felt that the ego is being fenced in. This attitude leads to a deficiency in those social qualities based on collective standards, an attitude that Hispanos do not consider negative because it manifests a measure of resistance to standardization in order to achieve a measure of individual freedom. Naturally, such an attitude has no *reglas fijas* [fixed rules].

Anglo-Americans who achieve a measure of success and security through 8 institutional guidance not only do not mind a few fixed rules but demand them. The lack of a concerted plan of action, whether in business or in politics, appears unreasonable to Anglo-Americans. They have a sense of individualism, but they achieve it through action and self-determination. Spanish individualism is based on feeling, on something that is the result not of rules and collective standards but of a person's momentary, emotional reaction. And it is subject to change when the mood changes. In contrast to Spanish emotional individualism, the Anglo-American strives for objectivity when choosing a course of action or making a decision.

The Southwestern Hispanos voiced strong objections to the lack of 9 courtesy of the Anglo-Americans when they first met them in the early days of the Santa Fe trade. The same accusation is leveled at the *Americanos* today in many quarters of the Hispanic world. Some of this results from their different conceptions of polite behavior. Here too one can say that the Spanish have no *reglas fijas* because for them courtesy is simply an expression of the way one person feels toward another. To some they extend the hand, to some they bow and for the more *intimos* there is the well-known *abrazo*. The concepts of "good or bad" or "right and wrong" in polite behavior are moral considerations of an absolutist culture.

Another cultural contrast appears in the way both cultures share part 10 of their material substance with others. The pragmatic Anglo-American contributes regularly to such institutions as the Red Cross, the United Fund and a myriad of associations. He also establishes foundations and quite often leaves millions to such institutions. The Hispano prefers to give his contribution directly to the recipient so he can see the person he is helping.

A century of association has inevitably acculturated both Hispanos and   11 Anglo-Americans to some extent, but there still persist a number of culture traits that neither group has relinquished altogether. Nothing is more disquieting to an Anglo-American who believes that time is money than the time perspective of Hispanos. They usually refer to this attitude as the "*mañana* psychology." Actually, it is more of a "today psychology," because Hispanos cultivate the present to the exclusion of the future; because the latter has not arrived yet, it is not a reality. They are reluctant to relinquish the present, so they hold on to it until it becomes the past. To an Hispano, nine is nine until it is ten, so when he arrives at nine-thirty, he jubilantly exclaims: "¡Justo!" [right on time]. This may be why the clock is slowed down to a walk in Spanish while in English it runs. In the United States, our future-oriented civilization plans our lives so far in advance that the present loses its meaning. January magazine issues are out in December; 1973 cars have been out since October; cemetery plots and even funeral arrangements are bought on the installment plan. To a person engrossed in living today the very idea of planning his funeral sounds like the tolling of the bells.

It is a natural corollary that a person who is present oriented should   12 be compensated by being good at improvising. An Anglo-American is told in advance to prepare for an "impromptu speech," but an Hispano usually can improvise a speech because *"Nosotros lo improvisamos todo"* [we improvise everything].

Another source of cultural conflict arises from the difference between   13 *being* and *doing*. Even when trying to be individualistic, the Anglo-American achieves it by what he does. Today's young generation decided to be themselves, to get away from standardization, so they let their hair grow, wore ragged clothes and even went barefoot in order to be different from the Establishment. As a result they all ended up doing the same things and created another stereotype. The freedom enjoyed by the individuality of *being* makes it unnecessary for Hispanos to strive to be different.

In 1963 a team of psychologists from the University of Guadalajara in   14 Mexico and the University of Michigan compared 74 upper-middle-class students from each university. Individualism and personalism were found to be central values for the Mexican students. This was explained by saying that a Mexican's value as a person lies in his *being* rather than, as is the case of the Anglo-Americans, in concrete accomplishments. Efficiency and accomplishments are derived characteristics that do not affect worthiness in the Mexican, whereas in the American it is equated with success, a value of highest priority in the American culture. Hispanic people disassociate themselves from material things or from actions that may impugn a person's sense of being, but the Anglo-American shows great concern for material things and assumes responsibility for his actions. This is expressed in the language of each culture. In Spanish one says, *"Se me cayó la taza"* [the cup fell away from me] instead of "I dropped the cup."

In English, one speaks of money, cash and all related transactions with   15 frankness because material things of this high order do not trouble Anglo-

Americans. In Spanish such materialistic concepts are circumvented by referring to cash as *efectivo* [effective] and when buying or selling as something *al contado* [counted out], and when without it by saying *No tengo fondos* [I have no funds]. This disassociation from material things is what produces *sobriedad* [sobriety] in the Spaniard according to Miguel de Unamuno, but in the Southwest the disassociation from materialism leads to *dejadez* [lassitude] and *desprendimiento* [disinterestedness]. A man may lose his life defending his honor but is unconcerned about the lack of material things. *Desprendimiento* causes a man to spend his last cent on a friend, which when added to lack of concern for the future may mean that tomorrow he will eat beans as a result of today's binge.

The implicit differences in words that appear to be identical in meaning   16
are astonishing. Versatile is a compliment in English and an insult in Spanish. An Hispano student who is told to apologize cannot do it, because the word doesn't exist in Spanish. *Apologia* means words in praise of a person. The Anglo-American either apologizes, which is a form of retraction abhorrent in Spanish, or compromises, another concept foreign to Hispanic culture. *Compromiso* means a date, not a compromise. In colonial Mexico City, two hidalgos once entered a narrow street from opposite sides, and when they could not go around, they sat in their coaches for three days until the viceroy ordered them to back out. All this because they could not work out a compromise.

It was that way then and to some extent now. Many of today's conflicts   17
in the Southwest have their roots in polarized cultural differences, which need not be irreconcilable when approached with mutual respect and understanding.

Questions to Start You Thinking

1. For what possible reason does Campa, near the beginning of his portrait of Anglos and Chicanos, examine the European cultures from which they came?

2. Have you ever noticed, yourself, any of the striking differences in attitude between Chicano and Anglo that this writer cites? Would you disagree with Campa on any points or perhaps interpret them differently?

3. Question for Anglos only: How does this essay help make you aware of your own values and assumptions?

4. What other groups of people can you think of who, examined by the method of comparing and contrasting, might illuminate each other? With which are you familiar enough to write?

LEARNING BY WRITING

The Assignment

Write a paper in which you compare and contrast two persons or two kinds of person; two places; or two things. Be sure you choose two subjects you care about and want to reveal. Let your aim in writing the paper be either to illuminate them or to illuminate them *and* choose between them. Like Maria Dixon and Arthur Campa, you might set out to write an impartial paper that distinctly portrays both subjects. Or instead, you might demonstrate why you favor one subject over the other.

Although the subjects should differ enough to throw each other into sharp relief, be sure they have enough in common to compare. A comparison of sports cars and racing cars might reveal much, but not a comparison of sports cars and oil tankers.

Among the most engaging and instructive recent student papers we've seen in answer to similar assignments are these:

> An American woman compared and contrasted her own home life with that of her roommate, a student from Nigeria. Her goal was to understand more deeply Nigerian society and her own.

> A man who had read some articles and books about comets contrasted the spectacular fly-by of Halley's Comet in 1910 with its less spectacular return in 1985–1986. He also compared and contrasted public responses to the comet's two twentieth-century appearances. He wished to demonstrate that the comet's latest performance had not really been a flop.

> For an economics course that asked for an explanation of a major idea of influential economist John Maynard Keynes, a woman student compared and contrasted Keynes's views of the causes of monetary inflation with those of Karl Marx on the same subject.

> A man compared the differences between traveling by airline and traveling by train. His purpose was to make a case for the continuation of intercontinental passenger rail service.

> A man, setting forth his understanding of George Orwell's novel *1984*, compared and contrasted two characters: O'Brien and Winston Smith.

In his freshman writing course, Eli Kavon, who had spent some time studying at an Israeli military seminary, wrote (from recall) an account of his experience for the information of his instructor and fellow students. In part of this account, he compared and contrasted himself (and his fellow American Jewish students in Israel) with Israeli students:

> We—the foreigners—shared much in common with our Israeli contemporaries: a history dating back thousands of years, a belief in one God, a love of Judaism and the Land of Israel. However, we would be in the country only for a year or two and would not be drafted with the Israelis, who devote two of five years in the seminary to military service. Unlike the average Israeli, none of us had grown up in a household where real weapons rested in closets and on top of refrigerators, ready for use. American teenagers know of war as either a childhood game with plastic weapons or as a memory of the battles and the body bags of a "television war." Israelis, on the other hand, have been forced to live a life of drafts, weapons, and fear. In Israel preparation for war is the norm.

As you can see from that passage, Kavon's comparing and contrasting is no meaningless exercise. Here, it is a way to think clearly and pointedly in order to explain an idea about which the writer deeply cares.

Generating Ideas

You first need a reason to place two subjects side by side—a reason that most readers will find compelling and worthwhile. Pick two subjects you can compare and contrast purposefully. An examination question may give them to you, ready-made: "Compare and contrast ancient Roman sculpture with that of the ancient Greeks" or "Discuss the main differences between the British system of higher education and the American system."

But suppose you have to find your subjects for yourself. You'll need to choose things that can sensibly be compared and contrasted—things clearly comparable. Find a basis for comparison: a common element. There is probably no point in comparing and contrasting moon rocks and stars, but it will make sense to bring together Springsteen and Dylan *as songwriters,* Dallas and Atlanta *as cities to consider settling in*, or Karl Barth and Søren Kierkegaard *as religious thinkers.*

Limit the territory your paper will encompass. If you proposed to write a comparison and contrast between Japanese literature and American literature in 750 words, probably you would be tackling a larger subject than you could bring to the ground. To explore it thoroughly, you might need to write a whole book. But to cut down the size of this promising subject, you might propose to compare and contrast, say, a haiku of Basho about a snake with a short poem about a snake by Emily Dickinson. You would then be dealing with a topic you could cover adequately in 750 words. Of course, the larger and more abstract topic might be manageable—if you had much time to read and more space.

For a start, why not do a little *brainstorming*—listing ideas as fast as they will come to mind? (This strategy is discussed in detail on p. 457.) Let your mind skitter around in search of pairs of words that seem to go together. Write them down in two columns as you think of them. Sometimes free association works. What comes to mind when you write "mothers"? "Fathers," perhaps. "Democrats"? "Republicans." "New York"? "Los Angeles." "King Kong"? "Godzilla." Or whatever. Continue listing pairs of words until you come to one that seems to offer possibilities. Star it. Then keep going until you have several pairs of starred words. From those you may be able to choose one pair that you feel able to develop into an informative paper. To help you zero in on one promising pair, ask a few questions about each as you consider it.

DISCOVERY CHECKLIST: COMPARING AND CONTRASTING

- What similarities between the two subjects immediately come to mind? (Write down these points of comparison—you may have the beginnings of a useful outline.) In what ways are the two strikingly different? (Again, write down these points of contrast.)
- To what extent do you prefer one over the other? What reasons can you find for doing so? (It's all right not to have a preference. Maria Dixon isn't arguing that Martina Navratilova is superior to Chris Evert Lloyd, or vice versa. The writer instead shows how each of her subjects throws the other into sharp relief.)

If your immediate answers to these questions are skimpy, or if you're less interested in them than you thought you'd be, you may want to pick a new pair and start again. Or it may be that with a little more imagination, some reading, observing, conversing, or recalling, you'll find you've made a good choice after all.

Shaping a Draft

Now that you are about to start writing your whole paper, remind yourself once more that, in comparing and contrasting two subjects, you have a goal. What is it you want to demonstrate, argue, or find out?

When you write a draft, an outline isn't always necessary. If you are setting forth something you can hold clearly in mind (such as a personal experience, written from recall), you may find you work best by just taking off and letting words flow. You may find you can compare and contrast without outlining. But in comparing and contrasting, most writers find that some prior planning helps speed the job. For one thing, an outline—even a rough scratch outline—enables you to keep track of all the points you want to make, which so easily may be lost or confused as you glance from side to side. You can make an outline in your head, of course, but it is probably easier to keep track of things on paper.

In comparing and contrasting, two ways of organizing an outline are usual.

The first way is *subject by subject*. You state all your observations about subject A and then do the same for subject B. This is the way Maria Dixon structures her short paper. She completes her remarks about Chris Evert Lloyd before going on to Martina Navratilova. As we read about Navratilova, it's not difficult to hold in mind what Dixon has said about Lloyd. This is a workable method for writing a short essay or a single paragraph, but for a long essay it has a drawback. A reader might find it hard to remember all the separate information about subject A while reading about subject B.

There's a better way to organize most papers of greater length: *point by point*. Working by this method, you take up one point at a time, applying it first to one subject and then to the other. Arthur Campa organizes his essay on Chicanos and Anglos point by point—an appropriate method because his topic (two ethnic groups) is larger than Dixon's (two individuals), and his task of comparing and contrasting is naturally more complicated. Setting forth only one point at a time, looking at each subject before moving on to the next point, Campa leads the reader along clearly and carefully. The beginning of his outline might have looked like this:

A. Plan: To show cultural differences that cause conflict in Southwest today
B. Historical differences in culture between English and Spanish people
    1. Geography and ethnic composition
        a. English—insular, integrated, zealous of racial "purity"
        b. Spanish—peninsular, individualistic, racial mingling
    2. Moral attitude
        a. English—absolute

b. Spanish—relative
3. Motive for coming to America
    a. Spanish—promise of route to India, treasures, souls to save
    b. English—escape religious persecution, make homes
4. Exploration
    a. Spanish—ambitious explorers because equestrians
    b. English—slow to explore because they went on foot

Notice that Campa reversed the order of English and Spanish people when he came to "Motive for coming to America." Perhaps he wanted to introduce a little variety.

Without even outlining, you can sometimes follow the point-by-point method informally. Mystery writer Raymond Chandler, for an essay likening English people and Americans (which he left unfinished in his notebooks), wrote this opening paragraph. It probably didn't require any outline at all.

> The keynote of American civilization is a sort of warm-hearted vulgarity. The Americans have none of the irony of the English, none of their cool poise, none of their manner. But they do have friendliness. Where an Englishman would give you his card, an American would very likely give you his shirt.

In its blast-off sentence, the paragraph announces its main idea. Then Chandler proceeds to compare the English and the Americans in two ways: (1) in manner, cool or friendly, and (2) in generosity. Like all generalizations about whole peoples (including Chicanos and Anglos), this one can be shot full of holes; but Chandler's paragraph states a memorable insight. A comparison and contrast can explain things neatly and intelligently, even though (like a one-paragraph description of Japanese and American literature) it might be wrong in many particulars.

In developing a meaty essay that compares and contrasts, an outline, however sketchy, will be your trusty friend. Keep your outline simple, and don't be ruled by it. If excellent thoughts come to you in writing your first draft, by all means let them in.

Rewriting

As you look over your early draft, you'll want to be sure that each comparison or contrast you include discusses similar elements. You'll only confuse your readers if, in considering the merits of two cities, you contrast New York's public transportation with Milwaukee's tree-lined streets; or if, in setting Springsteen and Dylan side by side, you deal with Springsteen's fondness for pizza and Dylan's politics. Go through your draft with a fine-tooth comb to make sure that, at every point you compare or contrast, you are looking at the same feature.

If your purpose in writing is to illuminate two subjects impartially, you can ask yourself: Have you given your reader a balanced view? Although you might well have more to say about one than about the other, obviously it would be unfair to set forth all the advantages of Oklahoma City and all the disadvantages of Honolulu and then conclude that Oklahoma City is superior to Honolulu on every count. If you haven't been fair, you may need to replan—perhaps make a new outline—and do some more discovering. (One useful way to tell whether you have done a thorough job of comparing and contrasting is to make an outline of your first draft and then give the outline a critical squint.)

Of course, if you love Oklahoma City and can't stand Honolulu, or vice versa, go ahead, don't be balanced, take a stand. Even so, you will probably want to admit, in all honesty, that Oklahoma City, unlike Eden, has its faults. (More about marshaling evidence will be offered in Chapter 14.)

Make sure, too, as you go over your draft, that you have escaped falling into a monotonous drone: A does this, B does that; A looks like this, B looks like that; A has these advantages, B has those. Comparison and contrast is a useful method, but it needn't result in a paper as symmetrical as a pair of sneakers. Revising and editing gives you a chance to add any lively details, interesting later thoughts, dashes of color, finishing touches that (with any luck) may occur to you.

In criticizing yourself as you rewrite, this checklist of points to test may prove handy.

REVISION CHECKLIST: COMPARING AND CONTRASTING

- Is your reason for doing all this comparing and contrasting unmistakably clear? (If not, and your paper seems an arbitrary exercise conducted in outer space, can you set out in a definite direction at the start of your paper or arrive somewhere at the end? Reexamine your goal: When you began this paper, what was it you wanted to demonstrate, argue for, or find out?)
- In discussing each feature you compare and contrast, do you always look at the very same thing? (Not contrasting American taste in clothes with English fondness for candy?)
- If you're making a judgment between your subjects, do you feel you have treated both fairly? Have you, for instance, left out any damning disadvantages or failures of the subject you're championing? Have you suppressed any of the losing subject's good points?
- Does your first draft look thin for lack of evidence? If so, from which resource might you draw more?
- Do you drop into a boringly mechanical style ("Now on one hand . . . now on the other hand")? (Show your paper to a friend and observe whether the friend begins to look glassy-eyed. If so, at what places can you break the monotony?)

Other Assignments

1. Easily and naturally, music reporter Michael Walsh falls into comparison and contrast as he reports the quarrel between music lovers who favor LPs (long-playing or analog recordings) and those who favor the new CDs (compact discs). If you will

read a little of his lively account of the conflict "The Great LP vs. CD War" (which is mostly devoted to comparing and contrasting the two sound media and the points claimed for each), you may feel like doing some comparing and contrasting yourself. Walsh first sums up a criticism that LP lovers have leveled at CDs: that the sound of a compact disc lacks warmth and makes individual instruments seem less distinct ("Digital audio is like McDonald's hamburgers—all alike"). Then he goes on, setting the two kinds of recording side by side:

> Analog defenders contend that there is nothing wrong with LPs that cannot be cured by a $1,000 Linn Sondek turntable, a $1,200 tone arm and an $850 rosewood cartridge, among other so-called high-end components. But it seems unlikely that the ordinary music lover will want to shell out $10,000 or more to experience the hidden delights of LPs. Despite their imperfections, CDs have overwhelming advantages. The sound is clear and bright. There is no surface noise, no turntable rumble, no pitch fluctuation. Says Leonard Feldman, who runs an audio laboratory on New York's Long Island, "I'll trade a metallic sound for the clicks, pops, and hisses of LPs any day." Even though they are recorded on only one side, CDs still have more potential playing time (75 minutes) than the average LP. Cuts can be programmed to play in any order, or skipped entirely, affording music lovers the opportunity to customize their listening.
>
> Worries about a vanishing repertory are more legitimate. The LP catalog has found a place for both the most familiar Beethoven symphonies and the most obscure baroque fugues. For now, classical and pop CDs run only to the best-known artists and material.

For this writing assignment, you will need access to a record collection containing both LPs and CDs and a stereo system that will reproduce them. (Perhaps your college has an audio room, or your college library has recordings and listening facilities.) Listen to two recordings of the same musical composition: one on an LP, one on a CD. Of course, the performances may differ, but the sound will be comparable. Then write (perhaps while you're listening) a paragraph or two comparing and contrasting what you hear.

2. If you don't have access to CDs and a player, here is an alternative. Listen to two different recordings (on LPs or on tape) of the same piece of music as performed by two different orchestras (or groups or singers). What elements of the music does each performer stress? What contrasting attitudes toward the music do you detect? In one paragraph or more, compare and contrast these versions.

3. Write a paragraph or two in which you compare and contrast the subjects in any of the following pairs, for the purpose of throwing light on both. In so short a paper, you can hope to trace only a few large similarities and differences, but don't hesitate to use your own recall or observation, go to the library, or converse with a friendly expert if you need material.

Women and men as single parents
Dormitory living and apartment living
Japanese and American workers
The coverage of a world event on a television newscast and in a newspaper
The state of cancer research at two moments in time: twenty years ago and today
Alexander Hamilton and Thomas Jefferson: their ideas of the role of the federal government

The playing styles of two major league pitchers (or two quarterbacks or two basketball players)

Cubist painting and abstract expressionist painting

English and another language

Your college and a rival college

Two differing views of a current controversy

Classic French cooking and *nouvelle cuisine*

The Odyssey and *The Iliad* (or F. Scott Fitzgerald's *The Great Gatsby* and Ernest Hemingway's *The Sun Also Rises,* or Walt Whitman's poem "To a Locomotive in Winter" and Emily Dickinson's poem about a locomotive "I like to see it lap the Miles,"·or two other comparable works of literature)

Northern California and southern California (or two other regions)

The experience of watching a film on a VCR and in a theater

Euclidean and non-Euclidean geometry

Two similar works of architecture (two churches, two skyscrapers, two city halls, two museums)

4.   In an essay either serious or nonserious, for the purpose of introducing yourself to other members of your class, compare and contrast yourself with someone else. You and this other person should have much in common: no sense comparing and contrasting yourself with Napoleon ("I admit to having less skill on the battlefield"). You might choose either a real person or a character in a film, a TV series, a novel, a comic strip. Choose a few points of comparison (an attitude, a habit, a way of life) and deal with each. Feel free to draw on your reading, your conversation with him or her (or with a mutual friend), your own observations, your imagination (what might it be like to be the other person?).

APPLYING WHAT YOU LEARN:
SOME USES OF COMPARING AND CONTRASTING

Because comparing and contrasting shows a reader how closely writers observe and how hard they think, comparison and contrast questions are great favorites on college essay exams of many kinds. "Compare and contrast earlier methods of treating heart attack victims with those that prevail today," you might be asked in a nursing course. At times, the examiner won't even mention the method of comparison and contrast by name. But when you get a request such as "Evaluate the relative merits of Norman Rockwell and Andrew Wyeth as realistic painters" (for a course in American art history) or "Consider the tax consequences of doing business as a small corporation and doing business as a partnership. How are they different, or similar?" (in a course in business law), then you can bet your bottom dollar that to compare and contrast is what the examiner hopes you will do.

Sometimes, in an exam or paper, you are asked to describe a person, a thing, or a scene. One good way to approach your response is to recall the useful method of comparison and contrast and to portray your subject by setting it next to something else, something similar but a little different. If asked to describe, for instance, a Cape Cod–style house, you might most clearly reveal its distinctive features by comparing and contrasting it with a Dutch colonial.

Often in your college writing, when you're called on to analyze, define, or argue, you'll find it useful, as Campa does, to use comparison, contrast, or both to make a point, even though your paper's main purpose may be other than comparing and contrasting. Although Arthur Campa in his essay compares and contrasts throughout, he also has another purpose, as his chosen title indicates ("Anglo vs. Chicano: Why?"). Campa is trying to unearth causes for the animosity that frequently exists between Chicano and Anglo. In an essay called "How to Make People Smaller Than They Are," Norman Cousins' purpose is to deplore "the increasing vocationalization of our colleges and universities." But in one paragraph in that essay, Cousins introduces a series of contrasts to strengthen his argument:

> The irony of the emphasis being placed on careers is that nothing is more valuable for anyone who has had a professional or vocational education than to be able to deal with abstractions or complexities, or to feel comfortable with subtleties of thought or language, or to think sequentially. The doctor who knows only disease is at a disadvantage alongside the doctor who knows at least as much about people as he does about pathological organisms. The lawyer who argues in court from a narrow legal base is no match for the lawyer who can connect legal precedents to historical experience and who employs wide-ranging intellectual resources. The business executive whose competence in general management is bolstered by an artistic ability to deal with people is of prime value to his company. For the technologist, the engineering of consent can be just as important as the engineering of moving parts. In all these respects, the liberal arts have much to offer. Just in terms of career preparation, therefore, a student is shortchanging himself by shortcutting the humanities.

In the sentence about the business executive, for variety's sake the contrast is implied rather than stated. As readers armed with the contrasts Cousins has already imagined, we have no difficulty inferring that this ideal business executive, like the liberally educated doctor and lawyer before him, has a less desirable counterpart: a business executive whose schooling has given him nothing more than job training.

Cousins, it would seem, directs his argument to a general audience. Let's look at two brief illustrations of comparing and contrasting found in writing more specialized and scholarly. William Broad and Nicholas Wade, in *Betrayers of the Truth: Fraud and Deceit in the Halls of Science,* a book-length study of scientists who have faked evidence in order to claim fictitious discoveries, contrast two influential opinions of what it is that keeps most scientists honest.

> The renowned German sociologist Max Weber saw science as a vocation. The individual scientist's devotion to the truth, in Weber's view, is what keeps science honest. His French contemporary Emile Durkheim, on the other hand, considered that it is the community of science, not the individual, that guarantees scientific integrity. Weber's view that scientists

are innately honest is still sometimes heard. "The scientists I have known ... have been in certain respects just perceptibly more morally admirable than most other groups of intelligent men," said the scientist and novelist C. P. Snow. ... But the opinion that scientists are somehow more honest than other people is not particularly fashionable. The prevailing view is that laid out by Robert Merton, the leading American sociologist of science, who like Durkheim attributes honesty in science to institutional mechanisms, not the personal virtue of scientists. The verifiability of results, the exacting scrutiny of fellow experts, the subjection of scientists' activities to "rigorous policing, to a degree perhaps unparalleled in any other field of activity"— these are features, says Merton, that ensure "the virtual absence of fraud in the annals of science. ..."

For a final example, Howard Gardner, in *Artful Scribbles,* an inquiry into what children's drawings mean, makes a sharp contrast between the drawings of younger children and those of older children.

When drawings made by eight- or nine-year-olds are juxtaposed to those produced by younger children, a striking contrast emerges. There is little doubt about which came from which group: works by the older children feature a kind of precision, a concern for detail, a command of geometrical form which are lacking in the attempts by younger artists. Schemas for familiar objects are readily recognized, and attempts at rendering less familiar objects can initially be decoded. And yet one hesitates to call the drawings by the older children "better"—indeed, most observers and sometimes even the youngsters themselves feel that something vital which is present at the age of six or seven has disappeared from the drawings by the older children. A certain freedom, flexibility, *joie de vivre* [zest for life], and a special fresh exploratory flavor which mark the childlike drawings of the six-year-old are gone; and instead of being replaced by adult mastery, this loss has merely been supplanted by a product that is at once more carefully wrought yet also more wooden and lifeless.

As you'll notice, Gardner, while giving the strong points of each age group of artists, apparently favors the work of the young, for all its faults.

These brief examples may suggest to you that comparing and contrasting aren't just meaningless academic calisthenics. Explaining devices, they appeal to writers who have a passion for making things clear.

CHAPTER 10

Explaining Step by Step: Analyzing a Process

When we analyze anything, we separate it into its parts, that we may better understand it and more easily explain it. A chemist analyzes an unknown compound, but you also can analyze less tangible things. News commentators analyze the news: they attempt to take an event apart and single out its elements. Did a riot break out in Bombay? Trying to make it understandable, the commentator discerns who the participants were, what the conflict was, what caused it, what resulted. Analyzing intangibles, too, one advertising firm tries to account for the success of a competitor's brand of personal computer by analyzing a rival ad agency's strategy. To analyze human affairs is a task more subjective and less certain than analyzing a chemical compound, but often no less necessary.

Not only can you analyze chemicals, riots, and advertising strategies, you can analyze an action, or a series of actions, as well. You can write a *process analysis,* a step-by-step explanation of either

> *How something happens* (an *informative* process analysis: how a new popular song is built into a national hit, how snakes shed their skins) or

> *How to do something* (a *directive* process analysis: directions written to a friend unacquainted with computers who is going to borrow yours for a paper she is writing; a magazine article "How to Conduct Yourself During a Job Interview").

LEARNING FROM OTHER WRITERS

Let's consider two illustrations, one written to each purpose. First, E. B. White, a writer admired for his insight and humor, will show you how something happens. For a number of years he raised sheep on his farm in Maine. From the experience, he derived a newfound respect for the instincts of animals.

A SHEPHERD'S LIFE
E. B. WHITE

This is a day of high winds and extravagant promises, a day of bright 1
skies and the sun on the white painted south sides of buildings, of lambs
on the warm slope of the barnyard, their forelegs folded neatly and on
their miniature faces a look of grave miniature content. Beneath the winter
cover of spruce boughs the tulip thrusts its spear. A white hen is chaper-
oning thirteen little black chicks all over the place, showing them the world's
fair with its lagoons and small worms. The wind is northwest and the bay
is on the march. Even on the surface of the watering fountain in the hen-
yard quite a sea is running. My goose will lay her seventh egg today, in the
nest she made for herself alongside the feed rack in the sheep shed, and
on cold nights the lambs will lie on the eggs to keep them from freezing
until such time as the goose decides to sit. It is an arrangement they have
worked out among themselves—the lambs enjoying the comfort of the
straw nest in return for a certain amount of body heat delivered to the
eggs—not enough to start the germ but enough to keep the frost out. Things
work out if you leave them alone. At first, when I found lambs sitting on
goose eggs I decided that my farm venture had got out of hand and that I
better quit before any more abortive combinations developed. "At least," I
thought, "you'll have to break up that nest and shift the goose." But I am
calmer than I used to be, and I kept clear of the situation. As I say, things
work out. This is a day of the supremacy of warmth over cold, of God over
the devil, of peace over war. There is still a little snow along the fence
rows, but it looks unreal, like the icing of a store cake. I am conducting
my own peace these days. It's like having a little business of my own. People
have quit calling me an escapist since learning what long hours I put in.

Lambs come in March, traditionally and actually. My ewes started drop- 2
ping their lambs in February, were at their peak of production in March,
and now are dribbling into April. At the moment of writing, thirteen have
lambed, two still await their hour. From the thirteen sheep I have eighteen
live lambs—six sets of twins and six single lambs. April is the big docking
and castrating month, and since I have named all my lambs for friends, I
wield the emasculatome with a somewhat finer flourish than most husband-
rymen. Tails come off best with a dull ax—the lambs bleed less than with
a sharp instrument. I never would have discovered that in a hundred years,
but a neighbor tipped me off. He also told me about black ash tea, without
which nobody should try to raise lambs. You peel some bark from a black
ash, steep it, and keep it handy in a bottle. Then when your lambs come
up from the pasture at night frothing at the mouth, poisoned from a too
sudden rush of springtime to the first, second, and third stomach, you just
put the tea to them. It makes them drunk, but it saves their lives.

That peerless organ of British pastoral life, *The Countryman,* published 3
at Idbury, recently printed a list of ancient Celtic sheep-counting numerals.
I was so moved by this evidence of Britain's incomparable poise during
her dark crisis that I gave the antique names to my fifteen modern ewes.
They are called Yain, Tain, Eddero, Peddero, Pitts, Tayter, Later, Overro,

Covvero, Dix, Yain-dix, Tain-dix, Eddero-dix, Peddero-dix, and Bumfitt. I think Yain is rather a pretty name. And I like Later too and Pitts. Bumfitt is a touch on the A. A. Milne side, but I guess it means fifteen all right. As a matter of fact, giving numerals for names is a handy system; I have named the ewes in the order of their lambing, and it helps me keep my records straight. Peddero-dix and Bumfitt are still fighting it out for last place.

When I invested in a band of sheep last fall (they cost seven dollars 4 apiece) I had no notion of what I was letting myself in for in the way of emotional involvements. I knew there would be lambs in spring, but they seemed remote. Lambing, I felt, would take place automatically and would be the sheep's business, not mine. I forgot that sheep come up in late fall and join the family circle. At first they visit the barn rather cautiously, eat some hay, and depart. But after one or two driving storms they abandon the pasture altogether, draw up chairs around the fire, and settle down for the winter. They become as much a part of your group as your dog, or your Aunt Maudie. Our house and barn are connected by a woodshed, like the Grand Central Station and the Yale Club; and without stepping out of doors you can reach any animal on the place, including the pig. This makes for greater intimacy than obtains in a layout where each farm building is a separate structure. We don't encourage animals to come into the house, but they get in once in a while, particularly the cosset lamb, who trotted through this living room not five minutes ago looking for an eight-ounce bottle. Anyway, in circumstances such as ours you find yourself growing close to sheep. You give them names not for whimsy but for convenience. And when one of them approaches her confinement you get almost as restless as she does.

The birth of a mammal was once a closed book to me. Except for the 5 famous "Birth of a Baby" picture and a couple of old receipted bills from an obstetrician, I was unacquainted with the more vivid aspects of birth. All that is changed. For the past six weeks I have been delivering babies with great frequency, moderate abandon, and no little success. Eighteen lambs from thirteen sheep isn't bad. I lost one pair of twins—they were dropped the first week of February, before I expected them, and they chilled. I also lost a single lamb, born dead.

A newcomer to the realm of parturition is inclined to err on the side 6 of being too helpful. I have no doubt my early ministrations were as distasteful to the ewe as those of the average night nurse are to an expectant mother. Sheep differ greatly in their ability to have a lamb and to care for it. They also differ in their attitude toward the shepherd. Some sheep enjoy having you mincing around, arranging flowers and adjusting the window. Others are annoyed beyond words. The latter, except in critical cases, should be left to work out their problem by themselves. They usually get along. If you've trimmed the wool around their udders the day before with a pair of desk shears, the chances are ten to one they will feed their lambs all right when they arrive.

At first, birth strikes one as the supreme example of bad planning—a 7 thoroughly mismanaged and ill-advised functional process, something thought up by a dirty-minded fiend. It appears cluttery, haphazard. But after you have been mixed up with it for a while, have spent nights squatting beneath a smoky lantern in a cold horse stall helping a weak lamb whose mother fails to own it; after you have grown accustomed to the odd trappings and by-products of mammalian reproduction and seen how marvelously they contribute to the finished product; after you've broken down an animal's reserve and have identified yourself with her and no longer pull your punches, then this strange phenomenon of birth becomes an absorbingly lustrous occasion, full of subdued emotion, like a great play, an occasion for which you unthinkingly give up any other occupation that might be demanding your attention. I've never before in my life put in such a month as this past month has been—a period of pure creation, vicarious in its nature, but extraordinarily moving.

I presume that everything a female does in connection with birthing 8 her young is largely instinctive, not rational. A sheep makes a hundred vital movements and performs a dozen indispensable and difficult tasks, blissfully oblivious of her role. Everything is important, but nothing is intelligent. Before the lamb is born she paws petulantly at the bedding. Even this is functional, for she manages to construct a sort of nest into which the lamb drops, somewhat to the lamb's advantage. Then comes the next miraculous reflex. In the first instant after a lamb is dropped, the ewe takes one step ahead, turns, and lowers her head to sniff eagerly at her little tomato surprise. This step ahead that she takes is a seemingly trivial thing, but I have been thinking about it and I guess it is not trivial at all. If she were to take one step backward it would be a different story—she would step on her lamb, and perhaps damage it. I have often seen a ewe step backward while laboring, but I never remember seeing one take a backward step after her lamb has arrived on the ground. This is the second instinctive incident.

The third is more important than either of the others. A lamb, newly 9 born, is in a state of considerable disrepair; it arrives weak and breathless, with its nose plugged with phlegm or covered with a sac. It sprawls, suffocated, on the ground, and after giving one convulsive shake, is to all appearances dead. Only quick action, well-directed, will save it and start it ticking. The ewe takes this action, does the next important thing, which is to open the lamb's nostrils. She goes for its nose with unerring aim and starts tearing off the cellophane. I can't believe that she is intelligently unstoppering these air passages for her child; she just naturally feels like licking a lamb on the nose. You wonder (or I do, anyway) what strange directional force impels her to begin at the nose, rather than at the other end. A lamb has two ends, all right, and before the ewe gets through she has attended to both of them; but she always begins with the nose, and with almost frenzied haste. I suppose Darwin is right, and that a long process of hereditary elimination finally produced sheep that began cleaning the forward end of a lamb, not the after end. It is an impressive sight, no matter what is responsible for it. It is literally life-giving, and you can see life take hold with the first in-draught of air in the freed nostril. The lamb twitches and utters a cry, as though from a long way off. The ewe answers with a stifled grunt, her sides still contracting with the spasms of birth; and in this answering cry the silver cord is complete and takes the place of the umbilicus, which has parted, its work done.

These are only the beginnings of the instinctive events in the maternal 10
program. The ewe goes on to dry her lamb and boost it to its feet. She
keeps it moving so that it doesn't lodge and chill. She finally works it into
position so that it locates, in an almost impenetrable jungle of wool, the
indispensable fountain and the early laxative. One gulp of this fluid (which
seems to have a liberal share of brandy in it) and the lamb is launched. Its
little tail wiggles and satisfaction is written all over it, and your heart leaps
up.

Even your own technique begins to grow more instinctive. When I was 11
a novice I used to work hard to make a lamb suck by forcing its mouth to
the teat. Now I just tickle it on the base of its tail.

Questions to Start You Thinking

1. At what point in "A Shepherd's Life" does White begin to describe a process? What
   purpose is served by all the material leading up to his process analysis?

2. How would you describe White's attitude toward his topic—awe-stricken, cool and
   detached, clinical, or what? Where in his essay do you find evidence of this attitude?

3. What general truth does White suggest in his final paragraph? State it in your own
   words.

4. Take a survey in your class. In what area does each class member have enough
   expertise to provide material for an informative process analysis?

Richard Polomsky, a student who knows a great deal about fossil collecting,
wrote the following paper to share his knowledge (gained in an area near
Chicago) with his English class. In it he gives us step-by-step directions for fossil
hunting and preservation.

COLLECTING THE PAST

RICHARD POLOMSKY

There are a wide variety of locations where one could search for fos- 1
silized remains of plant and animal life. One spot in particular, near Chicago, has yielded some of the world's most interesting varieties of fossilized
remains, and I will describe how to locate, reveal, clean, and care for them.

About forty miles southwest of Chicago lies an area that has been as- 2
sociated with geological interest for over a hundred years, the Braid-
wood–Coal City–Mazon Creek group of towns. Around 1865, coal was mined
extensively in quarries situated in and around these towns. The coal did
not last, however, and all that is left now are large gaping quarries filled
with water, not coal.

On the edges of some of the quarries, large mounds of shale protrude 3
from the ground with their layers of strata pointing perpendicular to the
ground's surface. Within the layers of shale, ironstone nodules can be found,
which look much like small to large hamburger patties that taper to the

edge. The fossilized remains contained within often are representative of the life that existed during the Pennsylvanian period, about 280 to 325 million years ago. If you want to collect the nodules, it's best to wait until after a strong thunderstorm passes through the area. Then the nodules are washed out of the surrounding shale and roll down the sides of the mounds, so that you may come by later to simply collect them, as though on an Easter egg hunt.

No special equipment is necessary to collect the nodules, except for a 4 heavy canvas sack to hold them and a hard hat to protect your head from any late arriving nodules. If you want to begin preparing the nodules in the field, you should be sure to bring a good-sized hammer (a 42-ounce one should be fine), eye protection goggles, and a brush with which to clean the fossils.

If you just collect them and bring them back to your "lab," you will 5 still need the same equipment, but you shouldn't attempt to work in the field without these tools.

Once back in the lab, set up a large piece of rock, to be used as an 6 anvil. Put on the safety goggles and pick up a nodule. Place it on the anvil so that the thinner edge is perpendicular to the anvil's surface. Next pick up the hammer and strike the nodule on the top edge. At first, don't use too much pressure applying the blows. If there is a delicately preserved fossil within the nodule, it would be a shame to crush it. If the first blows don't open it, gradually increase the pressure until the nodule splits to reveal the fossil, or absence of a fossil, as is sometimes the case.

From personal experience, I have discovered that you must be relent- 7 less in your search for fossils and collect several piles of rubble before you split the first fossil that reveals the approximately three-hundred-million-year-old impression of a tree fern, spider, jellyfish, shrimp, amphibian, or any of the other hundreds of species that once occupied the area when it was a steamy swamp at the edge of a saltwater sea. If you are fortunate enough to find a fossil, brush it lightly to remove any extraneous dirt from the specimen. You may then wish to glue both the positive and negative halves of the specimen side by side on a piece of corrugated cardboard with rubber cement. If collecting fossils is to become a serious endeavor for you, then you will probably want to build a cabinet with a series of drawers stacked one on top of the other. They should only be a couple of inches thick so that more drawers can fit into the cabinet. If you do not wish to glue the two halves of the fossil to a card, place them back together tightly and wrap them with several layers of soft paper. Then neatly stack them in the cabinet until you can get back to study and classify them. If you aren't motivated to build a cabinet, a shoebox would suffice for storage.

The act of collecting the nodules is extremely enjoyable if performed 8 on a nice day. It involves a healthy walk in the outdoors, generally for quite a few hours. You learn a little about patience as you sift through pile after pile of nodules only to have them yield a tiny handful of interesting specimens.

The greatest reward from collecting and studying the fossils is that if 9 you should happen to make a find that can be verified as being a previously undiscovered species by officials of the Field Museum of Natural History in Chicago, more than likely the new species would be named after you. This would be quite a feat for an amateur. Imagine being remembered through history as the discoverer of a new species of plant or animal that remained unknown for nearly three hundred million years, until you exposed it for the first time.

Questions to Start You Thinking

1. What details in Polomsky's essay convince you that he knows what he's talking about? What details reveal his love and enthusiasm for fossil hunting?

2. How clear are Polomsky's directions? If you had the opportunity to follow them, would you know what to do? Are there any places in the essay where the writer might be clearer, where you could use further advice?

3. What other uses of leisure time might lend themselves well to a written process analysis? Are you (or is anyone you know, whom you might talk with) a part-time expert in a special field of knowledge?

LEARNING BY WRITING

The Assignment

Write either an informative or a directive analysis of a process you know well (or want to find out about). Explain it to a reader who wants to learn that process. If you don't feel sufficiently informed to explain anything, or don't feel like explaining what you know, you can do some investigating in a fresh direction before you write. Still, everyone is an expert in *some* area. Often those essays in which a deeply caring writer tells from first-hand experience how to do something, or how something is done, are among the most engaging and instructive.

Among the lively student-written process analyses we've seen recently (some serious in tone, some lighter) were these:

> A man recommended techniques for finding rare record albums at bargain prices.
>
> A man who had dropped out of an airline's training program for flight attendants told the stages of training that an applicant goes through before receiving wings.
>
> A woman who had worked in a clinic guided her readers through the steps by which a doctor examines a heart patient and conducts diagnostic tests.
>
> A woman wrote a step-by-step account of how a lobbyist seeks to influence a legislator.
>
> A man shared what he had learned, in a season of knocking about the country holding odd jobs, about the skills needed to survive as a tramp.

A woman who had taken part in a summer seminar in wildlife management described, step by step, the process of banding birds in order to trace their patterns of migration.

A woman told how to make an excellent grilled cheese sandwich in a dorm room by using an electric iron.

Generating Ideas

What process will you analyze? It may be that at work, in the library, in a laboratory, or in a classroom, you have experienced, read about, or observed something done, or something happening. If that is the case, you're an expert right now; you're well equipped to write. But if a workable idea doesn't spring to mind, drum up ideas by asking yourself a few questions.

DISCOVERY CHECKLIST: ANALYZING A PROCESS

- What processes are you already familiar with?
- What ones might you go out and observe?
- What ones have you read about or would like to read about?
- From among your friends (perhaps including your instructors), whose expertise can you tap?
- What processes can you imagine happening, say, in the future?
- What processes have you learned about in classes other than English? Has anyone in your family or among your friends ever asked you to explain one of them?
- Is there a process you've wondered about but have never had the time to investigate thoroughly? Can you do so now?

For a start, do a little brainstorming. Jot down a list of titles that you figure you could develop into papers worth reading. For an *informative* process analysis (explaining how something happens), these might be "How a Hospital Emergency Room Responds to an Accident Case," "How a Large Telescope Functions," "How Glaciers Are Formed," "How an Artist Draws a Portrait," "What Would Have Happened If Halley's Comet Had Struck the Earth." (We'll get to the directive or "how to" kind of paper in a moment. For more suggestions on *brainstorming*, or rapidly listing ideas, see p. 457.)

What you include on such a list will depend, of course, on what you know or can find out. At this point, though, you don't have to know every detail. It's always possible, at any stage along the way, to fill in the gaps in your knowledge by reading, talking with experts, or (if possible) observing the process. What you need to do at first is just to choose a couple of paths for your thoughts to follow and eventually narrow your choices to one.

If your expertise involves a skill that you can teach your readers, you can write instead a *directive* process analysis. Do you know how to identify crystals with a microscope, navigate a sailboat, create graphs with a computer, teach someone how to drive, film a documentary, recognize the composer of a piece of chamber music, identify constellations? You'll find readers eager to learn those skills, and many more. What process do you know most about? Which one do you think you can most clearly explain? A list of possible topics might include "How to Renovate an Old House," "How to Choose Spreadsheet Software for a Small Business," "How to Record a Rock Group," "How to Train for Distance Running," "How to Silkscreen a Poster," "How to Recognize a Fourteenth-Century Italian Painting," "How to Repossess a Car."

When you decide on a topic, keep asking questions about it. Is there background material that your reader will have to know in order to understand the nature of the process? List the material. (Look back at Polomsky's "Collecting the Past" and note the amount of general information he includes at the start of his paper.)

If you're writing a "how to" essay, do you know any trade secrets that will make what you're teaching easier for your reader to master? Jot them down.

What preliminary steps, if any, will the reader need to take in order to follow your directions? ("Sharpen a pair of shears. . . .") What materials are needed to perform the skill you have in mind? List them: "a fifty-foot roll of sailcloth; a yardstick or measuring tape; one twelve-foot pine trunk at least twenty-four inches thick, trimmed of branches. . . ." Any ideas or information, however small, that you can put on paper now, you will soon be thankful for.

Shaping a Draft

If you have done enough thinking about your process analysis ahead of time, you'll have greatly lightened your next task: to map out the steps or stages in the process you are going to explain. You'll find such a list useful even if you're going to write just one paragraph.

Let's say you are writing an *informative* process analysis. Into what stages will you divide the process? Make a list. In what order do these stages generally occur?

If you're writing a *directive* or "how to" essay, what steps will the reader have to master in order to succeed in learning the skill? In what order do those steps need to be taken?

For either kind of process analysis, zero in on any parts that threaten to be complicated. Which stages or steps will take the most explaining? Underline or star these. This device will signal you, when you write your first draft, to slow down and cover that stage or step with special care. Does any stage include smaller stages or steps that you will need to cover one at a time? If so, list these carefully.

If you can, arrange all the stages or steps in chronological order. This will be easy if you're writing a "how to" essay, perhaps harder if you're writing an informative paper about an event in which everything seems to happen at once: say, how a tornado strikes. If you cannot explain your subject step by step, try explaining it part by part—the tornado's action observed at its center, its action observed at its edge—following the method of *dividing*, set forth in the next chapter.

Review your list once more, making sure you've included every small stage or step necessary.

Now your trusty list of steps or stages can serve you as an outline. As you write your first draft, concentrate on including every possible step in the process you're explaining, even if it seems so obvious as not to need mentioning. It's better at this point to put in too much detail than to put in too little. Later you can cross out what seems superfluous, but always keep in mind that what you're saying is probably news to your readers, who need more information about it than you might at first realize.

In drafting your paper, help your readers follow the steps in your analysis by putting in *time markers:* words and phrases like *then, next, soon, after, while, first, later, in two hours, by the following day, during the second week, as yet, at present.* By making clear exactly when some action occurs relative to other actions, time markers serve as signposts to keep your readers from getting lost in a forest of details. Look back at Richard Polomsky's essay about fossil hunting and notice how he uses time markers to keep his readers on the track: *Then* and *later* in paragraph 3, *Once back in the lab, Next,* and *At first* in paragraph 6, *then* (three times) in paragraph 7. Unobtrusively the time markers define each new stage of the process.

You needn't overload your writing with time markers. Use just enough so that the steps in the process will be clear. Not every sentence needs a time marker, and you'll want to avoid repeating the same ones too often ("After the seventh day ...," "After the eighth day ..."). Vary them, use them with care, and they will keep your reader with you every step of the way through even the most tangled time sequences.

Rewriting

Reread your draft in a picky, hard-to-please way. Put yourself in the place of a dim-bulb reader who can't follow any process without the writer leading him by the hand. This way, you'll notice any places where you (as a reader) need more help.

If you've written a directive or "how to" paper explaining a process that can readily be done in present circumstances (such as "How to Exercise for Relaxation"), ask a friend to try to follow your directions. If there are places where he or she meets difficulty, how can you rewrite to make such passages absolutely clear? If you've written an informative process analysis, ask the friend whether he or she can follow it, or if there are any points where the writer— that's you—could provide a little more help. If additional information is needed, add it patiently, giving each new point all the space it needs for clarity. The result just might be a process analysis that can provide your readers with information or a new skill that they will find truly valuable.

Check your paper for inconsistencies of person. Process analysis tempts writers to switch from *I* to *one* to *you* without reason. If you used *one* at the start of your paper, make sure you've used it throughout.

Too heavy use of the passive voice ("It is known that . . .") is another pit that too many process analyses fall into. Look for such constructions, and when you find any, try changing them to the active voice ("We all know that . . ."). An occasional passive is inevitable, but too many threaten to rob your writing of life. The exception to this advice occurs in scientific writing, where an objective tone is required and is generally achieved with the use of the passive voice.

Look too for language that might give your reader difficulty. Circle any specialized or technical words. Do they need defining?

Here are a few more questions to ask yourself while you read as a hard-to-please reader.

REVISION CHECKLIST: ANALYZING A PROCESS

- Is the nature of the process clear: what it will lead to, what it will accomplish?
- Have you put your steps or stages in the most logical possible order?
- If your process includes a number of smaller steps or stages, have you left any out?
- Wherever you have circled a technical word or piece of specialized language, can you put your point in any simpler terms?
- Have you included enough time markers so that your readers can easily follow the steps in the process you have analyzed?
- If you're writing a directive paper, is there any moment in the process when things are likely to go wrong? Can you alert your reader to possible problems and give advice for solving them?
- Does your own interest in the knowledge you're sharing with your readers shine through? If not, what can you do to make that interest evident?

Other Assignments

1. Write an informative paragraph or two, explaining how any of the following takes place (or took place):

> How a rumor starts
> How a bird learns to fly
> How a jury is selected
> How the Grand Canyon was formed
> How a cow dog does its job
> How the ozone layer has been damaged by chemical agents
> How someone becomes a Democrat or a Republican
> How a closed-end equity mutual fund operates
> How a psychiatrist diagnoses an illness
> How acid rain is formed
> How an expert detects an art forgery

2. For practice in writing a brief directive process analysis, explain in a page or two how to do one of the following:

    Judge the effectiveness of an advertisement
    Choose an academic major
    Win an election
    Write a news story
    Overcome an addiction
    Harness solar energy to perform a useful task
    Administer the Heimlich maneuver to someone choking on a bite of food
    Register a patent
    Take a market sampling
    Lodge a complaint with authorities
    Prevent a certain sports injury
    Dissect a frog

3. We've all bought items we have to assemble ourselves. Some of them come with instructions so confusing that even an engineer would be unable to follow them. If you can possibly unearth such a set of instructions, enter it into a classroom contest. You and your classmates can pick the winner—the most garbled, impossible-to-follow directions of the lot. Using the same illustrations (if there are any) as the original writer, try, singly or together, to rewrite the instructions so that they can be followed with ease.

4. From any textbook you are currently using in another course, choose a chapter in which a process is analyzed. Psychology, geology, chemistry, physics, biology, botany, zoology, engineering, computer programming, business, nursing, and education courses are likely candidates to supply processes.

    In a short paper of two or three paragraphs, including just the high points, explain the process to a fellow student who has not read the textbook or taken the course.

    This assignment is a matter of paraphrasing or nutshelling another writer's ideas and observations in your own words—a skill useful in many professional situations that involve writing from reading. (In a corporation, a senior executive might say, "Here, read all this stuff and write me a short report on what's in it.")

APPLYING WHAT YOU LEARN: SOME USES OF PROCESS ANALYSIS

Often in college writing you may be called on to set forth an informative process analysis, tracing the steps by which something takes place: the formation of a star, a mountain, or a human embryo; the fall of Rome, the awarding of child custody in a divorce case, or the election of a president. Generally, such a paper will be a process analysis from beginning to end.

Lab reports are good examples of such process analyses. For a marine biology course at his university, student Edward R. Parton did an experiment involving sea urchins, which he then described in a very fine lab report. He began the "Materials and Methods" section of his report with this paragraph, which reveals how to tell a male sea urchin from a female. (Evidently this is not a problem for sea urchins, but it is one for biologists.)

> Because sea urchins (*Strongylocentralus purpuratus*) do not have any distinguishing characteristics that identify their sex, several sea urchins were tested so that spermatozoa and eggs could be obtained. A sample of 4 or 5 sea urchins were injected with 2.0 ml of 0.5 M potassium chloride (0.5 MKCl) by a hypodermic syringe into the soft, fleshy area on each of the sea urchins' oral side. The injected sea urchins were set aside for 5 minutes with their oral sides facing up. The injected 0.5 MKCl made the gonad muscles of each sea urchin contract, thus releasing gametes to the external environment in a mucus-like fluid. If the fluid excreted was yellow, it signified the eggs of a female sea urchin. A male sea urchin excreted blue seminal fluid. But if the identification procedures didn't uncover both a male and female sea urchin from the sample of 4 or 5 sea urchins, additional sea urchins were injected with 2.0 ml of 0.5 MKCl each, following the same identification procedures until at least one male and one female were obtained.

Sometimes, though, process analysis will make up just *part* of what you are asked to write. You'll introduce it wherever in your essay, article, or report you need to explain how something comes about. Here, to take an example from a professional writer, is an informative process—a passage from *The Perceptual World of the Child* by T. G. R. Bower. The author finds it necessary to stop partway through the chapter he calls "Some Complex Effects of Simple Growth" to explain in brief the workings of the human eye.

> Finally we come to the most complex sensory system, the eye and its associated neural structures. The eye is an extremely intricate and complex organ. Light enters the eye through the cornea, passes through the anterior chamber and thence through the pupil to the lens. The lens is a soft transparent tissue than can stretch out and get thinner or shorten and thicken, thus focusing the rays of light and enabling images of objects at different distances to be seen clearly. The lens focuses the light on the retina, which is the thin membrane covering the posterior surface of the eyeball. The nerve cells in the retina itself are sensitive to spots of light. Each nerve cell at the next level of analysis in the brain receives inputs from a number of these retinal nerve cells and responds best to lines or long edges in particular orientations. Numbers of these nerve cells feed into the next level, where nerve cells are sensitive to movement of lines in particular orientations in particular directions. There are other levels that seem sensitive to size, and still others that respond to specific differences in the signals from the two eyes.

Process analysis, in a short passage, can define a thing or an idea. (In Chapter 13 we will discuss extended definition, a way of writing in which you draw exact boundaries around a thing or an idea. To know how to explain a process step by step may come in handy in definition writing.) The runner Jon Sinclair, to define the tactic called "surging," gives us a brief process analysis in an article in *Runner's World Annual:*

> To me, surging is the most fascinating aspect of the sport of road racing. It's the ultimate tactic, and it can be used in a variety of ways to weaken and eventually destroy your competition.
>
> I wait until I see a lapse, a hesitation in my competitors, before I start to surge. I'll go around a corner and blast away, or attack a small hill. Once I do that and get an indication that my competitor is faltering just the slightest bit, I'll put my head down and run as long and as hard as I feel I can maintain a hard pace. Then, I'll drop back to the pace that I was running before the surge.
>
> That's usually enough to break someone. Sometimes it's not enough and I'll have to do another surge and another to break a particularly tough opponent. Sooner or later he's not going to be able to react. Once I sense he's finished, I push it even more.

Other models of directive or "how to" writing are often found in textbooks such as *Surveying,* by Francis H. Moffitt and Harry Bouchard. The following passage instructs students in using a surveyor's telescope.

> When sighting through the telescope of a surveying instrument, whether it's a level, a transit, a theodolite, or an alidade, the observer must first focus the eyepiece system to *his individual eye.* This is most easily done by holding an opened field book about six inches in front of the objective lens and on a slant in order to obscure the view ahead of the telescope and to allow light to enter the objective lens. . . . The *eyepiece* is now twisted in or out until the cross hairs are sharp and distinct. Now, with the eyepiece system focused, the telescope is pointed at the object to be sighted, with the observer looking along the top of the telescope barrel (some telescopes are provided with peep sights with which to make this initial alignment). The rotational motion is then clamped. The object to be sighted should now be in the field of view. The tangent screw is then used to bring the line of sight directly on the point.

As you enter the world of work, you will probably find yourself called upon any number of times to analyze a process—in lab reports, technical writing of all sorts, business reports and memos, case studies, nursing records, treatment histories, and a host of other kinds of writing, depending on your career. You'll find it immensely useful to know how to explain a process from its beginning to its end.

CHAPTER 11

Slicing into Parts, Sorting into Kinds: Dividing and Classifying

Often in college writing you'll be asked to explain large and complicated matters: cellular metabolism, the Reformation, abstract expressionist painters, the Federal Reserve Bank, earthquakes and other natural phenomena, Marxism, nightmares, invertebrate animals, existentialist philosophers. Luckily, you have at your disposal two useful, easy-to-follow methods to render such subjects manageable. We'll explore them in this chapter—first division and then classification.

When you write by the method of *division,* you slice a whole thing into its component parts. You do so to explain a complicated subject more easily: by reducing it to its elements, you can then deal with it an element at a time. In a term paper for sociology about the ethnic composition of New York City, you might work through the city neighborhood by neighborhood—Chinatown, Harlem, Spanish Harlem, Little Italy, and so on—profiling the people who live there. In a paper for a course in art history, you might single out each element of a Rembrandt painting: perhaps its human figures, their clothing, the background, the light. This method helps your readers, too: they can more readily take in the subject in a series of bites than in one gulp. For this reason, college textbooks do a lot of dividing: an economics book divides a labor union into its components; an anatomy text divides the human hand into the bones, muscles, and ligaments that make it up.

Division, as you can see, is a kind of analysis: the breaking apart of something into its elements. If you have read the previous chapter, you have already met another kind of analysis: process analysis—breaking an action into steps, which you might do in explaining how to build a hang glider or how a river delta is formed. The method of division applies not only to cities and cars and countries but also to ideas and other intangibles. When you divide, you proceed from whole to parts. This is a plain and easy way to organize a paragraph or a whole paper.

Using *classification,* you start out not with just one thing, as you do in dividing, but with several things—perhaps hundreds. You group these things into categories on the basis of their similarities, as a postal worker does in sorting incoming letters into pigeonholes: grouping all the letters going to Main Street in one hole, all those going to Sunrise Avenue in another, and so on. A college writer classifies things, the better to write of them in a systematic way. An essay for a sociology course, for example, might classify workers by how they make their livings: farm workers, blue-collar workers, white-collar workers, professionals.

The method of classifying is a familiar way of making sense of the world. Zoologists classify species of animals, botanists classify plants, and their classifications help us make sense of that vast and complex subject life on earth. Librarians, to enable us to locate a book in a library, classify books into categories: fiction, biography, history, economics, and so on. Newspapers publish classified advertising, grouping small ads in categories such as FOR SALE and HELP WANTED. In everyday life, we classify continually. If we are well organized, we sort out a personal collection of tapes or records by musicians or by type of music; we sort out our clothes into different places, perhaps mentally classifying them by season (clothes for summer, clothes for winter) or by formality (dress-up clothes for formal occasions, sport clothes for stepping out, old duds for knocking around). Meeting individual people in the street, we might label them friends, acquaintances, or merely familiar faces. Those categories only begin to describe each individual, but they help us glimpse the composition of a crowd. Classifying, then, is a basic, everyday habit of thought.

The simplest method of classification is *binary* (or *two-part*) classification, in which the writer sorts things into two piles: things that possess a feature, things that don't possess that feature. This is the kind of classification a chemist makes, with the aid of litmus paper, in classifying solutions as either acids or bases. This method ignores fine gradations between two extremes, but sometimes it is clearly the right approach. You might classify people as scientists and nonscientists, literate and illiterate.

Both division and classification offer you ways to reduce complexity to an understandable order. To tell the two methods apart, remember: when you divide, you always start with only one thing (a university, a government, a whale, the theory of relativity). When you classify, you always start with many things (college students, senators, whales, theories). To see the difference, you need to look past words to what the words refer to. Although, for instance, the collective noun *humanity* treats all people in the world as one, if you separate humanity into swimmers and nonswimmers, you aren't dividing, you're classifying people according to their ability to swim.

Besides, your purposes are different in classifying and in dividing. When you divide you break a subject into parts so you can explain it one part at a time. You separate a thing into its components *on the basis of their differences.* Think of division as cutting a fish into head, body, fins, and tail, according to the different appearance and function of each part. When you classify, you try to make order out of a jumble of stuff: you take many things and, to simplify your view of them, group them *by their similarities*. Think of classification as sorting out a quart of marbles according to some common quality like color:

all the red ones in one pile, blue ones in another, yellow ones in a third. Cutting fish and sorting marbles may be a trivial way to view division and classification, those mighty instruments of thought, but perhaps these comparisons will help you remember them.

LEARNING FROM OTHER WRITERS

The following two essays show the two methods in action. In the first, a musician uses division to discuss listening to music; in the second, a student writer classifies the names of cars and their meanings.

In "How We Listen," from Aaron Copland's book *What to Listen for in Music*, the eminent American composer sets out to educate his readers in a skill: listening to music. As Copland makes clear, listening isn't a step-by-step activity, and so he does not try to treat it in chronological order as he might do in a process analysis. Rather, his essay explains by dividing the way we listen into three elements or planes. Though each is different from the others, all three exist simultaneously.

HOW WE LISTEN
AARON COPLAND

We all listen to music according to our separate capacities. But, for the sake of analysis, the whole listening process may become clearer if we break it up into its component parts, so to speak. In a certain sense we all listen to music on three separate planes. For lack of a better terminology, one might name these: (1) the sensuous plane, (2) the expressive plane, (3) the sheerly musical plane. The only advantage to be gained from mechanically splitting up the listening process into these hypothetical planes is the clearer view to be had of the way in which we listen.

The simplest way of listening to music is to listen for the sheer pleasure of the musical sound itself. That is the sensuous plane. It is the plane on which we hear music without thinking, without considering it in any way. One turns on the radio while doing something else and absent-mindedly bathes in the sound. A kind of brainless but attractive state of mind is engendered by the mere sound appeal of the music.

You may be sitting in a room reading this book. Imagine one note struck on the piano. Immediately that one note is enough to change the atmosphere of the room—proving that the sound element in music is a powerful and mysterious agent, which it would be foolish to deride or belittle.

The surprising thing is that many people who consider themselves qualified music lovers abuse that plane in listening. They go to concerts in order to lose themselves. They use music as a consolation or an escape. They enter an ideal world where one doesn't have to think of the realities of everyday life. Of course they aren't thinking about the music either. Music allows them to leave it, and they go off to a place to dream, dreaming because of and apropos of the music yet never quite listening to it.

Yes, the sound appeal of music is a potent and primitive force, but you 5 must not allow it to usurp a disproportionate share of your interest. The sensuous plane is an important one in music, a very important one, but it does not constitute the whole story.

There is no need to digress further on the sensuous plane. Its appeal 6 to every normal human being is self-evident. There is, however, such a thing as becoming more sensitive to the different kinds of sound stuff as used by various composers. For all composers do not use that sound stuff in the same way. Don't get the idea that the value of music is commensurate with its sensuous appeal or that the loveliest sounding music is made by the greatest composer. If that were so, Ravel would be a greater creator than Beethoven. The point is that the sound element varies with each composer, that his usage of sound forms an integral part of his style and must be taken into account when listening. The reader can see, therefore, that a more conscious approach is valuable even on this primary plane of music listening.

The second plane on which music exists is what I have called the 7 expressive one. Here, immediately, we tread on controversial ground. Composers have a way of shying away from any discussion of music's expressive side. Did not Stravinsky himself proclaim that his music was an "object," a "thing," with a life of its own, and with no other meaning than its own purely musical existence? This intransigent attitude of Stravinsky's may be due to the fact that so many people have tried to read different meanings into so many pieces. Heaven knows it is difficult enough to say precisely what it is that a piece of music means, to say it definitely, to say it finally so that everyone is satisfied with your explanation. But that should not lead one to the other extreme of denying to music the right to be "expressive."

My own belief is that all music has an expressive power, some more 8 and some less, but that all music has a certain meaning behind the notes and that that meaning behind the notes constitutes, after all, what the piece is saying, what the piece is about. This whole problem can be stated quite simply by asking, "Is there a meaning to music?" My answer to that would be, "Yes." And "Can you state in so many words what the meaning is?" My answer to that would be, "No." Therein lies the difficulty.

Simple-minded souls will never be satisfied with the answer to the 9 second of these questions. They always want music to have a meaning, and the more concrete it is the better they like it. The more the music reminds them of a train, a storm, a funeral, or any other familiar conception the more expressive it appears to be to them. This popular idea of music's meaning—stimulated and abetted by the usual run of musical commentator—should be discouraged wherever and whenever it is met. One timid lady once confessed to me that she suspected something seriously lacking in her appreciation of music because of her inability to connect it with anything definite. That is getting the whole thing backward, of course.

Still, the question remains, How close should the intelligent music lover 10 wish to come to pinning a definite meaning to any particular work? No closer than a general concept, I should say. Music expresses, at different moments, serenity or exuberance, regret or triumph, fury or delight. It expresses each of these moods, and many others, in a numberless variety of subtle shadings and differences. It may even express a state of meaning for which there exists no adequate word in any language. In that case, musicians often like to say that it has only a purely musical meaning. They sometimes go farther and say that *all* music has only a purely musical meaning. What they really mean is that no appropriate word can be found to express the music's meaning and that, even if it could, they do not feel the need of finding it.

But whatever the professional musician may hold, most musical novices 11 still search for specific words with which to pin down their musical reactions. That is why they always find Tschaikovsky easier to "understand" than Beethoven. In the first place, it is easier to pin a meaning-word on a Tschaikovsky piece than on a Beethoven one. Much easier. Moreover, with the Russian composer, every time you come back to a piece of his it almost always says the same thing to you, whereas with Beethoven it is often quite difficult to put your finger right on what he is saying. And any musician will tell you that that is why Beethoven is the greatest composer. Because music which always says the same thing to you will necessarily soon become dull music, but music whose meaning is slightly different with each hearing has a greater chance of remaining alive.

Listen, if you can, to the forty-eight fugue themes of Bach's *Well Tem-* 12 *pered Clavichord.* Listen to each theme, one after another. You will soon realize that each theme mirrors a different world of feeling. You will also soon realize that the more beautiful a theme seems to you the harder it is to find any word that will describe it to your complete satisfaction. Yes, you will certainly know whether it is a gay theme or a sad one. You will be able, in other words, in your own mind, to draw a frame of emotional feeling around your theme. Now study the sad one a little closer. Try to pin down the exact quality of its sadness. Is it pessimistically sad or resignedly sad; is it fatefully sad or smilingly sad?

Let us suppose that you are fortunate and can describe to your own 13 satisfaction in so many words the exact meaning of your chosen theme. There is still no guarantee that anyone else will be satisfied. Nor need they be. The important thing is that each one feel for himself the specific expressive quality of a theme or, similarly, an entire piece of music. And if it is a great work of art, don't expect it to mean exactly the same thing to you each time you return to it.

Themes or pieces need not express only one emotion, of course. Take 14 such a theme as the first main one of the *Ninth Symphony,*° for example. It is clearly made up of different elements. It does not say only one thing. Yet anyone hearing it immediately gets a feeling of strength, a feeling of power. It isn't a power that comes simply because the theme is played loudly. It is a power inherent in the theme itself. The extraordinary strength and vigor of the theme results in the listener's receiving an impression that a forceful statement has been made. But one should never try to boil it down to "the fateful hammer of life," etc. That is where the trouble begins.

Ninth Symphony: Final symphony of Ludwig van Beethoven (1770–1827).

The musician, in his exasperation, says it means nothing but the notes themselves, whereas the nonprofessional is only too anxious to hang on to any explanation that gives him the illusion of getting closer to the music's meaning.

Now, perhaps, the reader will know better what I mean when I say that 15
music does have an expressive meaning but that we cannot say in so many words what that meaning is.

The third plane on which music exists is the sheerly musical plane. 16
Besides the pleasurable sound of music and the expressive feeling that it gives off, music does exist in terms of the notes themselves and of their manipulation. Most listeners are not sufficiently conscious of this third plane. . . .

Professional musicians, on the other hand, are, if anything, too con- 17
scious of the mere notes themselves. They often fall into the error of be-coming so engrossed with their arpeggios° and staccatos° that they forget the deeper aspects of the music they are performing. But from the layman's standpoint, it is not so much a matter of getting over bad habits on the sheerly musical plane as of increasing one's awareness of what is going on, in so far as the notes are concerned.

When the man in the street listens to the "notes themselves" with any 18
degree of concentration, he is most likely to make some mention of the melody. Either he hears a pretty melody or he does not, and he generally lets it go at that. Rhythm is likely to gain his attention next, particularly if it seems exciting. But harmony and tone color are generally taken for granted, if they are thought of consciously at all. As for music's having a definite form of some kind, that idea seems never to have occurred to him.

It is very important for all of us to become more alive to music on its 19
sheerly musical plane. After all, an actual musical material is being used. The intelligent listener must be prepared to increase his awareness of the musical material and what happens to it. He must hear the melodies, the rhythms, the harmonies, the tone colors in a more conscious fashion. But above all he must, in order to follow the line of the composer's thought, know something of the principles of musical form. Listening to all of these elements is listening on the sheerly musical plane.

Let me repeat that I have split up mechanically the three separate planes 20
on which we listen merely for the sake of greater clarity. Actually, we never listen on one or the other of these planes. What we do is to correlate them—listening in all three ways at the same time. It takes no mental effort, for we do it instinctively.

Perhaps an analogy with what happens to us when we visit the theater 21
will make this instinctive correlation clearer. In the theater, you are aware of the actors and actresses, costumes and sets, sounds and movements. All these give one the sense that the theater is a pleasant place to be in. They constitute the sensuous plane in our theatrical reactions.

The expressive plane in the theater would be derived from the feeling 22
that you get from what is happening on the stage. You are moved to pity,

---

arpeggios: The playing of the tones of a chord in succession instead of together.
staccatos: Groups of disconnected notes played rapidly.

excitement, or gayety. It is this general feeling, generated aside from the particular words being spoken, a certain emotional something which exists on the stage, that is analogous to the expressive quality in music.

The plot and plot development is equivalent to our sheerly musical 23 plane. The playwright creates and develops a character in just the same way that a composer creates and develops a theme. According to the degree of your awareness of the way in which the artist in either field handles his material will you become a more intelligent listener.

It is easy enough to see that the theatergoer never is conscious of any 24 of these elements separately. He is aware of them all at the same time. The same is true of music listening. We simultaneously and without thinking listen on all three planes.

In a sense, the ideal listener is both inside and outside the music at 25 the same moment, judging it and enjoying it, wishing it would go one way and watching it go another—almost like the composer at the moment he composes it; because in order to write his music, the composer must also be inside and outside his music, carried away by it and yet coldly critical of it. A subjective and objective attitude is implied in both creating and listening to music.

What the reader should strive for, then, is a more *active* kind of listen- 26 ing. Whether you listen to Mozart or Duke Ellington,° you can deepen your understanding of music only by being a more conscious and aware listener—not someone who is just listening, but someone who is listening *for* something.

Duke Ellington: Edward Kennedy Ellington (1899–1974), American pianist, bandleader, and composer, whose innovative music profoundly influenced the history of jazz.

Questions to Start You Thinking

1.   What reason does the author give for dividing the way we listen into three separate components, or planes? What does the essay gain from his having done so?
2.   In paragraphs 21–24, the author makes an analogy to help explain what he's talking about. Can you think of other analogies that would make Copland's divisions clear?
3.   What, if anything, has Copland taught you about being an intelligent listener? Does he say anything that you disagree with, that doesn't coincide with your experience?
4.   What other large concepts might be most easily explained by the method of division?

For a humanities course Mary I. Linkowski wrote the following essay, both serious and entertaining. For the purpose of explaining how auto manufacturers try to sell us more than mere transportation, she classifies the names they give their products—and finds meanings in these revealing classifications.

THE NAMING OF CARS
MARY I. LINKOWSKI

Browsing through *Time,* one comes across an advertisement for the 1 Thunderbird that simply shows the car, with words such as "dauntless," "boundless," and "aggressive" displayed in the foreground. On another page, an advertisement for the Lancer calls this car "an American Revolution," while still another, for the Celebrity, states: "Warning: This car could change your lifestyle."

Evidently, car manufacturers aren't promoting the performance of their 2
automobiles but rather are attracting buyers by using car names that connote qualities people dream about possessing. The manufacturers utilize the slogan of a famous advertiser who said, "Don't sell the steak, sell the sizzle." Just as the car names Thunderbird, Lancer, and Celebrity connote animal, military, and personal qualities, a variety of car names can be classified according to themes. In turn, each theme can be broken down into two or more subclasses.

First, consider Lynx, Cougar, Bobcat, and Jaguar—animals of the cat 3
family. Documentaries, movies, and books have shown these animals fearlessly fighting their enemies and dominating their prey with sharp claws and teeth. Thus their very names provide the public with images of power. In addition, Skylark, Tercel, Eagle, Firebird, Sunbird, Skyhawk, and Phoenix are birds, but the names connote the quality of freedom as they soar and seem to float in midair, bounded only by the sky. Unlike birds, most people are earthbound and plagued with the pressures of school, families, or jobs. Most people would find flying an extraordinary feeling—enjoyable and worth experiencing. Buyers will purchase cars that convey this quality of freedom because they wish to be free of life's problems while driving a car. Names such as Rabbit, Impala, Pacer, Mustang, Colt, Pinto, and Charger all connote swiftness. The rabbit, a long-eared, short-tailed mammal, and the impala, an African antelope, both must be fast to avoid becoming the dinner for some hungry predator. In addition, names such as Pacer, Mustang, Colt, Pinto, and Charger denote horses and connote swiftness.

The Grand Prix and the Duster, obviously not names of animals, still 4
suggest the quality of speed. The French name for "great prize," Grand Prix, refers to a race many professional drivers compete in to see who has the fastest car. The Duster, a name that denotes a person who removes dust, also gives an image of swiftness: when animals run away, they may leave behind a field of dust just as a duster unsettles dirt when he cleans furniture. People buy these automobiles to feel swift in their life's endeavors.

Next, some cars connote qualities that relate to our past and suggest 5
military and government systems. Le Sabre and Cutlass, for example, are names for swords: weapons used in battle during the legendary King Arthur's reign. In addition, a Cavalier and a Lancer probably fought in these battles. While a cavalier is a gentleman trained in arms and horsemanship, a lancer is a knight who carries a steel spear. Knights would either defend their honor against a Challenge or achieve a Conquest. In battle, they would be Valiant, become a Champ, and receive a Citation. On the other hand, in the present, sometimes during negotiations between neighboring countries, an Alliance may end because a sudden Caprice, or impulsive action by a citizen, offends another country. For these Civic matters, a Diplomat comes and settles the dispute. During battle, an Escort or a Corvette, which are armed warships, protect a country from enemy attack. The military and the government try to be an invincible source of strength for their people,

and we, in turn, are attracted to these cars because they will fulfill our desires to be brave, uncompromising, and diplomatic.

Car names can relate to people. We often wish we were a Monarch, or 6 even Queen Victoria, wealthy and omnipotent (Omni), or all powerful, at one time. Such rulers reigned over Eldorados or places of great wealth, owned many gems, perhaps wore a Topaz in their crown or Corona, and tried to rule wisely and fairly. These qualities—wealth and power to rule— attract buyers by promising instant fulfillment of their dreams of imitating the lifestyles of the rich and influential.

Car manufacturers also often name their cars after glamorous places 7 people dream of visiting someday. Some people would like to go surfing at Malibu Beach or swim and bask in the sun at Daytona Beach in Florida. Others would rather go skiing in Aspen, Colorado, or tour Europe and experience its customs (Continental) in such places as Le Mans, France; Torino, or Turin, Italy; Seville or Granada, Spain, or meet a Parisienne in Paris. Many people wish to escape to such romantic places as Capri, an island in the Bay of Naples, and Firenza or Florence, Italy, or perhaps visit San Francisco and stay at the posh Fairmont Hotel. Car manufacturers hope that once you purchase their vehicle, you will go Trans Am or across America, perhaps meet a sophisticated New Yorker, and experience the place of your dreams, whether sunny and pleasant, cultural and exciting, cold and refreshing, or romantic and elegant.

In general, the names of cars connote admirable qualities we either 8 have or dream about one day possessing. Some of us would like to be a Celebrity whose popularity sometimes rests on whether or not an audience enjoyed his act and wants an Encore. Others yearn to be a Dasher, a spirited person, the life of the party or Fiesta. One person may want to be considered Reliant or responsible, while others are Mavericks, people who wish to be independent and lead their own, unconventional lives. Mavericks wouldn't enjoy living in a suburban Colony Park, a place where people might have common interests. Still other people are just like a Sirocco, or hot wind: their tempers reach the boiling point and eventually they are forced to let off steam. Other times, they're like a Zephyr, a gentle breeze; then they are kind, considerate, and willing to talk things out instead of shouting. Finally, when you finish reciting the Greek alphabet, you have reached Omega. Some people are like the Omega in that they want to be considered the ultimate or best in their particular professions.

Seen in this light, a car is not only a vehicle that transports us from 9 one place to another but an advertisement of what we wish to state about ourselves. We choose automobiles whose names add qualities to our lives that we did not previously possess. Literally, our car is a part of our being. Car manufacturers, aware of our dreams of desirable qualities, have named their cars accordingly, tempting us, the buyers, to succumb to the sizzle, not the steak.

Questions to Start You Thinking

1. On what basis does Linkowski do her classifying? What do all the car names that she groups have in common?

2. Comment on this essay's concluding paragraph. To what extent, do you believe, is it true that we "choose automobiles whose names add qualities to our lives that we did not previously possess"? What other considerations might a prospective buyer ponder as well? Is it a serious omission that Linkowski doesn't discuss those features?

3. Of the writer's five resources, which ones does Linkowski rely on most heavily? How can you tell?

4. What other topics could most easily be explained with the help of classification?

LEARNING BY WRITING

The Assignment

Choose a subject you would like to explain, one that you believe *needs* explaining to a student from overseas or to any other student not familiar with it. Decide whether the subject might better be explained by dividing or by classifying and then write an essay by that method.

Here are instances of college writers who successfully responded to this type of assignment.

WRITERS WHO DIVIDED

A man, for an economics course, divided the United States into geographic regions and discussed the present health of the economy in each.

A woman, for an introductory law course, divided a large city law firm into its departments, explaining the services that each performs: dealing with cases involving property, criminal defense, taxes and estates, civil rights, patents and copyrights, accident and indemnity claims, and other concerns.

A man, a student of geology, divided a typical earthquake into its geographic parts: the *focus*, or place where a layer of rock ruptures; the *epicenter*, or part of the earth's surface directly above the focus; and the *peripheral shock area*. Then he detailed what might be observed at each point.

A woman who plans a career as a consultant in time and motion study sliced a typical day in the life of a college student into the segments that compose it (class time, study time, feeding time, grooming time, recreation time, social time, waste time) and suggested ways to make more efficient use of the student's time.

A man, a student of psychology, divided the human brain into its parts and described the function of each.

WRITERS WHO CLASSIFIED

A man, a student of marketing, after inspecting twenty breakfast foods on sale in a supermarket, classified them into four kinds: TV-watching kid type, worried-about-health type, middle-aged citizen type (all-bran, high-fiber content, oatmeal), and noncommittal type (corn flakes, puffed rice). His paper gained interest from his astute comments on the pictures, special offers, slogans, and blurbs he found on the packages of each type—all clearly indicating how carefully the cereal manufacturers target their products toward specific consumers.

A woman who attends a college in which the students are predominantly male recalled various remarks addressed to her during the first week of classes by males she hadn't met before and sorted them into four categories: the innocent friendly line, the hostile line, the calculated opening gambit line, and the egotistical "look at me" line.

A man classified people he observed at a performance of *Don Giovanni* into four types: opera lovers, people who don't enjoy opera but who were dragged to it by opera lovers, people who wish to be seen at the opera, and amateur singers who dream of being opera stars (and who couldn't resist humming or singing along all through the arias). (He wrote for a journalism class in which he was assigned to write a feature article.)

A woman unseriously separated the students on her campus into three types: Ultra-Conservatives, Followers of Current Fads, and Jim Morrison Groupies "who refuse to admit that their namesake is no more."

A woman who had visited South Africa, writing for a course in political science, classified South Africans into angry blacks who demand change, passive blacks who try to live with the status quo, whites bitterly opposed to change, and whites sympathetic to change. She concluded that whites bitterly opposed to change are a dwindling minority.

A man, a drama major, classified well-known contemporary stand-up comedians into two kinds: insulters and insulted.

Generating Ideas

Your first task, as is usual in writing, is picking a subject you care about. The paper topics just listed may help start your own ideas flowing. Do some idle, relaxed thinking, with pencil and paper at hand. Or do some fast scribbling (see "Brainstorming," p. 457). Try to come up with something complicated that you think you understand and that you would really like to explain, or something that you would like to understand more clearly yourself.

When Mary Linkowski began to write "The Naming of Cars," she discovered a dazzling, nearly bewildering array of material. First she compiled a list of eighty-five car names (readily available in the car advertising pages of a newspaper). Then beside each she wrote the dictionary meaning of the name ("CUTLASS—a short curving sword formerly used by sailors on warships"). Later, this annotated list would prove immensely useful in her planning and in writing her draft.

Once the subject occurs to you, how do you decide the better way to explain it: to divide or to classify? Easy. Is it one thing that you might better explain part by part? Divide. Is it many things that you might sort into groups to make better sense of? Classify.

Then give your material (which you are going to organize) a careful, critical examination. Just spend some time looking it over, mulling it, and saying to yourself, How am I going to slice this up, or sort this?

The very act of slicing, or of sorting into kinds, will start ideas flowing. If, say, you set out to classify, deciding in what pigeonhole to place a thing involves deciding what it has in common with other things. If you are dividing, how is this segment of a whole subject distinctively different from the rest? To concern yourself with these matters is to observe more closely and so give yourself something to say when you write.

Suggestions for dividing. Right away, decide on the principle you will follow in taking slices. Just as you can slice a carrot in many ways, you can find many ways to divide a subject. You might divide the United States into geographical regions, or you might divide the country on the basis of different patterns of speech heard in each area. Firmly decide your reason for slicing before you begin. What differences are you trying to demonstrate?

When do you need to subdivide? Subdivide whenever a slice looks needlessly large and you could easily separate it into smaller parts. An anatomy textbook usually separates the human nervous system into the *central nervous system* (brain and spinal cord) and the *peripheral nervous system* (all other nerves in the body). But anatomists subdivide the peripheral nervous system into two smaller parts: the *somatic division* and the *autonomic division*. In explaining American food to a student from overseas, you might subdivide *fast food* into *hamburger, fried chicken, Chinese take-out,* and *pizza.*

Before you commit yourself to a subject, you may wish to leap ahead and do some planning to see whether your projected paper will work out. You might try making a rough outline (see p. 476) or perhaps writing a rough version of an opening paragraph. Then try to imagine yourself going on from there to write a finished paper. How well would your rough start lend itself to further development?

Suggestions for classifying. Classifications may be made to entertain or to make a serious point. To sort out cities according to their crime rates (high, medium, low), for example, might prove useful: it might even suggest to a reader where to settle. But whatever your purpose is, it's an excellent idea, from the start, to be sure you have a reason for classifying.

As you begin to classify, first decide on what basis you are going to sort. Your categories should exclude one another, not overlap. You should have just one principle of grouping your items, and it should be clear to you. If you were sorting feature films, you wouldn't list as two categories *movies for teenagers* and *science fiction movies* because the film *Back to the Future* might fit both categories. To sidestep this problem, you would reorganize your classification on a different principle. You could sort the films by audience (*children's movies, movies for teenagers, movies for mature audiences*) or by subject matter (*love-*

romance, mystery, science fiction, sports, exotic places). Back to the Future might fit either scheme of classification.

You'll save trouble later if you can decide early whether you'll need to *subclassify*. If, as you sort, you find that any group contains many examples, you might consider splitting it into smaller categories. In classifying feature films, the items in the category *mystery movies* might be regrouped: *detective movies, amateur detective movies, police movies, haunted house movies, monster movies*—all under the larger, more general category *mystery movies*.

You might ask yourself the following questions before you write.

DISCOVERY CHECKLIST: FOCUSING ON YOUR TASK

- Have you found a subject that interests you, one that seems worthwhile to slice or sort?
- Is your basis for dividing or classifying clear to you, so that you can make it clear to your readers?
- In dividing, have you left out any obvious parts that a reader might expect to find? A division of the electorate into Republicans and Democrats would omit some Independents as well as Socialist Labor Party or Prohibition Party members.
- In classifying, do any of your categories overlap? If so, try another basis for sorting things. Have you included all essential categories? It would be a major oversight to classify Americans according to their religious preferences and leave out members of a widely held faith or omit unbelievers. You may not care to explore in great detail every kind of thing that a reader might look for, but if you think it important, then at least you can mention it.
- Did you end with any spare parts—any remnants of pie or leftover marbles? If you did, fine, that's natural. A useful label for either a division or a classification may be *others*. Reality cannot always be neatly and completely sliced or perfectly pigeonholed. Don't try so hard to organize it that you distort it.
- In going through all this work, exactly what will you be trying to achieve? Make sure, before you begin, that your dividing or classifying is going to prove something or tell you or your readers something not known before. You don't divide and classify merely for the sake of fulfilling a writing assignment. Use these methods when they will help you explain something that matters to you and to your readers as well.

Shaping a Draft

In both dividing and classifying, the planning stage is crucial. Some kind of outline—whether extremely detailed or rough—will save you time and avoid confusion.

For dividing, your outline might be a pie-like circle with the slices labeled. If you make the slices larger or smaller according to their relative importance, the sketch might give you some notion of how much time to spend explaining each part. The pie outline for a paper analyzing the parts of a radio station's twenty-four-hour broadcast day might look like the illustration on page 195. If you need to subdivide any parts into smaller ones, clearly indicate it in your writing so that the reader won't get lost.

For classifying, you probably began by making a list of things to be sorted into categories. In planning your draft, you might try *clustering*, drawing lines to join similar items (as shown on p. 475). Mary Linkowski, in classifying car names, did much of her planning right on the list of car names (and their meanings) that she had made at the start. She worked down her list using colored pens. In the left-hand margin, she wrote *War* in blue ink next to names such as Alliance, Conquest, and Le Sabre; *Royalty* in orange ink next to Regal, Marquis, Monarch, and Crown Victoria; *Animal* in green ink next to Lynx, Cougar, and Rabbit, and so on. This system made it easy to sort the names into categories. Looking over her categories, Linkowski found that *Royalty* seemed to be only one of three themes relating to people. She made an outline of the themes she had discovered in all the car names:

Animals

Weapons and war

People
   1. Admirable qualities we want to possess
   2. Beautiful places we want to go to
   3. Advantages we envy—royalty, wealth

The animal names, she realized, could be subclassified according to their main suggestions: *strength, power, swiftness,* and *freedom.* On a new list arranged by categories, she noted each suggestion ("*Skylark*—freedom, *Jaguar*—power"). She began to set her findings down in a rough draft. It began:

First, twenty-two names of cars can be classified according to animal qualities. These attributes animals possess specifically define the quality a car company wants to convey about its product. Each animal quality can be broken down into the subclasses of strength, power, swiftness, and freedom.

Linkowski wrote this draft without trying to make it lively and entertaining. She simply tried to record her thinking and to put her ideas in order. Later, when she revised, she made her essay more readable.

Another way to plan your paper is to arrange the parts or the classifications of your subject from less important to more important or your divisions from smallest to largest—or any other order that makes sense to you. Some writers like to start a paper of either kind by telling their readers the divisions they are going to slice their subject into or the categories they are going to sort it into. That is one clear-cut way to go. Still, it takes some of the fun out of a paper, and some writers prefer to keep the reader guessing: what category or division is coming next?

Why are you going to go to all the trouble of dividing or classifying? Your readers might like to know. Right in the opening paragraph or paragraphs of your paper—the introduction—is the place to tell them. What are you trying to

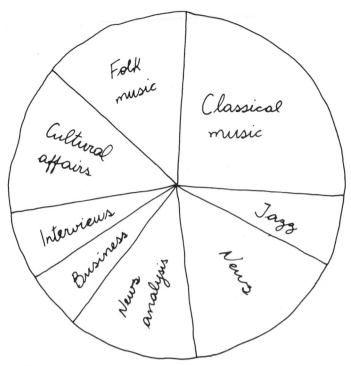

Pie outline of a radio station's broadcast day.

explain? What do you hope to accomplish by slicing it into parts or sorting it into kinds? Perhaps by dividing you'll make a complex thing more readily understandable, being able to see it part by part; or, by classifying, you'll reduce a sprawling array of things to an orderly set of categories. Make clear your purpose for dividing or classifying. Your paper should not be mistaken for a sterile academic exercise; by using either of these powerful methods, it should make a complexity or a confusion appear simpler and clearer.

While you slice or sort, the following suggestion may help you keep your material clearly in mind. If you haven't already done so, you might invent a name or label for each slice or each category you mention to distinguish it from all the others. This device will also help your reader to keep the divisions or categories straight. This is what the student did who classified her fellow students into Ultra-Conservatives, Followers of Current Fads, and Jim Morrison Groupies and what the student did who classified males' opening lines: the innocent friendly line, the calculated opening gambit, and so forth.

Rewriting

A paper that divides or classifies need not look (and read) like a lifeless stack of blocks. It may turn out that way if you just present each division or category as an item on a list ("9. Teenage Movies. Teenage movies are the kind that ..."). For one thing, you can put life into your paper and make it more readable by using transitions, those valuable words and phrases that introduce and connect ideas. (For more advice on this point, see "Using Transitions," p. 486.) Try to vary the way you start each paragraph. Don't be like the senator who in giving a speech made each new point one more number on a list: "And in the thirty-third place. . . ."

Here are questions to ask yourself.

REVISION CHECKLIST: DIVIDING

- Have you explained each part completely enough, so that a reader will understand it? (Try your paper on a peer reader.)
- Have you shown how each part functions, how it relates to the whole?
- If there are subdivisions—smaller slices—do you clearly identify them and clearly situate them within the larger division? One sample way to identify them: "In the typical editorial department of a city newspaper, you will find the city desk, the copy desk, the library or 'morgue.' . . ." Again, seek the aid of peer readers; they can help you notice whether any distinctions look blurry.
- Do you give your readers a sense of having beheld the subject as a whole? Perhaps your concluding paragraph affords you a chance to bring all the separate parts back together and affirm whatever your dividing has explained.

REVISION CHECKLIST: CLASSIFYING

- Do all members of each group have some trait in common?
- Do you illustrate each category with plenty of examples?
- If you have subclassified, do you make clear your subclassifications and relate them to a larger category?
- Does your paper read like a mechanical list? If you have had to use many pigeonholes, the danger of dullness is real. If as you are rereading you find yourself going to sleep, can you discover some lively and colorful details to add? In her final version, Mary Linkowski added this sentence to her paragraph about animals: "Documentaries, movies, and books have shown these animals fearlessly fighting their enemies and dominating their prey with sharp claws and teeth." That addition certainly enhanced her first draft, with its cut-and-dried description of categories. In adding it, Linkowski evidently discovered more sensory evidence just by searching her memory.

REVISION CHECKLIST: FOR DIVIDING OR CLASSIFYING

- Have you made clear your basis for dividing or classifying—the principle on which you slice, or sort?
- Have you led your readers along with helpful transitions?
- In your conclusion, do you show your readers that all this work has told them something?

Other Assignments

1. In a paragraph, analyze one of the following subjects by dividing it into its basic parts or elements:

> A symphony orchestra
> A colony of insects, a flock of birds, a school of fish
> The human heart
> The United Nations organization
> A computer or other technological device
> A basketball, football, or hockey team
> A painting or statue
> A radio telescope
> A hospital or other institution
> An essay, short story, novel, or play
> A scientific theory
> An era in history
> A child's first year
> A famous and influential idea

2. Write a paragraph in which you classify an assortment of individual things. Set forth three or four categories to enlighten your readers about any one of the following collective subjects:

> Inconsiderate people
> Contemporary styles of dress
> Students observed in a library or other gathering place
> Schools of twentieth-century painters or musicians
> Wars or episodes of violence
> Parents or children
> Techniques of sinking a shot in basketball or performing some other physical feat
> Inventions or discoveries
> Styles of architecture
> Neighborhoods in a city
> Special jobs within a career area
> Attitudes or opinions that you have heard from several different people
> Newspaper columnists
> Actors or singers

APPLYING WHAT YOU LEARN:
SOME USES OF DIVIDING AND CLASSIFYING

As you have probably seen already, many different college courses will give you an opportunity to divide or classify. In explaining for a political science course how the federal government works, you might divide the government into its branches, explaining each. You might write a geography paper in which you divide France into six regions and set forth the characteristics of each region. You might classify common kinds of nervous disease, classify schools of thought about a problem in economics, or classify familiar types of advertising.

You won't often write papers entirely devoted to dividing or classifying. But you may often find either method useful in writing *part* of an explanatory paper: a paragraph or a section. In the middle of his essay "Things Unflattened by Science," Lewis Thomas pauses to divide biology into three parts.

We can imagine three worlds of biology, corresponding roughly to the three worlds of physics: the very small world now being explored by the molecular geneticists and virologists, not yet as strange a place as quantum mechanics but well on its way to strangeness; an everyday, middle-sized world where things are as they are; and a world of the very large, which is the whole affair, the lovely conjoined biosphere, the vast embryo, the closed ecosystem in which we live as working parts, the place for which Lovelock and Margulis invented the term "Gaia" because of its extraordinary capacity to regulate itself. This world seems to me an even stranger one than the world of very small things in biology: it looks like the biggest organism I've ever heard of, and at the same time the most delicate and fragile, exactly the delicate and fragile creature it appeared to be in those first photographs taken from the surface of the moon.

We've mentioned that college textbooks divide and classify frequently. A psychology text classifies mental disorders into categories. A literature book customarily arranges works of literature into three genres or classes: stories, poems, and plays. In the following example, taken from the textbook *Human Development*, Kurt W. Fischer and Arlyne Lazerson describe a research project that sorted individual babies into three types:

The researchers also found that certain of these temperamental quali- ties tended to occur together. These clusters of characteristics generally fell into three types—the easy baby, the difficult baby, and the baby who was slow to warm up. The *easy infant* has regular patterns of eating and sleep- ing, readily approaches new objects and people, adapts easily to changes in the environment, generally reacts with low or moderate intensity, and typically is in a cheerful mood. The *difficult infant* usually shows irregular patterns of eating and sleeping, withdraws from new objects or people, adapts slowly to changes, reacts with great intensity, and is frequently cranky. The *slow-to-warm-up infant* typically has a low activity level, tends to with- draw when presented with an unfamiliar object, reacts with a low level of intensity, and adapts slowly to changes in the environment. Fortunately for parents, most healthy infants—40 percent or more—have an easy temper- ament. Only about 10 percent have a difficult temperament, and about 15 percent are slow to warm up. The remaining 35 percent do not easily fit one of the three types but show some other pattern.

Even if you don't write textbooks, you will be writing about the material your textbooks contain; and like the textbook writers, you can apply these methods.

A simple, straightforward way to begin many essays you may have to write is to explain your subject briefly by dividing ("A typical political party has these components . . ."). Julius Caesar opens his *Commentary on the Gallic War* with a famous division: "All Gaul is divided into three parts." Classifying, too, is a way to begin a paper. In the introductory paragraphs of Robertson Davies's essay "A Few Kind Words for Superstition," the Canadian writer explains his complicated subject by classifying familiar superstitions into four familiar and recognizable types: *vain observances*, such as not walking under a ladder or throwing a pinch of spilled salt over one's left shoulder; *divination,* such as consulting fortunetellers, astrology books, and the *I Ching; idolatry*, trusting in lucky charms; and *improper worship*, such as trying to bribe the Lord by tucking a two-dollar bill under an altar candle. After he sorts familiar superstitions into larger groups and makes their general nature more understandable, Davies goes on to the main business of his essay: to discuss how superstitions arise. Often, classifying at the beginning of your essay is a means of simplifying your writing task. Davies, for instance, might have set up four categories into which most superstitions fall and then dispensed with three of them and declared his intention to deal with only the fourth kind: improper worship. To take a classic example from psychology, Sigmund Freud, at the beginning of a chapter of *On Dreams,* classifies dreams into three types: (1) dreams that make sense; (2) dreams that make sense but that puzzle us; and (3) confused, seemingly meaningless dreams. He then proceeds to discuss what he believes even puzzling and meaningless dreams reveal.

In college writing, you can divide and classify whenever you need to take a complicated subject and organize it into smaller compartments so that you and your reader can make sense of it. This is putting either method to serious use. But we should add a small note about classification. Perhaps because of its gamelike quality, this method readily lends itself to humor and playfulness. Lighthearted writers have classified things for the fun of it, making a point but mainly trying to entertain readers. In a celebrated article for *Harper's,* "Highbrow, Middlebrow, Lowbrow," Russell Lynes classifies American tastes in matters such as food, drink, furniture, and entertainment according to the consumer's intellectual sophistication or lack of it. (In art, the highbrow likes an original work by a personal friend; the middlebrow, a reproduction of a Van Gogh painting; the lowbrow, a Norman Rockwell calendar. In drink, the highbrow likes "an adequate little red wine"; the middlebrow, mixed drinks with fruit in them; the lowbrow, beer.) In *Blue Highways,* William Least Heat Moon classifies the cafés he found on America's back roads:

> There is one almost infallible way to find honest food at just prices in blue-highway America: count the wall calendars in a cafe.
>
> No calendar: Same as an interstate pit stop.
>
> One calendar: Pre-processed food assembled in New Jersey.
>
> Two calendars: Only if fish trophies present.
>
> Three calendars: Can't miss on the farm-boy breakfast.
>
> Four calendars: Try the ho-made pie too.
>
> Five calendars: Keep it under your hat, or they'll franchise.
>
> One time I found a six-calendar cafe in the Ozarks, which served fried chicken, peach pie, and chocolate malts, that left me searching for another ever since. I've never seen a seven-calendar place. But old-time travelers— road men in a day when cars had running boards and lunchroom windows said AIR COOLED in blue letters with icicles dripping from the tops—those travelers have told me the golden legends of seven-calendar cafes.

CHAPTER 12

Asking Why: Looking for Cause and Effect

When a house burns down, an insurance company assigns a claims adjuster to look into the disaster and answer the question *Why?* The resulting answer—the *cause* of the fire, whether it be lightning, a forgotten cigar, or a match that the owner of the house deliberately struck—is given in a written report. The adjuster also details the *effects* of the fire: what was destroyed or damaged, what repairs will be needed, how much they will cost.

That's a common example of the kind of writing called *cause and effect*. This form of analysis divides the stream of events into the reasons something happens and the results of its happening. In college writing, you won't always be expected to do both tasks in one paper. You may need to ask only Why?— as in an exam question in a history course that calls for the causes of America's involvement in the Vietnam War. Or you may need to ask only What happened as a consequence?—as in a course in psychology in which you perform an experiment and then in a written report set forth the results.

In assigning you to write a paper tracing causes, no instructor will expect you to set forth a final and definitive explanation with absolute certainty. To ask why a huge phenomenon took place, such as continental drift or the Depression of the 1930s, is to propose long and serious toil. After decades of thought, historians are still trying to account for that remarkable burst of intellectual energy called the Italian Renaissance. When *you* write a paper, about the Italian Renaissance or anything else, don't blithely assign causes to things if you don't need to. Taken seriously, the simple statement "Herbert Hoover became un-popular because the stock market crashed" would call for months of effort to demonstrate for sure that the president's unpopularity resulted directly from the crash and from no other cause. Determining causes, even if a writer has all the time in the world, is at best an uncertain pursuit. "Causality," says French philosopher of history Paul Veyne, "is always accompanied by mental reservation."

If discovering causes is so difficult, why then are college students ever asked to try it? Because the attempt, whether wholly or only partly successful, is a powerful and effective means of explaining. When you challenge yourself to discover a *possible* answer, you venture into a subject deeply and critically; you gather information and ideas; you marshal evidence. In the process, both you and your reader learn a good deal and understand the subject more clearly. Effects, by the way, are usually easier than causes to demonstrate. The results of a fire are apparent to an onlooker the next day, though its cause may be obscure.

LEARNING FROM OTHER WRITERS

The following two essays explore causes and effects. The first is by a student, the second by a professional writer. "Why We Burned a Wilderness," the student-written paper, draws conclusions likely to surprise readers. A major in recreation management, Katie Kennedy had the opportunity to work for a season at a wildlife sanctuary near Naples, Florida. The experience changed one of her previous beliefs. Beginning with a vivid account drawn from experience, she explains why a fire in a cyprus swamp was set deliberately. You'll notice that she draws her material from all five basic resources: recalling, observing, reading, conversing, and imagining.

WHY WE BURNED A WILDERNESS
KATIE KENNEDY

Here I was, slogging through a Florida swamp with a lighted drip torch 1 in my hand, leaving behind me a trail of fire. I was going against everything I believed about fires in the outdoors. It had been ingrained in me to take the utmost caution in using fire in the woods, lest a blaze rage out of control. Yet now I was purposely setting fire to the surrounding grasses, vines, and scrubby trees with the intent of burning them to the ground.

I imagined the upcoming scene: clouds of insects rising, birds and 2 animals—snakes, frogs, turtles, deer, armadillos, raccoons, opossums, rabbits, and maybe a bobcat—fleeing the blaze. I tried not to think about the animals I was killing or leaving homeless. Smokey the Bear would be appalled.

Six of us had set out to do the day's burning, four naturalists including 3 myself, Greg the warden-biologist, and Ed the sanctuary manager. First we did a small practice burn along the side of the road, where Ed told us about the drip torches and how to use them. Drip torches are three-gallon tanks of gas mixed with diesel fuel, with a long spout and nozzle. When inverted and lit, they emit a thin stream of fire, as a watering can spouts water. "Today we're going to try to use the wind," Ed explained. "We'll try to keep it at our backs. Then it will spread the fire in the direction we're walking."

I lit my torch and pulled a bandana over my nose and mouth. We 4 spread out and tried to head in the same direction, burning as we went along. The vegetation was very thick, but I had to keep moving and rip through it, since the fire was close behind. The heat was intense and the smoke bothered my eyes. We couldn't see one another because of the dense vines and shrubs but had to keep yelling back and forth to make sure we were all still heading in the right direction and, most important, not trapping someone inside a ring of fire. Dry, crackling grass makes a lot of noise as it burns, so we had to yell loudly. Sometimes I'd find a mucky ditch in my way, or a thorny vine, but there wasn't time to ponder an alternate route. I just had to forge ahead, sinking up to my knees in cold, muddy water. I always found it nerve-racking to be followed so closely by the fire, although after my first ditch crossing I was somewhat comforted by the thought that my soaked jeans and boots probably wouldn't burn.

I never got over my uneasiness about being so close to the fire. I didn't 5 like going on controlled burns. Yet, as a seasonal naturalist at the National Audubon Society's Corkscrew Swamp Sanctuary in the Big Cypress Swamp region of South Florida, I soon learned that burns had to be done periodically to ensure the health of the swamp. One of my duties was to go along with the full-time staff to see how the burns were done. Another duty, one I hadn't expected, was to read books. I learned a lot from one of them, *Fire in South Florida Ecosystems,* by the staff of the Southeast Forest Experiment Station in Asheville, North Carolina (Washington, D.C.: U.S. Forest Service, 1980). It convinced me that trees and plants of the swamp need fire to survive.

The interrelationship of vegetation with fire has evolved over thousands 6 of years. In the past, when South Florida was covered with an unbroken canopy of vegetation, fires would start naturally by lightning. Sometimes, they would rage from one side of the Florida peninsula to the other and die only on reaching the coast. Or they might blaze until extinguished by the rains of the next wet season. Yet, in as little as two weeks, fresh green growth would begin to cover the ground again. When people started to discover the beauty of South Florida and began to chop it down to get to it, cutting through the wilderness with roads and housing developments, they brought their prejudices against fire with them. When natural fires were not allowed to take their course, the delicate balance was upset, causing havoc in the ecological system.

At Corkscrew Swamp Sanctuary, there are a diversity of habitats, in- 7 cluding pineland, marsh, wet prairie, bald cypress and pond cypress stands, and hardwood hammocks. What makes each distinct are the species of trees and plants found there, depending on how much water each area receives, its elevation, and other factors. Therefore, there are different animals associated with each habitat too. One goal of the sanctuary management is to keep this diversity of habitats available. Plant diversity ensures animal diversity, since certain animals prefer one habitat over another for food and shelter. Each habitat is burned on its own schedule. The wet prairie, for example, is burned every one to three years, while the pinelands, a more established plant community, are burned every five to seven years. If fire were kept out of an area, the natural progression would be toward hardwoods such as oaks. Eventually, all the areas would end up looking much the same, with the same plant composition. Burning ensures that areas such as marsh and wet prairie will remain that way.

In a wilderness, fire has still other valuable effects. Fire recycles nu- 8 trients. By reducing the vegetation to ash, the nutrients locked up in growing trees and plants are returned to the soil so that they may be used again. Without fire, some plants would not be able to reproduce. The seeds of certain plants must germinate through an ash layer. Other plants are stimulated to drop seeds only after feeling intense heat, ensuring that after a fire, new seeds are released to carry on the species.

Fire is a wonderful cleanser. It acts as a check on various diseases: the 9
heat and flames kill off harmful plant parasites and bacteria. Another reason for burning is to get rid of leaf litter. If all the fallen leaves and decaying vegetation were allowed to pile up, a natural fire would be a disaster for the sanctuary. Eliminating the extra fuel ensures that minimal damage will occur if an uncontrolled fire should accidentally start.

Through their long association with fire, South Florida's plants have 10
evolved many adaptations to its recurrences. Florida slash pines have a thick, spongy bark that contains much moisture. When a fire passes by, the bark may be singed, but the tree is protected. Saw palmettos have a long thick stem or "runner" that hugs the ground, so that a fire, unable to take hold from below, passes right over it. And I have to admit that nothing is wasted in a fire, not even the lives of the insects. Many birds come to a burned-over area to feed. Red-shouldered hawks love toasted grasshoppers.

I learned to unlearn my belief that fire and plants are enemies. Soaked 11
to mid-thigh, muscles sore, face and arms scratched, covered with seeds and burrs, I would emerge from a tangle of vines with a fire close on my heels. Taking the bandana from over my mouth and nose, I would gulp fresh air. I had to tell myself that I was giving the plants a hand. I was just helping a natural process that, until interrupted by humans, had been going on for centuries. The trees needed me. I looked across the fire lane at an area that had been burned a few weeks before, and already the ground was covered with light green. I'll have to have a talk with Smokey the Bear. He may have to change a few of his ideas if he ever retires to Florida.

Questions to Start You Thinking

1. By beginning and ending with the writer's personal experience, what does this essay gain? Can it be charged that the memories recalled in the first four paragraphs and the last paragraph don't serve the main purpose of the paper—to explain the "why" behind the burns?

2. At any point, do you get the sense that the writer is criticizing human beings? If so, what is her point? Do you agree or disagree?

3. What experience have you had lately whose causes or effects you might find worthwhile to explore?

Why all the dinosaurs perished at the same moment in time—about 65,000,000 years ago—has long challenged people who love to wonder. In 1963 a Princeton professor, Glenn Jepsen, made a list of forty-six theories—some persuasive, others crazy—that had been proposed to explain this sudden and mysterious disappearance. Since then, new theories have been suggested every year. In 1979, Fran Charig, a writer for the Natural History section of the British Museum,

surveyed the theories and concluded, "We can only confess our supreme ignorance of the real causes of dinosaur extinction and say, quite simply, 'We
don't know.' To do anything else would be unscientific."

Since Charig wrote, yet another explanation has been advanced, one that
did not begin as a theory about dinosaur extinction at all, but as an attempt to
discover the reason for interesting phenomena in rock strata. Nigel Calder, a
distinguished British science writer, former editor-in-chief of *New Scientist*, and
a creator of science programs for the BBC, believes it the best supported and
most convincing explanation to date. He sets it forth in the following account
from *The Comet Is Coming!* in which (like Katie Kennedy) he begins by recalling
an experience.

COFFIN OF THE DINOSAURS
NIGEL CALDER

It once encased the world and shrouded the bones of the last of the   1
dinosaur dynasties. In the sixty-five million years since the event, geological
processes have buried, eroded or mangled it. It is best preserved in an
accessible form where Earth movements have pushed up into the air the
well preserved sediments from the bed of a former sea. One such place is
Umbria in Italy, so I found myself there, in the small medieval city of
Gubbio.

A geologist from Perugia, Giampaolo Pialli, took me to the gorge just   2
outside Gubbio, where the river conveniently carved through the rocks and
exposed the layers of ancient pink limestone. They had been tilted at a
giddy angle, like a stack of playing cards towering beside the road, and they
recorded many millions of years of Earth history. Up the gorge we went,
through the layers of the geological periods called the Jurassic and Cretaceous. During all this time and more, the reptiles ruled the disintegrating
supercontinent of Pangaea.

My guide eradicated all vague conjecture as he pointed out the many   3
places where rock samples had been taken, for evidence of the repeated
reversals in the direction of the Earth's magnetism. Correlated from place
to place around the world, the patterns of flipping magnetism helped to
pinpoint corresponding events with great precision. Incidentally, they indicated that the death of the dinosaurs did not coincide, as some would
have it, with a geomagnetic reversal. The late Cretaceous rocks bore no
hint of the fate in store for the dinosaurs. And then there it was, sloping
up the wall of rock, neat as a line across a geologist's time-scale: the coffin
of the dinosaurs.

It was a layer of red-brown clay, barely a centimeter thick. Beyond it   4
the limestone layers resumed, but they were of the Tertiary period, when
the dinosaurs were extinct. By the roadside, the sample-points of the pa-
laeomagnetists bracketed the coffin-layer like bullet holes. When I reached
and picked out a flake of clay, I knew that it was rich in material not of this

Earth. Looking from the clay in my hand to the cloud-harassed Sun, I tried to visualize the clay as fine powder hurled into the air by a colliding comet or apollo,° and turning day to night.

The Case of the Disappearing Dinosaurs is of interest far beyond the 5 little realms of comet lovers and dinosaur hunters. At the end of the Cretaceous period the giant animals that had dominated the scenery for more than a hundred million years, munching leaves or chewing meat, suddenly were gone. Had that event not occurred, we the mammals would still be shrew-like beasts cowering in crevices and branches to avoid those cruel teeth and claws; our beady little eyes might not even have noticed the comets.

As soon as Victorian fossil-hunters appreciated the downfall of the di- 6 nosaurs, explanations proliferated. The most concise theory was that the dinosaurs were too large to fit into Noah's Ark. The most persistent said that they were too stupid to survive and British campaigners against nuclear weapons *circa* 1960 employed the slogan: "Dinosaurs died out: too much armor, too little brains." The libel lasted into the 1980s, in a notorious poster in which a German car manufacturer likened his rivals' products to decrepit dinosaurs destined for extinction; it provoked reptilian hisses from dinosaur lovers and the advertisement was withdrawn.

Hollywood producers had women cringing in deerskins while their 7 menfolk battled with the great brutes in the stone age, thus making good the sixty-million-year lacuna between the death of the dinosaurs and the rise of woman. And those who believed that God was an astronaut had no difficulty in imagining an alien Buffalo Bill massacring the herds of sauropods with laser beams, tossing his californium hand-grenades into the lairs of the tyrannosaurs, and loosing his surface-to-air missiles at the pterodactyls, which lost command of the air at the same time. But you would have to allow that this interloper also had a gargantuan appetite for shellfish.

A sea-change overtook the planet at the end of the Cretaceous perio . 8 The ammonites, well known to fossil collectors as coil-shelled jet-propelled creatures, perished just as decisively as the dinosaurs; so did other groups of small marine animals, and notable sea-monsters like the plesiosaurs. Monomania about the dinosaurs made people forget the ammonites, but the simultaneous termination of a wide variety of life on land and sea devalues any solutions peculiar to the dinosaurs. Thus even if the newly-evolved caterpillars destroyed vegetation as thoroughly as locusts, or rat-like mammals developed a hearty appetite for dinosaurs' eggs, as a couple of theories would have it, neither would affect life beyond the beaches. The same objection applies, unfortunately, to the most imaginative of all explanations of the dinosaurs' demise, which related it to the rise of the modern flowering plants. The involuntary change in diet, it was said, deprived the dinosaurs of the laxative oils that are present in the older conifers, ferns and cycads, so they all perished of constipation—no small matter in a dinosaur.

apollo: Minor planet, an asteroid that crosses the orbit of the earth.

Desperate problem-solvers turned to physical causes: a drastic fall in   9
sea-level, a global cooling, atomic radiation from space breaking in when
the Earth swapped its magnetism around, the explosion of a nearby star. A
phenomenon crying out for definitive explanation was just as creative of
theories as any comet. Ten years ago the same clutter of a hundred contradictory hypotheses had surrounded the ice ages. For them, the correct
explanation came largely from analyses of the atomic composition of seabed
fossils, which revealed the real rhythm of the ice ages. So I was prepared
to believe what the manuscripts had told me: that the atomic composition
of the red-brown clay from an ancient seabed, which I held in my hand in
the gorge at Gubbio, gave the definitive answer to the dinosaur problem.

Microfossils studied there and at similar sites by a generation of sci-   10
entists put the time-scale of the crisis between ever-narrower limits. At
Caravaca in south-eastern Spain, where the pattern in the rocks is very like
Gubbio, Jan Smit of Amsterdam recently established that the teeming marine life stopped suddenly. The plankton, constituting the pastures of the
sea, disappears in less than five millimeters of sediment—meaning about
a hundred years, at the longest. Thereafter the surface waters remained a
desert for ten thousand years. Before there was any appeal to atomic analysis the fossils themselves announced that the event that ended the Cretaceous period was quick and catastrophic, and dismissed all hypotheses
proposing gradual changes in climate, ecology or bowel-movements.

At the University of California at Berkeley, an eminent physicist, Luis   11
Alvarez, joined forces with his son, Walter Alvarez, a geologist who was
familiar with the crucial layers at Gubbio. Their initial idea was to use
delicate methods of chemical analysis as another way of finding out, not
what killed the dinosaurs, but how long the crisis lasted. They reasoned
that meteoritic dust, raining invisibly but continuously on to land and sea,
was comparatively rich in iridium, a metal that is very scarce in the ordinary
materials of the Earth's crust. The amount of iridium in the thin layer of
clay at the end of the Cretaceous might therefore indicate how long the
clay took to form. Samples from Gubbio went into a research reactor at
Berkeley, to make them radioactive, so that iridium and other elements
could be fingerprinted by the gamma rays they then gave off.

The result came as a shock: the amount of iridium jumped by a factor   12
of thirty in the Gubbio clay, compared with adjacent limestone. Either the
clay layer took an improbably long time to form, or the Earth was suddenly
swamped with iridium. Even more startling results came from the same
clayey layer at other places. Danish samples brought by Walter Alvarez to
Berkeley showed the amount of iridium increasing 160-fold. Then the
Dutchman, Jan Smit, collaborated with a Belgian atomic and meteoritic
expert, Jan Hertogen, and they found, in the bottom part of the Caravaca
boundary layer, iridium levels 460 times normal. The discovery was as
suspicious as finding traces of arsenic in a dying man, the patient in this
case being the sick planet Earth.

A forensic team consisting of Alvarez, Alvarez and two Berkeley space   13
scientists, Frank Asaro and Helen Michel, soon satisfied themselves that the
iridium could not have come from any plausible source on the Earth itself.

They considered whether the popular idea of an exploding star might explain a sudden influx of extraterrestrial material, but calculated that the star would need to be improbably close to account for so much iridium. In any case, the other symptoms of a stellar explosion were lacking, plutonium atoms for example. So they were led to suggest that an apollo object struck the Earth sixty-five million years ago.

The Berkeley scientists' sums led them repeatedly, by different routes, to an apollo about ten kilometers in diameter, just a little bigger than the largest known apollos. Hitting the dinosaurs' planet, it would have thrown up about a hundred times its own weight of material from the Earth's crust. A fraction of the debris, scattered as dust all around the world, made the layer of clay, doped to just the right degree with the tell-tale iridium from the apollo. 14

In accordance with the Krakatau Effect, the dust would take a long time to settle. When that volcanic island blew up in 1883, dust high in the atmosphere produced "glorious" sunsets all around the world for more than two years. A large apollo hitting the Earth causes an explosion more than a thousand times greater than Krakatau. A mushroom cloud sweeps material into the stratosphere, in the form of very fine grains that take years to fall out. The quantity of dust is more than sufficient to blot out the Sun completely and for about four years there is unending night. 15

Plants stop growing and the ensuing famine explains the disappearances among the fossil species. In the sea the microscopic plants die out almost completely and, if this is the true picture of the natural disaster at the end of the Cretaceous, the death of the oceans consigns to oblivion the ammonites, the plesiosaurs and other conspicuous marine animals; the survivors are presumably those that can scavenge in the mud for the remains of plants of former years. The putrefying remains of plants and animals, floating down the rivers, sustain some freshwater animal life and, as the sole survivors of the great reptiles, well may the crocodiles shed tears. 16

The plants on land are better equipped to recover afterwards, but during the fatal period all new growth ceases. Blundering about in pitch darkness the plant-eating dinosaurs strip every last leaf. The meat-eaters make a regal banquet of their herbivorous cousins and then, enraged by hunger, they turn cannibal. A few small animals—worms, insects, birds and so on—survive the four-year night feeding on decaying vegetation, seeds, nuts and one another. Among them are some of the diminutive mammals, which will found new dynasties in the depopulated world, when the sunlight breaks through again. 17

"Absolute nonsense," a friend of mine scoffed. As an authority on the great reptiles, he had read only the early press reports on the supposed impact. His immediate objection was that some quite large reptiles clung on, and survived for millions of years after the end of the Cretaceous period. "What about the pelomedusid turtles? Or the dyrosaurid crocodiles, six meters long? I've dug them up with my own hands." His eyes glowed like cinders, as if his manual labours settled the argument. 18

Quietly I told him how I had sampled the layer of comet clay at Gubbio with a finger. I rehearsed the evidence for a very large and unusual event and spoke of the same clayey layer showing up in Italy, Spain, Denmark, 19

Tunisia and France. "Oh, of course," he conceded, "it's obvious that something happened, but it can't be as simple as they say. We'll need palaeontological control." In less than five minutes my friend had switched from total disbelief to staking his specialism's claim to a piece of the action. He was quite right, of course: fossil hunters will have to trace the complicated consequences of the impact and make sense of the survival or disappearance of each kind of plant and animal. And to pretend that the story of life on Earth is just a succession of adaptations to catastrophic comet-shocks would be at least as foolish as to ignore the inevitability of intermittent events of that kind.

In 1980, when the Berkeley discoverers published their hypothesis, 20 they stressed that it was unproved. Jan Smit in Amsterdam called an impact "the most attractive" explanation. But the first severe test for the idea was soon fulfilled successfully. If dust was scattered all around the world by the impact, then the extraterrestrial iridium ought to show up on the other side of the globe, as far away as possible from Europe and North Africa. It duly did, in samples obtained near Canterbury, New Zealand. The best possible evidence would be the discovery of a crater of the right size (150–200 kilometers across) and the right age (sixty-five million years). There was no obvious candidate among the known craters on land, and the cosmic cannonball may have struck the sea, or a piece of land that is now submerged. For example, there is a suspicious ring-shaped feature in the seabed off the north coast of Australia. Before you rush for the map, let me mention that sixty-five million years ago the world was very different: Australia was still welded to Antarctica; the Atlantic was young and comparatively narrow; and the "Mediterranean" was an old ocean that was being squeezed as Africa and Europe converged.

The impacting object might have been a live comet, complete with its 21 ices and volatile material. Kenneth Hsü of Zurich argued a case for it and offered some different mechanisms for the slaughter: fierce heating of the air, poisoning of living things by cyanide brought in by the comet and spread by ocean currents, and a drastic increase in the carbon dioxide dissolved in the sea water. A seasoned investigator of cosmic impacts, Eugene Shoemaker, argued that it would be hard to account for the relative abundance of iridium, from a live comet of the right sort of size. Judged simply by the statistics of sky pollution, the odds are roughly fifty-fifty on whether so large an event would be caused by a comet or an apollo: massive apollos are much rarer than massive comets, but they blunder around for much longer. The intensive studies that the discovery is provoking in many laboratories may help to settle the issue. Some experts are not yet satisfied that the exploding-star hypothesis, which might account for both the origin of the iridium and the death of so many plants and animals, has been completely excluded. But perhaps the best argument in favour of a collision is the simplest: such an event must occur from time to time.

Questions to Start You Thinking

1. What does Calder do as a writer to convince us that the collision theory is worth taking seriously?

2. Are you entirely convinced by it? Can you find any flaws in it? Do you favor any other possible explanations for the disappearance of the dinosaurs?

3. On learning this selection is taken from Calder's book *The Comet Is Coming!* a student remarked: "Huh! No wonder Calder swallows the comet theory! Any other theory of the death of the dinosaurs wouldn't have fit into his book." Is this charge justified? Do you think Calder is fair or unfair to other, dissenting theorists?

4. Imagine your own explanation for the sudden death of the dinosaurs, one that Calder doesn't mention. Explain it in a paragraph and share it with your class.

LEARNING BY WRITING

The Assignment

The following assignment is designed to help you explain and understand some event or force that has deeply affected your life. It leaves you free to decide which method will be most useful in writing your paper: looking for causes, looking for effects, or looking for both.

First, point to some definite change that has taken place in your lifetime. It might be a change that has affected only you, such as a move to another location. It might be a change that has affected not only yourself but many other people in a city or region (the growth of high technology in the Silicon Valley of California) or in society at large (the arrival of the personal computer). Describe briefly the change that has taken place. That part of your paper is only an introduction. Don't make it longer than two or three paragraphs.

Then, in the body of your paper, go on to any one of the following tasks:

1. Explain the cause or causes of this change.
2. Explain its subsequent effects (on your life, or on the lives of others).
3. Explain both what caused the change and what resulted from it.

By "change," we mean a noticeable, lasting transformation, an alteration in your life (or people's lives), produced by some event, some definite new force, some new invention or discovery, some deep-down shift in the structure of society—not a trend or a passing fad likely to burn out in a year, like pet rocks, break dancing, Rambo games, or the grapefruit diet.

Write for an interested audience of your fellow students. If you write about a change in your own life, you can assume that they will care to know more about you. If you write about some change in a region or in society at large, assume that they will want to compare their own impressions of this change with yours.

Papers written in response to this assignment have included the following.

A woman's recollection of having lived for a year in rural Mexico, going on to show the effects of her stay on her outlook and opinions after her return to the United States.

A woman's view of a shift she has noticed in her lifetime: in male attitudes toward women. Now, she finds, women are treated with less "fake politeness" and with more respect. Her paper explores causes for this change besides the women's movement. One leading cause is that a shift in the economy from industry to service and technology has created more jobs in which women can shine.

A man's contention that, in quality of architectural design, new buildings constructed in Minneapolis have greatly improved over those designed before World War II. He surveys the reasons for this improvement, citing the influence of architects and city planners.

A woman's observation that America has seen a decline in popular interest in space travel. She arrays evidence to support this claim: children no longer want to be astronauts; the fact that people have walked on the moon is now rarely mentioned in the press. She then asks why and finds causes for the decline, including decreased funding for the space program and the Challenger disaster.

Generating Ideas

What change that has taken place in your lifetime would be enjoyable or instructive to explore? This assignment leaves you the option of writing either from personal experience or, if you or your instructor prefer, from what you know or can find out from the common experience of many people.

A random search of your memory may help get you started. You might let your thoughts wander back to how things were a few years ago or back when you were a child. Then ask yourself: In what respects are things different today?

These changes might be of any of the following kinds (or any others that occur to you).

DISCOVERY CHECKLIST: RECALLING CHANGES

- A change in how you live (caused by a new job; a fluctuation in income; personal or family upheaval caused by death, divorce, accident, illness, or good fortune; starting college).
- A change in where you live.
- A change in the environment (such as air pollution, natural causes such as a flood or a storm, the coming of new industry to a locality, or the failure of an old industry).
- A change caused by growing up or gaining in maturity.
- A change caused by a new invention (computers, microchips, pocket calculators, VCRs) or discovery (a wonder drug, a better design for reeds for woodwinds).
- A change in social opportunities (women now more readily accepted as corporate executives, judges, governors, candidates for other high political office; blacks and Hispanics increasingly prominent in sports as coaches and managers or media commentators).

Soon, when a few thoughts percolate, reach for a pencil and brainstorm— jot down a list of likely topics that immediately come to mind. (For more tips on brainstorming, see p. 457.) You might even make three lists, considering all the possibilities of the assignment:

1. Changes in your life
2. Changes in your locality
3. Changes in the whole country

Look over your lists. Ask yourself what you know most about, what you care most about. Then make your tentative choice. If it doesn't work out, you will soon realize that and be able to pick another.

As a next step, you'll probably need to decide whether to consider (1) the cause or causes of the change; or (2) the effects; or (3) both. Which of those tasks you pick will depend on your topic and on what you're trying to explain. A paper that confined itself to the causes of a family's move from New Jersey to Montana might be only one sentence long: "My father's company transferred him." But the subsequent effects of the move (on the writer and other family members) might require a whole paper. So the writer would probably choose to explain both causes and effects. Which—causes or effects—do you have more knowledge of? Which can you show with greater certainty?

Choose a topic you feel sure you can manage in the time you have. Unless you are writing a very long term paper, the causes of a change in women's roles during the past twenty years are likely to prove too many and too profound even to begin to sketch adequately in fewer than 10,000 words. Instead, can you narrow your topic? You might consider just one aspect of these changes: why more married women today hold full-time jobs. Or the effects of this situation on the economy (such as a rise in women's spending power and increased enrollments for schools of career education).

Your choice tentatively made, write for ten or fifteen minutes and set down likely causes and effects.

In looking for causes, look first for *immediate causes*—those evident and close at hand that clearly led to a situation or development. Then look for *remote causes:* underlying, more basic reasons for the situation, not always evident to an observing eye—perhaps causes that came earlier and led to immediate ones. The immediate cause of unemployment in a town might be the closing of a factory. But the more remote cause of unemployment might be competition from a foreign business, against which the local company couldn't survive. The immediate cause of an outbreak of sunburn cases might be a week of blazing sunshine. But the more remote cause of the problem, a writer could claim, might be the thinning of the ozone layer, causing a greater amount of harmful radiation to seep through.

Look back in time to seek causes only as far as seems necessary. A paper on the causes of the sexual revolution that began with the fall of Adam would probably be going back too far. The writer might better confine the inquiry to what has been happening since 1970 or 1980.

When jotting down possible causes or effects, you may find yourself generating other kinds of material, too—ideas, hunches, leads, information. Write down any stray thoughts that may be useful later.

In going over a list of possible causes, work with a pencil, and check, star, or underline any causes that stand out as extremely probable. One way to evaluate the items on your list is to ask: Is this an *essential* cause? Is it something without which the change couldn't have happened? (Then it deserves a big star.) Or, without it, might the change have taken place nevertheless, for some other reason? (It might still matter, but less importantly.)

If you haven't figured out enough causes to explain the change to your satisfaction, you need to do some more digging. Remember, you have five major resources.

DISCOVERY CHECKLIST: USING BASIC RESOURCES

- *Recall:* Do you remember having lived through this change? Can you remember life before it, and after?
- *Observation:* Can you go out right now and see the effects of this change in the world nearby?
- *Conversation:* Whom might you ask about it?
- *Reading:* Have any books or magazine articles on this change been published lately? (You might check a library card catalogue and the *Readers' Guide to Periodical Literature.*)
- *Imagining:* Can you imagine possible causes or effects for this change and then test your imaginings against reality? For instance, if you are writing about why married women want jobs, try putting yourself in the place of such a woman when she stays home full-time. What is her situation? Then talk to some such woman, either a homemaker or an ex-homemaker now employed. See how well you have imagined.

If your topic, such as increased opportunities for women as judges, calls on you to explain people's behavior, you might consider some suggestions from Kenneth Burke, a literary critic and philosopher. Burke has proposed a set of questions to help us understand the deep-down causes of a person's actions. While these questions can't solve every human mystery, for a writer they often generate insights, observations, and hunches worth pursuing. Take a look at "Seeking Motives" (p. 466).

Shaping a Draft

In guessing whether your topic will be manageable, you might do a little advance planning: deciding how thoroughly to show causes or effects and making an educated guess whether your paper would need to run 500 words—or 5000. If it looks likely to run too long, narrow that topic.

Katie Kennedy's "Why We Burned a Wilderness" follows a clear plan: in her first four paragraphs, the writer describes (by recall) the burning of the swamp; in the rest of the paper she shows why the swamp was burned. The essay was written from this brief scratch outline:

1. Going on the burn—I expected bad effects

2. Why was burn done?
   History of South Fla.—nature needs help
   Fire releases nutrients
   Some plants need fire to reproduce
   Diversify vegetation
   Check disease
   Get rid of leaf litter
   Guard against more serious fire

3. Bad effects not so bad at all
   Plants adapt
   Nothing wasted

The paper makes its point: it shows the reason for which professional naturalists act—to give nature a hand. And it shows that cause and effect are closely related: naturalists act in order to achieve desired effects. In paragraph 2, the writer *imagines* the disastrous effects of the fire: homeless creatures fleeing, some dying. Paragraph 6 sets forth the valuable effects of natural fires.

If in following your assignment you've decided to look for causes, many possible causes may present themselves. In planning your paper, try to assign them relative importance: classify them as major causes or minor ones. If you were writing about why more married women hold jobs now than they did ten years ago, you might make a list that included (1) boredom and (2) economic necessity—husbands don't earn enough. On reflection, you might decide that economic necessity is a major cause, while boredom is probably a minor one. Plan to give economic necessity more room.

Having finished the first part of your paper, the description of the change, you prepare to fulfill one of the three tasks (to explain causes, explain effects, or explain both). Your next sentence will probably write itself for you. Let it be a sentence that will make clear to your reader which task you are going to perform. We don't mean you ought to say, in a flat and mechanical fashion, something like "Now I am going to explain the causes of this change." You can announce your task more casually, more naturally, as if you were talking to someone: "At first, I didn't realize that keeping six pet cheetahs in our backyard would bother the neighbors." Or, in a paper about a writer's father's sudden move to a Trappist monastery: "The real reason for Father's decision didn't become clear to me for a long while." You might also indicate your choice of tasks by asking a straightforward question: "What caused this change in my life?" or "What followed this move?"

Rewriting

As you know by now, ascertaining causes and effects takes hard thought. You'll want to set aside an especially generous amount of time to look back over, ponder, and rewrite this paper.

In revising a paper that traces causes, you might ask yourself the following questions.

REVISION CHECKLIST: ASKING WHY

- Why are you going to all the work of demonstrating causes? Have you shown your reader that your paper has a point to it?
- Have you given any evidence to convince a reader that the causes you find are the true ones?
- If not, where can you discover more evidence? Look to your five basic resources: recalling, observing, reading, conversing, and imagining.
- Have you claimed remote causes you can't begin to prove? That's all right, but do indicate sheer guesswork.
- If you have set down pure hunches, are they convincing, or might they be left out? To find out, you might try your paper on a peer reader.
- Have you stated the causes with cocksure, swaggering certainty, when in all honesty you might admit that you're only guessing? "Thus it is obvious, as I have proved conclusively, that unemployment in Ohio is entirely due to the activities of pro-environment lobbyists." Like Nigel Calder, who sees merit in the exploding star theory of dinosaur disappearance, you can honestly admit that other explanations might be possible.
- Have you fallen into any logical fallacies, such as *oversimplification*—assuming that there was only one small cause for a large phenomenon? A simple oversimplification: "The revolution in sexual attitudes began because Marilyn Monroe posed in the nude for a calendar." A more subtle oversimplification has been detected by music scholar Donald Jay Grout. Many historians of music have claimed that the style and structure of Beethoven's symphonies have been "inevitable consequences of the class structure existing in Western Europe in the early nineteenth century." But, Grout remarks, "Co-existence is not causation."

  Another common mistake in logic is the *post hoc* fallacy, from the Latin *post hoc, ergo propter hoc*, meaning "after this, therefore because of this." In other words, don't assume that one thing caused another just because it preceded it. This is the error of a writer who declares, "Sandra Day O'Connor was appointed to the Supreme Court; in the following year, there was a noteworthy increase in the number of convicted rapists." (There seems no clear causal connection here: the Supreme Court doesn't try rapists. For more about logical fallacies, see p. 280.)

In revising a paper setting forth effects, you might ask yourself the following questions.

REVISION CHECKLIST: VERIFYING EFFECTS

- What possible further effects have you left out? Are any of them worth adding?
- Do you convince a reader that these effects have indeed occurred? (You might try your paper on a peer reader.) Have you given any evidence— perhaps reported any observations or testimony, perhaps quoted any opinions from authorities?
- Could any effect you mention have resulted not from the change you're writing of but from some other cause?

In writing a cause and effect paper, you may sometimes doubt your ability to find basic causes or real effects. In fulfilling this assignment, such self-doubt will probably be healthy. But remember, unless you are writing a paper that sets forth exact scientific findings (reporting, say, the effects of combining two chemicals), your instructor won't expect you to write a final and definitive explanation. You'll be expected only to do what lies within your capacity: to write an explanation that is thoughtful, searching, and reasonable.

Other Assignments

1. In a short paper, seek to explain *either* the causes *or* the effects of a situation that exists today in our society. Draw on your reading, your conversation, your memory, your observations—on any useful resource.

    Some existing situations might be the difficulty of getting admitted to law school, the shortage of highly qualified elementary school teachers in some areas, the recent willingness of businesses to hire college graduates with degrees in the liberal arts—or whatever interests and concerns you.

    Your readers for this paper won't be sociologists or other professionals who would expect a profound explanation, but fellow students with interests similar to your own, who might appreciate what you have to say.

2. Write an explanation of your own motives. Explore your reasons for taking some step or for doing something in a customary way. (All of us do some things without first reasoning. If you need help in pinning down reasons for your own behavior, some of Kenneth Burke's suggestions on p. 466 may be useful.)

3. In an introductory philosophy course at Loyola University in Maryland, Frank J. Cunningham asks his students to write, instead of a traditional research paper, a short original essay exploring their own ideas and opinions. The assignment calls for students first to describe an idea and then to ask themselves why they hold it:

    > Over the years, in the process of growing up and growing civilized, all of us have developed certain opinions about the way things happen, about what works and what doesn't work, about how things are. We have also developed certain expectations toward our world based on these opinions.
    >
    > Under ordinary circumstances, we live with these opinions and expectations unquestioningly, and, on the whole, we manage quite well with our lives. But . . . in philosophy we look at things we don't normally look at, question things we normally take for granted, analyze what we accept from day to day.

As preparation for this somewhat unusual (some would say perverse) activity, I would like you to think about your own opinions. Think about your views of the world, your expectations, your certainties, and decide on something of which you are absolutely certain. It may be a part of your normal life, a truth derived from your education, something that you have learned through your years of experience, something you were told, something you figured out on your own. Now write a short essay (no more than two pages) describing the one thing about which you are absolutely certain, and why this thing commands such certainty.

Remember that an essay such as this requires thought as preparation. You should not expect to sit down immediately at the typewriter and produce it. Remember too that there are at least two separate thinking tasks to be performed. First you must consider your stock of truths to find one in which you have utmost confidence. This will probably take some time and effort since we are willing to let a lot of truths pass without putting them to the test. Second, you must consider the reason for your certainty. In working out this part of the essay it might be useful to pretend that you are trying to convince a very reasonable but thoroughly doubting person of the truth of your position.

4. Glen Baxter, a humorous artist, specializes in the curious scene that cries out for an explanation. From the group of his drawings here, pick a drawing that interests you. In a paragraph, set forth the causes that might have led up to the scene depicted in it. Then in a second paragraph, give at least one effect that might follow from it. Give your imagination free rein.

IT WAS MRS. CRABTREE AND SHE WAS
IN NO MOOD FOR PLEASANTRIES

HELMUT CHECKED THE BOULDER AT TWELVE-
MINUTE INTERVALS THROUGHOUT THE NIGHT

"WE'LL HAVE NO ALLITERATION IN THIS
HERE BUNKHOUSE!" SNORTED McCULLOCH

217

APPLYING WHAT YOU LEARN:
SOME USES OF CAUSE AND EFFECT

Examination questions often pose a problem in causality: "Trace the causes of the decline of foreign sales of American automobiles." Equally familiar is the exam question that calls for a survey of effects: "What economic effects of the repeal of Prohibition were immediately evident in the early 1930s?" Problems of that very same sort, you'll find, will frequently turn up as paper topics.

But in fulfilling any kind of college writing assignment, even one that doesn't ask you to look for causes or effects, this method will be among your useful instruments. In writing a college paper that deals with any phenomenon—say, a sociology course assignment to write about an increase in teenage pregnancies among middle-class whites—you may wish to spend only a *part* of your paper in exploring the causes of that phenomenon or its effects. In a 1500-word essay setting forth her determination to become an engineer in spite of discouraging obstacles, Maria Ferrelli sought to report incidents of male chauvinism she had met but, more important, to explain why such an attitude exists. To show you how she fulfilled both purposes, we present a paragraph drawn from her re-called experiences and then the paragraph that immediately follows, exploring causes. Ferrelli has been remarking that she came to college confident that, as a high school student of mathematics, she had held her own successfully against male competition.

I soon began to experience what took me so long to abolish in high school: the chauvinistic attitudes of men. When I asked my physics teaching assistant to repeat the procedure for finding the magnetic field, guys looked down on me as if I were just a dumb blonde. They sighed and shook their heads. They acted superior because they supposedly knew what the teacher was saying. When I had a question about the computer program due Friday, they laughed at me. If I asked one of them a question about an assignment, he would either ignore me or answer me in an egotistical, superior tone of voice. Moreover, when working in a group design project, my three partners—all male—told me to take notes about the plans *they* were dis-cussing. When I tried to contribute an idea, they always had an excuse to throw my idea out the window. In other words, I was only considered capable of taking down notes like a secretary but not capable of thinking like an engineer. When I fight back now, the response is "Oh, you're so cute when you're mad." None of them takes me seriously. I don't believe any of them thinks I have a mind of my own.

Often I wonder how these men arrived at their conclusion that a woman is inferior. I believe that their upbringing caused much of the damage. Throughout their lives, their parents must have told them that men should excel in sports and school and that they must secure the highest-paying jobs in order to support a family. In school, textbooks reaffirm this idea. Children read about famous men and rarely study important women in history. Thus, students tend to see men as the most important people in the world and women as school teachers and nurses. They read about famous male scientists, doctors, lawyers, politicians. They begin to believe not only that men are dominant in society but that men ought to remain dominant in every field.

Luckily, my parents helped reduce the effects of those textbooks by encouraging me to chase after my dream.

There's more to that last paragraph, but we break it off here, for we just wanted to show you how Maria Ferrelli wove that previous paragraph discerning causes into the body of her essay. Although she does not pretend to give a thorough, final explanation of male chauvinism, her brief search for causes here lends her paper force. Not merely complaining about prejudice, she tries to understand some possible reasons for it. (Her paper concludes: "I will not tolerate their behavior nor will I be deflected from my goal. I will be an engineer.") As her essay demonstrates, a paragraph that even *begins* to seek causes or effects can lend a larger paper considerable effectiveness.

At any moment in a book or article that deals with some current phenomenon, the writer may ask why—in only a paragraph or a few paragraphs. In *The Economics of Public Issues,* a college textbook, Douglass C. North and Roger Leroy Miller make the surprising claim that the ban of cigarette advertising on television has had effects injurious to your health:

> The banning of advertising has had dramatic effects in other industries too. In 1976, Congress banned the advertising of cigarettes on television in response to the Surgeon General's finding that cigarette smoking could lead to lung cancer. It was argued that captive TV watchers should not be subjected to the advertising of a hazardous product. The results of such a ban were just the opposite of the desired effect. The lack of cigarette advertising on TV has caused two distinct phenomena, both of which have led to possible increased health problems. Prior to the banning of cigarette advertising on TV, the American Cancer Society and the antismoking lobbyists succeeded in forcing free antismoking ads on TV. Under the Fairness Doctrine promulgated by the Federal Communications Commission, networks are supposed to air *both* sides of the story (as if there were only two sides to every argument). Thus, if TV networks were accepting money for cigarette advertisements, it was argued they must also accept antismoking ads (and for free). Thus, prior to 1976, there were several antismoking ads a day on each network. After the ban on TV advertising of cigarettes, however, the networks were no longer obligated under the Fairness Doctrine to show antismoking ads for free. Thus, the number of antismoking ads dropped dramatically. Apparently such ads were having an effect, especially among teenagers and women, for the percentage of teenagers and women who smoke has been rising since the time cigarette TV ads were banned. Perhaps that is a coincidence, but perhaps not.
>
> The other phenomenon that may be leading to increased health hazards on the part of the American public results from the fact that TV advertising is a powerful, and perhaps the single most effective, means to introduce new cigarettes into the marketplace. Once people are set on smoking a particular brand of cigarette, it is hard to get them to change or to be aware

of new brands; but TV advertising did just that—it made them aware of what was available. Professor Ben Klein has found that since the banning of advertising on TV, the introduction of new low tar, low nicotine cigarettes has dropped by 42 percent. Presumably, smokers benefit by switching to low tar, low nicotine cigarettes because they reduce the probability of lung disease in the future. Thus, the banning of such advertising has led consumers to stick with their old brands of cigarettes, which are likely to have higher levels of tar and nicotine and, hence, are more of a health hazard.

In less formal writing, too, the method is used continually. Stephen King, in *Danse Macabre*, his study of horror movies, asks why the average American, living a life without terror or violence, will pay four or five dollars to see a horror movie. In several paragraphs, King considers "simple and obvious" reasons: to show that we aren't afraid, to have fun, to feel comfortable in our own essential normality. Then he considers a deeper reason for the films' appeal:

> The mythic horror movie, like the sick joke, has a dirty job to do. It deliberately appeals to all that is worst in us. It is morbidity unchained, our most base instincts let free, our nastiest fantasies realized—and it happens, fittingly enough, in the dark. For these reasons, good liberals often shy away from horror films. For myself, I like to see the most aggressive of them—*Dawn of the Dead*, for instance—as lifting a trapdoor in the civilized forebrain and throwing a basket of raw meat to the hungry alligators swimming around in that subterranean river beneath. Why bother? Because it keeps them from getting out, man. It keeps them down there and me up here. It was Lennon and McCartney who said that all you need is love, and I would agree with that. As long as you keep the gators fed.

To be sure, King's suggested explanation doesn't end the inquiry, but it offers a provocative answer to the question Why?

Looking for causes and effects has vital uses. The method enables the mind to discover order in a reality that otherwise seems chaotic. In his article "Causation of Terror," social historian Feliks Gross seeks to explain a difficult, complex, and vitally important matter: the reasons for political assassinations and terrorism in Europe and Russia in the nineteenth and twentieth centuries. Gross recalls cases of political parties who have used terrorist tactics to overthrow moderate and democratic governments; he remembers the victims of oppressive rule who have used terrorist tactics to fight back: the histories of the Armenians and Bulgarians under Turkish rule, the Serbs under Croatian Ustasha government, the Polish underground fighters who resisted the Nazi occupation. Tentatively, offering a vast generalization, Gross finds that economic hardship does not usually cause its victims to respond with terrorist tactics and political assassinations. Instead, the causes of terrorism appear to lie in ethnic tensions and clashes of political ideology.

"It is of paramount significance," Gross concludes, "to understand the conditions that are conducive to political assassination." By controlling such conditions, perhaps we might even prevent terrorism. Applied to such an end, exploring causes and effects is no mere game, but a way of seeking peace and ensuring it.

CHAPTER 13

Drawing Boundaries: Defining

When you *define* (from the Latin, meaning "to set bounds"), you indicate the meaning or meanings of a word, the nature of a thing, the limits around the territory of an idea. In any paper you write that explains something, you are likely to find definition a useful tool. With it, you can clarify an unfamiliar term or difficult concept and distinguish it from every other, thus helping your reader to understand its nature, habitat, or activities or to see its structure, the better to comprehend it.

Most of us on hearing the word *definition* think first of the kind of short, literal, and specific definition we find in a dictionary, which usually gives the general class to which a subject belongs, followed by any particular features that distinguish it: "**pro·leg** (prō′lĕg′) *n*. One of the stubby limbs on the abdominal segments of caterpillars and some other insect larvae." But writers of dictionaries aren't the only ones who write short definitions. At any moment, in writing a paper that explains, you may wish to define a word that you think your reader may not know: "Witches gather in a *coven*, a band or assembly usually numbering thirteen."

Writing a short definition is a simple art. To construct a short definition, one way to proceed is like a dictionary writer: first to state the general class to which the subject belongs ("An eland is an African antelope") and then to add some identifying characteristics ("resembling an ox or cow, with short, spiral-shaped horns"). Your subject also can be large and intangible: "Psychology is a study"—that's its general class—"that tries to explain the human mind and human behavior." This definition of *psychology*, short though it is, at least enables the reader to distinguish a certain field of knowledge from other fields such as metallurgy or pretzel-bending. To give a short, literal, dictionary-like definition can sometimes be a weary, clichéd way to begin: "This paper will deal with the idea of responsibility. Responsibility, according to *Webster's New Collegiate Dictionary*, is the quality or state of being responsible, as moral, legal, or mental accountability." Still, a short definition can be lively and thought-provoking, a way to say much in brief.

Short definitions, not always literal and not always built like a dictionary definition, can make a point humorously or express a writer's personal views. "Money," said economist John Maynard Keynes, "is that which one accepts only to get rid of it." "A riot," said Martin Luther King, Jr., referring to race riots in cities (and making an unforgettable metaphor), "is the language of the unheard."

In the rest of this chapter, we will be dealing not with short definitions but with another kind of definition: *extended definition*, a useful method of writing anything from a paragraph to a whole essay—or even a whole book, like Sol Gittleman's *From Shtetl to Suburbia* (1978), a survey tracing the migration of Yiddish literature to America. In the opening lines Gittleman defines a word and the idea it stands for:

> The Hebrew word *mishpoche* has found its way into every language spoken by Jews for the past two thousand years. Whether in Palestine or in African or European exile, this word for family has come to express the deepest sense of relationship that Jew can have to Jew. Its meaning transcends its application to merely narrow familial associations. There is a saying, "All Jews are *mishpoche*," and in this we see the intense feeling of common heritage, common obligations, and common values which often set apart historically persecuted minorities—Gypsies, Armenians, and Jews, for example—from their tormentors.

The definition here is valuable: *mishpoche* sums up a vital idea that will inform Gittleman's whole book.

Usually, in writing an essay by the method of extended definition, your purpose is to explain a word (*witch*) or an idea (*witchcraft*) or an entire phenomenon (the activity of self-proclaimed witches in contemporary America). When you write a definition, you're free to include any other method of explaining that you know: process analysis, comparison and contrast, cause and effect, division or classification. All of them, you will find, can serve you in arriving at the meaning of a word or a concept.

LEARNING FROM OTHER WRITERS

In the following essay from *Love and Will* by Rollo May, you'll see a well-known psychotherapist defining a rather subtle and unfamiliar concept—eros—by contrasting it with something more familiar—sex. May's essay clearly shows that for writing an extended definition, a method you have studied in a previous chapter, in this case comparison and contrast, can be handy.

WHAT IS EROS?
ROLLO MAY

Eros in our day is taken as a synonym for "eroticism" or sexual titillation. *Eros* was the name given to a journal of sexy arcana, containing   1

"Aphrodisiac Recipes" and posing such weighty question-and-answer articles as, "Q: How Do the Porcupines Do It? A: Carefully." One wonders whether everyone has forgotten the fact that eros, according to no less an authority than St. Augustine, is the power which drives men toward God. Such gross misunderstandings would tend to make the demise of eros unavoidable: for in our overstimulated age we have no need for titillation which no longer titillates. It is essential, therefore, that we clarify the meaning of this crucial term.

Eros created life on the earth, the early Greek mythology tells us. When 2 the world was barren and lifeless, it was Eros who "seized his life-giving arrows and pierced the cold bosom of the Earth," and "immediately the brown surface was covered with luxuriant verdure." This is an appealing symbolic picture of how Eros *incorporates* sex—those phallic arrows which pierce—as the instrument by which he creates life. Eros then breathed into the nostrils of the clay forms of man and woman and gave them the "spirit of life." Ever since, eros has been distinguished by the function of giving the spirit of life, in contrast to the function of sex as the release of tension. Eros was then one of the four original gods, the others being Chaos, Gaea (mother earth), and Tartarus (the dark pit of Hades below the earth). Eros, says Joseph Campbell, is always, regardless of guise, the progenitor, the original creator from which life comes.

Sex can be defined fairly adequately in physiological terms as consisting 3 of the building up of bodily tensions and their release. Eros, in contrast, is the experiencing of the personal intentions and meaning of the act. Whereas sex is a rhythm of stimulus and response, eros is a state of being. The pleasure in sex is described by Freud and others as the reduction of tension; in eros, on the contrary, we wish not to be released from the excitement but rather to hang on to it, to bask in it, and even to increase it. The end toward which sex points is gratification and relaxation, whereas eros is a desiring, longing, a forever reaching out, seeking to expand.

All this is in accord with the dictionary definitions. *Webster's* defines 4 sex (coming from the Latin *sexus*, meaning "split") as referring to "physiological distinctions. . . . the character of being male or female, or . . . the distinctive functions of male or female." Eros, in contrast, is defined with such terms as "ardent desire," "yearning," "aspiring self-fulfilling love often having a sensuous quality." The Latins and Greeks had two different words for sex and love, as we do; but the curious thing to our ears is how rarely the Latins speak of *sexus*. Sex, to them, was no issue; it was *amor* they were concerned about. Similarly, everyone knows the Greek word *eros*, but practically no one has ever heard of their term for "sex." It is φυλον, the word from which we derive the zoological term "phylon," tribe or race. This is an entirely different stem from the Greek word *philia*, which means love in the sense of friendship.

Sex is thus a zoological term and is rightly applied to all animals as 5 well as human beings. Kinsey° was a zoologist, and appropriately to his

---

Kinsey: Alfred C. Kinsey (1894–1956), who wrote with colleagues the widely known studies *Sexual Behavior in the Human Male* (1948) and *Sexual Behavior in the Human Female* (1953); founder of the University of Indiana's Institute for Sex Research.

profession, he studied human sexual behavior from a zoological point of view. Masters° is a gynecologist and studies sex from the viewpoint of sexual organs and how you manage and manipulate them: sex, then, is a pattern of neurophysiological functions and the sexual problem consists of what you do with organs.

Eros, on the other hand, takes wings from human imagination and is 6 forever transcending all techniques, giving the laugh to all the "how to" books by gaily swinging into orbit above our mechanical rules, making love rather than manipulating organs.

For eros is the power which *attracts* us. The essence of eros is that it 7 draws us from ahead, whereas sex pushes us from behind. This is revealed in our day-to-day language when I say a person "allures" me or "entices" me, or the possibilities of a new job "invite" me. Something in me responds to the other person, or the job, and pulls me toward him or it. I participate in forms, possibilities, higher levels of meaning, on neurophysiological dimensions but also on aesthetic and ethical dimensions as well. As the Greeks believed, knowledge and even ethical goodness exercise such a pull. Eros is the drive toward union with what we belong to—union with our own possibilities, union with significant other persons in our world in relation to whom we discover our own self-fulfillment. Eros is the yearning in man which leads him to dedicate himself to seeking *arête*, the noble and good life.

Sex, in short, is the mode of relating characterized by tumescence of 8 the organs (for which we seek the pleasurable relief) and filled gonads (for which we seek satisfying release). But eros is the mode of relating in which we do not seek release but rather to cultivate, procreate, and form the world. *In eros, we seek increase of stimulation.* Sex is a need, but eros is a desire; and it is this admixture of desire which complicates love. In regard to our preoccupation with the orgasm in American discussions of sex, it can be agreed that the aim of the sex act in its zoological and physiological sense is indeed the orgasm. But the aim of eros is not: eros seeks union with the other person in delight and passion, and the procreating of new dimensions of experience which broaden and deepen the being of both persons. It is common experience, backed up by folklore as well as the testimony of Freud and others, that after sexual release we tend to go to sleep—or, as the joke puts it, to get dressed, go home, and *then* go to sleep. But in eros, we want just the opposite: to stay awake thinking of the beloved, remembering, savoring, discovering ever-new facets of the prism of what the Chinese call the "many-splendored" experience.

It is this urge for union with the partner that is the occasion for human 9 tenderness. For eros—not sex as such—is the source of tenderness. Eros is the longing to establish union, full relationship. This may be, first, a union with abstract forms. The philosopher Charles S. Peirce sat alone in his house in Milford, Connecticut working out his mathematical logic, but this did not prevent his experiencing eros; the thinker must be "animated by a true

---

Masters: William H. Masters, M.D., contemporary gynecologist, who with his colleague (later wife) Virginia E. Johnson established an influential clinic and center for sex therapy in St. Louis.

eros," he wrote, "for the task of scientific investigation." Or it may be a union with aesthetic or philosophical forms, or a union with new ethical forms. But it is most obvious as the pull toward the union of two individuals sexually. The two persons, longing, as all individuals do, to overcome the separateness and isolation to which we all are heir as individuals, can participate in a relationship that, for the moment, is not made up of two isolated, individual experiences, but a genuine union. A sharing takes place which is a new *Gestalt*, a new being, a new field of magnetic force.

Questions to Start You Thinking

1.   In the process of defining eros, the author also redefines sex. How does his definition of sex differ from our usual understanding of the word?

2.   For discussion: Of what importance is eros? Why should anyone—especially a psychotherapist—bother defining it at all? Why should it matter if most people confuse eros with sex?

3.   From what resources, besides his own experience, does May draw his material?

4.   What unfamiliar concept other than eros do you think would make a good subject for an extended definition?

In a timely paper, written for a composition class, Matthew A. Munich doesn't give a short definition of his subject; he uses the methods of cause and effect and comparison and contrast to define a modern phenomenon. Notice too how extensively he illustrates his general statements.

THE NATURE OF MTV

MATTHEW A. MUNICH

The concept of the music video, a short film in which video images   1
interpret a song, is not a new one. The beginnings date as far back as the 1960s in the Beatles' full-length film *A Hard Day's Night* or later in the Rolling Stones' movie *Gimme Shelter*. With cable television and some of its subsidiary channels, however, the music video has received a tremendous amount of attention and popularity. MTV, a channel devoted solely to showing music videos twenty-four hours a day, has made the music video not only a new medium but also a new form of art. While it may not be fair to judge the popularity of the music video as a cultural step backward, neither can we consider it, in its display of violence and sexist attitudes, a cultural step forward. Music video can be thought of as a step timed to society, a form that meets a new criterion of entertainment.

Music video did for music what television did to radio; in fact, MTV is   2
a television station for videos. Before music video, listening was a more active process. The listener created a personal image of the song. With MTV, however, so compelling is the visual image that it imprints on the brain; the song cannot be divorced from the video. This phenomenon resembles

television's "laugh tracks" in that not only is the television showing us a picture but it's telling us what we should think is funny. In this sense, music videos do not require the viewer's active attention or imagination.

Music video does provide a place where new and important film tech- 3 niques can be tried and developed. The Cars' video, which won best video of 1984, exemplifies this stage of technological advancement. This video employed some of the most recent discoveries in film computer graphics. Music video can help exploit new ways of using film as an artistic expression.

While the methods used by music videos might be new and innovative, 4 the content seems stereotypical and trite. The figure of women in music videos is a large part of this stereotyped content. The "Spellbound" video by the group Triumph is a good example of the treatment of women. The video shows a man driving at night, and as he approaches a nebulous figure his car starts to break apart. When he sees that the figure is a woman with fluffed-out hair, wearing ripped white fabric, the car falls completely apart. He emerges from the wreckage and follows her in a trance. She stops to let him reach her, kisses him, and turns him into a statue. The video ends with the band playing the song on stage with the statue. The video suggests that, while women may be beautiful, they possess evil powers that will be the downfall of men. Modern props notwithstanding, this woman is a version of the Medusa who has been turning men to stone for centuries.

Regressing to an earlier stage than classical myth, people in music video 5 frequently dress in tribal garb. We see people in tattered clothing, non-human hair styles, jungle skins, and face paint. Although the medium is new, then, these painted creatures portray the primitive thrust of music video. A typical example is the "Talk to Me" video by the group Iam Siam, which shows a young girl taken by force to some tribal ritual where she is encircled by natives wearing face paint and loincloths. Watching this happen is a bald person painted blue and white from top to bottom. He decides to rescue this woman from the ceremony and, once he gets her back to safety, he touches her, instantly transforming her to a creature with the same paint job. Although music video advances technologies, it returns ideologically to a primitive state.

The concept of the music video invades our lives in other ways than 6 just on television. Movies that appear to be nothing more than two-hour music videos are becoming popular. The Talking Heads' movie *Stop Making Sense* is nothing more than an extended music video. Clearly the toleration for this new art form reflects popular taste; *Flashdance* and *Footloose* are other immense successes that reflect the music video mode. Who is the audience for the hard-imaged, fantastical, and sometimes amusing but always loud and rhythmic sounds? What, if anything, does the form tell us about our culture?

If music video is art, it is art you can do your homework to. It speaks 7 of a culture that loves gimmicks and quick fixes and noise. MTV has a mesmerizing effect, almost hypnotizing us and offering a visual counterpart to a drugged state. Like a dope peddler, the video station fosters addiction by promising total coverage: we can watch it all the time; we never have to give it up. It reflects our culture's fascination with and, more ominously, return to a more primitive state. There is no subtlety; every idea and theme is spelled out, not once but many times. Natives beat drums, beat their chests, and beat women. Women, conversely, are the stereotypical downfall of men. Music video is quintessentially modern because it's so thin: quickly replaced, dispassionate, disposable. In the nuclear age, MTV is us.

Questions to Start You Thinking

1. After reading Munich's *extended definition*, write a *short definition* of the music video in a sentence.
2. What knowledge other than an acquaintance with music videos does Munich bring to his essay?
3. What other modern phenomenon might be a promising subject for an extended definition?

LEARNING BY WRITING

The Assignment

Write an extended definition of one of the following:

An institution or an organization (such as a university, the Society of Friends, a corporation, the Dallas Cowboys, the Department of State)

A representative individual (a working woman, a redneck, a schizophrenic)

A phenomenon (fast food, rap music, acid rain)

A general idea (charisma, communism, an education)

These examples are given only to help set your own thoughts in motion.

Use details and concrete examples from any resource: recalling, observing, reading, conversing, imagining. Include in your paper any of the ways of explaining that will help you clarify meaning: process analysis, comparison and contrast, cause and effect, and division or classification. If you deal with an abstract idea, bring it down to earth.

A few successful recent student papers written by the method of extended definition include these:

In his definition of patriotism, a man quoted government officials who used the word *patriotism* to justify a military operation and charged that the operation did not reflect his own sense of the word.

A man, curious about the Rh-negative blood that had made his daughter's birth a difficult one, did some reading and came up with a working definition of the Rh factor. He explained it with the aid of examples, some from his own observation.

A woman explained what Christians mean when they call someone a saint.

A woman, taking examples from her reading (Franz Kafka's story "Friendship" and Susan Lee's essay "Friendship, Feminism, and Betrayal"), defined friendship by contrasting it with companionship.

A woman who disagreed with a chapter she had read in Jane Howard's book *Families* wrote her own definition of a family, recalling and observing groups of people she knew.

Generating Ideas

To begin, while you look for a topic, you might ask yourself the following questions.

DISCOVERY CHECKLIST: FINDING A TOPIC

- What do you have some knowledge of?
- What have you heard or read lately that you'd like to find out more about?
- Is there a word, a concept, or a general idea, now only vaguely clear to you, that you'd like to understand well enough to be able to explain it to someone else?
- What do you really *want* to write about?

Don't expect to pin down your topic immediately. Just tentatively pick a *possible* topic. Only when you have done some further exploring will you know whether you'll want to go on with it.

Before you write your definition, your main task is to make yourself aware of your subject's essential features. To help you see points that otherwise might escape your notice, here are a few more questions. And to show these questions in action, let's say you tentatively consider writing an extended definition of a current phenomenon: cable television.[1]

1. *Is this subject unique, or are there others of its kind? If it resembles others, in what ways?* Here you might admit that there are, after all, various cable TV services—that is, different companies in different localities. If you had enough information on the subject, you might compare and contrast their services—even though in this case you might conclude that they all have a certain similarity. All connect the home viewer's set to a cable and then supply access to the usual commercial channels and, for an extra fee, to certain channels available only to subscribers. Some throw in more channels with their basic, rock-bottom-priced service: a few channels in distant cities, perhaps channels in foreign languages.

2. *In what different forms does it occur, while keeping its own identity?* Here you might classify some of the various forms of cable TV programming: movie channels, all-sports, all-news, religious programming, local community programming, children's programming, X-rated or "adult" programming, and

---

[1]The six questions that follow are freely adapted from those first stated by Richard E. Young, Alton L. Becker, and Kenneth L. Pike, who have applied insights from psychology and linguistics to the writing process. To investigate subjects in greater depth, their own six questions may be used in nine possible combinations, as they explain in detail in *Rhetoric: Discovery and Change* (New York: Harcourt Brace Jovanovich, 1970).

more. You might consider forms of cable programming that have commercials and forms that don't. You might consider (or perhaps compare and contrast) professional programming and the local programs that amateurs can now produce and have screened in their localities.

3. *When and where do we find it? Under what circumstances and in what situations?* You find it in towns where the companies have decided to operate, where they have been authorized by the local government, and where they have completed laying the necessary cable.

4. *What is it at the present moment?* Here you might be inspired to voice your own opinion about the nature of cable TV. Or you might choose to give a straight, factual account of the present state of cable TV: how far the cable companies have progressed in their ambition to sign up most of the TV-viewing households in the nation.

5. *What does it do? What are its functions and activities?* Some people have attacked cable TV as a medium for soft-core pornography; others have defended it as a boon to education, an admirable improvement in television picture quality, a great thing for the aged and shut-ins, a blessing to members of minorities who can watch programs in their native languages, a benefit to local government (enabling the diffusion of programs about town and neighborhood issues), and so on.

6. *How is it put together? What parts make it up? What holds these parts together?* These questions could be taken to mean How do the cable companies go about assembling their services? How do they decide what people will watch? What effect do governments have on their selections? (This question might lead to further thoughts: In some places, X-rated channels may be banned. Some local governments may require that a certain percentage of cable channels be devoted to community service programs.) What part do viewers play in the programming by their very willingness to pay for certain channels?

There isn't always just one right answer to all these questions. You might interpret them variously. Although not every question will apply to every subject (and some may lead you nowhere), they will usually help get your thoughts in motion. They will sometimes reveal points that could use more finding out about.

Whether you work through that list of questions or just think randomly about your subject (preferably while observing it), work and think with your pencil moving. Get something down on paper, even a rough, partial list of your subject's standout features, and it will then be easier to notice any features you've left out. And you will have something to organize. In writing his definition of music videos, Matthew Munich began by jotting down (in no special order) thoughts that first came to mind:

Most videos are a showcase for the lead singer.

Artistic expression yes: new ways of utilizing TV as a medium helps promote
   artists who might not be noticed. Yet deceitful because a poor artist
   might be popularized because of good video, not good music.

Takes imagination out of listening to music. Downplays the act of listening. Images are force-fed.

"Billie Jean" video—one big commercial.

Reflection of the times—more violent, more sexist, more technological, more primitive.

A dozen more random notes followed. As you can see from Munich's finished paper, some of his first thoughts fell by the wayside as other features came to seem more important. That most videos showcase the lead singer did not seem as essential to his definition as his idea that the videos reflect our times. Other examples, more to the point than "Billie Jean," occurred to him as he wrote his first draft.

Shaping a Draft

If, like Matthew Munich, you will just get some preliminary thoughts on paper—the main features of your subject—you will have raw material, something to organize. Munich seems not to have made an outline on paper; evidently, he kept it in his head as he wrote a first draft based on his copious preliminary notes.

Methods of explaining occurred naturally as he wrote. In the second paragraph of his finished paper, he found himself recalling what listening to popular songs was like before music videos. Thus he was drawn to make a brief comparison between then and now. In extended definition, you may wish to call into service any method of explaining that you know. You might, if you were defining witchcraft in present-day America, do any of the following.

Analyze a process (how a new witch is initiated into a coven)

Compare and contrast (witches in Europe in the Middle Ages and witches in Palo Alto today)

Set forth causes (why do people proclaim themselves witches?) or *effects* (if one spouse joins a coven, what are the probable effects on a marriage?)

Divide (setting forth the component parts of a coven or a "service") or *classify* ("Contemporary Witches: Three Typical Varieties")

For suggestions on how to apply these methods, glance back over the past four chapters.

Still another method of defining—one of the best—is to give examples. What is the nature of a thing? Point to some illustrations of it. Matthew Munich's specific examples of videos add life to his paper. They assure us that the writer knows what he's writing about. If your subject is an abstract idea (like communism or conservatism), specific examples will be especially necessary. If you didn't come up with any when you did your preliminary discovering and note making, discover a few now.

Rewriting

You might start rewriting by looking over your paper to see if you have used any specialized word. If so, why not define it briefly, so that your readers will grasp its meaning? "Weather forecasters make use of *nephanalysis*, the tracking of clouds on a chart showing a large area of the earth."

You may find it helpful to try your draft on a peer reader to assure yourself that your paper really makes clear the subject you set out to define. A friendly critic can tell you if you've omitted some crucial bit of information or if your sequencing might be stronger if rearranged.

Then, as you read over your early draft, ask a few questions to see if you have made your definition as clear and as vivid as you can. The answers to these questions will depend, of course, on what you have chosen to define.

REVISION CHECKLIST: DEFINING

- Would what you're defining be more comprehensible to your readers if you had compared it with something familiar and similar?
- Is there a place in your paper where you could have amplified your definition of something by showing what it is *not*, as Rollo May did in his discussion of sex?
- Might your paper benefit from a process analysis that would show how the thing you're defining operates?
- If you're defining some large concept, did you break it into parts that could be dealt with one at a time? If you didn't, would it help to do some dividing now? Would classifying examples help your definition?
- Is there any reason to go into the causes or the effects of what you're defining? Did you do so?
- Have you included enough examples and illustrations to bring your paper to life?
- Have you made ample use of the five resources for writers: recalling, observing, reading, conversing, imagining?

No definition, of course, needs to include every resource and every writing method on the books. You just want to make sure that you have taken advantage of all those that can strengthen and enrich your paper.

Other Assignments

1. In a paragraph, define one of the following.

>A good or a bad horror movie
>A good or a bad high school
>A good or a bad salesperson
>A good or a bad newspaper
>A good or a bad leader
>A good or a bad therapy session
>A good or a bad student government

A good or a bad library
A good or a bad scientific experiment
A good or a bad housing development

2. From that list of good and bad subjects (or taking your own idea for a different good and bad subject), define the good by comparing and contrasting it with the bad. Plan to write more than one paragraph. For instance, you might write about a good salesperson versus a bad one, taking three paragraphs to compare and contrast them in three ways:

    a. In knowledge of what the salesperson is selling
    b. In consideration for the customer
    c. In honesty

    If you need any reminder on comparing and contrasting, look back over the discussion in Chapter 9.

3. In a paragraph or two, define one of the following. (Suggestion: Examples will help you make your definition clear, as will any of the other methods suggested in this chapter.)

    Neocolonialism
    A fugue
    Artificial intelligence
    Rococo architecture
    The Big Bang theory
    Parthenogenesis
    Art deco
    Lobotomy
    Laissez-faire
    A tribe
    Zero population growth
    The bourgeoisie
    Chemotherapy
    Machismo
    A wind tunnel

APPLYING WHAT YOU LEARN: SOME USES OF DEFINITION

A close friend wants a sense of what your college is like, so in a letter you try to define the whole institution. That's an everyday use for writing an extended definition. In college writing assignments, extended definitions are frequently required in any course in which large general ideas (or small general ideas) need explaining. An art history course might ask for a thorough definition of the Baroque or Surrealist style; a history course, for the meaning of feudalism. In a course in natural resources, you might be expected to define acid rain; in a course in accounting, to define a spread sheet and tell how it functions.

Read almost any newspaper or popular magazine, and examples of extended definition just might leap out at you. A sportswriter will try to define the unique team spirit of the Dallas Cowboys—what are its ingredients, what causes it to exist, and what are its effects on the team's opponents? A news commentator writes a feature on a representative individual, familiar in our time: the person who remains a celebrity for only a few days. Your college textbooks are constantly defining. This chapter has given an extended definition of definition. But crack open virtually any textbook in psychology and you'll find extended definitions on the order of this one from *Basic Psychology* by Henry Gleitman:

> In their milder form, manic states are often hard to distinguish from normal high spirits. The person seems to have shifted into some form of mental high gear; she is more lively and infectiously merry, is extremely talkative and always on the go, is charming, utterly self-confident, and indefatigable. It is hard to see that something is wrong unless one notices that she jumps from one plan to another, seems unable to sit still for a moment, and quickly shifts from unbounded elation to intense irritation if she meets even the smallest frustration. These pathological signs become greatly intensified as the manic episode becomes more severe (*acute mania*). Now the motor is racing and all brakes are off. There is an endless stream of talk that runs from one topic to another and knows no inhibitions of social or personal (or for that matter, sexual) propriety. Patients are incessantly busy. They rarely sleep, burst into shouts of song, smash furniture out of sheer overabundance of energy, do exercises, conceive grandiose plans for rebuilding the hospital or redirecting the nation's foreign policy or making millions in the stock market—a ceaseless torrent of activity that continues unabated over many days and sleepless nights and will eventually sap the patients' health (and that of those around them) if they are not sedated.

Technical and scientific writers continually define, for their definitions are vital to prevent misunderstanding. In *The Writer on His Own*, David Greenhood has explained why these definitions are necessary and why they have to be exact:

> In technology . . . definitions have a practical function: they fence in the meaning that must be used and they fence out all other meanings. When a science teacher or an artillery instructor says, "This definition will prevent error," he is implying, sagaciously too, that it forbids imagination. Or invention, or originality of any kind whatsoever.

Evidently, a chemist who creatively threw together elements would not produce the compound he wanted. Scientists all over the world, if they didn't agree on the meaning of a word or an idea, would find it difficult to share knowledge. For an example of a technical writer making his subject clear (to readers who can follow him), here is Gessner G. Hawley in an article, "A Chemist's Definition of pH." Though Hawley goes on to write an extended definition, he begins with a short definition:

pH is a value taken to represent the acidity or alkalinity of an aqueous solution; it is defined as the logarithm of the reciprocal of the hydrogen-ion concentration of a solution:

$$pH = 1n\frac{1}{[H^+]}$$

Often, in writing any paper explaining what you have learned, you'll pause occasionally to define, at least briefly, a word or a concept. Sometimes it's a standard word not often used. You define it to save your readers a trip to the dictionary. It might be a word or phrase you've coined yourself. Then you have to explain it or your readers won't know what you're talking about. Prolific word coiner and social prophet Alvin Toffler, in *The Third Wave*, for instance, invents (among many others) the word "techno-sphere," which he defines as follows:

> All societies—primitive, agricultural, or industrial—use energy; they make things; they distribute things. In all societies the energy system, the production system, and the distribution system are interrelated parts of something larger. This larger system is the *techno-sphere*.

In college and beyond, you'll find it useful to know how to write a short definition or an extended definition whenever issues are discussed or argued. What is equality? What is intelligence, socialism, preventive medical care, brand loyalty, a minimum wage, a holding corporation? Whenever you are asked to indicate the nature of an idea, a thing, a movement, a phenomenon, an organization—then the ability to write a definition, short or long, is a skill to have at your fingertips.

Further Writing Assignments: Combining Ways to Explain

In the world at large and in most college writing, few writers start out by saying, "I'm going to write an article in which I rely on the method of cause and effect" or "I'm going to write an essay by comparing and contrasting." Rather, they write because they have something to say. As they draft, they use whatever useful methods come to hand. Reading their work, we may find familiar ways of explaining rising and falling as naturally as waves in the sea. In one paragraph they will compare and contrast; in another, they'll analyze. They go along doing whatever will make their explanation clear to readers: dividing, classifying, looking for cause and effect, defining things.

In the last five chapters, to make these useful methods easy to learn, we have traced them one at a time. But often in fulfilling a college writing assignment, you will want to use more than one method. Most explanatory essays combine methods freely and include a number of examples and illustrations as well. Therefore, to give you extra practice in making something clear to your readers, we offer you a few assignments that call on you to use more than one way of explaining in the same paper.

Explain briefly the process by which some historic event unfolded: the Black Death, the influx of Irish immigrants into the United States during the 1840s, the U.S. civil rights movement of the 1960s, the new conservatism in American politics, or some other development that interests you. Then trace either some of the causes or some of the effects of this historic event.

Define socialized medicine by explaining how it works in Britain or another country and by contrasting it with the practice of medicine as we know it in this country.

Compare and contrast television news coverage of an event with newspaper coverage of the same event. Then explain what causes the two to differ so widely.

235

Here's an assignment that may help you make an important decision. Classify all the advantages and all the disadvantages you know in two careers you may be considering for yourself. On the basis of your classification, compare the two jobs and decide which is worth more, first to the person performing it and then to society.

Define your ideal college living arrangement. Then compare and contrast your ideal with the living arangement you actually have. If your actual situation could use some improvement, what could you do to make it better?

Explain how to do something that you're good at: dissecting a frog, photographing animals, taking lecture notes, identifying trees, showing cattle, or whatever, by comparing the process with another. Dissecting a frog, you might say, is a little like carving a turkey. Or telling one tree from another is not so different from telling one acquaintance from another. Your aim here is to explain as clearly as possible, so that your readers can easily grasp it, the process you follow in pursuing your chosen activity.

Divide into its component parts the skill of playing a musical instrument. In other words, how many things go on simultaneously while someone makes music? Then, concentrating on just one aspect of the skill—reading music, manipulating a violin bow, learning the proper fingering, responding to the conductor, or whatever—explain by process analysis how it's done.

FOR STILL MORE WRITING ASSIGNMENTS

When you write an extended definition, as you have seen in the last chapter, you can usefully combine methods: comparing and contrasting, analyzing a process, looking for cause and effect, dividing, classifying—doing anything that helps draw boundaries around your subject and explain its nature. In Chapter 13, glance again at "The Assignment" (p. 227) and "Other Assignments" (p. 231). Are there any assignments that you haven't tried that now appeal to you?

When you make a statement of opinion, or when you argue for an action, you will often find yourself explaining something, perhaps setting forth reasons for your view. Looking ahead to the next section of this book, "Writing to Persuade," we predict that you will want to keep the ways of explaining handy. In Chapters 14 and 15, "The Assignment" and "Other Assignments" will offer you still more opportunities to use the five methods you have just learned.

PART FOUR

Writing to Persuade

When you persuade, you convince others to change their minds. You invite them to substitute for a view they had held the view you offer them—perhaps also to act on it.

In daily life, you try to persuade a friend to take in a movie with you or a gas station attendant to fill up your tank even though he's about to close for the night. Often you are the object of persuasion too. Ministers, priests, rabbis, and parents try to persuade us to live better lives. Candidates for political office try to persuade us to give them our votes. And you meet an intense attempt at persuasion every time you watch a television commercial.

Unlike some advertisers on TV, college writers don't storm other people's minds. In college writing, you persuade by gentler means: by sharing your view with a reader willing to consider it. You'll find it important to know how to express that view clearly and forcefully so as to convince your reader that it is trustworthy. But it may be important to understand your reader's view as well. In so doing, you may find yourself, to your surprise, refining and improving and complicating the view you started with. If that should happen, then what you write won't become any less convincing, but probably more so.

In this section, two chapters will show you how to write persuasively. Chapter 14 will guide you in forming an opinion and expressing it. Chapter 15 will guide you in forming an opinion, expressing it, and going on to argue that something be done about it. At the end of this part, "A Note on Reasoning" will explain three useful methods of thinking devised in ancient and modern times. It will also provide a list of common varieties of logical error.

CHAPTER 14

Advancing a View:
The Statement of Opinion

Many times, your college instructors will ask you to take a stand in writing. Depending on the courses you take, you'll have numerous opportunities in college to state your views on anything from zero population growth to genetic engineering, from affirmative action to the influence of television on children, from ancient Greek philosophy to contemporary architecture. Doing so, you will find, will help you clarify for yourself what you think about important issues. It will also give you the chance to share what you believe.

In stating an opinion, you set forth the truth as you see it and feel it: "I think Picasso is a great artist" or "Picasso's art leaves me cold." To persuade your readers that your view makes good sense, you don't have to start out by trumpeting that your view is the one that, by God, ought to prevail. You may best convince your readers by seeking, first of all, to understand their own views. As writers, if we want to influence our readers to think as we do, then "we have to care more about communicating with them than about showing them the error of their ways," as writing specialist Maxine Hairston has said.

You don't just listen to opposing views in order to butter up the people who hold them. You listen in order to correct your own view, if need be. Seen in this light, persuasive writing isn't a way to manipulate others. Writer and reader become not foes, but two human beings seeking to agree. We think you will find that, whenever you set out to state your opinions in writing, this view of persuasion will relieve you of the crushing burden of having to be absolutely right.

A time-tested way to persuade a reader who doesn't share your view is *argument*. In one familiar sense of the word, argument is a fight—as in a news report, "Just before the shots rang out, neighbors heard the couple having a loud argument." Although an argument might have been part of that domestic rhubarb, for our purposes the word will mean something else. Let's call argument *reasoning:* making statements that lead to a conclusion. (A discussion of some *methods* of doing so is found in "A Note on Reasoning" on p. 277.)

The *conclusion* is whatever view or opinion you're going to set forth. When worded in a sentence, it is often called the *proposition* of an argument, the *thesis*, or the *claim*. Any facts, statistics, and expert opinions you offer in support of your conclusion make up your *data*, or *evidence*.

That's argument: reasoning from evidence to an opinion. But persuading—convincing your reader—isn't always a matter of such reasoning. You can also persuade in other powerful ways.

You can appeal to emotions. As advertisers well know, people can be persuaded to buy or do something by an appeal to their emotions. An ad for life insurance may show the wretched and wistful orphans of foolish parents who didn't buy a policy. Often, advertisers persuade by appealing to inner needs.

> You're somebody special the minute you step behind the wheel of a Saab 900.
>
> Feel at home in a Tamborg towel.
>
> Try a Parliament cigarette—she'll see you in a new light.

Often, emotional persuasion uses words that imply strong judgments, like the words in italics here: "You want to enjoy great art, don't you, and show the world that you're an *educated sophisticate*, right, and not an *ignorant boob?* Why not give Picasso another chance?" Jerome Michael, for many years a teacher at Columbia University's School of Law, used to end his course in advocacy (teaching lawyers how to plead before a court) by suggesting that, if all else fails, try an emotional appeal: "If you have the facts on your side, hammer the facts. If you have the law on your side, hammer the law. If you have neither the facts nor the law, hammer the table."

Appeals to emotion, though, are not always merely hard sells or courtroom tricks. All readers and listeners have emotions that a good writer or speaker cannot help rousing. Indeed, great emotional persuasion has been used in worthy causes. In 1776, Tom Paine's pamphlet *Common Sense* helped goad American colonists to revolution. In 1963, on the hundredth birthday of Abraham Lincoln's Emancipation Proclamation, the speech of Martin Luther King, Jr., "I Have a Dream," helped accelerate the civil rights movement. In truth, as long as writers and readers are human, thinking and feeling cannot be perfectly separated, nor need they be. The most persuasive writers reason with feeling. You might do so in writing a paper supporting the claim "Shooting seals for their furs is wrong" or "A handgun in every household is only right."

You can show your reader that you are trustworthy. One way to establish your credibility is to present yourself as an expert in your subject, someone who has studied it extensively. Perhaps you refer to your own experience: "As a lifeguard for two summers, I watched hundreds of people exhaust themselves in jumping the waves and once assisted a rescue crew in aiding the victim of a heart attack." This reference to first-hand knowledge might lend convincing support to the claim "To exercise strenuously is wrong." You can present yourself to your reader as an honest, modest, and careful claimer—as indeed you are. To make this clear to your reader, you might mention larger or more extreme claims that others have argued for, but not you—you're not going to claim all that much.

> Some have maintained that any exercise can be dangerous, citing the case of longtime runner Jim Fixx, who unexpectedly collapsed, and the many instances of heart attacks brought on by sudden exertion. Others have advised that no one be allowed to begin working out for any unfamiliar sport without the advice of a doctor and a complete physical. But it seems to me that doctors have enough busywork to do. Any reasonable person can safely exercise after taking a few precautions and making a few simple preparations.

You can show an awareness of your reader's opinions and feelings. Simply by doing so, you begin to persuade. If you know that people are likely to disagree with you, you can frankly acknowledge this fact. This, for instance, is the opening of Ott Reed's essay in favor of a tough-line foreign policy toward the Soviet Union.

> Although most of us intensely dread the threat of nuclear war and give top priority to working out peaceful coexistence, I believe from all I have read that an equal amount of dread exists on the Russian side. Like many who take a more conciliatory approach toward the Soviets, I know that we need to reduce nuclear armaments. I can only agree that we need to keep open the door to future negotiation. Yet, as I will suggest in this paper, it seems clear that while refusing to grant the Russians everything they ask and while maintaining our own defenses, we can stay within safe limits.

Like this writer, feel free to use the first person *I*. By this personal approach, you set forth your view not as absolute truth handed down from on high, but as the way things look to you.

Much of the time in writing to persuade, you spell out beliefs, values, and logical connections that might be taken for granted. By stating them, you lay them out in the open for your readers to examine. The reader who accepts them is already on your side. If you declare, "I oppose eating red meat because it contains fats and chemicals known to be harmful," you assert a claim and give evidence for it. The reader who responds, "That's right—I'm a vegetarian myself," is already on your side. Even the reader who responds at first, "Oh, I don't know—a couple of hamburgers never killed anyone!" may warm to your view *if* you will take the trouble to spell out the beliefs and values that underlie *his* (or hers). These might include the assumptions that a steak or a burger is delicious; that vegetables aren't; that red meat is a necessary part of one's diet; that the chemicals haven't conclusively been proven dangerous.

You could spell out all those assumptions, showing that you are aware of them, and you could consider them seriously. You might even agree with some of them, cheerfully accepting the first one—that meat tastes good. Then you might set forth, in a reasonable, even-tempered way, your own divergent views. In this fashion, by spelling out your assumptions and by imagining those of a dissenting reader, you will win—at the very least—a respectful hearing.

LEARNING FROM OTHER WRITERS

Like Russell Baker, whose "The Art of Eating Spaghetti" is reprinted in Chapter 4, Suzanne Britt is a southern-born writer of lively informal essays that set forth serious views. In this example, she voices an opinion that every college writer might consider. Notice where Britt states her claim: not only at the conclusion of her essay, but in her opening paragraph.

THE FIRST PERSON
SUZANNE BRITT

I have it on the good authority of a college freshman that English 1 teachers are still forbidding students the use of the first-person point of view. These teachers do so on the moral, not literary or grammatical, grounds that the middle letter in sin is "I." Well, I object. The admonition against "I" is absurd and will, I hope, come to an end in the waning decades of the twentieth century.

English teachers are foolish to deprive students of the only point of 2 view they have available to them: their own. In fact, people might have trouble writing well because, from an early age, they have received these binding, unexamined maxims, the rules that stifle or kill. Why should the "I" be so cruelly chastised by the puritanical, selfless set? After all, each person is the central figure in the drama of his own life, the point at which all that he is or becomes begins.

Our guilt about "I" arises from Christian pronouncements about the 3 sin of pride, Freudian theories about the tyranny of the ego and best-selling books about the dangers of narcissism, such as the one by Christopher Lasch.° We are all afraid that a clear, strong "I" might be neurotic or downright wicked.

Ironically, at the same time Lasch was lambasting us for our self-ab- 4 sorption, we were beginning to assert the "I." Ours is the century in which we have tried to find ourselves, to recover our identities, to become well-defined, individualistic non-conformists. We have been pleased to be different, to be ourselves, to unmask. Proponents of transactional analysis encouraged us to send I-messages, not You-messages. Psychologists picked up the TA refrain, pushing diffuse, fragmented people to face themselves; to depend on the "I" they had so long denied; to refer to, use and trust the "I."

So we have been torn. While the moralists were telling us the "I" was 5 the center of pride, the psychologists were telling us that a strong, healthy identity, a clear-cut "I," could make us feel and function better than a whole lifetime of tiresome selflessness.

I-messages were hardest for women. Women were raised to give in to 6 you. Some women, even in their early thirties, didn't have an "I." I was one. My messages were all for you. Where do you want to go, dear? What

one by Christopher Lasch: The Culture of Narcissism (New York: Norton, 1979).

do you want to do? What career plans do you have? What do you believe? How do you feel? What do you want for supper? When do you want to eat it? These questions determined my personality, behavior, ethics. I began to suspect that too many puritans had gotten hold of me, whereas the TA people had grabbed all the fellows. Women who had a strong "I" were arrogant and stuck up. Men who had a strong "I" were forthright, bold, brave, confident and determined.

When my English teacher forbade me to set foot in "I" country, I was 7 too well-indoctrinated to pose some obvious questions and challenges. The fact is, the strong, first-person "I" voice has been prevalent in every age, genre and circumstance of great literature and history: the "I" in St. Paul's letters, in *Pilgrim's Progress*, in *Moby Dick*, in Walt Whitman's *Song of Myself*, in Augustine's *Confessions*, in Sherwood Anderson's short stories, in Sylvia Plath's poems, in Lamb's essays, in Thoreau's *Walden*. The harder task is to find a piece of great literature that doesn't use the first-person point of view.

I think too, with some glee, of all the robust, oft-quoted I-messages 8 sent by great men and women in all ages: Julius Caesar's "I came, I saw, I conquered"; Descartes' "I think, therefore I am"; Tennyson's "I am the heir of all ages"; MacArthur's "I shall return"; Queen Victoria's "We are not amused"; Edna Millay's "I am not resigned."

The strong "I" voice is heard less and less in this age of the committee 9 decision, the corporate response, the governmental process. We hide behind the bland, safe, irresponsible wordiness of the passive voice. It is felt that bombs should be dropped, heads should be rolled, funds should be withdrawn, positions should be terminated. The subject, the doer, the "I" is gone. Truman may have been the last president to use the "I" responsibly. The only I-messages I can recall from recent presidents were either denials of responsibility or lies: Nixon's "I am not a crook"; Carter's "I will never lie to you."

I like "I" and have decided to use it. "I" is the place where every story 10 begins, every energy flows, every character emerges, every self achieves definition. "I" is autonomous. Maybe the people of this century are waiting for someone brave enough to speak, write and act in the first person and to take responsibility for those words and actions. If "I" is the center of sin, as some English teachers claim, then some of our greatest spiritual leaders were sinful. Example: I am the way, the truth and the life.

Questions to Start You Thinking

1. What impression of Suzanne Britt do you get from reading her essay? Would you call her an objective, detached, unemotional writer, or what? In your answer, draw evidence from her choice of words.

2. How does Britt show her awareness of people with different views, those who feel reluctant to use the first person?

3. Have any of your teachers encouraged or discouraged you to write in the first person? What is your opinion of first-person writing now that you have read Britt?

4. Where in her essay does Britt go beyond the realm of writing for her examples? Why do you suppose she does?

5.   What counterarguments to Britt's claim can you raise? Can you think of any writing
     situations in which this writer's insistence on the first person *I* might be bad advice?

     The pressure that many contemporary American women feel to live up to
the impossible standards of beauty extolled on television and in popular magazines is probably familiar to you. In the following essay, Susan C. Torres, a
student writer, offers some commonsense advice to women who want to fight
back.

SUPERWOMAN: AMERICA'S MYTHICAL HEROINE
SUSAN C. TORRES

     Toilet bowls and long enameled fingernails are not compatible, nor   1
are designer clothes and teething infants, but the media would have American women believe that they are. We American women are constantly
bombarded by the media with tips on how to be better wives, lovers, and
mothers and how to maintain showcase homes and prepare gourmet meals
while juggling careers and rearing children, but the media does not stop
there. We are led to believe that no matter how well we manage to fulfill
all these roles placed on us by our society, we can't be considered really
successful unless we are shapely, sexy, and beautiful to boot.
     Soap operas are great at portraying mythical superwomen who have it   2
all and do it all. In a typical scene, we find the heroine—beautiful, slender,
impeccably groomed and attired—lounging around her spotless and taste-
fully decorated home, gossiping with another superwoman. To look at her,
no one would guess she is a wife, mother, grandmother, career woman,
volunteer fire fighter, ex-nun, and alcoholic. We never see her children
clinging to her ankles, snagging her nylons, drooling on her silk dresses,
or drawing on her walls. We never see the sink full of dirty dishes, mud
tracks across the carpet, or toys strategically placed on the stairs so as to
do the most damage to an unsuspecting passer-by. We never see a lot of
the things that haunt real women in real life.
     Obviously, our heroine is not portraying a real housewife or mother,   3
or else her children are bound and gagged in a closet somewhere to be
displayed only on limited occasions. Yet, instead of laughing at this soap
opera invention, too many women believe in her and try to emulate her,
and when we fail to be perfect in fulfilling all these roles, we blame ourselves and feel like failures. The modern woman has enough trouble trying
to efficiently and effectively juggle her new career with the traditional roles
of matrimony, motherhood, and homemaking. She does not need any more
pressure or stress in her life, but instead of lessening her burden our society
expects her to find the time to live up to standards of beauty that are
unnatural and unrealistic and that can be detrimental to her overall health
and well-being.
     America's idea of a beautiful woman is unnatural. A popular beauty   4
image for American women is "the natural look." If a woman wishes to

acquire and maintain this "natural look," she should expect to spend several hundred dollars a year; she must set aside a separate room in her home to hold all the bottles, brushes, sponges, tubes, and miscellaneous other paraphernalia she will need; and she must devote a couple of hours a day every day for the rest of her life to its application, upkeep, and removal. Frankly, I would rather have a dog. I know a lot of women who feel naked without their makeup. In the daily rush, they may forget their keys, they may forget their purses, they may even forget to pick up their children from school, but they would never forget their beauty parlor appointments or their makeup kits. So what began as a way to enhance a woman's natural beauty has turned into a million-dollar industry and has left the American public with a distorted image of what natural feminine beauty is.

It is unrealistic to expect women to have figures that are so foreign to 5 the average female anatomy that maintenance takes hours of daily exercise, self-starvation, and masochism. I remember watching the *Mike Douglas Show* when he had several models as guests. I recall one model, in particular, because her appearance actually startled me. Dressed in tight jeans and a shirt, she appeared so thin as to have no discernible hips or bust. I thought she looked like a well-dressed skeleton with a pretty face. I could not believe that she could actually be a top model. I had never seen such a thin woman, yet this was what the fashion industry was parading before the public as an example of what fashion-conscious women everywhere should want to look like. Of course, Mike Douglas, who always raves about everything anyway, just raved about what a marvelous figure she had and wanted her to tell America how she managed to stay so wonderfully fit and trim. I was not startled by her answer. What she admitted to was lots and lots of strenuous exercise and basic starvation (carrot sticks, melba toast, an occasional banana, and lots of water). The fashion industry's choice of models, the model's excessive thinness, and Mr. Douglas's attitude can be summed up in the popular phrase "There is no such thing as being too thin."

Some people think that there is a correlation between the women's 6 movement and a growing subconscious desire to appear more physically manlike. Curves, a major distinguishing feature of the female anatomy, become less noticeable as a woman becomes thinner. I like actor Tony Randall's theory better, though. He thinks plump women went out of style when central heating came in. Men no longer need to cuddle up to something soft and warm to thaw them out after a frozen day on the job. Whatever the reason, for a lot of women this new ultrathin look means a constant battle against Mother Nature. In comparison to men, women have a higher percentage of body fat, tend to gain weight more easily and metabolize fat more slowly, and are blessed with things called hips. The problem is, unlike miniskirts and other seasonal attire that the fashion industry periodically trashes and then reestablishes, hips cannot be hung in the back of the closet to await their eventual return to style. Hips are like a Catholic marriage made in heaven—until death do you part. In fact, hips have a tendency to continue growing long after the rest of a woman's body has stopped. Diet, exercise, and prayer prove helpful in containing the ever-expanding molecules to a certain extent, but a lot depends on the individual woman's natural tendency toward curves.

So, superwomen that we are, we adopt an exercise regimen similar to   7
that of an Olympic hopeful, and as the sweat drips down our brow and our muscles scream for us to stop, we tell ourselves over and over again, "This feels good; this is fun," until eventually we really begin to believe it. After this type of torture session we ultimately end up in the kitchen for a little more torture. As the traditional food preparers, we women spend half of our lives in the kitchen surrounded by our number-one enemy—food. We have to look at it, touch it, smell it, serve it, watch others eat it, and not eat any of it ourselves. We really are gluttons for punishment.

Too many women are preoccupied with being thin. We are constantly   8
worried about what we can eat, what we cannot eat, and what we did eat. We feel guiltier about having a piece of chocolate cake than about telling a lie or stealing money from our husbands' wallets. We are always on a diet of some sort, or we feel guilty about not being on one. Doctors continually warn us that rapid weight loss and prolonged dieting deplete our body's supply of essential vitamins, minerals, and fluids. These same doctors tell us that we are better off maintaining one weight even if that weight is a heavier weight than we desire, instead of losing, regaining, and relosing it over and over again. But we ignore these warnings and try diet after diet, and our weight goes up and down like a yo-yo. Our closets are evidence of this yo-yo syndrome—left side for slim clothes and right side for fat clothes.

Our mental health suffers along with our physical health. When the   9
way we look becomes the most important thing about us, our self-confidence and basic sense of worth as human beings suffer. When we are unable to look the way we think we should, we become unhappy, anxious, and depressed. Some women even develop serious eating disorders such as bulimia and anorexia nervosa, both of which stem from preoccupation with food and obsession with controlling fat. We need to change our attitude or our physical and mental health will continue to suffer.

Exercise, watching our diet, and being attractive are healthy and desir-   10
able activities when we keep them in proper perspective. They should not be the major focus of our existence, though, as they seem to be for so many of us today. This is by no means a modern problem. Throughout history, women have tried to improve upon nature in an attempt to appear more attractive to the opposite sex. One hundred years ago, we were in corsets because we were convinced that men were attracted only to women who had exceptionally small waists. So we cinched ourselves in at the waist to the point of great discomfort, cutting off our circulation and very nearly our air supply as well, and all for vanity's sake. We laugh at this today and think that we would never go to such extremes, but actually we are not much beyond this behavior. Remember, one hundred years ago our corseted sisters would have considered a modern woman with her makeup a "painted" lady not fit for civilized society.

We are supposed to be fairly well educated now, and we have already   11
successfully managed to shed a lot of the traditional shackles placed on us as females. It is time we got rid of this one additional shackle, too. We need

to develop a healthier image of ourselves as women and a more natural and realistic approach to beauty. After all, we are not superbeings, and we have too many demands already on our precious time.

Questions to Start You Thinking

1. In a sentence, sum up Susan Torres's claim. Of the evidence this writer musters to support this view, what do you find most persuasive?

2. What remedies does Torres recommend for the uncomfortable dilemma faced by modern American women? Can you suggest a few additional ones she doesn't include?

3. After browsing through magazines and newspapers and doing a little brainstorming, what other problems in need of solutions seem to you and your classmates worth pursuing?

LEARNING BY WRITING

The Assignment

Converse with other students, in class discussion or outside of class, about a topic on which there is wide disagreement. This topic might be a controversial matter: is some attitude or policy desirable and right, reprehensible and wrong? (Is it right, for instance, that public clinics in some cities supply teenagers with contraceptives without the knowledge of their parents?) The topic might be something to attack or defend (such as the use of nuclear energy as a power source); it might be something to evaluate as excellent and admirable, good, mediocre, bad, terrible (such as a recent film).

After you have this conversation, write a paper in which you introduce your topic and sum up the view you have heard that seems farthest from your own. Show what attitudes and assumptions underlie this view. Consider anything in it that you are willing to accept as true or possibly true.

Then set forth your own view, showing where and why you differ with the other person or persons. Support your view with evidence.

Write for a reader or readers you know personally: the person or persons with whose view you disagree (not addressing them directly, of course). Your purpose in writing is to try to convert others to your view. You're trying to understand another view, show why you do not agree with it, and then set forth your own view honestly and clearly, together with your reasons for holding it.

Recently we have read good persuasive papers written by students at several colleges. Here are brief summaries of a few of them.

> A professional dancer, countering the view that "belly dancing" (a term she considers an unfortunate misnomer) is immoral, overtly sexual, and exploitive of women, wrote a serious defense of the art of Middle Eastern dance.
>
> A man, deploring the emotionalism that erupts after every assassination attempt on the life of a public figure, argued against gun control by

challenging some of the assumptions and statistics put forth by gun control advocates and by pointing out that many more people are killed by drunken drivers than by guns. He concluded that what is needed is not gun control but crime control.

A man, citing history and Christian doctrine, outlined his reasons for preferring to keep prayer out of public school classrooms.

A woman challenged the taste of the movie critics who praised *My Beautiful Laundrette* as high art and panned *Pee-Wee's Big Adventure*, a film that she claimed was more worthwhile.

A woman argued that to give federal aid to private and parochial schools would destroy public education in America.

A woman attacked her history textbook's account of the burning of Joan of Arc because the textbook author had characterized St. Joan as "an ignorant farm girl subject to religious hysteria."

Generating Ideas

This assignment begins in conversation. As you take part in the discussion of a controversial topic, take notes on any ideas you hear that startle you, arouse you, or enlighten you. Ask questions of anyone whose view intrigues you (whether or not you agree with it). Why does he or she hold this view? What beliefs underlie it? What is the person's ethnic or religious background? Is it likely that early environment or training naturally shaped his or her attitudes?

To change anyone's mind, it helps to understand the mind you are trying to change. Perhaps you will find that your view and the other person's view overlap in some places. You might be arguing with a member of a religious group to whom blood transfusions are wrong. In your view (let's say) when a person needs blood, a transfusion is desirable. Is a view so different from your own always false, or can you think of times and places when it might indeed be true—when, say, a blood transfusion might be foolish and undesirable? You might recall a doctor saying that some blood transfusions are unnecessary, that transfusions should be given only in extreme emergency. You might have read an article in a newspaper pointing out that in accepting blood a person risks accepting the diseases of its unknown donors. But don't pretend to side with anybody's view that you don't side with. In this case, you might agree that blood transfusions are sometimes wrong while sticking up for your view that in some cases they are desirable.

If you and the other person agree on *anything*, then you have a territory of agreement that you can work on enlarging. And at least you diminish hostility and mistrust, show your friendly antagonist that you are honestly trying to understand, perhaps open the way to a dialogue that will cause that other person if not to agree with you, at least to understand your position and take a friendly step nearer to it.

As you think over the conversation you have had, continuing to try to understand the other person's beliefs and feelings, you can even try to imagine yourself in that person's place. If you do so, you will probably think of more ideas—good points to make, objections to recognize and answer—than if you had thought only about your own view.

When you're done conversing, sift through your thoughts and recollections of your talk with people and any notes you may have jotted down. Your own view will probably have started taking shape. It will help you focus your argument if you state that view in a sentence: a thesis statement, a statement of your claim. Write it out and look it over. Here are some characteristics of a good, workable claim.

It is small enough to argue in the time and space you have. A broad statement such as "America's space program has been a success" (or "a qualified success") might be a fit topic for a book or a long research paper, but you couldn't expect to deal with it adequately in only a week. To argue it convincingly would call for too much evidence. A more manageable claim might be "The space program has had the valuable effect of encouraging the development of new lightweight foods."

It states only one view. "Drunken driving is dangerous" would be a clear statement of a single claim. But the following is a confused and two-headed claim-statement: "Driving while drunk is dangerous and reprehensible, but drinking on the job may be all right under certain circumstances—in fact, I am rather in favor of a beer with lunch on a hard day."

It should be clear to both you and your reader. There shouldn't be more than one way to interpret your claim. The statement "*Children of a Lesser God* is a very unusual film" does not make unmistakably clear whether the writer thinks the movie good or bad. Choose words that clearly imply an opinion: call the movie "a film I admire" or "the best film of its year." (For more advice about drafting a claim-statement, see "Stating a Thesis," p. 469.)

When you have your claim stated, you'll need evidence to support it. This matter is crucial, so let's take time right now to examine it.

Supplying evidence. The largest part of arguing is giving evidence; to supply it may take up most of your paper. What is evidence? Anything that demonstrates the truth of your claim: facts and figures, expert opinions, illustrations and examples, reported experience. Obviously, if you aren't writing a term paper on which you can spend months, you're limited in the amount of evidence you can collect by the amount of time you have. It will be a great help to you in collecting evidence if you can begin by stating your claim. Make it narrow enough to support in the time available. For a paper due a week from now, "The city's waterfront has become a stodgy, run-down disgrace" can probably be supported in part by your own observations. But to support the claim "The welfare program in this country has become a disgrace" would take much digging, perhaps the work of years.

At this point, we won't discuss those tremendous sources of evidence you can obtain by *deeply* exploring a library or by doing field research: actual legwork and first-hand reporting to find evidence that no one has published before. Those more ambitious tasks require more time. Surely they will concern you when you are writing a research paper, and we discuss them in detail in Part Five, "Investigating." For now, let's consider how you find evidence nearby. Let's see how you select what will be trustworthy and useful to you in supporting your claim. Evidence may be classified in the following categories.

1. *Facts.* Facts are statements that can be verified by objective means, such as going and looking. In actual life, of course, we take many of our facts from the testimony of other people. We can't possibly verify for ourselves every fact we accept. We may believe that the Great Wall of China exists, though we have never beheld it with our own eyes; and unless we have used a high-power microscope, we may accept the existence of bacteria though we may never have seen any. A fact is usually stated in an impersonal way: "Algonquin Indians still live in Old Orchard Beach"; "If you pump all the air out of a five-gallon varnish can, it will collapse." To convince your reader, a fact doesn't need to set a Guinness world record. Sometimes a small fact casts a piercing light. Claiming that the practice of strip-mining in his hometown had proved injurious to the environment, one student recalled taking a walk through local hills before a mining operation had moved in and being almost deafened by a din of birdcalls. The paper ended with a quiet statement of fact: "Yesterday, on that same walk, I heard no birds at all."

2. *Statistics.* Another valuable kind of evidence, statistics are facts expressed in numbers, gathered in answer to a question. What are the odds that you will be a murder victim? According to statistics compiled by the FBI in 1984, 1 in 100 if you are an American man, 1 in 323 if you are an American woman. (A student cited that statistic in an essay arguing that strict handgun control laws are desirable.) Most of us find numbers extremely convincing; that is why advertisers batter us with statistics: "Nine out of ten dentists recommend Periogel." Census takers ask questions of us; then the Bureau of the Census compiles the results, producing a remarkable profile of the nation's people, their characteristics, and the conditions of their lives. As you take notes, collect any promising statistics to use when you write. One student, who disputed the charge that his small college was a "party school," supplied a statistic to convince readers that it was a serious place: "Last Saturday evening, 115 students checked 284 books out of the library."

Most writers, without trying to be dishonest, interpret statistics to help their causes. The statement "Fifty percent of the populace have incomes above the poverty level" might be used to back the claim that the government of an African nation is doing a fine job of encouraging the economy. Putting the statement another way, "Fifty percent of the populace have incomes below the poverty level" might use the same statistic to show that the government's efforts are pitifully inadequate. A writer, of course, is free to interpret a statistic; and it is only human to try to present a case in a favorable light. But statistics should not be deliberately used to mislead. On the wrapper of a peanut bar, we read that one one-ounce serving contains only 150 calories and 70 milligrams of sodium. The claim is true, but the bar weighs 1.6 ounces. Eat the whole thing, as you are more likely to do than serving yourself exactly 62½ percent of it, and you'll ingest 240 calories and 112 milligrams of sodium—a heftier amount than the innocent statistic on the wrapper leads you to believe.

Such abuses make some readers automatically distrust statistics. To win your reader's confidence when you use figures, use them fairly, and make sure they are accurate. If you seriously doubt a statistic—or a fact—why not check it out? Compare it with facts and statistics reported by several other sources. A report that differs from every other report may well be true, but distrust it unless it is backed by further, incontrovertible evidence.

3. *The testimony of experts.* By *experts*, we mean people with knowledge of a particular field gained from study and experience. The test of an expert is whether his or her expertise stands up to the scrutiny of others knowledgeable in that field. Credentials, like college degrees, may indicate expertise, but usually a person's expertise is demonstrated by setting up a professional practice, publishing findings, giving public lectures, or in some other way subjecting his or her expertise to the scrutiny of the world. An essay by basketball player Akeem Olajuwon explaining how to play offense or by economist John Kenneth Galbraith setting forth the causes of inflation carries authority. Experts supply us not only with information but also with their opinions—these, too, may be admitted as evidence. If an opinion is couched in highly charged, emotional language ("City hall is a slime pit of corruption"), it is probably less trustworthy than if it is stated objectively ("City hall needs a thorough review of its executives' qualifications to hold office").

Does a self-alleged expert have any bias that would affect his or her reliability? Statistics on cases of lung cancer attributed to smoking might better be taken from government sources than from a representative for the tobacco industry. An advertisement for a new car might contain useful information about its horsepower, gas mileage, and trunk space, but even more useful (and probably more complete) would be information on the same car when it is evaluated in *Consumer Reports.*

The best way to know whether someone is a highly regarded expert is to ask others familiar with his or her field. Experts may disagree, but in general they treat one another with respect when respect is merited. For nearby experts who know the literature in their disciplines, consult professors at your college. Virtually all professors keep office hours, and most are glad to talk with you even though you may not be enrolled in any of their courses. Remember, too, another nearby source of expert testimony: any lecture notes you may have taken in classes.

4. *Memory and observation.* Obviously, first-hand experience and observation are persuasive. They add life to any paper. Often they will be more persuasive than many facts taken from reference books or tables of figures. As readers, most of us tend to trust, perhaps excessively, any writer who declares, "I was there. This is what I saw."

Although we urge you to draw evidence from your own experience and observation, here is one word of warning. Few writers have had enough personal experience or have done enough observing to support an extremely large claim. A writer might write, for instance, about the New England town meeting, in which citizens assemble to discuss matters of business and vote on them. If the writer were to advance the view that the town meeting is superior to any other form of local government, basing the claim only on having attended town meetings in Wellesley, Massachusetts, the argument would rest on insufficient foundation. To back such a claim, the writer would need to study other systems: the system of appointing a city manager, systems of electing representatives. But to do so would take much reading, perhaps more travel. When you can't assemble enough data to support a claim, your best resort is to pare down the claim: "I admire the town meeting form of government."

For this assignment, we assume you can find your evidence nearby—perhaps in the back of your mind or in the experience of a teacher or friend, perhaps in your observations of campus life or in a single visit to your library. If you'd like any questions to stimulate your search for evidence, try these.

DISCOVERY CHECKLIST: TAPPING RESOURCES

- What do you already know about this topic? What convinces *you* of the truth of your claim?
- What testimony can you provide from your own first-hand experience?
- What have you observed, or what might you observe, that would probably support your argument?
- What have you read about this topic? What else might you read? For a start, consult the card catalogue of your library and the *Readers' Guide to Periodical Literature* (discussed on pp. 340 and 349).
- What expert might you talk with?
- What illustrations and examples to back up your claim can you imagine? (Don't claim that these are facts, of course!)
- Try to imagine yourself as your reader—what further evidence might persuade you?

For this assignment, you can expect to write a relatively short paper and complete it within a week. You assemble a mass of evidence in written form. You take notes, in a notebook or on large, 4-by-6-inch or 5-by-7-inch index cards. (Cards have the advantage of being shufflable, easily arranged in an order for writing a draft.) Perhaps if you have found items in newspapers, magazines, and books, you'll have clippings or photocopies. Spread all this stuff out on a table and choose the evidence that best supports your claim. You'll need to decide which of it may be trusted, which of it may be really useful to your paper. Let's see in detail how you decide.

Testing evidence. When is evidence useful and trustworthy? When—

It is accurate. A writer assumes all responsibility for verifying facts and figures. Statistics from ten-year-old encyclopedias, such as population figures, are probably out of date. Take facts from latest sources and, especially when writing a paper in the sciences or social sciences, from latest research.

It is reliable. To decide whether you can trust it, you'll need to evaluate its source, as we have detailed. Whenever possible, do some reading. Compare information given in one source with information given in another. A *primary source* usually is more reliable than a *secondary source.* The very person who said something is a primary source; the reporter or writer who later summed up what the person said is a secondary source. Use primary sources whenever possible. In demonstrating that, more than a century ago, Frederick Douglass was a farsighted spokesman for the rights of black people, it is better to quote Douglass's very words than those of a later biographer who interprets them.

It is to the point. It backs the exact claim you're making in your paper. This point may seem too obvious to deserve mention, but you'd be surprised how many writers get hung up on an interesting fact or opinion that has nothing to do with what they're trying to demonstrate. Not long ago we read an argument on the need for greater public awareness of the dangers of recreational drugs. The article got sidetracked in an attack on the government of a South American country that supplies U.S. dealers with cocaine and cited various published opinions as evidence. The writer was trying to write two arguments at once, and they didn't blend. Sometimes a writer will leap from evidence to conclusion without reason, and the result is a *non sequitur* (Latin for "it does not follow"): "Benito Mussolini made the trains run on time. He was one of the world's leading statesmen." The evidence about trains doesn't support a judgment on Mussolini's statesmanship. (For more about errors in reasoning, see pp. 280–282.) If your evidence contradicts or belies your claim, your claim shouldn't be made.

It is truly representative. Any examples you select should be typical of all the things included in your claim. If you claim that, in general, students on your campus are well informed about their legal rights, don't talk just to prelaw majors, talk to an English major, an engineering major, a biology major, and others. Probably most writers, in the heat of persuading, can't help unconsciously stacking the evidence in their own favor. The writer who claims that "the films of George Lucas are successful both commercially and artistically" might skip hastily over *Howard the Duck.* But the best writers don't deliberately suppress evidence to the contrary. The writer for an airline magazine who tried to sell package tours to India by declaring, "India is an attractive land of sumptuous wealth and splendor," might give for evidence the Taj Mahal and a luxury hotel while ignoring the slums of Bombay and Calcutta. The result might be effective advertising, but hardly a full and faithful view.

It is sufficient and strong enough to back the claim. How much evidence you use depends on the size of your claim. Evidently, it will take less evidence to claim that a downtown park needs better maintenance than to claim that the Department of the Interior needs reorganizing. Find evidence solid enough to support your claim; if need be, you can always make your claim smaller. How much evidence you need may depend, too, on how much your reader already knows. A group of readers, all from Washington, D.C. and vicinity, will not need much evidence to be persuaded that the city's modern Metro Transit System is admirable in its efficiency, but more evidence may be needed to convince readers who don't know Washington. When lining up your evidence, it is generally a good idea to think of the reader you're trying to persuade.

Some writers fall into the error of *oversimplification*, supplying a too-easy explanation for a phenomenon that may be vast and complicated: "Of course our economy is in trouble. People aren't buying American-made cars." Both statements may be true, but the second seems insufficient to account for the first: there is obviously much more to the economy than cars alone. More information is called for. A paper that supplies too much evidence has a problem that's easy to cure: by a few snips of a scissors or cutting strokes of a pen. In a writing course, such a paper is a rarity, and most writing instructors will be happy to meet one. Much more common is the paper whose claims rest on scanty evidence. Whenever in doubt that you've given enough evidence to convince your readers, you are probably well advised to come up with more.

Not that mere quantity is enough. One piece of vivid and significant evidence—such as the first-hand testimony of an expert, given in that person's memorable words—may be more persuasive than a foot-high stack of statistics. Three pieces of vivid and significant evidence would be stronger still. In evaluating your evidence, you can ask yourself a few questions.

DISCOVERY CHECKLIST: TESTING EVIDENCE

- Does your evidence lead to the claim you want to make? (If it all leads you to a different opinion, then you'll want to revise your claim.)
- If you are writing about some current situation, is your evidence—especially any statistical information—up to date?
- Are facts and figures accurate? If you doubt a piece of information, try to check it against published sources. See reports by others, facts given in works of reference.
- If an important point rests on your quoting an opinion or citing information you receive from an expert, do you know that the person is respected in his or her field?
- Is your evidence complete? Does it at least reflect the full range of your topic? If it leads to a general claim ("Nursing homes in this city are firetraps"), does the general statement rest on a large and convincing number of examples?
- Do you have enough evidence to persuade a reader? (Talk with fellow students, show them your evidence.)
- If you were to read an argument based on this evidence, would you be convinced? Imagine your paper all written and yourself in a reader's place.

Shaping a Draft

Once you have looked over your written evidence and sifted out the useful part, you will probably find it falling into some shape. Notes, if you have taken them on cards, can be grouped into the order you'll follow in writing your draft.

Having written your statement of your claim, keep writing. Summarize your reasons for holding this view. List the supporting evidence. You will find this writing growing into an argument. The result may even be a short but shapely condensed version of the essay you plan to write. (For a three-part model of such a condensed version, see p. 279.)

If you prefer, instead of a condensed version, you might make an informal outline. (For methods, see p. 476.) Your claim—your statement of your view—will most likely come early in the paper. Then you might give your evidence and any further reasons for holding your view. At the end of your paper, you will probably want to restate your claim firmly.

As you start to write your draft, make clear any questionable terms used in your claim. If your claim reads, "Humanists are dangerous" or "Humanists are admirable," you had better give a short definition of *humanists* early on. Your terms need to be clear, to you and to your reader, for they help determine the course of your argument. "At the very start," says Kenneth Burke, "one's terms leap to conclusions."

Our assignment, remember, asks you to sum up someone else's view. The most persuasive thing you can do is to be honest and fair in that summary. If you trumpet your opinions loudly, in a tone of absolute authority that will stand for no dissent, or if you call names, you risk alienating your readers—driving them into a corner, prepared to fight back. This is certainly a risk that Suzanne Britt runs in her essay championing the first-person *I:* she calls an admonition against the pronoun "absurd" and "foolish." If her essay persuades, it does so by stating an opinion with vigor and humor and by enlisting our agreement in friendly fashion. A writer who thunders at us (as Britt doesn't) tempts us to defy him or her and rebel: "All intelligent readers will agree that Mick Jagger is surely the greatest rock singer of our century." (For another view of this matter, see "A Writer's Tone," p. 505.)

Just as you want to make clear your friendly antagonist's reason for holding a certain view, you have to make clear your own. Why do *you* believe what you do? Are there any beliefs and assumptions you grew up on, or learned in school, or thought out for yourself? Write them out and see where they might usefully fit in.

As you write, make your sources of evidence clear. If an expert whom you quote has outstanding credentials, you may easily be able to put in a brief citation of those credentials: "Lewis Thomas, chancellor of the Memorial Sloan-Kettering Cancer Center," "Michael Scammell, author of the award-winning biography *Solzhenitsyn*." If you have personally talked to your experts and are convinced of their authority, state why you believe your experts know their onions. "From conversation with Mr. Dworshak, who showed me six model wind tunnels he has built, I can testify to his extensive knowledge of aeronautics." In the opening sentence of "The First Person," Suzanne Britt refers to a convincing authority: a college freshman.

In supplying evidence, form the habit of citing exact numbers whenever you can. To report that a condition holds true "in thirty-four cases out of fifty" is more convincing than to say "in many cases." At least it shows that you haven't taken a mere woolly-eyed gawp at a scene but have taken the trouble to count.

Rewriting

You should now have before you a rough draft of an assignment in two parts: (1) a summary of another's view and (2) a statement of your own view with evidence supporting it.

Does writing a persuasive paper seem harder than some earlier assignments? Most people find that it is. This assignment is a particularly tough one for anyone accustomed to thinking of a *different* view as an *opposing* view. As we've been trying to suggest, a view not your own can do you friendly service: it can help you in generating ideas and evidence and in improving the accuracy of your own view.

If you feel the need for special help with this assignment, find out whether your college has a writing laboratory or a tutoring facility where peers help peers. You may be able to call on it for help in criticizing your draft. If your college doesn't have such a thing, enlist a couple of other students to read your draft critically and tell you whether they accept your argument. If there are moments in your paper when your readers feel doubtful, ask them to spell out why. (For more suggestions along these lines, glance back at Chapter 3.)

Speaking of peer editors, be sure to show your friendly antagonist your summary of his or her view. Ask if you've got it right. Revise as necessary.

A temptation, when you're writing a paper like this, is to fall in love with the evidence you have gone to such trouble to collect. Some of it won't help your case; some may just seem boring and likely to persuade nobody. If so, give it a pitch. Sometimes you can have too much evidence, and if you throw some out, a stronger argument will remain. Sometimes you can become so attached to old evidence that, when new evidence or new thoughts come along, you won't want to discard what you have on hand. But in writing an argument, as in any other writing, second thoughts, especially the ones that come from the careful gathering of ideas and information, often surpass the thoughts that come at first. Be willing to revise not only your words but your original view.

In writing an early draft of "Superwoman: America's Mythical Heroine," Susan Torres had later thoughts she wanted to add. To do so, she used a common and convenient technique: she wrote them out on separate sheets, then indicated in her draft (by writing in a margin INSERT #1, INSERT #2, ...) exactly where they should go. Then, when she wrote her final draft, she was able to insert the new material with ease.

When you're taking a last look over your paper, proofread with care. Wherever you have given facts and figures as evidence, check for errors in names and numbers. This advice may seem trivial, but between "10,000 people" and "100,000 people" there's a considerable difference. To refer to Sigmund Frued or Alvin Einstein won't persuade a reader that you know what you're talking about.

As you rewrite, here are some points to consider.

REVISION CHECKLIST: ADVANCING A VIEW

- Does your view convince you? Or do you think you need still more evidence?
- Have you fairly and accurately summed up your reader's different point of view? Have you asked your prospective reader to look at your summary?
- In the later part of your paper, have you tried to keep your readers and what would appeal to them in mind?
- Might the points in your argument seem stronger if arranged in a different sequence?
- Have you unfairly omitted any evidence that would hurt your case? If so, you might make your paper more persuasive if you acknowledge it.
- In rereading your paper, do any excellent, fresh thoughts occur to you? If so, be willing to shove aside what you have written and make room for them.

Other Assignments

1. Write a letter to the editor of your local newspaper or of a national news magazine (*Time, Newsweek, U.S. News & World Report*) in which you disagree with the publication's editorial stance on a current issue, with a new development in local, national or international affairs, or with the recent words or actions of some public figure. Be sure to make clear your reasons for dissenting and for holding a different view.

2. Write a paragraph or two in which you agree or disagree with one of the following suggestions—or some other you have lately read that interests you. You need not propose an alternative action; just give your opinion of the suggestion.

    Creationism and evolution should be given equal importance in high school science courses.
    Public television should be allowed to die a natural death.
    To protect certain endangered species of ocean fish, fish rationing should be imposed on consumers.
    The United States should invade Cuba.

3. Write a short paper in which you express your view on one of the following topics or another that comes to mind. Make clear your reasons for believing as you do.

    Bilingual education
    Smokers' rights
    The Miss America contest
    Chemical castration for rapists
    The fitness movement
    The minimum wage
    Mandatory drug testing for athletes

4. Write a short comment in which you agree or disagree with the following quotation from Gilbert and Sullivan's musical comedy *Ruddigore*. Use examples and evidence to support your view.

    > If you wish in this world to advance
    > Your merits you're bound to enhance;
    >   You must stir it and stump it,
    >   And blow your own trumpet,
    > Or, trust me, you haven't a chance.

5. Writing in *Weekly World News*, columnist Ed Anger headlines his claim "Junk Food Made Our Country Great." After all, he reasons, American heroes have grown up on hamburgers, french fries, potato chips, beer, Twinkies, Snickers, and Coke. "You never saw The Duke [John Wayne] strolling around munching a pita bread sandwich stuffed with alfalfa sprouts."

    > Ever see one of those parsley puffs punching a herd of cattle, operating an endloader, putting up a roof, or doing some other kind of he-man's work? Every one of them is skinny, beady-eyed, and yellow-skinned. You call that healthy? I call it sick. If all Americans looked as washed-out and wimpy as those broccoli Bruces, the Ruskies would be dropping down on us and taking over right now.

    And he concludes:

    > If American foods are so bad, how come all those foreign countries are building McDonald's and Burger Kings in their countries? Because they want their people to get tough and smart too—by eating like Americans.

    Write a paragraph or two in reply to Ed Anger, discovering evidence for your own view, whatever it may be. If you care to dissent with Anger and analyze his remarks, the catalogue of logical fallacies on page 280 may be of help to you.

APPLYING WHAT YOU LEARN:
SOME USES OF ADVANCING A VIEW

As you may have found out by now, college is a place where you are often called on to voice your opinions—and sometimes to put them in writing. Not only paper assignments but also college examination questions sometimes ask you to demonstrate your opinion on a controversial or disputed matter:

> Criticize the statement "There's too much science and not enough caring in the modern practice of medicine."
> Respond to the view that "there's no need to be concerned about carbon dioxide heating up the earth's atmosphere because a warmer climate, by increasing farm production, would be preferable to the one we have now."

Your answers to such questions can indicate clearly to your instructor how firm a grasp you have on the material.

In your daily life, too, you'll sometimes feel the need to advance a view in writing. You never know when you'll be called on to represent your fellow tenants by writing a letter of protest to a landlord who wants to raise your rent or when you'll feel moved to write to a store manager complaining about the treatment you received. As an active citizen, you'll surely wish from time to time to write a letter to the editor of your local newspaper or of a national news magazine. At times you may want to write to those who represent you in Congress and in the presidency, making clear your view about some course of action they have taken.

When you enter the working world, you'll find great importance attached to knowing how to present your views clearly in writing. Newspaper editors are called on every day to state on the editorial page their opinions about the day's news events. Lawyers prepare countless briefs before arguing their cases in court. Business executives regularly put into writing their reactions to new ideas for products, new financial ventures, new office procedures, evaluations of their employees. There is hardly a professional position in which you won't be invited from time to time to state and support your views about some important matter, often for the benefit of others in your profession. Here is a sample of such writing, in which Mary Anne Raywid, in the *Journal of Teacher Education* (Sept.–Oct. 1978) defends professors of education against the constant charge that they use jargon when ordinary English would do:

> This is not to deny that educators speak a language of their own. Indeed they do; and it is very much a part of their specialized knowledge. These words become a way first to select out certain qualities, events, and phenomena for attention; and they expedite communication via shorthand references to particular combinations of these. To cite a familiar example, when an educationist talks about a *meaningful learning experience*, s/he is not just spouting jargon, but distinguishing out of all the events and phenomena of a given time and place, a particular set. Moreover, a substantial list of things is being asserted about what is going on—e.g., the words *learning experience* suggest that it is, or it is meant to be, an episode from which learning results. The term *meaningful* is not superfluous but does a specific job: it adds that it is likely to be or was (depending on temporal perspective) a successful exercise in learning—which not all learning experiences proffered by teachers can claim. To qualify as *meaningful* in advance—in other words, well calculated to succeed—a number of conditions must be met, ordinarily including learner comprehension, interest, motivation, capacity, and likely retention.
>
> If it sounds like an awkward list to summarize and transmit, that is exactly why a term was brought into service to do so. Voilà—*meaningful learning experience*. Thus, when educationists invoke the term, it is not merely jargon or vacuous talk, but a quick way to communicate some information of particular professional concern to them.

Scientists who do original research face the task of persuading the scientific community that their findings are valid. Routinely, they write and publish accounts of their work in scientific journals for evaluation by their peers. In such articles they not only report new facts, they often state opinions. Some scientists and medical people, to be sure, write not only for their professional peers but for us general readers. Here, for instance, is Gerald Weissmann, in an essay called "Foucault and the Bag Lady," airing his views on the recent trend to deinstitutionalize the mentally ill:

> Motivated by the observation that the overt aberrancy of the badly disturbed can be managed by the wonders of psychopharmacology, our asylums have evolved over the past decades into homes of only temporary detainment. The therapeutic rescue fantasy—as current in Paris as in Glasgow, in London as in Albany—has been joined to the concept that the diagnostically insane will be more humanely treated, or achieve greater personal integration, if they are permitted freely to mix with the "community."
>
> It has always seemed to me to constitute a fantastic notion that the social landscape of our large cities bears any direct relationship to that kind of stable, nurturing community which would support the fragile psyche of the mentally ill. Cast into an environment limited by the welfare hotel or park bench, lacking adequate outpatient services, prey to climatic extremes and urban criminals, the deinstitutionalized patients wind up as conscripts in an army of the homeless. Indeed, only this winter was the city of New York forced to open temporary shelters in church basements, armories, and lodging houses for thousands of half-frozen street dwellers. A psychiatrist of my acquaintance has summarized the experience of a generation in treating the mentally deranged: "In the nineteen-fifties, the mad people were warehoused in heated public hospitals with occasional access to trained professionals. In the sixties and seventies, they were released into the community and permitted to wander the streets without access to psychiatric care. In the eighties, we have made progress, however. When the mentally ill become too cold to wander the streets, we can warehouse them in heated church basements without supervision."

Weissmann's statement is a good illustration of a specialist writing for the rest of us—and reasoning with feeling.

CHAPTER 15

Arguing for an Action: The Proposal

Sometimes, in reading a newspaper or watching a newscast, learning of a problem such as acid rain or nuclear fallout, seeing about the plight of abandoned pets or the still more appalling plight of famine victims, you say to yourself, "Something should be done about that." This chapter will show you one way to do something about it yourself: by the powerful and persuasive activity of writing.

Writing, as political leaders and advertisers well know, can rouse people to action. Thomas Jefferson and his cohorts who wrote the Declaration of Independence proved as much, and even in your daily life at college you find chances to demonstrate this truth often. Does some policy of your college administrators irk you? Do you suffer from the obtuseness of fellow students who play their stereos at top volume in the hours before dawn? Do you want to urge students to attend a rally for a charity? Write a letter to your college newspaper or to someone in authority, in which you try to stir your readers to action.

The uses of arguing for action go far beyond these immediate applications, as we will see, and, accordingly, a college course (of any kind) will sometimes ask you to write a *proposal:* a recommendation that something be done about a problem. What you write cannot always stir people to action, as Thomas Jefferson's declaration did. After all, the people who read what you write may not have the power to carry out your suggestions. Usually it is enough to outline a course of action, as editorial writers do, and give so many good reasons for the wisdom of your recommendations that you will persuade your readers to agree that the course of action you suggest is the best one possible. It is, after all, from such agreement that actions eventually grow.

In the previous chapter, you stated an opinion and supported it with evidence. Now you will find that from stating an opinion to urging an action takes only a short step more. If you have made the claim "Our national parks are in a sad state of neglect," you may conclude that your next step is to urge readers to write to their congressional representatives or contribute funds to save endangered species or go to a national park and pick up trash. Or instead you

261

may want to suggest that the Department of the Interior be given a budget increase to hire more park rangers, purchase additional park land to accommodate the increasing horde of visitors to the national parks, and buy more clean-up equipment. The first paper would be a call to immediate action on the part of your readers; the second, an attempt to forge a consensus about what needs to be done.

Some statements of view *imply* that something ought to be done; the writer hasn't come out and urged any action specifically. But in making a proposal you do just that. You clearly set forth what needs to be done, and you urge action by using words like *should, ought,* and *must:* "This city ought to have a Bureau of Missing Persons"; "Small private aircraft should be banned from flying closer than one mile to a major passenger airport"; "Every consumer must refuse to buy South African apples." Then you lay out, clearly and concisely, all the convincing reasons you can muster to persuade your readers that your solution deserves to be implemented.

LEARNING FROM OTHER WRITERS

In recent years, some people have complained that certain rock lyrics incite listeners to violence. Rock singers and composers and listeners have protested against any attempt at censorship. In an article from the *Boston Globe*, Caryl Rivers, novelist and professor of journalism at Boston University, sets forth her own view of the question, together with pointed suggestions for action. Notice how much painstaking care (and how much space) she devotes to defining the problem she sees.

WHAT SHOULD BE DONE ABOUT ROCK LYRICS?
CARYL RIVERS

After a grisly series of murders in California, possibly inspired by the lyrics of a rock song, we are hearing a familiar chorus: Don't blame rock and roll. Kids will be kids. They love to rebel, and the more shocking the stuff, the better they like it.   1

There's some truth in this, of course. I loved to watch Elvis shake his torso when I was a teen-ager, and it was even more fun when Ed Sullivan wouldn't let the cameras show him below the waist. I snickered at the forbidden "Rock with Me, Annie" lyrics by a black Rhythm and Blues group, which were deliciously naughty. But I am sorry, rock fans, that is not the same thing as hearing lyrics about how a man is going to force a woman to perform oral sex on him at gunpoint in a little number called "Eat Me Alive." It is not in the same league with a song about the delights of slipping into a woman's room while she is sleeping and murdering her, the theme of an AC/DC ballad that allegedly inspired the California slayer.   2

Make no mistake, it is not sex we are talking about here, but violence. Violence against women. Most rock songs are not violent—they are funky,   3 sexy, rebellious, and sometimes witty. Please do not mistake me for a Mrs. Grundy. If Prince wants to leap about wearing only a purple jock strap, fine. Let Mick Jagger unzip his fly as he gyrates, if he wants to. But when either one of them starts garroting, beating, or sodomizing a woman in their number, that is another story.

I always find myself annoyed when "intellectual" men dismiss violence 4 against women with a yawn, as if it were beneath their dignity to notice. I wonder if the reaction would be the same if the violence were directed against someone other than women. How many people would yawn and say, "Oh, kids will be kids," if a rock group did a nifty little number called "Lynchin'," in which stringing up and stomping on black people were set to music? Who would chuckle and say, "Oh, just a little adolescent rebellion" if a group of rockers went on MTV dressed as Nazis, desecrating synagogues and beating up Jews to the beat of twanging guitars?

I'll tell you what would happen. Prestigious dailies would thunder on 5 editorial pages; senators would fall over each other to get denunciations into the Congressional Record. The president would appoint a commission to clean up the music business.

But violence against women is greeted by silence. It shouldn't be.   6

This does not mean censorship, or book (or record) burning. In a 7 society that protects free expression, we understand a lot of stuff will float up out of the sewer. Usually, we recognize the ugly stuff that advocates violence against any group as the garbage it is, and we consider its purveyors as moral lepers. We hold our nose and tolerate it, but we speak out against the values it proffers.

But images of violence against women are not staying on the fringes 8 of society. No longer are they found only in tattered, paper-covered books or in movie houses where winos snooze and the scent of urine fills the air. They are entering the mainstream at a rapid rate. This is happening at a time when the media, more and more, set the agenda for the public debate. It is a powerful legitimizing force—especially television. Many people regard what they see on TV as the truth; Walter Cronkite once topped a poll as the most trusted man in America.

Now, with the advent of rock videos and all-music channels, rock music 9 has grabbed a big chunk of legitimacy. American teen-agers have instant access, in their living rooms, to the messages of rock, on the same vehicle that brought them Sesame Street. Who can blame them if they believe that the images they see are accurate reflections of adult reality, approved by adults? After all, Big Bird used to give them lessons on the same little box. Adults, by their silence, sanction the images. Do we really want our kids to think that rape and violence are what sexuality is all about?

This is not a trivial issue. Violence against women is a major social 10 problem, one that's more than a cerebral issue to me. I teach at Boston University, and one of my most promising young journalism students was raped and murdered. Two others told me of being raped. Recently, one female student was assaulted and beaten so badly she had $5,000 worth of medical bills and permanent damage to her back and eyes.

It's nearly impossible, of course, to make a cause-and-effect link be- 11 tween lyrics and images and acts of violence. But images have a tremendous power to create an atmosphere in which violence against certain people is sanctioned. Nazi propagandists knew that full well when they portrayed Jews as ugly, greedy, and powerful.

The outcry over violence against women, particularly in a sexual con-   12
text, is being legitimized in two ways: by the increasing movement of these images into the mainstream of the media in TV, films, magazines, albums, videos, and by the silence about it.

Violence, of course, is rampant in the media. But it is usually set in   13
some kind of moral context. It's usually only the bad guys who commit violent acts against the innocent. When the good guys get violent, it's against those who deserve it. Dirty Harry blows away the scum, he doesn't walk up to a toddler and say, "Make my day." The A Team does not shoot up suburban shopping malls.

But in some rock songs, it's the "heroes" who commit the acts. The   14
people we are programmed to identify with are the ones being violent, with women on the receiving end. In a society where rape and assaults on women are endemic, this is no small problem, with millions of young boys watching on their TV screens and listening on their Walkmans.

I think something needs to be done. I'd like to see people in the   15
industry respond to the problem. I'd love to see some women rock stars speak out against violence against women. I would like to see disc jockeys refuse air play to records and videos that contain such violence. At the very least, I want to see the end of the silence. I want journalists and parents and critics and performing artists to keep this issue alive in the public forum. I don't want people who are concerned about this issue labeled as bluenoses and bookburners and ignored.

And I wish it wasn't always just women who were speaking out. Men   16
have as large a stake in the quality of our civilization as women do in the long run. Violence is a contagion that infects at random. Let's hear something, please, from the men.

Questions to Start You Thinking

1. Does Rivers persuade you that action is necessary? Do you think she takes rock lyrics too seriously?

2. Can you recall from your own experience any other evidence that might support her argument?

3. Where in her essay does Rivers present, even sympathize with, views opposed to her own? By doing so, does she strengthen or weaken her case?

4. What unspoken values and assumptions do you discern in Rivers that make her argue as she does?

5. Where in her essay does Rivers use the resource of imagination? For what purpose?

After pondering an old problem—people who mix drinking and driving—Jeffrey Ting came up with an original solution. For a freshman writing seminar called Contemporary Social Problems, he wrote the following proposal.

THE DRINKING AGE:
HOW WE SHOULD DETERMINE IT

JEFFREY TING

Recent history has shown that the big problem when the driver mixes 1 alcohol and gasoline comes from people between the ages of sixteen and twenty. The reason for this problem is not that young people are irresponsible. After the Vietnam War an old point was popularly raised: "Well, if a person can be old enough to fight in a war why isn't he old enough to drink?" So in the 1970s the drinking age was lowered in most states to eighteen. This proved an experiment that failed. Fatalities rose on the highways. That is why the federal government in 1984 passed the law requiring states to raise the drinking age to twenty-one or else lose federal funding for their highways. Many states promptly reacted and in early 1985 raised the drinking age to twenty-one.

Some individuals will be ready to drink at seventeen, and others never 2 will be if they live to be ninety. Instead of penalizing all the twenty-one-year-olds who have been spoiling for a beer ever since they were seventeen and who would be perfectly well qualified to handle it, I would like to propose a completely new solution to the problem. It is a drinking license.

We have a driver's license now, which is given out to persons who 3 demonstrate their ability to drive, and this has proven an effective system. Why then do we not license drinking to those who can prove their competence? I do not suggest that, to win one's drinking license, it should be necessary to chug-a-lug a pitcher of beer and then walk a straight line. It seems to me that the best way to determine the ability to handle alcohol would be to relate this ability to the ability to drive.

Let me imagine the plan like this. Let us say that the driver's license, 4 in a certain state, may be obtained at seventeen. Then should follow a period of eighteen months in which the young driver proves that he can keep an unblemished record—no drinking-related accidents. This caution would be necessary, for you may be sure that seventeen-year-olds who drive can find someone to buy beer for them. If at the end of that eighteen months the driver's record is clean, he can apply for a drinking license. A written test should be administered, like the one most states require for a driving license, to determine that the applicant has at least a basic knowledge of alcohol and its effects. Questions should be included such as "How many drinks does it take to get a person weighing 150 pounds over the point at which he can be declared legally inebriated?" "How long does it take, after that many drinks, to sober up?" "What is the best cure for a hangover?" (Answer: Honey.) And "How many people were killed last year in alcohol-related car accidents?" The applicant, if he can pass all this, receives a temporary drinking license good for six months of beer and wine, with hard liquor not yet permitted. If at the end of that six months he can both drink and drive and not have any accidents, he gets a permanent drinking license. I say "permanent," but this license can always be revoked. If the person is involved in a drinking-related accident he loses both driver's license and drinking license. No drinking license will be required for people over twenty-one.

At least two objections, I realize, can be leveled against this plan. It will 5 require more paperwork and more bureaucracy. I don't see this as a serious problem. Indeed, compared to the work that the present unworkable system creates for our courts, what with the charging of people for violating the drinking laws and the crushing burden of trials resulting from accidents, I believe this extra work would be relatively small. The states could charge a small fee for a drinking license, which the teenager would pay willingly, thus making money for the state.

A more serious objection is that this plan would tie drinking licenses 6 to drivers' licenses, and what about people who don't drive? Would they never be able to drink? That is a good objection, and I propose that, for those individuals without wheels, a different means be created for them to prove their ability to drink without causing any problems for society. They would be required to affirm that they are not going to obtain drivers' licenses. They would have to keep this pledge or else have to fall subject to the usual requirements for drivers. They would have an eighteen-month period following their seventeenth birthdays, during which they would be required to keep a clean police record. At the end of this eighteen months, if they had shown themselves to be good citizens, they could apply for and receive their drinking licenses. They would be required to take the same written test as anyone else.

While, like all official attempts to regulate unpredictable humans, the 7 plan I suggest would not work perfectly, I expect that it would work much more efficiently in keeping drunken drivers off the roads than the present confusion of laws and drinking ages. It would view the growing individual as going through a series of gauntlets in taking his or her rightful place as a responsible member of adult society. Right now the law unfairly discriminates against those who are willing and able to assume responsibility early. My plan would trust those individuals who can show society that they are ready to be trusted.

Questions to Start You Thinking

1. What, to your mind, is Ting's most convincing point in favor of his proposal? Which is least convincing?
2. Are there other objections to Ting's plan that he fails to deal with? If so, what are they?
3. Which of the writer's five resources—recalling, observing, reading, conversing, imagining—does Ting use in his essay? On which one does he rely most heavily?
4. What other possible solutions to this same problem can you imagine?

LEARNING BY WRITING

The Assignment

In this essay, you're going to accomplish two things. First, you'll carefully describe a social, economic, political, civic, environmental, or administrative problem—a problem you care about, one that irritates you or angers you, one that you strongly wish to see resolved. The problem may be large or small, but it shouldn't be trivial. (No comic essays about the awful problem of catsup that squirts from Big Macs, please. For this assignment you'll want to probe deeper and engage your thinking with other people's real concerns.) The problem may be one that affects the whole country, or it may be one that affects mainly people in your locality: your city, your campus, or your dormitory. Show your readers that this problem really exists and that it concerns them. Show them why it ought to arouse them, not only you.

After setting forth this problem, go on to propose a way to solve it or at least alleviate it. What should be done? Supply evidence that your proposal is reasonable, that it can work, that a way to improve the existing state of affairs is within our grasp.

Some recent student papers that cogently argued for actions include the following.

A woman argued that SAT, ACT, and achievement test scores should be abolished as criteria for college acceptance. She demonstrated that the tests favor aggressive students from affluent families, who can afford to take courses (and buy software programs) designed to improve their scores.

A woman made a case for drafting all eighteen-year-olds for a year and putting them to work at such tasks as feeding the homeless, tutoring students who need special help, eliminating litter and graffiti, teaching the illiterate to read, planting trees and flowers, helping patients in nursing homes, and staffing day-care centers.

A student of education, suggesting that students in sixth through ninth grades are ill served by the big, faceless middle schools and junior high schools they now attend, proposed a return to small, personal elementary schools that teach children from kindergarten through eighth grade.

A man, stressing the humanizing influence of light, sunshine, and green space, argued for a moratorium on the construction of all high-rise buildings.

A woman, setting forth her belief in the importance of new frontiers, advocated more and better-funded research into space travel.

Generating Ideas

In selecting a topic, why not go to your five familiar resources? They can supply you with knowledge of a problem that needs to be cured. Here are a few questions to help ideas start flowing.

DISCOVERY CHECKLIST: DRAWING FROM RESOURCES

- Can you recall any such problem you have met in your own experience? If your topic is a problem you are well acquainted with, your writing task will be easier by far. Ask yourself what problems you meet every day or occasionally, or what problems concern people near you.

- Consider how to improve systems (or ways of doing things) that you believe to be flawed. Can you think of a better way for your college to run its course registration? A better way for your state or community to control dangerous drugs?
- Have you observed a problem recently? What have you seen or heard, on television or on your daily rounds, that needs improvement? What action is called for?
- Have you read of any such problem in a newspaper or news magazine?
- Have you heard of any problem in recent conversation or class discussion? (If not, you might go talk with somebody.)
- By trying to put yourself in the position of another person, perhaps some-one of a different ethnic background, someone with fewer advantages, can you imagine some problem that no doubt exists? (This last suggestion in-vites you also to do some reading about it.)

Surely one of the most convenient sources of information about real and current problems is a daily newspaper or a news magazine such as *Time, News-week,* or *U.S. News & World Report*. Any copy of such a publication will abound with the cares of multitudes. In a single copy of a newspaper published on the morning we wrote these words, we found discussions of the problems of acid rain, teenage pregnancy, the high school dropout rate, famine in the Sudan, hunger in America, a spurt in the highway death toll due to drunken drivers, an increase in medical malpractice suits (causing some obstetricians to quit their practices), unemployment, cases of abuse of the drug called crack, the difficulty of apprehending parents suspected of child abuse, traffic congestion, a surplus of wine produced by California vintners, terrorist hijackings of air-liners, swindlers who sell worthless franchises, the disposal of toxic waste, a sharp increase in severe injuries in professional football (prompting debate over whether the rules of the game need to be changed), and the long-lasting problem of how the United States and the Soviet Union can agree to reduce their nuclear missile stockpiles.

Brainstorming—compiling a list of possible writing topics—is another good way to begin. (See p. 457 for more advice on this useful strategy.)

Once you've chosen a problem, think about solutions. Some problems—such as that of reducing international tensions—present no easy solutions. Still, why not give some thought to any problem that you feel seriously concerned with? You can't be expected to solve, in one college writing assignment, a problem that may have thwarted teams of scientists and government experts. But sometimes a solution to a problem will reveal itself to a novice thinker. And for some problems, like the problem of reducing armaments, even a small contribution to a partial solution will be worth offering. You will want to think about the problem analytically. Here are a few questions to start your thoughts.

DISCOVERY CHECKLIST: UNDERSTANDING A PROBLEM

- How urgent is this problem? Does something need to be done about it immediately?
- For how long has this problem been going on?

- What causes for this problem can you find? What have been its effects? (For more ideas, glance back through Chapter 12.)
- In the past, have any problems like this been solved or eliminated?
- How does this problem affect the reader's health, well-being, conscience, or pocketbook?
- How many possible solutions to it can you imagine?

Think, too, of your readers—the persons you seek to persuade. If you are addressing your fellow students, maybe they haven't had occasion to think about this problem before. If you can discover any way to bring it home to them, any evidence to show that it affects and concerns them, your paper is likely to be effective. Do some more brainstorming. Try *freewriting*, the useful strategy of starting out to write steadily, thinking as you write (see p. 459 for more advice about it). As you write any preliminary notes, here are points to consider.

DISCOVERY CHECKLIST: UNDERSTANDING YOUR READERS

- Why should your readers care? Why is this a problem that concerns them personally?
- In the past, have they expressed any interest in this problem that you can recall?
- Do they belong to any organization, religious group, minority, or other segment of society that might make them especially likely to agree or disagree? What assumptions and values do they hold that you should be aware of?
- What attitudes have you in common with them? Do you and your readers already agree on anything?

To show that this problem that concerns you really exists, you'll need evidence and examples. Again, draw on your five familiar resources. While you think, scribble notes to yourself. Keep your pencil moving. If you feel that further reading in the library will help you know what you're talking about, now is the time. The *Readers' Guide to Periodical Literature* and the card catalogue are trusty sources of relevant reading—the former to locate magazine articles on a subject that interests you, the latter to locate books. (For advice on using these aids, see Chapter 17.)

Shaping a Draft

In writing this paper, you may find use for the ways of explaining that appear in Part Three. If, for instance, your claim is "We should outlaw the possession of handguns by private citizens," you might argue that the free possession of handguns, as the law now stands, *causes* a high murder rate. You might examine the undesirable *effects* of the present policy or foresee the desirable *effects* that you believe would result from a ban. You might *compare and contrast* the present situation with the course of action you recommend. You might trace the *process* by which lobbyists have prevented the passage of legislation banning handguns or the *process* by which the change that you urge might come about. You might give a *short definition* of a handgun, or an *extended definition* of the present law, showing its limits. To understand your opposition, you might *classify* opponents of the ban, or you might *divide* the case against the ban into parts and then discuss each part. Try applying any of these useful methods to your topic and you may find yourself generating unexpected, valuable ideas.

A basic way to organize a paper like this is to state your proposal in a sentence: "A law should be passed enabling couples to divorce without having to go to court"; "The United States should secede from the United Nations." From that statement at the beginning of the paper, the rest of the argument may start to unfold. Usually a paper of this kind falls naturally into a simple shape with the following two parts.

1. A claim that a problem exists. This is a long introductory part, describing the problem and supplying evidence to suggest that it is intolerable.
2. A claim that something ought to be done about it. This part is the proposal.

You can make your proposal more persuasive by including some or all of the following elements.

The knowledge or experience you have or the thinking you have done that qualifies you to propose a solution to this problem.

The values, beliefs, or assumptions that have caused you to feel strongly about the need for action. (Sample statement: "I believe persons of fifteen are old enough to chart their own destinies, that it is morally wrong for them to remain under their parents' control with no say in the matter.")

What will be required—an estimate of money, people, skills, material. This part might include a list or enumeration of what is readily available now and what else will have to be obtained.

Exactly what must be done, step by step, to enact your solution. (For help here, browse again through Chapter 10, about analyzing a process.)

How long the solution is likely to take.

What possible obstacles or difficulties may need to be overcome.

Why your solution to the problem is better than others that have been proposed in the past or tried already.

What tests, controls, or quality checks might be used to make sure that your solution is proceeding as expected.

Any other evidence to show that what you suggest is practical, reasonable in cost, and likely to be effective.

If you can imagine your way into your reader's mind, then perhaps you can think of possible objections he or she might raise: reservations about the high cost, the complexity, or the workability of your plan, for instance. It is wonderfully persuasive to anticipate the very objection that might occur to your reader and to deal with it and lay it to rest. Jonathan Swift, in "A Modest Proposal," is aware of this rhetorical strategy. After arguing that it will greatly help the poor of Ireland to sell their babies to rich landlords for meat (he's being ironic, savagely condemning the landlords' lack of feeling), Swift goes on:

> I can think of no one objection that will possibly be raised against this proposal, unless it should be urged that the number of people will be thereby much lessened in the kingdom. This I freely own, and it was indeed one principal design in offering it to the world.

How to open your paper? You might think of a scene or incident that will put the problem into a reader's mind's eye. Beginning an essay entitled "Why Don't We Complain?," in which he argues that Americans should vigorously protest inconveniences and inefficiencies, William F. Buckley starts by recalling how he and other commuters sat roasting in an overheated train coach, too docile to complain to the conductor. Buckley draws the scene in memorable detail: "I took off my overcoat, and a few minutes later my jacket, and noticed that the car was flecked with the white shirts of the passengers. I soon found my hand moving to loosen my tie." Reading his essay, we too feel ourselves sympathetically sweltering.

When you come to set forth your proposal, you will increase the likelihood of its acceptance if you make the first step simple and inviting. A claim that national parks need better care might begin by suggesting that the reader head for such a park and personally size up the situation.

If as you go along you find you don't know enough about a certain point, don't hesitate to backtrack to the library, or to converse with others, or to give your memory another rummage, or to go out and observe, or to do some more imagining.

When you collect ideas and evidence from outside sources, whether books and periodicals or nonprint sources, you'll need to document your evidence, that is, tell where you got everything. Check with your instructor on the documentation method he or she wants you to use. Chapter 19 contains extensive information on documentation systems, but for a short paper like the one assigned in this chapter, it will probably be enough to introduce brief lines and phrases to identify sources.

> According to *Newsweek* correspondent Josie Fair . . .
>
> . . . as 1980 census figures indicate . . .
>
> In his biography *FDR: The New Deal Years*, Kenneth S. Davis reports . . .
>
> While working as a Senate page in the summer of 1986, I observed . . .

Rewriting

Try your draft on other students. Are they convinced that the problem you are talking about is of vital concern to them? If not, why don't they care? Are they persuaded that your solution is likely and workable?

Exaggerated claims for your solution will not persuade. Don't be afraid to express your own reasonable doubts that your solution will root out the problem forever. If you have ended your draft with a sort of resounding trumpet call or a horrific vision of what will happen if your plea should go unheard, ask yourself whether you have gone too far and whether a reader might protest, "Aaah, this won't mean the end of the world."

A temptation in writing a paper like this is to simplify the problem so that the solution will seem all the more likely to apply. In looking back over your draft, if you have proposed an easy, three-step way to end war, famine, or pestilence, perhaps you have fallen into oversimplification. You may need to rethink both the problem and your solution.

In looking back over your draft once more, review these points.

REVISION CHECKLIST: ARGUING FOR AN ACTION

- Have you made the problem clear?
- Have you made it of immediate concern to your readers, so that they will feel it is their business?
- Have you anticipated the doubts they may have?
- Have you made clear the steps that must be taken?
- Have you demonstrated that your solution to the problem will confer benefits?
- Have you considered other possible solutions to the problem before rejecting them in favor of your own?
- Have you come on as the well-meaning, reasonable writer that you are, one willing to admit, "I don't know everything"?
- Have you made a reasonable claim, not promised that your solution will do more than it can possibly do? Have you made believable predictions for the success of your plan, not wild ones?

Other Assignments

1. If in working in Chapter 14 you followed the assignment and stated a view, now write a few additional paragraphs extending the paper you have already written, going on to argue for an action. Obviously some evaluations will not work for this assignment, if nothing need be done about them. The claim that Pavarotti is a fine singer leads to no action other than listening to the man sing. But if you wrote a paper pointing out the existence of a problem ("American opera is hamstrung by too little funding"), you will now find it natural to ponder ways to solve or alleviate that problem.

2. Write an editorial in which you propose to your town or city fathers an innovation you think would benefit the whole community. Here are a few suggestions to get your own thoughts working:

    A drug and alcohol education program in the schools
    A network of bicycle paths
    Conversion of a vacant lot into a park
    After-school programs for children of working parents
    A neighborhood program for crime prevention

   Low- or moderate-income housing
   A drop-in center for old people
   More recreational facilities for teenagers
   Tests of the local water supply
   A law against the dumping of hazardous wastes
   An adult education program

3.   Write a letter to your congressional representative or your senator in which you
     object to some government policy with which you disagree. End your letter with a
     proposal for righting the wrong that concerns you.

4.   Choose from the following list a practice that seems to you to represent an ineffi-
     cient, unethical, unfair, or morally wrong solution to a problem. In a few paragraphs,
     give reasons for your objections. Then propose a better solution. (You might prefer
     not to choose a topic from the list, but let the list prompt you to think of another,
     different wrong solution.)

   Censorship
   Corporal punishment for children
   Laboratory experiments on animals
   Strip-mining
   Surrogate motherhood
   State lotteries
   The arms buildup

APPLYING WHAT YOU LEARN: SOME USES OF PROPOSALS

      In college we often think of a proposal as a specific thing: as a written plan
submitted to someone in authority who must approve it before we go ahead
with it. Students embarking on a thesis are usually required to submit a proposal
to an adviser or a committee, in which they set forth what they intend to
investigate and how they will approach a chosen topic. Students who want
academic credit for an internship or permission to carry on independent study
often have to write a proposal laying out why they deserve it. Like writers of
persuasive essays, they state a claim and supply evidence in its support. Seniors
and postgraduates who apply for a grant or fellowship from a federal or private
agency have to write proposals that will convince that agency to support their
work or research.

      In business, proposals for action are commonly useful: for persuading a
prospective customer to buy a product or service, for recommending a change
in procedure, suggesting a new project, or urging an outlay of funds to purchase
new equipment. An office manager might use a proposal as a means to achieve
harmony with co-workers: first discussing with the staff a certain problem—
poor morale, a conflict between smokers and nonsmokers—and then writing
a proposal to outline the solution on which the group has agreed. Copies of
the proposal go to the people who agreed on it so they can put it into action.

      Throughout this chapter, we have looked at proposals as more general than
plans in need of okaying. We have seen them as any arguments with which we

try to influence readers to act on our ideas or, at the very least, to agree with them. Most of us have ideas for doing something more effectively than it has been done in the past, for improving a situation in which we discern some annoying fault, for abolishing a practice that strikes us as unfair or outmoded. We are often given opportunities, in college and beyond, to propose a solution to a problem. Sometimes we're given such an opportunity when we answer a question on an exam or when we are assigned to write a paper arguing for an action. "How can environmentalists change people's attitudes and therefore their actions toward the natural world?" "What suggestions can you make to alleviate the plight of women who want to work but cannot afford day care for their children?"

Thoughtful, imaginative answers to such questions can be the first crucial step toward solving some of the world's knottiest problems. By laying out possible solutions, writers can at the very least encourage fruitful debate. Every day in the world around us, we see samples of proposals—on the editorial pages of newspapers and magazines, in books new and old. For example, in this paragraph from an editorial written for a 1979 textbook to urge more funding for research on alternative energy sources, nuclear physicist David Rittenhouse endorses the value and practicality of harnessing the wind:

> As another example of inadequate effort, no one is building a giant windmill. One prototype, built on a limited experimental basis during World War II, fed 1,000 kilowatts into the electricity grid in Vermont. That experiment came just at the dawn of the atomic age and was not followed up, probably because of early rosy hopes for infinite, cheap, and trouble-free nuclear power. Now that those early dreams have faded, it is high time to follow up on wind power development. The potential is enormous—almost limitless. Modern engineering stands ready, without awaiting further research and development, to build large numbers of giant windmills either in the sparsely settled parts of the Great Plains or offshore near the edge of the continental shelf, where they will bother almost no one. They can generate hydrogen to be stored and provide a steady source of power. The immediate need is for a few million dollars to build the first full-scale prototypes to convince decision makers that thousands of windmills would provide as much power as the nuclear plants that are being proposed.

Sometimes an entire article, essay, or other document is devoted to arguing for an action. In other cases, a writer's chief purpose may be to explain something or perhaps to express an opinion. Such an article can *end* with a proposal, a call to action. Carl Sagan, David Duncan Professor of Astronomy and Space Sciences at Cornell, in an article for the September 1985 issue of *Discover*, gives his reasons for believing that the Strategic Defense Initiative (nicknamed Star Wars), proposed by the Reagan administration in 1983, will not work. Near the end of his article, Sagan proposes an alternative.

> But if strategic defense isn't the solution, what is? The only alternative for the U.S. and the U.S.S.R. is to act in what is clearly their mutual inter-

est: to negotiate both a moratorium on the development and deployment of new nuclear weapons systems, and to make massive, bilateral, and verifiable reductions in the present nuclear arsenals. Because the arsenals are so bloated—a single American missile-carrying submarine can destroy 192 Soviet cities—deep cuts can be made without compromising strategic deterrence. This is a task that does not require, as Star Wars does, a whole series of technological breakthroughs; it requires only political will. The two nations can take major steps now and create a climate for subsequent joint action to reduce the peril in which they have placed our species.

Like many proposals that you will read during your college years and beyond, Sagan's is controversial. Whether Sagan persuades you or fails to persuade you, he performs a useful service. By giving us a thoughtful proposal on this crucial issue, he challenges us to think, too.

In time, some calls to action that at first are controversial become generally accepted. This has certainly been true of Dr. Elisabeth Kübler-Ross's views about how dying patients and their loved ones ought to be treated. Before she wrote her landmark book *On Death and Dying* (1969), terminally ill patients in hospitals were seldom told when they were close to death, and little was done to help them die with dignity. Their families felt uncomfortable about the silences and deceptions imposed on the dying. After studying the problem, Kübler-Ross evolved a number of suggestions that would ease a patient's transition into death—easing pain for the caregivers as well as for the patient. Among them is this one.

> There is a time in a patient's life when the pain ceases to be, when the mind slips off into a dreamless state, when the need for food becomes minimal and the awareness of the environment all but disappears into darkness. This is the time when the relatives walk up and down the hospital hallways, tormented by the waiting, not knowing if they should leave to attend the living or stay to be around for the moment of death. This is the time when it is too late for words, and yet the time when the relatives cry the loudest for help—with or without words. It is too late for medical interventions (and too cruel, though well meant, when they do occur), but it is also too early for a final separation from the dying. It is the hardest time for the next of kin as he either wishes to take off, to get it over with; or he desperately clings to something that he is in the process of losing forever. It is the time for the therapy of silence with the patient and availability for the relatives.
>
> The doctor, nurse, social worker, or chaplain can be of great help during these final moments if they can understand the family's conflicts at this time and help select the one person who feels most comfortable staying with the dying patient. This person then becomes in effect the patient's therapist. Those who feel too uncomfortable can be assisted by alleviating their guilt and by the reassurance that someone will stay with the dying until his death has occurred. They can then return home knowing that

the patient did not die alone, yet not feeling ashamed or guilty for having avoided this moment which for many people is so difficult to face.

Proposals of various kinds can be valuable and powerful instruments. At their best, like Kübler-Ross's pioneering recommendations for facing death and dying, they're often the advance guard that comes before useful action.

A Note on Reasoning

When we argue (rationally, not with fists), we *reason*—that is, we make statements that lead to a conclusion. From Aristotle's time down to our own day, many methods of going from statements to conclusion have been devised. The following section will tell you of a recent, informal method and also of two traditional ones.

DATA, WARRANT, AND CLAIM

In recent years, a simple, practical method of reasoning has been devised by the British philosopher Stephen Toulmin. Helpfully, Toulmin has divided a typical argument into three parts:

1. *The data*, or evidence to prove something
2. *The claim*, what you are proving with the data
3. *The warrant*, the thinking that leads from data to claim

Any clear, explicit argument has to have all three parts. Toulmin's own example of such an argument is this:

Harry was born in Bermuda ——————— Harry is a British subject
(*Data*)   (*Claim*)

Since a man born in Bermuda
will be a British subject
(*Warrant*)

Of course, the data for a larger, more controversial claim will be more extensive. Here are some claims that would call for much more data, perhaps thousands of words.

Abortion should be forbidden by law.

Huckleberry Finn is the greatest American novel.

People who invest in South African mines are contemptible.

The warrant, that middle term, is often crucially important. It tells *why* the claim follows from the data. Often a writer won't bother to state a warrant because it is obvious: "In his bid for reelection, Mayor Perkins failed miserably. Out of five thousand votes cast for both candidates, he received only two hundred." The warrant might be stated, "To make what I would consider a strong showing, he would have had to receive two thousand votes or more," but it is clear that 200 out of 5000 is a small minority, and no further explanation seems necessary.

A flaw in many arguments, though, is that the warrant is not clear. A good clear warrant is essential. To be persuaded, a reader needs to understand your assumptions and the thinking that follows from them. If you were to argue, "In *Huckleberry Finn*, Mark Twain tells the story of how civilization spread westward and tamed the frontier. Therefore, *Huckleberry Finn* is the greatest American novel," then your reader might well be left wondering why the second statement follows from the first. But if you were to add, between the statements, "Because civilization's westward spread is the most important fact in American history, I believe that any American novel called 'greatest' ought to take it in," then you supply a warrant. You show why your claim follows from your data—from what you have observed in Mark Twain's book.

At times, though, your warrant may be perfectly clear without your even stating it. Say you are writing a paper about the recent problem of malicious people who uncap patent medicines in drugstores and slip in poison. If in giving your data you declare, "Packages of headache remedies sold in drugstores have sometimes been tampered with," and then right away go on to state your claim, "and so tamper-proof packaging is desirable," your warrant is already clear. You wouldn't even need to spell it out. If you did state it, it might be "I assume that to let people introduce dangerous substances into medicines in drugstores is a bad idea." Most readers will need no such statement; they will have heard news reports of poisonings that resulted from such tampering, or they will readily imagine the bad results that tampering can produce.

Let's say, though, that you write a paper that starts by reporting the tampering and then states your claim, or opinion: "I find exercise the most admirable form of headache relief." To most readers, just how you went from that data to that claim might not be clear. You would need to make your warrant explicit. Perhaps it might be stated, "I think it's wise to avoid the risk of taking poisoned medicine by instead doing relaxation exercises whenever a headache strikes" (or you might state your warrant in any one of a dozen other ways).

Think of Toulmin's scheme and you will recognize when an argument is in trouble—either your own or another writer's. Then, apparently, the warrant needs to be expressed. To be sure, your readers may not accept your warrant. They may disagree about your definition of the most important fact in American history, or they may object that a great novel ought to do more than reflect history. But at least they will understand your reasoning.

In an assignment for her second-semester course in English composition, Maire Flynn was asked to set forth in three short paragraphs a condensed argument. The first paragraph was to set forth some data; the second, a claim; and the third, a warrant. The result became a kind of outline that the writer could then expand into a whole essay. Here is Flynn's.

DATA

Over the past five years in the state of Illinois, assistance in the form of food stamps has had the effect of increasing the number of people on welfare instead of reducing it. Despite this help, 95 percent of long-term recipients remain below the poverty line today.

CLAIM

I maintain that the present system of distributing food stamps is a dismal failure, a less effective way to help the needy than other possible ways.

WARRANT

No one is happy to receive charity. We need to encourage people to quit the welfare rolls; we need to make sure that government aid goes only to the deserving. More effective than giving out food might be to help untrained young people learn job skills, to help single mothers with small children to obtain child care, freeing them for the job market; and to enlarge and improve our state employment counseling and job-placement services. The problem of poverty will be helped only if more people will find jobs and become self-sufficient.

In her warrant paragraph, Flynn spells out her reasons for holding her opinion—the one she states in her claim. "The warrant," she found, "was the hardest part to write," but hers turned out to be clear. Like any good warrant, hers expresses those thoughts that her data set in motion. Another way of looking at the warrant: it is the thinking that led the writer on to the opinion she holds. In this statement of her warrant, Flynn makes clear her assumptions: that people who can support themselves don't deserve food stamps and that a person is better off (and happier) holding a job than receiving charity. By generating more ideas and evidence, she was easily able to expand both data paragraph and warrant paragraph, and the result was a coherent essay of 700 words.

How, by the way, would someone who didn't accept Flynn's warrant argue with her? What about old, infirm, or handicapped persons who cannot work? What quite different assumptions about poverty might be possible?

Writing Exercise: Data, Warrant, and Claim

On the model of Maire Flynn's three-part condensed argument, write a condensed argument in three paragraphs demonstrating data, warrant, and claim. For a topic, consider any problem or controversy in this morning's newspaper and form an opinion on it.

DEDUCTION AND INDUCTION

One traditional method of reasoning may be stated in a *syllogism*, a three-step form like this:

All trees have roots. (Major premise)
An oak is a tree. (Minor premise)
Therefore, an oak has roots. (Conclusion)

Few writers arrange their statements in this strict form, favored by Aristotle in his *Rhetoric*, a classical guide to argument so brilliant that it remains useful today. And yet all of us still employ, at times, the same method of reasoning found in a syllogism: *deductive reasoning*. This kind of reasoning begins with a statement of general truth ("All trees have roots") and moves to a statement about an individual ("An oak has roots"). Deductive reasoning is commonly applied to college writing. If, for an economics paper, you remark that all liberal senators favor a federally funded program of medical care for all citizens, then identify Edward M. Kennedy as a liberal senator, and conclude that he may be expected to favor the program, you reason deductively.

But you might argue the other way around. If instead of starting with a general statement ("All liberal senators favor..."), you were to interview Senator Kennedy and a score of other liberal senators, find them unanimous in favoring the program, and then conclude that liberal senators favor the program, you would follow the opposite method: *inductive reasoning*. Inductive reasoning is sometimes called "scientific method." Scientists commonly work in this way: by observing particulars and then drawing general conclusions. Either method of reasoning is only as trustworthy as the observations on which it is based. In *Zen and the Art of Motorcycle Maintenance*, Robert M. Pirsig gives memorable short illustrations of the two kinds of reasoning:

> If the cycle goes over a bump and the engine misfires, and then goes over another bump and the engine misfires, and then goes over another bump and the engine misfires, and then goes over a long smooth stretch of road and there is no misfiring, and then goes over a fourth bump and the engine misfires again, one can logically conclude that the misfiring is caused by the bumps. That is induction: reasoning from particular experiences to general truths.

> Deductive inferences do the reverse. They start with general knowledge and predict a specific observation. For example if, from reading the hierarchy of facts about the machine, the mechanic knows the horn of the cycle is powered exclusively by electricity from the battery, then he can logically infer that if the battery is dead the horn will not work. That is deduction.

LOGICAL FALLACIES

Most students of logic today would agree that there is no universal and infallible method of reasoning. Still, some ways of reasoning are evidently more fallible than others. In arguments we hear (and sometimes read and sometimes write), we often meet *logical fallacies*, common mistakes in thinking—generally, the making of statements that lead to demonstrably wrong conclusions. Here is a list of the most familiar, to help you recognize them when you see or hear them and so guard against them when you write. (Some arguments can exhibit more than one fallacy at once.)

Non sequitur (from the Latin, "it does not follow"). Stating a claim that doesn't follow from the first premise (the statement you begin with). "Jergus will make an excellent husband for Marge. Why, in high school he got all A's." The problem with a non sequitur, if we invoke Toulmin's terms, is that its warrant isn't clear.[1]

Oversimplification. Supplying neat and easy explanations for large and complicated phenomena: "We have a lot of unemployment in this country because people are too lazy to work." Oversimplified solutions are also popular: "If we want to do away with drug abuse, let's get tough: let's sentence every drug user to death."

Either/or reasoning is a special kind of oversimplified thinking: assuming that a reality may be divided into only two parts, that there are only two sides to a question, that all statements are either true or false, that all questions demand either a yes or a no answer. "The nonbiologist," comments Eric B. Lenneberg, "mistakenly thinks of genes as being directly responsible for one property or another; this leads him to the fallacy of dichotomizing everything as being dependent on either genes or environment." Other adherents to the either/or principle divide reality into either mind or body, sense or intellect, intelligence or stupidity, public or private, finite or infinite, humanity or nature, good or evil, competence or incompetence. An either/or reasoner assumes that a problem has only two possible solutions, only one of which is acceptable. "What are we going to do about acid rain? Either we shut down all the factories that cause it, or we just forget about acid rain and learn to live with it. We've got no choice, right?"

Argument from dubious authority. An unidentified authority can be used unfairly to shore up a quaking argument: "According to some of the most knowing scientists in America, smoking two packs a day is as harmless as eating a couple of oatmeal cookies."

Argument ad hominem (from the Latin, "against the man"). Attacking people's opinions by attacking their character. "Carruthers may argue that we need to save the whales, but Carruthers is the kind of person who always gets

---

[1]Professor Patricia Bizzell has pointed out that with enough thought, it might be possible to invent a warrant to link those two statements: "Someone smart enought to get all A's ought to be able to figure out how to live with someone else amicably." Supply such a warrant and the non sequitur disappears.

excited over nothing." A person's circumstances can also be turned against him: "Carruthers would have us spend millions to save whales, but I happen to know that he owns a yacht from which he selfishly enjoys watching whales."

Argument from ignorance. Maintaining that, because a conclusion has not been disproved, it has to be accepted. "Despite years of effort, no one has conclusively proved that ghosts don't exist; therefore, we should expect to see them at any time." The converse is also an error: that, because a conclusion has not been proved, it should be rejected. "No one has ever shown that there is life on any other planet. Evidently the notion of other living things in the universe is unthinkable."

Begging the question. Setting out to prove a statement already taken for granted. When you reason in a logical way, you state that because something is true, then, as a result, another truth follows. But when you beg the question, you repeat that what is true is true. If, for instance, you argue that rapists are a menace because they are dangerous, you don't prove a thing. Beggars of questions just repeat what they already believe, in different words. Sometimes a question can exhibit this fallacy. Interrogating a witness to determine whether she had ever served a prison term, a trial lawyer unfairly asked, "How much time did you spend in the penitentiary?" This fallacy sometimes takes the form of *arguing in a circle*, demonstrating a premise by a conclusion and a conclusion by a premise: "He is a liar because he simply is not telling the truth."

Post hoc ergo propter hoc (from the Latin, "after this, therefore because of this"). Confusing cause and effect, as in the remark "Because President Carter was obliged to leave office, the problem of inflation has been cured."

Arguing by analogy. Using a metaphor as though it were evidence. An analogy explains a complicated idea in terms of something familiar: for instance, shooting a spacecraft to another planet is like placing a golf ball with uncanny accuracy into a hole a half mile away. But in argument, it has a weakness. Dwelling only on similarities, a writer doesn't consider differences (since to admit them would weaken the analogy). "People were born as free as the birds. It's wrong and cruel to expect them to work." Hold on, there—human society and bird society have more differences than similarities. Because they may be alike in one way doesn't mean that in every way they should be alike. In 1633, Scipio Chiaramonti, professor of philosophy at the University of Pisa, argued against Galileo: "Animals, which move, have limbs and muscles. The earth has no limbs and muscles, hence it does not move."

As you can see from these examples, listening and reading for logical fallacies can supply enjoyable exercise for the mind.

For Further Reading

In late years, the study of *logic*, or systematic reasoning, has seen exciting developments. If you care to venture more deeply into its fascinating territory, a good, lively (but challenging) introductory textbook is Albert E. Blumberg's *Logic* (New York: Knopf, 1976). Stephen Toulmin, in *The Uses of Argument* (Cambridge, Eng.: Cambridge University Press, 1969), sets forth his own system in detail. His views are further explained and applied by Douglas Ehninger and Wayne Brockriede in *Decision by Debate*, 2nd ed. (New York: Harper & Row, 1978) and by Toulmin himself, with Richard Rieke and Allan Janik, in *An Introduction to Reasoning*, 2nd ed. (New York: Macmillan, 1984).

PART FIVE

Investigating

What is research? *The word comes from the Middle French* recherchier, *"to investigate thoroughly." To do research is, in a sense, to venture into the unknown: to explore, to experiment, to discover facts and laws, to revise earlier thinking. When its object is to probe the mysterious recesses of the human brain or the far galaxies, research can be thrilling. That may be why some people devote their lives to such investigation—in libraries, in the field, in laboratories.*

In one college research paper due in a month, you won't be expected to unfold the secrets of the brain or the Spiral Nebula. Still, in your college research, you just might find a little excitement. It can occur when a writer, interviewing a dozen people and collecting their answers, suddenly realizes that a meaningful pattern is emerging. ("Six people say they'd like to own a Sun-yu-san sports car; eight people dislike that make of car intensely. What do the groups have in common? Hmmmm-m-m—the eight haters all come from Detroit!") Excitement can happen in a library's stacks where, looking up the facts of a long-past event and thinking about them, a writer might come to understand what actually took place, perhaps even realize that a history book needs to be corrected. ("I'm sure of it—Leon Trotsky's assassin wasn't an agent of the government but a personal friend!")

In writing a college research paper, you may not make any earthshaking discoveries. Even so, you won't just stack up facts: you'll arrive at your own fresh view. In doing research, you don't merely paste together information and opinions taken from other people; you use that material to think for yourself.

If in browsing through the next four chapters you glance at the sample research papers, you may expect that the task of writing such a paper yourself will be quite different from other college writing, and more intimidating. But for much of the time you'll find it like any other kind—full of backtracking, twists and turns, and surprises. Distracted by the vastness of a card catalogue, perplexed by the intricacies of a microfilm projector, weighed down by an obligation to cast citations into a style approved by the American Psychological Association or the Modern Language Association, you can easily forget that, most importantly, a research paper needs to say something you believe is worth saying.

To help you find your own view and express it convincingly, our assignment for a library research paper in Chapter 16 is fairly simple. If you take our advice, you will make a short investigation, not an extremely deep one. But you will *learn how to do research in a library, how to use various useful sources, and how to bring together your findings in a readable, trustworthy paper.*

The second chapter in this section, "Knowing Your Library," is merely informative. It doesn't insist that you write anything. It explains the many sources available in a library, and we offer it just to guide any writer who will be doing further research than Chapter 16 calls for. If you go on to take specialized courses in a major field, you will undoubtedly find helpful information there.

Chapter 18 will take you into field research, often done by observing and conversing with people, by finding out something brand-new. This chapter includes a paper by a college student who broke new ground: he revealed new knowledge about a little-known, much-maligned, sometimes glamorized business—bail bonding.

Last in this section is Chapter 19, "Documenting Sources," which need not be read through but is there to be consulted when you document your sources and when you type up your paper in finished form.

286

The purpose of citing and listing your sources is to enable any interested reader to look them up and verify what you say. The mechanics of documentation may seem fussy, but the obligation to cite and list sources keeps research writers truthful and responsible.

CHAPTER 16

Writing from Library Research

All around us, information keeps exploding. From day to day, software and the video screen, books, newspapers, and magazines shower us with facts and figures, statements and reports, views and opinions—some of them half-baked, some revealing and trustworthy. College gives you experience in sorting through this massive burst of wordage. It calls on you to tell data from opinion, off-the-wall claims from knowing interpretations. It asks you to sort out what matters to you. To help you acquire such skills is usually one purpose of writing a library research paper.

You'll have to do more than just squirrel up acorns of information. You'll need to ask a question you really want to answer and then start living with that question, thinking about it. Otherwise, though your finished product may look neat and may keep all its notes in order, it will be just a stack of accurately despoiled paper. Some writers start writing a library research paper feeling like slaves to a library, obliged to collect a lot of pieces of books and magazines—for no good reason except to make a tall pile. But a library isn't your boss; it exists to serve you. Regard your work as a chance to expand the frontiers of what you know already.

Back in Chapter 6, if you did the main assignment, you read five or six works by other writers and wrote a paper that one of your readings inspired. When you wrote, you gave credit to other writers in an informal way. That experience will prove good preparation for writing a research paper. This new task, though, will be different in at least the following ways.

All your reading will point in one direction.

You'll do more interpreting, more piecing together, more evaluating, more throwing away of the unnecessary.

You'll learn to cite and list your sources in the exact form that many scholars and other professionals follow in writing research papers.

To be able to write a library research paper is a useful skill. This kind of writing is essential not only in an academic community but in business and the professions. At the end of this chapter, we'll supply more evidence of its usefulness. If you feel the need to be convinced, page ahead and glance over "Applying What You Learn" on page 335.

Naturally, in doing research and in writing it, you'll find yourself taking certain steps ahead of certain others. Until you take notes and see what material you gather, you probably won't want to outline—you won't have anything to organize yet. But the process isn't lockstep; it's often recursive: you can back-track or jump ahead when it makes sense to do so. You might find, in the midst of writing, that you need to reorganize your outline. Or in rewriting, you might find you need more material on a certain point; in that case, back you go to the library. Early on, you'll need to plan your time and block out the work to be done, but you won't follow any inflexible track laid down for you. Like detective work, research sometimes will lead to an insurmountable obstacle. When stopped on one path, you can turn around, or go sideways, and set out on another.

To give you a sense of what one student encountered in fulfilling a typical research paper assignment, we will tell you a true story. It's about a freshman who began her investigation with enthusiasm, found herself stopped in her tracks, and had to start out in a fresh direction. Her story will give you an idea of how a typical research paper is written.

LEARNING FROM ANOTHER WRITER: ONE STUDENT'S EXPERIENCE

At first, Lisa Chickos wasn't daunted to find herself taking English 102 that spring, even though it was a course many students dreaded. Its notorious re-quirement—a research paper—made some people register for it unhappily. But in high school back in Apollo, Pennsylvania, Chickos had coped with more than one writing assignment that had taken her into the library. Research, in her experience, hadn't been cause for despair.

Even so, the English 102 assignment presented challenges. As often happens in college, the nature of the course itself suggested a direction for its students' research papers. That spring, Ms. Miller's section was centered on a theme: the changing roles of men and women in contemporary society. To start their thinking along that broad and promising line, the students had been reading *On the Contrary,* a collection of essays on male and female role playing. Within the large area of that topic, the research paper assignment left the way wide open: "Write a paper of at least 1500 words on a subject that has its source in our discussions and on which we have agreed."

A month would be an awfully short time to go from a tentative topic to a finished research paper. But along the way, the instructor would meet with each student at least twice in conference to follow the student's progress and offer counsel.

Right at the start, Chickos's investigation ran head-on into its tallest obstacle. Chickos had decided on a general direction: to find out more about women who make movies, their roles as producers, directors, and workers behind the scenes. That subject keenly appealed to her, but it led to immediate discouragement. In her college library, she made a preliminary search of the card catalogue and the *Readers' Guide to Periodical Literature* but turned up very little recent material. It may have been that she wasn't looking in the right places or that the best sources weren't available to her. Had she consulted a specialized index, such as *Film Literature Index,* she might have found more leads. She did find articles on women filmmakers and skimmed through them, but they struck her as too slight—lacking in facts and figures, in clearly stated views. From them, she couldn't get a clear sense of the extent of women's influence on filmmaking. Besides, what could her conclusion be? Probably something obvious: "Hooray for women filmmakers—more power to them!" Disappointed, Chickos realized that in the time she had, she probably couldn't write a strong paper on that interesting subject.

All wasn't lost. In the reference room, she dug into indexes. In the *Readers' Guide* she found a promising article listed: "A Bright Woman Is Caught in a Double Bind." She looked up the article in *Psychology Today* and found it thought-provoking. Some women, said psychologist Matina Horner, won't aspire to administrative positions because they fear success: if they succeed, they might find themselves cast out from society. This point confirmed an idea Chickos had met in her introductory psychology course. The textbook contained a discussion about some women's feelings that to deviate from traditional sex roles is more frightening than to fail. Ideas were coinciding. Chickos began to take notes.

Although she was moving in a clearer direction, she didn't have a definite topic yet. Administration—that seemed a discouragingly broad subject to investigate. What particular field of endeavor for bright women might she concentrate on? She looked over the anthology of essays her English class had discussed, and she did some random thinking. In elementary and secondary schools, most teachers are women. But what about their administrators—the principals, the superintendents? She reasoned, "We tend to think that a school administrator has to be a man." But was that necessarily the case?

She decided to find out. With the aid of the library card catalogue, she tracked down two books that promised to light the way: collections of essays by various writers, entitled *Women and Educational Leadership* and *Academic Women on the Move.* When she looked into them, she found helpful comments by the fistful. Her research began to soar off in its new direction.

In the second book, she came across a passage that annoyed her and made her want to keep investigating. Patricia Albjerg Graham, a teacher of history and education at Columbia University, made a revealing comment:

> Administrators are expected to be independent and assertive, behaviors understood as "tough and bitchy" when displayed by women, but "clearheaded and attentive to detail" when found in a man.

Graham's remark indicated sex discrimination in the hiring of school administrators, and Chickos felt her resentment continue to rise. Just how prevalent was this attitude? She read further. By happenstance, a kind of luck that sometimes favors research paper writers, she soon met (in *Women and Educational Leadership*) another quotation that fruitfully irritated her. A male administrator frankly admitted, "It's easier to work without women. Principals and superintendents are a management team. . . . I wonder if we could hang together so well if some of us were women."

Chickos was beginning to feel involved personally. This paper would be well worth writing! Could she find out more about this outrageous situation, even suggest what might be done about it? If so, maybe the toil of shuffling note cards, outlining, and citing sources would all be justified. She set to work with confidence. A couple of times Ms. Miller met with Chickos to monitor her progress and offer advice. "But she didn't try to tell me what avenues to follow," Chickos recalls. "The direction of my research had to be original."

When Chickos did some early drafting, she set down her points as they occurred to her. As she reviewed her draft, one idea stood out from the rest. Educator Jacqueline Clement had posed a problem: "Administrators usually start out as teachers and move up through the ranks. Why, then, if women make up the pool of potential educational leaders, are so few of them at the top?" On her draft, Chickos penned a red star next to this thought. She had found her basic research question, and the remainder of her paper would try to answer it.

In this chapter, we'll show you some of the research materials Lisa Chickos consulted, some notes she took, and some of her experiences along the way. Finally we'll give you her completed paper, "Educational Leadership: A Man's World."

LEARNING BY WRITING

Lisa Chickos's experience of getting momentarily stopped at the start could have happened to anyone at any college. As a rule, in any composition course a research paper is your most complicated job.

Some of our advice in this chapter may be old news to you. You may have learned in high school how to take research notes or how to make a working bibliography. At times, as we guide you through writing your paper, we'll pause to explain those special skills. To master them, if you haven't mastered them already, will speed you toward that triumphant day when you bang a final staple through your paper. But if at any moment you find us telling you more than you care to know, just skip over that part and go on. Later, should you want that information, you can always return to it.

The Assignment

Two kinds of library research papers are commonly required in college courses. We'll briefly discuss both of them.

A survey of what is thought or known. This kind of paper is a summing-up of knowledge in some area or discipline: modern methods of treating burns, the effects of tax revision, what music historians know about Mozart's family life, the theories of archeologists to account for the building of the Egyptian pyramids. In writing such a paper, you don't argue for any view of your own; you impartially report and carefully interpret what other writers have written.

A persuasive essay. In this kind of research paper, a writer might just state and support a view: that erosion of coastal shorelines is a desirable natural process or that color-tinted prints of classic black-and-white movies are deplorable. Or a writer might both advance a view *and* propose an action: that we should remove artificial barriers on our beaches and let erosion take its course or that there ought to be a law against tinting great old movies like *Casablanca.* Unlike the persuasive papers you may have written when studying Part Four, persuasive research papers call for investigation and thorough documentation of sources.

In this assignment, we suggest the second kind of research paper: a persuasive one. (An assignment for the first kind, a survey paper, will be found on p. 335.) Here's what you do, in more or less this order. In the following sections we carefully explain each of these tasks.

1. Choose a general subject you care to investigate.
2. Do a little reading around in it, to see exactly what aspects of the subject most keenly interest you.

(If you know, from early on, exactly what interests you, you can skip the first two steps.)

3. State, in the form of a question, exactly what you care to find out.
4. By means of library research, find an answer to your question. This answer may be tentative—just a healthy hunch—but if it is your best hunch, go ahead and stick up for it.
5. Then, in a paper of at least 1500 words, set forth your view. Give evidence to support it, drawn from your research.

If you like, and if your topic seems to call for it, add a further step:

6. Propose some action that should be taken.

This paper, as you can see, will be more than a stack of facts. It will set forth an opinion you originate or, if you didn't think it up yourself, an opinion that you decide to accept after reading at least ten or twelve other writers and considering their various views.

Among student research papers we have seen recently, the following are a few that made enjoyable, persuasive reading.

PAPERS ADVANCING A VIEW

A man, tracing Rambo's rise to the status of American hero, gave reasons for his view that the character falls short of standards set by earlier American heroes like Davy Crockett and Daniel Boone.

A woman praised the British system of supplying drug addicts with drugs, thus making business for drug dealers less profitable.

A woman wrote a brief analysis of a controversy involving the news commentator Walter Lippmann: his having argued in favor of interning Japanese-Americans during World War II. Lippmann's argument, she concluded, had been biased and ill informed.

A man studied unemployment in a large eastern city and found one of its causes to be racial discrimination. He condemned this discrimination without feeling able to propose any definite solution.

A man studied the process through which an unpublished song by an unknown composer might be recorded and go on to hit the top of the charts. He concluded that if you are an unknown composer, your chances of such success are remote, but the odds aren't hopeless.

PAPERS ADVANCING A VIEW
AND ARGUING FOR ACTION

A man, after considering several possible solutions to the problem of America's national debt, came to the conclusion that the best would be a national lottery. He supported his proposal with evidence from his research into national lotteries held in other countries.

A woman studied the forces that deprive today's children of their innocence at earlier and earlier ages, including television, adult movies, VCRs, drugs, and changing sexual mores. She pleaded that parents take steps to allow their children to remain children until they are emotionally ready to cope with adult problems.

After investigating studies showing that treatment with bright light helps patients suffering from depression, a woman argued that this treatment should be adopted in every hospital.

A note about schedules. Along with the assignment to write a research paper, some instructors will suggest a schedule. Lisa Chickos's instructor blocked out the students' obligations like this:

March 26   Topic due (the question to be answered)

April 3   Thesis statement due (a one-sentence statement of opinion: what the paper will demonstrate)

April 9   Preliminary outline due

April 18   Draft due

April 25   Completed paper due

But if your instructor doesn't give you a series of deadlines, you'll be wise to set some for yourself. You can depend on this: a research paper will require more time than you expect. When putting it into its final draft, you'll need hours to cite all your sources accurately. You'll need time, then, to look it all over and proofread it, not be forced to toss everything together in a desperate all-night siege. A clear-cut schedule will help.

Generating Ideas

> How can we most effectively help long-term prisoners, on their release, to return to society?
>
> Did Walt Disney make any admirable and original contributions to American art, or was he a mere imitator, a purveyor of slick schlock, as some of his critics have charged?
>
> What should be done about acid rain?
>
> Should the U.S. State Department act to prevent American soldiers of fortune—hired mercenaries—from fighting in Africa?

If you already have a narrowly defined research question in mind, such as the preceding examples—congratulations. You can just skip to the Discovery Checklist on page 297. But if you don't have a question yet, read on.

Choosing your territory. To explore, you need a territory—a subject that interests you. Perhaps, as Lisa Chickos found, your work in this very course, or in another course, will suggest an appropriate territory. Chickos wrote a paper suggested by a theme that ran through all the readings and discussions in her writing course. A psychology course might encourage you to investigate mental disorders; a sociology course, labor relations.

You'll have an easier time from the start if you can make your territory smaller than "mental disorders" or "labor relations." "Schizophrenia" or "steelworkers' strikes" would be smaller, more readily explorable territories. But if you don't feel that you can make your topic so narrow and definite yet, go ahead, start with "mental disorders" or "labor relations."

For finding your general subject, the following questions may help you at the start. They'll send you back once more to every writer's five basic resources.

DISCOVERY CHECKLIST: CHOOSING YOUR TERRITORY

- Can you recall from your work or leisure experience, from travel or study, something you'd care to read more about?
- What have you observed recently that you could more thoroughly investigate with the aid of books and magazines? (Suggestion: try watching the evening news, taking notes as you watch.)
- What have you recently read that has left you still wondering?
- In recent conversation with friends, in class discussions, what topics have arisen that you'd care to explore?

- What can you imagine that might be confirmed or denied by your reading? If, for instance, you can imagine life as a peasant on a feudal manor or as a slave on a plantation, you might go to some history books to have your mental picture corrected and enlarged. If you can imagine yourself living on a space station in orbit, you might learn from recent science writers what such a space station will probably be like.

Your next move is to take an overall look at your subject, to see what's in it for you.

Taking an overview. Before launching an expedition into a little-known territory, a smart explorer first makes a reconnaissance flight and takes an overview. Having seen the terrain, the explorer then chooses the very spot to set up camp: the point on the map that looks most promising.

Research writers do something like that, too. Before committing themselves to a topic, they first look over a broader territory to see what in it looks most attractive. How do you take an overview?

You might look up your subject in an encyclopedia and read the general article about it—*unions* or *labor relations, mental illness* or *schizophrenia* or (still more general) *psychiatry.* By now, you are a veteran reader of encyclopedias, but if you care for any useful tips on using both general encyclopedias and specialized ones, see Chapter 17 (pp. 345–347).

You might look at an article in a popular, nonspecialized magazine. In your library's reference room, check the *Readers' Guide to Periodical Literature,* that green-bound index of recent articles in popular magazines. It will direct you to the latest information and opinion, classified by many subjects. You probably know the *Readers' Guide;* if not, go look at it. Very soon, we'll tell you more about its usefulness. (There's also a whole discussion of it and other indexes on pp. 348–352.)

You might browse in an introductory textbook, if any seems likely to help. For the general subjects we've been using, labor relations and mental illness, you might go to a textbook in political science or psychology. Articles in encyclopedias and books, usually wide-ranging and general, will contain smaller ideas, some of them more manageable for your research project.

When Lisa Chickos began investigating women in school administration, she had only a large, vague subject in mind. But as she kept reading and thinking, she saw a smaller idea she wanted to concentrate on: "discrimination against women school and college administrators." That seemed plenty to consider in a 1500-word research paper. As you read, keep a lookout for any ideas that intrigue you, that you might like to explore.

How much time should you devote to your overview? Many students find that they can make such a reconnaissance flight in an evening or a few hours. At this point, your investigation need go only far enough to suggest a question you'd care to answer—one like Chickos's "In educational administration, why are so few women at the top?" Let's see what goes into a workable, researchable question.

Stating your question. Once you have zeroed in on part of a territory to explore, you can ask a definite question. Ask what you want to find out, and your task will leap into focus. Having begun with a broad, general interest in (let's say) social problems in large cities, a writer might then ask, "What happens to teenage runaways on the streets of Manhattan?" Or, if a writer has started with a general yen to know more about contemporary architecture, a definite question might be "Who in America today is good at designing sports arenas?"

You might start with a brainstorming session. For fifteen or twenty minutes, let your thoughts revolve, and jot down whatever questions come to mind—even useless ones. Then, looking over your list, you may find one that appears promising.

In generating questions, you may find it helpful to review the various ways of explaining presented in Part Three. If, for instance, you go back over the method of comparing and contrasting (Chapter 9), you might think of a question that naturally calls for that method. Can you recall two individuals in public life—two leading members of any profession you're interested in, two artists, two authors, two economists, two heads of state—who might be interesting to compare and contrast with the aid of research? Pick influential thinkers or persons prominent in international affairs rather than recently popular entertainers or sports stars so that you can find some *books* about your subject. Just to get your thoughts started, here are sample research questions suggested by the methods of explaining.

Comparing and contrasting. What differences and similarities exist between Elie Wiesel and Bruno Bettelheim as historians of the Holocaust?

Analyzing a process. How does a forger go about painting and selling an "original" Old Master?

Dividing. Into what groups of supporters can the Republican (or the Democratic) party in your state be divided?

Classifying. What various kinds of software are currently available for small business?

Looking for causes. What causes stammering?

Looking for effects. What effects has the growth of videotape rentals had on American family life?

Defining. What is a "hyperactive" child?

In the course of answering any of these questions by research, you would be highly likely to arrive at a personal opinion on the subject. You would then be ready to fulfill the fifth step suggested in the assignment: to state a view.

A workable question has to be narrow enough to allow a fruitful investigation in the library. A question can be too immense and the research it would call for be too overwhelming to complete in a month—"How is the climate of the earth changing?" "Who are the world's best living storytellers?" "Why are there poor among us?" "What's going on in outer space?"

On the other hand, a question can be too narrow. If a mere source or two could answer it, the resulting research paper may be thin and uninteresting.

"How does the First Lady do her hair?" would be a shallow question to research. It would turn up facts but few opinions. All you would need to answer it would be one popular magazine interview with a White House hairdresser. But even if you were to find such an interview, you would lack for material. The subject has provoked a lot of gossip, but little thought. Probably you could either search out an answer to that question in fifteen minutes or waste days and find nothing worth taking a note about. So instead, ask a question that will lead you to a lot of meaty books and articles. "How does the First Lady influence the politics of this administration?" That might be worth a research paper.

A caution: if you pick a topic currently in the news, you may have trouble finding valuable material—deep analysis, critical thought, ample historical background, intelligent controversy. For many up-to-the-minute topics, the only printed sources may be recent newspapers and news magazines. The topic may be too new for anyone yet to have done a book or a really thorough magazine analysis about it.

Try to keep the wording of your question as simple as you can: set yourself one thing to find out, not several. If the question reads "How does current art and music still reflect the cultural revolution of the 1960s?" it is too big. Split it into two questions and then pick one of them: "How does art still reflect the cultural revolution of the 1960s?" or "How does music . . . ?" By qualifying the word *music,* you might cut the question still further down to size: "How does last year's rock music . . . ?" Focus on whatever you most keenly wish to learn.

A well-wrought research question suggests ways to answer it. Say the question is "What has caused a shortage of low-income housing in northeastern cities?" The wording suggests subject headings that may be found in the card catalogue or the *Readers' Guide: housing, housing shortage, low-income housing, urban housing.*

Until you start working in the library, of course, you can't know for certain how fruitful your question will be. If it doesn't lead you to any definite facts, if it doesn't help you form a clear opinion, you'll need to reword it or throw it out and ask a new question. But at the very least, the question you first ask will give you a definite direction in which to start looking.

When you have tentatively stated your question, you can test it by asking other questions about it.

DISCOVERY CHECKLIST: QUESTIONING YOUR QUESTION

- Is this question answerable—at least partly answerable—in the time you have? Does it need to be reduced or expanded?
- Does the question refer to a matter that has been written about only lately? Or, like a more promising question for library research, will it send you to books and magazines of at least a year earlier?
- Have you worded your question as plainly and simply as you can? Do you understand exactly what you'll be looking for?
- Does the question ask for just one answer, not many?

- Does your question interest you? Do you honestly crave the answer to it? If so, your research is likely to cruise along at a great rate and you will find yourself enjoying a sense of discovery. Interest yourself and you are also likely to interest your reader.

Making a preliminary search. You can put your question to the acid test and quickly see whether it is likely to lead to an ample research paper. You can conduct a short, fast search that shouldn't take you more than an hour. You just check the card catalogue to see what books appear under your subject heading and if possible go into the stacks and look over the shelves. You take a quick check of magazine articles: consult the last annual *Readers' Guide,* looking under the subject heading closest to your special concern. Don't look up the articles yet; just see how many there are and whether their titles sound promising. If your subject is "Women: School Administrators," an article called "Iona Dawes Honored with Birthday Cake for Fourteen Years as Principal" is probably going to be too specific to help.

You don't have to take notes yet, if you don't want to—just look around and get a sense of the sources available. This preliminary search has a simple purpose: to ascertain that you'll have enough material to do the job. If the material looks so skimpy that you won't have anything to choose from, and you'll need to force every crumb of it into your paper to get 1500 words, you might better ask another question. If your first trip into the stacks reveals ten yards of books that probably deal with your question, alarm bells should start ringing in your ears. Did someone other than Shakespeare write Shakespeare's plays? A thousand books have issued from that question. What caused the Civil War? Every United States history book offers a few explanations. You might want to ask a different question. It would be too easy to say nothing on those subjects except what has already been said. Instead of a question that only two books might answer or a question that a hundred books might answer, pick a question that a dozen or twenty might.

If you ask a neighboring student, "What can I write a research paper on?" and he gives you a topic, fine. But before committing yourself to it, you had better do some preliminary reading in the library. Otherwise, you could get stuck with a topic full of more problems than you realize, including a shortage of helpful material.

Making a working bibliography. Before going on with your investigation, you need a working bibliography: a detailed list of books and articles you plan to consult.

Your overview and your preliminary search may have given you a good rough notion of where your most promising material lies. Now you need titles and information. Some writers keep track of everything in a notebook small enough to fit a pocket. Others find that the most convenient way to compile such a working bibliography is on 3-by-5-inch note cards, one source to a card. Cards are handy: you can arrange and shuffle them, even use a stack of well-ordered cards for your working outline. The more care you take in listing your tentative sources, the more time you'll save later, when at the end of your paper you compile a list of works cited. At that point, you'll be grateful to find all the necessary information at your fingertips.

What should each source card contain? Everything necessary to write the final list of sources to be placed at the end of your paper. Include the following for books (see Figure 16.1).

1. The library call number, in the upper left corner of the card.
2. In the upper right corner, in uppercase letters, just the last name of the book's author so that you can identify the source at a glance.
3. The author's full name.
4. The book's title, including its subtitle if there is one.
5. The publication information: publisher, place, and year of publication.

For a magazine article, your source card need contain no library call number, but you'll need the following data (see Figure 16.2).

1. In the upper right corner, in uppercase letters, the identifier: the last name of the person who wrote the article.
2. The author's full name.
3. The title of the article, in quotation marks, followed by the name of the publication, underlined.
4. For a scholarly journal, the series number (if there is one) and the volume number (sometimes followed by the issue number).
5. The date of the issue: for a journal, the year in parentheses; for a monthly magazine, the month and year; for a weekly or daily publication, the month, day, and year.
6. The page numbers of the article. (The "+" indicates that the article covers more than one page, but not consecutive pages.)

```
BF          WORTMAN, LOFTUS, & MARSHALL
121
.W67        Wortman, Camille B., Elizabeth F.
1981
            Loftus, and Mary Marshall.

            Psychology. New York: Knopf,

            1981.
```

Figure 16.1 A Bibliography Card for a Book in MLA Style

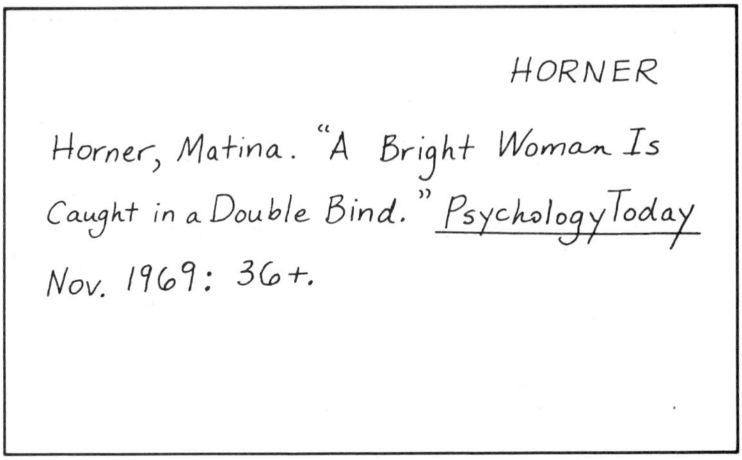

HORNER

Horner, Matina. "A Bright Woman Is Caught in a Double Bind." Psychology Today Nov. 1969: 36+.

Figure 16.2 A Bibliography Card for an Article in MLA Style

This may seem like a lot of record keeping. But now, as you begin your research, it will take you less time to jot down all this information in full than to make future trips to the library. As you will see, you're going to need every last bit of this information. You will need it in citing your sources and in making your list of works cited. On the night before your paper is due, you will thank your stars you've got all this stuff.

To fill your bibliography cards with promising titles to look for, what sources do you consult? The following three are essential. You probably know them already, but if you don't, you will quickly get some hands-on experience. (They are also discussed in detail in the next chapter.)

1. *The card catalogue,* for the titles and locations of books. Early on, you'll no doubt consult this master listing of every book and bound periodical in the library. Are you acquainted with the *Library of Congress Subject Headings?* This useful directory can help you find a particular subject in the card catalogue even if you don't know exactly what to call it. For more about this helpful aid, see page 340. For a basic description of the card catalogue, how it works, and how it can serve you, see pages 340–343.

2. *An index to periodicals,* for the titles of magazine articles. In high school, you probably used at least the *Readers' Guide to Periodical Literature,* which covers popular magazines, but if your subject falls into the category of art, music, theater, film, architecture, law, business, or education, other indexes are likely to be helpful. Some cover specialized magazines and scholarly journals. If you'd like a short description of these indexes—there may be one just right for your project—see page 350.

3. *A ready-made bibliography,* for a list of books and articles on a certain subject, often with a brief descriptive opinion of each item. Imagine what a big job you'll be spared if someone has already drawn up a bibliography for your subject. For more about such bibliographies, see page 348.

For your present short-range investigation, those three basic sources will probably lead to more books and articles than you can weave into 1500 or 2000 words. But what if they don't, and you need still more material? In that case, you can find thumbnail descriptions of other likely sources in Chapter 17. Whenever a college course calls on you to do a longer and deeper research paper, such as a term paper at the end of a course or an honors thesis, you will surely need more sources than the three basic ones suggested here. These will be only places to begin. Your present task, though more limited, is still large: to think with the aid of printed sources and, with their help, to speak your mind.

 Evaluating your sources. With any luck, in making your working bibliography you will have turned up some books and articles by writers of deep knowledge and high integrity. You may also have turned up a few hasty hunks of verbiage written by hacks or some material written with biases—which may be perfectly good as long as you recognize the biases. How do you know what sources are trustworthy? We realize that, in the short while you have to work, you can't spend a lot of time running background checks on all the writers you're quoting. But you can look them over. Here are a few suggestions.

 A *primary source,* the writer or speaker who said something originally, is generally more reliable than a *secondary source,* a writer or speaker who refers to the primary source at second hand. An eyewitness account of a fire is a primary source; a secondary source is a reporter's account based on the testimony of eyewitnesses. In a research paper, a book by child psychologist Jean Piaget would be a primary source; a secondary source might be a book by another writer discussing Piaget's theories.

 Another evidence of reliability is a recent date of publication. If you are using a book that has been revised, use the latest edition. Try to use at least some material that has appeared this year or in recent years.

 Still another test of a source is a writer's reputation. How will you know if the writer is a recognized authority? See whether any credentials are given in a *blurb,* or biographical note, at the beginning or end of a book or article. If still in doubt, you might check whether the writer is listed in the card catalogue as the author of other books on the subject and in *Who's Who, Contemporary Authors,* or reference works covering specialized fields, such as *Who's Who in Science.* Inclusion in such works isn't a guarantee that the writer is absolutely trustworthy, but you may be able to get an idea of the author's background. Ask your reference librarian whether the writer's name is familiar. But ultimately, the best test of a writer's authority is whether his or her work meets the critical demands of other authorities. You might find some authorities on campus to talk with. Your instructor is an authority on some things. And you might do some more reading in the field and start becoming an authority yourself.

 If your source is a weekly news magazine like *Time, Newsweek,* or *U.S. News & World Report,* the writer of an article is likely to be a reporter, not always a famous name, perhaps not a world-renowned authority. Such magazines do, however, feature some articles by experts; and all such magazines have a good reputation for checking their facts carefully. They try to present a range of opinions but sometimes *select* facts to mirror the opinions of their editors. In a serious, reputable periodical of general interest, other than a news weekly—a magazine such as *New York Review of Books,* the *Atlantic, Harper's,* or the *American Scholar*—articles are often written by distinguished authorities.

In testing another writer's statements to see whether they hold water, it helps to notice the audience for which they were written. Does the periodical have a predictable point of view? Is it written toward any special community? How can you find out, if you don't already know, the general outlook of the periodical you're examining? The *Nation,* a magazine of commentary from a left-leaning political point of view, is likely to give you a different picture of the world from that found in the *National Review,* edited by conservative William F. Buckley. To find out a magazine's stance, or stand, we make the following suggestions.

Read the advertisements, if any. These are usually the surest guide to a magazine's audience. If you can size up the readers, you will know where the magazine's views are coming from and to whom its editors are trying to appeal. *Time, Newsweek,* and *U.S. News & World Report* address mostly college-educated professionals. A large part of this audience consists of businesspeople—as shown by the many ads for office copiers, freight and delivery services, hotels that welcome the business traveler, and corporations trumpeting their own importance. To take a periodical of another extreme, weekly tabloids such as the *National Enquirer,* the *Star,* and *Weekly World News* specialize in scandal and sensation, with headlines like SEX-CHANGE NUN TURNS TV WRESTLER and ELVIS ALIVE ON FLYING SAUCER. The ads offer fortune-telling rocks, courses in hypnosis that make a member of the opposite sex do your bidding, and cold creams that promise to wipe twenty years from a wrinkled face with one quick smear. These tabloids probably appeal to two audiences: the gullible and people who like to say, "My land! What will they think up next?"

Read more than one issue of the magazine. Browse, at least, through several issues—as many as necessary to understand the magazine's assumptions and its audience. The more you read of the magazine the clearer will be your sense of where it stands.

Read the editorials, in which the editors, making no pretense of being impartial, set forth their views. In most magazines, these will be in a front section and may not even be signed, since the name of the editor is on the masthead, near the contents. If you can find an editorial commenting on a familiar issue, you may soon know the magazine's bias.

Read any featured columnists who appear regularly. Usually their jobs depend on their voicing opinions congenial to the magazine's editors and publishers. Apparently columnist Damon Runyon was aware of this situation, for he wrote in a newspaper published by tycoon William Randolph Hearst: "Whose bread I eat, his songs I sing." Discount Runyon's songs accordingly. We should admit, though, that this test isn't foolproof. Sometimes a dissenting columnist will be hired to lend variety.

Read with an analytic eye the lead features or news stories (those most prominently placed in the front of the issue), paying special attention to the last paragraph, in which the writer reveals what it all means. Sometimes some advice or directive or hope will tip you off to where the magazine stands. "Despite the stern criticisms leveled at Centro Oil by environmentalists, the company has weathered this small storm and no doubt will outlast many to come." The voice is clearly that of a friend of the oil company.

Read the letters to the editor. Some magazines, like *Time,* strive to offer space to a diversity of opinion. (When *Time* prints two letters, one is generally pro and one is con.) You can often get a line on the level of schooling and intelligence shown by who writes in and thereby understand something about the magazine's readers.

A helpful work of reference that evaluates magazines is *Magazines for Libraries.* It mentions biases, tells what sort of material the magazine customarily prints, and gives circulation figures.

For still more advice on evaluating evidence, turn back to "Testing Evidence," on pages 252–254.

Setting out: Note taking. Once you have a strong working bibliography and have evaluated your sources and winnowed out any you don't trust, you need to begin reading and accumulating material for your paper. What will you look for? Examples and illustrations of the ideas you're pursuing as well as evidence to support them—and to refute them. Start with the sources that seem most promising—those most recent, most authoritative, most complete in their coverage of your chosen subject.

As you read, decide whether to take notes and, if so, how extensively. You can't always guess the usefulness of a source in advance. Sometimes a likely source turns out to yield nothing much, and a book that had promised to be a juicy plum shrivels to a prune right in your hands.

If you do take notes while you read, take ample ones. Many a writer has come to grief by setting down sketchy jottings and trusting memory to fill in the blanks. You'll probably find that using note cards will work better than taking notes on pieces of paper. Then, when the time comes to organize the material you've gathered, you can shuffle your cards into an order that makes most sense to you. Roomy 4-by-6-inch or 5-by-8-inch cards will hold more than the 3-by-5-inch cards you used for your working bibliography. Even a meaty idea ought to fit on one card. Use one card per idea. Putting two or more ideas on the same card complicates your task when you reach the drafting stage.

Some research writers insist that the invention of photocopying has done away with the need to take notes. Indeed, judicious photocopying can save you time as you gather materials for your paper, but the key word here is *judicious.* Simply photocopying everything you read with the vague notion that some of it contains material valuable for your essay is likely in the end to cost you more time rather than less. Much of it won't be worth saving. Most important, you won't have digested and evaluated what was on the page; you will merely have copied it. Selecting what is essential, transcribing it by hand, perhaps nutshelling or paraphrasing it, helps make it yours. When later you start drafting, unless your paper is to be very short, it will take you longer to decode great bundles of photocopied material than to work from carefully thought-out note cards. Indiscriminate photocopying may also cost you a lot of money.

If, however, you're using a source that doesn't circulate, such as a reference book always kept in the reference room, you may want to photocopy the relevant pages so that you can use them whenever and wherever is convenient for you. Just make sure that the name of the source and the page number appear on your copy so that you can make a source card for it. If not, pencil it on the photocopy. When you start organizing your notes, you may find it convenient to scissor out of a photocopied page what you're going to use and to stick it onto a note card.

A good rule is to make your notes and citations full enough so that, once they're written, you're totally independent of the source from which they came. That way you'll avoid having to rush back to the library in a panic trying to find again, in a book or periodical you returned weeks ago, some nugget of material you want to include in your paper. Good, thoughtful notes can sometimes be copied verbatim from note card to first draft. But often they will take rewriting to fit them in so they don't stand out like boulders in the stream of your prose.

A useful note card includes three elements:

An identifier, usually the last name of the author whose work you're citing, followed by *the page number or numbers* on which the information can be found

A subject heading, some key word or phrase you make up yourself to help you decide where in your paper the information will best fit

The fact, idea, or quotation you plan to use in your paper

You'll need all these elements so that later, when it's time to incorporate your notes into your paper or develop your ideas from multiple sources, you'll have an accurate record of what you found in each source. You'll also know exactly where you found it, and you will be able to cite every source without difficulty. (For sample note cards, see Figures 16.3, 16.4, and 16.5.)

While you're taking notes, you can keep on evaluating. You can be deciding whether the stuff is going to be greatly valuable, fairly valuable, or only a little bit valuable. Some note takers put a star at the top of any note they assign great value to, a question mark on a note that might or might not be useful. Later, when they're organizing their material, they can see what especially stands out and will need emphasis. In reading the material you are collecting, you need not regard it all as holy writ. In fact, if you can look at it a little sourly and suspiciously, that might be to your advantage. Mary-Claire van Leunen, author of *A Handbook for Scholars* (New York: Knopf, 1979), has advised researchers who must read much scholarly writing: "Do not smile sweetly as you read through pages of graceless, stilted, maundering bombast. Fume, fuss, be angry. Your anger will keep you up to the mark when you turn to writing yourself."

How many notes are enough? When you find that the sources you consult are mostly repeating what you've learned from previous sources, you have probably done enough reading and note taking. But before you reach that point, we'd like to remind you of three ways of setting down notes that will help you write a good, meaty paper. (You have met them before in Chapter 6.)

Quoting, nutshelling, paraphrasing. Preparing to write her paper on women in educational administration, Lisa Chickos found a thought-provoking paragraph in Patricia Albjerg Graham's "Status Transitions of Women Students, Faculty, and Administrators," a chapter in *Academic Women on the Move.*

> Violation of cultural stereotypes may be another factor working against women faculty members moving into upper-level administrative positions. It generally is assumed that women can make their best contributions in positions subordinate to men. Hence the university administrator's job description is almost invariably drawn with a man in mind, particularly a married man whose wife can provide auxiliary social support. Moreover, administrators are expected to be independent and assertive, behaviors understood as "tough and bitchy" when displayed by women, but "clear-headed and attentive to detail" when found in a man. Tolerance for men's behavior is a good deal broader than it is for that of women. Men are permitted their idiosyncracies of whatever sort, but women are expected to maintain a much more precarious balance between conspicuous competence and tactful femininity. Manifestations of independence and autonomy are expected in a male executive; their presence in women makes some male colleagues cringe.

Figures 16.3, 16.4, and 16.5 illustrate note cards for quoting, nutshelling, and paraphrasing material from this paragraph.

To quote selectively—to choose the words with life and pith in them—is one convincing way to demonstrate and refute ideas and to marshal evidence. To do so, you'll need to copy a brief quotation carefully onto a card, making sure to reproduce exactly the spelling and punctuation, even if they're unusual. Take the trouble to go back over what you've written to make sure that you've copied it correctly. Put quotation marks around the material so that when you come to include it in your paper, you'll remember that it's a direct quotation. You might also want to remind yourself in a bracketed note that you intend to use the author's words in a quotation. Lisa Chickos wrote herself the note card shown in Figure 16.3 to extract a lively quotation.

Sometimes it doesn't pay to transcribe a quotation word for word. Parts may fail to serve your purpose, such as transitions ("as the reader will recall from Chapter 14"), parenthetical remarks ("which data slightly modifies the earlier view of Pflug"), and other information useless to you. Lisa Chickos, quoting a sentence on her note card shown in Figure 16.3, doesn't bother to take down the transition word, "Moreover," with which the sentence begins. But she faithfully indicates the omission by using an ellipsis mark (. . .).

Nutshelling, or summarizing, takes less room than quoting extensively. To give your reader just the sense of a passage from another writer, you can

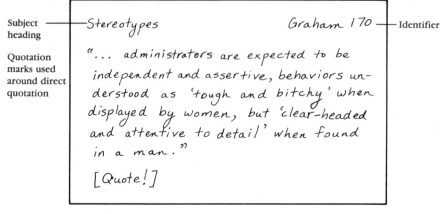

Stereotypes   Graham 170 — Identifier

Quotation
marks used
around direct
quotation

"... administrators are expected to be
independent and assertive, behaviors understood as 'tough and bitchy' when
displayed by women, but 'clear-headed
and attentive to detail' when found
in a man."
[Quote!]

Figure 16.3 A Sample Note Card Giving a Direct Quotation from a Source

Attitudes that limit women   Graham 170-171

Job descriptions for administrators have married
men in mind. Works against women in two
ways: (1) Women don't have wives to help
with social aspects of job; (2) the traits
essential for administrators are also
considered unfeminine.

Figure 16.4 Nutshelling, or Summarizing, a Paragraph

condense it in your own words. If Lisa Chickos had put into nutshell form the essential ideas she wished to take from the paragraph in Graham's article, her note card might have looked like Figure 16.4.

Paraphrasing, a third strategy useful in taking research notes, also transforms an author's ideas into your own words. Unlike nutshelling, though, paraphrasing doesn't necessarily make your notes any briefer. Why paraphrase? It is especially helpful when the language of another writer isn't particularly vivid and memorable (unlike the phrase from Graham that Lisa Chickos quotes: "tough and bitchy"). When the writer's ideas look valuable but the words seem not worth preserving in the original, render them in paraphrase. Don't hover so close to the writer's very words that your paraphrase is merely an echo. If your source writes, "In staging an ancient Greek tragedy today, most directors do not mask the actors," and you write, merely changing the word order, "Most directors, in staging an ancient Greek tragedy today, do not mask the actors," you have stuck too closely to the original. Write instead: "Few contemporary directors of Greek tragedy insist that their actors wear masks." When you paraphrase, also avoid the temptation to merely substitute a synonym here and there. That way lies madness—and perhaps a charge of plagiarism. The style in paraphrasing, as in nutshelling, has to be yours. If Lisa Chickos had chosen to paraphrase rather than to quote Graham, her note card might have looked like Figure 16.5.

How do you abstract the main idea from another writer's thoughts? Before you nutshell or paraphrase, we'd suggest that you do the following.

1. Read the original passage over a couple of times.
2. Without looking at it, try to state its gist, the point it makes, the main sense you remember.
3. Go back and reread the original passage one more time, making sure you got its gist faithfully. Revise as necessary.

If you have dealt carefully with the material, you won't have to put quotation marks around anything in your paraphrase.

Unless an assignment strictly confines you to library sources, which it might, no law forbids your using any promising, good-looking nonlibrary materials in your research paper. To make a point, you can recall your own experience, observations, conversations, past reading. And why park your imagination outside the library? You might want to bring together sources not usually related. One fine research paper we have read, by a pre-law student, compared gambling laws in ancient Rome with gambling laws in present-day Atlantic City. Placing Rome and Atlantic City cheek to cheek took imagination.

Honest borrowing. You have an obligation to repay the researchers, scholars, and writers who came before you. That is why, in doing research, you cite

Roadblocks   Graham 170–171

Women aspiring to administrative positions in education are limited by the assumption that administrators are married men whose wives can provide social support. Because job descriptions are written with such men in mind, they also call for skills considered natural for men but unfeminine for women. On the job men are given latitude in how they carry out their duties, but there is pressure on women to walk a fine line between competence and femininity.

Figure 16.5 Paraphrasing the Quotation from Graham's Article

your source materials so carefully, mentioning the names of all other writers you borrow from. You do this not only for quotations you take but also for ideas, even though you have nutshelled or paraphrased them in your own words. Sometimes, because a student failed to acknowledge all sources, he or she is blamed for plagiarism. Or the writer failed to paraphrase but used the original writer's words without quotation marks. The writer is suspected of a rip-off, when he or she merely failed to make a debt clear.

In Chapter 19, we offer detailed information about how to cite and list sources so that, like any good scholar, you will know exactly how to pay your debts in full.

Shaping a Draft

From question to answer. At this point, we're going to take time out for (1) a look back at where you've come from and (2) a look ahead to where you still have to go.

You began gathering material with a question in mind. It asked what you wanted to find out. By now, if your research has been thorough and fruitful, you know the answer. The moment has come to weave the material you have gathered into a rough whole.

First, look over your material. See the general configuration of it. It's a good idea, at this point, to throw out any of it that won't help you write.

Then, having taken a quick survey of your material, you have a choice of at least two ways to proceed.

The thesis method. This way, a time-proven method of shaping a research paper, is to decide right now what your research has shown. What does it all mean? Or what's your own view of it? You sum up that view in a sentence. It is your thesis, the one main idea your paper will demonstrate. Lisa Chickos's thesis sentence might be "The scarcity of women school administrators is deplorable." (For more advice on composing such a sentence, see "Stating a Thesis," p. 469.) You then start writing your draft, including only material that supports your thesis, concentrating from beginning to end on making that thesis clear.

The answer method. Some writers have an easier time of writing if they plunge in and start writing without first trying to state any thesis at all. If you care to try this method, recall your original question. What's the answer to it— what have you found out? Start writing with the purpose of making that answer clear.

The resulting draft will be only the main body of your paper. It won't have any head or tail. We suggest you don't worry about writing your introduction (the opening paragraph or paragraphs) or your conclusion (the last paragraph or paragraphs) until you have written that middle part. The start and finish may be easier to write once you see what you say in between.

When your draft of the main body is complete and you have set forth what you've learned, then ask yourself another question: How do you feel about your findings? Or what do you think it all means? Then write a beginning and ending that will make your opinion clear.

If you don't know quite how to express your opinion yet, start writing anyway. Perhaps, while you thoughtfully write, your view will become clear.

Evaluating your material. About now, you will probably wish to sift through all the evidence you have collected, separating wheat from chaff. If you've been taking notes on cards, the labor of sorting the cards into piles will be made easier. But thinking will be the hardest part of sorting: you'll need to reflect on each item, imagining it as a piece of your finished paper. You might classify your notes into three categories:

essential material
good but less important material
material not worth the powder to blow it up

How to decide what is essential? *A useful note will plainly help answer your original question.* If that question was "How far advanced is Soviet computer technology?" then a comment by a Norwegian engineer who was permitted to use a large computer at the Soviet Academy of Sciences and who evaluated its performance would obviously be very valuable. Of lesser import might be an American tourist's recollection of seeing a large computer in Moscow being unloaded from a truck. Yet, if for any reason the latter note seemed memorable, you should hang on to it, at least until writing a draft.

Of course, just as you evaluated sources from the time you started collecting their titles ("Is this writer an expert? Will this article really help?"), you go on evaluating your material all the while you write, and all the while you rewrite besides.

You aren't trying to impose your will on your material to line it up so that it proves only what you want to prove. Still, the only rough rule we can offer for evaluating your material is this: *Does this note help you say what you now want to say?*

Organizing your ideas. Either the thesis method or the answer method will have the effect of pulling your miscellaneous material into shape. But if your material seems not to want to shape up, you may find it helpful to outline. You might arrange all your note cards in an order that makes sense. Then the stack of cards becomes your outline, and as you write, turning over card after card, you follow it. Or you can make an informal outline on paper (see p. 476). That's what Lisa Chickos did at first. She made a rough preliminary listing of the points she planned to cover.

Introduction

Leadership in American education

Barriers to women who might go into administration
 Perceptions of women's ability
 Socialization

        "Fear of success"
        Departure from traditional roles
        Family and geographic ties
        Female stereotypes
    Solutions
        Mutual support
        Support from male colleagues
        Encouragement of children
        Support from family
        Openness of employers
        Support from organizations and legislation

As you can see, Chickos included the heading "Fear of success," and at that point she found the outline prompting her ideas. Next to "Fear of success" she wrote, "Say something about deviating from prescribed roles." Obviously young women in educational administration might be afraid of being branded as "tough and bitchy" (to quote Graham again). "I may need another category," Chickos realized, noting to herself, "Women who have reached positions. Maybe a separate category for barriers that inhibit both women from rising in administration and employers from hiring them." Just looking over her rough outline proved stimulating: it made thoughts start to flow.

    From notes to outline to draft. Note cards are only the raw material for a research paper. If they are to end up in a readable, unified whole, they need shaping and polishing. Much wordage in your notes probably won't need to go into your paper. When you draft, you'll find yourself summarizing your notes or selecting just the useful parts of them.

    When you look over your outline, if you use one, it's a good idea to compare each section with the notes you have on hand for it. If for a certain section you have no notes, or only a single note, your research has a gap to fill. Back to the library.

    When you are satisfied that your notes fall into some kind of order and your outline has some notes for every part of it, you start to write. If things don't fall into perfect order, start writing anyway. Get something down on paper so that you will have something to revise.

    All the while you're writing, you keep citing: referring your reader exactly to the sources of your material. To cite your sources is easy—it just takes time and care. In the body of your paper, right after every fact, idea, or quotation you have borrowed, you tell your reader where you found it. In Chapter 19, we show you in detail how to cite. It's probably easiest to cite your sources carefully *while you're drafting your paper*. Although to do so takes a little extra time as you write, it saves fuss when you're putting your paper into final form.

    Right now, probably all you need to do is to note in your draft, right after each borrowed item, the name of the author and the page of the book you took it from. If you're using two or more works by the same author, you need one more detail to tell them apart. Assign each one a short title—the first word or phrase of a title will do.

> An assassin outrages us not only by his deed but also by offering an unacceptable reason for violence. Nearly as offensive as his act of wounding President Reagan was Hinckley's explanation that he fired in order to impress screen star Jody Foster. (Szasz, "Intentionality," 5)

This citation is short for an article by Thomas Szasz, "Intentionality and Insanity," to distinguish it from another work by Szasz that the writer also cites: *The Myth of Mental Illness.*

When in writing a draft you include a direct quotation, you might as well save copying time. Just paste or tape in the whole note card bearing the quotation. Your draft may look sloppy, but who cares? You're going to recopy the quotation anyway when you type your final version.

If, when you lay the quotation into place, a few words to introduce it spring to mind, by all means put them in. A brief transition might go something like "A more negative view of standardized intelligence tests is that of Harry S. Baum, director of the Sooner Research Center." Then comes Baum's opinion, that IQ tests aren't very reliable. The transition announces why Baum will be quoted. Evidently, you have previously written about somebody else's praise of IQ tests; now Baum will cast cold water on them. And the transition, brief as it is, tells us a little about Baum: his professional title. Indicating that he is a recognized authority, this bit of information makes us more willing to accept his expert view. (For more suggestions on introducing ideas, see "Using Transitions," p. 486.)

But if no transition occurs at the moment, don't sit around waiting for it. Slap that card into place and keep writing while the spirit is moving you along. Later, when you rewrite, you can always add connective tissue. Just remember to add it, though—a series of slapped-in cards would make rough reading.

Using sources (not letting sources use you). Sometimes you can get drawn into discussing something that really doesn't have anything much to do with your investigation, perhaps because the material is interesting and you happen to have a heap of it. It's a great temptation, when a note has cost you time and toil, to want to include it at all costs. Resist. Include only material that answers your research question. Your paper will be far stronger as a result. A note dragged in by force always sticks out like a pig in the belly of a boa constrictor.

Quoting needs to be done sparingly, and for good reason—to add support and authority to your assertions. Otherwise, it raises needless complications. Some writers of college research papers do much pointless quoting. This notion is understandable, but dubious. Mary-Claire van Leunen in *Handbook for Scholars* gives cogent advice:

> Quote only the quotable. Quote for color; quote for evidence. Otherwise, don't quote. When you are writing well, your sentences should join each other like rows of knitting, each sentence pulling up what went before it,

each sentence supporting what comes after. Quotation introduces an alien pattern—someone else's diction, someone else's voice, someone else's links before and afterward. Even necessary quotations are difficult to knit smoothly into your structure. Overquotation will result in something more like a bird's nest than like fine handiwork.

That quotation, by the way, seems to us worth quoting. Its words are memorable, worth taking to heart.

Nutshell and paraphrase again: Using long passages. Nutshell and paraphrase are fine ways to avoid quoting excessively. We first talked about these useful methods on page 101, and earlier in this chapter we saw how Lisa Chickos used them. Both methods translate another writer's ideas into your own words.

If, to save time in the library, you made photocopies of long passages, you now have to face the task of selecting from them, boiling them down, and weaving them into your paper. To illustrate once again how nutshelling and paraphrasing can serve you, let's first look at a passage from historian Barbara W. Tuchman. In *The Distant Mirror: The Calamitous 14th Century*, Tuchman sets forth the effects of that famous plague the Black Death. In her foreword to her study, she admits that any historian dealing with the Middle Ages faces difficulties. For one, large gaps exist in the supply of recorded information:

> A greater hazard, built into the very nature of recorded history, is overload of the negative: the disproportionate survival of the bad side—of evil, misery, contention, and harm. In history this is exactly the same as in the daily newspaper. The normal does not make news. History is made by the documents that survive, and these lean heavily on crisis and calamity, crime and misbehavior, because such things are the subject matter of the documentary process—of lawsuits, treaties, moralists' denunciations, literary satire, papal Bulls. No Pope ever issued a Bull to approve of something. Negative overload can be seen at work in the religious reformer Nicolas de Clamanges, who, in denouncing unfit and worldly prelates in 1401, said that in his anxiety for reform he would not discuss the good clerics because "they do not count beside the perverse men."
>
> Disaster is rarely as pervasive as it seems from recorded accounts. The fact of being on the record makes it appear continuous and ubiquitous whereas it is more likely to have been sporadic both in time and place. Besides, persistence of the normal is usually greater than the effect of disturbance, as we know from our own times. After absorbing the news of today, one expects to face a world consisting entirely of strikes, crimes, power failures, broken water mains, stalled trains, school shutdowns, muggers, drug addicts, neo-Nazis, and rapists. The fact is that one can come home in the evening—on a lucky day—without having encountered more than one or two of these phenomena.

This passage in a nutshell, or summary, might become as follows:

> Tuchman reminds us that history lays stress on misery and misdeeds because these negative events attracted notice in their time and so were

reported in writing; just as in a newspaper today, bad news predominates. But we should remember that suffering and disaster didn't prevail everywhere all the time.

As you can see, this nutshell merely abstracts from the original. Not everything in the original has been preserved: not Tuchman's thought about papal bulls, not the specific examples such as Nicolas de Clamanges and the modern neo-Nazis and rapists. But the gist—the summary of the main idea—echoes Tuchman faithfully.

Now here is Tuchman's passage in paraphrase. The writer has put Tuchman's ideas into other words but retained her major points. Note that the writer gives Tuchman credit for the ideas.

> Tuchman points out that historians find some distortion of the truth hard to avoid, for more documentation exists for crimes, suffering, and calamities than for the events of ordinary life. As a result, history may overplay the negative. The author reminds us that we are familiar with this process from our contemporary newspapers, in which bad news is played up as being of greater interest than good news. If we believed that newspapers told all the truth, we would think ourselves threatened at all times by technical failures, strikes, crime, and violence—but we are threatened only some of the time, and normal life goes on. The good, dull, ordinary parts of our lives do not make the front page, and praiseworthy things tend to be ignored. "No Pope," says Tuchman, "ever issued a Bull to approve of something." But in truth, disaster did not prevail as widely as we might think from the surviving documents of medieval life. Nor, the author observes, can we agree with a critic of the church, Nicolas de Clamanges, in whose sour view evildoers in the clergy mattered more than men of goodwill.

In that reasonably complete and accurate paraphrase, most of Tuchman's points have been preserved and spelled out more fully, though they have been rearranged. Paraphrasing enables the writer to emphasize the ideas important to his research, makes the reader more aware of them as support for his thesis than if the whole passage had been quoted directly. But notice that Tuchman's great remark about papal bulls has been kept a direct quotation because the statement is short and memorable, and it would be hard to improve on her words.

Make sure that, like the writer of the nutshell and the paraphrase just given, you indicate your original source. You can pay due credit in a terse phrase: "Barbara W. Tuchman believes that . . ." or "According to Barbara W. Tuchman. . . ."

Often you paraphrase to emphasize one essential point. Here is an original passage from Evelyn Underhill's classic study, *Mysticism*:

> In the evidence given during the process for St. Teresa's beatification, Maria de San Francisco of Medina, one of her early nuns, stated that on entering the saint's cell whilst she was writing this same "Interior Castle" she found her [St. Teresa] so absorbed in contemplation as to be unaware

of the external world. "If we made a noise close to her," said another, Maria del Nacimiento, "she neither ceased to write nor complained of being disturbed." Both these nuns, and also Ana de la Encarnacion, prioress of Granada, affirmed that she wrote with immense speed, never stopping to erase or to correct, being anxious, as she said, to write what the Lord had given her before she forgot it.

Suppose that the names of the witnesses do not matter, but the researcher wishes to emphasize, in fewer words, the celebrated mystic's writing habits. To bring out that point, the passage might be paraphrased (and quoted in part) like this:

> Evelyn Underhill has recalled the testimony of those who saw St. Teresa at work on *The Interior Castle*. Oblivious to noise, the celebrated mystic appeared to write in a state of complete absorption, driving her pen "with immense speed, never stopping to erase or to correct, being anxious, as she said, to write what the Lord had given her before she forgot it."

Ending (also beginning). Perhaps, as we have suggested, only after you have written the body of your paper will a good beginning and a concluding paragraph or paragraphs occur to you. The head and tail of your paper might then make clear your opinion of whatever you have found out. But that is not the only way to begin and end a research paper. Lisa Chickos begins with a short summary of what her investigation had revealed:

> Whoever first said, "It's lonely at the top," must have had the field of education in mind—more specifically, women in education. Although women predominate at the lower levels in education, the "top" of the educational field is overwhelmingly composed of men.

With facts and figures, Chickos goes on to support her view. That's a strong, concise beginning, and it makes the situation clear. A different opening paragraph might have answered the question she had investigated ("Why do so few women become educational leaders?").

> For a woman to become a school administrator, she must battle stereotyped attitudes. This obstacle defeats many teachers who try to rise in their profession and discourages many others from trying.

That opening may not be as lively as the one Chickos actually wrote, but it would do. Still another way to begin a research paper is to sum up the findings of other scholars. One research biologist, Edgar F. Warner, has reduced this kind of opening to a formula:

> First, in one or two paragraphs, you review everything that has been said about your topic, naming the most prominent earlier commentators. Next you declare why all of them are wrong. Then you set forth your own claim, and you spend the rest of your paper supporting it.

That pattern may seem cut and dried, but it is clear and useful. If you browse in specialized journals in many fields—literary criticism, social studies, the sciences—you may be surprised how many articles begin and go on in that very way. To use this method yourself, you don't need to damn every earlier commentator. Should you find reason to disagree, one or two other writers may be enough to argue with. Erika Wahr, a student writing on the American poet Charles Olson, starts her research paper by disputing two views of him:

> To Cid Corman, Charles Olson of Gloucester, Massachusetts, is "the one dynamic and original epic poet twentieth-century America has produced" (116). To Allen Tate, Olson is "a loquacious charlatan" (McFinnery 92). In my opinion, the truth lies between these two extremes, nearer to Corman's view.

At the end of her paper, Wahr returns to the point she made in her opening and sums up the reasons for her own view. She concludes:

> Far from being a charlatan, Olson is one of the poets of our times who has captured the truth about real people.

Whether or not you have stated your view in your beginning, you will certainly need to make it clear in your closing paragaph or paragraphs. A suggestion: before writing the last lines of your paper, read back over what you have written earlier. Then, without looking at your paper, try to put your view into writing. (For more suggestions on starting and finishing, see pp. 489 and 491.)

Rewriting

Because in writing a library research paper it is easy to lose sight of what you're saying, why not ask a fellow student to read over your draft and give you reactions? If your reader gets lost at any point, take it as a sign that you need to give him or her more guidance along the way. Ask your reader to indicate on your draft at what points it becomes hard to follow. Then, when you set about the task of rewriting, you can work on binding your paper together and keeping your reader with you by backtracking for a moment at those trouble spots and briefly summarizing the discussion so far. By so doing, you remind your reader of what you have already said. This strategy might seem pompous in a paper of 500 words, when the reader has hardly had time to forget what you have said; but it can come in handy in a longer paper when, after a few pages, the reader's memory may need refreshing, and a summary of the argument so far will be welcome. Such a brief summary might go like this: "As we can infer from the previous examples, most veteran career counselors are reluctant to encourage women undergraduates to apply for jobs as principals in elementary schools." (For more about transitions—which are, among other things, devices of organization—see p. 486.)

When you look over your draft, here are a few other points you can inspect critically (and if need be, try to fix).

REVISION CHECKLIST: LOOKING OVER EVERYTHING

- Do you honestly feel you have said something, not just heaped facts and statements by other writers that don't add up to anything? If your answer is no, a mere heap of meaningless stuff is all you've got, then you face a painful decision. Take a long walk and try to define what your research has shown you. Don't despair: talk to other students, talk to your instructor. It may be that you need a whole new question whose answer you care about. Or it may be that you need to do deeper research.
- Does your paper make clear the research question it began with? Does it reveal, early on, what you wanted to find out and why this might be important to the reader?
- Does it sum up your findings? Because your paper is short, perhaps it doesn't need a formal concluding summary. In that case, does it clearly present your findings as it goes along?
- Have you included only library materials that told you something and left out any that seem useless (even though they took you work to look them up)?
- Have you digressed in any places from answering the question you set out to answer? If so, does the digression help your reader understand the nature of the problem, or does it add extraneous material that might simply be omitted? (Although it is a shock to discover you have written, say, six pages that don't advance your research, be brave—use that scissors, feed that wastebasket.)
- Does each new idea or piece of information seem to follow from the one before it? Can you see any stronger order to arrange things in?
- Is the source of every quotation, every fact, every idea you have borrowed made unmistakably clear? If your readers care to look up your sources, could they readily find them in a library?

You may find it helpful at this point to check your paper against the outline you made before you started to write. Or, even better, make a new outline that sets forth your points in the order in which they appear in your paper. Any outline that lays out in order what you have written can be an invaluable revision tool. It doesn't have to be formal or complicated to help you see at a glance whether you have made your points in a sensible and logical order, easy for your readers to follow. It can also reveal whether you've put into your paper material that doesn't belong or if you've left out a point that would clarify what one idea has to do with the one that comes after it.

If you find that your outline makes it obvious that you've included extraneous material, reveals gaps in your thinking, or shows that in your paper you presented your ideas in haphazard, hard-to-follow sequence, keep revising your outline until it makes perfect sense. Then go back to your paper and, in light of what your new outline reveals, try moving paragraphs around (with scissors and tape if it helps) until the order of the ideas in your paper conforms to their order in your outline. Add new ideas if they appear to be needed, even if it means a trip back to your sources. After making all the changes that seem called for, you'll need to go over your paper carefully at least one more time, putting in new transitions between paragraphs that you've put into some new sequence.

Preparing your manuscript. At the back of this book is an appendix that tells you how to prepare a finished manuscript. Its advice applies not only to library research papers but to any other college papers you may write. A research paper calls on you to follow special rules in documenting your sources— in citing them as you write and in listing them at the end of your paper. At first, these rules may seem fiendishly fussy, but for good reason professional writers of research papers swear by them and follow them to a T. The rules will make sense if you imagine a world in which scholarly and professional writers could prepare their research papers in any old way they pleased. The result would be a new tower of Babel. Research papers go by the rules in order to be easily readable, easily set into type. The rules also ensure that all necessary information is there to enable any reader interested in the same subject to look up the original sources.

In humanities courses and the social sciences, most writers of research papers follow the style of the Modern Language Association (MLA) or the American Psychological Association (APA). Your instructor will probably suggest which style to observe; if you are not told, use MLA. The first time you prepare a research paper according to MLA or APA rules, you'll need extra time to look up just what to do in each situation. Chapter 19 gives examples of most of the usual situations.

When you use a direct quotation from one of your sources, ordinarily you simply put into quotation marks, in the body of your paper, the words you're using, along with the name of the person who said them.

It was Patrick Henry who said, "Give me liberty or give me death."

Johnson puts heavy emphasis on the importance of "giving the child what she needs at the precise moment in her life when it will do the most good."

When you include a quotation longer than four typed lines, you set it off in your text by indenting the whole quotation ten spaces from the margin if you're following MLA style, five for APA style. You double-space the quotation, just as you do the rest of your paper. Don't place quotation marks around an indented quotation and, if the quotation is a paragraph or less, don't indent its first line. (For detailed instructions about quoting sources, see Chapter 19.)

At the very end of a library research paper, you supply a list of all the sources you have cited: books, periodicals, and any other materials. Usually this list is the last thing you write. It will be easy to make if, when you compiled your working bibliography, you included on each note card all the necessary information (as shown in Figures 16.1 and 16.2). If you did, you can now simply shuffle those cards into alphabetical order and then type the information on each item, following the MLA or APA guidelines (given in Chapter 19, pp. 394 and 401). The MLA specifies that you entitle your list "Works Cited"; the APA, "References." Any leftover parts—cards for sources you haven't used after all—

may now be sailed into the wastebasket. Resist the temptation to transcribe them, too, and impressively lengthen your list.

Before you hand in your final revision, go over it one last time for typographical and mechanical errors. If you have written your paper on a word processor, it's an easy matter to correct errors right on the screen before you print it. If you find any mistakes in a paper you have typewritten, don't despair. Your instructor knows how difficult and frustrating it would be to retype a whole page to fix one flyspeck error. Correct it neatly in ink. (How to be neat? See p. 524 in the appendix.)

A COMPLETED LIBRARY RESEARCH PAPER

Lisa Chickos's irritation at men who would call a hard-working woman school administrator "tough and bitchy" led to her writing a paper she strongly cared about. The completed paper is more than a compilation of facts, more than a string of quotations. Chickos takes a definite, personal view. She argues that something ought to be done, and, moreover, she proposes action.

To help her instructor follow her thoughts, she prefaced her paper with a formal outline. Written in complete statements, it is the kind called a *sentence outline*—a document not for the writer's own use but meant to be read. (If your instructor asks for such an outline, see the advice on formal outlines on p. 478.)

In her later college life, Chickos found, the training she acquired as a freshman researcher proved valuable. "Now that I'm a history major," she says today, "I'm *always* doing research papers."

Title page contains, on separate lines, centered and double-spaced, the title of the paper, the writer's name, the course number, and the date.

Educational Leadership: A Man's World

Lisa Chickos

Professor Laura Miller

English 102

May 12, 198–

Outline

Thesis: Women are not fairly represented in
educational administration, and to achieve
equity they must overcome the restrictions
imposed by the current system.

I.   Women make up most of the staff but men
make up most of the administration of
public school systems.

A.   In 1972, 62 percent of all teachers
were women, but 99 percent of superintendents, 98 percent of high school
principals, and 80 percent of elementary school principals were men.

B.   Today, two-thirds of teachers are
women, but the great majority of administrators are men.

II.   Why do so few women become educational
leaders?

A.   Women do not seem to have less ability than men to be effective leaders.

1.   One study showed that women principals were viewed as no less
competent than men principals.

2.   Another study indicated that men
in competitive situations become
aggressive and self-interested
while women consider the interests
of all involved.

3.   Women administrators have been
described as "conscientious, sen-

All pages after the title page are numbered in the upper right corner half an inch from the top. The writer's name appears before the page number. Outline pages are numbered with small roman numerals (the title page is counted but is not numbered).

Type "Outline" centered, one inch from the top. Double-space to the first line of text.

The thesis states the main idea of the paper.

This outline is in sentence form rather than in the shorter topic form.

sitive..., reliable, adaptable,
and tactful."

B. Women may have been socialized not to
    aspire to positions of leadership.

    1. Boys are encouraged to be compet-
        itive, whereas girls are taught
        merely to look and act nice but
        not to reach for high goals.

    2. Women may fear success and the
        social rejection that may accom-
        pany success.

    3. Women may fear the consequences
        of "unfeminine" behavior--that is,
        independence and assertiveness,
        particularly in nontraditional
        professions such as administra-
        tion.

    4. Women lack role models in posi-
        tions of educational leadership;
        men in such positions do not pro-
        vide adequate role models for
        young girls and women.

C. Family and geographic ties may pre-
    vent women from seeking or being of-
    fered high-level positions.

    1. Women's jobs are seen as provid-
        ing a second, not a primary, in-
        come for their families, so women
        have less incentive to seek
        higher-level positions.

    2. Women are not considered as geo-

graphically mobile as men and are
therefore overlooked for positions
that may require relocating.

D. The female stereotype, which categorizes women as emotional and
non-task-oriented, prevents women from
advancing.

   1. Women are considered capable of
obeying rules and taking orders
but not of making rules and giving
orders.

   2. Women are not offered administrative positions because men control
the hiring process.

   3. Women in responsible positions
are seen merely as tokens and are
inhibited from performing naturally and effectively, thereby
creating a negative image of women
administrators.

III. Women can break the negative stereotypes
and can try to change the system that
prevents them from advancing.

A. Women must provide support for other
women in administrative positions and
for women seeking to advance.

B. Women need the support of their male
colleagues, who are in positions of
power and are able to make changes.

C. Boys and girls need to be encouraged

Chickos v

to reach for their own goals, even if
they include nontraditional careers.

D. Women need the cooperation of their
husbands and children so that they are
freer to pursue more responsible
positions.

E. Employers must not consider women applicants differently from men applicants and should include more women in
the hiring process.

F. Organizations and legislation can
support women seeking administrative
positions.

Educational Leadership: A Man's World

Whoever first said, "It's lonely at the top," must have had the field of education in mind--more specifically, women in education. Although women predominate at the lower levels in education, the "top" of the educational field is overwhelmingly composed of men. If women are to be more fairly represented in educational administration, they must overcome the restrictions imposed by the current system, which is built on outdated ideas about women's work and on stereotypes about women's abilities.

In 1972, 62 percent of the professional staff of the public schools were female. Yet 99 percent of the superintendents, 98 percent of the high school principals, and 80 percent of the elementary school principals were male (Schmuck 244). Unfortunately, these figures haven't improved much. Today, two-thirds of the public school teachers are women, but the great majority of the administrative positions are still held by men (Truett 1).

Could it be that men have more ability than women to be effective leaders? This hardly seems the case. A research study conducted by Fischel and Pottker asking teachers to evaluate women principals showed no significant differences in the behavior of women principals compared with that of men principals, and the women

Chickos 2

were certainly viewed as competent leaders (qtd. in Biklen 10).

In fact, some studies show that women are likely to be more effective educational leaders than men. One study, for example, indicated that when placed in competitive situations, men become very aggressive and tend to act in ways that are most advantageous for themselves. Women usually try to consider the interests of all those involved, not just their own (Conoley 39).

Furthermore, the study showed that in educational settings, groups accomplish more when they have a leader who works with them rather than ruling over them--someone who listens to the opinions of all the group members and tries to do what's best for all involved (Conoley 40).

In another survey, which measured the attitudes toward women as school district administrators, "conscientious, sensitive to the needs of others, reliable, adaptable, and tactful" were some of the terms used to describe the most effective administrators (Temmen 9).

Clearly, women do have the ability to be effective educational leaders. Therefore, the reasons that more men reach higher positions must lie elsewhere.

One possibility may be that women simply do not aspire to positions of leadership. From early childhood, boys are encouraged to be competitive. Organized sports and other games

Chickos 3

send young boys a clear message—be the best.
For young girls, however, the emphasis is placed
mainly on looks and personality. They are not
encouraged to reach high goals (Clement 134).
For this reason, a woman may not attach the same
importance to an administrative position as a
man would.

Women also may not aspire to administrative
positions because of a "fear of success." Society's concept of femininity tells young girls
that achievement is a masculine quality. It
doesn't mix with a pretty face and pleasant
personality. This gives many girls the fear
that they will be socially rejected if they
succeed in reaching a position of authority
(Horner 36).

Others have suggested that women may not
actually have a fear of success. Women who
were tested for fear of success showed a fear of
losing love or of being socially rejected. The
small number of men who showed some fear of
success questioned the value of the success
rather than showing any fears about possible
rejection (Johnson 176). For this reason, it
has been speculated that women have a fear of
what might happen if they deviated from traditional sex roles, not a fear of succeeding
(Wortman, Loftus, and Marshall 368).

Fear of the consequences of "unfeminine"
behavior is certainly legitimate. Society's
attitudes are unfavorable toward women in tra-

Citation of work by
two or three authors
gives the names of all
authors.

Chickos 4

ditionally male professions. As Dr. Patricia
Albjerg Graham, a member of the history and education faculty at Barnard College and Teachers
College, Columbia University, states, "administrators are expected to be independent and assertive, behaviors understood as 'tough and
bitchy' when displayed by women, but 'clear-
headed and attentive to detail' when found in a
man" (170).

Obviously, no woman (or man, for that matter) would want to be described as "tough and
bitchy." Young girls need to see that they can
fill administrative positions and still gain
approval. What better place for this to start
than in the educational system? Unfortunately,
because there are so few women already in higher
positions, young girls have no role models to
follow. There are plenty of men for girls to
pattern themselves after, but it is easier for
children to model themselves after someone they
can identify with and, in most cases, a young
girl can most easily identify with a woman
(Antonucci 186).

Young women in college and entering the job
market also need role models. They need to see
that other women have succeeded and that they
too can succeed and thus strive to seek better
jobs (Antonucci 188).

Perhaps the major reason women don't reach
for administrative jobs is family. If a woman
is a wife and mother, she has added responsi-

Direct quotation
rather than paraphras-
ing for the source's
strong, effective lan-
guage. Title and
credentials establish
the source as an au-
thority.

Source's name men-
tioned at the begin-
ning of the quotation,
so the citation gives
only the page num-
ber.

Chickos 5

bilities and may not be able to put as much time
as she would like into a demanding job (Graham
170).

Also, it is rare to find a family woman
working in the educational system who is the
sole or main breadwinner. In a survey of public school administrators, the working husbands
of the female administrators made more money
than their wives, while the working wives of
male administrators made less money than their
husbands (Truett 9). It can be speculated that
men see their jobs as the main source of family
income and, therefore, go after the highest-
paying positions, while women view their jobs as
a second income and have no financial need for a
better position.

A woman's geographic mobility may also influence her decision not to advance in her
field. There is nothing strange about a family
relocating because of the father's job transfer,
but it is not commonplace for a family to move
to a new location for the mother's job. Not
only does the possibility of relocating keep
some women from pursuing jobs, but women's supposed immobility also keeps women who do pursue
such jobs from being hired. Employers assume
that a man would be able to relocate and a woman
would not and simply do not consider women for
certain positions. Interestingly, however, the
survey of public school administrators revealed
that the person who had moved the most (three

Chickos gives her in-
terpretation of some
data in sentence form
and then presents the
statistics themselves.

Chickos 6

times in the past five years) was a woman
(Truett 13). This same survey showed no real
difference between men and women in willingness
to relocate; 16.7 percent of the men anticipated
a future move to obtain a better job, as did
14 percent of the women (Truett 15). Actually,
neither men nor women seem very eager to relocate for a higher position, but women are certainly no less willing to relocate than men
(Truett 22).

Other factors keep women from reaching
higher positions that they desire and also inhibit other women from pursuing similar positions. The female stereotype, which
categorizes women as being emotional and non-
task-oriented, can cause many problems. This
stereotype holds that women can be part of the
system, obeying its rules and taking orders,
but that they are not capable of running the
system--making the rules and giving the orders
(Biklen 10). This societal attitude convinces
some women that they don't have what it takes to
be a leader. As Sari Knopp Biklen states,
"People's perceptions about their ability influence achievement more than their actual
ability or level of aspiration" (8). But, as
mentioned earlier, women do have the ability to
become successful leaders.

The female stereotype also keeps women from
being hired. Many men have this image of all
women, and because the educational leaders are

Chickos 7

primarily men, they may not even consider hiring
women for administrative positions (Schmuck
248). An interview with male administrators
revealed their feelings:

Quotation of more
than four typed lines
is indented ten spaces
from the left margin
and is double-spaced
with no quotation
marks. Citation is in
parentheses following
the end punctuation
of the quotation.

> It's easier to work without women.
> Principals and superintendents are a
> management team. It fosters interde-
> pendence and mutual support. We need
> each other for survival. It's no
> evil liaison--it's just pure politics.
> I wonder if we could hang together so
> well if some of us were women. (Bik-
> len 12)

This brings up another difficulty that
women must confront. Because there are so few
women in educational administration, a woman who
reaches such a position may see herself (and may
be seen by others) as a token or representative
of all women. This makes it very difficult to
perform naturally (Biklen 16). Because she is
in the spotlight and because she may feel like
an outsider in a male-dominated profession, a
woman may adopt a "female behavior" (passive,
compromising, and so on), which in turn gives
her role as a female administrator a negative
image (Clement 136).

Women must work to break these negative
stereotypes. Women who are already in administrative positions must consciously try to
project a positive image to their male colleagues (Schmuck 249). The women in these po-

Chickos 8

sitions must also encourage women who are on the
way up, and they all need to support one another. One female administrator pointed out:

> It used to be when I walked into a
> room full of men and only one woman I
> would tend to ignore her. Now when I
> walk into a similar situation the
> woman and I at least have eye-contact.
> There's too damn few of us women; we
> found out we need to support each
> other. If there were more of us we
> would be free to act just as folks,
> but because there are so few of us,
> there is the common bond of being
> women. (Schmuck 254)

But women cannot just join forces and try
to overthrow the system. They need to have the
support of their male colleagues, too, because
the men are in the power positions and have the
ability to make changes. Also, if women banded
together and excluded men from their efforts,
that in itself would be discrimination, which is
exactly what must be overcome (Schmuck 251).

Outside forces can also aid in changing the
present situation. During the school years,
boys and girls can be taught that there is
nothing wrong with pursuing untraditional careers and can be encouraged to reach for their
own goals--not the goals society has set for
them (Johnson 180).

Chickos 9

In addition, family support can be a great help. If a career woman is also a wife and mother, she is actually carrying two jobs. Support from her husband and the independent behavior of her children may give a woman a chance to pursue a position she thought was not within her reach (Biklen 14).

The system also must change if women are ever to become an equal part of educational administrations. Those who review applications should not consider marital status and family because, as discussed earlier, employers often consider a family to be a burden for a woman's career but not for a man's. Also, since administrative staffs are essentially male, and they tend to hire men over women, some women need to be involved in selection processes (Weitzman 485).

Organizations are common knowledge, and no source is needed.

A number of organizations and some legislation, such as Sex Equity in Educational Leadership (SEEL), the National Council of Administrative Women in Education (NCAWE), the Leadership and Learning Cooperative (LLC), and the Women's Educational Equity Act (WEEA), have been designed to facilitate the changes that are necessary to ensure equity in educational leadership.

With the help of such groups and legislation, along with an enlightened public, perhaps equality in educational administration will soon be realized.

Chickos 10

Works Cited

Antonucci, Toni. "The Need for Female Role
    Models in Education." Biklen and Branni-
    gan 185—195.

Biklen, Sari Knopp. "Introduction: Barriers to
    Equity——Women, Educational Leadership, and
    Social Change." Biklen and Brannigan
    1—23.

Biklen, Sari Knopp, and Marilyn B. Brannigan.
    Women and Educational Leadership. Lexing-
    ton, MA: Heath, 1980.

Clement, Jacqueline. "Sex Bias in School
    Administration." Biklen and Brannigan
    131—137.

Conoley, Jane Close. "The Psychology of Lead-
    ership: Implications for Women." Biklen
    and Brannigan 35—46.

Graham, Patricia Albjerg. "Status Transitions
    of Women Students, Faculty, and Adminis-
    trators." Academic Women on the Move.
    Ed. Alice S. Rossi and Ann Calderwood.
    New York: Russell Sage Foundation, 1973.
    163—72.

Horner, Matina. "A Bright Woman Is Caught in a
    Double Bind." Psychology Today Nov. 1969:
    36+.

Johnson, Marilyn. "How Real Is Fear of Suc-
    cess?" Biklen and Brannigan 175—82.

Schmuck, Patricia A. "Changing Women's Repre-
    sentation in School Management: A Systems

Works cited paren-
thetically in text of
paper are listed here
alphabetically by au-
thor's last name. Type
"Works Cited" cen-
tered, one inch from
top. Double-space to
first entry and double-
space within and be-
tween entries. Indent
turn lines five spaces.

Book itself is not
cited parenthetically
in text of paper, but
more than two entries
in the list of works
cited are taken from
it. Publication infor-
mation is given here,
and short cross-refer-
ences to it are used in
the other entries.

Chapter in an edited
book with publication
information given in
this entry.

Article in a monthly
magazine.

Chapter in an edited
book. Note cross-ref-
erence to another
book in the list of
works cited.

Chickos 11

Perspective." Biklen and Brannigan 239–59.

Study sponsored by a corporation.

Temmen, Karen. "A Research Study of Selected Successful Women Administrators in the Educational Field." St. Louis: CEMREL, 1982.

Paper presented at a conference.

Truett, Carol. "Professional and Geographic Mobility of a Selected Sample of Nebraska Public School Administrators: Differences between Men and Women." Paper. Annual Meeting of the National Conference of Professors of Educational Administration. San Marcos, TX, 1982.

Weitzman, Lenore J. "Affirmative Action Plans for Eliminating Sex Discrimination in Academe." Academic Women on the Move. Ed. Alice S. Rossi and Ann Calderwood. New York: Russell Sage Foundation, 1973. 463–504.

Book with more than one author.

Wortman, Camille B., Elizabeth F. Loftus, and Mary Marshall. Psychology. New York: Knopf, 1981.

Questions to Start You Thinking

1. Which of the reasons given in this paper for women's failure to advance in the field of education seems to you the strongest? What makes it hard to refute?

2. Do any of the points that Chickos includes for support seem to you less convincing? What are they? If you were her peer critic, what suggestions would you make that might strengthen her main point?

3. What other professions can you name in which men hold most positions of leadership? Why do you think this is so?

Other Assignments

The main assignment in this chapter asks you to write a library research paper in which you state your own views about a subject important to you. The suggestions listed here invite you instead to do the other kind of library research, the kind that you do when your purpose is to learn what is thought or known about a subject that interests you and then explain it to your readers. Using your library sources, write a short research paper, under 3000 words, in which you give a rough survey of the state of current knowledge on one of the following topics or on another that you and your instructor agree offers promising opportunities for research. Proceed as if you had chosen to work on the main assignment (except that you need not advance an opinion).

1. The health of the economy or the stability of the government in a third world country.

2. Career opportunities in a certain line of work that interests you.

3. Another planet in the solar system, or comets, novas, black holes, perhaps even a neighboring star.

4. Progress in the cure and prevention of a disease or syndrome.

5. Treatment of drug abuse or the rehabilitation of users.

6. The "greenhouse effect" (a phenomenon causing a change in worldwide climate).

7. The possibility of an accord between the United States and the Soviet Union in reducing stockpiles of nuclear weapons.

8. Present methods of disposing of nuclear wastes and a comparison of their relative effectiveness.

9. Attempts to ban smoking in public places.

10. The growth of telecommuting: the tendency of people to work in their own homes, keeping in touch by phone and computer modem with the main office.

APPLYING WHAT YOU LEARN: SOME USES OF LIBRARY RESEARCH

In many courses beyond your English course you will be asked to write papers from library research. The more deeply you move into core requirements and specialized courses for your major, the more independent research and thinking you will do. At some liberal arts and technical colleges, a long research paper is required of all seniors in order to graduate. Beyond college, the demand for writing based on library research is evident. Scholars explore issues that absorb and trouble them and the community of scholars to which they belong. In the business world, large companies often maintain their own specialized libraries on the premises since information and opinions are worth money and decisions have to be based on them. If you should take an entry-level job in the headquarters of a large corporation, don't be surprised to be told, "We're opening a branch office in Sri Lanka and Graham (the executive vice-president) doesn't know a thing about the place. Can you write a report on it? Customs, geography, climate, government, state of the economy, political stability, religion, lifestyle, and all that?" In the office of a large city newspaper, reporters and feature writers continually do library research (as well as field research), and the newspaper's library of clippings on subjects covered in the past ("the morgue") is in constant use. Many popular magazine articles were obviously researched in a library: "The Strangest Career in Movies" (for which the writer looked up all the biographies and biographical facts about Greta Garbo), "New Findings About Sunburn" (for which the writer went through the past year's crop of medical journals).

As one of the ways they become prominent in their disciplines, academics and professionals in many fields—law, medicine, English, geography, social studies, art and music history, the history of science—write and publish papers and whole books based on library research in specialized and scholarly journals. In an exciting study of urban architecture, *Spaces: Dimensions of the Human Landscape* (New Haven: Yale University Press, 1981), Barrie B. Greenbie draws connections between our notion of "self"—a personal universe bounded by the skin—and our sense of the kind of dwelling we feel at home in. In exploring this relationship (and the need to build dwellings that correspond to our psychic needs), Greenbie brings together sources in psychology, architecture, economics, and literature (the poetry of Emily Dickinson). This passage from the beginning of his book may give you a sense of his way of weaving together disparate materials:

> The psychoanalyst Carl Jung placed great emphasis on the house as a symbol of self, and many others have elaborated this idea.[1] Of course Jung considered "self" both in a social as well as individual sense, and in fact the concept of *self* has no meaning except in the context of *others*. Most of us share our houses with some sort of family group during most of our lives, and while parts of an adequately sized house may belong primarily to one or another individual, the boundaries of the home are usually those of a cluster of selves which form a domestic unit. Even people who by choice or circumstance live alone express in their homes the images and traditions formed at one time in a family group.
>
> The architects Kent C. Bloomer and Charles W. Moore view buildings as the projection into space of our awareness of our own bodies. Fundamental and obvious as this relationship might seem, it has been to a great

extent ignored in contemporary architecture. Bloomer and Moore sum up the personal situation very well in their book, *Body, Memory, and Architecture:*

> One tell-tale sign remains, in modern America, of a world based not on a Cartesian abstraction, but on our sense of ourselves extended beyond the boundaries of our bodies to the world around: that is the single-family house, free-standing like ourselves, with a face and a back, a hearth (like a heart) and a chimney, an attic full of recollections of *up*, and a basement harboring implications of *down*.[2]

> Many North American tract houses fit this characterization less adequately than they might. But whatever the deficiencies of domestic and other kinds of contemporary architecture may be, they are as nothing compared to the shortcomings of most urban design. ... This book will focus on the hierarchical structures that extend from the "skin" of the family home to the street and beyond.

Notice that Greenbie uses endnote form because he has much to put in his notes, which might have interrupted the flow of his prose. Endnote 1, for instance, reads:

> [1]Carl G. Jung, *Memories, Dreams, and Reflections* (London: Fontana Library Series, 1969). For an exceptionally good summary and elaboration, see Clare Cooper, "The House as Symbol of the Self," in *Designing for Human Behavior,* ed. J. Lang et al. (Stroudsburg, Pa.: Dowden, Hutchinson, and Ross, 1974).

Earlier, we pointed out that unless your assignment specifically confines you to library materials, your research paper may certainly draw on any other sources you have: recall of your personal experience, observation, conversation, previous reading, even imagination. Here is a memorable example of two professional writers on biology, Anne and Paul Ehrlich, combining library materials with their own experience.

> The direct benefits supplied to humanity by other species are often little appreciated, but nonetheless they can be very dramatic. In 1955 Paul's father died after a grim thirteen-year battle with Hodgkin's disease, a leukemia-like disorder of the lymphatic system. Just after his death, some Canadian scientists discovered that an extract of the leaves of a periwinkle plant from Madagascar caused a decrease in the white blood cell count of rats. Chemists at Eli Lilly and Company analyzed the chemistry of periwinkle leaves, and the analysis turned up a large number of alkaloids, poisonous chemicals that plants apparently have evolved to protect themselves from animals that eat them and parasites that infest them.[1] Two of these alkaloids, vincristine and vinblastine, have proven to be effective in treating Hodgkin's disease. Indeed, treatment with vincristine in combination with other chemical agents now gives a very high remission rate and long periods where no further treatment is required in patients even in the advanced stage of the disease.

> Thus a chemical found in a plant species might have helped greatly to prolong Bill Ehrlich's life—and is now available to help the five to six

thousand people in the United States alone who contract Hodgkin's disease annually. As some measure of its economic value, total sales of vincristine worldwide in 1979 were $35 million.[2] Vincristine also is used along with other compounds to fight a wide variety of cancers and cancerlike diseases, including one form of leukemia, breast cancer, and cancers that afflict children. Had the periwinkle plant been wiped out before 1950, humanity would have suffered a loss—even though no one would have realized it. (*Extinction: The Causes and Consequences of the Disappearance of Species* [New York: Random House, 1981], 53–54.)

---

[1]P. R. Ehrlich and P. H. Raven, "Butterflies and Plants: a Study of Coevolution," *Evolution* 18 (1964): 586–608.

[2]Information on origins of vincristine is from G. E. Trease and W. C. Evans, *Pharmacognosy,* 10th ed. (Baltimore: Williams and Wilkins, 1972). The figure on the value of sales is from Norman Myers, "What Is a Species Worth?" manuscript for *Science Digest,* 1980.

As you can see from that remarkable illustration, these writers care very much about a topic for library research. In a personal way, they combine what they discover with what they already know.

CHAPTER 17

Knowing Your Library: A Directory of Sources

Back in Chapter 11, you saw the usefulness of dividing a complicated subject into its parts, when that subject is sliceable. Now we'll apply that method of explaining to a subject that richly deserves it: your library.

In the previous chapter, we didn't want to bore you with anything you know already. Neither did we want to ply you with additional information, lest you lose sight of what library research is all about. But there is a good deal that most of us ordinary citizens not trained in library school don't know about a large library. Now that you have seen the process of thoughtful writing that goes into a library research paper, perhaps you would like to see in greater depth what your library has to offer.

Lately, public service announcements on television have urged us to find out what our libraries contain besides those dry old fossils, books. It is true: nowadays most libraries also lend recordings, software, videotapes, musical scores, works of art, and sometimes (as our hometown's public library lends to responsible children) even pet animals. Through a computer terminal, a library may have access to a data bank, bringing a world of information to your fingertips. Unfortunately, at the moment, to lay a hand on this world will cost you about $30 an hour.

Yet for all these changes, in a college library books are still indispensable properties. Technology may have altered our methods of storing, retrieving, and transmitting ideas, but the book still remains a compact and relatively inexpensive source. It is also easier than a computer to curl up with.

Most libraries have a reference librarian who can find anything from a two-letter word for "ancient Egyptian sun god" (for a distraught crossword puzzle addict) to an 1898 news story stored on microfilm. Know your reference librarian. You might be surprised where this learned specialist can direct you. Still, it is part of your education to be able to find usual, everyday sources. James A. Michener, who writes huge novels and nonfiction books from library research (works such as *Poland*, *Space*, and *Texas*), gives pointed advice: "Don't waste the time of this expert by asking silly questions you ought to solve yourself. Save the reference librarian for the really big ones."

By the way, when you set out to do college research, don't forget your *local* library. In large towns and cities, it may be less busy than your college library. Some of its facilities—reference room, current newspapers, and popular magazines—may be just as extensive as your college's, if not more extensive.

Whatever library you use, you'll save time if you first know your way around in it. You'll need to locate the centers of action: circulation desk where you charge out books; reference room; card catalogue (drawers of cards or a computer terminal); microfilm projectors; special collections of materials on specific subjects; current newspapers and periodicals; back issues. Here are five small questions worth knowing the answers to. If any stumps you, ask a librarian.

CHECKLIST: FIVE PRACTICAL MATTERS

- If another borrower has a book out, how can you get it held for you on its return?
- If this library doesn't have a certain book you need, can you order it on interlibrary loan?
- If you haven't previously taken a guided tour of your college library, is one available?
- Is there a pamphlet mapping the library's rooms and explaining its services?
- Are there any available study carrels—usually small cubicles with desks in the stacks—that you can use while working on your research paper?

CONSULTING THE CARD CATALOGUE

Like the ignition key that starts the car, a card catalogue starts your book search moving. You consult it for detailed information on every book in the library.

If your library's card catalogue is a traditional sort, it is housed in file drawers, on 3-by-5-inch cards. In many libraries nowadays, although a catalogue still has cards, you view them on a screen. They are filed on microfilm or microfiche or on a computer, and you scroll through them.

The catalogue lets you look up a book in any of three ways: (1) by author, (2) by title, or (3) by subject. Here's some special advice about subject headings.

Library of Congress Subject Headings

Sometimes, if you go straight to the card catalogue, you can't find the subject heading you're after, or helpful books don't seem to be listed under the subject headings you do find. You look up, say, "Women school administrators" in the card catalogue and there isn't any such subject. In fact, the library may own several books on the subject, but they are listed in the card catalogue under "School administrators" and "Women in education." Now how do you find out that useful information? You can look up "Women school administrators" in a copy of *Library of Congress Subject Headings*, usually on hand near the card catalogue. (If your library is an older or smaller one that files books under the Dewey decimal system instead of the Library of Congress system, you can consult instead the *Dewey Decimal Classification and Relative Index*.) Figure 17.1 shows how entries look in the *Library of Congress Subject Headings*.

Finding a Book

In some libraries, author cards are contained in one file, title cards in a second, subject cards in a third. In other libraries, all cards are filed together alphabetically. On the author card, the main card for each book, you find the following information—which often will give you some ideas about the book before you look for it. (Figure 17.2 shows a typical author card.)

1. The call number. The combination of letters and numbers tells you exactly where to find the book.
2. The author's full name, last name first, with birth and death dates (if known).
3. The title as it appears on the book's title page; the fact that the book has been revised in a second (or later) edition if that is the case.
4. Publication information: city, name of publisher, and date of publication.
5. The number of pages, the height of the book, and mention of any maps, charts, or illustrations the book may contain.
6. A list of whatever special features the book may have—bibliographies, appendices, indexes, illustrations.
7. All subject headings under which the book is filed in the library.
8. The International Standard Book Number used by librarians to order books. (You need pay no attention to it.)

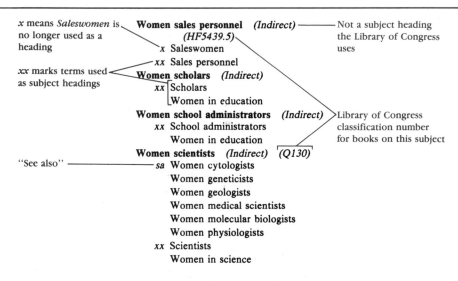

Figure 17.1 Entries from the *Library of Congress Subject Headings*

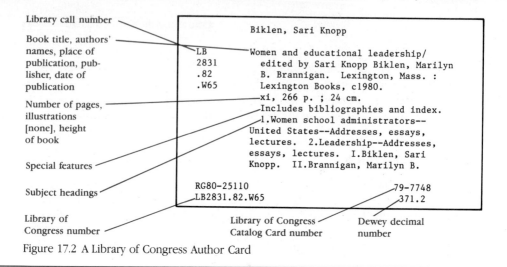

Library call number

Book title, authors'
names, place of
publication, pub-
lisher, date of
publication

Number of pages,
illustrations
[none], height
of book

Special features

Subject headings

Library of
Congress number

```
                    Biklen, Sari Knopp

        LB      Women and educational leadership/
        2831        edited by Sari Knopp Biklen, Marilyn
        .82         B. Brannigan.  Lexington, Mass. :
        .W65        Lexington Books, c1980.
                    xi, 266 p. ; 24 cm.
                    Includes bibliographies and index.
                    1.Women school administrators--
                    United States--Addresses, essays,
                    lectures.  2.Leadership--Addresses,
                    essays, lectures.  I.Biklen, Sari
                    Knopp.  II.Brannigan, Marilyn B.

        RG80-25110                          79-7748
        LB2831.82.W65                        371.2
```

Library of Congress   Dewey decimal
Catalog Card number   number

Figure 17.2 A Library of Congress Author Card

```
        LB       Women and educational leadership/
        2831         edited by Sari Knopp Biklen, Marilyn
        .82          B. Brannigan.  Lexington, Mass. :
        .W65         Lexington Books, c1980.
                     xi, 266 p. ; 24 cm.
                     Includes bibliographies and index.
                     1.Women school administrators--
                     United States--Addresses, essays,
                     lectures.  2.Leadership--Addresses,
                     essays, lectures.  I.Biklen, Sari
                     Knopp.  II.Brannigan, Marilyn B.

        RG80-25110                            79-7748
        LB2831.82.W65                          371.2
```

Figure 17.3 A Library of Congress Title Card

The title card looks like the main card except that it lists the book's title at the top, above the name of the author (see Figure 17.3).

When you start your research, you may find subject cards more useful than author cards. They will often lead you to useful titles. Also, the subject you look under may direct you to related subjects and thus to still more titles. The subject card looks just like the author card except the author's name appears under a subject heading (see Figure 17.4).

Assuming that your book is in the library, you can expect its call number to help you find it. The first letter or letters of that call number point you to its neighborhood. A book, for instance, whose call number starts with an *S* is about agriculture or forestry. (For a rundown of the Library of Congress system

342

```
┌─────────────────────────────────────────────────────────────┐
│        LEADERSHIP--ADDRESSES, ESSAYS,                         │
│        LECTURES.                                              │
│                                                              │
│  LB       Women and educational leadership/                  │
│  2831         edited by Sari Knopp Biklen, Marilyn           │
│  .82          B. Brannigan.  Lexington, Mass. :             │
│  .W65         Lexington Books, c1980.                        │
│               xi, 266 p. ; 24 cm.                            │
│ ┌───────────────────────────────────────────────────────────┐
│ │          WOMEN SCHOOL ADMINISTRATORS--UNITED              │
│ │            STATES--ADDRESSES, ESSAYS, LECTURES.            │
│ │                                                           │
│ │   LB       Women and educational leadership/              │
│ │   2831         edited by Sari Knopp Biklen, Marilyn       │
│ │   .82          B. Brannigan.  Lexington, Mass. :         │
│ │   .W65         Lexington Books, c1980.                    │
│ │                xi, 266 p. ; 24 cm.                        │
│ │                Includes bibliographies and index.         │
│ │                1. Women school administrators--            │
│ │           United States--Addresses, essays,              │
│ │           lectures.  2.Leadership--Addresses,             │
│ │           essays, lectures.  I.Biklen, Sari              │
│ │           Knopp.  II.Brannigan, Marilyn B.               │
│ │                                                           │
│ │   RG80-25110                              79-7748         │
│ │   LB2831.82.W65                           371.2          │
│ └───────────────────────────────────────────────────────────┘
```

Figure 17.4 Library of Congress Subject Cards with Subject Subdivisions

---

of classifying books, see the next section. Or look for a location chart posted prominently in your library.)

If your library lets you wander freely in the stacks, you're lucky. Shelved near the book you've come for may be others by the same author or on the same subject. Browse around in the neighborhood. Lisa Chickos, who discovered *Women and Educational Leadership* in the card catalogue, might have found on the same shelf another title full of promise for her research: *Academic Women on the Move*. The golden rule for research in the stacks is this: *To do right unto others, don't put a book back in place hastily.* Replace it wrong and no one else will be able to locate it.

UNDERSTANDING SYSTEMS OF CLASSIFICATION

To help you find books easily, every library organizes its shelves by a system of classification. We will look at the two most prevalent. Some people claim that it pays to memorize these systems; then when you have to trek from one section of the library to another, looking for books, your head will save your feet. At least, you may care to recognize the call numbers of books in the category of your investigation.

Library of Congress System

Most college libraries use the same system of book classification used by the Library of Congress in Washington, D.C. If your library does, you'll find that call numbers and letters direct you to books gathered together in subject areas.

A	General Works		M	Music
B	Philosophy, Psychology, Religion		N	Fine Arts
			P	Language and Literature
C–D	Foreign History and Topography		Q	Science
			R	Medicine
E–F	America		S	Agriculture and Forestry
G	Geography, Anthropology, Sports and Games		T	Engineering, Technology
H	Social Sciences		U	Military Science
J	Political Science		V	Naval Science
K	Law		Z	Bibliography and Library Science
L	Education			

Dewey Decimal System

Small libraries often still use the older Dewey decimal system of classifying books. Other libraries, in transition, have some books filed according to the Dewey decimal system and some filed according to the Library of Congress method. The Dewey decimal system files books into large categories by numbers.

000–099	General Works
100–199	Philosophy
200–299	Religion
300–399	Social Sciences, Government, Customs
400–499	Philology
500–599	Natural Sciences
600–699	Applied Sciences
700–799	Fine and Decorative Arts
800–899	Literature
900–999	History, Travel, Biography

Incidentally, neither Admiral George Dewey, who took Manila, nor educator John Dewey started the Dewey decimal system. The credit goes to Melvil Dewey (1851–1931), founder of the American Library Association.

USING THE PERIODICALS ROOM

The periodicals room houses current and recent issues of magazines and newspapers. Many of the items on your working bibliography that you found listed in the latest *Readers' Guide to Periodical Literature* will be there. Older issues, bound into volumes for previous years, are shelved by call numbers. Some are kept on microfiche or microfilm (see p. 354). A list or file of periodicals' names and their call numbers is usually posted conspicuously in the periodicals room; if you can't find it, look up the name of the periodical in your card catalogue.

In the periodicals room, too, current newspapers are available. Even in most small libraries, you'll find at least the *New York Times* and your nearest big city's daily, probably also the *Washington Post* and the *Christian Science Monitor*, two newspapers noted for their coverage of national and international affairs. Most libraries have back issues of the *New York Times* on microfilm, and the *New York Times Index* (see "News Indexes," p. 350). The *Wall Street Journal*, an extremely well written and edited daily newspaper, not only covers business news but reviews films and books and often features articles of interest to the general public.

SURVEYING THE REFERENCE SECTION

Make your own tour of that treasure trove for researchers: the reference section. See what is available. Interesting reference books exist on subjects you may never have dreamed had been covered. You may find whole shelves devoted to general areas in which you plan to do research.

Here is a short tour of a few groups of reference books.

Encyclopedias

Back in high school when you had to do a research paper, you shot like a comet straight to an encyclopedia. (Sometimes you read *two* encyclopedias, and that was all the research required.) An encyclopedia (the word comes from the Greek, meaning "a general education") can still help you get an overview of your subject and may be especially valuable when you are first casting around for a topic. But when you start investigating more deeply, you will need to go to other sources as well.

General encyclopedias are written for the reader who isn't a specialist, who wants a decent smattering of information, or who wants some fact he or she is missing. In all but the cheapest encyclopedias, notable experts write the longer and more important articles. The *New Encyclopaedia Britannica*, now published in Chicago, is the largest general (that is, unspecialized) encyclopedia on the shelves. More sprightly in style, and sometimes beating the *Britannica* to the shelves with recent information, are other popular encyclopedias: *Encyclopedia Americana, Collier's, New Columbia, World Book*, and several more.

All encyclopedias struggle with a problem: how to give a reader not only specific facts but a broader, more inclusive view. If you look something up, how do you find out that your subject relates to larger matters that also might interest you? If, for instance, you look up Marie Curie, how do you learn that she and her work are discussed under "Chemistry," "Curie, Pierre," "Physics," "Polonium," "Radiation," "Radioactivity," and "Uranium" as well? To help you find all the places where a topic will be discussed, some encyclopedias offer an index in a separate volume, referring to other articles. *World Book* gives cross-references after an article ("See also . . ."). The *Britannica* now comes in two parts. A ten-volume *Micropaedia* (which you consult first, like any other encyclopedia) offers a concise, pointed article and may also refer you to other places in a nineteen-volume *Macropaedia* containing longer articles, wider in scope.

Specialized Encyclopedias

Specialized encyclopedias are written for the searcher interested in a single area: art, movies, music, religion, science, rock and roll. How do you know that someone has prepared one in the very field you are investigating? Look up your subject in the card catalogue. If a specialized encyclopedia about your subject exists, you will find it indicated on a subject card. The *Encyclopedia of World Art*, for instance, is usually listed under "Art—Dictionaries." (Specialized encyclopedias are often classified as dictionaries, even though they contain much more than short definitions.) Better yet, dwell a while in the area of the reference room that involves your subject and glance at the books shelved there. If your subject is from science, see the *McGraw-Hill Encyclopedia of Science and Technology* or *Van Nostrand's Scientific Encyclopedia*. If you are writing about some aspect of life in a less industrialized, developing nation, the *Encyclopedia of the Third World* might be valuable. If existentialism is your subject, likely places to look might be the *Dictionary of the History of Ideas*, the *Encyclopedia of Philosophy*, and the *Harper Dictionary of Modern Thought*. The *Encyclopedia Judaica* and the *New Catholic Encyclopedia* concentrate on matters of faith, tradition, ritual, history, philosophy, and theology. Just to give you a notion of the variety of other specialized encyclopedias, here is a sampling of titles:

Black's Law Dictionary
Encyclopedia of Banking and Finance

Encyclopedia of Biochemistry

Encyclopedia of Pop, Rock, and Soul

Harper's Bible Dictionary

International Encyclopedia of the Social Sciences

New Grove Dictionary of Music and Musicians

Oxford Companion to American Literature

Oxford Dictionary of the Christian Church

Dictionaries

Besides desk dictionaries, of the kind on every college student's desk, your library's reference section stocks large and specialized dictionaries. You'll find dictionaries of foreign languages; dictionaries of slang; dictionaries of regionalisms; dictionaries of medical, scientific, and other specialized terms. If you don't know what NATO or RSVP stands for, a specialized dictionary such as the *Acronyms, Initialisms, and Abbreviations Dictionary* might help. An unabridged dictionary, such as *Webster's Third New International*—the kind so hefty it sits on a stand of its own, tied down with a chain—tries to include every word and phrase in current use in the language. The *New Century Cyclopedia of Names*, a dictionary of names of people and peoples, places, works of art, and other proper names of every kind, is useful for tracking down allusions—mentions of things that a writer believes are common knowledge but that you may not happen to know.

The massive and monumental *Oxford English Dictionary* (OED) is a historical dictionary: that is, it lists words with dated examples of their occurrences in the language, from the twelfth century to the twentieth, arranged in chronological order. Any shade of meaning an English word ever had is there, making it a beloved treasure for any word freak (who probably owns the two-volume edition in reduced print, which comes with a magnifying glass). It is invaluable if you are tracing the history of an idea through the centuries: you can see how the meaning of a word may have changed. Along with those changes, sometimes, go major changes in society and its people. One student, writing a paper on pollution in the environment, looked up the word *pollution* in the OED and as a result was able to reinvigorate the contemporary meaning of the word with earlier meanings of shame and sin. If, in defining terms used in your paper, you need a definition of *freedom*, consult the OED and an immense storehouse will swing open to you. You'll find quotations using this luminous word in a whole spectrum of ways, starting with its earliest recorded appearance in the language.

Because the original OED was completed in 1933, it does not cover many new words that have since entered the language. *A Supplement to the Oxford English Dictionary,* in four volumes, is now available. Its latest volume includes relatively modern additions to the language, such as *slapstick* (see Figure 17.5).

sla.pstick. orig. *U.S.* Also **slap-stick.** [f. SLAP *v.*[1] + STICK *sb.*[1]] **1.** Two flat pieces of wood joined together at one end, used to produce a loud slapping noise; *spec.* such a device used in pantomime and low comedy to make a great noise with the pretence of dealing a heavy blow (see also quot. 1950).

1896 *N.Y. Dramatic News* 4 July 9/3 What a relief, truly, from the slap-sticks, rough-and-tumble comedy couples abounding in the variety ranks. **1907** *Weekly Budget* 19 Oct. 1/2 The special officer in the gallery, armed with a 'slap-stick', the customary weapon in American theatre galleries, made himself very officious amongst the small boys. **1925** M. W. DISHER *Clowns & Pantomimes* 13 What has caused the playgoers' sudden callousness? The slapstick. Towards the end of the seventeenth century Arlequin had introduced into England the double-lath of castigation, which made the maximum amount of noise with the minimum of injury. **1937** M. COVARRUBIAS *Island of Bali* iv. 77 Life-size scarecrows are erected, but soon the birds become familiar with them... Then watchmen circulate among the fields beating bamboo drums and cracking loud bamboo slapsticks. **1950** *Sun* (Baltimore) 10 Apr. 3/1 The 50-year-old clown..said that when he bent over another funnyman accidentally hit him with the wrong side of a slap-stick. He explained that a slap-stick contains a blank ·38-caliber cartridge on one side to make a bang.

2. a. *attrib.* passing into *adj.* Of or pertaining to a slapstick; of or reminiscent of knockabout comedy.

1906 *N.Y. Even. Post* 25 Oct. 10 It required all the untiring efforts of an industrious 'slap-stick' coterie..to keep the enthusiasm up to a respectable degree. **1914** *Photoplay* Sept. 91 (*heading*) Making slap-stick comedy.

1923 *Weekly Dispatch* 4 Mar. 9 He likes good comedies.. but thinks the slapstick ones ridiculous. **1928** *Daily Sketch* 7 Aug. 4/3 The jokes..are rapier-like in their keenness, not the usual rolling-pin or slapstick form of humour. **1936** W. HOLTBY *South Riding* iv. v. 258 She took a one-and-threepenny ticket, sat in comfort, and watched a Mickey Mouse film, a slapstick comedy, and the tragedy of Greta Garbo acting Mata Hari. **1944** [see *POCHO]. **1962** A. NISBETT *Technique Sound Studio* x. 173 Decidedly unobvious effects, such as the cork-and-resin 'creak' or the hinged slapstick 'whip'. **1977** R. L. WOLFF *Gains & Losses* II. iv. 296 The prevailing tone of the book is highly satirical, with strong overtones of slapstick farce.

b. *absol.* Knockabout comedy or humour, farce, horseplay.

1926 *Amer. Speech* I. 437/2 *Slap-stick*, low comedy in its simplest form. Named from the double paddles formerly used by circus clowns to beat each other. **1930** *Publishers' Weekly* 25 Jan. 420/2 The slapstick of 1929 was often exciting. The Joan Lowell episode was regarded as exposing the gullibility of the critics... The popularity of 'The Specialist' made the whole book business look cockeyed. **1955** *Times* 6 June 9/1 A comic parson (Mr. Noel Howlett) is added for good measure, mainly to play on the piano while other people crawl under it. Even on the level of slapstick the farce seemed to keep in motion with some difficulty and raised but moderate laughter. **1967** M. KENYON *Whole Hog* xxv. 253 A contest which had promised..to be short and cruel, had become slapstick. **1976** *Oxf. Compan. Film* 640/1 As it developed in the decade 1910–20..slapstick depended on frenzied, often disorganized, motion that increased in tempo as visual gags proliferated.

Figure 17.5 Entry from *A Supplement to the Oxford English Dictionary*

Bibliographies

It takes work to make a working bibliography. Wouldn't it be great if a bibliography came ready-made for you? Perhaps it does.

Each field of knowledge has its own bibliography, often more than one, which may appear in an issue of a learned journal or appear as a separate publication, like the *International Bibliography of Sociology.* Is there a bibliography in your area of interest? Consult the latest *Bibliographic Index: A Cumulative Bibliography of Bibliographies.* A quarterly, it is gathered together into one volume each year. Turn to it for listings, by subject, of specialized bibliographies and also of books and articles that contain specialized bibliographies. Some bibliographies you track down will be *annotated;* that is, they will give a short summary of what a book or article contains. Sometimes the bibliographer will venture a judgment about a book's worth.

Some encyclopedias, after the end of an article, will also give you a short list of relevant works worth reading. Often such a list will include the best-known and most popular books on a subject. Such lists are usually directed to a reader who knows nothing much about the subject rather than to a specialist, and they may be long out of date. We recommend that you look first into the *Bibliographic Index.* It's a wonderful instrument for the serious specialist.

Indexes to Periodicals

Magazines, because they can be published faster than books, often print the latest information and opinions months before they appear in book form. Look to them for the most up-to-date material.

To find recent articles on any subject you're investigating, start with the *Readers' Guide to Periodical Literature,* issued monthly, collected into thicker issues quarterly, and bound into a heavyweight volume in each new year. The *Readers' Guide* classifies, by author and subject, recent articles from popular magazines aimed toward general readers—*Time, The New Yorker, Psychology Today*—but not scholarly or professional magazines such as *American Zoologist, Harvard Business Review, Physics Today,* or *Journal of Music Theory,* which address specialized audiences. It gives cross-references so that with a little digging you can usually find headings that will lead you to useful articles. Under each heading, entries give you the title and author of an article and the name of the periodical, its volume number and date, and the pages on which the article can be found.

When you're making a working bibliography with the aid of the *Readers' Guide* and you want the most up-to-date material, begin with the most recent issue, then work backward through previous issues or annual volumes. If, like Lisa Chickos, you had decided to investigate why so few educational administrators are women, you would have found in the February 1986 issue of the *Readers' Guide* the headings "Women school administrators" and "Women school superintendents and principals." Under both you would have found indexed an article from the December 1985 issue of a periodical called the *Phi Delta Kappan* that seemed promising enough to follow up (see Figure 17.6). After combing through earlier issues of the *Readers' Guide* for more leads, you would have amassed a list of perhaps seven or eight articles that seemed to promise valuable information on your topic. At that point, you'd be ready to check out your library's collection of periodicals to see how many of the listed articles you could find and read.

Naturally, the *Readers' Guide* falls short of including every periodical your investigation might call for. To supplement it, *Access: The Supplementary Index to Periodicals* has, since 1975, been listing the contents of many regional and city magazines not found in the *Readers' Guide.* It includes the periodicals listed on the next page as well as dozens more.

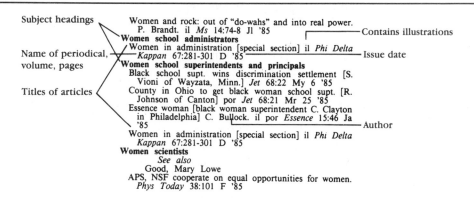

Figure 17.6 Entries from the *Readers' Guide*

Alaska
Analog Science Fiction
Horn Book
Hot Rod
Mother Jones
Poetry
Sporting News
TV Guide
Western Horseman
Whole Earth Software Review

Articles in more magazines than are included in either the *Readers' Guide* or *Access* are indexed in a data base, *Magazine Index*. In some libraries, you can view it on a computer monitor. But you probably won't need it, and wouldn't want to pay its hourly fee, for usual college assignments. (Data bases are discussed further on p. 355.)

If you find too few leads in the *Readers' Guide* or *Access* or not enough solid information in popular magazine articles, you may want to consult a selected subject index for more scholarly or professional materials. Here is a short list of some indexes widely available.

Art Index
Bioresearch Index
Business Periodicals Index
Criminology Index
Education Index
Environment Index
Film Literature Index
General Science Index
Humanities Index
Social Sciences Index

Art Index is broader in scope than its name implies: it lists not only articles on graphic art but many on archeology, architecture, city planning, crafts, films, industrial design, interior design, and photography. For a research paper on women as school and college administrators, the relevant section of *Education Index* for November 1985 is illustrated in Figure 17.7.

News Indexes

To locate a newspaper account of virtually any recent event or development, your most likely printed aid is the *New York Times Index*. Most libraries subscribe to the *Times*, and many keep back years of it on microfilm. Its semimonthly *Index*, bound into a volume each year, directs you to stories in daily and Sunday issues all the way back to the newspaper's founding in 1851.

Women as college presidents *See* Women as educators
Women as educators
  California more receptive to hiring female school ad-
    ministrators—despite impinging environmental factors.
    R. Nava. bibl *Education* 105:398-402 Summ '85
  Comparative career accomplishments of two decades of
    women and men doctoral graduates in education. J.
    S. Stark and others. bibl *Res Higher Educ* 22 no3:219-49
    '85
  Number of woman college presidents has doubled in
    decade, study finds. B. T. Watkins. *Chron Higher Educ*
    31:1+ S 18 '85
  San Diego State U. fires the only woman to head sports
    in top NCAA division. C. S. Farrell. *Chron Higher
    Educ* 31:79 S 4 '85
  Women said to hold fewer coaching positions and
    administrative jobs than in the early 1970's. C. S.
    Farrell. *Chron Higher Educ* 31:35+ S 25 '85

Figure 17.7 Entry from *Education Index*

Say you're pursuing the question of why relatively few women hold top
jobs as administrators in schools and colleges. "Women" might seem your
largest, most central idea, so in the 1984 volume you look up "Women" and
under it find the subheading "Education." This is a mere cross-reference that
lists the dates of five stories about women in education; it doesn't have room
to tell you what the stories are about. It directs you to a larger category, "Education and Schools," where you find listed and briefly summarized all the
stories about education, in chronological order. You skim down the listing and
check the five dates that interest you. For November 26 three stories about
education are listed (see Figure 17.8). Clearly, the last one will be the most
promising story for this topic. And the story will be easy to find. The legend
"N 26,II,12:2" indicates that it appeared on November 26 in section II of the
newspaper, page 12, column 2. The length of the story is also indicated: "L" for
a long story (more than three columns), "M" for a story of medium length
(between one and three columns), "S" for a short item (less than a column
long). This system points you to substantial stories especially worth looking up
and (if your time is scarce) saves you from bothering with short items that
might or might not prove worthwhile.

Article on program in Toledo, Ohio, under which experienced teachers are subjected to peer evaluation by
consulting teachers who are paid extra $1,000 annually;
illustrations (M), N 26,I,14:2
New York City and its school system, trying to prevent
teen-age girls from leaving school to care for their out-of-
wedlock babies, are financing day care centers for young
mothers in 17 high schools; photos (M), N 26,II,1:4
Drop in enrollment at nation's private schools has resulted
in many school mergers and, in ensuing years, boards of
trustees at private schools have named men to their top
positions in belief that men cope best with problems of
recruitment, administration and fund-raising; result has been
that fewer women head private schools now (M), N 26,II,
12:2

Figure 17.8 Entry from the *New York Times Index*

351

Other newspapers that publish indexes include the *Wall Street Journal*, the *Washington Post*, and the *Times* of London. *Facts on File* (discussed on p. 353) publishes an index twice a month to help readers locate its summaries of recent news. Also, some libraries now receive computerized indexes, such as *National Newspaper Index*, which lists the contents not only of the *New York Times* but also of the *Christian Science Monitor* and the *Wall Street Journal*. Ask your reference librarian whether your library makes any computerized index available without your having to pay a steep fee for it.

Abstracts

To cope with the information explosion, many collections of abstracts (or condensed versions) are available. Specialists can keep up with their changing territories with the aid of (for instance) *Abstracts of English Studies*, *Biological Abstracts*, *Chemical Abstracts*, *Journal of Economic Abstracts*, and *Sociological Abstracts*. Such periodicals can help you see, without much legwork, another researcher's principal findings and can direct you to sources worth consulting in their entirety.

For summaries of doctoral theses, see *Dissertation Abstracts*. Although these are usually read only by doctoral candidates looking for a topic that hasn't been exhausted, they could perhaps be useful for research on a specialized topic. A doctoral thesis not published in book form is generally available on microfilm.

Before you go to the trouble of searching for a book, *Book Review Digest* can give you a notion of it. This publication doesn't exactly abstract books—doesn't nutshell their kernels—but it does describe them briefly and then supply quotations from critics who reviewed the books in newspapers or magazines.

Biographical Sources

If you want to know about someone's life and work, you have a rich array of sources. To find quickly the names and dates of famous people now dead, *Webster's New Biographical Dictionary* can be handy. For more extensive treatment of outstanding Americans (dead ones only), see the *Dictionary of American Biography* (DAB) in 20 volumes (1928–36 and later supplements). The British equivalent is the *Dictionary of National Biography*. Lately, a four-volume set has filled many gaps in the DAB: *Notable American Women, 1607–1950*. See if your library also has *Who Was Who Among Black Americans*.

For the lives of living celebrities of all nations, see *Current Biography* (published monthly and gathered together each year), a highly readable and entertaining compilation. Bare facts, but many of them, about celebrities and people prominent in their fields, are listed in *Who's Who* (for Britain), *Who's Who in America*, and *Who's Who in the World*. Regional American editions (*Who's Who in the West* as well as volumes for the Midwest, South and Southwest, and East) and *Who's Who of American Women* encapsulate people not included in the nationwide volume. *Who Was Who* (for Britain) and *Who Was Who in America* preserve facts on those cut down by the grim reaper. Marquis, publisher of *Who's Who in America*, also offers specialized *Who's Whos*: *Who's Who in American Law* and similar volumes for finance and industry, frontier science and technology, religion, and science.

The lives of writers are usually well documented. For early writers' biographies, see *American Authors, 1600–1900*, *British Authors before 1800*, *British Authors of the Nineteenth Century*, *Twentieth Century Authors* and its supplement, and *World Authors, 1950–1970*. Writers from all countries, including hundreds not found in encyclopedias, are usually to be found in *Contemporary Authors* and its revisions, a vast series that covers not just poets and fiction writers but popular writers in every field. *Contemporary Novelists*, *Contemporary Poets*, and *Contemporary Dramatists* contain not only biographies and bibliographies but critical estimates.

Yearbooks and Almanacs

Encyclopedia publishers, realizing that time gallops on and that their product rapidly becomes obsolete, bring out an annual yearbook of recent events and discoveries in an attempt to look up to date. We consider these to be rather cumbersomely organized sources, designed to extract more money from owners of encyclopedias. If you want a short account of a recent event or development, try *Facts on File*. Calling itself a "Weekly World News Digest, with Cumulative Index," it is a concise list of news events. Important events rate more space. Twice a month it publishes an index on blue paper, and then quarterly yellow indexes supersede the blue ones. Librarians gather the weekly issues into a binder every year.

Many miscellaneous facts—news events, winners of prizes, athletic records—are compiled in a yearly almanac such as the *World Almanac and Book of Facts*, a popular, variously useful work that many people like to have as a desktop reference. In it you can find out everything from the population of Bloomington, Indiana, to information about job openings and current earnings, from the locations of hazardous waste sites to the time the moon rises on any given date—and much more. Your library may also offer specialized almanacs: *American Jewish Year Book*, *Catholic Almanac*, *Canadian Almanac and Directory*.

Gazetteers and Atlases

Gazetteers list places and give basic facts about them: the *Columbia Lippincott Gazetteer of the World*, *Webster's New Geographical Dictionary*.

For maps, see atlases such as *The Times Atlas of the World*, *National Atlas of the United States of America*, and (for maps that show political boundaries in the past—fascinating!) the *Historical Atlas*.

EXPLORING OTHER SOURCES

Besides reference books, your library may have other sources that will supply you with ideas and information not available elsewhere.

Microfilm and Microfiche

Most libraries now take advantage of microfilm to store newspapers and other materials that would otherwise take up acres of valuable shelf space. If you aren't acquainted with the stuff, if the projector in the reference room has looked like an intimidating mystery, you should get to know it, for marvelous research opportunities are available to you if you do. If, for instance, you are writing a paper on World War II, wouldn't it be great to see the front page of a newspaper for December 8, 1941, the day the U.S. Congress declared war? Or to quote from an editorial published on that fateful day? (To this question, one researcher, Professor John Ruszkiewicz, ruefully replied, "Sure—if the bulb works, the image will focus, the reels will take up the film, and the film is in the right box." Clearly, microfilm has problems that still need ironing out.)

Microfilm is small photographic film that contains the images of printed pages in reduced form. A whole week's file of daily newspapers can be preserved on a strip of microfilm two inches wide and seven or eight feet long. Wound into a roll and stashed in a small, labeled box, the microfilm can be stored in a few square inches of space. Microfilm saves books that otherwise might be lost: it crumbles more slowly than paper does. It also permits the publication of monographs and dissertations, which have small audiences, for less cost than printing.

Complete files of historically important magazines that are now practically impossible to obtain are currently at the service of a small library. In many reference rooms, files of the *New York Times* and other frequently consulted newspapers and periodicals sit in microfilm boxes next to a viewing projector. The machine bears instructions, but if you need help getting the thing to work, ask a librarian. Once you have the film on the machine, you crank till you come to the very page you are looking for. Some projection machines will print out a photocopy of any page.

A *microfiche* is a card containing a sheet of translucent microfilm bearing many frames: images of printed pages reduced 20:1. Sixty to a hundred book pages can fit on one microfiche card. Copies of rare books and manuscripts can now be obtained cheaply and stored safely in a small space. While in the past only a library with $30,000 to spare could own a copy of Francis Bacon's *Novum Organum*, now any library can own a microfiche copy for a small fraction of that sum. One file cabinet can hold the contents of a rare-book room. A projector shows each frame of the microfiche on a viewing screen. A reader-printer can produce a photocopy of any page you require.

Data Bases

Data bases, great troves of information obtainable over telephone wires and run on computers, are now available in many libraries. Particularly useful for research on a cross-curricular subject that spans several disciplines (such as medical ethics or legal language), computer searching may be used instead of rummaging through indexes, books, and periodicals by hand. There is a charge—generally $30–40 an hour—but by zeroing in on what you most want, this expense might save your looking through hundreds of scattered sources.

On some campuses where the computer stations are connected to a large mainframe computer, hundreds of data bases may be available. To use a data base, first talk with your reference librarian about the search you have in mind and determine which data base would be of most use to you. After you log in to the computer, you can ask a question—for instance, "What has been written about famine in Africa?" Or ask for rundowns on key words: "famine," "Africa." Within a minute the computer will list indexed words and phrases that are similar and the number of items it has titles for.

FAMINE, 346 ITEMS

FAMINE, IN CAMBODIA, 34 ITEMS

FAMINE, IN CONGO, 27 ITEMS

FAMINE, IN ETHIOPIA, 43 ITEMS

FAMINE, IN INDIA, 34 ITEMS

FAMINE, IN MIDDLE AGES, 4 ITEMS

FAMINE RELIEF, 63 ITEMS

FAMINE VICTIMS, MEDICAL STUDIES OF, 52 ITEMS

Your next move is to ask the computer to show you citations under any subject heading or headings (called *descriptors*) that look promising. Each cited item has an identifying number. Entered into the computer, this number brings you bibliographical facts on the book, article, or other printed source, a brief abstract (a summary of the item), and a list of all the various descriptors that identify it ("famine victims, medical studies; famine relief organizations; International Red Cross; Oxfam; India"). For an extra fee, some will even supply a printout of the item itself.

To a serious researcher, a data base can be a wonderful means of sifting through a world of information in a hurry. Still, a computer search has its limitations. Most data bases, being recent innovations, go back no further than to books and articles published in the last ten or twenty years. To find earlier items, you will still need earlier printed volumes of specialized indexes.

A further problem in using data bases is that unless you find the right descriptors, you can spend an enormous amount of money needlessly. If you are seeking nothing but items about famine relief in India, tell the computer to search only for items with two descriptors: "India" and "famine relief." You might then receive only 12 articles. Otherwise, the computer will deliver too much: the descriptor "famine relief" alone would bring you 63 descriptions, while "India" alone might bring you thousands. In using some data bases, you need to instruct the computer to supply you only with items written in English or other languages you can read, or you may be overwhelmed with titles in languages you do not know.

At this writing, more than five hundred data bases are available, with names like PsyInfo (for sources in psychology), ABI/Inform (for business and finance), and SCISEARCH (for biological and applied sciences). If interested, first decide very clearly the exact subject of your investigation. To help you narrow your search, nearly every data base supplies a current, alphabetical list of its own descriptors. You can inspect this list (generally called a *thesaurus*) before you begin searching. Unless you have money to burn, don't select a data base and don't try using one without the help of a patient expert—most likely your research librarian.

Government Documents

"A glance at the organization of our government documents," says Mary-Claire van Leunen, author of *A Handbook for Scholars* (New York: Knopf, 1979), "may suggest that the United States is neither a democracy nor a republic, but an anarchy. Writing a good reference to a federal document would be simple if only one of those brainy forefathers of ours had thought to write at the bottom of the Declaration of Independence, 'Serial #1,' but it's too late now." It is true that because government documents differ widely in format, depending on which branch of the government published them, they are sometimes hard to find; but often they contain valuable material worth searching for.

Among major American publishers is the United States Congress. Its primary publications include the *Congressional Record*, a daily transcript of what is said in both the House and the Senate, together with anything else members of Congress wish inserted; bills, acts, laws, and statutes (after a bill is enacted into law it is bound into *Statutes at Large*); and the minutes of congressional committee hearings. Most college libraries carry at least the *Congressional Record*.

The judicial branch of the government doesn't publish anything except cases. But other executive departments and state governments publish prolifically, as do various agencies of the United Nations. John L. Andriot's *Guide to U.S. Government Publications* lists and explains the printed products of most federal agencies. The U.S. Government Printing Office in Washington, D.C., publishes and distributes some popular works, including *Your Child From 1 to 6* and the *Government Manual*, an explanation of how the government is organized.

There is, by the way, a *Monthly Catalog of United States Government Publications*, compiled into one volume annually. Matthew Lesko's guidebook *Information U.S.A.* (New York: Viking-Penguin, 1983) is valuable for both library and field research. It lists federal libraries open to the public (some offering free telephone reference service) and free government publications and how to order them. It also tells where and how to inquire for information (with phone numbers).

Brochures, Handouts, and Annual Reports

For other kinds of printed material, your library may be helpful—or you may need to round it up on your own. Often, on a visit to a museum or historic site, you are given (along with your ticket of admission) a pamphlet to carry with you, containing a terse history of the place and perhaps a map of its exhibits. This kind of material can prove valuable to researchers. Usually it is the work of curators and other dedicated experts who know their locales, and sometimes it is hard to find anywhere else. If, say, you are making a field trip to a computer museum before writing about the history of early computers, you might carefully save any handout. You might also peruse the gift shop or the pamphlet rack at the information desk, even if the offerings cost money. If you can't visit the museum or historic site, a phone call might tell you how to mail order its publications.

Many concerned organizations, such as the American Cancer Society, the American Heart Association, Physicians for Social Responsibility, and others, sometimes publish surveys and reports that they will send you on request. Some of their valuable handouts are made known through public service announcements on radio and television. The U.S. government's Consumer Information Center in Pueblo, Colorado, sends free pamphlets (*Occupations in Demand, Being Your Own Boss*) and sells larger brochures at low prices (*The Job Outlook in Brief, Exercise and Weight Control*). A list of publications with an order form is available on request; the zip code is 81002.

Most large corporations produce hefty annual reports, copies of which are yours for the asking. Few people except investors write to a corporation for an annual report, but the corporations are willing to give a copy to practically anyone seriously interested in their activities. You are likely to receive a vast, handsomely printed document favorably portraying the past year's operations and future expectations of the company so that present stockholders will be reassured and future investors will be attracted; the report usually contains graphs, charts, photographs, and other documents. Writing a research paper on recent developments in artificial intelligence, a student we know requested the annual reports of several computer and software firms. For the cost of a few postage stamps, he received hundreds of pages of up-to-date information and professional opinion that would have been difficult to find elsewhere.

CHAPTER 18

Writing from Research in the Field

Finding material in a library is only one way to do research. You can also generate your own ideas and information—in other words, tap your own primary sources.

Most often in college, field research is required in upper-level courses. For a term paper in the social sciences, education, or business studies, you may be expected to interview people or gather statistics. Usually, course assignments in field research are directed toward specific ends. A psychology assignment for the purpose of testing a hypothesis, for example, might ask you to observe people in a situation of stress and to report their behavior.

If you enjoy meeting and talking with people and don't mind what news reporters call "legwork," you will relish the fun and satisfaction of obtaining ideas and information at first hand. Perhaps you will even investigate matters that few researchers have investigated before. Many rich, unprinted sources of ideas and information lie beyond library walls. This chapter will reveal a few of them. It will show you how to write a research paper by observing, conversing with people, remembering, and doing some practical imagining—so that in the future, library researchers may be able to cite *you*.

Like library research, field research should be more than a squirreling-up of facts—or else you may end up with a great heap of rotting acorns and no nourishment. Field research (and kindly underline this sentence) has to be the sensitive, intelligent, and critical selection of *meaningful* ideas and information. As the chapter proceeds, we'll give you more specific suggestions for picking out what is meaningful from what isn't. Right now, it is sufficient to note that you can expect to change your initial hunches while at work out in the field. You'll be sifting evidence, revising and correcting your early thoughts, forming clearer ideas. When you begin a project on identical twins, say, you might seek evidence to back up your hunch that identical twins are likely to enter the very same line of career work in later life. Perhaps, though, the evidence will refuse to march in the path you want it to follow. You might end up disproving your hunch and coming to a fresh realization after all: that some twins, perhaps, develop in independent directions.

LEARNING FROM ANOTHER WRITER:
ONE STUDENT'S EXPERIENCE

To show you a student thinking and solving problems in the field, changing his mind while collecting material and coming to fresh realizations, let us tell the story of Jamie Merisotis. A political science major, Merisotis became interested in studying the lives and work of people engaged in an unusual profession: bail bonding. He grew increasingly curious about this business of supplying bail money for suspected criminals who have been arrested.

Whatever your field research topic, you will probably have an easier time gathering ideas and information than Jamie Merisotis had. First, because he found little recent published research on his topic, he decided to try to interview every bondsman practicing in an East Coast state he knew well, where the bail bond system still thrives. His labors were complicated by the fact that while attending college in Maine, he pursued his research in another state. It took him most of a year to obtain his evidence, for he had only weekends and vacations for interviewing.

"The hardest part," Merisotis recalls, "was getting the bondsmen to talk to me." Busy people who shun publicity, many bondsmen flatly turned down the student's request for interviews. At first, Merisotis had trouble even getting in touch with the bondsmen, since many publish only their phone numbers, not their addresses. The phone numbers connect to an answering service that relays only calls from people in need of bail money. Luckily, a friendly bail commissioner took an interest in Merisotis's study and encouraged the bondsmen to talk to him. Even with this help, one bondsman had to be called ten times before he consented to an interview. "I think he finally broke down just to get rid of me," Merisotis says. In the end, he succeeded in interviewing eighteen bail bondsmen—about half of all those practicing in the state, perhaps the largest number ever interviewed by any researcher, student or professional.

Although the bail bondsman is a familiar figure in detective movies and fiction, surprisingly little about his life has been documented. A few facts may help you glimpse the nature of Merisotis's project. In effect, a bail bond is a promissory note stating that if the defendant does not appear in court to stand trial, he or she will forfeit a sum of money. When a person arrested and charged with a crime has to post bail, needs money to do so, and cannot raise it alone, he or she calls a bail bondsman. In some commentaries Merisotis read, the bondsmen are "mindless thugs," "moronic leeches," "cigar-chomping social parasites living off the misfortunes of others." Reports have circulated that bondsmen use guns and brass knuckles to whip their errant clients into submission. On television they are romanticized: in the series *The Fall Guy*, glamorous bondswoman Big Jack sometimes sends muscle man Lee Majors to track down missing clients for her.

Curious to learn the truth behind the stereotypes, Merisotis formulated his question for research: *What is an accurate description of the life and work of a typical bail bondsman?* As he interviewed practicing bondsmen, he found his preliminary ideas changing. In some cases, he learned, bondsmen do indeed threaten violence against clients they suspect will fail to appear ("I'll break your legs," "I'll get a gorilla over to take you in") or they threaten financial disaster ("Your mother will pay if you don't show"). Empowered to arrest clients who run out on them, they sometimes (but seldom) risk their necks tracking down a fugitive. Compared to their stereotypes on television, however, their lives are quiet. If some of their tactics are unpleasant, bondsmen do provide useful service. Slow to risk their money, suspicious of some prospects, they nevertheless assist many low-income people who otherwise would languish in jail. They help make the legal system work. Because they assume responsibility for their clients' appearing in court, they often pester a client, browbeat him, and see that he shows up for trial.

In our legal system, then, bondsmen are valuable people. Yet to his surprise Merisotis found little recent literature on the topic in his college library. We'll continue to trace his story in this chapter and finally show you a chapter from his completed paper.

LEARNING BY WRITING

The Assignment

Here is a typical *general* writing assignment for a field research paper, one that leaves up to you the task of finding a specific topic. Try to find a topic that, because you care about it, will elicit your desire to write.

Consider some group of people in our society about whose lives and activities you would like deeper knowledge. The group you choose should be one whose members you would be able to engage in conversation—vagrants, amateur rock musicians, members of the Society of Friends, aspiring painters, women construction workers, model-railroad buffs, hospital patients, people who live in a certain locality, or any other group of people that for any reason keenly interests you. Find out as much as you can about the group by observing, by conversing with people, by questioning them, by seeking any other evidence that you do not find in print but discover for yourself.

From what you have learned, draw some conclusion or make some generalization. Present it in a paper, supporting it with evidence you have collected.

Among successful papers we have seen written from this assignment are the following.

> Using her own observations, a questionnaire she had devised, and a series of interviews, a woman set out to test the validity of something she had read: that the tradition of the family dinner was fast disappearing from middle-class life. She wrote this paper for a freshman English course centering on the theme "The Way We Live Now."
>
> A man studying child development, after observing two- and three-year-olds at a day-care center and keeping a log of his observations for three

weeks, wrote about the many ways in which the two groups of children differed from each other.

In a sociology course, a man sought out and interviewed people in the helping professions who worked with street people in his city. He also talked with some of the homeless people themselves, in an effort to find out what forces had driven them to the streets and what was being done for them.

A man conducted a survey among his fellow students to learn their reasons for choosing the college they attended. He sorted out their answers, emerging with a varied list and increased respect for his college's reputation.

A woman who had recently moved from Baltimore to Portland, Oregon, relied on recall, observation, and conversation to record and interpret cultural differences between easterners and westerners. After writing the paper for an English class, she sold part of it to a newspaper as a feature article.

Generating Ideas

Before you set out to study the later lives of identical twins or the various methods of designing hang gliders, you first have to decide that that is the subject you want to investigate. Start by casually looking into something that appeals to you, seeing whether to persist in further investigation. Those trusty resources for writers discussed in Part Two may prove their usefulness. You might observe your subject in action (twins, hang gliders, or whatever) and recall what you already know about it. You might talk with anyone familiar with it, do some reading about it in a library, and imagine yourself doing field research into it (interviewing twins or builders of hang gliders). The more you look into a subject, the more it is likely to interest you.

Once you feel sure of your direction, state a question—exactly what are you trying to find out? How to word such a question is discussed in Chapter 16 on page 296. That's the central question to ask yourself and to keep living with; the following are other, smaller ones.

DISCOVERY CHECKLIST: WEIGHING POSSIBILITIES

- Where will you find more ideas and information about this subject? Whom might you consult for suggestions?
- What places should you visit?
- Whom should you talk with?
- How much time and effort is this investigation likely to take? Is your project reasonable?

You may not be able to answer this last question accurately until you start investigating, but make a rough guess. Set yourself a schedule, with deadlines for completing your research, for drafting, for rewriting. For any project in which you interview people, an excellent rule of thumb is to allow 50 percent more time than you might reasonably think necessary. People may be out when you call or you may find that one interview didn't supply all you need and that you'll have to do a follow-up. For a college paper, a field research project has to be humanly possible. If you begin with the intention of interviewing all the identical twins in your county, you might take a look at your deadline (and your course load) and then decide to limit your research to a sampling of, say, twenty individuals. Robert A. Day, author of *How to Write and Publish a Scientific Paper*, offers this sound advice: "Don't start vast projects with half-vast ideas." Don't start half-vast projects, either.

Reading for background. Jamie Merisotis didn't plunge blindly into field research. Even though it was slim, his reading gave him leads to follow up. Books such as Roy B. Flemming's *Punishment Before Trial: An Organizational Perspective of Felony Bail Processes* (New York: Longman, 1982) helped fill him in on how the bail bond business operates. He also found a few helpful articles on bail bonding in professional law journals, such as *Criminal Law Bulletin, Justice System Journal*, and *Law and Society Review*.

A useful question for you before you start to do field research is, What helpful background material on your topic can you find first of all in your library?

Directing an interview. People in all walks of life are often willing, sometimes even eager, to talk to a college student writing a research paper. Many, you may find, will seem flattered by your attention. Interviews—conversations with a purpose—may prove to be your main source of material. In Chapter 7 (p. 115), we gave advice that once again may come in handy. Make sure your prospect is willing to be quoted in writing. Fix an appointment for a moment when this person will have enough time—if possible, an hour—to have a thorough talk with you. Appear promptly, with carefully thought-out questions to ask. Really listen. Let the person open up. If a question draws no response, don't persist and make a nuisance of yourself; just go on to the next question. Make additional notes right after the interview ends to preserve anything you didn't have time to record during the interviews.

Despite bondsmen's initial reluctance to talk to him, in the end Jamie Merisotis came up with a trove of exciting material. His interviews were never shorter than forty-five minutes. Some bondsmen, apparently gratified by his taking their work seriously, opened up and talked candidly for as long as two hours. As is usual in studies of criminal justice, Merisotis's research paper gave the bondsmen anonymity. Because some bondsmen's activities (such as coercing clients to appear) hover on the borderline of the law, Merisotis had to assure them that he would not cite their names. He wouldn't even identify the state they practiced in. Some bondsmen, in fact, would agree to be interviewed only on the condition that their voices not be tape-recorded.

For his own guidance, Merisotis first made himself a list of questions he wanted to ask. To persuade the bondsmen to trust him, he began with questions that voiced his genuine interest in them as people:

> Tell me about yourself—where you live, where you grew up, your personal background.
>
> How long have you been working as a bondsman? Do you plan to stay in the business?
>
> Let's suppose you're having an average day. Could you tell me what this average day as a bondsman is like? In other words, what happens that you consider "regular"?

Then he probed more deeply, pursuing his main interest in his paper: how the bondsman operates. He asked questions to zero in on the bondsman's activities and reveal certain parts of them in detail:

> What do you consider when deciding to post bond for a defendant?
>
> Do you consider his or her ties to the community?
>
> His past record?
>
> His financial situation?
>
> The offense he is charged with?
>
> Are there any other things you take into account?

To round out his view of the bondsmen's activities, Merisotis sought interviews with other legal professionals. To his disappointment, although he asked them many times, no judges would consent to be interviewed. But Merisotis persisted. He talked with others in the legal system: police, prosecutors, public defenders, private attorneys, sheriffs, and bail commissioners. They confirmed, and sometimes supplemented, what the bondsmen had told him in confidence.

As Merisotis collected more and more evidence, not only his ideas changed but also the language he couched them in. From reading about bail bondsmen in legal journals, he had picked up the term *deposit bail*, which he used in his first interviews. But he soon found that the phrase belonged to classrooms and law offices, not to bondsmen in the field. He had to change it to *ten percent bail* so that the bondsmen would understand him.

Preparing a questionnaire. From each of the eighteen bail bondsmen who consented to talk with him, Jamie Merisotis sought even more evidence than his interview alone would bring. When the conversation came to an end, he would hand each person a questionnaire to fill out and return.

Questionnaires, as you know, are part of contemporary life. You probably filled out one the last time you applied for a job or for college. Many people, in our experience, enjoy having their knowledge tapped or their opinion solicited. Indeed, filling out a questionnaire has a gamelike appeal, as you can tell from the frequency with which self-quiz features appear in popular magazines: "How Rigid Are You?" followed by a thirty-question quiz to score yourself.

```
                              Questionnaire

Interview number_____

Age:

Marital status:

Number of dependents:

Father's occupation:

Mother's occupation:

How old were you when you became a bondsman?

How did you learn to become a bondsman?

       _____ family member was a bondsman      _____ taught myself
       _____ friend was a bondsman             _____ other  (Please explain)


How long, in months and years, would you estimate it took you to learn about
bail bonding?

How many days a week do you work as a bondsman?

Do you hold another job?

Estimate your earnings as a bondsman last year:

       _____ less than $10,000               _____ $20,000 to $30,000
       _____ $10,000 to $15,000              _____ more than $30,000
       _____ $15,000 to $20,000

How many employees do you have (excluding other bondsmen)?

In what state were you born?

In what state have you lived the most number of years?

How long have you been a resident of this state?

Do you speak any foreign languages?

If so, which?

Estimate the percentage of your clients who do not speak English:

       _____ less than 10 percent
       _____ 10 percent to 50 percent
       _____ more than 50 percent

Which best describes the education you have received?

       _____ some high school                _____ some four-year college
       _____ graduated high school           _____ graduated four-year college
       _____ some two-year college           _____ post-college or graduate study

List the schools and colleges you have attended, starting with high school:


What newspapers and magazines do you read regularly?
```

Figure 18.1 Jamie Merisotis's Questionnaire to Bail Bondsmen

As a rule, when researching a particular question professional pollsters, opinion testers, and survey takers survey thousands of individuals, chosen to represent a certain segment of society or perhaps a broad range of the populace (widely diversified in geography, income, ethnic background, and education). Their purpose may be to inform manufacturers who are test-marketing new products or trying to identify a new market. It may be to help a politician in

---

Questionnaire / page 2

Which of the following best describes your partisan political preference?

_____	sometimes vote Democrat	_____	always vote Republican
_____	usually vote Democrat	_____	independent
_____	always vote Democrat	_____	don't vote
_____	sometimes vote Republican	_____	usually vote for another
_____	usually vote Republican		party (Please name)

Which word best describes your political beliefs?

_____	left-liberal	_____	moderate conservative
_____	liberal	_____	conservative
_____	middle-of-the-road		

Are you a veteran of any U.S. wars?   If so, which ones?

How many of the following kinds of organizations do you belong to?

_____ veterans' organizations (VFW, American Legion, etc.)
_____ religious organizations (Knights of Columbus, etc.)
_____ fraternal and service organizations (Masons, Elks, etc.)
_____ service organizations (Kiwanis, Boy Scout leader, etc.)
_____ business organizations (Chamber of Commerce, etc.)
_____ advocate or lobbyist organizations (National Rifle Association,
          Greenpeace, Common Cause, etc.)

Please indicate any you contribute to or otherwise actively support.

What is your religious affiliation?

_____	Protestant	_____	Muslim
_____	Roman Catholic	_____	Other (Please name)
_____	Eastern Orthodox	_____	None
_____	Jewish		

How often do you attend religious services?

_____	very regularly	_____	infrequently
_____	fairly regularly	_____	never

Please list any hobbies or special interests:

Figure 18.1 (Continued)

planning a campaign. Questionnaires are widely used because they deliver large stores of useful information quickly and efficiently.

To make it easy for his interviewees to return his questionnaire, Merisotis provided each with a stamped, addressed envelope. Apparently, the bondsmen, after they opened up and talked, felt involved in his research and became willing also to reply to written questions.

Merisotis's questionnaire is reprinted in Figure 18.1. The questions call for short answers, easy to supply. He had used his most complicated questions in his interviews. This questionnaire asks for information revealing the bondsman's personal history, his family circumstances and background, his income, his education, his religious and political views. In keeping with his promise to the bondsmen to keep them anonymous, Merisotis identified each questionnaire by a number and did not use the respondent's name.

What is this questionnaire trying to discover? Since bail bondsmen often are asked to aid disadvantaged minorities, people who don't have personal lawyers or large bank accounts, Merisotis correctly guessed that the bondsmen's views, allegiances, education, and personal circumstances might well throw some light on their policies in deciding whether or not to take a risk on a client and write a bond. Why did Merisotis's questionnaire deliver good results? It addressed the questions its author wanted answered. It was directed to the people able to answer it.

By using this questionnaire, Merisotis soon found a clear picture of typical bondsmen emerging—one quite different from the image in the popular mind. Most bondsmen, the responses indicated, are not lone wolves, glamorously racing around cornering fugitives, but are cautious middle-class citizens: most of them married, with children, people of more education than he had expected, churchgoers and templegoers involved in community activities. From the responses to his questionnaire, he concluded that most bondsmen are not pistol-packing vigilantes but "day-to-day businessmen determined to make a living within the limits of the law."

You too will want to define the purpose of your questionnaire and then thoughtfully invent questions to fulfill it. If, for instance, you want to know how effective a day-care center is in the eyes of working mothers who entrust their children to it, you might ask questions like these: Do your children report that they are happy there? Have you ever had reason to complain? If so, about what?

Any questionnaire you design has to be one that people are willing to answer. The main point to remember in writing a questionnaire is to make it easy and inviting to fill out. If you make it too complex and time-consuming, the recipient will throw it away. Ask questions that call for a simple yes or no, for a word or a few words. Ask yourself as you write each question what information you want to acquire with the question. Then read it over to be sure that it will work the way it is written. It's a good idea to ask for just one piece of information per question. Like Merisotis, keep it simple: list alternative answers with blanks for your respondent to check.

You'll be especially lucky if you can assemble a group of people (at, say, an evening coffee for parents or children in a day-care center) and have them fill out your questionnaire on the spot. Facing the group, you can explain the purpose of your research, and, to enlist their confidence, you can invite questions and answer them. If you must send your questionnaire to people, include a concise letter or note explaining what you are trying to do and what use you will make of the replies. You might say, "This questionnaire should take no more than ten minutes of your time to complete" or give some such estimate that will make the task look reasonable to the respondent. Some professional questioners offer a morsel of bait: a small check or a coupon good for a free jar of pickles. You might promise a copy of your finished paper or article, a brief report of the results, or a listing of each respondent's name in an acknowledgment.

Even with such little enticements, professional poll takers and opinion testers find that a 40 percent response to a mailed questionnaire is unusually high. That is why they often conduct surveys by telephone, with the phone caller filling in the questionnaire for the respondent. Better results will come if you distribute your questionnaire in person, laying a copy in your prospects' hands. In this regard, an especially valuable use for a questionnaire is to follow up an interview, as Jamie Merisotis did.

If you can't interview a person, you might find it worthwhile to add to your questionnaire some "open questions," questions that call for short written responses. Although you are likely to get a smaller response to these, they might supply you with something worth quoting or might suggest facts for you to consider when you mull over the findings. Urge your recipients to flip over the questionnaire and use the back side if they need more room.

When you get back all your questionnaires, sit down and tally the results. That is easy enough to do if you are just counting short answers ("Republican," "Democrat"), but longer answers to open questions ("What is your goal in life?") will need to be summed up in paraphrase and then sorted into rough categories ("To grow rich," "To serve humanity," "To travel," "To save own soul"). By this means, you can count similar replies and accurately measure the extent of a pattern of responses.

Making a field trip. A visit to observe at first hand may well be essential in field research, as it certainly was in Jamie Merisotis's study. Merisotis visited four criminal courts, where he observed the bondsmen in action. In his paper, his observations supplied the evidence for his contention that the work of a bondsman has some socially redeeming use:

> In the crowded, often disorganized environment of a lower criminal court, bondsmen are a stabilizing influence. Their presence is unmistakable. They can be seen conferring with family and friends of defendants in courthouse corridors, speaking with prosecutors during a court recess, and keeping track of defendants still to be presented in court. Bondsmen help keep order in the courtroom, and they locate people. One bondsman was frequently observed assisting in translating for Spanish-speaking defendants when the official courtroom interpreter was unavailable.

Merisotis also observed the bondsmen on their daily rounds. He accompanied several as they made calls, observing them talking with clients and writing bonds. This firsthand experience supplied authentic details from which his writing profited.

In making an observational visit of your own, you may care to recall the suggestions we give in Chapter 5. You may need to make an appointment. Right away when you arrive, identify yourself and your business. Some receptionists will insist on identification. You might ask your instructor for a statement on college letterhead, declaring that you are a bona fide student doing field research. (If this document doesn't get you in, you can always return in overalls and say you have come to replace a fluorescent light. Seriously, unless your topic is bail bondsmen, you will probably be surprised how helpful most people will be.) Follow-up field trips may be necessary if, while you are writing, you find gaps in your research or if new ideas occur that you'll need to test by further observation.

Inquiring by telephone. If you can't talk to an expert in person, your next best resource may be a telephone interview. A busy person whom you call during a working day may not be able to give you a half hour of conversation on the spur of a moment, and it is polite to ask for a time when you may call again. You will waste the person's time (and yours) if you try to wing your interview; have written questions in hand before you dial. Take notes.

Federal regulations, by the way, forbid recording an interview over the phone without notifying the person who is talking that you are recording his or her remarks and without using a recorder-connector with a warning device that emits a beep signal every fifteen seconds. For a charge, some telephone companies will now make a beep-punctuated recording of your conversation and mail you a tape cassette; ask your operator whether this service is available.

The telephone, of course, has other uses besides interviewing. Early in his project Jamie Merisotis placed scores of phone calls to set up his face-to-face interviews. Later he checked some facts by making further calls.

Interviews, questionnaires, visits, and telephone inquiries are the sources of evidence you are likely to find most useful in field research. (If at this point you would care to see a self-contained chapter of Jamie Merisotis's honors thesis, which drew from all these sources, please turn to p. 375.) But other sources of ideas and information will serve you, too, for other kinds of field research. Briefly, we'll run through them.

Letter writing. Do you know a person whose knowledge or opinions you need but who lives too far away to interview? Write him or her a letter. Make it short and polite, keep your questions brief and pointed, and enclose a stamped, self-addressed envelope for a reply.

Large corporations, huge organizations such as the Red Cross and the National Wildlife Federation, and branches of the military and the federal government are accustomed to getting such mail. In fact, many of them employ public relations officers whose duty is to answer you. Sometimes they will unexpectedly supply you with a bonus: free brochures, press releases, or other material that they think might interest you. Many such nuggets of material valuable for research are to be had for nothing, from people trying hard to give it away.

Using television and radio programs, films, recordings. As Drew Cook demonstrated in his paper about James Bond (in Chapter 1), intriguing possibilities for writing lie in the media. If you ever care to do a research paper about television, radio, movies, or contemporary theater or music, you may find yourself doing field research as original as if you went out and interviewed eighteen bail bondsmen. Because your material lies close at hand (in the case of television, it may be yours at the twist of a knob), our only advice to you is to get plenty of it. Watch (or listen to) a large amount of it and draw conclusions.

Successful papers based on such research are legion. One student we know wrote an excellent research paper on public service commercials, free time devoted to good causes (like accident prevention and saving whales), which all television channels are required by law to make available. She classified the different causes being promoted and their different pitches or appeals, and she found an interesting correlation between the causes given air time and the presumed interests of a station's advertisers. For example, one station that aired many beer commercials rarely aired a public service message about the dangers of alcohol. Another student fruitfully compared the news coverage of an election by three major networks and the Public Broadcasting System by first recording a dozen televised newscasts with the aid of a VCR. Her main finding was that the networks seemed determined to cast the election into a more dramatic form—similar to a prizefight or a football game—than Public Broadcasting did, even though the outcome became clear very early.

Program guides (*TV Guide*, a station's own guide, or a daily newspaper) can save you time by directing you to the most relevant programs. For easy reference, the script of a broadcast or telecast may be available on request (or for a small charge) from a station or network; if an announcer does not proclaim that it is available, you can write to inquire.

In writing about movies or plays, don't forget to check out reviews in magazines and newspapers. In writing about a recording, inspect any information supplied on an insert or on the sleeve. Record labels, too, sometimes provide dates, names of members of a group, and song composers.

Attending lectures and conferences. Professionals in virtually every walk of life—and also special-interest groups—will sometimes convene for a regional or national conference. Such conferences bring together doctors, lawyers, engineers, scientists, librarians, teachers, and assorted people bound together by some mutual concern (a conference to protest acid rain, a convention of science fiction fans). These meetings can be fertile sources of fresh ideas.

Fortunately, college campuses sometimes welcome such conferences, and if there are any of possible use to you, go take them in. An idea for a field research paper might result. At some conferences, lectures and panel discussions are open to the public. At others, to gain admission you might have to enroll in the conference, for a fee. This drawback might discourage a casual researcher, but if your honors thesis depends on material to be discussed at the conference, or if you are thinking of a possible career in that profession, you might find it worthwhile to pay the fee. To attend a professional conference, to meet and talk with speakers and fellow attendees, can be an excellent way to learn the language of a discipline. If you plan to be an ornithologist, start thinking and talking and writing like an ornithologist. Learn the vocabulary, the habits of mind. To steep yourself in the language of a specialized conference is one way to begin. You can take notes on the lectures, which are given by speakers who usually are distinguished in their specialties, and thus get some firsthand live opinions. You may even be able to ask questions from the audience or corner the speakers later for informal talk.

Proceedings of important conferences may be published later (unfortunately, often months or years later) and eventually can be tracked down in a library. A paper presented at one such conference of professors of educational administration is cited in the research paper by Lisa Chickos on page 324.

Check the weekly schedules of events listed on your college bulletin boards and in your campus newspaper. These may alert you to other lectures (besides those delivered at conferences) that may hold ideas and information useful to you.

Shaping a Draft

All the while you have been gathering material, you have been evaluating it, deciding what to trust, which evidence looks most likely to answer your basic research question. Presumably, you have been doing some heavy sifting and discarding along the way. If you have, you will have saved yourself much toil at the present moment, when you are ready to shape your material into a paper.

At this point, as you glance over what you have collected, you can again be critical of it. Do you have *enough* material to demonstrate what you hope to demonstrate? If not, you may need to go out and get more. How much is enough? To answer that, we can't lay down any hard-and-fast rule. But the larger the generalization you make from your evidence, the more evidence it calls for in support. Clearly, you cannot decide that all day-care centers in the state of Washington are safe, well-managed facilities from having visited only five of them in Seattle; and in a research project bounded by the limited time of a college course, you may need to trim down your generalization: "The day-care centers *I visited in Seattle* impressed me by their safety and professional management" [emphasis ours].

Most college writers find, at the moment they begin to shape a first draft, that they have collected a bewildering array of material. If you've done much legwork, the amount and variety of your evidence may dismay you. Do you feel frozen as you contemplate your difficulties? Don't know how you will ever pull this jumble into shape? Stop trying to plan; start writing. Don't worry about which part of your paper to write first—start with anything at all. If you just get something down on paper, then later you can decide where to place it. Absorb yourself in your task. Maybe your material will start falling into shape as you write.

Organizing your ideas. With any luck, your material may fall readily into shape, but if it is various and extensive, you may find you'll need to outline beforehand. In Part Seven, we offer detailed advice on outlining (p. 476). For some writers, a dependable-looking outline inspires confidence.

In organizing their field research, writers need to remember that, as is true of most other kinds of writing, some intuitive art is called for. It is not enough to relate the steps you took in answering your research question: you aren't writing a memoir, you're reporting what you found out. And it may be that a reader will take in your material more readily if you try putting it together in various combinations until you find out what seems most engaging and clear. In a guidebook titled *How to Write and Publish Engineering Papers and Reports* (Philadelphia: ISI Press, 1982), Herbert B. Michaelson remarks:

> Because there is no one best way to organize all engineering manuscripts, the role of the imagination cannot be overemphasized. Writing progress seldom follows the same sequence as progress on an engineering project. Designing a device or developing a process may get off to a false start, or may be sidetracked into a wrong approach, or may undergo modifications before the work is completed. A manuscript describing all these stages of the design or process would be difficult to read. After the problems have been solved in the laboratory, it is time for a new exercise of the imagination: the design of the manuscript.

If you began with a clear, carefully worded question for research (first discussed on p. 296), you will generally have an easier time in organizing your evidence to answer it. Of course, research questions often may change and re-form while you're at work in the field. Don't be afraid, when the time comes to organize, to junk an original question that no longer works and to try to reorganize your material around a newly formed question.

Interpreting your evidence. To be sure, organizing the facts you collect is an important part of your task. You might easily mistake that part for the most important part of field research. But still more important is to *interpret* those facts. What do they indicate? In themselves, facts and statistics may not always make much sense. Much more likely to communicate meaning to your reader is what you make of your figures—your summaries of what statistics mean. Instead of reporting that 34.1 percent of your respondents favor capital punishment (with no further comment on the statistic), it might make more sense to write, "More than a third of the people I questioned said that they believe capital punishment is sometimes justified, although many of these people qualified their answers. They said they believed in it only to punish violent crimes such as murder and rape."

When you are finished collecting evidence, read back over your notes. With pencil in hand, think about what you have gathered. Try to answer the basic research question you began with. You will want to put this answer into the conclusion of your paper. Obviously, this final part of your paper is highly important. In it, you try to draw some generalization about what you have learned. An example: "I find, therefore, that sky divers, far from being reckless and suicidal as some people think, are responsible experts who carefully prepare for their jumps and observe every safety precaution."

Evaluate your sources. You can probably trust anyone you interviewed who has a high reputation among other experts in the same field. Did some person you interviewed seem indifferent, half asleep? Did he appear not to know what he was talking about? Discard his testimony or give it only a passing mention. Did any others impress you with their competence? Rely on them more heavily.

If you used a questionnaire and tabulated the replies, show them to fellow students whose opinions you respect. What conclusions do they draw? Test their interpretations against your own.

Here are some evidence-testing questions.

CHECKLIST: EVALUATING EVIDENCE

- Is any of your evidence hearsay ("I understand she was a pretty reckless driver in her younger days")? If so, can you support or discount a speaker's view by comparing it with any other evidence?
- Was anyone who described an important event actually on the scene? Is it likely that the passage of time has distorted his or her memory?
- Does the testimony agree with published accounts—in books, magazines, and newspapers?
- Have you compared different people's opinions or accounts of the same thing? In general, the more people, the better.
- Do you base any large generalization on a single example, one fact, one individual opinion? If so, reconsider your claim.
- If you have tried to question a random sampling of people, do you feel they are truly representative?
- Did an interviewee exhibit prejudice or bias? Some remarks may need to be discounted.
- How detailed is your evidence? How extensive?

For more suggestions on evaluating facts and testimony, glance back over the section "Testing Evidence" in Chapter 14 (pp. 252–254).

Using sources (not letting sources use you). While you write, it is easy to get distracted from your central inquiry—from your attempt to answer the research question you started out with. No doubt you will have collected experiences, comments from people, and miscellaneous delightful facts that you think you just have to include in your paper. Maybe they belong in an informal paper—a memoir, say, of your life as a field researcher—but be willing to omit them in writing up your field research. Some material that you may have taken great pains to collect may not prove useful when you draft. If it doesn't serve your inquiry, leave it out—don't yank it in by the heels.

A common danger, besides letting sources dominate a draft and receive undeserved prominence, is for a writer to swagger in triumph over what he or she discovered. Cultivate a certain detachment. Make no exorbitant claims for what you have discovered ("Thus I have shown that day-care centers universally deserve the trust of any parent in the state of Washington"). You have probably not answered your research question for all time; you need not claim to be irrefutable. Norman Tallent, in his guidebook *Psychological Report Writing*, quotes a professional reader of reports in the field of psychology: "I have seen some reports which affected me adversely because of a tendency to sound pompous with the implication 'This is the final word!' rather than 'This is an opinion intended to be helpful in understanding the whole.' "

As you write, introduce pieces of evidence with transitions, such as *"Two other bail bondsmen disagreed* that first-time offenders make the best risks" or *"Elsewhere, in the southwest end, a more ethnically various part of the city*, few respondents felt that the problem of unemployment was serious." On the art of smoothly weaving quotations and other material into your paper, Chapter 16 makes a few suggestions (pp. 305–307).

Rewriting

As in writing a library research paper, you will probably find it easier to write the beginning and ending of your paper after you have done your research and written it up. You'll now better understand what you have demonstrated.

Looking over your evidence and your draft, you may quite possibly find your conclusion changing. Don't be afraid of making a whole new interpretation.

Not every spoken remark you've collected will be worth quoting, and if you faithfully introduce every one, word for word, the result may sound like drivel. In that case, summarize and paraphrase in your own words. To test whether a quotation is worth quoting, ask yourself:

Are these words memorable? Would you recall them if you hadn't written them down? If not, away with them!

Does the speaker's remark support any point you're trying to make? Or does it seem mere maundering chin music? If so, out with it!

When you sit down to rewrite, here are other, possibly useful questions to ask yourself.

REVISION CHECKLIST: LOOKING OVER YOUR RESULTS

- Have you put in only evidence that makes a point?
- Have you ever yielded to the temptation to put in some fact or quotation just because it cost effort to obtain?
- Are your sources of information trustworthy? Do you have lingering doubts about anything anyone told you? (If so, whom might you consult to verify it?)

- Did you take advantage of any library material that supplied background information or helped you test the validity of your evidence?
- Is your conclusion (or generalization) made clear? (Ask a peer editor to read your work.)
- Do you spend much space announcing what you are going to do or in repeating what you demonstrated? (If you do, consider whether such passages might be whittled down or done without.)
- If you include observations made on a field trip or visit, do you now need to make any follow-up visit?
- Do you need more evidence to back up any point? If so, where might you obtain it?

Preparing your manuscript. The form of your field research paper isn't much different from that of a library research paper (whose final preparation is discussed briefly on pp. 317–318). One difference may occur when, if you are following APA style, you come to prepare a list of your sources ("References") at the end of your paper. You do not list personal communications such as letters, interviews, and phone conversations. You need list only sources that a reader can verify: published works and public records. For specific advice on citing and listing your sources, see Chapter 19.

Proofreading a field research paper calls for checking information carefully—not against neatly printed sources, which are easier to check, but against your original notes and jottings. Allow yourself ample time to give your paper a final going-over. (For further instructions, see also the appendix at the back of this book.)

A COMPLETED FIELD RESEARCH PAPER

When Jamie Merisotis completed his honors thesis, it caused a local stir. Friends and roommates who read it were greatly intrigued and impressed by it. As his academic department required, large parts of his thesis were devoted to explaining recent and pending legislation as it affected the bail bond business and to giving an account of his methods of research (which account we have already summarized). But let us show you one short, self-contained chapter of the thesis, which illustrates how Merisotis put his field research to use. The paper is written in APA style, so both direct quotations and indirect quotations, taken from interviews, are dated. Unlike most field research papers, this one contains no names, for in order to persuade the bondsmen to talk freely, Merisotis had to agree to keep them all anonymous. In preserving anonymity, he followed the practice of *Law and Society Review*, a professional journal that sometimes publishes articles quoting criminals who want to conceal their identities. He dated all facts and quotations he obtained from interviews, but lest anyone see a pattern in the responses and try to identify the speakers, he did not distinguish one speaker from another.

How a Bondsman Decides to Post Bail
Jamie Merisotis

The bail bondsman's decision whether or not
to post bond for a defendant is probably the
single greatest power he wields in the legal
system. People who seek the services of a
bondsman normally do not have the means to raise
the full bond amount themselves. Thus the
bondsman is often the deciding factor in determining a defendant's pretrial status. Defendants unable to secure the services of a bondsman
often remain in the custody of the state until
the trial, which may be several months later.

When a bondsman is asked to write a bond,
he considers several factors. This decision-
making process is complex, and most bondsmen
stress that each client is considered on his own
terms. Nevertheless, from this research several clear patterns have emerged. (All evidence cited in this study is from personal
communications.)

By far the most important factor, at least
initially, is the amount of the bond. After
all, it is the bond amount that ultimately
yields the bondsman's fee. Of course, the
bondsman is also aware that the greater fee
carries the greater risk. One telltale sign of
the importance of the bond amount may be seen
from the bondsman's method of screening prospective clients. A defendant, or someone

2

close to him, can call the bondsman by looking under "Bonds--Bail" in the telephone book or requesting the list of bondsmen from the police station. But a phone call does not bring direct access to the bondsman. In most cases, a professional answering service fields calls for the bondsman, then notifies him through an electronic beeper. The bondsman then calls the answering service and takes the message. What is interesting is that the answering service asks callers only three questions: (1) name, (2) where they are at the moment, and (3) the bond amount. Clearly this amount is of tantamount importance to the bondsman, and he makes note of it immediately when taking the message. Bondsmen concur that the bond amount is very important in their decision-making process, as these comments reveal:

> Let's say I get a call at three
> o'clock a.m. I've just gotten into bed
> and the service beeps me with a call.
> It's late but I take the call and find out
> it's for a five hundred dollar bond out in
> [a town about 20 miles from the bondsman's
> house]. My answer to that is simple. No.
> There's no way I drag myself out of bed for
> a 50 dollar fee. As a matter of fact, I
> might even call the service back and tell
> them not to bother me with nickel fees.
> (November 29, 1985)

3

> I don't write bonds for under five
> hundred. Whether I'm taking a call or
> sitting in court during arraignments, I
> can't—won't—even sneeze at a guy who
> wants my services on a two-fifty bond.
> It's not worth my time. (December 27, 1985)
> Do you know how much paperwork there
> is on a bond? Do you? I'm not saying I
> won't write a bond because of the paper-
> work, but any bondsman will tell you that
> paperwork is the worst part of this job.
> If I write only a few bonds a week, you
> better believe they're good risks for good
> money. (November 9, 1985)

Bondsmen who have a large bond volume, but deal
in very low bonds, rarely survive in the modern
bail bond business.

Bondsmen consider another important factor:
the alleged offense. It tells them something
about the defendant, which in turn gives them an
idea of the likelihood that he will appear.
Probably the single offense that causes greatest
apprehension to bondsmen is a failure to appear,
also referred to as FTA. Obviously, a defendant who did not face the court in a previous
case is not a good risk. Failing to appear is
a sin that many bondsmen will not forgive, and
thus recidivist criminals may often find that
they have no benefactors in the community of
bondsmen. In other cases, bondsmen have personal preferences for not wanting to bond out

4

certain defendants. Sample responses demonstrate this eclecticism:

> I don't bond sex offenders. Perverts
> don't deserve to be free. (November 29,
> 1985)

> I try to stay away from people who are
> charged with violent crimes, especially if
> it involves a gun. Will he turn around
> and use it on me? I don't want to find
> out. (January 11, 1986)

> No prostitutes, and no one that deals
> in heroin. You never know where those
> kind of people will be in the morning.
> (October 5, 1985)

Another factor that bondsmen take into account is the defendant's community ties. Most
bondsmen ask the defendant where he lives, what
kind of job he has, and how long he has lived in
the area. This information is important to a
bondsman because it gives him an idea of the
likelihood of a defendant's returning for trial;
it also gives him some information about how
difficult the client would be to trace if he
failed to appear in court. Bondsmen are wary
of out-of-state defendants because the costs of
retrieving a client from a long distance are
naturally higher. But information on community
ties can also be used to measure the client's
credibility. As one bondsman stated, "A guy
who's got a good job, wife, kids, whatever, is a

5

lot better risk than some chump with no address"
(October 5, 1985).

Some bondsmen express no apprehensions
about career criminals if they "know the guy or
his family" (November 16, 1985; January 4,
1986). Others, however, are unwilling to assume the risk for repeat offenders. "If I'm in
another business," one bondsman said, "steady
clients are great. In this business, steady
clients are bad news" (December 30, 1985).

Several bondsmen said they take the defendant's age into consideration because they
believe that young clients have high rates of
failure to appear. That the defendant is living with his parents, however, bondsmen take as
a sign of stability. One bondsman noted that
if a parent has "gone down" (engaged a bondsman
before), "you know the kid will have someone
around making sure he gets to court" (November
6, 1985).

It should be noted that a majority of
bondsmen denied that race is a factor in their
decisions. Others, quite vocal about their racial preferences, said they do not bond out
black defendants. The reasons offered were
mostly stereotypes:

I'll bond out a black person if he
comes from a good neighborhood. But I
definitely check the address. A lot of
the time, I read [the name of a predominantly black area] and say to myself, "If

6

> this guy skips, are you gonna go in there
> and drag him out?" Unless I'm in a daring
> mood, there's no way. (January 11, 1986)

Women defendants are also approached cautiously
by some bondsmen. One remarked that women are
sometimes difficult to trace because "once the
case comes up, months or even a year later, she
could be married and change her name. That
makes tracing difficult" (November 6, 1985).

In many cases the bondsman requires an indemnitor on the bond. This person is often a
relative or friend, usually the person who
called the bondsman. The indemnitor agrees to
compensate the bondsman for his losses in the
event of forfeiture or to deposit collateral
with the bondsman. The bondsman's decision to
post bond is often contingent on who the indemnitor is and what he has to offer as security
or collateral. Only in extenuating circumstances—if he knows the defendant well or is
feeling extraordinarily compassionate—will the
bondsman not require an indemnitor. Indeed,
the indemnitor in some ways plays a more important role in the bondsman's business than does
the defendant, as the following comments show:

> I deal strictly with the indemnitor.
> I want to know who this person is, how much
> money he's got, and what he can offer me
> for collateral. Otherwise, no deal. (No-
> vember 8, 1985)

7

> Really, my financial leverage--you
> know, how I'm gonna get my money back if
> the client skips--is with the indemnitor.
> As co-signer, they're putting their butt on
> the line for this guy.... Most times, I
> don't even see the defendant until it's
> time to sign the papers. (December 30,
> 1985)

Bondsmen accept an array of things as security or collateral: for example, stocks, savings account passbooks, real estate, and car titles. A bondsman wants to know how much leverage he will have with a defendant in the event of forfeiture. Clearly, a majority of this leverage is with the indemnitor, the person who has the most to lose (at least financially) if the client absconds.

Whether any of these factors that bondsmen consider really affects the defendant's likelihood of appearance for trial--a most important question in every bondsman's mind--goes beyond the scope of the present study. Nevertheless, each bondsman perceives these factors and weighs them differently. His analysis ultimately yields the decision whether or not to assume the risk for a defendant.

Unlike a library research paper, this field research paper has no listing of its sources entitled "References." Merisotis's information came entirely from personal communications, mostly from interviews and responses to his questionnaire, which he distributed privately. But if, using the APA style, you were writing a field research paper that referred to public sources, such as a lecture to an audience or records in courthouses, which are open for anyone's inspection, then at the end of your paper you would add a list of "References."

Questions to Start You Thinking

1. How does the life of a bail bondsman appear similar to the lives of any other businesspeople you know? In what ways is it strikingly different?
2. How does Merisotis demonstrate his opening contention that the bondsman wields great power within the legal system?
3. In his concluding paragraph, how does he separate his own view from the views of the bondsmen? With what opinions that the bondsmen have expressed (and which he has quoted) do you suppose he might disagree?
4. What other interesting, unusual, or unfamiliar occupations come to mind about which you might enjoy doing field research?

Other Assignments

1. As Jamie Merisotis did, investigate a job or profession. Interview people in this line of work, explain what they do, and try to characterize them. Your topic need not be as colorful and hard to research as bail bonding; just pick a profession you care to know more about, perhaps one that you consider a career possibility. Suggested collateral reading: Studs Turkel's *Working* (New York: Pantheon, 1974), a fascinating series of interviews with people in various occupations.
2. Write a portrait of life in your town or neighborhood, as it was in the past, from interviews with senior citizens. Any photographs or other visual evidence you can gather might be valuable to include. If possible, try to verify any testimony you receive by comparing it with a file of old newspapers (probably available at a local newspaper office) or by talking with a local historian.
3. Avail yourself of experts on your college faculty. Interview at least three recognized authorities in their disciplines, asking them all the same questions on a specific topic, and then compare their answers and draw conclusions. For instance, you might ask three professors of political science, "What do you foresee as the outcome of the next presidential election?" Or three English professors might be asked, "Do you agree with poet-critic Stanley Kunitz's remark that American poetry of the last twenty-five years has become harder to remember?"
4. Write a short history of your immediate family from interviews, photographs, scrapbooks, old letters, written but unpublished records, and any other sources available.
5. Investigate a current trend you have noticed on television (collecting evidence by observing news programs, other programs, or commercials).
6. Write a survey of recent films of a certain kind (detective movies, horror movies, science fiction movies, comedies, love stories), making generalizations that you support with evidence from your own film watching.

7. Study the lyrics of contemporary popular songs and draw a conclusion about them, citing a dozen or more examples. (Suggestions: Your research might support the argument of Caryl Rivers, whose article "What Should Be Done about Rock Lyrics?" appears on pp. 262–264—or it might enable you to argue with her.)

8. Review the writing assignments in Chapter 5 and Chapter 7. Among them, you might find the germ for a field research paper. Choose a subject you haven't investigated before. Understand, however, that, to be the outcome of true field research, such a paper will require more extensive evidence than those assignments call for.

APPLYING WHAT YOU LEARN: SOME USES OF FIELD RESEARCH

Opportunities may arise to do field research in almost any college course, at any level, in which you are called on to collect evidence and to observe. If you happen to be a student of journalism, you may be sent out to cover news stories: one of the most practical applied kinds of field research. In education and social studies courses, field trips and observational visits are commonplace. (Columbia College offers a well-known undergraduate course in the sociology of New York City that includes trips to police lockups, morgues, and charity hospitals.) In a course in psychology, medical care, or political science, you may have to observe people's behavior and interpret it.

In the world beyond the campus, to carry out useful field research is an enormous and bustling concern. Sociologists seek to explain the components of the population. Bankers and stockbrokers and businesspeople seek to predict trends in the economy. Businesspeople seek new products that will sell, or they try to learn why an established product isn't selling better. Often they seek to understand a potential market and how to appeal to it. Professionals who conduct research often set forth their findings in reports and articles—that is why specialized technical and professional journals abound. Anthropologists and sociologists study how people live, archeologists dig up evidence of how people lived in the past, biologists and students of the environment collect evidence about the behavior of species of wildlife.

Here, for instance, is the anthropologist E. Richard Sorenson reporting his observations of children of the Fore, a tribal people in New Guinea who live by agriculture. Taking movies with a concealed camera that went unnoticed and taking still pictures without alerting the tribesmen in advance, Sorenson photographed growing children and their families in their daily activities. From the pictures and his notes, he formed several interesting generalizations about the Fore people's practices in childrearing.

> The core discovery was that young infants remained in almost continual bodily contact with their mother, her housemates, or her gardening associates. At first, mothers' laps were the center of activity, and infants occupied themselves there by nursing, sleeping, and playing with their own bodies or those of their caretakers. The infants were not put aside for the sake of

other activities, as when food was being prepared or heavy loads were being carried. While they remained in close, uninterrupted physical contact with those around them, their basic needs, such as rest, nourishment, stimulation, and security, were continuously satisfied without obstacle. . . .

A second crucial thread running from infancy through childhood was the unrestricted manner in which exploratory activity and pursuit of interest were left to the initiative of the child. As the infant's awareness increased, his interests broadened to the things his mother and other caretakers did and to the objects and materials they used. Then these youngsters began crawling out to explore things nearby that attracted their attention. By the time they were toddling, their interests continually took them on short sorties to nearby objects and persons. As soon as they could walk well, the excursions extended to the entire hamlet and its gardens, and then beyond with other children. Developing without interference or supervision, this personal exploratory quest freely touched on whatever was around—even axes, knives, machetes, and fire [Figure 18.2].

Initially astonished by the ability of young children to manage so independently without being hurt, I eventually began to see how this capability

Figure 18.2 A generally practiced deference to the desires of the young in the choice of play objects permitted them to investigate and handle knives and other potentially harmful objects frequently. They were expected to make use of the tools and materials which belonged to their adult associates and were indulged in this expectation. As a result, use of knives was common, particularly for exploratory play.

also emerged from the infants' milieu of close human physical proximity and tactile interaction. Touch and bodily contact lent themselves naturally to satisfying the basic needs of the babies, and provided the basis for an early kind of communicative experience based on touch. In continual physical touch with people engaged in daily pursuits, infants and toddlers began to learn the forms of behavior and response characteristic of Fore life. Muscle tone, movement, and mood were components of this learning process; formal instruction was not. . . . Competence with the tools of life developed quickly, and by the time they were able to walk, Fore youngsters could safely handle axes, knives, and fire.

The early pattern of exploratory activity included frequent return to one of the "mothers." Serving as a home base, the bastion of security, a woman might occasionally give the youngster a nod of encouragement, if he glanced in her direction with uncertainty. Yet rarely did anyone attempt to control or direct, nor did they participate in a child's quests or jaunts.

At first I found it quite remarkable that toddlers did not recklessly thrust themselves into unappreciated dangers, the way our own children tend to do. Eventually I came to see that they had no reason to do so. From their earliest days, they enjoyed a benevolent sanctuary from which the world could be confidently viewed, tested, and appreciated. These human bases were neither demanding nor restrictive, so there was no need to escape or evade them in the manner so frequently seen in Western culture. Confidently, not furtively, the youngsters were able to extend their inquiry, widening their understanding as they chose. There was no need to play tricks or deceive in order to pursue life. Nor did they have to act out impulsively to break through subliminal fears induced by punishment or parental anxiety. Such children could safely move out on their own, unsupervised and unrestricted.

Most of us may never go on a field research expedition to New Guinea, but the techniques that Sorenson demonstrates—patiently collecting evidence, laying aside his own unwarranted assumptions, and finally making generalizations about the behavior patterns he observed—may serve for any investigation of the unfamiliar. You might try emulating Sorenson's accuracy, patience, and open-mindedness the next time you write a paper about people or a lifestyle different from your own.

In the sciences, social sciences, and fields of business (such as marketing or advertising), writers of articles frequently report on still another kind of study: their observations of tests and practical inquiries they have made. People in the helping professions, after testing and observing their patients, interviewing their families, and studying information from other professionals who have known them, often write case studies, which they keep on file and sometimes share with their colleagues. Only rarely are case studies meant for publication. Here, from a mental health center, is an example of one such case study.

Debbie is a twelve and a half-year-old girl from a broken home (father deserted six years ago and continues to upset the family by calling to complain to Debbie's mother about his present wife). Debbie is thought to be underachieving in school. Her teachers see her as an angry, troubled child. Debbie herself complains that schoolwork overwhelms her, tires her out. The following report seeks to achieve an understanding of Debbie as a basis for taking further action.

Debbie's intellectual status is above average. Her observations are accurate and there is originality of thought. She is an insecure child who has many fears. She fears the loss of her integrity, attack from others, and her own impulses. Debbie has a great need for acceptance and affection, but is inhibited by an overpowering fear of being rejected and hurt. There seems to be hostility directed to the mother. The relationship has not been mutually satisfying, often leaving Debbie frustrated. It is my impression that the mother's inconsistencies in handling the child may be a source of anger. Now she wants her own way and is conflicted about her dependency. Her attitudes to men are also unwholesome. They are seen as weak and mutilated. And she is confused about herself. She feels inadequate, and having a specific learning disability she requires more guidance and love than most children her age. However, not being able successfully to reach out to others has only left her more frustrated. Since Debbie finds it difficult to relate to people and because her own feelings are threatening to her, she withdraws to an immature fantasy world that provides little refuge. Even her fantasy is fearful, involving aggression and fear of being injured emotionally. Debbie is a very unhappy child.

In one memorable college paper, a business student reported the results of his attempt to give out free samples of a new margarine to supermarket customers. When he spread globs of the stuff on soft white bread, he had very little luck trying to give away samples. But when he dabbed the stuff daintily on tempting-looking crackers studded with sesame seeds, it moved well. He then tried dainty dabs of margarine on bread (with a little more success, but not much) and sometimes fat globs on the crackers (which moved fairly well). His conclusion: the crackers were the catalyst that made the margarine move. But in margarine samples, he decided, smaller offerings had proved more appealing than generous ones. These findings may not seem earthshaking to you, but to a merchant of margarine they might prove worth their weight in butter.

Anybody, in practically any field, can conduct an experiment. You might even ask yourself, What experiment might I conduct that might produce interesting results? In fact, what experiments might you conduct in order to write an interesting paper *for this very course?* Once again, you'll need your imagination.

CHAPTER 19

Documenting Sources: Using a Style Book

In newspaper language, a *style book* is a list of usages that every writer for the paper observes. A style book might instruct reporters, for instance, to refer to women as *Ms.,* to use a lowercase letter and not a capital on names of the seasons (*spring*, not *Spring*), to put quotation marks around the title of a book, a film, or a song. Every newspaper makes up its own style book and every staff writer has a copy. The style book helps determine the personality of a newspaper. For years, the *Chicago Tribune* insisted on spelling *philosophy* "filosofy," while the New York *Daily News* referred to no woman as a *lady* unless she was a convicted prostitute. More important, a style book saves each writer from having to deliberate about every fussy little thing: to capitalize or not to capitalize? It keeps all the articles in a newspaper consistent and so makes the paper more easily readable.

A similar logic operates in scholarly writing. Writers of college research papers most often follow the rules from either of two handbooks, one compiled by the Modern Language Association (MLA), the other by the American Psychological Association (APA). The style of the MLA is generally observed in papers for English composition, literature, and foreign language courses. APA style usually prevails in papers for the social sciences and business. If your research takes you into any scholarly or professional journals in those special areas, you will probably find all the articles following a recognizable style.

In other disciplines, other handbooks prescribe style: *CBE Style Manual* of the Council of Biology Editors (1983), for instance, is used in the biological sciences and medicine. You will need to familiarize yourself with it, or with other manuals, if you ever do much research writing in those or another discipline.

This chapter is here for handy reference. We try to tell you no more than you will need to know to write a freshman research paper. You won't have to worry about many of these matters until you are typing your paper in finished form. Then you can refer to this advice. To know MLA style or APA style will be useful at these moments:

In citing while you write—at any time when you want to document, often on a note card, exactly where you obtained a fact, idea, opinion, or quotation.

In listing all your sources—that is, in adding a final bibliography, a list entitled "Works Cited" or "References."

CITING: MLA STYLE

As you write, you need to indicate what you borrowed and where you found it. The *MLA Handbook for Writers of Research Papers, 2nd ed.* (New York: Modern Language Association of America, 1984) has extensive and exact recommendations. If you want more detailed advice than that given here, you can purchase a copy of the *MLA Handbook* or see a copy in the reference room of your college library.

Citing Printed Sources

To cite a book or a periodical in the text of a paper, you usually place in parentheses the author's last name and the number of the page containing the information cited. You do this as close as possible to your mention of the information you have borrowed, as in the following examples.

A WORK BY A SINGLE AUTHOR

At least one critic maintains that Dean Rusk's exposure to Nazi power in Europe in the 1930s permanently influenced his attitude toward appeasement:

> In contrast to Acheson, who had attended Groton, Yale, and Harvard despite his family's genteel poverty, Rusk was sheer Horatio Alger stuff. He had grown up barefoot, the son of a tenant farmer in Georgia's Cherokee county, and had worked his way through Davidson.... Then came the moment that transformed his life and his thinking. He won a Rhodes scholarship to Oxford. More important, his exposure to Europe in the early 1930s, as the Nazis consolidated their power in Germany, scarred his mind, leading him to share Acheson's hostility to appeasement in any form anywhere. (Karnow 179)

One reason we admire Simone de Beauvoir is that "she lived the life she believed" (Morgan 58).

For complete information about your source, the reader can then turn to the end of your paper and refer to your list entitled "Works Cited" (see p. 394). Notice that a long direct quotation is indented and needs no quotation marks to set it off from the text of your paper.

For the sake of readability, you'll sometimes want to mention an author or authors in your text, putting only the page number in parentheses.

A WORK BY TWO OR MORE AUTHORS

```
Taylor and Wheeler present yet another view (25).
```

A WORK BY A CORPORATE AUTHOR

```
The American Red Cross lists three signs of oxygen depri-
vation: blue tongue, lips, and fingernails; loss of con-
sciousness; and dilated pupils (181).
```

A GOVERNMENT DOCUMENT

```
The Department of Health and Human Services sets forth
several methods for combating future outbreaks of mos-
quito-borne diseases (25).
```

AN ANONYMOUS WORK

When no author is mentioned on the title page of the work you're citing, refer to your source with a shortened version of the title (the first word or phrase).

```
In Alcoholism, we find a list of questions people can ask
themselves if they suspect their drinking has gotten out
of hand (3).
```

MULTIPLE WORKS BY THE SAME AUTHOR

If you have used two works by the same author (or authors), you need to indicate with an abbreviated title which one you are citing in the text. In a paper that uses as sources two books by Iona and Peter Opie, *The Lore and Language of Schoolchildren* and *The Oxford Nursery Rhyme Book*, you would cite the first book as follows:

```
The Opies found that the children they interviewed were
more straightforward when asked about their "magic prac-
tices" or their "ways of obtaining luck or averting ill-
luck" than when asked about their "superstitions" (Lore
210).
```

MULTIPLE WORKS IN THE SAME CITATION

If you refer to more than one source, separate the two citations with a semicolon.

> The love between Aylmer and Georgiana, in Hawthorne's
> story "The Birthmark," has been called rare, pure, and
> beautiful (Matthiessen 254; Van Doren 131).

WORKS WITH EDITORS, TRANSLATORS, OR COMPILERS

When you cite a writer whose work appears in a book that has an editor, translator, or compiler, you need cite only the writer's name (and, of course, the page number). Due credit to the editor, translator, or compiler will be given in your list of works cited.

> Critic Denis Donoghue refers to Randall Jarrell's "won-
> derful feeling for dreams and for the children who attend
> them" (57).

A MULTIVOLUME WORK

For a work with multiple volumes, show the author's name and the volume number followed by a colon and the page number.

> In ancient times, astrological predictions were sometimes
> used as a kind of black magic (Sarton 2: 319).

Citing Nonprint Sources

In both library and field research, it is likely that some of your material will be drawn from nonprint sources: interviews, questionnaires, phone calls, tapes and recordings, personal letters, films, filmstrips, slide programs, video-tapes, computer programs. Finding material in the field (as in an interview) means that *you* are the source. You should document all your material as faithfully as you credit books, newspapers, and periodicals. Probably the easiest way to do that is to weave your mention of each source into the body of your paper.

> Hearing Yeats read "The Song of the Old Mother" on tape
> sheds new light on several lines in the poem.

> On the H.L. Mencken recording, journalist Donald Howe
> Kirkley, Sr., was able to persuade the veteran writer to
> talk about his defeats as well as his triumphs.

In your list of works cited you give complete information about each source. Transitions—phrases to introduce quotations, statistical tables, and other blocks of material—can also serve you well. (For weaving material in gracefully, see the suggestions in Chapter 16, p. 311.)

Using Endnotes to Cite Printed Sources

Some students and instructors continue to prefer notes rather than parenthetical citations for documentation, especially when the citations need to be long. The *MLA Handbook*, after giving detailed instructions for the newer, simpler way of citing sources that it now recommends, still contains instructions for doing it the old way.

If you use endnotes, you number your citations consecutively in the body of your text, like this.[1] You roll your typewriter platen up a notch or learn the command in your word processing program for superscripts. Then, at the end of the text, on a new page, you center the title "Notes," skip two spaces, and cite each source, in sequence, with a corresponding number. Double-space the entire list. Unless your instructor prefers otherwise, this method can eliminate the need for a "Works Cited" list since it contains the same publishing information, merely adding the specific page number for each citation. Only the form is slightly different. The note for the sentence above would look like this.

FIRST REFERENCE TO A BOOK

[1] Joseph Gibaldi and Walter S. Achtert, <u>MLA Handbook for Writers of Research Papers</u>, 2nd ed. (New York: MLA, 1984) 166.

The first line of each note is indented five spaces from the left-hand margin. A comma separates the authors' names from the title. The publishing information is in parentheses, and the number of the page containing the borrowed information is not set off with a comma or any other punctuation. *Notice that this example also shows how to cite a book that is in a second or later edition.*

SUBSEQUENT REFERENCE

Should you cite the same work a second time, you use just the authors' last names and a page number.

[2] Gibaldi and Achtert 181.

A WORK WITH A CORPORATE AUTHOR

[3] American Red Cross, <u>Lifesaving: Rescue and Water Safety</u> (New York: Doubleday, 1974) 181.

A GOVERNMENT DOCUMENT

    4 United States, Department of Health and Human
Services, <u>Mosquito Control Measures in Gulf Coast States</u>
(Washington: GPO, 1986) 25.

AN ANONYMOUS WORK

    5 <u>Alcoholism and You</u> (Pearl Island: Okra, 1986) 3.

MULTIPLE WORKS BY THE SAME AUTHOR

If you have consulted more than one work by the same author (or authors),
give full documentation for each one the first time it is mentioned. In subsequent references, include an abbreviated title after the author's name. For instance, if you have previously referred to both Opie books mentioned above,
your next citation might look like this:

    6 Opie and Opie, <u>Lore</u> 192.

A WORK IN AN EDITED COLLECTION

When you document one item from a work in an edited collection, begin
with the name of the author of the individual work. "The Example of *Billy
Budd*" is the name of an article written by Werner Berthoff (*Billy Budd* is the
title of a short novel by Herman Melville). *Twentieth Century Interpretations of
Billy Budd* is the name of Howard P. Vincent's collection of essays about *Billy
Budd*, written by various people.

    7 Werner Berthoff, "The Example of <u>Billy Budd</u>,"
<u>Twentieth Century Interpretations of</u> Billy Budd: <u>A Col-
lection of Critical Essays</u>, ed. Howard P. Vincent (Englewood Cliffs: Prentice, 1971) 58–60.

A MULTIVOLUME WORK

When you cite a multivolume work, indicate which volume contains the
pages from which you have borrowed.

    8 Francis James Child, ed., <u>The English and Scottish
Popular Ballads</u>, 5 vols. (New York: Cooper Square, 1962)
2: 373–76.

A JOURNAL ARTICLE

The following is the usual form for citing information from a journal article.

    9 Carol Cook, "'The Sign and Semblance of Her
Honor': Reading Gender Difference in <u>Much Ado about Noth-
ing</u>," <u>PMLA</u> 101 (1986): 200.

NEWSPAPER AND MAGAZINE ARTICLES

Newspaper and magazine articles are treated very much like journal articles.

> 10 Richard D. Lamm, "English Comes First," New York Times 1 July 1986, natl. ed.: A23.
> 11 Robin Morgan, "The World without de Beauvoir," Ms. July 1986: 58.

Using Endnotes to Cite Nonprint Sources

The endnotes for nonprint sources appear in the same list, titled "Notes," as the printed sources.

AUDIOTAPES AND RECORDINGS

> 1 H. L. Mencken, H. L. Mencken Speaking, Caedmon, TC 1082, 1960.
> 2 William Butler Yeats, "The Song of the Old Mother," The Poems of William Butler Yeats, audiotape, read by William Butler Yeats, Siobhan McKenna, and Michael MacLiammoir, Spoken Arts, SAC 8044, 1974.

FILMSTRIPS, SLIDE PROGRAMS, VIDEOTAPES

Document a filmstrip, slide program, or videotape by including the name of the director or producer.

> 3 Wildlife Conservation, sound filmstrip, prod. Wildlife Research Group, 1986 (87 fr., 11 min.).

COMPUTER PROGRAMS

To document a computer program, include the name of the company that produced the program and the date.

> 4 Business Systems, computer software, Regis Software, 1985.

LECTURES

To cite a lecture, speech, or address, first give the speaker's name and the title of the talk (if any—see the official program), and then state where you heard it.

> 5 Lois DeBakey, "The Intolerable Wrestle with Words and Meaning," International Technical Communication Conference, Washington, 2 May 1971.

PERSONAL COMMUNICATIONS

You would document a personal letter received from one of your sources by including your correspondent's name and the date of the letter. The entries for a personal interview and a telephone interview are similar.

> [6] Helen Nearing, personal interview, 12 Nov. 1985.
> [7] John Bowlby, telephone interview, 3 June 1983.
> [8] Charles G. Sherwood, letter to the author, 29 Sept. 1986.

For more detailed information about citing nonprint sources, see the *MLA Handbook for Writers of Research Papers.*

LISTING: MLA STYLE

At the end of your paper, you will be expected to provide a list of sources from which you have gleaned ideas or information. The usual procedure in an English course is to follow the guidelines set forth by the Modern Language Association. We include here a brief rundown of the advice you are most likely to find useful as you set about the task of listing your sources.

Begin by starting a new page, continuing the page numbering of your paper. Under the title "Works Cited," skip two spaces and, starting flush with the left-hand margin, list your sources alphabetically by author, last name first; if there is no author, alphabetize by title. Double-space between entries and between lines within entries. When an entry exceeds one line, indent subsequent lines five spaces.

Listing Printed Sources

Notice that the information about each source appears in three sections, each followed by a period: author or agency's name (if there is one), title, and publishing information. Give the author's name and the title in full as they appear on the title page. If the publisher lists more than one city, include just the first. Use just the first name of a publisher with multiple names: not Holt, Rinehart and Winston, but simply Holt. Omit initials too. For J. B. Lippincott Co., simply write Lippincott.

A WORK BY A SINGLE AUTHOR

Karnow, Stanley. <u>Vietnam: A History</u>. New York: Viking, 1983.

A WORK BY TWO OR MORE AUTHORS

For a work with more than one author, reverse only the first author's name.

```
Taylor, Edwin F., and John A. Wheeler.  Spacetime
     Physics.  San Francisco: Freeman, 1966.
```

A WORK BY A CORPORATE AUTHOR

```
American Red Cross.  Lifesaving: Rescue and Water Safety.
     New York: Doubleday, 1974.
```

A GOVERNMENT DOCUMENT

To list a government document in accordance with MLA guidelines is much like listing any work that has a corporate author. Start with the name of the government, then the department or agency that put out the document, then the title of the publication, identifying information, and publication information (the place, publisher, and date).

```
United States.  Department of Health and Human Services.
     Mosquito Control Measures in Gulf Coast States.
     Washington: GPO, 1986.
```

AN ANONYMOUS WORK

```
Alcoholism and You.  Pearl Island: Okra, 1986.
```

MULTIPLE WORKS BY THE SAME AUTHOR

When listing successive books by the same author, put the titles in alphabetical order and include the author's name in full for the first entry only. In subsequent entries, indicate the author's name by using three hyphens and a period.

```
Opie, Iona, and Peter Opie.  The Lore and Language of
     Schoolchildren.  Oxford: Clarendon-Oxford UP, 1960.
---, eds.  The Oxford Nursery Rhyme Book.  Oxford: Clar-
     endon-Oxford UP, 1955.
```

A WORK WITH AN EDITOR, COMPILER, OR TRANSLATOR

Follow the name of an editor, compiler, or translator with a comma and a standard abbreviation (ed., comp., trans.). *Note too the standard way to list a multivolume work and the way to signal a university press.*

```
Child, Francis James, ed.  The English and Scottish Popu-
     lar Ballads.  5 vols.  New York: Cooper Square,
     1962.
```

> Glen, Duncan, ed.   Selected Essays of Hugh MacDiarmid.
>   Berkeley: U of California P, 1970.
> Williams, Miller, trans.   Sonnets of Giuseppe Belli.   Ba-
>   ton Rouge: Louisiana State UP, 1981.

A WORK IN AN EDITED COLLECTION

To quote a work that you find in an edited collection, begin with the name of the writer who wrote the individual work.

> Berthoff, Werner.   "The Example of Billy Budd."   Twen-
>   tieth Century Interpretations of Billy Budd: A Col-
>   lection of Critical Essays.   Ed. Howard P. Vincent.
>   Englewood Cliffs: Prentice, 1971.
> Donoghue, Denis.   "The Lost World."   Randall Jarrell:
>   1914—1965.   Ed. Robert Lowell, Peter Taylor, and
>   Robert Penn Warren.   New York: Farrar, 1967.

AN ENTRY IN A REFERENCE BOOK

Most research at the college level moves quickly beyond encyclopedias. If for some good reason you do cite an entry from a reference book, enter it under the name of its author or, if it is unsigned, under the name of the article's title. If the reference book is well known, enter only its title and edition.

> Fuller, R. Buckminster.   "Geodesic Dome."   Encyclopedia
>   Americana.   1985 ed.
> "Stichomythia."   American Heritage Dictionary.   1979 ed.

A JOURNAL ARTICLE

Begin with the author's name, and place in quotation marks the title of a journal article. Follow with the journal's title, underlined, and the volume number (if there is one). The year of publication belongs in parentheses, followed by a colon and the page numbers.

> Cook, Carol.   "'The Sign and Semblance of Her Honor':
>   Reading Gender Difference in Much Ado about Noth-
>   ing."   PMLA 101 (1986): 186—202.

A NEWSPAPER ARTICLE

List a newspaper article with the author's name first, then the title of the article, the name, date, and edition of the newspaper, and the page number. Notice that the day comes before the month.

> Lamm, Richard D. "English Comes First."   New York Times 1
>   July 1986, natl. ed.: A23.

A MAGAZINE ARTICLE

The entry for a magazine article is similar to that for a journal article. If a newspaper or a magazine article is printed on more than one page and the pages are not consecutive, simply put a " + " after the first page number.

```
Morgan, Robin. "The World without de Beauvoir." Ms. July
     1986: 58+.
```

Listing Nonprint Sources

If you're using the MLA guidelines, your "Works Cited" page will list non-print sources alphabetically along with print sources.

AUDIOTAPES AND RECORDINGS

For tapes and recordings, entries begin with the name of the speaker, the writer, or the production director, depending on what you want to emphasize.

```
Mencken, H. L.  H. L. Mencken Speaking.  Caedmon, TC
     1082, 1960.
Yeats, William Butler.  "The Song of the Old Mother."
          The Poems of William Butler Yeats.  Audiotape.  Read
          by William Butler Yeats, Siobhan McKenna, and Mi-
          chael MacLiammoir.  Spoken Arts, SAC 8044, 1974.
```

FILMSTRIPS, SLIDE PROGRAMS, VIDEOTAPES

Citations for filmstrips, slide programs, and videotapes generally start with the title, underlined. Enter other information—writer, performers, producer—if it seems pertinent. Information about the size and length of the film or program follows the date.

```
Wildlife Conservation.  Sound filmstrip.  Prod. Wildlife
     Research Group, 1986.  87 fr., 11 min.
```

COMPUTER PROGRAMS

```
Business Systems.  Computer software.  Regis Software,
     1985.
```

LECTURES

```
James Hurley.  Address.  Opening General Sess., American
     Bar Association Convention.  Chicago, 17 Jan. 1987.
```

PERSONAL COMMUNICATIONS

Telephone interviews, interviews that you conduct in person, and comments you have obtained by letter are listed as follows.

```
Bowlby, John.  Telephone interview.  3 June 1983.
```

```
Nearing, Helen.  Personal interview.  12 Nov. 1985.
Sherwood, Charles G.  Letter to the author.  29 Sept.
     1986.
```

CITING: APA STYLE

The American Psychological Association (APA) supplies a guide to the style most commonly used in the social sciences. This style is set forth in its *Publication Manual*, 3rd ed. (Washington, DC: APA, 1983). As in the newest MLA style, APA citations are made in parentheses in the body of the text.

Citing Printed Sources

A WORK BY A SINGLE AUTHOR

```
A number of experts now believe that cognitive develop-
ment begins much earlier than Piaget had thought (Gelman,
1978).
```

Notice that, because it is often necessary to refer to a whole study, only the author's name and the publication year are generally included in the citation. If the author's name appears in the body of the text, only the date is given in parentheses.

```
As Gelman (1978) points out, a number of experts now be-
lieve that cognitive development begins much earlier than
Piaget had thought.
```

If you do refer to a specific page, use "p." and set it off with a comma.

```
Dean Rusk's exposure to Nazi power in Europe in the 1930s
seems to have permanently influenced his attitude toward
appeasement (Karnow, 1983, p. 179).
```

When the author's name appears in the text, the page number still belongs in parentheses after the cited material.

```
Karnow (1983) maintains that Dean Rusk's exposure to Nazi
power in Europe in the 1930s "scarred his mind" (p. 179).
```

If you set off a long quotation in a block, the author's name and the publication year can follow the quotation, with no additional period. (These are Karnow's actual words about Dean Rusk, former U.S. secretary of state.)

Then came the moment that transformed his life and his
thinking. He won a Rhodes scholarship to Oxford. More
important, his exposure to Europe in the early 1930s, as
the Nazis consolidated their power in Germany, scarred
his mind, leading him to share Acheson's hostility to appeasement in any form anywhere. (Karnow, 1983)

A WORK WITH TWO AUTHORS

Refer to coauthors by their last names, in the order in which they appear
in the book or article you cite. (This is especially important in the sciences,
where the person whose name comes first is generally the main researcher.)
Join the names by "and" if they appear in the body of the text, by an ampersand
(&) if they are in parentheses.

Ex-mental patients released from institutions but given
no follow-up care will almost surely fail to cope with
the stresses of living on their own (Bassuk & Gerson,
1978).

Bassuk and Gerson (1978) hold out little hope for ex-mental patients who are released from institutions but are
given no follow-up care.

A WORK WITH MULTIPLE AUTHORS

When a book or article you cite has three or more authors (but fewer than
six), include all the last names in your first reference only. In referring to the
same source again, use the first author's name only, followed by "et al.," which
means "and others." For *more* than six authors, use "et al." even in the first
reference.

In one study, the IQs of adopted children were found to
correlate more closely with the IQs of their biological
mothers than with those of their adoptive mothers (Horn,
Loehlin, & Wellerman, 1975).

Later studies have challenged the genetic view advanced
by Wesson et al. (1978) by citing, among other things,
selective placement on the part of adoption agencies.

A WORK BY A CORPORATE AUTHOR

In the first citation, use the full name of the corporate author in parentheses.
There are three signs of oxygen deprivation (American Red
Cross, 1974).

A GOVERNMENT DOCUMENT

A citation in your text, at the end of a sentence, would simply identify the document by originating agency, as given in the reference list, followed by its abbreviation (if any) and year of publication (and page number, if appropriate).

> Clearly, it is of paramount importance to stop the spread of mosquito-borne diseases (Department of Health and Human Services [DHHS], 1986, p. 25).

Later citations would use just the abbreviation for the agency and the date (DHHS, 1986).

AN ANONYMOUS WORK

When you cite an anonymous work, such as a pamphlet or an unsigned newspaper article, identify it with a short title and a date.

> There are questions people can ask themselves if they suspect their drinking has gotten out of hand (Alcoholism, 1986).

MULTIPLE WORKS BY THE SAME AUTHOR

Identifying sources with dates is especially useful when you need to cite more than one work by the same author.

> One nuclear energy proponent for years has insisted on the importance of tight controls for the industry (Weinberg, 1972).... He goes so far as to call on utility companies to insure each reactor with their own funds (Weinberg, 1977).

When citing two or more sources written by the same author during the same year, arrange the titles alphabetically in the reference list (see p. 402) and identify each with a lowercase letter placed after the date (1976a, 1976b, 1976c, and so on). Identify them the same way in your text. Here the book referred to is Stephen H. Schneider's *The Genesis Strategy* (see p. 402).

> Those who advocate the "genesis strategy" would have the world store up food in preparation for future climatic changes (Schneider, 1976b).

MULTIPLE WORKS IN THE SAME ENTRY

Refer to works by different authors in alphabetical order, and include the dates of the studies you cite.

```
Several studies (Bassuk & Gerson, 1978; Miller, 1977;
Thompson, 1980) blame society for the plight of homeless
mental patients.
```

Citing Nonprint Sources

You mention nonprint sources in the same style as print sources.

PERSONAL INTERVIEWS

Personal communications are not given in the reference list according to APA style. But in the text of your paper, you should include the initials and surname of your communicator, with the date remembered as exactly as possible.

```
C. G. Sherwood (personal communication, September 29,
1986) has specific suggestions about the market in
Belgium.
```

```
It is important to keep in mind the cultural differences
between countries, especially in this case the differ-
ences between the United States and Belgium (C. G. Sher-
wood, personal communication, September 29, 1986).
```

LISTING: APA STYLE

If you're using APA guidelines (which you might do in listing both field and library materials), each entry should contain most of the same information given in an MLA citation, but the format will be slightly different. In the APA style, the list of works cited is called "References" and appears at the end of the text. For entries that run past the first line, indent subsequent lines three spaces.

Listing Printed Sources

Organize your list alphabetically by author. The year appears immediately following the author's name, in parentheses. In the title only the first word, proper names, and the word following a colon are capitalized. For the author's first and middle names, only initials are used. Note that APA style uses a more complete name for a publisher (including "Press") than does MLA style.

A WORK BY A SINGLE AUTHOR

```
Karnow, S. (1983).  Vietnam: A history.  New York: Viking
     Press.
```

A WORK WITH TWO OR MORE AUTHORS

In a work with multiple authors, all authors' names are inverted and they are separated by commas.

```
Miller, G. A., Galanter, E., & Pribram, K. H. (1960).
     Plans and the structure of behavior.  New York: Holt,
     Rinehart and Winston.
```

A WORK BY A CORPORATE AUTHOR

Books with corporate authors are treated very much like books with individual authors.

```
American Red Cross. (1974).  Lifesaving: Rescue and water
     safety.  New York: Doubleday.
```

A GOVERNMENT DOCUMENT

To list a government publication in your "References" in accord with APA style, start with the name of the department and then give the date of publication, the title (and author, if any), identifying number, and publisher.

```
Department of Health and Human Services. (1986).  Mos-
     quito control measures in Gulf Coast states (DHHW Pub-
     lication No. F 82-06000).  Washington, DC: U.S.
     Government Printing Office.
```

AN ANONYMOUS WORK

List an anonymous book, pamphlet, or news article by its full title.

```
Alcoholism and you. (1986).  Pearl Island: Okra Press.
```

MULTIPLE WORKS BY THE SAME AUTHOR, PUBLISHED DURING THE SAME YEAR

Arrange the titles alphabetically and identify their order with lowercase letters beginning with "a."

```
Schneider, S. H. (1976a).  Climate change and the world
     predicament: A case study for interdisciplinary re-
     search.  Boulder, CO: National Center for Atmospheric
     Research.
Schneider, S. H. (1976b).  The genesis strategy: Climate
     and global survival.  New York: Plenum Press.
```

A WORK IN AN EDITED COLLECTION

For one selection from a book with an editor, proceed as follows.

```
Lewontin, R. C. (1976).  Race and intelligence.  In N. J.
    Block & G. Dworkin (Eds.), The IQ controversy (pp.
    78–92).  New York: Pantheon.
```

AN ARTICLE IN A PERIODICAL

If in your paper you cited an article from a periodical that paginates continuously throughout a single year, the reference listing looks as follows. Note that the volume number is underlined.

```
Gelman, R. (1978).  Cognitive development.  Annual Review
    of Psychology, 29, 297–332.
```

If a periodical paginates each issue separately, the listing should be as follows.

```
Bassuk, E. L., & Gerson, S.  (1978, February).  Deinsti-
    tutionalization and mental health services.  Scien-
    tific American, pp. 46–53.
```

A NEWSPAPER ARTICLE

```
Auerbach, J. D. (1986, June 22).  Nuclear freeze at a
    crossroads.  The Boston Globe, p. A19.
```

Listing Nonprint Sources

Nonprint sources appear alphabetically in your "References" along with printed works.

RECORDINGS

```
Mencken, H. L. (Interviewee), with Donald Howe Kirkley,
    Sr. (Interviewer).  (1960).  H. L. Mencken speaking
    (Record No. TC 1082).  New York: Caedmon.
```

VIDEOTAPES, AUDIOTAPES, SLIDES

```
Wildlife Research Group (Producer).  (1986).  Wildlife
    conservation.  [Sound filmstrip].
```

The location and name of the distributor, if they are known, appear at the end of the citation.

COMPUTER PROGRAMS

When documenting computer programs, you include the same information as in the MLA citations, with the addition of the city of origin. If the author is known, his or her name appears first, and the title of the software appears after the date, followed immediately (without an intervening period) by the bracketed description of the source.

> <u>Business systems</u>.   (1985).   [Computer program].   Barton,
> CA: Regis Software.

PERSONAL COMMUNICATIONS

The newest APA guidelines suggest omitting personal communications (interviews, letters, memos, phone conversations, and so on) from the reference list because they do not provide recoverable data. You would of course mention such sources in the body of your paper—even if you do so simply, as Jamie Merisotis does in reporting his conversations with bail bondsmen ("One bondsman stated . . .").

PART SIX

Special Writing Situations

As a college writer you are likely to meet three challenges that we have not dealt with yet. These call for special attention.

First let's consider one that surely concerns every college student: how to write quizzes, tests, exams, and impromptu essay assignments. In Chapter 20 we try to show you how to meet and survive the demands of such situations.

Second, if you take a literature course (or a course that combines reading literature and writing), you can expect it to keep your pen or your keyboard racing. Such courses usually call for critical papers that analyze, explain, or evaluate stories, poems, and plays. Critical writing calls for close and imaginative reading and for a special vocabulary to report your insights. Chapter 21 briefly explains the process of criticizing literature.

In Chapter 22 we offer practical advice on a kind of writing that may seem more useful outside college than within: business writing—the writing of memoranda, business letters, and applications. But some of this information may serve you right away or in the near future. You may need to apply in writing for a job and turn in a résumé with your application. And you may need to write business letters and reports while holding a job in the summer or in your noncollege hours.

CHAPTER 20

Writing in Class

So far, we've been considering how you write when *you* control your writing circumstances. We've assumed that in writing anything from a brief account of a remembered experience to a hefty research paper, you can write lying down or standing up, write in the quiet of a library or write in a clattering cafeteria. Although an instructor may have handed you a deadline to meet, nobody has been timing you with a stopwatch.

But as you know, often in college you do need to write on the spot. You face quizzes to finish in twenty minutes, final exams to deliver in three or four hours, an impromptu essay to dash off in one class period. Just how do you discover, shape, and put across your ideas in a limited time, with the least possible agony?

First let's consider the techniques of writing an essay exam—in most courses the most important kind of in-class writing. Although lately multiple-choice tests, scored by computer, have been whittling down the number of essay exams that college students write, still the tradition of the essay exam endures. Instructors believe that such writing shows you haven't just memorized a bale of material but that you understand it, can think with it, and can make your thoughts clear to someone else. To prepare for an essay exam and to write it are seen as ways to lift knowledge out of textbook or notebook and bring it alive.

PREPARING FOR AN ESSAY EXAMINATION

The days before an examination offer you a chance to review what you have learned, to fill in any blank spots that remain. Such reviewing enables you to think deeply about your course work, to see how its scattered parts all fit together. Sometimes the whole drift and purpose of a course may be invisible until you look back over it.

As you review your reading and any notes gleaned from lectures and class discussion, it's a good idea—if the exam will be closed book—to fix in memory any vitally important names, dates, and definitions. We said "vitally important"—

you don't want to clutter your mind with a lot of spare parts selected at random. You might well be glad, on the day of the exam, to have a few apt quotations at your command. But preparation isn't merely a matter of decorating a vast glacier of ignorance with a few spring flowers of dates and quotations. When you review, look for the main ideas or themes in each textbook chapter. Then ask yourself: What do these main ideas have to do with each other? How might they be combined? This kind of thinking is a practical form of imagining.

Some instructors favor open-book exams, in which you bring your books to class for reference, and perhaps your notes as well. In an open-book exam, ability to memorize is less important than ability to reason and to select what matters most. In such a writing situation, you have more opportunity than in a closed-book exam to generate ideas and to discover material on the spot.

When you study for either type of exam, you generate ideas. After all, what are you doing but discovering much more material than you'll be asked to use? The chief resource for most essay exams is your memory. What you remember may include observations, conversation, reading (usually important), and perhaps some imagination.

A good way to prepare in advance for any exam, whether the books are to be closed or open, is to imagine questions you might be asked. Then plan answers. We don't mean to suggest that you should try to psyche out your instructor. You're only slightly more likely to guess all the questions in advance than you are to clean out a slot machine in Las Vegas, but by thinking up your own questions, you review much material, imaginatively bring some of it together, and gain valuable experience in shaping answers. Sometimes, to help you get ready for an exam, the instructor will supply a few questions asked in former years. If you are given such examples, you can pattern new questions after them.

As you probably don't need to be told, trying to cram by going without sleep and food, consuming gallons of coffee, and reducing yourself to a wreck with red-rimmed eyes is no way to prepare. You can learn more in little bites than in huge gulps. Psychologists testify that if you study something for fifteen minutes a day for eight days, you'll remember far more than if you study the same material in one unbroken sprint of two hours.

The secret of writing good exams, if it is any secret, lies in keeping your cool—which you can do by preparing thoroughly, so that you feel confident.

TAKING AN ESSAY EXAMINATION

Learning from Another Writer

To start looking at techniques of answering *any* exam question, let's take one concrete example. A final exam in developmental psychology posed this question:

> What evidence indicates innate factors in perceptual organization? You might find it useful to recall any research that shows how infants perceive depth and forms.

In response, David Ian Cohn sat back in his chair for ten minutes and thought over the reading he'd done for the course. What perception research had he heard about that used babies for subjects? He spent another five minutes jotting down ideas, crossed out a couple of weak ones, and drew lines connecting ideas that went together. (For an illustration of this handy technique, see "Linking," p. 473.) Then he took a deep breath and, without revising (except to cross out a few words of a sentence that seemed a false start), wrote this straightforward grade A answer:

> Research on infants is probably the best way to demonstrate that some factors in perceptual organization are innate. In the cliff box experiment, an infant will avoid what looks like a drop-off, even though its mother calls it and even though it can feel glass covering the drop-off area. The same infant will crawl to the other end of the box, which appears (and is) safe. Apparently infants do not have to be taught what a cliff looks like.
>
> Psychologists have also observed that infants are aware of size constancy. They recognize a difference in size between a 10-cm box at a distance of one meter and a 20-cm box at a distance of two meters. If this phenomenon is not innate, it is at least learned early, for the subjects of the experiment were infants of sixteen to eighteen months.
>
> When shown various patterns, infants tend to respond more noticeably to patterns that resemble the human face than to those that appear random. This seemingly innate recognition helps the infant identify people (such as its mother) from less important inanimate objects.
>
> Infants also seem to have an innate ability to match sight with sound. When simultaneously shown two television screens, each depicting a different subject, while being played a tape that sometimes matched one screen and sometimes the other, infants looked at whichever screen matched what they heard—not always, but at least twice as often.

Questions to Start You Thinking

1. If you were the psychology instructor, how could you immediately see from this answer that Cohn had thoroughly dealt with the question, and only with the question?
2. In what places is his answer concrete and specific, not vague and general?
3. Suppose Cohn had tacked on a concluding paragraph: "Thus I have conclusively proved that there are innate factors in perceptional organization, by citing much evidence showing that infants definitely can perceive depth and forms." Would that have strengthened his answer?
4. Do you have any tried-and-true exam-answering techniques of your own that might have worked on that question or one like it? If so, why not share them with the class?

Generating Ideas

When, at last in the classroom, you begin your neck-and-neck race with the clock, you may feel tempted to start scribbling away frantically. Resist the temptation. First read over all the questions carefully. Notice whether you are expected to make any choices, and decide which questions to answer. Choices are luxuries: they let you ignore questions you are less well prepared to answer in favor of those you can tackle with more confidence. If you are offered a choice, just X out any questions you are *not* going to answer so you don't waste time answering them by mistake. And if you don't understand what a question calls for, ask your instructor right away.

Few people can dash off an excellent essay exam answer without first taking time to discover a few ideas. So take a deep breath, get comfortable, sit back, and spend a few moments in thought. Instructors prefer answers that are concrete and specific to answers that stay up in the clouds of generality. To come up with specific details may first take thought. David Cohn's answer to the psychology question cites evidence all the way through: particular experiments in which infants were subjects. A little time taken to generate concrete examples—as Cohn did—may be time wisely spent.

Some people have a rare talent for rapidly putting their thoughts in order. Many, however, will start writing an exam with a burst of speed, like race horses sprinting out of a paddock, only to find that, although they are moving fast, they don't know which way to run. Your pen will move more smoothly if you have a few thoughts in mind. These thoughts don't have to be definitive—only something to start you writing. You can keep on thinking and shaping your thoughts while you write.

Often a question will suggest a way to start your answer. Thought-provoking essay questions, to be sure, call for more than a regurgitation of your reading, but they often contain directive words that help define your task for you: *evaluate, compare, discuss, consider, explain, describe, isolate, summarize, trace the development of.* You can put yourself on the right track if you incorporate such a directive word in your first sentence.

Typical Exam Questions

Most examination questions fall into recognizable types, and if you can recognize them you will know how to organize them and begin to write. Here are specimens.

The cause-and-effect question. In general, these questions are easy to recognize: they usually mention *causes* and *effects*.

What were the immediate causes of the stock market crash of 1929?

Set forth the principal effects on the economy commonly noticed as a result of a low prime rate of interest.

The first question invites you to recall specific forces and events in history; the second question (from an economics course) invites an account of what usually takes place. For specific advice on writing to show cause or effect, see Chapter 12.

The compare-and-contrast question. One of the most popular types of examination question, this demands a writer to throw into sharp relief not one subject but two subjects. By pointing out similarities (comparing) and discussing differences (contrasting), you can explain both.

> Compare and contrast *iconic memory* and *eidetic imagery*. (1) Define the two terms, indicating the ways in which they differ, and (2) state the way or ways in which they are related or alike.

After supplying a one-sentence definition of each term, a student proceeded first to contrast and then to compare, for full credit:

> *Iconic memory* is a picturelike impression that lasts for only a fraction of a second in short-term memory. *Eidetic imagery* is the ability to take a mental photograph, exact in detail, which later can be recalled and studied in detail, as though its subject were still present. But iconic memory soon disappears. Unlike an eidetic image, it does not last long enough to enter long-term memory. IM is common, EI is unusual: very few people have it. Both iconic memory and eidetic imagery are similar, however: both record visual images, and every sighted person of normal intelligence has both abilities to some degree.

A question of this kind doesn't always use the words *compare* and *contrast*. Consider this question from a midterm exam in basic astronomy:

> Signal at least three differences between Copernicus's and Kepler's models of the solar system. In what respects was Kepler's model an improvement on that of Copernicus?

What is that question but good old comparison and contrast? The three differences all point to the superior accuracy of Kepler's model, so all a writer would need to do is list each difference and, in a few words, indicate Kepler's superiority.

> Distinguish between *agnosia* and *receptive aphasia*. In what ways are the two conditions similar?

Again, without using the words *comparison* and *contrast*, the question asks for both. When you distinguish, you contrast, or point out differences; when you tell how two things are similar, you compare.

> Briefly explain the duplex theory of memory. What are the main differences between short-term memory and long-term memory?

In this two-part question, the second part calls on the student to contrast (but not compare).

> Which bryophyta resemble vascular plants? In what ways? How do these bryophyta *differ* from the vascular plants?

Writers of comparison and contrast answers sometimes fall into a trap: in this case, they might get all wound up about bryophyta and fail to give vascular plants more than a few words. When you compare and contrast two things, pay attention to both. (For further specific advice on comparison and contrast writing, see Chapter 9).

The demonstration question. In this kind of question, you are given a statement and asked to back it up.

> Demonstrate the truth of Freud's contention that laughter may contain elements of aggression.

In other words, supply evidence to support Freud's claim. You might refer to crowd scenes you have experienced, perhaps quote and analyze a joke, perhaps analyze a scene in a recent TV show or film. Or use examples from your reading.

The discussion question. A discussion question may tempt an unwary writer to shoot the breeze.

> Name and discuss three events that precipitated Lyndon B. Johnson's withdrawal from the 1968 presidential race.

This question looks like an open invitation to ramble aimlessly about Johnson and Vietnam, but it isn't. Whenever a question says "discuss," you will be wise to plan your discussion. What it asks is "Why did President Johnson decide not to seek another term? List three causes and explain each a little."

> Discuss the economic uses of algae.

Here you might write a sentence or two on every use of pond scum you can think of ("Algae, when processed with yogurt cultures, become a main ingredient for a palatable low-calorie mayonnaise"). To deepen the discussion you might also tell how or why that use is important to the economy ("Last year, the sale of such mayonnaise increased by about thirty percent"). Sometimes a discussion question won't announce itself with the word *discuss*, but with *describe* or *explore:*

> Describe the national experience following passage of the Eighteenth Amendment to the Constitution. What did most Americans learn from it?

Provided you knew that the Eighteenth Amendment (Prohibition) banned the sale, manufacture, and transportation of alcoholic drinks and that it was finally repealed, you could discuss its effects—or perhaps the reasons for its repeal. (You might also assert that the amendment taught many Americans how to make whiskey out of rotten potatoes or how to fold a complete jazz band into a suitcase when the police raided a speakeasy, but probably that isn't what the instructor is after.)

The divide-or-classify question. Sometimes you are asked to slice a subject into parts, or sort things into kinds.

> Enumerate the ways in which each inhabitant of the United States uses, on the average, 1,595 gallons of water a day. How and to what degree might each person cut down on this amount?

This two-part question invites you, for a start, to divide up water use into several parts: drinking, cooking, bathing, washing clothes, brushing teeth, washing cars, and so on. Then after you divide them, you might go on to give tips for water conservation and tell how effective they are ("By putting two builder's bricks inside a toilet tank, each household would save 15–20% of the water required for a flush").

> What different genres of film did King Vidor direct? Name at least one outstanding example of each kind.

In this classification question, you sort things out into categories—films into general kinds—possibly comedy, war, adventure, mystery, musical, western. (See Chapter 11 for more tips on both dividing and classifying.)

The definition question. To write an extended definition is a task you'll often meet on an essay exam.

> Explain the three dominant styles of parenting: *permissive, authoritarian-restrictive*, and *authoritative*.

This question calls for a trio of definitions. It might help to illustrate each definition with an example, whether recalled or imagined.

> Define the Stanislavsky method of acting, citing outstanding actors who have followed it.

As part of your definition, again you'd give examples. (For specific advice on writing by the method of definition, see Chapter 13; for writing short definitions, see pp. 221–222.)

The evaluation question. This is another favorite kind of question, much beloved by instructors because it calls on students to think critically.

> Set forth and evaluate the most widely accepted theories to account for the disappearance of the dinosaurs.

> Evaluate *two* of the following suggestions, giving reasons for your judgments:
> a. Cities should stop building highways to the suburbs and instead build public monorail systems.
> b. Houses and public buildings should be constructed to last no longer than twenty years.
> c. Freeways leading to the core of the city should have marked express lanes for buses and carpooling drivers and narrow lanes designed to punish with long delays individual commuters who drive their cars.

This last three-part question calls on you to argue for or against. Other argument questions might begin "Defend the idea of ..." or "Show weaknesses in the idea of ..." or otherwise call on the writer to take a stand.

The respond-to-the-quotation question. "Test the validity of this statement," a question might begin, and then it might go on to supply a quotation for close reading. In another familiar form, such a question might begin:

> Discuss the following statement: High-minded opposition to slavery was only one cause, and not a very important one, of the animosity between North and South that in 1861 escalated into civil war.

The question asks you to test the writer's opinion against what you know. You would begin by reading that statement a couple of times carefully and then seeing whether you can pick a fight with it. It's a good idea to jot down any contrary evidence you can discover. If you end up agreeing with the statement, then try to supply evidence to support it. (Sometimes the passage is the invention of the instructor, who hopes to provoke you to argument.)

Another illustration is the following question from an examination in women's literature:

> Was the following passage written by Gertrude Stein, Kate Chopin, or Tillie Olsen? On what evidence do you base your answer?
>
> > She waited for the material pictures which she thought would gather and blaze before her imagination. She waited in vain. She saw no pictures of solitude, of hope, of longing, or of despair. But the very passions themselves were aroused within her soul, swaying it, lashing it, as the waves daily beat upon her splendid body. She trembled, she was choking, and the tears blinded her.

The passage is taken from a story by an earlier writer than either Stein or Olsen: Kate Chopin (1851–1904). If you knew Chopin, who specializes in physical and emotional descriptions of impassioned women, you would know the answer to the examination question, and you might point to language (*swaying, lashing*) that marks it as her own.

The process analysis question. Often, you can spot this kind of question by the word *trace:*

> Trace the stages through which a bill becomes a federal law.
> Trace the development of the medieval Italian city-state.

Both questions invite you to tell how something occurs or occurred. The other familiar type of process analysis, the "how to" variety, is called for in this question:

> An employee has been consistently late for work, varying from fifteen minutes to a half hour daily. This employee has been on the job only five

months but shows promise of learning skills that your firm needs badly. How would you deal with this situation?

For pointers on writing a process analysis, see Chapter 10. In brief, you divide the process into steps and detail each step.

The far-out question. Sometimes, to invite you to use your imagination, an instructor will throw in a question that at first glance might seem bizarre.

> Imagine yourself to be a trial lawyer in 1921, charged with defending Nicola Sacco and Bartolomeo Vanzetti, two anarchists accused of murder. Argue for their acquittal on whatever grounds you can justify.

On second glance, the question will be seen to reach deep. It calls on a prelaw student to show familiarity with a famous case (which ended with the execution of the defendants). In addition, it calls for knowledge of the law and of trial procedure. Such a question might be fun to answer; moreover, in being obliged to imagine a time, a place, and dramatic circumstances, the student might learn something. If you were to answer that question, you'd be employing a method you have learned if you worked through Chapter 15: proposing an action. The following is another far-out question, this time from a philosophy course:

> What might an ancient Roman Stoic philosopher have thought of Jean-Paul Sartre's doctrine of anguish?

In response, you might try to remember what the Stoics had to say about enduring suffering, define Sartre's view and define theirs, compare their views with Sartre's, imagine how they would agree (or, more probably, differ) with him.

Shaping a Draft (or the Only Version)

When the clock on the wall is ticking away, generating ideas and shaping an answer are seldom two distinct, leisurely processes: they often take place pretty much at the same time, and on scratch paper. Does your instructor hand you your own copy of the exam questions? If so, see if there's room on it to jot down ideas and roughly put them in order. If you can do your preliminary work right on the exam sheet, you'll have fewer pieces of scratch paper rattling around. Besides, you can annotate questions, underline points you think important, scribble short definitions. Write reminders that you will notice while you work: TWO PARTS TO THIS QUES.! or GET IN EXAMPLE OF ABORIGINES. To make sure that you include all necessary information without padding or repetition, you may care to jot down a brief, informal outline before setting pen to examination booklet. This was David Cohn's outline:

cliff box— kid fears drop despite glass, mother, knows
        shallow side safe
size constancy — learned early if not intrinsic
shapes— infants respond more/better to face shape than nonformed

match sound w/sight— 2 TVs, look twice as much at right one

When you have two or more essay questions to answer, block out your time at least roughly. Sometimes your instructor will suggest how many minutes to devote to each question or will declare that one question counts twenty points, another ten, and so on. Obviously a twenty-point question deserves twice as much time and work as a ten-pointer. If the instructor doesn't specify, then after you have read the questions, decide for yourself how much time each question is worth. Make a little schedule so that you'll know that at 10:30 it's time to wrap up Question 2 and move on. Allot extra minutes to a question that looks complicated (such as one with several parts: a, b, c . . .) and fewer minutes to a simpler one. Otherwise, give every answer equal time. Then pace yourself as you write. A watch with an alarm you can set to buzz at the end of twenty or thirty minutes, alerting you that it's time to move on, might help— unless it would prompt your neighbors to start beating on you for buzzing.

Many students find it helps their morale to start with the question they feel best able to answer. Unless your instructor specifies that you have to answer the questions in their given order, why not skip around? Just make sure you clearly number the questions and begin each answer in such a way that the instructor will immediately recognize which question you're answering. If the task is "Compare and contrast the depression of the 1930s with the recession of the 1970s," an answer might begin:

> Compared to the paralyzing depression that began in 1929, the recession of the 1970s seems a bad case of measles.

The instructor would recognize that question, all right, whether you answered it first or last. If you have a choice of questions, you can label your answer *a* or *b* or restate the question at the start of your essay so that your instructor will have no doubt which alternative you have chosen, as in the following example:

> Question: Discuss *one* of the following quotations from the writings of Voltaire:
>
> a. "The truths of religion are never so well understood as by those who have lost the power of reasoning."
> b. "All roads lead to Rome."
>
> Answer: When, in September 1750, Voltaire wrote in a letter to Mme. de Fontaine, "All roads lead to Rome," his remark referred to more than the vast network of roads the ancient Romans had built—and built so well— throughout Europe. . . .

Some students find it useful to make their opening sentence a thesis state-ment—a sentence that makes clear right away the main point they're going to make. Then they proceed in the rest of the answer to back that statement up. This method often makes good sense. With a clear thesis statement to begin with, you will be unlikely to ramble into byways that carry you miles away from your main point. (See "Stating a Thesis," p. 469.) That's how David Cohn opens his answer to the psychology question. One easy way to start with such a thesis statement is to take the question itself and turn it around into a declarative statement.

> Can adequate reasons for leasing cars and office equipment, instead of purchasing them, be cited for a two-person partnership?

You might turn that question around and *transform it into the start of an answer:*

> I can cite at least four adequate reasons for a two-person partnership to lease cars and office equipment. For one thing, under present tax laws, the entire cost of a regular payment under a leasing agreement may be deducted. . . .

Stick to the point of the question. It's a temptation to want to throw into your answer everything you have learned in the course. But to do so defeats the purpose of the examination: not to parade your knowledge, but to put your knowledge to use. So when you answer an exam question cogently, you select *what matters* from what you know, at the same time shaping it.

Often a question will have two parts: it will ask you, say, to name the most common styles of contemporary architecture and then to evaluate one of them. Or it might say, "List three differences between the landscape paintings of Monet and those of Van Gogh" and then add, "Which of the two shows the greater influence of eighteenth-century neoclassicism?" When the dragon of a question has two heads, make sure you cut off both.

Pressed for time, some harried exam takers think, "I haven't got time to get specific here—I'll just sum up this idea in general." Usually that's a mistake. Every time you throw in a large, general statement ("The Industrial Revolution was a beneficial thing for the peasant"), take time to include specific examples ("In Dusseldorf, as Taine tells us, the mortality rate from starvation among displaced Prussian farm workers now dropped to nearly zero, although once it had reached almost ten percent a year").

Incidentally, it's foresighted to write on only one side of the page in your examination booklet. Leave space between lines. Then later, should you wish to add words or sentences or even a whole paragraph, you can do so with ease. Give yourself room for second thoughts and last-minute inspirations. As you write and as you revise, you may well do further discovering.

Rewriting

If you have paced yourself, you'll have at least a few minutes left at the end of your examination period when, while some around you are still agonizingly trying to finish, you can relax a moment and look over your work with a critical eye.

Even if you should stop writing with an hour to spare, it probably won't be worth your time to recopy your whole exam. Use any time you have left not merely to improve your penmanship but to test your ideas and how well they hang together. Add any large points you may have overlooked in writing your draft.

Your foresight in skipping every other line will now pay off. You can add sentences wherever you think new ones are needed. Cross out any hopelessly garbled sentences and rewrite them in the blank lines. (David Cohn crossed out and rewrote part of his last sentence. Originally it read, "When simultaneously shown two television screens, each depicting a different subject, while being played *a tape that oscillated between which TV it was in time with.* ..." He rethought the last words, which we have italicized, found them confusing, crossed them out, and instead wrote on the line above: "a tape that sometimes matched one screen and sometimes the other.") If you recall an important point you forgot to put in, you can add a paragraph or two on a left-hand page that you left blank. So the grader will not miss it, draw an arrow indicating where it goes. If you find that you have gone off on a big digression or have thrown in knowledge merely to show it off, boldly X out that block of wordage. Your answer may look sloppier, but your instructor will think the better of it.

Naturally, errors occur oftener when you write under pressure than when you have time to edit and proofread carefully. Most instructors will take into consideration your haste and your human fallibility. On an exam, what you say and how forcefully you say it matter most. Still, to get the small details right will just make your answer look all the sharper. No instructor will object to careful corrections. You can easily add words with carets:

foreign

I *sraeli* ^ *policy*

Or you can neatly strike out a word by drawing a line through it. Some students like to use an erasable pen for in-class writing. With the aid of this wonder of writing technology, they can hand in an exam of amazing cleanliness: a little smeary, maybe, but free of crossed-out words.

We don't expect you to memorize these questions and carry them like crib notes into an examination. But when you receive your paper or blue book back and you look it over, you might learn more about writing essay exams if you ask them of yourself.

POSTEXAM CHECKLIST: EVALUATING YOUR PERFORMANCE

- Did you understand the question and what was expected?
- Did you answer the whole question, not just part of it?
- Did you stick to the point, not throw in information the question doesn't call for?
- Did you make your general statements clear by citing evidence or examples?
- Does your answer sprawl, or does it look shaped?

- Does your answer, at any place, show a need for more knowledge and more ideas? Did you inflate your answer with hot air, or did you stay close to earth, giving plenty of facts, examples, and illustrations?
- On what question or questions do you feel you did a good job that satisfies you, no matter what grade you received?
- If you had to write this exam over again, how would you *now* go about the job?

Let's end with a few tips on two other common kinds of in-class writing.

THE SHORT-ANSWER EXAMINATION

Requiring answers much terser than an essay exam does, the *short-answer exam* may call on you to identify names or phrases from your reading, in a sentence or less.

Identify the following: Clemenceau, Treaty of Versailles, Maginot line, Dreyfus affair.

You might begin your answer to such a question:

Clemenceau—premier of France in World War I.

Or, if a fuller identification is called for:

Georges Clemenceau—This French premier, nicknamed The Tiger, headed a popular coalition cabinet during World War I and at the Paris Peace Conference demanded stronger penalties against Germany.

Writing a short identification is much like writing a short definition (see p. 221). Be sure to mention the general class to which a thing belongs:

Clemenceau—*French premier* who . . .
Treaty of Versailles—*pact* between Germany and the Allies that . . .
Maginot line—*fortifications* which . . .

If you do so, you won't lose points for an answer like this, which fails to make clear the nature of the thing being identified:

Maginot line—The Germans went around it.

THE IN-CLASS ESSAY

Some instructors, to give you laboratory experience in writing on demand, may assign an impromptu essay to be written in class. The topic might be assigned in advance or at the start of the class. Being obliged to write such an impromptu essay, after getting used to a deadline a week or a month away, is a little like being told to drive a subcompact car when you're accustomed to a Lincoln Continental. But the way you write an essay in class need not differ greatly from the way you write anywhere else. Your usual methods of working can serve you well, even though you may have to apply them in a hurry.

If you have forty-five minutes to write an in-class essay, a good rule of thumb is to spend ten minutes preparing, thirty minutes writing, and five minutes rereading and making last-minute changes and additions. In the act of writing, you may find new ideas occurring to you and perhaps those exact proportions of time will need to change. Even so, a rough schedule like that will help you to allocate your time.

When you write, write carefully and deliberately. You can revise while you work—make cross-outs and small corrections as you go along. Your instructor won't mind, as long as your essay is legible. If you double-space your essay, skipping every other line, you'll have room to add further thoughts later. Those last few minutes you leave yourself to review your work may be the best-spent minutes of all.

CHAPTER 21

Criticizing Literature:
Essays about Stories and Poems

To be a *critic* doesn't mean to spread blame on everything. The word, from the Greek *kritikos*, means "one who can judge and discern." A critical essay usually deals with a work of art or literature, a film, a concert, a piece of music. Most often in college, the subject for critical writing is literature, and so this chapter will guide you in writing a critical essay about a poem or a story.

Most such college essays are written for one of these purposes:

1. To reveal the theme (the main idea or insight the work reveals). Often a theme is at the heart of a story or poem: any essential truth that its author tries to put across. (Some authors, though, don't have much essential truth to tell. Some works of literature, even pretty good ones, will just take a reader on an emotional trip and contain little or no theme—for instance, some of Edgar Allan Poe's horror stories.)

2. To analyze a work for some other element or elements (such as language, plot, setting, character, symbol, or point of view). To show what goes on in a work, you break it down into parts or isolate a single part of it.

3. To interpret or explain the work so that another reader can understand it or more keenly appreciate it. To some degree, works of literature cannot help meaning what readers wish to see in them, but don't claim that a work can mean anything you wish—that, for instance, Poe's poem about the raven that croaks "Nevermore" is a prophecy of nuclear disaster. Otherwise you can run wild and find in the tale of "The Three Little Pigs" or a Nancy Drew book deep symbolic significance. Neither is a work of literature a locked box with a hidden key that, if located, will make the box swing wide. There is no one right interpretation. In interpreting, all you can do is read carefully, try to clear up difficulties, and arrive at an interpretation (and evidence for it) with which most people will agree.

4. To evaluate (that is, to judge whether the work is any good and, if so, how good). Usually there is not much point in evaluating a universally acclaimed masterpiece ("Tolstoy's *Anna Karenina* is certainly a good book"); evaluation is most useful for new or neglected works. "But how can I judge stories, poems,

or plays?" the hesitant student may ask. "I can't honestly say I'm capable myself of writing 'literature.'" Samuel Johnson, great eighteenth-century critic, talker, and pioneer dictionary maker, once made a classic reply to this objection: "You may scold a carpenter who has made you a bad table, though you cannot make a table."

The four purposes can coincide. When you analyze a work, you may find yourself also stating its theme, interpreting it, and making a judgment on it.

LEARNING FROM OTHER WRITERS

Criticizing Fiction

To see how a student critic responds to a short story, here is one of the most widely reprinted works of an acclaimed American storyteller, Kate Chopin (1851–1904), followed by a student's analysis of the story. Chopin's work has lately been enjoying a revival of interest, after long neglect. *The Awakening* (1899), a novel about a woman who seeks sexual and professional independence, caused shock and anger in its day, and its author was able to find few magazines willing to print her work after the book was published. Even in our day, "The Story of an Hour" has had its detractors, and in reply to them English major Jane Betz has written a sensitive defense of it.

THE STORY OF AN HOUR
KATE CHOPIN

Knowing that Mrs. Mallard was afflicted with a heart trouble, great care   1
was taken to break to her as gently as possible the news of her husband's death.

It was her sister Josephine who told her, in broken sentences, veiled   2
hints that revealed in half concealing. Her husband's friend Richards was there, too, near her. It was he who had been in the newspaper office when intelligence of the railroad disaster was received, with Brently Mallard's name leading the list of "killed." He had only taken the time to assure himself of its truth by a second telegram, and had hastened to forestall any less careful, less tender friend in bearing the sad message.

She did not hear the story as many women have heard the same, with   3
a paralyzed inability to accept its significance. She wept at once, with sudden, wild abandonment, in her sister's arms. When the storm of grief had spent itself she went away to her room alone. She would have no one follow her.

There stood, facing the open window, a comfortable, roomy armchair.   4
Into this she sank, pressed down by a physical exhaustion that haunted her body and seemed to reach into her soul.

She could see in the open square before her house the tops of trees   5
that were all aquiver with the new spring life. The delicious breath of rain

was in the air. In the street below a peddler was crying his wares. The notes of a distant song which some one was singing reached her faintly, and countless sparrows were twittering in the eaves.

There were patches of blue sky showing here and there through the 6 clouds that had met and piled one above the other in the west facing her window.

She sat with her head thrown back upon the cushion of the chair, quite 7 motionless, except when a sob came up into her throat and shook her, as a child who has cried itself to sleep continues to sob in its dreams.

She was young, with a fair, calm face, whose lines bespoke repression 8 and even a certain strength. But now there was a dull stare in her eyes, whose gaze was fixed away off yonder on one of those patches of blue sky. It was not a glance of reflection, but rather indicated a suspension of intelligent thought.

There was something coming to her and she was waiting for it, fearfully. 9 What was it? She did not know; it was too subtle and elusive to name. But she felt it, creeping out of the sky, reaching toward her through the sounds, the scents, the color that filled the air.

Now her bosom rose and fell tumultuously. She was beginning to 10 recognize this thing that was approaching to possess her, and she was striving to beat it back with her will—as powerless as her two white slender hands would have been.

When she abandoned herself a little whispered word escaped her slightly 11 parted lips. She said it over and over under her breath: "Free, free, free!" The vacant stare and the look of terror that had followed it went from her eyes. They stayed keen and bright. Her pulses beat fast, and the coursing blood warmed and relaxed every inch of her body.

She did not stop to ask if it were not a monstrous joy that held her. A 12 clear and exalted perception enabled her to dismiss the suggestion as trivial.

She knew that she would weep again when she saw the kind, tender 13 hands folded in death; the face that had never looked save with love upon her, fixed and gray and dead. But she saw beyond that bitter moment a long procession of years to come that would belong to her absolutely. And she opened and spread her arms out to them in welcome.

There would be no one to live for during those coming years; she 14 would live for herself. There would be no powerful will bending her in that blind persistence with which men and women believe they have a right to impose a private will upon a fellow creature. A kind intention or a cruel intention made the act seem no less a crime as she looked upon it in that brief moment of illumination.

And yet she had loved him—sometimes. Often she had not. What did 15 it matter! What could love, the unsolved mystery, count for in face of this possession of self-assertion which she suddenly recognized as the strongest impulse of her being.

"Free! Body and soul free!" she kept whispering. 16

Josephine was kneeling before the closed door with her lips to the 17 keyhole, imploring for admission. "Louise, open the door! I beg; open the door—you will make yourself ill. What are you doing, Louise? For heaven's sake open the door."

"Go away. I am not making myself ill." No; she was drinking in a very 18
elixir of life through that open window.

Her fancy was running riot along those days ahead of her. Spring days, 19
and summer days, and all sorts of days that would be her own. She breathed
a quick prayer that life might be long. It was only yesterday she had thought
with a shudder that life might be long.

She arose at length and opened the door to her sister's importunities. 20
There was a feverish triumph in her eyes, and she carried herself unwittingly like a goddess of Victory. She clasped her sister's waist, and together
they descended the stairs. Richards stood waiting for them at the bottom.

Some one was opening the front door with a latchkey. It was Brently 21
Mallard who entered, a little travel-stained, composedly carrying his grip-
sack and umbrella. He had been far from the scene of accident, and did
not even know there had been one. He stood amazed at Josephine's piercing cry; at Richards' quick motion to screen him from the view of his wife.

But Richards was too late.   22

When the doctors came they said she had died of heart disease—of joy 23
that kills.

Questions to Start You Thinking

1. How heartfelt is the "storm of grief" that sweeps over Mrs. Mallard when first she
    hears the report of her husband's death? Why then, only minutes later, does she
    whisper "Free, free, free!"? Do you find this account of a woman's emotions true
    to life or hard to believe? Discuss.

2. An opinion: "There's a simple reason why Mrs. Mallard dies. As we are told in the
    opening sentence, she has heart trouble and can't stand the slightest shock." What
    other reason for Mrs. Mallard's collapse does this explanation fail to take into ac-
    count?

3. What does Kate Chopin tell us about love and marriage? How would you sum up
    her theme (the main idea or insight the story reveals)? Write it out in a sentence
    to read in class.

4. Would you call this a "trick ending" story, one containing an artificial surprise that
    the writer whips out at the end like a rabbit out of a hat? Or would you defend the
    ending as logical, natural, convincing, prepared for? (After you have thought about
    this, read on and see how Jane Betz explains the ending and why she praises it.)

A DEFENSE OF THE ENDING
OF "THE STORY OF AN HOUR"

JANE BETZ

Some readers complain that the ending to Kate Chopin's "The Story of 1
an Hour" is a cheap trick, an unwanted surprise that comes like a killer
through an old woman's bedroom window in a low-grade horror movie.
Probably such readers are confused by Mrs. Mallard's behavior throughout
the story, for they must not see how the author prepares her readers for
the ending. Mrs. Mallard spends her last hour getting acquainted with death:

she meets it, visits with it, understands it, and finally—logically—she knows it. In the course of an hour Louise Mallard is gracefully initiated into the world outside her window. Chopin gives us the most clearly inevitable conclusion possible and still manages to surprise us with it. The "trick" to the story does not lie in the ending but in the author's talent for giving "veiled hints that reveal in half-concealing." She reveals enough hints not only to justify the ending but to necessitate it, and she holds enough back to keep the reader from knowing what's coming.

Louise Mallard does not react to her husband's death the way another 2 wife would. Instead of rejecting the news, ignoring it, or slowly taking it in with a muddled and dull acceptance, Mrs. Mallard recognizes its significance at once. She regards the news with sadness and terror, knowing what she sees.

After her "storm of grief" Mrs. Mallard looks at the world as she never 3 has before. She goes upstairs and surveys the view from her western window through blank, fixed eyes. Exhaustion presses her into her armchair and she throws her head back and sobs like "a child who has cried itself to sleep." She colors the view from her window with mixed feelings of youth and age: simultaneously she is seeing its beauty for the first time and saying good-bye to its comfortable familiarity for the last. The easy chair, the western window, the sleep of a child, and the suspension of intelligent thought call to her like the sirens.

Mrs. Mallard resists seeing paradise in that view: even through her 4 exhaustion and her fuzzy inability to think she resists it instinctively. She tries to close her eyes to the blue sky, her ears to the sparrows, and her mind to the thought of how much she would like to melt into that picture.

She holds on to the life she knows with white knuckles, but her two 5 slender white hands are powerless. The most salient and appealing offer of the world outside her window fights its way through to her and releases her grip; the sirens will have her understand that they're offering her freedom. As soon as she sees the possibility of freedom Mrs. Mallard frees herself from the petty distinctions that were weighing her down. Important and unimportant are sorted out. It does not matter to her if her joy is "monstrous" or not: it is joy. It makes no difference whether someone else's will to control her life was kind or cruel: it was unjustified. There's no point in asking if she always loved her husband or if she didn't sometimes; he's gone now. Mrs. Mallard concentrates upon the word *free*, which only has meaning as an absolute.

But absolutes do not exist on earth, and Mrs. Mallard is yearning for a 6 freedom that she cannot attain. In our lives the word *freedom* is always qualified, and the pressure to cater to the desires of others comes down hard on even the "most free." The vision for the future that has grabbed Mrs. Mallard with such a firm grip can lead her nowhere but to death.

Unaware that she faces the choice between life and death, Mrs. Mallard 7 descends the stairs "like a goddess of Victory," already more immortal than earthly. Armed with her vision of perfection and prepared to fuse that vision on to her everyday world, she goes down to meet the others. At the bottom of the stairs Louise Mallard confronts the crowded world where our dreams are constantly compromised by our realities, and she does not care to stay.

Questions to Start You Thinking

1. How convincing do you find Jane Betz's point about Mrs. Mallard's moving closer to the absolute, or eternity, as the story proceeds? To what evidence in the story does Betz point?

2. Whether or not you agree with Betz's interpretation, what did this student critic help you notice in the story or realize about it?

Criticizing Poetry

Now let's look at a famous poem by William Butler Yeats, Irish poet and playwright (1865–1939). To know a little about his life may help you make sense of "A Prayer for My Daughter." In February 1919, when Yeats was fifty-four, the birth of his first child, Anne, was a tremendous event to him; and shortly afterward, he began the poem. When in June he finished it, he and his family were living in an ancient stone tower that he had bought and had had rebuilt. Square and drafty, the tower stood on a riverbank in Ballylee, near Galway Bay. The "great gloom" that the poet tells us had settled on his mind was his fear that civilization was nearing its downfall. The violent Irish uprising of 1916 and the execution of its leaders, the terrible carnage of World War I— these had seemed to Yeats signs of increasing chaos. (If you imagine the setting of the poem, you might suspect, too, that anyone who had just moved with a three-month-old baby into a cold, windswept, stone tower might be susceptible to gloom.)

Other references in the poem are explained in notes at the bottom of each page, if you feel any need to look at them. "A Prayer for My Daughter" is a wonderful, richly musical poem, but we don't present it as holy scripture. Indeed, in her thoughtful essay that follows this famous poem, Joyce Carol Oates will find fault with it.

A PRAYER FOR MY DAUGHTER
WILLIAM BUTLER YEATS

Once more the storm is howling, and half hid
Under this cradle-hood and coverlid
My child sleeps on. There is no obstacle
But Gregory's° wood and one bare hill
Whereby the haystack- and roof-levelling wind,
Bred on the Atlantic, can be stayed;
And for an hour I have walked and prayed
Because of the great gloom that is in my mind.

I have walked and prayed for this young child an hour
And heard the sea-wind scream upon the tower,   10
And under the arches of the bridge, and scream

Gregory's wood: Yeats's tower stood near the estate of Lady Gregory, his patron and friend.

In the elms above the flooded stream;
Imagining in excited reverie
That the future years had come,
Dancing to a frenzied drum,
Out of the murderous innocence of the sea.

May she be granted beauty and yet not
Beauty to make a stranger's eye distraught,
Or hers before a looking-glass, for such,
Being made beautiful overmuch,   20
Consider beauty a sufficient end,
Lose natural kindness and maybe
The heart-revealing intimacy
That chooses right, and never find a friend.

Helen being chosen found life flat and dull
And later had much trouble from a fool,°
While that great Queen, that rose out of the spray,
Being fatherless could have her way
Yet chose a bandy-leggèd smith for man.°
It's certain that fine women eat   30
A crazy salad with their meat
Whereby the Horn of Plenty° is undone.

In courtesy I'd have her chiefly learned;
Hearts are not had as a gift but hearts are earned
By those that are not entirely beautiful;
Yet many, that have played the fool
For beauty's very self, has charm made wise,
And many a poor man that has roved,
Loved and thought himself beloved,
From a glad kindness cannot take his eyes.   40

May she become a flourishing hidden tree
That all her thoughts may like the linnet° be,
And have no business but dispensing round
Their magnanimities of sound,
Nor but in merriment begin a chase,
Nor but in merriment a quarrel.
O may she live like some green laurel°
Rooted in one dear perpetual place.

Helen . . . fool: Probably the fool who troubled Helen of Troy (over whom a war was fought, as Homer recounts in *The Iliad*) was her husband Menelaus.

that great Queen . . . a bandy-leggèd smith for man: Aphrodite, Greek goddess of love and beauty, born from the sea, married Hephaestus, god of fire, usually depicted as a blacksmith. He had a disabled leg.

Horn of Plenty: In Greek mythology, the god Zeus was suckled by a goat, who made him a gift of the cornucopia, one of her magical horns. Food and drink flowed from it on demand. Even today, a familiar symbol, especially at Thanksgiving, is a curved horn spilling fruits and vegetables.

linnet: A songbird common in Ireland.

laurel: Leaves of this tree, sacred to Apollo, god of poetry and the arts, signify victory. In classical times, laurel wreaths were given to winning poets and athletes.

My mind, because the minds that I have loved,
The sort of beauty that I have approved,   50
Prosper but little, has dried up of late,
Yet knows that to be choked with hate
May well be of all evil chances chief.
If there's no hatred in a mind
Assault and battery of the wind
Can never tear the linnet from the leaf.

An intellectual hatred is the worst,
So let her think opinions are accursed.
Have I not seen the loveliest woman born°
Out of the mouth of Plenty's horn,   60
Because of her opinionated mind
Barter that horn and every good
By quiet natures understood
For an old bellows full of angry wind?

Considering that, all hatred driven hence,
The soul recovers radical innocence
And learns at last that it is self-delighting,
Self-appeasing, self-affrighting,
And that its own sweet will is Heaven's will;
She can, though every face should scowl   70
And every windy quarter howl
Or every bellows burst, be happy still.

And may her bridegroom bring her to a house
Where all's accustomed, ceremonious;
For arrogance and hatred are the wares
Peddled in the thoroughfares.
How but in custom and in ceremony
Are innocence and beauty born?
Ceremony's a name for the rich horn,
And custom for the spreading laurel tree.   80

loveliest woman born: Maud Gonne, Irish patriot whom Yeats had long and unsuccessfully courted. He thought she had worn herself out working for political causes and (in those days without sound systems) had wrecked her voice by delivering fiery speeches before crowds.

Questions to Start You Thinking

1. What traits does the poet pray his infant daughter will have? Why do you suppose he hopes she won't be "beautiful overmuch" (line 20)? Why might he want her to "think opinions are accursed" (line 58)?

2. What reason or reasons does the poet give for wanting his daughter to value courtesy, custom, and ceremony?

3. The howling wind mentioned in the opening line, and again and again in the lines that follow, is a *symbol:* a thing full of hints and suggestions. Recall the biographical facts: If Yeats was expecting civilization to end, that "roof-levelling wind" may be

more than a literal wind; it may suggest whatever forces of chaos and destruction are going to destroy the social order. (More suggestions emerge as the wind is recalled in lines 55–56 and 64.) What other things does Yeats name that seem full of suggestions? What do they suggest to you?

4. What do you notice about the sound and rhythm of "A Prayer for My Daughter"? Is the poem written in free verse or formal verse? How can you tell? Does the musical shape of the poem seem in harmony with its content, or at odds? Explain.

YEATS'S "A PRAYER FOR MY DAUGHTER"

JOYCE CAROL OATES

One of the most highly regarded of Modernist poems is Yeats's "A 1 Prayer for My Daughter," written in 1919. If we examine it closely we see that it carries both a blessing and a curse, though it is the blessing critics always recall:

> I have walked and prayed for this young child an hour
> And heard the sea-wind scream upon the tower,
> And under the arches of the bridge, and scream
> In the elms above the flooded stream;
> Imagining in excited reverie
> That the future years had come,
> Dancing to a frenzied drum,
> Out of the murderous innocence of the sea.
>
> May she be granted beauty and yet not
> Beauty to make a stranger's eye distraught,
> Or hers before a looking-glass, for such,
> Being made beautiful overmuch,
> Consider beauty a sufficient end,
> Lose natural kindness and maybe
> The heart-revealing intimacy
> That chooses right, and never find a friend.

It is rarely remarked that Yeats's first concern for his daughter is her physical appearance. He prays that she will be beautiful—but not *too* beautiful—for such beauty might arouse in her a sense of her own autonomy: her existence in a "looking-glass" rather than in a man's eyes. Yeats goes on to hope, like many another anxious father, that his daughter will be spared passion and sensuality, for "It's certain that fine women eat / A crazy salad with their meat / Whereby the Horn of Plenty is undone." (The Horn of Plenty being, one must assume, an unintentional pun.)

Yeats had been in love, as all the world knows, with the beautiful and 2 passionate Maud Gonne for many years, and had been so aroused by her revolutionary political views that, for a time, he had belonged to a secret extremist revolutionary group called the Irish Republican Brotherhood—in a remarkable defiance, in fact, of his own deeply introspective nature. Yet his prayer for his daughter is that she be chiefly learned in *courtesy*. And:

> May she become a flourishing hidden tree
> That all her thoughts may like the linnet be,
> And have no business but dispensing round
> Their magnanimities of sound,
> Nor but in merriment begin a chase,
> Nor but in merriment a quarrel.
> O may she live like some green laurel
> Rooted in one dear perpetual place.

This celebrated poet would have his daughter an object in nature for others'—which is to say male—delectation. She is not even an animal or a bird in his imagination but a vegetable: immobile, unthinking, placid, "hidden." The activity of her brain is analogous to the linnet's song—no distracting evidence of mental powers, only a "magnanimity" of sound, a kind of background music. The linnet with its modest brown plumage is surely not an accidental choice; a nightingale might have been summoned, too—except that the nightingale has been used too frequently in English poetry and is, in any case, a nocturnal creature. The poet's lifework is the creation of a distinct voice in which sound and sense are harmoniously wedded: the poet's daughter is to be brainless and voiceless, *rooted*.

So crushingly conventional is Yeats's imagination—and he is writing several decades after the despised Victorian women novelists—that he cannot conclude his prayer with this wish for his infant daughter; he must look into the future and anticipate her marriage. Though the ideal woman is childlike, in fact vegetative, with no passion, sensuality, or intelligence, it is the case that she must be given in marriage to a man: she will be incomplete unless she is joined "in custom and ceremony" to a husband.

> And may her bridegroom bring her to a house
> Where all's accustomed, ceremonious;
> For arrogance and hatred are the wares
> Peddled in the thoroughfares.
> How but in custom and in ceremony
> Are innocence and beauty born?
> Ceremony's a name for the rich horn,
> And custom for the spreading laurel tree.

This is the sentiment, not undercut but confirmed by the pat rhyming, of many a sentimental, "inspirational" poem of the nineteenth century. And the ideals of innocence and beauty, docility, spiritual muteness—altogether familiar to any student of popular literature.

This famous poem is not, however, solely a father's prayer, a gesture of sanctification: it is also a curse, an instrument of revenge. Though Yeats had written numberless poems celebrating Maud Gonne, primarily for her beauty ("Pallas Athene in that straight back and arrogant head"), he now says, in a stanza that strikes the ear as arbitrary:

> An intellectual hatred is the worst,
> So let her think opinions are accursed.
> Have I not seen the loveliest woman born
> Out of the mouth of Plenty's horn,

> Because of her opinionated mind
> Barter that horn and every good
> By quiet natures understood
> For an old bellows full of angry wind?

(One notes again the horn, and now the betrayal of the horn—the independent woman's most unspeakable act. But Yeats's imagery is for once not at his conscious command.)

The feminine soul must be "self-delighting, self-appeasing, self-affright- 6 ing"—affecting a kind of autism of the spirit "though every face should scowl / And every windy quarter howl / Or every bellows burst. . . ."

Yeats's feminine ideal is of course not exclusively his: it is *the* feminine 7 ideal of centuries, the mythic being (or function) of which another poet, Robert Graves, so confidently speaks in declaring: "A woman is a Muse, or she is nothing." What is most unsettling about this sentimental vision is the anger that any "betrayal" arouses in the male. The female is not to concern herself with history, with action; it is her role to simply exist; even her beauty must not be too extreme, so that men will not be disturbed. When Woman fails to conform to this stereotype she is bitterly and savagely denounced: she is "an old bellows full of angry wind." Constance Markievicz also draws forth the poet's disapproval, in "Easter 1916," for, like Maud Gonne, she has violated masculine expectations:

> That woman's days were spent
> In ignorant good-will
> Her nights in argument
> Until her voice grew shrill.
> What voice more sweet than hers
> When, young and beautiful,
> She rode to harriers?

This crude division between good girl and shrill (hysterical?) woman 8 differs very little from the stereotyping associated with popular or mass culture. But so skillful is Yeats's employment of language that the self-mesmerizing function of his poetry disguises the simplicity of his thought.

Perhaps, too, the poet assumes a masculine privilege by way of his role 9 as a poet, a manipulator of language. For it seems to be a deep-seated prejudice that written language belongs to men, and that any woman who attempts it is violating a natural law. As Thoreau argues with evident reasonableness in the chapter "Reading," in *Walden:*

> Books must be read as deliberately and reservedly as they were written. It is not enough even to be able to speak the language of that nation by which they were written, for there is a memorable interval between the spoken and the written language, the language heard and the language read. The one is commonly transitory, a sound, a tongue, a dialect merely, almost brutish, and we learn it unconsciously, like the brutes, of our mothers. The other is the maturity and experience of that; if that is our mother tongue, this is our father tongue, a reserved and select expression, too significant to be heard by the ear, which we must be born again in order to speak.

If either of our "languages"—spoken or written—is a language of brutes, naturally it will be imagined a Mother Tongue; for the Father Tongue, that "reserved and select expression," necessitates a religious initiation. One must be born again—which is to say, born male.

Questions to Start You Thinking

1. Consider Oates's charge that Yeats doesn't want his daughter to be too beautiful because "such beauty might arouse in her a sense of her own autonomy." Think about her claim "This celebrated poet would have his daughter an object in nature for others'—which is to say male—delectation." On what evidence does she base each of these conclusions?

2. What does Oates see as the poet's main impetus for wanting his daughter to be as different as possible from Maud Gonne, the woman with whom he had been in love?

3. For what purpose does the author quote the stanza about Constance Markievicz (Irish patriot and political leader, married to a Polish count), from Yeats's "Easter 1916"?

4. What do you think Oates is trying to accomplish? How well does she accomplish it?

5. How would you answer the student who objected, "It's not fair for Joyce Carol Oates to accuse Yeats of male chauvinism because he lived before the women's movement raised everyone's consciousness"?

LEARNING BY WRITING

The Assignment

Read some other story or poem suggested by your instructor, or find one that you especially want to write about (and that your instructor agrees might be worth your effort). Then write a short critical essay setting forth your understanding of it. Let your purpose be to explain the story or poem. Write so that another student will better understand and appreciate it.

In recent student papers we have read, the following stood out as among the most perceptive critical essays on literature.

A man wrote an essay on William Faulkner's short story "A Rose for Emily" in which he suggested that the main character's fate symbolized the fate of the Old South.

After reading the story "Wild Swans," by the contemporary Canadian writer Alice Munro, a woman explained the symbolism in the story and showed how it cast light on the characters.

A women, after several careful readings of the Flannery O'Connor story "A Good Man Is Hard to Find," demonstrated that the story's central character, an old grandmother, died a Christian martyr's death.

A man worked through "Ariel," a complicated poem by Sylvia Plath, found a narrative, and made it clear.

A woman shed light on English poet George Meredith's sonnet "Lucifer in Starlight" by finding out that Lucifer is a name both for the devil and for the planet Venus and then interpreting the poem in terms of her discovery.

Generating Ideas

If you can just light upon a work that intrigues and excites you, your task as a critic will be a pleasure. In making your choice you may find it helpful to talk with your instructor or with other students or to browse in a library. Once you have made your choice, you will want to reread the poem or story more carefully.

But probably your best source of ideas will be your own thoughtful reading, conducted with pencil in hand. Read the text at least three times, each time for a different reason:

First, read for the big picture, for an overall idea of what the story, poem, or play is about.

Then read for pleasure.

Then go back and read for detail. In this last reading, read with pencil in hand and make notes—right on the margins of the work itself if the copy is yours and if it isn't, on paper or index cards. But don't get lost in note taking: notes that are too dutiful and extensive can crush any interest you have in the work, and you want to leave something for your unconscious mind to contribute when the time comes to write. Try paraphrasing hard parts—aloud or (better still) in writing. If you're writing about a poem, make sure you understand the meaning of every word in it, and here, of course, your trusty ally is your dictionary. Sometimes reading a poem aloud to yourself will help it make sense to you.

If a story, poem, or play you are explaining is difficult and you feel an urgent need for help, you might—just might—want to read other critics. We recommend turning to other critics only after you have thought good and hard about the work on your own and formed some opinions of it. It is *your* views, and not some professional critic's, that will matter. But if you need help, go ahead and look: there may be plenty to be found. Your library's card catalogue can direct you to critical books about your chosen author. For a list of both books and articles about a short story, see Warren S. Walker, *Twentieth-Century Short Story Explication: Interpretations, 1900–1975, of Short Fiction Since 1800*, 3rd ed. (Hamden, CT: Shoe String Press, 1977) and its later supplements (1980, 1984). For criticism of a poem, see Joseph M. Kuntz and Nancy C. Martinez, *Poetry Explication: A Checklist of Interpretation Since 1925 of British and American Poems Past and Present*, 3rd ed. (Boston: G. K. Hall, 1980).

Of course, you will want to acknowledge any critical ideas you derive from elsewhere. A word of caution about those crib books, sometimes sold in college bookstores, that offer outlines and notes on famous, frequently assigned novels, plays, and epic poems: we never saw one that got the plot straight. And when a student heavily relies on one in writing a paper, generally the student's prose goes as dead and stale as the crib book writer's.

Before you start writing, here are some questions you might ask yourself.

DISCOVERY CHECKLIST: APPROACHING A STORY OR POEM

- What do you find in the story or poem that you most greatly care about and wish to explore? Whether it is the theme, some other element, an assumption on the writer's part (that men are a superior race, as Oates finds Yeats assuming)—that is the thing to concentrate on.
- Do you know any background information that may help you understand the literary work? Some facts, such as the writer's biography, can prove helpful in some cases, as in that of Yeats's "A Prayer for My Daughter." You might ask some of the following questions.
- Who is the author? What can you find out about him or her? Helpful information lurks in standard works in your library's reference room, such as *American Authors, World Literature, Contemporary Poets*, and encyclopedias.
- When was the work written? In what region or country? That may tell you something about its content and its author's attitude: that "A Prayer for My Daughter" was written in Ireland in 1919 may help account for its author's view of a woman's place in society.
- Finally, what is there in this story or poem that you don't understand so far? If you are still having trouble with all or part of it, you are within your rights to discuss it with a fellow student or with your instructor.

Literary Language: A Brief Glossary

To find ideas for a critical essay, you need a language in which to conceive and express them. Just as you have to learn the vocabulary of a specialized field (economics, say, or computer programming) to write in it, you will find it easier to seize hold of a story, poem, or play and write about it if you know a few useful terms. Some of these words you have already met in the questions on Chopin and Yeats. If any are unfamiliar, skim through the following glossary and refresh yourself (or fill yourself in). Don't feel obliged to memorize all these terms: most of them will be familiar to you anyhow. They are given here mainly to suggest possibilities to write about.

Characters in a story, play, or narrative poem are recognizable human beings (or memorable nonhumans, like King Kong or Shakespeare's Caliban). If the story, play, or poem is well crafted, they behave consistently and have some *motivation:* good reason to act or react as they do—as, according to Jane Betz, Mrs. Mallard has.

Connotations are meanings that a word suggests, over and above its denotation, or literal dictionary meaning. The word *skeleton* denotes the bone-structure of a vertebrate animal, but its connotations might include thoughts of ghosts, battlefields, or medical school lecture halls. In a poem, much of the poetry is often expressed in connotations: in *"casements* opening on the *foam* of perilous *seas"* the connotations of the words in italics are far richer than if the poet had written *"windows* opening on the *scum* of perilous *salt water."* In Yeats's "A Prayer for My Daughter," rich suggestions surround the word *laurel* (in line 47): hints of triumph, of prize-winning poetry, of athletic prowess, of gardens and green forests.

Conventions are trappings you can expect to find in a certain kind of story, poem, or play. It is conventional for a Gothic horror story to be set in a moldering mansion full of antiques and half-heard screams in the night. It is also conventional for a *sonnet* to contain fourteen lines divided into an octave (a group of eight lines, riming with one another and raising a problem or question, such as "Does she love me?") and a sestet (a group of six lines riming with one another and containing an answer to the problem or question).

Diction is a writer's choice of words. Kinds of diction include *standard English* (language that native-born speakers use in formal writing), *nonstandard English* (words that we often hear spoken but that are not acceptable in standard written English), *slang* ("That dress looks wicked on her," *coffin nails* for *cigarettes*), *regional words* (heard in a locality, such as *spritzing* for *raining* in Pennsylvania Dutch country), *dialect* (usually spoken language, differing from standard English because of the geography, education, or social background of the speaker), *technical terms, jargon* (specialized language applied to general use; see p. 520), and *euphemisms* (ways of putting unpleasant things pleasantly; see p. 519). Any diction may be the right diction for an occasion: choice of words depends on a writer's purpose and audience.

Figures of speech are departures from the literal, dictionary definition meanings of words. When in Shakespeare's *As You Like It* Jaques declares, "All the world's a stage," we do not look for boards under our feet; we realize that the statement is an imaginative comparison. It is an example of a *metaphor*, a figure of speech that identifies one thing with another. An identification made with a connective word is often called a *simile* ("The world is *like* a stage," "is *as* a stage," "is more changeable *than* a stage," *"resembles* a stage"). (Jaques's later remark that all men and women "have their exits and their entrances" is an *implied metaphor*, a statement that doesn't say the world is a stage but just takes the identification for granted.) Other familiar figures of speech include the *pun*, or playful use of words that sound like other words but have different meanings ("The pun is mightier than the sword"); *personification*, or humanizing an object, animal, or abstraction ("Inspiration rang the doorbell"); and *hyperbole*, or overstatement ("I could eat a million sandwiches"). As in that last example, a figure of speech can lend emphasis. (See "Growing a Metaphor," p. 495.)

The *form* of a poem is its structure of sounds and rhythms: whatever shape you can see on the page, whatever structure you can hear if the poem is read aloud. The kind of poetry called *formal verse* comes in rime, meter, and stanzas, but actually, all poetry has some kind of form to it, whether it is a sonnet or a work of free verse that looks as if words were slung off a shovel and onto the page. *Free verse,* or verse in *open form,* is usually defined by what it does not have: rime, meter, stanzas. Consider Walt Whitman's lines from "Song of Myself":

> I think I could turn and live with animals, they are so placid and self-
>   contain'd,
> I stand and look at them long and long.
>
> They do not sweat and whine about their condition,
> They do not lie awake in the dark and weep for their sins,
> They do not make me sick discussing their duty to God,
> Not one is dissatisfied, not one is demented with the mania of owning
>   things,
> Not one kneels to another, nor to his kind that lived thousands of years
>   ago,
> Not one is respectable or unhappy over the whole earth.

Although these lines may seem to go on for as long as the author wishes, a little inspection will show them to be under control. They produce a rhythm by repeating words at the beginnings of lines (*I, They, Not one*). They contain interesting sounds (assonance, alliteration). Most contemporary American poets write in free verse, which freedom enables them to get effects—rhythms, emphases—by where they break their lines.

Images are words or groups of words that refer to any sense experience. Though *image* suggests a picture, an image doesn't always evoke seeing (a window "diamonded with panes") but may refer to hearing ("snarling trumpets"), smelling ("incense sweet"), tasting ("him whose strenuous tongue can burst Joy's grape against his palate fine"), touching ("damp and slippery footing"), feeling heat or cold ("numb were the Beadsman's fingers"), or feeling pain or thirst ("a burning forehead and a parching tongue")—all examples from John Keats. If one image can't be isolated from others, we speak of *imagery:* two or more images taken together. When Keats writes, "The murmurous haunt of flies on summer eves," sight, sound, and warmth blend, and the result is not a single image but a line rich in imagery. (On writing sense impressions into prose, see Chapter 5.)

Irony results from our sense of a discrepancy. A simple form of verbal irony, *sarcasm,* occurs when we say a thing sourly but mean the opposite: "Oh, scratching poison ivy blisters is my favorite sport." The discrepancy lies between what is said and what is meant. But other kinds of irony inform literature: an *ironic situation* is one that contains some wry contrast or incongruity, such as occurs in Poe's story "The Cask of Amontillado," where the setting of a grim murder is a Mardi Gras celebration and a murder victim is dressed as a clown. When we notice a sharp difference between a character who tells the story and the author, we say the story has an *ironic point of view.* William Faulkner tells part of his novel *The Sound and the Fury* through the eyes of an idiot, but the author is not an idiot. *Irony of fate* or *cosmic irony* occurs in any grim twist of events: in Stephen Crane's story "The Open Boat," some survivors of a shipwreck get within sight of the shore, which they yearn for, only to be forced (for a time) to head back out to sea.

Myth is any idea people believe that enables them to find meaning in their lives. Myth doesn't mean "a cock-and-bull story"; any religion contains myths, which many regard as true. Thus when we speak of "the Christian myth" or "the myth of Eden," we are simply naming a belief; we do not imply contempt. Classical mythology, that of Greece and Rome, is full of stories of the gods and goddesses; some myths were invented to explain phenomena in the natural world (spring returns because Persephone has come back from the underworld for her annual visit), but not all. Traditional myths supply poets and storytellers and playwrights with an endlessly useful source of material; other writers invent new myths of their own, as J. R. R. Tolkien does in *Lord of the Rings*.

Point of view is the angle from which a story is told. Who is the *narrator* of the story—that is, who tells it? What part does he or she play in it, and what limits does the author place on that character's knowing what is going on? Answer those questions and you define the point of view. The two most usual points of view from which to tell a story are those of the first-person narrator ("I"), who takes part in the action as a character, and the third-person narrator, who doesn't take part in the action but relates it from outside.

The third-person narrator may be the all-knowing (or omniscient) godlike author who can see into the mind of any character; the limited, partly knowing narrator who sees into the mind of only one character; or the complete outsider or objective narrator who can't see into any character's mind but, like a movie camera, can depict only surfaces.

Plot in a story or play means the way events are arranged. Some plots unfold in *chronological order* (from earliest happenings to latest); others begin with an interesting event to hook our attention and then, with the aid of *flash-backs,* or scenes relived in memory, fill us in on what happened earlier. The opening portion, or *exposition,* sets the scene, introduces the *protagonist* (main character), and probably draws a *dramatic situation* (in which the character is shown in conflict with some opposing person or force). Any new conflict is a *complication.* A *crisis* is the moment of highest tension, or a turning point in the action. Events reach their *climax:* the moment when the outcome is to be decided. The outcome itself is the *resolution* or *conclusion.*

Rhythm refers to any regular, recurrent movement: the rhythms of the heart-beat, of the seasons, of the tides, of a lead guitar. In poetry, rhythm is the regular recurrence of accented and unaccented syllables. If every line in a poem follows a basic, fixed pattern (departing at times but always coming back to it), the poem is written in a pattern called a *meter.* The most frequent meter found in traditional English poetry is *iambic,* a series of *iambs* (pairs of syllables, the first not accented, the second accented), as in these lines from Elizabeth Barrett Browning (with the accented syllables in italics):

> My *let*·ters! *all dead pa*·per, *mute* and *white!*
> And *yet* they *seem* a·*live* and *quiv*·er·ing

> A·*gainst* my *trem*·u·lous *hands* which *loose* the *string*
> And *let* them *drop down* on my *knee* to·*night*.

If you read these lines aloud, you'll notice that, while you can feel a basic *da-DUM da-DUM* beat in them, the poet doesn't stick to her pattern like a marching robot but keeps departing and returning to it like a dancer throwing in a fresh, original step here and there. The word *tremulous* shatters the chain of da-DUMs and our expectations: at that point, the rhythm of the line trembles, meaningfully, like the hands untying the packet of love letters. Prose, especially when it is full of feeling and close to poetry, as in passages in Melville's *Moby-Dick*, can employ rhythms too.

Setting in a story, play, or narrative poem is the time and place where events transpire; sometimes the season or the weather is part of it. Setting isn't a mere painted backdrop; in fiction it often makes things happen. An old, spooky mansion may provide atmosphere for a horror story, but it can also provide ghosts.

Poets, mostly, and also storytellers with musical ears revel in *sound* effects, which are effective if they harmonize with and enforce the meaning of what a writer is saying. The pattern called *alliteration* oc urs when a consonant is repeated, whether at the beginnings of words ("Peter Piper picked a peck of pickled peppers") or inside words (called *internal alliteration:* all those *k* sounds in that same line). When a vowel sound is repeated, the effect is called *assonance* ("An awful and august law," "How now, brown cow"). Words that name a thing or action by imitating its sound (*zoom, whiz, crash, buzz, ding-dong, whoosh, yakety-yak*) are said to produce *onomatopoeia. Rime* (also spelled *rhyme*) is a device of poetry left over from medieval days, when most poems in English were songs. Strictly speaking, rime occurs when two or more words or phrases contain an identical or similar vowel sound, usually accented, and when the consonant sounds that follow are identical: *ripe* and *snipe, prairie schooner* and *piano tuner*. When the vowel sounds are different but the final consonants (if any) are the same (*love* riming with *cave, flame* with *dim, thigh* with *bee*) the result is *off-rime* (or *near rime* or *slant rime*).

Style, usually an element noticed in works of prose ("Mencken's salty and erudite style"), is the distinctive manner in which a writer writes. Many things make it up, especially word choice and structure of sentences (their length, complexity, and variety). Two writers may write on the same subject, perhaps even state similar ideas, but it is style that gives each one's work a personality.

Symbol in literature is a verbal account of a visible object or action that hints at many meanings besides itself. A symbol doesn't "stand for" or "represent" any one meaning; it hints at practically endless meanings. In William Faulkner's story "The Bear," the huge old beast with the trap-injured foot sug gests not only himself but the vanishing wilderness being driven into a corner, a challenge a boy must conquer to become a man, and much more. In a short story, as in "The Bear," the main symbol usually clearly points you to the story's central theme. Figure out what the symbol suggests and you will find yourself stating the theme. At the end of Yeats's "A Prayer for My Daughter," the spreading laurel tree points to what the poet is saying: may his daughter grow up triumphantly.

Theme is the main idea or insight a work of literature contains. Usually after you have read and understood a work of literature, you can sum up its theme in a sentence. In a short fable, such as Aesop's "The Fox and the Grapes," after the fox can't jump high enough to get the fruit he covets and he goes off muttering, "Those grapes were probably sour anyway," the theme is stated for us at the end: "Moral: It is easy to scorn what cannot be attained." In a longer work, the theme is seldom as obvious; we may have to grope around for it, and we might word it in different ways. Kate Chopin's "The Story of an Hour" is about the death of a woman from shock—but that is the story's subject. The theme is something else, and one way to state it is "Marriage can trap a woman in a prison." Another way: "For a woman, the death of her husband can be an unexpected delight."

Tone is the author's attitude toward the characters or other material or, strictly speaking, whatever we can find in a story or poem that makes this attitude clear to us. In *David Copperfield*, Charles Dickens clearly detests Uriah Heep for his faked humility and portrays Heep in such a way that we are bound to detest him too. Like tone of voice, tone in literature conveys feelings: friendly or angry, sympathetic or aloof, playful or grimly earnest. (See also p. 505.)

How can this glossary help you generate ideas? After you have chosen the story or poem to write about, cruise through the glossary again, asking yourself whether you'd have anything to say about its characters, the connotations of its language, its conventions, and so on—until you can imagine yourself having enough to say. Some of these terms indicate things that go together: *theme* and *symbol*. Some refer especially to language: *connotations, diction, figures of speech, images, rhythm, rime, sound, style.* An essay on "The Language of Kate Chopin" might go into those things, or some of them, or just one.

Shaping a Draft

When you write a memoir of a crucial experience in your life or a description of a familiar place, you have only to capture in words what you vividly recall. In doing so, you can probably work with only a quick, scribbled outline or with no outline at all.

But writing about literature is seldom that simple. It calls for careful thought and continual rereading of the work you have chosen to discuss; it probably calls for more planning before you set out. If you can put the main point of your essay into the form of a thesis statement (and we have some advice on doing this on p. 469), you will find much of your planning accomplished. Oates might have made the thesis statement "William Butler Yeats is a male chauvinist." Then look back over your annotated reading and any notes you've made, to see what material you have on hand that will make this main point clear. Make a list or (if your material consists of index cards, photocopies, or loose pieces of paper) stack the material up in an order you mean to follow, with your opening point on top. If you feel the need for further advice on organizing your paper, see "Grouping Your Ideas" (p. 473), and "Outlining" (p. 476).

Rather than planning you can, of course, just work through a story paragraph by paragraph, or a poem line by line, explaining any difficulties you meet as you go along. But that way of working can easily become so mechanical that it will put you to sleep ("Now, in the forty-seventh paragraph, we find . . ."). You'll probably write with more vigor if you follow the order of *what you most want to say*—the points you crave to make—even if that order means you will discuss paragraph 25 ahead of paragraph 1.

As you write, don't worry about being brilliant. Although you need a critical vocabulary at your fingertips (for which reason we offered the glossary of literary terms), you don't want to sling words around merely to show off. Those terms, we think, are immensely useful; but they can easily be misused. Use only those terms that are part of you. The writer who writes "The myth imagery in this story is symbolic in tone" is about as clear as corned beef hash. Just say as plainly as you can what you most want to say. If you are dishing out helpful insights, though your language may be ordinary, your reader will gladly follow you.

You can assume, by the way, that your reader has read the story or poem you're discussing. This assumption will save you many words: you don't need to summarize the work. When you write as a critic, we suggest that you regard your reader as a friend in whose company you are looking over something already familiar to both of you.

In giving evidence for your claims, you can't do better than to quote the author's text. Literary critics might well post this sign over their desks: KEEP LOOKING AGAIN AND AGAIN AT THE AUTHOR'S WORDS. Lest you retranscribe all the author's words, you'll sometimes want to summarize or paraphrase. When dealing with a story, you can often summarize a long passage in only a few words— recalling a scene or event just fully enough to help your reader recognize it. For instance: "In the solitude of her room, Mrs. Mallard's meditation brings her to realize her new freedom." The habit of making such brief references as you write will keep your discussion on the track, for you will be obliged to keep returning to the writer's printed page. (More suggestions for summarizing and paraphrasing are offered on pp. 101–102.)

When you deal with a short poem, it's an excellent plan to quote the entire text of the poem at the start of your paper, numbering the lines so that you may easily refer to them. Apt quotations can enliven your commentary, pointing to moments in a poem that you consider important but that a reader might miss. Quoting a poem is slightly trickier than quoting a story. A poem is written in lines, those meaningful units whose exact shape a conscientious critic preserves. When you quote several lines, quote them just the way they look in the poem, observing the same spacing and indentations:

It's certain that fine women eat
A crazy salad with their meat
Whereby the Horn of Plenty is undone.

When you quote just a few words, use a virgule, or slash (/), to show where a line breaks:

In Yeats's view, some women, like the political crusader Maud Gonne, "eat / A crazy salad with their meat"—meaning, perhaps, that they consume radical ideas, which drive them wild.

Rewriting

Before you rewrite a draft, an excellent thing to do is to reread the story or poem you have explained. If you haven't looked at it lately, you may be surprised what fresh thoughts you now can bring to it. Sometimes in the act of writing, a critic becomes so enthralled with spinning a fresh web of ideas that the result isn't criticism but a new work of self-sufficient art, which has nothing to do with the work under discussion. The results can be wonderful, but in a basic literature course your first task is to pay attention to the literature you're interpreting. So as not to fly off into outer space, we suggest you reread the author's work before you reread your own. When you inspect your draft, you might look for the following points.

REVISION CHECKLIST: CRITICIZING A STORY OR POEM

- Have you read the original work carefully enough, and thought about it long enough, to supply some insights of your own?
- Do you need any more evidence to make a point clear: brief quotations, summary, paraphrase?
- Do you fill up too much of your essay with long quotations from the original work, which presumably your reader has read too?
- In an essay on a short story or play, do you spend all your time summing up the plot? (If so, slice.)
- Do you clearly acknowledge your debt to any other critics who lent you their ideas?
- If you quote any critics and don't agree with their views, do you fearlessly differ with them?
- Do you ever say a writer said something that he or she did not say?
- Do you pretend to know or understand anything you really don't?

In criticizing a story or poem, watch out for tense troubles. Switching back and forth between the author's text and your own, you can easily confuse past and present: "After her sister breaks the news of the railroad disaster, Mrs. Mallard wept." *Wept* should be *weeps*. In critical writing it is conventional to use the "historical present" when discussing the action that takes place in a story or poem.

When Jane Betz looked over a late draft of her essay she felt dissatisfied with her opening sentence. She had written:

> Some readers complain that Kate Chopin's "The Story of an Hour" is a trick-ending story, that the ending is tacked on only to surprise, and that Mrs. Mallard's behavior. . . .

The sentence, as it lengthened, seemed to grow wordy. Betz apparently decided to make it more definite and concrete. She tried to enliven it with a figure of speech, a colorful comparison:

> Some readers complain that the ending to Kate Chopin's "The Story of an Hour" is a cheap trick, a tacked-on surprise that comes like a killer out of a dark alley in a low-grade horror movie.

Looking over this rewrite, she scribbled a complaint to herself: "No wait—don't we *expect* that, in a horror movie?" In one more try, she kept the idea of the horror movie and introduced a more surprising surprise. The sentence now ended (as it appears in the essay):

> . . . a cheap trick, an unwanted surprise that comes like a killer through an old woman's bedroom window in a low-grade horror movie.

One more thing: In transcribing quotations, it is easy to garble them. It's good policy, if you have a few minutes to spare, to check them one last time against the original.

Other Assignments

1. Write a short critical essay evaluating a story or a poem (other than Chopin's story or Yeats's poem). (For suggestions on evaluating, see p. 421.) Your instructor can offer suggestions for stories or poems to consider. In evaluating, you argue for a view. Like Jane Betz, you may care to defend a work against possible attack; or, like Joyce Carol Oates, you might charge the work with failure in some regard.

2. Read the following storytelling poem by Charlotte Mew (an English poet, 1869–1928, whose work is just now gaining the appreciation it deserves). The poem was first published in 1916. Write a short interpretation of it: Who is the speaker? What happens? What would the poet have us think of it?

THE FARMER'S BRIDE

Three Summers since I chose a maid,
Too young maybe—but more's to do
At harvest-time than bide and woo.
    When us was wed she turned afraid
Of love and me and all things human;
Like the shut of a winter's day.
Her smile went out, and 'twasn't a woman—
    More like a little frightened fay.
        One night, in the Fall, she runned away.

"Out 'mong the sheep, her be," they said,
'Should properly have been abed;
But sure enough she wasn't there
Lying awake with her wide brown stare.
So over seven-acre field and up-along across the down
We chased her, flying like a hare
Before our lanterns. To Church-Town
All in a shiver and a scare
We caught her, fetched her home at last
And turned the key upon her, fast.

She does the work about the house
As well as most, but like a mouse:
Happy enough to chat and play
With birds and rabbits and such as they,
So long as men-folk keep away.
"Not near, not near!" her eyes beseech
When one of us comes within reach.
The women say that beasts in stall
Look round like children at her call.
I've hardly heard her speak at all.

Shy as a leveret, swift as he,
Straight and slight as a young larch tree,
Sweet as the first wild violets, she,
To her wild self. But what to me?

The short days shorten and the oaks are brown,
The blue smoke rises to the low grey sky,
One leaf in the still air falls slowly down,
A magpie's spotted feathers lie
On the black earth spread white with rime,
The berries redden up to Christmas-time.
What's Christmas-time without there be
Some other in the house than we!

She sleeps up in the attic there
Alone, poor maid. 'Tis but a stair
Betwixt us. Oh! my God! the down,
The soft young down of her, the brown,
The brown of her—her eyes, her hair, her hair!

3. In this assignment (and the next one) you will fulfill the purpose of a critical essay—
to analyze a work of literature—while writing in a more creative form. In a paragraph or more, write a parody (or humorous take-off) of Chopin's story, or Yeats's
poem, or some other story or poem, or some kind of literature (the horror story,
the western, the paperback Harlequin romance). In a good parody or take-off, a
writer picks out characteristics of the original but exaggerates them. The reader
should feel that, although much is familiar (probably plot, characters, and style),
something is absurdly different. As well as you can, remind your reader of the
language found in the original. For instance, detective fiction writer Raymond Chandler wrote this parody of what he believed to be a typical science fiction story.

I checked out with K 19 on Aldabaran III, and stepped out through the crummalite hatch on my 22 Model Sirus Hardtop. I cocked the timejector in secondary and waded through the bright blue manda grass. My breath froze into pink pretzels. I flicked on the heat bars and the Brylls ran swiftly on five legs using their other two to send out crylon vibrations. The pressure was almost unbearable, but I caught the range on my wrist computer through the transparent cysicites. I pressed the trigger. The thin violet glow was icecold against the rust-colored mountains. The Brylls shrank to half an inch long and I worked fast stepping on them with the poltex. But it wasn't enough. The sudden brightness swung me around and the Fourth Moon had already risen. I had exactly four seconds to hop up the disintegrator and Google had told me it wasn't enough. He was right.

4. For another challenging exercise in analysis, rewrite a short story (Kate Chopin's or another) as a one-act play. You will be limited to dialogue that can actually be heard and will be unable to express thoughts within the characters' heads (unless you invent some device to have these thoughts spoken). For written models, see the printed version of any classic modern play (Arthur Miller's *Death of a Salesman* and Tennessee Williams's *The Glass Menagerie* are interesting for their stage techniques, among other things) or a collection of contemporary plays. After you finish your script, why let it languish in a bottom drawer? Cast it and stage a reading-performance of it for the class.

APPLYING WHAT YOU LEARN:
SOME USES OF CRITICIZING LITERATURE

Outside of a literature course (whether in English or in a foreign language), you'll seldom be asked to write an essay in literary criticism in college. Once in a while a sociology or a philosophy professor might assign a critical report on a book in his or her discipline. You might possibly be asked for a critical essay in a film study course or a course in music appreciation. Otherwise, your skills in such writing may languish, unless you review books, films, plays, lectures, or concerts for your college newspaper.

Writing the critical essay, then, might seem a strictly academic exercise, one of limited usefulness. But the skills you learn in writing about literature can carry over to your writing and thinking in other disciplines. When you write a critical essay about a story or poem, you live with language closely, and such experience has practical value in other liberal arts and social science courses—not to mention its usefulness in life after college. Richard Gummere, for nineteen years director of placement and career services at Columbia University, reports: "Employers tell us one of the skills they look for most is good use of the language, spoken and written." Gummere recalls a conversation with a recruiter for E. F. Hutton, who phoned with jobs for two liberal arts graduates. "The company wanted to train them in corporate bond research—sizing up companies that want their bonds sold by Hutton. The man said, 'Any major, provided they can analyze things skeptically.'"

One evident way to get experience in such analysis is to write a critical essay taking apart a story, play, or poem. In an interview in 1979, U.S. Supreme Court Justice John Paul Stevens remarked that the best preparation for the study of law is the study of lyric poetry. After discussing this observation with Justice Stevens, lawyer and English professor George D. Gopen concluded that, indeed, some of the methods of critical reading and writing of poetry directly apply to what a student does in law school:

> No other discipline so closely replicates the central question asked in the study of legal thinking: "Here is a text; in how many ways can it have meaning?" . . . No other discipline concentrates as much on the effects of ambiguity of individual words and phrases.

Many business executives affirm that, among job applicants, students of literature have a decided advantage. "The study of literature is the study of human behavior," remarks Harris Shane, vice-president of Pullman, Inc., adding that the student of English trained in literary analysis "has probably done more thinking about why people act as they do than a major in any other subject." Surely Jane Betz had to analyze human motivations in writing her analysis of "The Story of an Hour." Stressing his belief that the study of literature helps deepen a business executive's practical understanding of human nature, Richard Hankinson, personnel director for Blue Cross–Blue Shield of Iowa, has argued:

> Understanding requires almost gut level feeling. How do you teach this to managers? I think that one answer lies within literature, for literature is the only vicarious source of the feeling and understanding that comes through identification and introspection. . . . Sometime in the not too distant future we are going to experiment in a course in management development based on literature. I can't help feeling that any individual . . . who is capable of understanding the source of desperation in Willie Loman [in Arthur Miller's play *Death of a Salesman*] and the course of his ultimate destruction will be a more effective servant of his people. Too many times our managers understand only the theoretical basis of behavior without understanding the way it may affect the individual. I think the study of literature may overcome some of this handicap.

CHAPTER 22

Business Writing

Most of the world's business communication still takes place in writing. The reasons are easy to discover. Although a telephone message may conveniently be forgotten or ignored, a letter or a memorandum is a physical thing that sits on a desk, calling for some action—if only to crumple it up and pitch it into a wastebasket. Written documents can be kept on file, to be consulted again. In every business, people are continually writing: producing instructions, proposals, announcements, plans for sales campaigns, annual reports to stockholders, reports for the information of executives. Even where people work elbow to elbow, you will sometimes hear: "That's a bright idea. Write me a memo about it, will you?"

That is why personnel managers of large corporations, the people who do the hiring, tend to be keenly interested in applicants who can write clearly, accurately, and effectively. Recently, a survey conducted at Cornell University asked business executives to rate in importance the qualities they would like their employees to possess. Skill in writing was ranked in fourth place, ahead of managerial skill, ahead of skill in analysis. This fact may be worth recalling if you ever wonder what practical good you can do your career by taking a writing course.

In this chapter, we will show you three kinds of business writing soon likely to prove useful to you.

BUSINESS LETTERS

In most college courses, you know your readers well—usually they are your instructor and other students—but the reader you address in a business letter may be unknown to you. If you write to a personnel manager seeking a job interview, chances are that you aren't personally acquainted with that mysterious functionary. Still, you can try to imagine him or her and supply information that this person needs to know: that you are capable of doing the job, how soon you will be available to go to work, and how you can be contacted.

A good business letter supplies whatever information the reader needs, no more.

Each of us, at least once in a while, has to write a letter for a business purpose: if not to apply for a job, then to apply for a scholarship or for acceptance at a graduate school; to request help, advice, or information; to order something by mail; to complain about a product or service; to answer a newspaper ad; or to express an opinion, as in a letter to the editor of a newspaper or to some elected official. Those are only a few common uses of a business letter in everyday life. Most college students enter the world of business on graduation, at which time they may find that writing business correspondence is daily bread. But whether or not you plan a business career, knowing how to draft a good business letter is a skill that can serve you well.

Learning from Other Writers

An effective business letter is straightforward, forceful, but polite and considerate, concise, neat, and legible. Figure 22.1 contains a sample letter, its parts labeled and explained.

In this case, the *cc* at the end of the letter indicates that the writer is sending a copy of her letter to an organization called the Fair Housing Committee. Another common reference at the end of a letter is *Enc.* (if the writer is enclosing some document in the envelope along with the letter). If the letter, composed by someone whose initials are W.F., has been typed by someone whose initials are B.R., the legend *WF/br* usually appears below the signature, at the left margin.

Notice the tone of Liggett's letter: the attitude she takes toward her hard-timing landlady. Scrupulously, she avoids calling the skinflint names, and she proposes a reasonable way for the landlady to satisfy herself that her tenants haven't done $500 worth of damage. The letter shows gumption, but it is diplomatic and considerate of the recipient's feelings.

The envelope for Jennifer Liggett's letter is shown in Figure 22.2.

When you don't know the name of the person who will read your letter, as when you write to someone at a large organization, it is acceptable to word your salutation "Dear Sir or Madam," "Dear Editor," or "Dear Angell's Bakery." "Gentlemen" has become too sexist for contemporary tastes.

In a letter requesting information, try to be clear but brief and to the point, as in Figure 22.3.

If you ever find yourself on the opposite side of the desk, writing letters as a spokesperson for a company, you will face a special problem: do you write in the voice of an individual human being or try to write as an impersonal organization? Obviously you can't write to a complaining customer as though addressing a personal friend ("Keep your shirt on, old buddy . . .") or answer a request for information about a product line with an unwanted personal opinion ("Aren't these simulated oak cabinets cool-looking? I just love them!"). On the other hand, writing impersonally, you might risk sounding stuffy ("It is

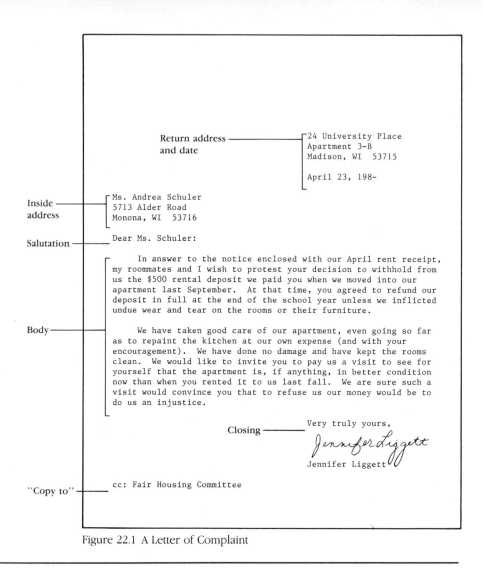

Figure 22.1 A Letter of Complaint

the earnest wish of this agency ...”). Hesitant to speak your own mind, you may render your thoughts obscure.

The solution to this dilemma is threefold: (1) to keep clearly in mind the reason for the letter; (2) to try to size up the recipient of the letter and his or her needs; and (3) to adopt a tone appropriate to the occasion: friendly, but not backslapping; objective, but not cold or haughty. (For more advice on tone, see “A Writer's Tone,” p. 505.) The letter writer who rejected a job applicant with the sentence “Sorry, but we have found someone better qualified than you are” was guilty of taking the wrong tone—cruelly frank—and it is no wonder that the recipient felt crushed and resentful. A better reply might have thanked the applicant for applying, explained that another applicant with more experience had come along, and wished the recipient good fortune on another application. “Too often,” notes a professor of business English, “inexperienced

24 University Place
Apartment 3-B
Madison, WI 53715

Ms. Andrea Schuler

5713 Alder Road

Monona, WI 53716

Figure 22.2 Envelope for a Business Letter

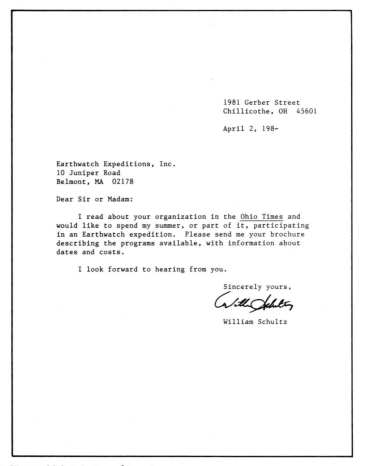

1981 Gerber Street
Chillicothe, OH 45601

April 2, 198-

Earthwatch Expeditions, Inc.
10 Juniper Road
Belmont, MA 02178

Dear Sir or Madam:

I read about your organization in the Ohio Times and
would like to spend my summer, or part of it, participating
in an Earthwatch expedition. Please send me your brochure
describing the programs available, with information about
dates and costs.

I look forward to hearing from you.

Sincerely yours,

William Schultz

Figure 22.3 A Letter of Inquiry

writers in the corporate world equate 'professional' with 'bureaucratic,' forgetting that every good writer—in or out of business—writes as one human being to another."

Formatting a Business Letter

Standard procedure suggests that in writing a business letter you observe these points.

Type your letter single-spaced, on good 8½-by-11-inch bond paper or, if the letter is short, on 5½-by-8½-inch paper.

Type on only one side of the paper.

Skip a line between the return address and the date, the date and the inside address, the inside address and the salutation, the salutation and the body of the letter, and between paragraphs.

Skip two to four lines between the body and the closing, four lines between the closing and the typed signature.

Sign your name above the typed signature.

Letters look best if they are centered on the page, but there is more than one correct format for a business letter. It is not wrong, for instance, to indent your paragraphs, though you will usually find that letters written in large offices contain no such indentations. Some business letter writers line up all parts, including the addresses and salutation, date, and closing, and the signature along the left-hand margin. Others prefer the return address and date, the closing, and the signature closer to the right-hand margin. Let whatever pleases your eye govern your choices concerning such details, unless you're working for a company that prescribes a special form to follow. For your records, keep a carbon copy or photocopy of every business letter you write.

When addressing a woman, unless you are aware that the recipient prefers *Miss* or *Mrs.*, use *Ms.* in your inside address and salutation.

LETTERS OF APPLICATION AND RÉSUMÉS

The most momentous business letter you write in your life may be a letter applying for a job. Start by telling your prospective employer where and how you heard about the position for which you are applying. Don't be shy about setting forth your reasons for wanting the job and your qualifications. You can enlarge on both in the résumé you send along with your letter. Show your willingness to appear for an interview.

It's a good idea to take pains with both letter and résumé. They will enable a busy personnel manager to decide quickly whether or not your application deserves any follow-up. Direct, persuasive, grammatically correct prose can help you stand out above the crowd. (See Figure 22.4.)

"Enc." at the end of Baker's letter alerts her reader to look for an enclosure, the accompanying résumé.

```
                                        Box 1277 Living/Learning
                                        University of Vermont
                                        Burlington, VT  05405

                                        February 4, 198-

        Educational Coordinator
        Programs and Facilities Branch
        Land Between the Lakes, TVA
        Golden Pond, KY  42231

        Dear Sir or Madam:

            I wish to apply for one of the summer internships you offer to college
        students.  I became keenly interested in your internship program after
        reading the Land Between the Lakes brochure on file in the placement office
        at the University of Vermont's School of Natural Resources.  The practical
        experience of working in your campground during June, July, and August would,
        I feel sure, offer excellent preparation for my chosen career in recreation
        management.  At the same time, I believe I could serve your program well by
        bringing to it some skills and experience in working with teenagers and
        young children.

            As a high school student I was a full-time counselor for two summers in
        my hometown's day camp, where I worked first with fifth graders and later
        with seventh and eighth graders who took week-long canoe trips and bicycle
        trips.  Last summer I volunteered as a nature guide at Hale Reservation in
        Westwood, Massachusetts, and within a few weeks began receiving both
        additional duties and pay for my efforts there.

            I am currently a sophomore at the University of Vermont, where I major
        in recreation management.  During the third week in March, I will be in
        Paducah, Kentucky, for a family visit and would be available for an inter-
        view any time during that week.  My telephone number in Vermont is
        (802) 650-3985.

                                        Very truly yours,

                                        Laura Baker

                                        Laura Baker

        Enc.
```

Figure 22.4 A Letter to Apply for a Summer Job

Surely every time you write a letter of application, you'll want to make the thing gleam like a jewel. Probably you'll draft it, ponder it, make any changes, and rewrite it in the smooth. Here are some key questions to ask yourself when you revise.

REVISION CHECKLIST: WRITING A LETTER OF APPLICATION

- Is your letter brief? A long-winded life history will quickly land in the wastebasket. Your purpose in writing is to make the recipient want to interview you. Accordingly your letter need do little more than introduce yourself in a sentence ("I expect to be graduated in June from Clark Community College with a certificate in dental hygiene"), tell what sort of position you're seeking, when you will be available, and when and how you may be contacted for an interview. You need not repeat your qualifications in detail; they appear on your résumé. Keep your letter down to two or three short paragraphs.

451

- Does your letter make clear which job you're applying for? If you're responding to an ad, refer to it. If no job has been advertised, then describe briefly—but not too narrowly—what kind of job you seek: "I can meet people, take phone calls, and keep track of schedules—in short, handle most front-desk office assignments."

- Do you leave yourself open to *other* possible jobs, in case the one you want is filled? Unless you are applying for a very specialized job that has been advertised, one in which you are highly trained, you might be wise not to make your aim too specific at this early stage: "I would be able to train new employees in methods of thread-waxing . . ." Perhaps the recipient has more than one job available. You might occur as a likely prospect for some job quite different from what you have in mind.

- Do you respect yourself? Delete any statement that might seem hangdog: "Although I realize that I have not taken the necessary college courses to qualify me . . . ," "However young and inexperienced I may seem. . . ." Let the employer decide whether you lack the qualifications for the job. Why give him or her reasons to turn you down? Delete any statement such as "Any entry-level job you may have available, however temporary and low-paying . . ." or "I would be happy to work for you in any capacity. . . ." This last leaves the impression that the letter writer would thankfully lick boots. If you're worth hiring, you deserve a decent job.

- Do you sound like yourself? If you don't happen to feel brilliant, you don't need to radiate brilliance—all you are trying to gain is an invitation for an interview. And there's no need to force humor and charm. If jokes fall flat, they will only turn off the recipient's sympathy. Let the facts in your résumé do the charming for you.

- Do you leave the salary open to discussion? Better keep silent on this point. If you ask for too much, you will cut yourself out; if you ask for too little, you will seem to come cheap. If a prospective employer is interested in you, an offer is likely to follow.

- The résumé you enclose with your letter of application lets a prospective employer see at a glance your qualifications for the job. Let it set forth as full a picture of you as possible in one page. Figure 22.5 shows a résumé that, making clear the applicant's professional skills and experience, projects a positive impression.

References are the names of people who know you well and who would respond favorably to your request for a letter of recommendation. Valerie Brunn apparently intends to supply the names of references only to a prospective employer seriously interested in her. There is nothing wrong, though, with listing names, addresses, and phone numbers in your résumé. The recipient may find such a list helpful. If your references are on file in your college placement office, mention this fact in your letter or résumé. Don't forget to obtain permission from the people whose recommendations you seek before you submit their names. This is both common courtesy and wise policy. If you request a recommendation from someone who happens to be less than enthusiastic about you, he or she can refuse to write it or can spell out any reservations to you on the spot rather than in a letter to your prospective employer.

RÉSUMÉ

```
                                    RÉSUMÉ

        Valerie L. Brunn
        21525 Saltair Avenue, #506
        Los Angeles, CA  90025
        (213) 816-3688

        Career Objective    A position in advertising with special interest in
                            new product marketing.

        Education           University of California, Los Angeles
                            B.A., Psychology/Business Administration
                            Expected date of graduation:  April 1987

                            Courses in Business:  Accounting, Principles of
                            Economics, Practical Business Writing, Computer
                            Programming, Statistics

                            Courses in Human Behavior:  Work Behaviors of Women
                            and Men, Human Information Processing, Fundamentals
                            of Learning, Psychology of Gender, Research Methods

        Experience          The Best Service Company
                            Los Angeles, CA
        1/86 to present     Collector.  Responsible for auto lease accounts.
                            Prepare and approve affidavits for lawsuits.  Confer
                            with debtors and attorneys.  Review correspondence
                            and write replies.  Created new form letter that
                            increased debtor response and payments.

        1/85-1/86           Mail Clerk.  Responsible for postal distribution to
                            accounts from more than two dozen banks.  Supervised
                            form letter input/output on word processor.  Ran
                            amortization and interest prime rate charts.
                            Conducted investigations to locate debtors.

        Summer 1984         K-Mart
                            La Verne, CA
                            Cashier.  Developed public relations skills in a
                            fast-paced environment.  Reconciled receipts with
                            sales.

        Computer Skills     Experienced with IBM personal computer and Wordplex
                            word processor.

        Interests           Aerobics, racquetball, and jazz music.

        References          Will be furnished on request.
```

Figure 22.5 A Résumé

Without having done yourself any harm, you will then be free to ask someone else instead.

Brunn further strengthens her résumé by including relevant courses she has taken in college.

MEMORANDA

The *memorandum*, or *memo* for short, is a form of communication used within a company to request or exchange information, to announce meetings or new policies, or to confirm what has passed in conversation. Memoranda tend to be written in the first person *I* or *we*, with headings if they are long, in simple, direct paragraphs if they are short. Be clear; be brief. Assume that your

453

recipients will be busy people wanting a quick but accurate grasp of a single point.

The subject of a memo is always stated in very few words. Make this statement short and exact, and confine your memo to that subject and no other. In writing a memo, keep your probable reader in mind. Obviously, if you are writing a memo to Old Man Barker, the president and chairman of the board, you will keep it formal and respectful; if you address a memo to a fellow worker you know well, friendliness and even a touch of humor may be appropriate.

Sometimes memo sheets come preprinted in a standard form, with spaces to fill in the names of sender and recipient, the date, and the subject under discussion. Usually, instead of signing the memo, the writer simply initials it, in the space after his or her typewritten name. (See Figure 22.6.)

```
                         MEMORANDUM


        TO:   Sarah Uschold, Vice President for Sales
        FROM: James E. Kessler, Sales Representative  J.E.K.
        DATE: May 28, 198-
        SUBJECT: Retailers' Reactions to Our Line of Corkscrews

             As you suggested in our conversation on May 2, I have conducted an
        informal survey among the hardware store owners in my territory about
        our current line of corkscrews.  Their sentiments are best summed up by
        Al Gaulke in Marshfield:  "You have to be a French waiter to get the
        cork out of a bottle of wine with one of these."  He presented me with
        this wing-type corkscrew (sample enclosed) as an example of the one he
        recommends to his customers because it works easily, anyone can use it,
        and it never drops bits of cork into the wine.  I tried it and, you
        know, Al is right!



        Enc.
```

Figure 22.6 A Sample Memorandum

PART SEVEN

Strategies:
A Reference Manual

The following three chapters constitute a manual offering special advice on strategies. The word strategy *may remind you of warfare: in the original Greek sense of the word, it is a way to win a battle. Writing a college paper, you'll probably agree, is a battle of a kind. In this manual you'll find an array of small weapons you may want to use—and perhaps some heavy artillery.*

Here are techniques you can learn, methods you can follow, good practices you can observe in writing more effectively. Earlier in this book, you saw many of these strategies briefly mentioned. At moments when we didn't want to slow you down by explaining them in detail, we gave them a mere passing glance. These techniques and practices can assist you in many different writing tasks. We would now like to give them the discussion they deserve.

To help you locate what you're looking for, this manual classifies the strategies according to the three familiar phases of the writing process that we trace in earlier chapters:

Generating ideas
Shaping a draft
Rewriting

We have placed each strategy where we think you'll find it useful, but don't feel bound by the arrangement we have made. As you know, stages of writing can overlap. Sometimes as you write you backtrack, or you leap forward. In the middle of rewriting you sometimes need more material, and go back to generating ideas.

No strategy will appeal to every writer. Outlining is a strategy that has rescued many a writer from getting lost, but we know writers who never outline except to make (sometimes) the roughest of lists.

You won't need to read this manual all the way through. It is meant only to refer to when you need it. If you care to browse in it, we trust you'll find reward—especially if you try out some of these strategies.

CHAPTER 23

Strategies for Generating Ideas

First, here are two useful techniques for starting ideas flowing and recalling information: brainstorming and freewriting. Then comes advice on the valuable habit of journal keeping, a great way to insure a constant supply of ideas. Last in this chapter, "Asking a Reporter's Questions" and "Seeking Motives" suggest ways to probe deeply into events, phenomena, and human acts.

BRAINSTORMING

When you brainstorm, you start with a word or phrase that might launch your thoughts in some direction. For a set length of time, putting the conscious, analytical part of your mind on hold, you scribble a list of ideas as rapidly as possible. Then you look over the often surprising results.

For a college writing assignment, you might brainstorm to find a specific topic for a paper. If at any time in writing you need to generate some needed piece of material such as an illustration or example, you can brainstorm. If you have already written a paper, you can brainstorm to come up with a title for it.

Brainstorming can be a group activity. In the business world, brainstorming sessions are common strategies to fill a specific need: a name for a product, a corporate emblem, a slogan for an advertising campaign. Members of a group sit facing one another. They designate one person as the recording secretary to take down on paper or a blackboard whatever suggestions the others offer. If the suggestions fly too thick and fast, the secretary jots down the best one in the air at that moment. For several minutes, people call out ideas. Then they look over the secretary's list in hopes of finding useful results.

You can try group brainstorming like that with a few other students. But you may find brainstorming also useful when, all by yourself, you need to shake an idea out of your unconscious. Here is how one student did just that. On the opening day of a writing course, Martha Calbick's instructor assigned a paper from recall: "Demonstrate that the invention of the computer has significantly changed our lives." Following the instructor's advice, Calbick went home and brainstormed. First, she wrote the key word *computer* at the top of a sheet of paper. Then she set her alarm clock to sound in fifteen minutes and began to scribble away. The first thing she recalled was how her kid brother sits by the hour in front of a home computer playing Wizardry, a Dungeons and Dragons kind of game. This first recollection quickly led, by free association, to several more.

> Wizardry
> my kid bro. thinks computers are for kids
> always trading games with other kids—software pirates
> Mother says it's too bad kids don't play Wiffle Ball anymore
> in 3rd grade they teach programming
> hackers
> some get rich
> Ed's brother-in-law—wrote a program for accountants
> become a programmer? big future?
> guided missiles
> computers in subway stations—print tickets
> banks—shove in your plastic card
> a man lucked out—deposited $100—computer credited him with $10,000
> sort mail—zip codes
> computers print out grades
> my report card showed a D instead of a B—big fight to correct it
> are we just numbers now?

When her alarm clock rang, Calbick dropped her pencil and took a coffee break. When she returned to her desk, she was pleased to find that a few of her random thoughts suggested directions that interested her. Much of the list she immediately discarded, going through it with a pencil and crossing out most entries. She didn't have any interest in Wizardry, and she didn't feel she knew enough to write about missiles. She circled the question "are we just numbers now?" Maybe some of the other ideas she had listed might express that very idea, such as the mindlessness of the computer that had credited the man with $10,000. As she looked over the list, she began jotting down more thoughts, making notes on the list and adding to it. "Dealing with computers isn't dealing with people," she wrote next to the circled question. From her rough-and-ready list, an idea was beginning to emerge.

Calbick was later to write a whole paper on the simple computer error in her high school office that had momentarily robbed her of a good grade. She recalled how time-consuming it had been to have that error corrected. She mentioned a few other cases of computer error, including that of the man who had struck it rich at the bank. Her conclusion was a wry complaint about computerized society: "A computer knows your name and number, but it doesn't know who you are."

You can see how brainstorming typically works and how it started one student going. Whenever you try brainstorming, you might follow these bits of advice.

1. Start with a key word or phrase—one that will head your thoughts in the direction you wish to pursue.

2. Set yourself a time limit. Fifteen or twenty minutes is long enough—brainstorming can be strenuous.

3. Write rapidly. List any other words, any thoughts, phrases, fragments, or short sentences that surface in connection with your key word. Keep your entries brief.

4. While you're brainstorming, don't worry about misspelling, repetition, absurdity, or irrelevance. Write down whatever comes into your head, as fast as your pencil will go. Now is not the time to analyze or to throw any suggestion away. Let your unconscious run free. Never mind if it comes up with ideas that seem crazy or far out. Don't judge, don't arrange—just produce. If your mind goes blank, keep your pencil moving, even if you are only repeating what you've just written.

When you finish, look over your list to see what may be interesting. Circle or check anything you want to think about further. If anything looks useless, scratch it out.

Look over your edited list. You can now do some conscious organizing. Do any of the thoughts you have generated link together? Can you group them? If so, maybe they will suggest a topic. If you succeed in finding a topic from your brainstorming session, you might then wish to try another technique—*freewriting* (the next strategy we discuss).

If you are writing and you need an example, some specific thing, you can brainstorm at any time. In writing her paper on computers Martha Calbick couldn't think of a name for a typical computer store. She wrote down some real names she knew (Computer World, Computerland, OnLine Computers Plus), and those triggered a few imaginary ones. Within three minutes, she hit on one she liked: Byte City.

Whether you brainstorm at your writing desk or in a lounge with a group of friends, you will find this strategy calling up a rich array of thoughts from knowledge and memory. Try it and see.

FREEWRITING

Like brainstorming, freewriting is a way to fight writer's block by tapping your unconscious. To freewrite, you simply begin writing in the hope that good ideas will assert themselves. You write without stopping for fifteen or twenty minutes, trying to keep words pouring forth in a steady flow. Freewriting differs from brainstorming: in freewriting you write not a list but a series of sentences. They don't have to be grammatical or coherent or stylish sentences; just let them leap to paper and keep them flowing along. When you have just the beginning of an idea, freewriting can help open it up and show you what it contains. When you have an assignment that looks difficult, freewriting can get you under way.

Generally, freewriting is most productive if it has an aim. You have in mind—at least roughly—some topic, a purpose, or a question you want answered. Before you begin, you write a sentence or two summing up the idea you're starting out with. Martha Calbick, who found a topic by brainstorming (p. 457), headed the page on which she freewrote with the topic she had decided to pursue: "How life in the computer age seems impersonal." Then, exploring some of the rough ideas she had jotted down in her brainstorming session, she let words flow rapidly.

> Computers—so how do they make life impersonal? There's something impersonal about the screen of a monitor. You look at it in the bank when you push in your plastic card and try to get some cash. Just a glassy screen. Like TV, which tends to become smudged with fingerprints and needs a wipe every now and then. That's different—not like looking at a human teller behind a window. But somehow when you put in your plastic card and the computer tells you you have no money left in your account, that's terrible, frightening. Worse than when a person won't cash your check. At least the person looks you in the face, maybe even gives you a faint smile. Computers make mistakes, don't they? Sometimes people get lucky. That story in the paper about a man—in Utica, was it? I can't remember—who deposited a hundred dollars to his account and the computer misplaced a decimal point and said he had put in $10,000. But the error turned up when people at the bank found a shortage. So what did the bank people do? Guess they went over the printouts. Probably called him and told him about the mistake. What if he had gone out and made a down payment on a new car! Could be embarrassing. Not a good idea to go on a spending spree if a computer did that to you.

The result, as you can see, wasn't polished prose. It was full of false starts down distracting alleys ("Like TV, which tends to become smudged with fingerprints") and little asides to herself ("in Utica, was it? I can't remember") that she later crossed out. Still, in twenty minutes she produced a rough draft that served (with much rewriting) as the basis for her finished essay.

If you want to try freewriting for yourself, here's what you do.

1. Write a sentence or two at the top of your page: the idea you plan to develop by freewriting.

2. For at least ten minutes, write steadily without stopping. Start by expressing whatever comes to mind, even if it is only "I don't want to write a paper because I have nothing at all to say about any subject in the universe." If your mind goes blank, write, "My mind is a blank, I have nothing to say, I don't know where to go next," and keep at it until some new thought floats into view.

3. Don't stop to cross out false starts, misspellings, or grammatical errors. Never mind if your ideas have gaps between them. Later, when you look them over, some of the gaps may close. If you can't think of the word that perfectly expresses your meaning, put in a substitute. At least it will keep your pencil moving.

4. That sentence (or those sentences) you started with can serve as a rough guide, but they shouldn't be a straitjacket. If as you write you stray from your original idea, that change in direction may possibly be valuable. Sometimes, you may discover a more promising idea.

Some writers prepare for freewriting. They find it pays to spend a few prior minutes in thought. While you wait for the moment when your pencil is to start racing, some of these questions may be worth asking yourself.

What interests you about this topic? What aspects of it do you most care about?

What does this topic have to do with you?

What do you recall about it from your own experience? What do you know about it that the next person doesn't?

What have you read about it?

What have you observed about it for yourself?

Have you ever talked with anyone about it? If you have, what did you find out?

How might you feel about this topic if you were someone else? (You might try thinking about it from the imagined point of view of a friend, a parent, an instructor, a person of the opposite sex, a person from another country.)

At the very least, your freewriting session may give you something to rewrite and make stronger. You can prod and poke at the parts that look most interesting to see if they will further unfold. In expanding and developing what you have produced by freewriting, here are a few questions you might ask.

What do you mean by that?

What interests you in that idea?

If that is true, what then?

What other examples or evidence does this statement call to mind?

What objections might your reader raise to this?

How might you answer them?

KEEPING A JOURNAL

If you are already in the habit of keeping a journal, consider yourself lucky. If not, now is a good time to begin. Journal writing offers rich rewards to anyone who engages in it every day or several times a week. All you need is a notebook, a writing implement, and a few minutes for each entry; and you can write anywhere. There are students whose observations, jotted down during a bus ride, turned into remarkable journal entries. Not only is journal writing satisfying in itself, a journal can also be a storehouse of material to write about.

What do you write? The main thing to remember is that a journal is not a diary. When you make a journal entry, the emphasis is less on recording what happened than on *reflecting* about what you do or see, hear or read, learn or believe. A journal is a record of your thoughts, for an audience of one: yourself.

In a journal you can plan your life, try out ideas, vent fears and frustrations. The following passage is from the journal of the poet Sylvia Plath, written in the early 1950s when she was a college freshman. Uncommonly sensitive and colorful, her journal exhibits the freedom and frankness of a writer who was writing for only her own eyes. In this entry she contrasts the happy fantasy world she inhabited as a child with the harsher realities of college life.

> After being conditioned as a child to the lovely never-never land of magic, of fairy queens and virginal maidens, of little princes and their rosebushes, of poignant bears and Eeyore-ish donkeys, of life personalized as the pagans loved it, of the magic wand, and the faultless illustrations—the beautiful dark-haired child (who was you) winging through the midnight sky on a star-path . . . of the Hobbit and the dwarves, gold-belted with blue and purple hoods, drinking ale and singing of dragons in the caverns of the valley— all this I knew, and felt, and believed. All this was my life when I was young. To go from this to the world of grown-up reality. . . . To feel the sex organs develop and call loud to the flesh; to become aware of school, exams (the very words as unlovely as the sound of chalk shrilling on the blackboard), bread and butter, marriage, sex, compatibility, war, economics, death, and self. What a pathetic blighting of the beauty and reality of childhood. Not to be sentimental, as I sound, but why the hell are we conditioned into the smoothstrawberry-and-cream Mother Goose world, Alice-in-Wonderland fable, only to be broken on the wheel as we grow older and become aware of ourselves as individuals with a dull responsibility in life? To learn snide and smutty meanings of words you once loved, like "fairy." To go to college fraternity parties where a boy buries his face in your neck or tries to rape you if he isn't satisfied with burying his fingers in the flesh of your breast. To learn that there are a million girls who are beautiful and that each day more leave behind the awkward teenage stage, as you once did, and embark on the adventure of being loved. . . . To be aware that you must compete somehow, and yet that wealth and beauty are not in your realm.

Like Plath, to write a valuable journal you need only the honesty and the willingness to set down what you *genuinely think and feel*. When you first face that blank journal page, plunge boldly into your task by writing down whatever observation or reaction comes to mind, in any order you like. No one will criticize your spelling or punctuation, the way you organize or the way you express yourself. A journal entry can be a list or an outline, a paragraph or a full-blown essay.

To know what to put into your journal, you have only to *un*cover, *re*cover, *dis*cover what is happening both inside and outside your head. Describe a person or a place. As accurately as you can, set down a conversation you have heard, complete with slang or dialect or colloquialisms. Record any insights you have gained into your actions or those of others. Make comparisons. Respond to something you have read or to something mentioned in a class. Do you agree with it? Disagree? Why? What was wrong with the last movie or television show you watched? What was good about it? Have you or has someone you know faced a moral dilemma? Was it resolved? If so, how?

Perhaps you have some pet peeves. List them. What do you treasure? Have you had an interesting dream or daydream? What would the world be like if you were in charge? What are your religious convictions? What do you think about the current political scene or about this nation's priorities? Have you visited any foreign countries? Did you learn anything of worth from your travels?

On days when your mind is sluggish, when you can come up with no observations or insights to record, do a stint of freewriting or of brainstorming in your journal, or just describe a scene, an object, or a person present before you. Any of those activities may result in at least a few good thoughts to follow up in future entries.

One further benefit rewards the faithful journal keeper. Well done, a journal is a mine studded with priceless nuggets: thoughts and observations, reactions and revelations that are yours for the taking. When you have an essay to write, chances are you will find that a well-stocked journal is a treasure indeed. Rifle it freely—not only for writing topics, but for insights and material. It can make your writing assignments far easier to fulfill. "This book is my savings bank," wrote Ralph Waldo Emerson in his journal. "I grow richer because I have somewhere to deposit my earnings; and fractions are worth more to me because corresponding fractions are waiting here that shall be made integers by their addition." Emerson refers to his personal writing process. In many of his lectures and essays, he would combine thoughts that had begun as disconnected entries. From the savings bank of his journal, the nineteenth-century Yankee philosopher made heavy withdrawals.

Your journal can also be used for the warm-up writing you do when you start collecting your thoughts in preparation for any assignment, whether short or long. In it you can freewrite, brainstorm, group ideas, scribble outlines, sketch beginnings, capture stray thoughts, record relevant material from any one of the writer's five resources (recalling, observing, reading, conversing, imagining) that bear on your assignment.

A journal can be a catch-all or miscellany, like Emerson's, or it can be a focused, directed thing. Some instructors assign students to keep journals of their readings in a certain discipline. Faced with a long paper to write, and weeks or months to do it in, you might wish to assign *yourself* to keep a specialized journal. If, say, you were going to write a survey of current economic theories or an account of the bird life of your locality, you might keep a journal of economists whose work you read or the birds you are able to observe. Then, when the time comes to write your paper, you will have plenty of material to quarry.

ASKING A REPORTER'S QUESTIONS

News reporters, assembling facts with which to write the story of a news event, ask themselves six simple questions, the five W's—

Who?
What?
Where?
When?
Why?

—and an *H:* How? In the *lead,* or opening (and most important) paragraph of a good news story, where the writer tries to condense the whole story into a sentence, you will find simple answers to all six questions:

The ascent of a giant homemade fire balloon (*what*) startled residents of
   Costa Mesa (*where*)
last night (*when*)
as Ambrose Barker, 79, (*who*)
in an attempt to set a new altitude record, (*why*)
zigzagged across the sky at a speed of nearly 300 miles per hour (*how*).

Such answers don't go deep. In a few words, they give only the bare bones of the story. If readers want to learn more, they keep reading. But they enable the writer to seize all the essentials of the story and give them to us in brief.

Later in a news story, the reporter will tell us in greater detail what happened. He or she can dig and probe and make the story more interesting. With a little thought on the reporter's part, the six basic questions can lead to further questions, generating more to write about than space will allow.

WHO is Ambrose Barker, anyway? (An amateur balloonist? A jack-of-all-trades? A retired professional aeronautical engineer?) Is he a major figure in balloonist circles? (Call a professional balloonist and ask, "Who is this Ambrose Barker? Ever hear of him?") What kind of person is he: a serious student of ballooning or a reckless nitwit? What do his neighbors and his family think of him? (Interview them.) What words spoken by Barker himself will show the kind of person he is? Is he proud of his flight? Humble? Disappointed? Determined to try again? What was his mental state at the moment he took off? (Elated and determined? Crazed? Inebriated?)

WHAT happened, exactly? Was Barker, or anyone else, hurt? What did his craft look like from close up? (How big was it? Any distinguishing features?)

What did it look like to a spectator on the ground? (Did it resemble a shooting star? A glowing speck? Did it light up the whole sky?) Did Barker's flight terrify anybody? Did the police receive any phone calls? Did the nearest observatory? What has happened since the flight? (Will anyone sue Barker for endangering life and property? Will the police press charges against him? Has he received any threats, any offers to endorse products?)

WHERE did Barker take off from? (A ballfield? A parking lot? His back yard? What is his exact street address?) From where to where did he fly? Where did he land? Where did the onlookers live? In what neighborhoods? How far off was the most distant observer who sighted Barker's balloon? (Was it visible, say, from forty miles?)

WHEN, by the clock, did the flight take place? (What time did Barker take off? How long was he aloft? Exactly when did he touch down again?) Was the choice of evening for the flight deliberate? (Barker could have gone up in the daytime. Did he want to fly by night to be more noticeable?) Did he deliberately choose this particular time of year? When did Barker first conceive his plan to tour Costa Mesa in a fire balloon? (Just the other day? Or has he been planning his trip for thirty years?)

WHY did Barker want to set a record? What impelled him? What reasons did he give? (And might he have had any reasons other than the ones he gave?) Why did he wait till he was 79 to take off? Was making such a flight a lifelong dream? Did he feel the need to soar above the crowd? Did he want his neighbors to stop laughing at him ("That thing will never get off the ground...")? Why did his balloon zigzag around the sky, not sail in a straight line? Why were spectators terrified (if they were)?

HOW did Barker make his odd craft airborne? What propelled it into the sky? (A bonfire? Jet fuel? Gunpowder?) Did he take off without aid, or did his wife or a friend assist? How did he construct the balloon: where did he get the parts? Did he make the whole thing with his own two hands or have help? How did he steer the craft? How did he land it? Was the landing smooth or did he come down in a heap? How was he greeted when he arrived?

Your topic in a college writing task may be less spectacular than a fire balloon ascent: a team winning or losing a pennant, an experience of your own, an ancestor's arrival in America. It might be what happened at some moment in history (the firing on Fort Sumter at the start of the Civil War) or in social history (the rise of rock music). The six basic questions will work in discovering how to write about all sorts of events and phenomena; and, given thought, your six basic questions can lead to many more.

Don't worry if some of the questions lead nowhere. Just try answering any that look promising: jot down any thoughts and information that come to you. At first, you can record these unselectively. You are just trying to gather a big bunch of ideas and material. Later, before you start to write, you'll want to weed out the bunch and keep only those buds that look as though they might just open wide.

SEEKING MOTIVES

In a surprisingly large part of your college writing, you try to explain human behavior. In a paper for history, you might show why Lyndon Baines Johnson decided not to seek a second full term as president. In a report for a psychology course, you might try to explain the behavior of people in an experimental situation. In a literature course, writing of Nathaniel Hawthorne's *The Scarlet Letter*, you might analyze the motives of Hester Prynne: why does she conceal the name of her illegitimate child's father? Because people, including characters in fiction, are so complex, this task is challenging. But here is a strategy useful in seeking out human motives.

If you want to better understand any human act, according to philosopher-critic Kenneth Burke, you can analyze its components. To do so, you ask five questions. (To produce useful answers, your subject has to be an act performed for a reason, not a mere automatic reaction like a sneeze.)

What was done?

Who did it?

What means did the person use to make it happen?

Where and when did it happen and in what circumstances?

What possible purpose or motive can you attribute to the person?

Answering those questions starts a writer generating ideas. Burke names the five components as follows.

1. The *act.*
2. The *actor:* the person who acted.
3. The *agency:* the means or instrument the actor used to make the act happen. (If the act is an insult, the agency might be words or a slap in the face; if it is murder, the agency might be a sawed-off shotgun.)
4. The *scene:* where the act took place, when, and in what circumstances.
5. The *purpose:* the motive for acting.

As you can see, Burke's *pentad*, or set of five categories, covers much the same ground as the news reporter's five *W*'s and an *H*. But Burke's method differs in that it can show how these components of a human act affect one another. This line of thought can take you deeper into the motives for human behavior than most reporters' investigations ever go.

How might the method be applied? Say you are writing a paper to explain your own reasons for taking some action. Burke's list of the components of an act may come in handy. But let's take, for example, the topic "Why I Enrolled in Prelaw Courses." You might analyze it like this:

1. The *act* is your decision.
2. The *actor*—that's you.
3. The *agency* is your enrolling in college and beginning a program of study.

4. The *scene* is your home last spring (where the circumstances might have included many earnest, knock-down, drag-out discussions with your family on the subject of what you should study in college).

5. The *purpose* is at least twofold: to make comfortable money and to enter a career you expect to find satisfying.

What happens when you start thinking about what each of these factors had to do with any other? What if you ask, say, "How did the *scene* of my decision influence the *actor* (me)?"

You may then recall that your father, who always wanted to be a racing car driver himself, tried to talk you out of your decision and urged you to hang around racetracks instead. In arguing with him you were forced to defend your notion of studying law. You came to see that, yes, by George, being a lawyer would be a great life for you. Maybe your brother was on the scene, too, and he said, "Why don't you go to law school? You always were a hard-liner in arguments." Maybe that was a factor in your decision. You can pursue this line of thought. Then maybe you can try making another link: between scene and purpose. Ask, "How did my home motivate me?" Maybe then you realize that your brother gave you a real purpose: to show the world how well you can argue. Maybe you realize that your decision to go to law school was a way to prove to your father that you don't need to be a racing car driver—you can make good in a different career.

This example, to be sure, may not fit you personally. Perhaps you don't live with a father or a brother, and you can't stand the thought of studying law. But the point is that you can begin all sorts of fruitful lines of inquiry simply by asking questions that team up these components. Following Burke's method, you can pair them in ten ways:

actor to act	act to scene	scene to agency
actor to scene	act to agency	scene to purpose
actor to agency	act to purpose	agency to purpose
actor to purpose		

If you wish to understand this strategy, try writing one question for each pair; for example, for the first pair, "What does the actor have to do with the scene?" If you were writing about your move to study law, this question might be put: "Before I made my move, what connection existed, if any, between me and this college?" Try to answer that question and you may sense ideas beginning to percolate. "Why," you might say, "I came here because I know a good lawyer who graduated from the place." You'll get a head start on your writing assignment if, while trying to answer the questions, you take notes.

The questions will serve equally well for analyzing someone else's motives. If you were trying to explain, for a history course, why President Johnson chose not to run again, the five elements might perhaps be these.

Act: Announcing the decision to leave office without standing for reelection.

Actor: President Johnson.

Agency: A televised address to the nation.

Scene (including circumstances at the time): Washington, D.C., March 31, 1968. Protesters against the nation's involvement in Vietnam were gaining in numbers and influence. The press was increasing its criticism of the president's escalation of the war. Senator Eugene McCarthy, an antiwar candidate for president, had made a strong showing against Johnson in the New Hampshire primary election.

Purpose: Think of any *possible* purposes: to avoid a probable political defeat, to escape further personal attacks, to spare his family, to make it easier for his successor to pull the country out of the war, to ease bitter dissent among Americans.

If you started asking questions such as "What did the actor have to do with the agency?" you might come up with an answer like "Johnson apparently enjoyed facing the nation on television. Commanding the attention of a vast audience, he must have felt he was in control—even though his ability to control the situation in Vietnam was slipping."

Do you see the possibilities? The value of Burke's questions is that they can start you writing. Not all the questions will prove fruitful, and some may not even apply. But one or two might reveal valuable answers. Try them and see.

CHAPTER 24

Strategies for Shaping a Draft

Starting to write often seems a chaotic activity, but when you shape a draft, you try to reduce the chaos and create order. In doing so, you can use the strategies in this chapter.

Sometimes, especially when writing a persuasive paper or a research paper, you can shape your draft around one central point (see "Stating a Thesis"). In nearly any kind of writing task, you can also organize your thoughts by various strategies (see "Grouping Your Ideas" and "Outlining"). You can develop good, meaty, well-unified paragraphs, trying for an opening that will enlist your readers' attention and a conclusion that will satisfy them. You can supply clear, pointed examples. (All these matters will be dealt with under "Paragraphing.") Another way to give an example will be briefly discussed in "Telling a Story." Finally, in "Growing a Metaphor," we suggest one more strategy to lend your writing color, concreteness, and life.

STATING A THESIS

Many pieces of effective writing make one main point. In "What Is a Hunter?" (p. 54), Robert G. Schreiner maintains that anyone who knows no more than how to fire a rifle makes a cruel and stupid hunter. In "Coffin of the Dinosaurs" (p. 204), Nigel Calder sets forth what he believes to be the most likely explanation for the dinosaurs' sudden extinction. In "The First Person" (p. 242) Suzanne Britt advances the view that writers may use the pronoun *I* without apology. After you have read such an essay, you could sum up its writer's main point in a sentence or (if the idea is large and complicated) in two or three sentences. You might call your summary a *thesis statement*.

Often a thesis—the writer's main point—will be plainly stated in the piece of writing itself. In her defense of the first person, Britt clearly spells out her thesis in her opening paragraph:

> The admonition against "I" is absurd and will, I hope, come to an end in the waning decades of the twentieth century.

Such a thesis statement, which often comes at the beginning or at the end of an essay, helps the reader see the main point unmistakably. In some writing, though, a thesis may simply be implied. Nowhere in David Quammen's "A Republic of Cockroaches" (p. 88) will you find it said that, in order to survive, the human race must avert nuclear holocaust. But Quammen's whole essay, in demonstrating that cockroaches could inherit the earth, makes the main point painfully evident. You too can imply rather than state your main point in what you write. If you can keep your main idea clearly posted on the bulletin board of your mind, you need not set it down, even for yourself.

At some moment in the writing process, though, many writers find it helpful to jot down a thesis statement. The statement may help them clarify a main idea in their own minds. It may help guide them as they write by reminding them of the point they're driving at. Sometimes, before even setting a word on paper, writers know what main point they intend to make. Such writers feel reassured to know where they are going; for them, as we suggest on page 29, to state a thesis may be a good way to break the ice and start words flowing. Other writers will not know their main point until they write. For them, writing is in part an act of discovering a thesis.

Often, during the interplay of a writer's mind, the English language, and a piece of paper, an insight will appear. If this discovery occurs to you, you might wish—at that moment when in the midst of your work your thesis becomes clear to you—to set it down in a statement, even post i. over your desk as a friendly reminder. Then it won't get away; and when you finish your draft, the thesis statement will make it easier for you to evaluate what you have written. As you revise, you can reconsider your thesis statement and ask yourself, "Have I made that main point clear?"

Not all writing tasks call for a thesis statement. You may not need one in recalling, say, a memorable personal experience. In telling an entertaining story, writing a letter to a friend, reviewing a book, analyzing a process into its stages, you are not necessarily driving toward a single point. In writing "If I Could Found a College" (p. 130), Jennifer Bowe has no thesis; she simply describes her imagined ideal.

But stating a thesis will often be a useful strategy in explaining and arguing. A thesis statement can help you stay on track and, incorporated into your essay, can help your reader readily see your point. Most writers of research papers find that they can clearly organize their thoughts and their material if they state a thesis (at least to themselves) just as soon as they can decide what their research demonstrates.

Often a good, clear, ample statement of thesis will suggest to you an organization for your ideas. Say you plan to write a paper from the thesis "Despite the several disadvantages of living in a downtown business district, I wouldn't live anywhere else." That thesis statement suggests how to organize an essay. You might start with several paragraphs, each discussing a disadvantage of living in the business district, and then move on to a few paragraphs that discuss advantages. Then close with an affirmation of your fondness for downtown city life.

How do you arrive at a thesis? You have heard a similar question before, worded differently: How do you discover what you want to say? We are back to the age-old problem of college writers that Part Two of this book tries to resolve. In every writer's resources—recalling, observing, conversing, reading, and imagining—you can find ideas, including likely main ideas for papers. We have traced the variable, not entirely predictable ways in which you can turn a rough idea into a draft and on into finished writing (in Chapters 4 through 8). For specific techniques to start ideas flowing, you'll find more suggestions in Chapter 23, "Strategies for Generating Ideas."

If you decide to write on the topic "The decline of old-fashioned formal courtesy toward women," you indicate the area to be explored. Still, that topic doesn't really tell you the main point of your paper. What will you try to do in your paper, anyhow? Will you perhaps affirm something, or deny, or recommend? If you stick with that topic about old-fashioned formal courtesy— how women don't need coats or chairs held for them anymore—then (at some point in your writing) you might state a thesis like this: "The new, less formal manners make men respect women more." Or "The new, less formal manners make women respect themselves more because they no longer need to pretend to be helpless." Or (taking a personal view) "I miss the old formal courtesy."

If, to change topics, you plan to describe an old hotel, what possible point will you demonstrate? If you have one already in mind when you start to write, perhaps a thesis sentence might read: "I love the old Raccoon Racket Club: it's quaint and funny, even if it is falling apart, as my description will show." If you are going to compare and contrast two things—for instance, two local newspapers in their coverage of a Senate election—what is the point of that comparison and contrast? One possible thesis statement might be "The *Herald*'s coverage of the Senate elections was more thorough than the *Courier*'s."

As you write, you don't have to cling to a thesis for dear life. Neither must you force every fact to support your thesis, if some facts are reluctant to. You might want to change your thesis while you write. A thesis statement can be tentative. Just to put your *trial* thesis into words can help you to stake out the territory you need to know better. Before you look up more information about wolves, you might guess that you're probably going to maintain the thesis "Wolves are a menace to people and farm animals and ought to be exterminated." Suppose, though, that further reading and conversation don't support that statement at all. Suppose what you learn contradicts it. Your thesis statement isn't chiseled in marble. You can change it to "The wolf, a relatively peace-abiding animal useful in nature's scheme of things, ought to be protected and encouraged to multiply." That's what a thesis is for: to guide you on a quest, not to steer you on a foolish and unheeding march to doom. You can restate it at any time: as you write, as you rewrite, as you rewrite again.

As Suzanne Britt's "The First Person" demonstrates, if you insert your thesis statement into your paper it will alert your reader to your main idea. Perhaps you will want to state your thesis in your opening sentence: "Computers are the greatest help for bashful lovers since Cupid first shot darts." Or you might want to place this main idea at the very end: "As we have seen, without computer networks, which have proven to be a tremendous boon to shy intellectuals, some poor hackers would probably never find their soulmates at all."

Here are four suggestions for writing a workable thesis statement.

1. *State it exactly* in as detailed and down-to-earth a way as you can. The thesis statement "There are a lot of troubles with chemical wastes" is too huge and general. Are you going to deal with all chemical wastes, through all of history, all over the world? Make the statement more specific: "Careless dumping of leftover paint is to blame for a recent skin rash in Georgia."

2. *State just one central idea.* This proposed thesis sentence has one idea too many: "Careless dumping of leftover paint has caused a serious problem in Georgia, and a new kind of biodegradable paint now looks promising." Either the first half (before the *and*) or the second half of the statement would suffice.

3. *State your thesis positively.* Write "The causes of breast cancer remain a challenge for medical scientists" instead of "Medical scientists do not know what causes breast cancer." The former statement might lead to a paper about an exciting quest. But the latter statement seems to reflect a halfhearted attitude by the writer toward the subject. Besides, to demonstrate that some medical scientists are still working on the problem would be relatively easy: you could show that after an hour doing research in a library. To prove the negative statement, that no medical scientist knows the answer, would be a harder task.

4. *Limit your thesis statement to what it is possible to demonstrate.* A thesis statement should stake out enough territory for you to cover thoroughly inside the assigned word length, and no more. To maintain throughout a 700-word paper the thesis "My favorite tune is 'Manic Monday' by the Bangles" would be a difficult task unless you could go into voluminous (and interesting) detail. "For centuries, popular music has been indicative of vital trends in Western society" wouldn't do for a 700-word paper either: that thesis would be large enough to inform a whole encyclopedia of music in twelve volumes. "In the past two years, a rise in the number of pre-teenagers has resulted in a comeback for heavy metal on our local concert scene"—now, that idea sounds much more likely.

To take a few more examples of thesis statements:

"Indian blankets are very beautiful." That statement seems too vague and hard to demonstrate for a usual college writing assignment of 400 to 1000 words.

"American Indians have adapted to modern civilization." That sounds too large, unless you plan to write a 5000-word term paper in sociology.

"Members of the Apache tribe have become celebrated as skilled workers in high-rise construction." All right; you could probably find support for that thesis by spending two hours doing research in a library.

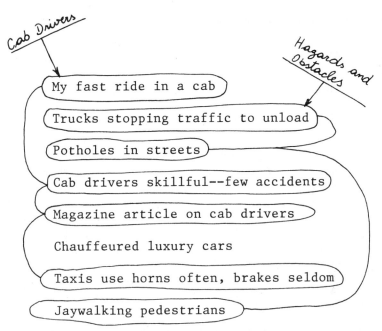

Figure 24.1 The Linking Method for Grouping Ideas

GROUPING YOUR IDEAS

In any bale of scribblings you have made while exploring a topic, you will usually find a few ideas that seem to belong together. They make the same point ("Just what I need," you think, "*two* examples of how New Yorkers drive"). They might follow one another ("Here are facts on the frequency of New York traffic jams—from this, I can go to the point that New York drivers are frustrated").

As you look over these preliminary notes, you'll want to indicate to yourself any connections you find between your materials. You'll need to sort your notes into groups, arrange them in sequences. Here are six common ways to work.

1. *Rainbow connections.* Some writers list on a sheet of paper all the main points they're going to express. (They don't recopy all their material—they just list each main point briefly.) Then, taking colored pencils, they circle with the same color any points that seem to go together. When they write, they can follow the color code and deal with similar ideas at the same time.

2. *Linking.* Other writers, though they work in black and white, also start by making a list of major points. They draw lines that link similar ideas. Then they number each linked group, to remember in what sequence to deal with it. Figure 24.1 is an illustration of a linked list. This particular list was produced in a one-person brainstorming session. It is nothing but a brief jotting-down of points the writer wants to make in an essay to be called "Manhattan Driving." The writer has drawn lines between points that seem to go together. He has

numbered each linked group in the order he plans to follow when writing and has supplied each with an outline heading. When he writes his draft, each heading will probably inspire a topic sentence or a few lines to introduce each major division of his essay. One point failed to relate to any other: "Chauffeured luxury cars." In the finished paper, it probably will be left out. This rough plan, if expanded three or four times, would make a workable outline for a short paper. It sifts out useless material; it arranges what remains.

3. *Solitaire.* Some writers, especially scholars, collect notes and ideas on roomy (5-by-7-inch) file cards. When they organize, they spread out the cards and arrange them in an order, as in a game of solitaire. When the order looks worth keeping, when each idea seems to lead to the next, they gather all the cards into a deck once more and wrap a rubber band around them. Then when they write, they deal themselves a card at a time and translate its contents into readable writing.

4. *Scissors and tape.* Other writers swear by scissors and Scotch tape. They lay out their rough notes before them. Then they group any notes that refer to the same point and that probably belong in the same vicinity. With scissors, they separate items that don't belong together. They shuffle the pieces around, trying for the most promising order. After throwing out any ideas that don't belong anywhere, they lock up the material into a structure. They join all the parts with tape. They may find places in the grand design where ideas and information are lacking. If so, they make a note of what's missing and tape that note into place. Although this taped-together construction of cards or slips of paper may look sloppy, it can serve as a workable outline to follow.

Some writers use this strategy not merely for planning, but for planning and drafting simultaneously. They tape together not just notes, but passages they have written separately. If you follow this method, you write whatever part you want to write first, then write the next most tempting part, and so on until you have enough rough stuff to arrange into a whole piece of writing. You'll need to add missing parts and to supply transitions (discussed on p. 486).

5. *Clustering.* In clustering, you take a piece of paper and in the middle of it write your topic in one or a few words. Put a circle around the topic. Then think of the major divisions into which this topic might be sliced. For an essay "Manhattan Drivers," the major divisions might be (1) taxi drivers, (2) bus drivers, (3) truck drivers, (4) drivers of private cars—New Yorkers, and (5) drivers of private cars—out-of-town visitors. Write these divisions on your page, clustering them around your topic, and circle them, too. You now have the beginning of a rough plan for an essay.

Now, around each division, make another cluster of points you're going to include: examples, illustrations, facts, statistics, bits of evidence, opinions, whatever. On your page, identify each item with a brief label ("My taxi ride," "Talk with New York friend," "Statistic on accidents").

What makes clustering especially useful is that when you cluster, you don't just plan. Your chart shows you at a glance where you need to generate ideas

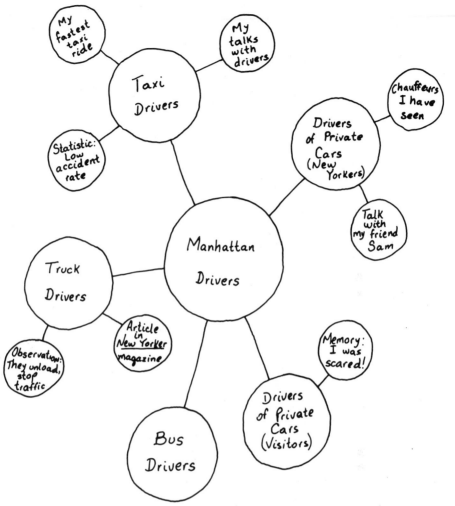

Figure 24.2 The Clustering Method for Generating Ideas

and information. If any major divisions look lonesome, evidently you need to come up with more material to surround them.

Clustering is a particularly valuable strategy for any writing assignment that calls for much evidence, such as a persuasive essay or a research paper. Figure 24.2 presents a cluster for "Manhattan Drivers." For a long paper (of, say, 1000 words), it would need more material. The division "Bus Drivers" hasn't any.

6. *The electronic game.* With the advent of word processing, many writers now arrange their rough notes into groups right on a computer screen, moving items from place to place until they like the resulting plan. Much computer software is dedicated to outlining, making it possible for the user to try out different schemes of organization before deciding on any one of them. (For detailed suggestions on writing with the aid of a computer, see "A Note on Word Processing," p. 43.)

OUTLINING

Some writers start writing without any plan. "When I work," says novelist Norman Mailer, "I don't like to know where I'm going." In college, you are often obliged to write with little advance planning—as when, on a final exam, you are given fifteen minutes to discuss the effects of World War II on patterns of world trade. Yet whether they lay out extensive plans on paper or arrange ideas in their heads as they go along, good writers organize what they write.

In the previous section, "Grouping Your Ideas," we set forth ways to bring related thoughts together. Another perhaps more familiar means to organize ideas is to outline. For most writing, most of the time, most college writers find it enough to make a scratch outline—perhaps just a list of points to make. A written outline, whether brief or greatly detailed, serves as guide and friend. If you forget where you are going or what you are trying to say, you can always pause to consult it. An outline can be like a map that you make before setting out on a journey. It shows where to set out from, where to stop along the way, and where at last to arrive. Unlike highway maps, outlines can be flexible. While you drive along, occasionally consulting your map, you can easily revise your route.

How detailed an outline will you need? The answer depends in part on the kind of writer you are. Some writers feel most comfortable when writing with a highly detailed outline: buoyed up as though by a pair of water wings. Others feel inhibited by such a thing, as though they were trying to swim in a strait-jacket. Some writers like to lay out the job very carefully in advance; others prefer to lay it out more loosely and follow an outline more casually. Do people tell you your writing isn't well organized and that they can't follow you? Then maybe you need a more detailed outline. Do they tell you your writing sounds tired and mechanical, as if you're ticking off your note cards in numerical order? Maybe your outline is constricting you and you should keep it brief.

Sometimes, when you have written the first draft of a paper that you suspect doesn't quite make sense, outlining can help you apply first aid. If you can't easily make an outline of what you have written, then probably your reader will have a hard time following you. Something is wrong with the paper's basic construction. Perhaps the main points don't follow clearly. Maybe the sequence of ideas needs rearranging. Maybe too many ideas are jammed into too few paragraphs. It is often easier to operate on your outline than on your ailing paper. Work on the outline until you get it into strong shape and then rewrite the paper to follow it.

An outline, even a detailed one, shouldn't say *everything* you plan to write in your paper. You shouldn't use up all your thought and energy on your outline. If yours gets too detailed, stop and set it aside with your notes.

Informal Outlines

For in-class writing and for brief essays, often a *short* or *informal outline,* also called a *scratch outline,* will serve your needs. It is just a brief list of points to make, in the order you plan to make them. The short outline is only for your own eyes. When the writing job is done, you pitch the outline into the trash basket.

The following is an informal outline for a 600-word paper on the topic "Los Angelenos versus New Yorkers: Who Are Better Drivers?" Its thesis statement reads, "Los Angelenos are better drivers than New Yorkers because they are healthier, more skillful, and more considerate." (You'd need plenty of facts, observations, and other specific evidence to back up *those* claims, of course!) One obvious way to proceed would be to list the three points you want to compare (physical fitness, skill, and consideration). Then, for each quality, you might plan to discuss (1) New Yorkers and (2) Los Angelenos: how they do or don't exhibit it. You could put this plan in simple outline form, like this:

1. An old controversy
2. Physical fitness
   —New Yorkers: less time and space in which to exercise
   —Los Angelenos: outdoor lifestyle conducive to physical and mental ease
3. Skill at the wheel: both highly skilled
   —New Yorkers: more small, crowded streets
   —Los Angelenos: a lot of freeway driving
4. Consideration for others
   —New Yorkers: tendency to vent their aggressions at the wheel
   —Los Angelenos: laid-back attitude toward life reflected in driving habits
5. Conclusion: Los Angelenos win.

A simple five-point outline like that could easily fall into a five-paragraph essay. If you have a great deal to say about New Yorkers and Los Angelenos, though, the essay might well run longer—perhaps to eight paragraphs: introduction, conclusion, and three pairs of paragraphs in between. But outline and essay won't always correlate neatly. You may not know until you write exactly how many paragraphs you'll need.

An informal outline can be even less formal than the preceding one. If you were writing an in-class essay, an answer to an examination question, or a very short paper, your outline might be no more than three or four phrases jotted down in a list.

Physical fitness

Skill

Consideration for others

Often a clear thesis statement (discussed on p. 469) will suggest a way to outline. Let's say you are assigned, for an anthroplogy course, a paper on the people of Melanesia. A thesis statement reads, "The Melanesian pattern of family life may look strange to westerners, but it fosters a degree of independence that rivals our own." Laying out ideas in the same order as they follow in that thesis statement, you might make a short, simple outline like this:

1. Features that appear strange:
   A woman supported by her brother, not her husband
   Trial marriages usual
   Divorce from her children possible for any mother

2. Admirable results of system:
   Wives not dependent on husbands for support
   Divorce between mates uncommon
   Greater freedom for parents and children

This informal outline might result in an essay that naturally falls into two parts: strange features, admirable results. In writing and thinking further, you might want to flesh out that outline with more material. The outline might expand accordingly.

Say you plan to write a "how-to" essay on buying a used car. Your thesis statement might read: "Despite traps that lie in wait for the unwary, you can get a good deal if you first read car magazines and *Consumer Reports,* check ads in the papers, make phone calls to several dealers, test-drive critically, and take along a friend who's a mechanic." Follow this same sequence of ideas in your outline, and you will probably start out your paper with some horror stories about people who get taken by car sharks and then proceed to list, point by point, your bits of advice. Of course, you can always change the sequence or revise your thesis statement if you find it makes sense to do so as you go along.

Formal Outlines

A *formal outline* is the Mercedes-Benz of outlines: an elaborate job built with time and care and meant for showing off. As a plan to be used for everyday writing jobs, it would take too much time—probably more than it would be worth.

In college, a formal outline is occasionally used for term papers, research papers, honors theses, doctoral dissertations, and other ambitious projects. As a rule, it isn't meant for a writer's own guidance, but for an instructor or a committee to ponder before (or after) the writer writes. Because research papers and theses require so much work, some academic departments ask a writer to submit a formal outline before going ahead and toiling for months, perhaps in vain. Some instructors in assigning a research paper ask for a special kind of formal outline—a sentence outline—to make the paper's organization easier to appreciate and to discuss. For an example, see Lisa Chickos's sentence outline on page 320. Writing such a detailed outline can pay off: with only a little more work, it can turn into a finished paper. In business, a formal outline for a research project (or for a program of matters to be discussed) might be offered to a meeting of a board of directors—meant to impress the top brass with how logical the bottom brass can be.

A formal outline offers the greatest amount of guidance that an outline can give. In a clear, logical way, it spells out where you are going to go. It shows how ideas relate, one to another: how large points lead to smaller. It ranks the points to be made according to their importance and inclusiveness: a roman numeral I point is a major point that takes in more territory than the letter A point under it.

When you make a formal outline, you place your thesis statement at the beginning. Then you list your most important points—those that most directly bear upon your thesis—in roman numerals: I, II, III. These points support and develop the main idea of your whole paper. Then you break down these points into divisions that take capital letters: A, B, C. You subdivide those into divisions with arabic numbers—1, 2, 3—and you further subdivide those into divisions with small letters: a, b, c. Be sure to cast all headings in parallel grammatical form: phrases or sentences but not both. If you have so much material that you have to subdivide still further, small arabic numerals and small letters, both in parentheses, are commonly used. But it will take a hugely complicated writing project to need subdividing that far.

A formal outline for a long, thoroughly researched paper about New York and Los Angeles drivers might start like this:

Thesis statement: Driving habits in New York City and Los Angeles reflect basic cultural and behavioral differences between Easterners and Westerners.

I. New York drivers aggressive and impatient
   A. Manifestations of these traits
      1. Horn-blowing and shouting
      2. Running red lights
      3. Disregard for pedestrians
   B. Reasons for their behavior
      1. New York an old city
      2. Population density
         a. Limited contact with nature for most people
         b. Little time and space for exercise
      3. Fast-paced lifestyle
      4. Traffic laws not rigidly enforced
         a. Not enough police
         b. General acceptance of status quo
         c. A certain pride in survival skills—pedestrians and drivers alike

II. Los Angeles drivers laid back and relaxed
   A. Contributing factors
      1. Los Angeles a comparatively new and sprawling city
         a. More room for cars
         b. Fewer pedestrians
         c. Vast network of freeways—little need to drive far on narrow streets
      2. Outdoor living year-round
         a. Fewer frustrations
         b. A slower-paced life
   B. Less frenzy on L.A. roads
      1. Laws generally enforced and obeyed
      2. Consideration on the part of most drivers for pedestrians and other drivers

This outline would continue, but from this much of it you can see how a formal outline unfolds. Some readers will grow wrathful if you list only one lonesome item in a subcategory, as in this formal outline for an essay on earthquakes:

> D. Probable results of an earthquake
>   1. Houses stripped of their paint

If that point is all you have to say, then why not just combine your categories?

> D. Houses stripped of paint during an earthquake

But more likely, the lack of more than one subpoint indicates that more thinking needs to be done, more evidence discovered. With a little more thought or reading, the outline might grow:

> D. Probable results of an earthquake
>   1. Broken water mains
>   2. Collapsed bridges
>   3. Gaps in road surfaces
>   4. Cracks in foundations
>   5. Houses stripped of their paint

Not only has this writer come up with more points, she has ranked them in an order of diminishing importance. This careful planning will save her some decisions when she comes to write ("Now, which of these results do I deal with first?").

Often written after the paper, meant for the benefit of the reader and not the writer, a formal outline can also be a planning strategy. If you do write it in advance for your own guidance, let it be tentative. You will want to revise it to include any new ideas you may discover as you go along.

PARAGRAPHING

Even your most willing readers need occasionally to pause, to digest what you tell them. This is why essays are written not in large, indigestible lumps of prose but in *paragraphs*—small units, each indented, each more or less self-contained, each contributing something new in support of your essay's main idea.

Paragraphs can be as short as one sentence or as long as a page. Sometimes their length is governed by the audience for whom they are written or by the medium in which they appear. News writers, for instance, tend to write in brief, one- or two-sentence paragraphs to make their stories easy to cut to fit a page. Newspaper readers, consuming facts like popcorn, seem not to mind this style of skimpy paragraphing. (To find long, meaty paragraphs in a newspaper, you have to read the editorials.) Academic writers, on the other hand, assume some willingness on the part of their colleagues to read through long paragraphs in a specialized treatise.

Most paragraphs are organized around one idea or event and form sections of a larger whole. As we will show on page 488, sometimes a paragraph serves as a bridge, a *transition,* between the paragraph preceding and the one following. Effective paragraphs are both well organized and unified. They seem to go somewhere.

Ideally, a paragraph indentation signifies a pause, as if the writer were taking a breath, finished making one point and ready to begin another. In real life, when they slice their thoughts into paragraphs, probably no two writers work by exactly the same principles. Certain writers dwell on one idea at a time. They state a point and develop it amply: illustrate it with an example or a story, perhaps give a few facts to support it. Then, all done with that point, they indent and start making a further point in a fresh paragraph. Their prose seems to fall into paragraphs naturally. At the opposite extreme are those writers who don't even think about where to break their paragraphs until they finish a first draft. Then they go back over their work and mark a paragraph at each place where an important new point starts. Such slicing isn't always logical. Inspect the articles in some current magazine and, indeed, you'll meet writers who begin a new paragraph for no apparent reason except that they feel the old paragraph has run on long enough. As for readers, they tend not even to notice where a writer's paragraph breaks fall. Readers care only about whether the writer's thoughts follow in a sensible line and interest them.

Why, then, pay attention to paragraphs? You have to keep your readers with you every step of the way. This involves developing each of your main points fully and clearly, using examples and abundant evidence, before going on to the next. It means taking your readers by the hand and not only telling but *showing* them, with plenty of detailed evidence, exactly what you mean.

Using Topic Sentences

One tried-and-true way to draft an effective paragraph is to write down in advance one sentence that spells out what the paragraph's central point is to be. We call such a sentence a *topic sentence.* It supplies the foundation on which to build the rest of the paragraph.

Often when you read good clear prose, especially writing that explains or argues, you can pick out a given paragraph's topic sentence. Usually, as in this example from James David Barber's *The Presidential Character: Predicting Performance in the White House,* it appears first in the paragraph, followed by sentences that illustrate and support what it says. (In all the following examples, we have put the topic sentences in *italics.*)

> *The first baseline in defining Presidential types is activity-passivity.* How much energy does the man invest in his Presidency? Lyndon Johnson went at his day like a human cyclone, coming to rest long after the sun went down. Calvin Coolidge often slept eleven hours a night and still needed a nap in the middle of the day. In between, the Presidents array themselves on the high or low side of the activity line.

Here the topic sentence clearly shows at the outset what the paragraph is to be about. The second sentence defines *activity-passivity*. The third and fourth sentences, by citing extremes at either end of the baseline, supply illustrations: active Johnson, passive Coolidge. The final sentence makes a generalization that reinforces the central point.

Not every topic sentence stands at the beginning of its paragraph. Sometimes the first sentence of a new paragraph functions as a transition, linking what is to come with what has gone before, as in the following illustration from the essay "On Societies as Organisms" by science writer and physician Lewis Thomas. In such a paragraph the *second* sentence might be the topic sentence. The paragraph quoted here follows one about insects that ends, ". . . and we violate science when we try to read human meanings in their arrangements."

> It is hard for a bystander not to do so. *Ants are so much like human beings as to be an embarrassment.* They farm fungi, raise aphids as livestock, launch armies into wars, use chemical sprays to alarm and confuse enemies, capture slaves. The families of weaver ants engage in child labor, holding their larvae like shuttles to spin out the thread that sews the leaves together for their fungus gardens. They exchange information ceaselessly. They do everything but watch television.

Occasionally a writer, especially one attempting to persuade the reader to agree, piles detail upon detail throughout a paragraph. Then, with a dramatic flourish, the writer *concludes* with the topic sentence. You can see this technique in the following paragraph, from Heidi Kessler's paper in response to a writing assignment in sociology: to report on a contemporary social problem and voice an opinion on it.

> A fourteen-year-old writes to an advice columnist in my hometown newspaper that she has "done it" lots of times and sex is "no big deal." At the neighborhood clinic where my aunt works, a hardened sixteen-year-old requests her third abortion. A girl-child I know has two children of her own, but no husband. A college student in my dorm now finds herself sterile from a "social disease" picked up during casual sexual encounters. Multiply these examples by thousands. *It seems clear to me that women, who fought so hard for sexual freedom equal to that of men, have emerged from the battle not as joyous free spirits but as the sexual revolution's walking wounded.*

By the time you come to the end of the paragraph, you might be ready to accept the conclusion in the topic sentence. Reversing the most usual order of paragraph development (to make a general statement and back it up with particulars), this paragraph moves instead from the particular to the general: from the examples of individual girl-children and women to the larger statement about American women made in the topic sentence.

The topic sentence, then, can appear anywhere in the paragraph. It is also possible to find a perfectly unified, well-organized paragraph that has no topic sentence at all, like this one from "New York" by Gay Talese.

> Each afternoon in New York a rather seedy saxophone player, his cheeks blown out like a spinnaker, stands on the sidewalk playing *Danny Boy* in such a sad, sensitive way that he soon has half the neighborhood peeking out of windows tossing nickels, dimes and quarters at his feet. Some of the coins roll under parked cars, but most of them are caught in his out-stretched hand. The saxophone player is a street musician named Joe Gabler; for the past thirty years he has serenaded every block in New York and has sometimes been tossed as much as $100 a day in coins. He is also hit with buckets of water, empty beer cans and eggs, and chased by wild dogs. He is believed to be the last of New York's ancient street musicians.

No one sentence neatly sums up the writer's idea. Like most effective paragraphs that lack a topic sentence, Talese's paragraph contains something just as good: a topic idea. The author doesn't allow his paragraph to wander aimlessly. He knows exactly what he wants to achieve: a description of how Joe Gabler, a famous New York street musician, plies his trade. Because Talese succeeds in keeping this main purpose firmly in mind, the main point—that Gabler meets both reward and abuse—is clear to the reader as well.

A paragraph is likely to have a strong topic idea, too, if you begin it with a question. You'll probably find it easy to organize the rest of the paragraph around the answer to that question. Here is a paragraph, by psychoanalyst Erik Erikson, organized by the question-and-answer method.

> Is the sense of identity conscious? At times, of course, it seems only too conscious. For between the double prongs of vital inner need and inexorable outer demand, the as yet experimenting individual may become the victim of a transitory extreme identity consciousness, which is the common core of the many forms of "self-consciousness" typical for youth. Where the processes of identity formation are prolonged (a factor which can bring creative gain), such preoccupation with the "self-image" also prevails. We are thus most aware of our identity when we are just about to gain it and when we (with that startle which motion pictures call a "double take") are somewhat surprised to make its acquaintance; or, again, when we are just about to enter a crisis and feel the encroachment of identity confusion. . . .

Evidently to write by the topic sentence method won't help every writer; some find it inhibiting. But if you generally have trouble organizing an essay, you might try it. One foolproof way to plan is to make a sentence outline (see p. 478) and then write a paragraph enlarging on every sentence.

With practice, organizing a paragraph around one main point can become almost second nature. A writer accustomed to this method can see exactly where more examples and illustrations are called for: if a paragraph looks skimpy and consists of little besides the topic sentence, then it probably needs more beef.

The more pointed and lively your topic sentence, the more interesting the paragraph that is likely to surround it. If your topic sentence leads off your paragraph, think of it as bait to hook your readers and tow them along with you. "There are many things wrong with television" may be a little dull and vague, but at least it's a start for a paragraph. Zero in on one specific fault, change the sentence to "Of all television's faults, the one I can't stand is its nightly melodramatization of the news" and go on to illustrate your point with two or three melodramatic newscasts that you remember. An arresting paragraph—and an arresting paper—will probably result from that topic sentence.

Giving Examples

An example—the word comes from the Latin *exemplum,* meaning "one thing chosen from among many"—is a typical instance that illustrates a whole type or kind. Here's an example, from *In Search of Excellence* by Thomas J. Peters and Robert H. Waterman, Jr., explaining why America's top corporations are so successful:

> Although he's not a company, our favorite illustration of closeness to the customer is car salesman Joe Girard. He sold more new cars and trucks each year, for eleven years running, than any other human being. . . . Why start with Joe? Because his magic is the magic of IBM and many of the rest of the excellent companies. It is simply service, overpowering service. Joe noted, "There's one thing that I do that a lot of salesmen don't, and that's believe the sale really begins after the sale—not before. The customer ain't out the door, and my son has made up a thank-you note."

Had a writer in love with generalities written that paragraph, he might have begun in the same way, with a generalization about "closeness to the customer." But then, instead of giving the example of Joe the car salesman and a sample of his speech, he might have gone on, still staying up in the clouds: "The need to consider the customer as an individual is very important to the operation of a successful business. The retailer is well advised to consider the purchaser as a person with whom he will have a continuing relationship," and so on, vaguely and boringly. Not only do examples make your ideas clear, they also interest your reader. Writers who stay up in the clouds of generality may have bright ideas, but in the end a reader may not care.

Giving examples, as Peters and Waterman do, is one way to back up a general statement of the sort you make in a topic sentence. On page 481 James David Barber illustrates the main idea of his paragraph (that "activity-passivity" characterizes presidents) with examples of different presidential types: the drowsy Coolidge, the energetic Johnson.

To find your own examples, do a little brainstorming or thinking. Review whatever you know. You can begin with your own experience, with whatever is near you. When you set out to draft a paragraph on a topic that you think you know nothing about—the psychology of gift giving, let's say—revolve it slowly in your mind. Maybe you will find yourself an expert on it. Did you ever know a person who gave large gifts people didn't want and felt uncomfortable accepting? Now why do you suppose he or she behaved that way? Was the gift giver looking for gratitude? A feeling of importance? Power over the recipient? How might you tell? If necessary, you might discover still more examples from conversation with others, from your reading, from digging in the library. By using examples, you make an idea more concrete and tangible. Examples aren't trivial doodads you add to a paragraph for decoration; they are what holds your readers' attention and shows them that your writing makes sense.

In truth, examples are only one kind of *evidence*—the factual basis for an argument or an explanation. Besides pointing to the example of President Coolidge, James David Barber gives a little evidence to show that Coolidge was sleepy: the report that he would sleep eleven hours a night and then take a nap in midday besides. To back up your general statements, you would do well to supply such statements of fact, bits of historical record, your own observations. Mary Harris "Mother" Jones in old age published the story of her life as a labor organizer, *The Autobiography of Mother Jones*. In this view of a Pennsylvania coal miner's lot at the turn of the century, she makes a general statement and then with ample evidence lends conviction to her words.

> Mining at its best is wretched work, and the life and surroundings of the miner are hard and ugly. His work is down in the black depths of the earth. He works alone in a drift. There can be little friendly companionship as there is in the factory; as there is among men who build bridges and houses, working together in groups. The work is dirty. Coal dust grinds itself into the skin, never to be removed. The miner must stoop as he works in the drift. He becomes bent like a gnome.
>
> His work is utterly fatiguing. Muscles and bones ache. His lungs breathe coal dust and the strange, damp air of places that are never filled with sunlight. His house is a poor makeshift and there is little to encourage him to make it attractive. The company owns the ground it stands on, and the miner feels the precariousness of his hold. Around his house is mud and slush. Great mounds of culm [the refuse left after coal is screened], black and sullen, surround him. His children are perpetually grimy from playing on the culm mounds. The wife struggles with dirt, with inadequate water supply, with small wages, with overcrowded shacks.
>
> The miner's wife, who in the majority of cases worked from childhood in the nearby silk mills, is overburdened with child bearing. She ages young. She knows much illness. Many a time I have been in a home where the poor wife was sick in bed, the children crawling over her, quarreling and playing in the room, often the only warm room in the house.

Mother Jones, who was not a learned writer, wrote these memoirs in her mid-nineties. Her style may be heavy with short, simple sentences ("She ages young. She knows much illness"), but her writing is clear and powerful. She knows the strength of a well-chosen verb: "Coal dust *grinds* itself into the skin." Notice how she opens her description by making two general statements: (1) "Mining is wretched work" and (2) the miner's life and surroundings are "hard and ugly." Then she supports these generalizations with an overwhelming barrage of facts from her own experience. The result is a moving, convincingly detailed portrait of the miner and his family.

Here's a revealing experiment you can make easily to test your skill at using examples. Glance back over the last essay you wrote for your writing course.

How long are its paragraphs? Are they solid and stout? Or are they skimpy, undernourished: is there hardly a paragraph longer than three sentences? If indeed you find your paragraphs tending toward frailty, ask why. Maybe you need to be more generous in giving examples.

To give plenty of examples is one of the writer's chief tasks. We can't stress this truth enough. Most beginning writers don't give a reader enough examples. You'll want to cultivate the habit of example giving. Do something to remember its importance. Put a ring around this paragraph, or star it, or paint this motto over your writing desk: USE EXAMPLES! Or engrave it on your brain screen in letters of gold.

Using Transitions

Effective writing is well organized. It proceeds in some sensible order, each sentence following naturally from the one before it. Yet even well-organized prose can be hard to read unless it contains *transitions:* devices that tie together words in a sentence, sentences in a paragraph, paragraphs in an essay.

You already use transitions every day, in both your writing and your speech. You can't help it. Instinctively you realize that certain words and phrases help your audience follow your line of thought. But some writers, in a rush to get through what they have to say, omit important linkages between thoughts. Hastily, they assume that because a connection is clear to them it will automatically be clear to their readers.

If your readers sometimes have trouble following you, you may find it useful to pay attention to transitions. Often just a word, phrase, or sentence of transition inserted in the right place will transform a seemingly disconnected passage into a coherent one.

Back in Chapter 10, we discussed time markers, those transitions especially useful for telling a story or analyzing a process because they make clear *when* one thing happens in relation to another. Time markers include words and phrases like *then, soon, the following day,* and *in a little while.* (For that discussion, see p. 176.) But not all transitions mark time. The English language contains many words and phrases that make clear other connections between or within sentences. Consider choosing one of the following transitions to fit your purpose. (We'll group them here by purposes.)

SUMMARIZE OR RESTATE	in other words, to put it another way, in brief, in simpler terms, on the whole, in fact, in a word, to sum up, in short, in conclusion
RELATE CAUSE AND EFFECT	therefore, accordingly, hence, thus, thereupon, consequently, as a result, because of, for
AMPLIFY OR COMPARE	and, also, too, besides, as well, in addition, moreover, furthermore, likewise, similarly, in effect
CONCEDE OR CONTRAST	on the other hand, whereas, but, however, nevertheless, still, and yet, or, even so, although, unlike, in spite of, on the contrary, at least

GIVE EXAMPLES	in particular, for instance, for example
QUALIFY	for the most part, by and large, with few exceptions, mainly, in most cases, sometimes
LEND EMPHASIS	it is true, indeed, of course, certainly, to be sure, obviously, without doubt, evidently, clearly, understandably
MARK THE PLACE	in the distance, close by, near at hand, far away, above, below, to the right, on the other side, opposite, to the west, next door

Occasionally a whole sentence serves as a transition. Often, but not always, it is the first sentence of a new paragraph. When the transitional sentence appears in that position, it harks back to the contents of the previous paragraph while simultaneously hinting at the direction the new paragraph is to take. Here is a sample, excerpted from an essay by Marsha Traugot about adopting older and handicapped children, in which the transitional sentence (*in italics*) begins a new paragraph.

> .... Some exchanges hold monthly meetings where placement workers looking for a match can discuss waiting children or families, and they also sponsor parties where children, workers, and prospective parents meet informally.
>
> *And if a match still cannot be made?* Exchanges and other child welfare organizations now employ media blitzes as aggressive as those of commercial advertising. ...

By repeating the key word *match* in her transitional sentence and by inserting the word *still,* Traugot makes clear that in what follows she will build on what has gone before. At the same time, by making the transitional sentence a rhetorical question, Traugot promises that the new paragraph will introduce fresh material, in this case answering the question.

As we see in Traugot's passage about adoption, still another way to make clear the relationship between two sentences, two paragraphs, or two ideas is to *repeat* a key word or phrase. Such repetition, purposefully done, almost guarantees that the reader will understand how all the parts of even a complicated passage fit together. Note the transitional force of the word *anger* in the following paragraph, from *Of Woman Born* by poet Adrienne Rich, in which the writer explores her relationship with her mother:

> And I know there must be deep reservoirs of anger in her; every mother has known overwhelming, unacceptable anger at her children. When I think of the conditions under which my mother became a mother, the impossible expectations, my father's distaste for pregnant women, his hatred of all that he could not control, my anger at her dissolves into grief and anger *for* her, and then dissolves back again into anger at her: the ancient, unpurged anger of the child.

The repetition of the one word in several contexts—those of a mother's anger toward her children and a child's anger, past and present, toward her mother—holds all the parts of this complex paragraph together, makes clear the unity and coherence of its ideas. Repetition of the word *mother* performs the same binding function.

Pronouns, too, because they always refer back to the nouns they stand for, serve as transitions by making the reader refer back as well. Note how certain pronouns (indicated by *italics*) hold together the following paragraph by columnist Ellen Goodman.

> I have two friends who moved in together many years ago. *He* looked upon *this* step as a trial marriage. *She* looked upon *it* as, well, moving in together. *He* was sure that in a matter of time, after *they* had built up trust and confidence, *she* would agree that marriage was the next logical step. *She,* on the other hand, was thrilled that here at last was a man *who* would never push *her* back to the altar.

Goodman's paragraph contains transitions other than pronouns, too: time markers like "many years ago," "in a matter of time," and "after they had built up trust"; "on the other hand," which makes clear that what follows will represent a contrast from what has gone before; and repetition. All serve the main purpose of transitions: keeping readers on track.

Transitions may be even longer than sentences. When you write an essay, especially one that is long and complicated, you'll find that to move clearly from one idea to the next will sometimes require an entire paragraph of transition:

> So far, we have been dwelling on the physical and psychological effects of driving nonstop for more than two hundred miles. Now let's reflect on causes. Why do people become addicted to their steering wheels?

Usually, such a paragraph will be shorter than its neighbors, but you'll want to allow it whatever space it may require. Often, as in the preceding example, it makes a comment on the structure of the essay. The writer is taking time out to explain what she is doing so that her readers may readily follow her.

Let a transition paragraph come to your aid, too, whenever you go off on one branch of argument and then return to your main trunk. Here's an example from a masterly writer, Lewis Thomas, in an essay, "Things Unflattened by Science." A medical doctor, Thomas has been complaining in his essay that biologists keep expecting medical researchers to come up with quick answers to intractable problems: cancer, schizophrenia, stress. He takes most of a paragraph to explain why he doesn't think medical science can solve the problem of stress: "Stress is simply the condition of being human." Now, to turn again to the main idea of his essay—what biological problems he would like to see solved—Thomas inserts a transition paragraph:

> But I digress. What I wish to get at is an imaginary situation in which I am allowed three or four questions to ask the world of biomedical science to settle for me by research, as soon as possible. Can I make a short list of top-priority puzzles, things I am more puzzled by than anything else? I can.

In a new paragraph, he continues: "First, I want to know what goes on in the mind of a honeybee." He wonders if a bee is just a sort of programmed robot or if it can think and imagine, even a little bit. Neatly and effectively, the transition paragraph has led to this speculation and to several further paragraphs that will come.

One word of warning. If you find yourself using a great many transition paragraphs in a short essay or if you find a transition paragraph growing to ten or twelve sentences, you are turning into a boring gasser, probably. Some writers so enjoy explaining what they are doing that they explain even though what they are doing is self-evident. If you can do without transition paragraphs, do. Sometimes a question at the start of a paragraph will supply enough connection: "Why do people become addicted to their steering wheels?" That question neatly introduces a whole new idea. If the essay is short and clear, the question saves a whole transition paragraph. Use such a paragraph only when you sense that your readers might get lost if you don't patiently lead them by the hand.

Opening Paragraphs

Even writers with something to say occasionally find it hard to begin. Often they are so intent on writing a brilliant opening paragraph that they freeze, unable to write anything at all. Brilliant beginnings are fine if you can get them, but they may be gifts of God. "Start with a bang," Richard Strauss advised his fellow composers, and he opened his symphonic poem "Thus Spake Zarathustra" with a sunrise: the whole orchestra delivers a tremendous explosion of sound. But in most writing, brilliance and orchestral explosions are neither expected nor required. In truth, when you sit down to draft an essay, you can ease your way into the job by simply deciding to set words—any words—on paper, without trying at all for an arresting or witty opening. A time-honored approach to your opening paragraphs is to write them *last,* after you have written the body of your essay and know exactly in what direction it is headed. Some writers like to write a first draft with a long, driveling beginning and then in rewriting cut it down to the most dramatic, exciting, or interesting statement, discarding everything that has gone before.

At whatever point in the writing process you set about fashioning an opening paragraph on your own, remember that your chief aim is to persuade your readers to lay aside their preoccupations and enter, with you as guide, the world set forth in your essay. Often a simple anecdote, by capturing your readers' interest, serves as a good beginning. Here is how Harry Crews opens his essay "The Car":

> The other day, there arrived in the mail a clipping sent by a friend of mine. It had been cut from a Long Beach, California, newspaper and dealt with a young man who had eluded police for fifty-five minutes while he raced over freeways and through city streets at speeds up to 130 miles per hour. During the entire time, he ripped his clothes off and threw them out

the window bit by bit. It finally took twenty-five patrol cars and a helicopter to catch him. When they did, he said that God had given him the car, and that he had "found God."

Most of us, reading such an anecdote, want to read on. What will the author say next? What has the anecdote to do with the essay as a whole? Crews has aroused our curiosity.

In some essays, the author introduces a subject and then turns momentarily away from it to bring in a vital bit of detail, as in this opening paragraph by A. Alvarez from "Shiprock," an essay about climbing a mountain:

> I suppose the first sight of a mountain is always the best. Later, when you are waiting to start, you may grow to hate the brute, because you are afraid. And when, finally, you are climbing, you are never aware of the mountain as a mountain: it is merely so many little areas of rock to be worked out in terms of hand-holds, foot-holds and effort, like so many chess problems. But when you first see it in the distance, remote and beautiful and unknown, then there seems some reason for climbing.

That paragraph establishes the author as someone with firsthand knowledge. Alvarez proceeds smoothly from the opening paragraph about mountain climbing in general to the heart of his essay, with a sentence of transition at the start of his second paragraph: "I first saw Shiprock on a midsummer day."

A well-written essay can also begin with a short definition, as James H. Austin begins "Four Kinds of Chance":

> What is chance? Dictionaries define it as something fortuitous that happens unpredictably without discernible human intention. Chance is unintentional and capricious, but we needn't conclude that chance is immune from human intervention. Indeed, chance plays several distinct roles when humans react creatively with one another and with their environment.

To ask a question like that is often an effective way to begin. The reader will expect the essay to supply an answer.

To challenge readers, a writer may begin with a controversial opinion.

> Unlike any other sport, football is played solely for the benefit of the spectator. If you take the spectator away from any other game, the game could still survive on its own. Thus tennis players love tennis, whether or not anyone is watching. Golfers are almost churlish in their dedication to their game. Ping-pong players never look around. Basketball players can dribble and shoot for hours without hearing a single cheer. Even baseball might survive the deprivation, despite the lack of parks. Soft-ball surely would. But if you took away the spectators, if you demolished the grandstands and boarded up the stadium, it is inconceivable to think that any football would be played in the eerie privacy of the field itself. No football team ever plays another team just for the fun of playing football. Army plays Navy, Michigan plays Purdue, P.S. 123 plays P.S. 124, only with the prospect of a loud crowd on hand.

After his first, startling remark, the writer, Wade Thompson, generalizes about games unlike football: "If you take the spectator away from any other game, the game could still survive on its own." Then the author backs up his generalization with examples of such games: tennis, golf, Ping-Pong, basketball, baseball, softball. Finally Thompson returns to his original point, thus emphasizing the direction his essay will take.

An effective opening paragraph often ends, as does Thompson's, with a statement of the essay's main point. To end your opening paragraph this way, after first having captured your readers' attention, is to take your readers by the hand and lead them in exactly the direction your essay is to go. No one can ask more of any introduction. Such a statement can be brief, as in the second sentence of this powerful opening of an essay by educator George B. Leonard called "No School?":

> The most obvious barrier between our children and the kind of education that can free their enormous potential seems to be the educational system itself: a vast, suffocating web of people, practices and presumptions, kindly in intent, ponderous in response. Now, when true educational alternatives are at last becoming clear, we may overlook the simplest: no school.

We suggest these points to keep in mind when constructing opening paragraphs.

1. Don't worry too hard about capturing and transfixing your readers with your opening paragraphs. Getting their attention is enough.
2. Open with an anecdote, a description, a comparison, a definition, a quotation, a question, or some vital background.
3. Set forth your thesis at the end of your introduction.
4. Lead into the body of your essay with a transitional word or phrase.

Concluding Paragraphs

The final paragraphs of an essay linger longest in the reader's mind. Here is a conclusion that certainly does so. In "Once More to the Lake," about returning with his young son to a vacation spot the author had known and loved as a child, E. B. White conveys his confused feeling that he has gone back in time to his own childhood, that he and his son are one. Then, at the end of the essay, in an unforgettable image, he remembers how old he really is:

> When the others went swimming my son said he was going in, too. He pulled his dripping trunks from the line where they had hung all through the shower and wrung them out. Languidly, and with no thought of going in, I watched him, his hard little body, skinny and bare, saw him wince slightly as he pulled up around his vitals the small, soggy, icy garment. As he buckled the swollen belt, suddenly my groin felt the chill of death.

White's concluding paragraph is a classic example of an effective way to end. It begins with a sentence of transition that points back to what has gone before and at the same time looks ahead. (He might just as easily have put a transitional sentence at the end of the preceding paragraph.) After the transition, White leads us quickly to his final, chilling insight. Then he stops.

Yet even a quiet ending can be effective, as long as it signals clearly that the essay is finished. Sometimes the best way to conclude a story, for instance, is simply to stop when the story is over. This is what Martin Gansberg does in his true account of the fatal beating of a young woman, Kitty Genovese, in full view of residents of a Queens, New York, apartment house, who, unwilling to become involved, did nothing to interfere. Here is the last paragraph of his account, "38 Who Saw Murder Didn't Call Police":

> It was 4:25 A.M. when the ambulance arrived to take the body of Miss Genovese. It drove off. "Then," a solemn police detective said, "the people came out."

Similarly, a process analysis can simply end when you have finished explaining the final step in a process. A description, when the picture it paints is complete, need draw no special conclusion. But for an essay that traces causes or effects, compares and contrasts, classifies or divides, defines, or argues, a deft concluding thought performs the worthy function of reinforcing your main idea. Notice the definite click with which former heavyweight champion Gene Tunney closes the door on "The Long Count," an analysis of his two victorious fights with Jack Dempsey, whose boxing style differed markedly from Tunney's own.

> Jack Dempsey was a great fighter—possibly the greatest that ever entered a ring. Looking back objectively, one has to conclude that he was more valuable to the sport or "The Game" than any prizefighter of his time. Whether you consider it from his worth as a gladiator or from the point of view of the box office, he was tops. His name in his most glorious days was magic among his people, and today, twenty years after, the name Jack Dempsey is still magic. This tells a volume in itself. As one who has always had pride in his profession as well as his professional theories, and possessing a fair share of Celtic romanticism, I wish that we could have met when we were both at our unquestionable best. We could have decided many questions, to me the most important of which is whether "a good boxer can always lick a good fighter."
> I still say yes.

It's easy to suggest what *not* to do at the end of an essay. Don't leave your readers suspended in midair, half expecting you to go on. Don't introduce a brand-new topic that leads away from the true topic of your essay. And don't feel you have to introduce your final paragraph with an obvious signal that the end is near. Words and phrases like "In conclusion," "As I have said," or "So, as we see," have their place, but do without them and your essay is likely to end more gracefully. In a long, complicated paper, a terse summation of your main points right before your concluding sentences may help your reader grasp your ideas; but a short paper usually requires either no summary at all or little more than a single sentence.

"How *do* you write an ending, then?" you might well ask. An apt quotation can neatly round out an essay, as Malcolm Cowley demonstrates at the end of an essay in *The View from Eighty,* his discussion of the pitfalls and compensations of old age.

> "Eighty years old!" the great Catholic poet Paul Claudel wrote in his journal. "No eyes left, no ears, no teeth, no legs, no wind! And when all is said and done, how astonishingly well one does without them!"

In a sharp criticism of American schools, humorist Russell Baker uses another technique for ending his essay "School vs. Education": that of stating or restating his claim. Baker's main point is that schools do not educate, and he concludes:

> Afterward, the former student's destiny fulfilled, his life rich with Oriental carpets, rare porcelain and full bank accounts, he may one day find himself with the leisure and the inclination to open a book with a curious mind, and start to become educated.

It is also possible to introduce at the end of your essay not new topics that you haven't time to go into, but a few new implications concerning the topic you *have* covered. As you draw to a close and are restating your main point, ask yourself, "What now?" Why not try to leave your reader with one or two provocative thoughts to ponder? The obstreperous 1920s debunker H. L. Mencken uses this technique in "The Libido for the Ugly," an essay about the ugliness of American cities and towns.

> Here is something that the psychologists have so far neglected: the love of ugliness for its own sake, the lust to make the world intolerable. Its habitat is the United States. Out of the melting pot emerges a race which hates beauty as it hates truth. The etiology of this madness deserves a great deal more study than it has got. There must be causes behind it; it arises and flourishes in obedience to biological laws, and not as a mere act of God. What, precisely, are the terms of those laws? And why do they run stronger in America than elsewhere? Let some honest *Privat Dozent*[1] in pathological sociology apply himself to the problem.

TELLING A STORY

Telling a story is a vivid and convincing way to give an example, or to illustrate what a writer is saying. Mahatma Gandhi, in *An Autobiography,* makes the point that a truly independent man tends to his own personal needs. To illustrate this principle, he tells a story: an incident that happened when he was a young lawyer in South Africa.

[1]*Privat Dozent:* A lecturer at a German university.

In the same way as I freed myself from slavery to the washerman, I threw off dependence on the barber. All people who go to England learn there at least the art of shaving, but none, to my knowledge, cut their own hair. I had to learn that too. I once went to an English hair-cutter in Pretoria. He contemptuously refused to cut my hair. I certainly felt hurt, but immediately purchased a pair of clippers and cut my hair before the mirror. I succeeded more or less in cutting the front hair, but I spoiled the back. The friends in the court shook with laughter—"What's wrong with your hair, Gandhi? Rats have been at it?" "No, the white barber would not condescend to touch my black hair," said I, "so I preferred to cut it myself, no matter how badly."

A simple story. Why is it so powerful? In his opening sentence, Gandhi promises to tell us about some kind of revolution ("I threw off dependence on the barber"). Out of curiosity, we read on. We soon find the writer telling us of something even more gripping: a confrontation with a racial bigot. We sympathize with the writer, with his attempts to cut his own hair, with his experience of ridicule (especially if we have ever had friends make fun of us). The clincher of the story comes in the last line: Gandhi, with an apt comeback, turns humiliation into triumph. Bigotry has taught him something.

Effective writers, like Gandhi, often tell stories to illustrate their ideas. They know that narration, or storytelling, is a powerful means to engage and hold a reader's interest. They know that, with the aid of a story, a general point can become more persuasively clear.

Narratives come in all lengths, from hefty novels like Leo Tolstoy's *War and Peace* to this ghost story in a sentence: "Before going to bed one night, a man hung his wig on the bedpost; in the morning, he found it had turned white." But in most essay writing, a story will take only a paragraph. Like Gandhi's haircutting story, it may be just an *anecdote:* a brief, entertaining account of a single incident.

Whatever its length, every good story has a purpose, even if the purpose is simply to entertain. As in Gandhi's story, this purpose may be to illustrate a point. It may be to supply evidence to clinch an argument; it may be—if the story is a joke—merely to amuse. To think for a moment, "Why do I want to tell this story? What am I trying to achieve?" may repay you when you come to write.

Let's say you're writing a paper for a psychology course. Your central idea is "Few people, witnessing some swift, unexpected event, can remember it accurately without adding to it." You could go on about that in an abstract way ("The natural tendency is to reinforce our memories with additional elements by which we make sense out of our perceptions"). But the point might come across much more memorably, clearly, and effectively if you could tell the story of three witnesses to a car accident, all of them honest and well intentioned, who gave wildly different accounts of it.

Before you write a story, make sure you have a whole story to tell. Like a newspaper reporter, you can ask yourself certain questions: What happened?

Who took part? When? Where? Why did these events take place? How did they happen? (See p. 464.)

If you have plenty of time and space, you can tell a story by *scene* (or scenes), like a fiction writer. To do so, you first imagine each event and the persons involved in it so clearly and fully and in such great detail that you might be watching the event in a movie. You then try to draw the scene or scenes in words. You don't merely mention people, you portray them. You can include dialogue and description.

A more concise method is to tell the story by *summary*. You sum up what happened, briefly, just telling of events in general rather than presenting them in detail. Summary, though it may produce writing with less detail and vividness, isn't an inferior method to the method of drawing scenes. Most stories are told by this method, for it takes less time and fewer words. Novelists, writing to keep readers enthralled, can afford to draw detailed scenes in the hundreds of pages at their disposal; someone telling several stories in the course of a short argumentative essay will want instead to summarize them. If you tell your story in a single paragraph, then most likely you'll use the method of summary.

Some storytellers change methods in mid-story. They'll begin by drawing elaborate scenes and then they'll say, "Well, to make a long story short . . ." and wrap up everything in a hasty summary. They would be well advised to stick to one method or the other.

A usual way to tell a story, an easy one for a writer to follow, is to tell it in chronological order—that is, in the same sequence the events followed in time. But when you see some good reason not to stick to chronology, you can depart from it. You might, for instance, return to earlier events by *flashback,* departing from chronology to hark back to an earlier scene. That earlier scene, you might decide, is more vivid and arresting than later scenes, and you would be more likely to capture your reader's interest if you started with it. A rule of thumb is to tell a story in chronological order *unless* a different order would make a better story.

When you're writing a whole essay, not just a paragraph, narration will often serve you together with other methods. When you explain or try to persuade, feel free to tell stories. Well-chosen ones will help make your meaning clearer and harder to forget.

GROWING A METAPHOR

Readers pay attention to writers who use metaphors. Write "He's always shooting off his mouth," and you employ a metaphor, a figure of speech that calls one thing another. Evidently, you assume that a mouth, like a gun, can be loaded and thoughtlessly fired.

All over the English language, such metaphors sprout. To be aware of them and to seize them when they naturally occur is one of a writer's most valuable strategies. An apt metaphor can cause a statement to leap to life and to stay in a reader's memory. Describing a group of sailors suddenly arriving at an inn, Herman Melville (in *Moby-Dick*) remarks: "Enveloped in their shaggy coats, . . . their beards stiff with icicles, they seemed an eruption of bears from Labrador." In a Sherlock Holmes story, Arthur Conan Doyle characterizes one rugby player as "the hinge the whole team turns on." When singer Mabel Mercer died, a friend paid tribute to her: "She got to the root of a song."

A *simile* is a kind of metaphor usually introduced by *like* or *as:* "a glue that holds *like* iron," "easy *as* falling off a log." Here is magazine writer John Domini, describing the colorful, neonlike paint jobs of some vintage cars: "Street rods and classics stand in rows, gleaming like fireworks frozen and lacquered in mid-explosion." Referring to professional gambler Amarillo Slim Preston, trying to convey his lean build (and perhaps also his look of menace), a reporter wrote: "He looks like an advance man for a famine."

In an *implied metaphor*, you don't bother to say that a thing *is* or *seems* something else; you simply speak of it as though it were. Write "The new city administration *slithers* into office," and you imply that a newly elected mayor is a snake. (Say "*slink* into office," and you hint that the new officials are jackals or other predators descending on their prey.) Explaining why he hadn't replied to a slander, Mark Twain remarked, "Few slanders can stand the wear of silence." What makes Twain's sentence memorable is that implied metaphor, *stand the wear*. It turns a slander into a physical thing that silence, like an abrasive force, will grind down and annihilate. Movie queen Mae West made a famous remark in which a metaphor is implied: "I used to be Snow White, but I drifted."

A good metaphor doesn't merely enliven—it renders an idea clear. Trying to explain the effect a certain sermon had on him, Thomas Hardy remarked (in his notebook), "The rector in his sermon delivers himself of mean images in a very sublime voice, and the effect is that of a glowing landscape in which clothes are hung out to dry." That there's a contrast between the preacher's high and pompous delivery and the pedestrian nature of his statements is made clear to us. "A camel," according to a British epigram, "is a horse designed by a committee"—thus making clear the camel's awkward, unsymmetrical look (and also taking a poke at the way things get done by committees).

Metaphors are so basic to our language that often we use them unconsciously. Some are *dead metaphors,* once new and vivid, now common words that no longer call to mind physical images. We speak of the brow of a hill, the arms of a chair, the foundation of a government—even though a hill isn't really a creature with a forehead, nor a chair a person with arms, nor a government a house with a foundation under it. As metaphors, those phrases may be "dead," yet they remain useful parts of our living vocabulary.

Trouble occurs when metaphors that had been safely dead unexpectedly spring to life and start to quarrel.

> To succeed in business, you have to keep your eye on the ball, your feet on the ground, your nose to the grindstone, and your shoulder to the wheel.

The problem with such *mixed metaphors* is that a reader might try to visualize what the writer depicts. To succeed in business, it would seem, you have to be a contortionist. Consider this mixture.

> Going down the list of names with a fine-tooth comb, we left no stone unturned.

Is that list made of hair or of rocks? The writer might better flatly say, "We looked through the list of names carefully." That sentence may not gleam with any bright figures of speech, but at least it is short and clear. In writing, one good rule is never to trust a metaphor you have just invented unless you first call it before your mind's eye. Another is to distrust any metaphor you've heard or seen before.

For all their dangers, metaphors can lend life to your writing and vividness to your ideas. Lately, in a journal written for a composition class, one student struck a metaphor to express a feeling of impatience: "If my life were a VCR, I'd set it on fast forward." Metaphors like that arise from living, from actual observation.

Many excellent writers don't try for metaphors, yet their writing is forceful. Don't strong-arm a metaphor into your writing. It will work for you only when it comes naturally. If it wants to come, though, by all means welcome it.

CHAPTER 25

Strategies for Rewriting

The advice in this chapter is meant to lend you support in revising your paper, whether you change all its main ideas or only polish its words and phrases.

Some of these strategies will prove useful to you in doing a thorough, top-to-bottom revision. In "A Writer's Tone," you will become aware of the attitude that informs a whole essay. In "Stressing What Counts," we suggest how you can emphasize important ideas. That advice surely applies to rewriting whole essays; the section also gives hints for rewriting just *parts* of essays: sentences and paragraphs.

Other strategies included here will prove useful mainly for editing: for that final going-over that makes your work clearer, less wordy, and more vigorous. In editing you look for small mistakes, cut a surplus word here and there, recast a sentence, replace a cliché ("dead as a doornail") or a bit of jargon ("student-administration interfacing") with fresher and plainer words. These editing strategies won't help you rework a paper extensively, when not only sentences but also main ideas need polishing. Still, they can make your writing far more readable.

REVISING DEEPLY

When you look back over your draft, how do you know what you need to rewrite? In previous chapters of this book, in the "Rewriting" sections, you found specific advice for such decision making. Here now are three *general* checklists of questions you might ask yourself in preparing to rewrite. You can use these questions in revising drafts written for practically any paper assignment. But the questions will prove useful only if you allow time to give your work a thorough going over. When you have a few hours to spare, they will help you find opportunities to make not just slight, cosmetic touchings-up, but major improvements.

REVISION CHECKLIST: REACHING YOUR GOAL

- Have you accomplished what you set out to do? If not, what still needs doing?
- Has your paper said everything that you believe needs to be said?
- Do you still believe everything you say? In writing the paper, have you changed your mind, rethought your assumptions, made a discovery? Do any of your interpretations or statements of opinion now need to be revised?
- Have you tried to take in too much territory, with the result that your coverage of your topic seems too thin? How might you—even now—reduce the scope of your paper? Could you cut material, perhaps write a new introduction making clear exactly what you propose to do?
- Do you know enough about your subject? Does more evidence seem called for? If so, try recalling, observing, reading, conversing, and imagining.
- If you have taken ideas and information from other writers, have you always given credit where it is due?
- If you have written to persuade readers, can you sum up in a sentence the claim your paper sets forth? (For help, see "Stating a Thesis," p. 469.)
- Have you emphasized what matters most? Have you kept the essential idea or ideas from being obscured by a lot of useless details and distracting secondary thoughts? (For "Stressing What Counts," see p. 500.)

REVISION CHECKLIST: TESTING STRUCTURE

- Would any paragraphs make more sense or follow better if arranged in a different order? Try imagining how a paragraph might look and sound in a new location. Scissor it out and stick it into a different place; reread and see whether it works well there.
- Does your topic make itself clear early in the paper, or must the reader plow through much distracting material in order to come to it? Later on in the draft, is there any passage that would make a better beginning?
- Can you cut any long-winded asides?
- Does everything follow clearly? Does one point lead to the next? If connections aren't clear, see "Using Transitions," page 486.
- Does the conclusion follow from what has gone before? It doesn't seem arbitrarily tacked on, does it? (See "Concluding Paragraphs," p. 491.)
- Do you suspect your paper is somewhat confused? If you suspect it, you are probably right. Suggestion: Make an informal outline of the paper as it now stands. Then look over the outline and try to spot places to make improvements. Revise the outline, then revise the paper. (For advice on outlining, see p. 476.)

REVISION CHECKLIST: CONSIDERING YOUR READERS

- Who will read this paper? Does the paper tell them what they will want to know? Or does it tell them only what they probably know already?
- Does the beginning of the paper promise your readers anything that the paper never delivers?
- Are there any places where readers might go to sleep? If so, can such passages be shortened or deleted? Do you take ample time and space to unfold each idea in enough detail to make it both clear and interesting? Would more detailed evidence help—perhaps an interesting brief story or a concrete example? (See "Giving Examples," p. 484.)

- Are there places where readers might raise serious objections? How might you recognize these objections, maybe even answer them?
- Have you used any specialized or technical language that your readers might not understand? If so, can you work in brief definitions?
- What attitude toward your readers do you seem to take? Are you overly chummy, needlessly angry, cockily superior, apologetic? Do you still feel that way? (For more suggestions, see "A Writer's Tone," p. 505.)
- From your conclusion, and from your paper as a whole, will your readers be convinced that you have told them something worth knowing?

STRESSING WHAT COUNTS

A boring writer writes as though every idea is no more important than any other. An effective writer cares what matters, decides what matters most, and shines a bright light on it.

You can't emphasize merely by underlining things or by throwing them into CAPITAL LETTERS. Such devices soon grow monotonous, and a writer who works them hard ends up stressing nothing at all, like a speaker whose every second word is a curse. One Navy boatswain's mate, according to folklore, couldn't talk without emphasizing every noun with an obscene adjective. To talk that way cost him great effort. By the time he could get out an order to his crew to bail, the boat had swamped. Emphasis wasn't all that was lost.

An essential of good writing, then, is to emphasize things that count. How? This section offers four suggestions.

Stating First or Last

One way to stress what counts is to put important things first or last. The most emphatic positions in an essay, or in a single sentence, are two: the beginning and the end. Let's consider each.

Stating first. In an essay, you might state in your opening paragraph what matters most. Writing a paper for an economics course in which students had been assigned to explain the consequences of import quotas (such as a limit on the number of foreign cars allowed into a country), Donna Waite began by summing up her findings:

> Although an import quota has many effects, both for the nation imposing the quota and the nation whose industries must suffer it, I believe that the most important is generally felt at home. A native industry gains a chance to thrive in a marketplace of lessened competition.

Her paper goes on to illustrate her general observation with evidence. Summing up the most important point right at the start is, by the way, a good strategy for answering a question in an essay examination. It immediately shows the instructor that you know the answer.

A persuasive paper might open with a statement of what the writer believes.

> Our state's antiquated system of justices of the peace is inefficient.

> For urgent reasons, I recommend that the United States place a human observer in temporary orbit around the planet Mars.

The body of the paper would set forth the writer's reasons for holding the view, and probably the writer would hammer the claim or thesis again at the end.

That advice refers to whole essays. Now let's see how in a single sentence you can stress things at the start. Consider the following unemphatic sentence.

> When Congress debates the Hall-Hayes Act removing existing legal protections for endangered species, as now seems likely to occur on May 12, it will be a considerable misfortune if this bill should pass, since the extinction of many rare birds and animals would certainly be the result.

The coming debate, and its probable date, take up the start of the sentence. The writer might have made better use of this emphatic position.

> The extinction of many rare birds and animals will follow passage of the Hall-Hayes Act.

Now the writer stresses what he most fears: dire consequences. (In a further sentence, he might add the date of the coming debate in Congress and his opinion that passage of the legislation would be a misfortune.)

Consider these further examples (a sentence in rough draft and in a revision):

> It may be argued that the best method of choosing software for a small business is to call in a professional consultant, who is likely to be familiar with the many systems available and can give helpful advice.

> The best method to choose software for a small business is to call in a professional consultant.

In the second version, the paper might go on: "Familiar with the many systems available, such an expert can give helpful advice." Notice that in the revision, the two most important ingredients of the idea are placed first and last. *Best method* is placed up front, and *professional consultant,* standing last in the sentence, is also given emphasis.

Stating last. In your reader's mind, an explosion of silence follows the final statement in your paper. To place an idea last can throw weight on it. One way to assemble your ideas in an emphatic order is to proceed from least important to most important.

This order is more dramatic: it builds up and up. Not all writing assignments call for drama, of course. In the papers on import quotas and justices of the peace, any attempt at a big dramatic buildup might look artificial and contrived. Still, this strategy is worth considering. Perhaps in an essay on city parks and how they lure shoppers to the city, the claim or thesis sentence—summing up the whole point of the argument—might stand at the very end: "For the inner city, to improve city parks will bring about a new era of prosperity." Ask yourself: "Just where in my essay have I made my one main point, the point I most want to make?" Once you find it, see if you can place it last by cutting or shifting what comes after it.

Arranging ideas in ascending order of importance can work not only for a whole essay but for single sentences. A memorable sentence will end, as William Butler Yeats said a poem should end, "with a click like a closing box." Here's a sentence that fails to click:

> The car crashed head-on into a brick wall after leading two police cruisers on a long chase through rush-hour traffic while sirens sounded.

Which idea most matters? That sirens sounded? No, the fact that the car crashed into a wall. Let's revise to make that fact stand last.

> Sirens roaring, two police cruisers chased the car through thick rush-hour traffic until it crashed head-on into a brick wall.

Not only is that sentence more emphatic, it is also more readable, for it comes to a point. In each of the following sentences, what takes the emphasis?

> Harum College's campus is green and beautiful as an April morning in a wilderness, although it sits in a neighborhood of junkyards, prowling cats, and a smoldering glue factory.
>
> Although Harum College sits in a neighborhood of junkyards, prowling cats, and a smoldering glue factory, its campus is green and beautiful as an April morning in a wilderness.

Both sentences work. The first lays weight on the grim surroundings; the second, on the beauty of the campus. The first starts with the beauty, then dwindles away from it, and ends on negative notes (junkyards, cats, and factory) that leave a reader likely to forget that the campus is beautiful. The first sentence (only the name of the college has been changed) comes from an early draft of a student paper; the second is her revision. She decided to revise because her purpose was to show how the college overcomes its disadvantages.

Usually, it will pay you to place the most important point in your sentence as close as possible to the end. That end position is a highly valuable piece of real estate, and you want to build something strong on it. Writers sometimes end a sentence with an unimportant aside, a weak qualifier, or some fussy minor detail:

> The car skidded for a hundred yards and crashed into a brick wall, or so the witness, who lives upstairs from my aunt, claimed.
>
> The car skidded for a hundred yards and crashed into a brick wall, according to a report in the *Morristown Daily Record*, a newspaper that is generally reliable in my opinion.
>
> The car skidded for a hundred yards and crashed into a brick wall, resulting in considerable broken glass lying around and a good deal of spilled oil also.

Try to amputate any such tacked-on ending. If you can't, and you believe some fact matters, embed it earlier in the sentence.

> The car, according to a report in the *Daily Record*, skidded for a hundred yards and crashed into a brick wall.

Like a well-aimed pitch, a well-turned sentence seems to arrive in the catcher's mitt with a smack. Our statement about the car crash, as revised, seems to land with blunt force in its reader's mind, just by stopping at that brick wall.

Subordinating

> Jason has a keen sense of humor. He has an obnoxious, braying laugh.

From that pair of sentences, a reader doesn't know what to feel about Jason. One trait seems to cancel out the other. The writer needs to decide whether to like Jason and then to indicate which trait matters more.

> Although Jason has a keen sense of humor, he has an obnoxious, braying laugh.

The revision makes Jason's sense of humor less important than the annoying hee-haw this lad emits. The less important idea is stated as a dependent clause ("Although . . ."), the more important idea as the main clause. But we could combine the two separate ideas quite differently:

> Although Jason has an obnoxious, braying laugh, he has a keen sense of humor.

That version reverses the meaning. It makes Jason sound fun to be with, despite his mannerism. The main clause states the main idea: "he has a keen sense of humor."

In both combined versions of the original two separate sentences, the reviser takes a definite stand. We know what to make of Jason. We know how the writer wants us to feel. What has happened? One of the two ideas—the idea the writer considers less important—has taken a backseat to the one that matters more. Through sentence combining, we have unfolded the information in one statement into another.

This way of combining sentences, *subordination*, is one of the most useful of all writing strategies. To subordinate one idea to another enables you to stress what counts. Besides, it gives your writing a certain professionalism. In truth, to subordinate is easy. Anyone can do it who can rewrite carefully. When sentences in a draft are short and simple, they are candidates for subordination.

> You can hold a tarantula in your hand. Be gentle with it. It probably will not attack you. Anyway, its bite is relatively harmless. It is like a hornet's sting.

This passage moves along like a freight train in which no boxcar stands out. The five sentences might be blended effectively into two sentences:

> If you hold a tarantula gently in your hand, it probably will not attack. Even if it does, its bite is no more harmful than a hornet's sting.

In this revision, the two most essential ideas become main clauses: (1) the tarantula probably won't attack and (2) its bite is relatively harmless. One whole sentence ("Be gentle with it") shrinks to an adverb: *gently.*

In scores of different ways, you can subordinate one idea to another. Perhaps the best method to learn these ways is to read, with pencil in hand, a professional writer like Joan Didion, Russell Baker, Alan Lightman, or another in this book, noticing how, in the longer sentences, the writer blends subordinate clauses with main clauses.

When you rewrite your own work and find many short or simple sentences, ask yourself: "What do I most want to stress?" Underline it and see whether it might become a main clause in a more complex sentence.

Is it already a main clause? If so, let it be. See what you might distill from the surrounding sentences to add to it.

What sentences state information that seems less important? Circle them. See if you can play them down: make them subordinate clauses or perhaps only phrases in longer sentences.

This advice on subordinating shouldn't be taken to mean that you should always yoke together all short, simple sentences. You need a few for variety. And a short, simple sentence can make a point with force. Sometimes, following a longer sentence or sentences, it can lend special emphasis.

> Some people, going without sleep for twenty-two hours at a stretch, subsisting on popcorn and french fries, drinking heavily and ignoring the need to exercise, think they can always pay attention to their health at a later date. They can't.

The last two-word sentence seems to land like a short jab to the jaw. Of course, you don't want to write in sentences so short and simple all the time. If you do, nothing you say will take emphasis.

Repeating

In general, it's economical to say a thing once. But at times a repetition can be valuable. One such time is when a repetition serves as a transition: it recalls something said earlier. (We discuss such repetition on p. 487.)

Repetition can be valuable, too, when it lends emphasis. When Robert Frost ends his poem "Stopping by Woods on a Snowy Evening" by repeating a line, he does so deliberately:

> The woods are lovely, dark and deep,
> But I have promises to keep,
> And miles to go before I sleep,
> And miles to go before I sleep.

The effect of this repetition is to lay weight on the fact that, for the speaker, a long, weary journey remains.

This device—repeating the words that most matter—is more often heard in a speech than found in writing. Recall Lincoln's Gettysburg Address, with its promise that "government of the people, by the people, and for the people" will endure; and Martin Luther King's famous speech with the insistent refrain "I have a dream." This is a powerful device for emphasis. Break it out only when an occasion calls for it.

A WRITER'S TONE

Like a speaking voice, a writer's voice may seem warm and friendly or cool and aloof, angry or merely annoyed, playful or grimly serious. Its quality depends on how the writer feels toward his or her material and toward the reader.

Whatever shows the writer's attitudes toward the topic and the reader is called the *tone* of a piece of writing. Tone may include choice of formal or informal language, colorful or bland words, dispassionate, coolly objective words or words loaded with emotional connotations ("You swine!" "You lover!"). A tone that seems right (to a reader) comes when the writer has written with an accurate sense of how the reader will react. If the writer is unaware of the reader or is wrong about the reader's responses, then the writer writes in an inappropriate voice. If a writer, for example, decides to take a humorous approach to the dread disease of leprosy, and the reader doesn't think that topic funny, the piece of writing will fall flat because the reader will read without sympathy.

In everyday life, when you talk to someone in person, you can look that person in the face. You know pretty well how your listener is taking what you say, and often the person's responses shape your words. If your listener smiles at your humor, you go on being humorous; if the person frowns, you cut the comedy, alter your tone of voice, and become more serious. In writing, knowing the responses of your audience is more difficult. Usually you have to imagine them.

From time to time, as you gather material and as you write, you may wish to consider your reader. Will a certain bit of evidence be convincing? Is a word too strong, likely to turn a reader off, or too weak, not likely to be persuasive? But probably you do most of your imagining of your reader's responses as you reread what you have written. If your first draft projects a tone that now seems inappropriate, then you'll need to rewrite.

Awareness of your reader helps you choose words neither too formal nor too informal. By *formal* language we mean the impersonal language of educated persons, usually only written but perhaps spoken on dignified occasions, such as college commencements. It is the language of writers for scholarly and professional journals. In general, it is marked by longer and more complicated sentences and by a large vocabulary including learned words and phrases (*libido, ethnology, in flagrante delicto*). It doesn't use contractions (like *doesn't*) and its attitude toward its topic is serious.

Informal (or colloquial) language is found in the writing of educated people in letters to friends and in books, essays, or articles that address general readers. Its sentences are less involved and may include contractions, slang (*nerd, to freak out*), and references to humble objects (*pants, cheeseburger*). It may address the reader as *you*, and it more closely resembles ordinary conversation.

A tone that your readers just can't stand will certainly kill any attempt at communication. Here are three varieties of tone that can murder any piece of writing.

1. The *superior* tone. The writer who takes this attitude writes in a cocksure manner, as though he thinks himself a superior being who can't be wrong, as any fool can see.

> Obviously, it is a fallacy to think that a new sales tax is needed. As all informed people are well aware, such a measure would undoubtedly suffer a crushing defeat, as a recent poll of fifty members of Congress has proved conclusively.

Revised, taking out all that trumpeting certainty and that painful attempt to flatter the reader ("As all informed people are well aware"), the passage might read:

> I believe it is a mistake to think that a new sales tax is necessary. A recent poll of fifty members of Congress indicates that this measure would suffer defeat by a large margin.

More likeable in its modest affirmation of an opinion, that revision also saves words.

2. The *inferior* tone. In contrast to the superior tone, some writers make themselves sound like kicked dogs, cringing and apologizing.

> Of course, the present writer does not know anything about this and probably should not even dare to venture an opinion. If the reader will forgive him, he would like to say, although well aware that he may be wrong. . . .

This writer needs to find out more about his topic. Then he won't have to apologize.

3. The *outraged* tone. Once in a while you'll meet a writer—usually in the service of some extreme political cause—who adopts a tone too fervent or too ferociously angry to be believed.

> Conservatives, licking their chops in anticipation, are lining up in favor of this outrageous legislation.

> Mealy-mouthed liberals swarm forth, their tender hearts ready to bleed for every unwed mother on welfare.

The emotion in such statements is too extreme. The writers sound as though they are foaming at the mouth. They display more rage than is necessary for their purposes—apparently, to criticize the opposition. In these cases, revision seems hardly enough. Perhaps these writers could use a quick immersion in ice water.

A writer who successfully adopted such a tone of outrage, but who did so for comic effect, was the Waco, Texas, newspaperman of the 1890s, William Cowper Brann. Brann once called someone's children "worthless spawn whose syphilitic carcasses are not worth a cent a pound for soap grease" and remarked of an enemy:

> He has cirrhosis of the soul. His heart is a green worm that feeds on gall. His bowels of compassion are petrified. If his milk of human kindness were churned, the product would be limburger cheese.

But the people Brann wrote about took him seriously, and the acid-penned writer's career ended suddenly when a bullet struck him—according to a witness, "right where his suspenders crossed."

Perhaps the best advice about tone is very simple. Pretend to no feelings you don't feel, and write in whatever words come naturally. Grace Paley, a fiction writer, always tells her students when she begins teaching a writing course, "If you say what's on your mind in the language that comes to you from your parents and your street and friends, you'll probably say something beautiful."

CUTTING AND WHITTLING

Like pea pickers who throw out dirt and pebbles, good writers remove needless words that clog their prose. They like to. One of the chief joys of revising is to watch 200 paunchy words shrink to a svelte 150. To see how saving words helps, let's first look at some wordiness. In what she imagined to be a gracious, Oriental style, a New York socialite once sent this dinner invitation to Hu Shi, the Chinese ambassador:

> O learned sage and distinguished representative of the numerous Chinese nation, pray deign to honor my humble abode with your noble presence at a pouring of libations, to be followed by a modest evening repast, on the forthcoming Friday, June Eighteenth, in this Year of the Pig, at the approximate hour of eight o'clock, Eastern Standard Time. Kindly be assured furthermore, O most illustrious sire, that a favorable reply at your earliest convenience will be received most humbly and gratefully by the undersigned unworthy suppliant.

In reply, the witty diplomat sent this telegram:

CAN DO. HU SHI.

Hu Shi's reply disputes a common assumption: that the more words an idea takes, the more impressive it will seem. Most good contemporary writers know that the more succinctly they can state an idea, the clearer and more forceful it will be.

Ever since the sixteenth century, some English writers have favored prolixity and, like the woman who invited Hu Shi, have deliberately ornamented their prose. George Orwell, a more recent writer who favored concision, thought English writing in his day had set a new record for wind. Perhaps the verbosity he disliked has been due in part to progress in the technology of writing. Quill pens that had to be dipped have given way to pens with ball points or felt tips, to electric typewriters and word processors. These strides have made words easier to seize and perhaps have made them matter less. As a printer-reporter in Virginia City, Nevada, Mark Twain sometimes wrote while he set type, transferring letters of lead from a case to a composing stick in his hand. An editorial might weigh ten pounds. Twain said the experience taught him the weight of a word. He soon learned to use no word that didn't matter.

Some writers may begin by writing a long first draft, putting in every scrap of material, spelling out their every thought in detail. They know that later it will be easier to trim away the surplus than to add missing essentials. But they mean to work back through the jungle of their prose with a merciless machete. In their revising habits, such writers may be like sculptor Auguste Rodin, who when an admirer asked, "Oh, Monsieur Rodin, is sculpture difficult?" answered lightly, "Not at all! I merely behold the statue in the block of stone. Then I chip away everything else."

Let us see how writers chip away. Often, a wordy introduction can just go.

As far as getting ready for winter is concerned, I put antifreeze in my car.

Why would anybody put antifreeze in a car if not to get ready for winter? Out with that needless explanation.

I put antifreeze in my car.

Some writers can't utter an idea without first sounding trumpets before it.

The point should be made that . . .
I might hasten to add that . . .
Let me make it perfectly clear that . . .
It is important for the reader to note that . . .

Cut the fanfare. Why bother to announce that you're going to say something? We aren't, by the way, attacking the usefulness of transitions that lead a reader along. You wouldn't chop a sentence like "Because, as we have seen, Chomsky's theory fails to account for the phenomenon of stuttering, let us consider the work of speech psychologist Wendell Johnson."

The phrases *on the subject of, in regard to, in terms of, as far as . . . is concerned,* and their ilk, often lead to wind.

He is more or less a pretty outstanding person in regard to good looks.

Write instead, "He is strikingly handsome" or "In looks, he stands out." Here's an especially grim example of corporate prose (before cutting and after):

Regarding trainees' personal life in relation to domestic status, it is not the intention of the management to object to the marriage of any of its trainees at their own individual discretions.

Trainees may marry if they like.

Words also tend to abound after *There is* or *There are*.

There are many people who dislike flying.

This construction provides an easy way to open a sentence, but it takes words. You can cut it.

Many people dislike flying.

You could even write, "Many dislike flying."
Another instance:

There is a lack of a sense of beauty in Wallace.

Make this "Wallace lacks a sense of beauty" or "Wallace is insensitive to beauty." Indeed, the verb *to be* can make a statement wordy when a noun or an adjective follows it.

This construction is conducive to wordiness.
The Akron game was a disappointment to the fans.

Replace *to be* by an active verb and revise the sentences:

This construction leads to wordiness.
The Akron game disappointed the fans.

Such changes not only save words, they strengthen a verb and enliven a sentence.

Often, when a clause begins with a relative pronoun (*who, which, that*), you can whittle it to a phrase:

Venus, which is the second planet of the solar system, is called the evening star.

Venus, the second planet of the solar system, is called the evening star.

Bert, who is a prize-winning violist, played a work of Brahms.

Bert, a prize-winning violist, played a work of Brahms.

The more you revise, the more shortcuts you'll discover. The following sentences have words that can just be cut (indicated in *italics*). Try reading each sentence without them.

Howell spoke for the sophomores and Janet *also spoke* for the seniors.
Professor Lombardi is *one of the most* amazing *men*.
He is *somewhat of* a clown, but *sort of the* lovable *type*.
As a major in *the field of* economics, I plan to concentrate on *the area of* international banking.

> *The decision as to* whether *or not* to go is up to you.
> The vice-chairman *very much* regrets that he is *very* busy.

Overused, *very* before a word won't strengthen that word but will detract from it. William Allen White, a Kansas newspaper editor who detested the little modifier, told his reporters, "Every time you feel you must write *very*, write *damn* instead." (He knew that his copy editor would delete any *damn*.)

Adjectives and adverbs are often dispensable. Consider the difference between these two versions.

> Johnson's extremely significant research led to highly important major discoveries.
>
> Johnson's research led to major discoveries.

Sometimes a foliage of words deliberately hides a sour apple of sense.

> As pertaining to your request for an increase in terms of the amount of your salary, we regret to inform you that in the considered opinion of the management such an increase does not seem feasible at the present moment. In terms of the amount of service performed by the requestee in relation to the comparable amount performed by his co-workers, the requestee's current scale of compensation seems to adequately reflect the approximate level of his output.

Hard to read, that paragraph chooses specialized, highfalutin words in place of simple ones (*the management* for *I, requestee* for *you, scale of compensation* for *pay, output* for *work*. We touch here on the problem of jargon, explored on page 520. In plain English, the passage might read:

> We have thought about your request for a pay raise. We can't approve it now. We think you make enough for the work you do. You don't deserve more than your co-workers.

Of course, that would be a shockingly plainspoken letter to receive, and the recipient might feel so hurt that he would quit immediately. Less severe revision might produce a message both plain and considerate:

> We have thought carefully about your request for a pay raise and are sorry to say we can't approve it now. We have to think of your co-workers and how to pay everyone fairly.

(And a sympathetic manager who valued the employee might add, "Why don't you drop by and discuss this with me? If you badly need more money, perhaps we can find a way.")

While sometimes a long word conveys a shade of meaning that its shorter synonym doesn't, in general it's a good idea to shun a long word or phrase when you can pick a short one. Instead of *the remainder,* try to write *the rest;* instead of *activate, start* or *begin;* instead of *expedite, rush;* instead of *adequate* or *sufficient, enough.* Wordiness, to be sure, doesn't always come from slinging overlarge words. Sometimes it comes from not knowing a right word—one that wraps an idea in a smaller package. The cumbersome expression *persons who are new to the sport of skiing* could be replaced by *novice skiers*. Consider these two remarks about a boxer:

Andy has a left fist that has a lot of power in it.

Andy has a potent left.

By the way, it pays to read. From reading, you absorb words like *potent* and *novice* and set them to work for you.

Here are a few more windy statements and whittled revisions of them:

WINDY	Mr. Pratt demonstrated to us the proper procedure by which to put the strings on a guitar.
WHITTLED	Mr. Pratt showed us how to string a guitar.
WINDY	Unemployment is one of the several considerable contributing factors producing a noticeable decline in the birth rate.
WHITTLED	Unemployment contributes to a lower birth rate.
OR	People out of work have fewer children.

Here is a final list of questions to use in slimming your writing.

REVISION CHECKLIST: CUTTING AND WHITTLING

- Do you announce an idea before you utter it? If so, consider giving the announcement a chop.
- Can you recast any sentence that begins *There is* or *There are?*
- What will happen if, wherever you use *to be*, you substitute an active verb?
- Can you reduce to a phrase any clause beginning with *which is, who is,* or *that is?*
- Do you see any useless words that might go? Try omitting them.
- Have you used any windy words or phrases that have shorter equivalents? (See the list in the next section.)

Checklist of Windy Words and Phrases

Here is a list of common words and phrases that take up more room than they deserve. For each, there's a shorter substitute.

Don't worry if this list contains some of your favorite expressions. No human being can write with perfect terseness, and even the best professional writers can't help using a few windy words. Still, the list may prove helpful for self-editing, especially if you ever need to write within a strict word limit. If, for instance, you write for a college newspaper where space is tight or have to do a laboratory report and squeeze all your findings into the blank spaces of a standard worksheet or face an assignment that insists on no more than 600 (or however many) words, then you can use this list to pare your prose to the bone.

WINDY WORDS	SUBSTITUTE
adequate enough	adequate
a period of a week	a week
approximately	about
area of, field of	(*omit*)
arrive at an agreement, conclude an agreement	agree
as a result of	because
as far as . . . is concerned	about
as to whether	whether
as you are already well aware	as you know
at an earlier point in time	before, earlier
at a later moment	after, later
at the present moment, at this point in time	now
basic rudiments, basic fundamentals	rudiments, fundamentals
brief in duration	brief
consensus of opinion	consensus *or* opinion
concerning the subject of, in connection with the subject of, with respect to the matter of	about
continuing on, continuing along	continuing
considerable amount of	much
considerable number of	many
despite the fact that, regardless (*or* irregardless) of the fact that	though, although
drive in a reckless manner (*or* fashion)	drive recklessly
due to the fact that, for the reason that, on account of the fact that	because
each individual person	each, each person
feel the necessity for	need
first beginnings, early beginnings	beginnings
for the most part	mostly
for the purpose of, in order to	to
for the reason that	because
from my own personal point of view	to me
give consideration to	consider, think about
great amount of, large amount of	much
great number of, large number of	many

WINDY WORDS	SUBSTITUTE
I am of the opinion that, it is my personal opinion that	I think
if it is agreeable to you	if you agree
in color (*as in* "red in color")	(*omit*)
in regard to, with reference to	about
in such a way that	so that
in terms of	(*Omit and rewrite; for advice, see p. 508.*)
in the last analysis	in the end, finally
in the likely (*or* unlikely) event that	if
in the not-too-distant future	soon
in this modern world, in the world of today, in contemporary society	now, today
in view of the fact that	because, since
it is my considered opinion that	I believe
I would like to request that you please send me	please send me
join (*two things*) together	join
kind of, sort of, type of	(*omit*)
large in size, large-sized	large
lend assistance to	assist, aid, help
main essentials	essentials
make contact with	call, talk with
members of the opposition	opponents
merge together	merge
numerous	many
numerous and sundry	many different
on the occasion of his birthday	on his birthday
on a once-a-month schedule	monthly
past experience, past history	experience, history
persons of the female gender	women
persons of the homosexual inclination	gays, homosexuals
persons of the Methodist faith	Methodists
pertaining to	about, on
plan ahead for the future	plan
prior to	before
put an end to, terminate	end
rarely ever, seldom ever	rarely, seldom

WINDY WORDS	SUBSTITUTE
rather a large number of	many
strongly urge	urge
sufficient amount of	enough
the reason why	the reason
refer to by the name of	call, name
refer back to	refer to
reinvite again	reinvite
remarks of a humorous nature, remarks on the humorous side	humorous remarks
render completely inoperative	break, smash
repeat again	repeat
resemble in appearance	look like
returning back	returning
similar to	like
subsequent to	after
subsequently	later, then
true facts	facts, truth
utilize, make use of	use
very	(*Omit unless you very much need it!*)

AVOIDING SEXISM

Among the prime targets of American feminists in the 1960s and 1970s was the deplorable tendency of the English language to relegate women to second-class status. Why, they asked, do we talk about *prehistoric man, manpower, the common man,* and *the brotherhood of man,* when by *man* we mean the entire human race? Why do we denigrate a woman's accomplishment by calling her a *poetess* or a *lady doctor?* Why does a letter to a corporation have to begin, "Gentlemen:"?

Early efforts to provide alternatives to the sexism of the language occasionally led to awkward, even ungrammatical solutions. To substitute "Everyone prefers their own customs" for "Everyone prefers *his* own customs" is to replace sexism with bad grammar. "Everyone prefers his or her [or *his/her*] own customs" is correct, but sometimes clumsy. Even clumsier is "Was it George or Jane who submitted his or her [*his/her*] resignation?" *Chairperson, policeperson, businessperson, spokesperson,* and *congressperson* do not flow easily from tongue or pen; and some readers object to *chairwoman, policewoman,* and similar words because they call attention to gender where gender ought not to matter. *Male nurse* elicits the same objection.

Some writers try to eliminate sexual bias by alternating between the masculine and feminine genders every few sentences. Dr. Benjamin Spock, when referring to babies, uses *he* and *she* in roughly equal numbers throughout later revisions of his well-known *Baby and Child Care.* Some readers find this approach refreshing. Why should we, after all, think of every baby as a boy, every parent as a woman? Other readers find such gender switches confusing.

Well-meaning attempts to invent or borrow neutral third-person pronouns (*thon asks* instead of *he asks* or *she asks,* for instance) have not gained general acceptance. How then can we as sensitive writers minimize the sexist constraints that the English language places in our path? There are no hard-and-fast rules, no perfect solutions. At best, we can be aware of the potholes and try to steer around them as smoothly as possible.

1. For *mankind,* why not substitute *people, human beings, humanity,* or *human race?*

2. Sometimes you can avoid sexism by making a singular subject plural. Instead of "Today's student values his education," write, "Today's students value their education."

3. Where possible, sidestep the problem. If you find you've written a sentence like "For optimal results, there must be rapport between a stockbroker and his client, a teacher and his student, a doctor and his patient," why not simply substitute "stockbroker and client, teacher and student, doctor and patient," thus eliminating the offending masculine pronouns?

4. Be on the lookout for sexual stereotypes. If you find you have written, "Astronauts have little time to spend with their wives and children," consider substituting, "Astronauts have little time to spend with their families."

5. When writing a letter to a woman, consider addressing her as *Ms.*—a wonderfully useful form of address comparable to *Mr.* for a man and easier to use than either *Miss* or *Mrs.* for someone whose marital status you don't know or when marital status doesn't matter—which in professional life is usually.

6. Accept your inability to change the English language overnight, single-handedly. As more men and women come to regard themselves as equals, the language will increasingly reflect the reality. Meanwhile, in your writing, try to be fair to both sexes without succumbing either to clumsiness or to grammatical error.

WEEDING OUT CLICHÉS

A *cliché* is a trite expression, worn out from too much use. Like a coin fresh from the mint, it may have glinted once, but now it is dull and flat from years of passing from hand to hand. If a story begins, "It was a dark and stormy night" and introduces a "tall, dark, and handsome" man and a woman who is "a vision of loveliness," then its author is obviously running low on change.

Sometimes a cliché is an old dull expression whose writer assumes it is bright. "Let's run this up the flagpole and see if anyone salutes it," says the executive, proposing an idea—not realizing that the expression she thinks so smart went out with the great white auk. Stale, too, would be a suggestion to put an idea *on the back burner.* Clichés abound when writers and speakers try hard to sound vigorous and colorful but don't trouble to invent anything vigorous, colorful, and new.

George Orwell once complained about prose made up of phrases "tacked together like the sections of a prefabricated henhouse." Newspaper readers keep meeting such ready-made constructions. A strike is usually settled after "a marathon bargaining session" that "narrowly averts a walkout," often "at the eleventh hour." For years, practically no reporter has been able to refer to Rose Kennedy as other than "the ninety-six-year-old matriarch of the Kennedy clan" (or however many years old she has been). Fires customarily "race" and "gut." For a feast of still more blatant clichés, open any issue of a weekly tabloid newspaper sold in supermarkets. Clichés will shriek at you. This headline has three shrieks in a row.

AN *UGLY LIGHT* ON *THE BEAUTIFUL
PEOPLE* AS *SCANDALS ROCK SOCIETY*

Some writers use clichés to exaggerate, giving a statement more force than they feel. The writer to whom everything is *fantastic* or *terrific* arouses a reader's suspicion that it isn't. Such word inflation once drew a protest from sports writer Ray Fitzgerald to his fellow baseball writers in the press box at Boston's Fenway Park.

The word you hear around here is *incredible.* Everything is incredible this or incredible that. Every other play is incredible. Do you know what's incredible? If that guy turns into a swan while he's sliding into second base, that's incredible.

Though Fitzgerald's remark was leveled at baseball writers, college writers also can take it to heart. If in presenting evidence and illustrations you overwork words like *remarkable, unique,* or *significant,* you probably exaggerate.

A writer who relies on clichés sometimes pays too little notice to words even to spell them right. In such writers' prefabricated henhouses, you will find "died (instead of *dyed*) in the wool" and mention of a leading citizen who is a "pillow (instead of a *pillar*) of her community."

You can worry too hard, though, about writing a cliché now and then. To write a really disturbingly stale cliché takes effort—not much effort, but a little. You have to try for a colorful, vivid figure of speech and then fail because only a worn-out drab and dreary expression comes to mind. No writer can entirely avoid clichés or avoid echoing scraps of colorful language. Such is the case with proverbs ("It takes a thief to catch a thief"), well-worked quotations from Shakespeare ("Neither a borrower nor a lender be"), and other faintly dusty wares from the storehouse of our language. "Looking for a needle in a haystack" may be a well-worn phrase, yet who can put that idea any more memorably? Don't fear that every familiar expression is a cliché. "Wait a minute," "what time is it?" "excuse me," "hold the mustard"—these are old, dull, familiar expressions, to be sure; but they are not clichés, for they don't try to be vivid or figurative. Inevitably, we all rely on them.

When editing your writing, you will usually recognize any really annoying cliché you'll want to eradicate. If you feel a sudden guilty desire to surround an expression with quotation marks, as if to apologize for it, then strike it out.

> In his campaign speeches for his seventh term, Senator Pratt shows that he cannot "cut the mustard" any longer.

Think again: what do you want to say? Recast your idea more clearly, more exactly.

> At the age of seventy-seven, Senator Pratt no longer can hold a crowd with an impassioned, hour-long speech, as he could when he first ran for Congress.

By what other means can you spot a cliché? It may help to show your papers to friends, asking them to look for anything trite. As you go on in college, your awareness of clichés will grow with reading. The more you read, the easier it is to spot an old-hat expression on sight, for you will have met it often before. You can then prune from your writing anything dried up, seedy, and shedding.

Writers who use a word processor now have access to software programs that detect clichés. Whenever the writer uses a cliché that matches any of hundreds the program has on file, the stale words are highlighted on the screen, and alternatives are offered.

A Cliché Checklist

Here is a list of a few clichés still in circulation. If any is a favorite of yours, try replacing it with something new and more vivid and original.

Achilles' heel
acid test
add insult to injury
apple of one's eye
as American as apple pie
an astronomical sum
behind the eight ball
beyond a shadow of a doubt
the Big Apple (*name for New York City*)
born with a silver spoon in one's mouth

bosom companions (*or* bosom buddies)
burn the midnight oil
burn one's bridges behind
busy as a beaver [*or* a bee]
But that's another story.
callow youth
come hell or high water
cool as a cucumber
cream of the crop
cross the Rubicon
dead as a doornail

do a land-office business

do your own thing

dressed fit to kill

dry as dust

eager beaver

easy as taking candy from a baby

easy as falling off a log

a face that would stop a clock

feeling on top of the world

few and far between

fiddle while Rome burns

fine and dandy

fly in the ointment

fresh as a daisy

from time immemorial

going like a house afire

golden years

greased lightning

hands-on learning experience

hard as a rock

high as a kite

holler bloody murder

honest as the day is long

hot and heavy

I couldn't have imagined in my
    wildest dreams . . .

In conclusion, I would like to
    say . . .

last but not least

Little did I dream . . .

mad as a wet hen

make a long story short

marital woes

a name to conjure with

natural inclination

neat as a pin

nice as pie

nutty as a fruitcake

old as the hills

on the ball

on the brink of disaster

one for the book

over and above the call of duty

pay through the nose

piece of cake

point with pride

proud as a peacock

pull the wool over someone's
    eyes

pure as the driven snow

read the riot act

salad days

sell like hotcakes

a sheepish grin

since the dawn of time

skating on thin ice

a skeleton in the closet

slow as molasses

smell a rat

a sneaking suspicion

sound as a dollar

stack the deck

stagger the imagination

stick out like a sore thumb

sweet as honey

That's the way the ball bounces
    (*or* the cookie crumbles).

thin edge of the wedge

tip of the iceberg

through thick and thin

time-honored

too little, too late

tried but true

unimpeachable authority

The worm turns.

You could have knocked me over
    with a feather.

RECOGNIZING EUPHEMISMS

Euphemisms are plain truths dressed in attractive words, sometimes hard facts stated gently and pleasantly. To say that someone "passed away" instead of "died" is a common euphemism—useful and humane, perhaps, in breaking terrible news to an anxious family. In such shock-absorbing language, an army that retreats "makes a strategic withdrawal"; a poor old man becomes a "disadvantaged senior citizen." But euphemisms aren't always oversized words. If you call someone "slim" instead of "underweight" or "skinny" you use a euphemism, though it has only one syllable.

Because they can bathe glum truths in a kindly glow, euphemisms are beloved by some advertisers—like the mortician (a euphemism for "undertaker") who offered "preneed arrangements." Some acne medications treat not pimples but "blemishes." Euphemisms can make ordinary things sound more impressive. "Dental cream," the invention of a writer of advertising copy, glorifies toothpaste ever so slightly. In Madison, Wisconsin, a theater renamed its candy counter the "patron assistance center." In everyday use, some euphemisms are so familiar that we don't notice that they disguise anything. Life insurance might well be called "death insurance" since it prevents financial hardship only on the death of the insured. (Imagine how much harder it would be to sell "death insurance"!)

Official spokespersons love euphemisms. Knowing that nobody likes paying taxes, the federal Office of Management and Budget once referred to a tax hike as "revenue enhancement" and "tax-base erosion control." William Safire has recorded a memorable euphemism uttered in Grand Canyon Park, where at the time wild burros were destroying too much scrub. Asked by a reporter if he intended to shoot the burros, a park officer replied, "Well, sir, we call it *direct reduction.*" In similarly indirect official language, one hospital recorded every death as a "Negative Patient Care Outcome." That must have looked better on the books. Whenever a recruiter describes a company with a job opening as "running a tight ship" or declares, "We're a close-knit team," the applicant should probably beware. According to former executive Roger Axtell, such euphemisms mean "We don't employ enough people to do all the work there is to do."

Euphemisms may serve grimmer purposes. During World War II, Jewish prisoners sent to Nazi extermination camps carried papers stamped *Rückkehr Unerwünscht* ("Return Unwanted"). In 1984, the Doublespeak Award of the National Council of Teachers of English went to the State Department for its announcement that it would no longer use the word *killing* in its official reports, but substitute "unlawful or arbitrary deprivation of life." The following year, the award went to the Central Intelligence Agency, which prepared a manual for rebels fighting the government of Nicaragua. In the manual, the rebels were told how to join a peaceful demonstration and, equipped with "knives, razors, chains, clubs, bludgeons," march along "slightly behind the innocent and gullible participants." Asked about this manual, CIA director William Casey said that its purpose was "to make every guerrilla persuasive in face-to-face communication." At times, Pentagon spokespersons have referred to civilian casualties in nuclear war as "collateral damage" and have measured the radiation from a nuclear blast in "sunshine units." Some writers, to be sure, use euphemisms ironically. As readers, we then enjoy noticing a discrepancy between humble truth and a lofty way of putting it. The result is a comic effect—as when Mark Twain, in *Life on the Mississippi*, refers to a "fragrant town drunkard." With tongue in cheek, a sports writer calls first base "the initial hassock." Mechanically contrived, though, such euphemisms won't be funny. Most of the time, a euphemism is far less effective than direct words.

Few college writers have the problem of using too many euphemisms. But all need to be wary of euphemisms when they read, especially when collecting evidence from biased sources and official spokespersons.

CHOOSING COMMON WORDS OVER JARGON

People in special disciplines—music, carpentry, the law, computer programming—speak and write with the aid of special terms. Baseball players, for instance, have their own professional language. When he faces a dangerous batter, says pitcher Dennis Eckersley, he thinks, "If I throw him *the heater,* maybe he *juices it out* on me." (Translation: "If I throw him a fastball, he might hit a home run.") Among people who converse on citizens band radio, "What's your *twenty?*" means "Tell me your whereabouts," while "I'm going *double nickel*" means "I'm going the speed limit: 55 miles per hour." In any new job, you may need to learn a new vocabulary—as newspaper reporter Benjamin Taylor soon found on being assigned to cover the White House:

> White House officials talk to the press under any number of arrangements of qualified anonymity, and reporters have to learn the difference between *off the record, background, deep background,* and *for guidance only. Off the record* apparently means "I'll tell you this but you can't use it." *Background* means that you can use it but only if you attribute it to an administration or a White House source. *Deep background,* I am told, means you can use it but not attribute it to anyone connected with the administration. And *guidance* is usually furnished by a White House official who wants to steer a reporter in the right direction but who does not want to be quoted.

To a specialist addressing other specialists, such language is convenient and necessary. Given "deep background," reporters know that if they want to hold their jobs, they can't say, "The press secretary declared . . . ," but have to say, "Observers believe. . . ." Without technical terms, after all, two surgeons could hardly discuss a patient's anatomy. To an outsider, such terms are *jargon* (from the Middle English: *jargoun,* "meaningless chatter").

Commonly, we apply the name *jargon* to any private, pretentious, or needlessly specialized language that blurs meaning and confuses us. When, to save money, a top executive of Apple Computer pared the company's work force from 5300 to 4600, *Time* reported that he called the massive firings "infrastructure phasedown." Statesmen and bureaucrats, too, seek to bedazzle us commoners. In the language of the Defense Department, a hammer is a "manually powered fastener-driving impact device." Some official spokespersons make a noun into a verb—"Let us *prioritize* our objectives"—tacking the suffix *-ize* on to any noun in sight. Less stuffy than *to prioritize* would be "to decide what to give priority" or "to rank our aims" or "to put certain goals first." In 1983 a much-worked verb from federalese entered a Merriam-Webster dictionary; still, it wears the look and shares the feel of a jargon word:

The government intends to *privatize* federal landholdings.

The statement means that the government plans to sell public land to private owners—as might occur, say, were a national park to be auctioned off to developers. (That example might also be called a *euphemism,* which is any high-falutin language that masks real meanings. See p. 519.) In jargon, another favorite suffix is *-wise:*

Voterwise, many minorities were represented.

To slash its jargon, this sentence might be recast: "Many minorities in the electorate were represented." Or better still: "Many minorities voted."

Jargon blights writing whenever a writer uses specialized terms loosely and inaccurately, without considering readers. As if addressing fellow specialists, such a writer bombards general readers with technical terms. Recently, high technology has given new meanings to the familiar verbs *to access, to boot,* and *to format* and has invented the new verb *to interface.* Used in ordinary discourse, these may result in jargon as hard to make sense of as *prioritize.* To tell how computers work, such terms may serve; but when thoughtlessly applied to abstract or intellectual ideas, they can result in bepiddlements: "A democracy needs the electorate's *input.*"

One trouble with such language is that it is inaccurate: it transforms people into components in a system of processes. "Information is lost, not gained," declares semanticist Robert W. Hunt, "when we are told that 'feedback was obtained,' rather than 'the students complained about the policy.'"

People who sling technical words may not know much about technology, but they probably think that specialized terms lend their writing an air of knowledge. Among other expressions that hamper understanding, we sometimes hear the vague phrase *x amount of* and the specialized terms *data base* and *random access.* Mathematicians have almost lost control of the noun *parameters* (meaning "certain numbers that determine the shape of a curve or other mathematical object"). As one scientist has complained, "*Parameters* is a useful word. If people want to say 'limits,' I wish they wouldn't use *parameters.* I am quite sure many scientific people join me in that weary wish."

Many other specialists have yearned for plainer and more common language in the scholarly writing of their own professions. "Be brave," urge Maeve O'Connor and F. Peter Woodford in *Writing Scientific Papers in English*, in their

DOONESBURY
by Garry Trudeau

advice to medical researchers. "Say, 'It is most often found in the heart,' not 'The most frequent among its localizations is the cardiac one.'" In a recent professional journal, Hanan C. Selvin and Everett K. Wilson warn their fellow sociologists against using larger words than necessary. The short word *methods,* they point out, sometimes "suffers an attack of syllabitis" and swells to *methodology.* This larger term is often too broad: it takes in not only the tactics and strategy of investigating but also the grounds for those tactics and strategies.

While a variety of methodologies have been employed to answer this question. . . .

Selvin and Wilson would suggest instead:

Although various methods have been employed. . . .

Like slang, jargon words shift into fashion and out again. Lately, *ongoing* has had its vogue: "ongoing efforts," "an ongoing project," "This university is making ongoing upgradings of dormitory habitability." Usually, a writer can just cut *ongoing;* for as William Zinsser has noted, everything alive continues: "When we cease to be ongoing, we are dead."

Here's how to shun needless jargon.

1. Beware of any flashy new word that seems the in thing when a perfectly good old word will do.

2. In particular, before using a new word ending in *-ize* or *-wise,* count to ten. This will give you time to think of a different word.

3. Lapse not into the vocabulary of a special discipline (say, psychology or fly-fishing) unless you write of psychological or fly-fishing matters and you know for sure that your reader, too, is familiar with them. If you're writing about some specialty you're expert in, for an audience of general readers—if, for instance, you're explaining the fundamentals of hang gliding—define any specialized terms. Even if you're writing to fellow adepts at hang gliding, use plain words and you'll rarely go wrong.

Do these things, and you too may help realize the vision of historian Thomas Carlyle—of a day "when jargon might abate, and genuine speech begin."

Appendix:
Manuscript Style

Some instructors are sticklers in detailing how your paper ought to look; others maintain a benign indifference to such commonplaces. In writing for an instructor of either stripe, it is only considerate to turn in a paper easy to read and to comment on.

In case you have received no particular instructions for the form of your paper, here are some general, all-purpose specifications.

1. Write or type on just one side of standard letter-size paper ($8\frac{1}{2}$-by-11 inches). Erasable typing paper, however helpful to a mistake-prone typist, may be irksome to an instructor who needs to write comments. The paper is easily smeared, and it won't take certain brands of pen.

2. Use a black ribbon if you type, blue or black ink if you write. Don't hand in a paper printed on a dot matrix printer or done in italic type. Both are hard to read.

3. For a paper without a separate title page, place your name, together with your instructor's name, the number and section of the course, and the date in the upper left corner of the first page, each item on a new line even with the left margin. Double-space between lines. Number your pages consecutively (do not type a page number on the first page). For a paper of two or more pages, put your last name in the upper right corner of each sheet after page 1 along with the page number. Staples are the best bet; paper clips quit their posts. By the way, don't ever try to bind your pages together by ripping a little tab in them and folding it. This method never works; the pages always come apart.

4. Double-space again and center your title on the line. Don't underline the title; don't put it in quotation marks or type the title all in uppercase letters; and don't put a period after it. Double-space twice between your title and the first line of your text.

5. Make sure you give your instructor plenty of room to write in, if need be. Leave ample margins—at least an inch—left and right, top and bottom. If you type, double-space your manuscript; if you write, use wide-ruled paper or skip every other line.

6. Indent each new paragraph five spaces.

7. Leave two spaces after every period or other end stop, one after a comma or semicolon.

8. Long quotations should be double-spaced like the rest of your paper but indented from the left margin—ten spaces if you're following Modern Language Association (MLA) guidelines, five if you're using American Psychological Association (APA) guidelines. Citations appear in parentheses two spaces after the final punctuation mark of the block quotation. (For more about citing sources, see Chapter 19.)

9. Covering a short essay—one of, say, five pages—in a hefty binder or giving it a title page with a blank sheet or two after it is unnecessary. Title pages are generally reserved for research papers and other bulky works.

10. For safety's sake and peace of mind, make a copy of your paper.

Additional Suggestions for Research Papers

For research papers the format is the same with the following additional specifications.

1. Type a title page, with the title of your paper centered about a third of the way down the page. Then go down two to four more spaces and type your name, then the instructor's name, the number and section of the course, and the date, each on a separate line. Repeat your title on the first page of your paper.

2. Do not number your title page; your outline, if you submit one with your paper, is numbered with small roman numerals (ii, iii, and so on).

3. Don't put a number on the first page of your text (page 1); all subsequent pages through your notes and works cited pages are numbered consecutively with arabic numerals in the upper right corner of the page.

4. Double-space your notes and your list of works cited. (For more instructions for making such a list, see Chapter 19.)

5. If you are asked to hand in your note cards along with your paper, be sure that they are in order and securely bound with a rubber band or placed in an envelope.

How to Make a Correction

Although you will want to make any large changes in your rough draft, not in your final copy, don't be afraid to make small corrections in pen when you give your paper a last once-over. No writer is error-free; neither is any typist. In making such corrections, you may find it handy to use certain symbols used by printers and proofreaders.

A transposition mark (ꙮ) reverses the positions of two words or two letters:

```
The nearby star Tau Ceti closely resﬔbles our sun.
```

Close-up marks (⌒) bring together the parts of a word accidentally split when a typewriter stutters. A separation mark (⌐) inserts a space where one is needed:

```
The nearby star Tau Ceti closely re⌒sembles our⌐sun.
```

To delete a letter or a punctuation mark, draw a slanted line through it:

```
The nearby star Tau Ceti closely res/embles our sun.
```

When you insert a word or letter, use a caret (∧) to indicate where the insertion belongs:

```
                                   s
The nearby star Tau Ceti closely reembles our sun.
                                   ∧
```

The symbol ¶ before a word or a line means "start a new paragraph":

```
But lately, astronomers have slackened their efforts to
study dark nebulae. ¶ That other solar systems may support
life as we know it makes for still another fascinating
speculation.
```

Finally, you can always cross out a word neatly and write a better one over it:

```
                          closely
The nearby star Tau Ceti somewhat resembles our sun.
```

Abbreviations

A good rule is to spell out most words in full, limiting your use of abbreviations to those that are most common, as in the case of a title or designation that goes before a name.

```
Mr. Collins     Dr. Jordan
St. Matthew     Ms. Boudreau
```

Some abbreviated titles, set off by commas, follow the proper name: Jr., Sr., M.D., D.D.S., C.P.A., M.A., Ph.D., Litt. D., S.J. You can abbreviate academic degrees even when they appear without proper names.

```
My sister has a B.A. in economics.
```

Spell out other titles when they appear without proper names.

```
Hawkins is studying to be a doctor.
```

Abbreviations are commonly used with exact dates and numbers.

```
9:05 a.m.      4:40 p.m.
2000 B.C.      A.D. 1066
```

A few common Latin abbreviations will get by in everyday writing (or in hasty notes to yourself); but in formal writing, unless you are addressing an audience of ancient Romans, you had best translate the terms.

ABBREVIATION	LATIN	ENGLISH
c.	*circa*	about, around, approximately
etc.	*et cetera*	and so forth, and others, and whatnot, and several other things
i.e.	*id est*	that is
e.g.	*exempli gratia*	for example

You can use acronyms, or words formed from the first letters of other words, for organizations and corporations. If they are very familiar, you need not use periods: FBI, IBM, NATO, UCLA.

To avoid possible misunderstandings on the part of your reader, write out the acronym the first time you use it and include its abbreviation in parentheses. In later references, you can rely on the acronym alone.

Mothers Against Drunk Drivers (MADD) led to the formation of Students Against Drunk Drivers (SADD). In persuading legislators to stiffen the penalties meted out to intoxicated drivers, both MADD and SADD have been forceful influences.

If you don't know whether to abbreviate, don't abbreviate. When in doubt, spell it out.

Capital Letters

The main thing to remember about capital letters is to use them only with reason. Capitalize the proper names of people, places, and things.

```
Charles Darwin
Sequoia National Park
a Volkswagen
```

Capitalize adjectives derived from proper names unless they are used with a specialized meaning.

```
Australian beer          but: french fries
Shakespearean comedy          roman numerals
```

Capitalize a rank or title in front of a name.

```
As a rule, Senator Wilimczyk serves his constituents well.
In her last lecture Professor Jones dealt with eugenics.
```

Some writers also capitalize a rank or title when using it instead of the name of an individual.

```
The Senator voted for the appropriation.
The Doctor will see you now.
```

Unless a title or rank substitutes for a proper name, don't capitalize it.

```
Trebor consulted a doctor about his rash.
Nezbrun is the art department's only full professor.
```

Academic and professional degrees that follow a person's name take capitals and periods.

```
Donna B. McLean, M.D.
Jack Elmo Stalnaker, D.Ed.
```

Capitalize a family relationship only when it is part of a proper name or when it takes the place of a name.

```
He cited the old Irish song about Mother Machree.
A student of ceramics, Mother is an internationally known
authority on Ming vases.
```

Capitalize the names of religions and their followers: *Christianity, Islam; Muslims, Methodists.* Capitalize nouns referring to the deity: *Jehovah, Messiah, Allah, Krishna, the Holy Spirit.*
Use capital letters for the titles of papers, books, and articles and for the titles of works of art. Do not capitalize articles, conjunctions, or prepositions unless they come first or last in the title or follow a colon.

```
"Once More to the Lake" (an essay)
Of Mice and Men (a novel)
W. D. Snodgrass's "The Operation" (a poem)
```

Don't capitalize *north, south, east,* and *west* unless they are parts of proper names (*West Virginia, South Orange*).

```
Go west, young man.
Drive south to Chicago, then on to East Cleveland.
```

Some writers capitalize those direction words when they refer to geographic regions: *the mysterious East, the economic growth of the South.*
A common noun, such as *street, avenue, boulevard, park,* and *hill,* is capitalized when it is part of a proper name.

```
Meinecke Avenue      Diversey Boulevard
Hamilton Park        Briar Lane
```

Capitalize the days of the week and the names of months but not seasons. Don't capitalize names of academic years and terms.

```
Monday's child                spring term
the January study plan        junior year abroad
```

Numbers

When do you write out a number (twenty-seven) and when do you use figures (27)? In general, when writing an essay and not an income tax return, use words. But if it would take *several* words, use figures instead.

```
More than two hundred people paid $25 apiece for a cheap
plastic novelty worth $1.05.
A frog's tongue has 970,000 taste buds, one-sixth as many
as a human's.
```

If, however, a figure falls at the start of a sentence, good practice is to write it out—or move it deeper into the sentence. By so doing, you help your reader's eye to recognize a new sentence by capitalizing the first word of it. You can't capitalize a figure. Try to begin your sentences with words.

```
Nine hundred seventy thousand taste buds help the frog
distinguish sweet flies from salty ones.
```

Figures are usually the shortest way to give dates, prices, percentages, scores, and page numbers.

```
As Smith notes on page 197, the 1984 Little League World
Series saw South Korea beat the team from Altamonte
Springs, Florida, 6-2 before a throng of 7500.
```

If a given time is exact to the minute, use figures: 2:29 p.m.; if it is a round or approximate number, write it out (*half-past two in the afternoon* or *between two and three o'clock*).

Italics

Italic type—as in this line—slants to the right. Italics are usually saved for brief occasions: for a word or several words. In writing or typewriting, indicate italics by underlining.

Underline words when you mean "Look here—these words are words."

```
The word orthodoxy means "conformity."
Psychologists now prefer the term unconscious to
subconscious.
```

```
The rhythmic, wavelike motion of the walls of the
alimentary canal is called peristalsis.
```

Underline words or phrases from another language unless they're in everyday use.

```
Gandhi taught the principles of satya and ahimsa: truth
and nonviolence.
```

But if you write, "That view is passé" or "Most students like pizza," you need not underline. Such terms have become familiar English words.

Underline the titles of magazines, newspapers, and long literary works (books, pamphlets, plays); the titles of films; the titles of paintings and other works of art; the titles of long musical works (operas or symphonies).

```
Before it came out as a book, John Hersey's Hiroshima
first appeared in the New Yorker.
The Broadway musical My Fair Lady was based on Shaw's
play Pygmalion.
The Cleveland Philharmonic played Dvořák's New World.
Pete regularly reads the Washington Post and Newsweek
magazine.
```

Note that in giving titles of newspapers and magazines, you underline the publication's exact title—nothing more. (*Newsweek* isn't called *Newsweek Magazine*.) The titles of short poems and short stories usually appear in quotation marks.

```
Generations of readers have shivered over Poe's poem "The
Raven" and his short story "The Fall of the House of
Usher."
```

The name of the Bible is not italicized; neither is that of any of its books (Genesis, Matthew) or of any other sacred book (the Koran, the Rig-Veda).

Underline the names of record albums, ships, boats, trains, airplanes, and spacecraft.

```
The Who's In Orbit features a song about Mariner IX.
```

Finally, if you absolutely *have* to place special emphasis on a word, you can underline it; but do so sparingly. Throw weight on things with italics only if you must.

Acknowledgments (continued from p. iv)

Arthur L. Campa. "Anglo vs. Chicano: Why?" *Western Review,* vol. IX, Spring 1972. Reprinted by permission of the estate of Arthur L. Campa.

Raymond Chandler. From *Selected Letters of Raymond Chandler,* edited by Frank MacShane. Copyright © 1981 Columbia University Press, New York.

Aaron Copland. "How We Listen" from *What to Listen for in Music* by Aaron Copland. Copyright © 1964 McGraw-Hill Book Company, New York. Reprinted by permission of McGraw-Hill.

Norman Cousins. "How to Make People Smaller Than They Are." © 1978 *Saturday Review* Magazine. Reprinted by permission.

Harry Crews. "The Car" from *Florida Frenzy* by Harry Crews. University Presses of Florida. Copyright © 1982 by Harry Crews. Reprinted by permission of John Hawkins & Associates, Inc.

Pers Crowell. From *Cavalcade of American Horses* by Pers Crowell. Copyright © 1951 McGraw-Hill Book Company. Reprinted by permission of McGraw-Hill.

Frank J. Cunningham. "Writing Philosophy: Sequential Essays and Objective Tests." *College Composition and Communication* 36 (May 1985). Copyright © 1985 by the National Council of Teachers of English. Reprinted by permission of the publisher and the author.

Joan Didion. "Marrying Absurd" from *Slouching Toward Bethlehem* by Joan Didion. Copyright © 1961, 1964, 1965, 1966, 1967, 1968 by Joan Didion. Reprinted by permission of Farrar, Straus & Giroux, Inc.

Paul R. Ehrlich and Anne H. Ehrlich. Excerpt from *Extinction: The Causes and Consequences of the Disappearance of Species.* Copyright © 1981 Random House, Inc., New York.

Robert Finch. "The Tactile Land" from *Outlands: Journeys to the Outer Edges of Cape Cod* by Robert Finch. Copyright © 1986 by Robert Finch. Reprinted by permission of David R. Godine, Publisher, Inc. Originally published in *Sanctuary,* the Bulletin of the Massachusetts Audubon Society.

Robert Frost. From "Stopping by Woods on a Snowy Evening" by Robert Frost. Copyright 1923, © 1969 by Holt, Rinehart and Winston. Copyright 1951 by Robert Frost. Reprinted from *The Poetry of Robert Frost,* edited by Edward Connery Lathem, by permission of Henry Holt and Company, Inc.

Ellen Goodman. "Misunderstood Michelle" from *At Large* by Ellen Goodman. Copyright © 1981, The Boston Globe Newspaper Company/Washington Post Writers Group. Reprinted with permission.

Stephen Jay Gould. From "Sex and Size." Reprinted from *The Flamingo's Smile: Reflections in Natural History* by Stephen Jay Gould, by permission of W. W. Norton & Company, Inc. Copyright © 1985 by Stephen Jay Gould.

Patricia Albjerg Graham. From "Status Transitions of Women Students, Faculty, and Administrators" in *Academic Women on the Move,* edited by Alice S. Rossi and Ann Calderwood. Copyright © 1973 Russell Sage Foundation. Reprinted by permission of Basic Books, Inc., Publishers.

Barrie B. Greenbie. From *Spaces: Dimensions of the Human Landscape* by Barrie B. Greenbie. Copyright © 1981. Reprinted by permission of Yale University Press, New Haven.

Garret Hardin. "Naked Emperors." Reprinted with permission from *Essays of a Taboo-Stalker* by Garret Hardin. Copyright © 1982 by William Kaufmann, Inc., Los Altos, CA 94022. All rights reserved.

Robert Hershon. From "John The Printer." Copyright © 1986 by Robert Hershon. Reprinted from *Images* 11:2.

Mary Harris "Mother" Jones. From *The Autobiography of Mother Jones,* edited by Mary F. Parton. Copyright © 1980 Charles H. Kerr Publishing Company.

Philip C. Kolin and Janeen L. Kolin. From *Models for Technical Writing* by Philip C. Kolin and Janeen L. Kolin. Copyright © 1985 by St. Martin's Press, Inc., and used with permission of the publisher.

Elisabeth Kübler-Ross. Reprinted with permission of Macmillan Publishing Company from *On Death and Dying* by Elisabeth Kübler-Ross. Copyright © 1970 by Elisabeth Kübler-Ross.

Martha Weinman Lear. From "The Art of Interviewing." Reprinted by permission of the author.

William Least Heat Moon. "A View of Prejudice" and the photograph of Barbara Pierre from *Blue Highways* by William Least Heat Moon. Copyright © 1982 by William Least Heat Moon. By permission of Little, Brown and Company in association with the Atlantic Monthly Press.

Alan P. Lightman. Excerpted from "Time Travel and Papa Joe's Pipe" from *Time Travel and Papa Joe's Pipe: Essays on the Human Side of Science.* Copyright © 1984 Alan P. Lightman. Reprinted with the permission of Charles Scribner's Sons.

Rollo May. "What Is Eros?" Selection reprinted from *Love and Will* by Rollo May by permission of W. W. Norton & Company, Inc. Copyright © 1969 by W. W. Norton & Company, Inc.

H. L. Mencken. "Libido for the Ugly" from *A Mencken Chrestomathy,* edited and annotated by H. L. Mencken. Copyright © 1949 by Alfred A. Knopf, Inc. Reprinted by permission of Random House, Inc.

Charlotte Mew. "The Farmer's Bride." *Collected Poems and Prose,* edited by Val Warner. Copyright © 1981 Carcanet Press Limited. Reprinted by permission.

Leigh Montville. From a column on Ray Fitzgerald that appeared August 4, 1982. Reprinted courtesy of the *Boston Globe.*

Douglass C. North and Roger Leroy Miller. Excerpt from pp. 74–75 from *The Economics of Public Issues,* Sixth Edition. Copyright © 1983 by Harper & Row, Publishers, Inc. Reprinted by permission of Harper & Row, Publishers, Inc.

Joyce Carol Oates. "Yeats's 'A Prayer for My Daughter' " from *The Profane Art* by Joyce Carol Oates. Copyright © 1983 by the Ontario Review, Inc. Reprinted by permission of the publisher, E. P. Dutton, a division of New American Library.

Sylvia Plath. "Northampton" from *The Journals of Sylvia Plath,* edited by Ted Hughes and Frances McCullough. Copyright © 1982 Doubleday Publishing Company. Reprinted with permission.

David Quammen. "A Republic of Cockroaches." © 1985 by David Quammen. Excerpted from *Natural Acts,* published by Nick Lyons Books, 31 West 21st Street, New York, NY 10010.

Mary Anne Raywid. "Power to Jargon, for Jargon Is Power," *Journal of Teacher Education* (Sept./Oct. 1978). Reprinted with permission.

Caryl Rivers. "What Should Be Done About Rock Lyrics?" (Original title: "Issue Isn't Sex, It's Violence"). Reprinted from the *Boston Globe* and with permission of the author.

Carl Sagan. From "The Case Against SDI." Copyright © 1985 Dr. Carl Sagan. First appeared in the September 1985 issue of *Discover.* Reprinted by permission of the author and the author's agents, Scott Meredith Literary Agency, Inc., 845 Third Avenue, New York, NY, 10022.

Sociology Writing Group. From *A Guide to Writing Sociology Papers,* by the Sociology Writing Group, University of California at Los Angeles. Copyright © 1986 St. Martin's Press, Inc., and used with publisher's permission.

E. Richard Sorenson. "Cooperation and Freedom Among the Fore in New Guinea" and Figure 18.2 from *Learning Non-Aggression: The Experience of Non-Literate Societies,* edited by Ashley Montagu. Copyright © 1978 by Ashley Montagu. Reprinted by permission of Oxford University Press, Inc.

Ann Swidler. From *Habits of the Heart: Individualism and Commitment in American Life* by Robert N. Bellah, Richard Madsen, Ann Swidler, William M. Sullivan, and Steven M. Tipton. Copyright © 1985 University of California Press, Berkeley. Reprinted by permission.

Norman Tallent. From *Psychological Report Writing,* Second Edition, © 1983, pp. 190–192. Reprinted with permission of Prentice-Hall, Inc., Englewood Cliffs, New Jersey.

Benjamin Taylor. "In This Corner" by Benjamin Taylor, February 14, 1983. Reprinted courtesy of the *Boston Globe.*

Wade Thompson. From "My Crusade Against Football" by Wade Thompson. *The Nation,* April 11, 1959. Reprinted by permission of The Nation Magazine/The Nation Associates, Inc.

Barbara W. Tuchman. From *A Distant Mirror: The Calamitous 14th Century.* Copyright © 1978 by Alfred A. Knopf, Inc. Reprinted by permission of Alfred A. Knopf, Inc.

Michael Walsh. Excerpts from "The Great LP vs. CD War." Copyright © 1986 Time Inc. All rights reserved. Reprinted by permission from *Time.*

Gerald Weissmann. Excerpt from "Foucault and the Bag Lady." Reprinted by permission of Dodd, Mead & Company, Inc., from *The Woods Hole Cantata: Essays on Science and Society* by Gerald Weissmann. Copyright © 1985 by Gerald Weissmann, M.D.

E. B. White. "A Shepherd's Life" from *One Man's Meat* by E. B. White. Copyright © 1940, renewed 1968 by E. B. White. Reprinted by permission of Harper & Row, Publishers, Inc.

Bob Wischnia. From "Twenty Top Runners and Coaches Give Advice on How You Can Improve Your Running." *Runner's World Annual,* 1983. Reprinted by permission of the author.

William Butler Yeats. "A Prayer for My Daughter" reprinted with permission of Macmillan Publishing Company from *Collected Poems* by William Butler Yeats. Copyright 1924 by Macmillan Publishing Company, renewed 1952 by Bertha Georgie Yeats. Reprinted by permission of A. P. Watt Ltd. on behalf of Michael B. Yeats and Macmillan London Limited.

Philip Zaleski. "The Superstars of Heart Research," *Boston* Magazine, December 1982. Copyright © 1982 by Philip Zaleski. Reprinted by permission of the author.

Art and Photograph Credits

pages 78–79: The Master I.B. with the Bird and Forgery. *How Prints Look* by William M. Ivins. Beacon Press, Boston.

page 83 (top): Peter Vandermark/Stock Boston. *(bottom):* J. R. Holland/Stock Boston.

page 84: Eva M. Demjen/Stock Boston.

page 97: Excerpt from *Eating Disorders: The Facts* by Suzanne Abraham and Derek Llewellyn-Jones. Oxford University Press, 1984. Reprinted with permission of Oxford University Press.

pages 216–217: Atlas, © 1979, by Glen Baxter/De Harmonie, Amsterdam.

Figure 17.5: Reproduction of entry "slapstick" from *The Supplement to the Oxford English Dictionary,* edited by R. W. Burchfield, vol. IV, Se–Z, 1986.

Index